MAYA
CIVILIZATION

MAYA
CIVILIZATION

EDITED BY
PETER SCHMIDT
MERCEDES DE LA GARZA
ENRIQUE NALDA

THAMES AND HUDSON

First published in Great Britain in 1998
by Thames and Hudson Ltd, London

Copyright © 1998 RCS Libri – CNCA INAH

British Library Cataloguing-in-Publication Data
A catalogue record for this book is available
from the British Library

ISBN 0-500-01889-8

Printed in Italy

With the patronage of

the President
of the United States of Mexico
Ernesto Zedillo Ponce de León

the President
of the Italian Republic
Oscar Luigi Scalfaro

PALAZZOGRASSI

Palazzo Grassi S.p.A.
San Samuele 3231, Venice

After centuries of relative oblivion, the great civilization of the Maya peoples has resurfaced
to impart a cogent message from the distant past.

For the specialists, the exhibition poses a vital occasion for analysis and comparison.

For the public it will be an astounding discovery, as the Maya speak to us from such distance
in time in the unique language of symbols, idols, and ideas of which their culture was constituted.
This rediscovery does not simply involve our admiration of the vast compass of Maya art,
but allows us to delve into the Maya's innermost secrets and relive their message by means
of their monuments and art.

Behind that message is an engrossing history. The remote origins of the Maya lie in Asia, whence
they crossed over the then frozen Bering Straits to the new continent and made their way down
the Pacific coast to Central America. During this transition, the Maya shed many traditions
but gained new ones, conserving the primitive expression of their forebears while creating
a new, wholly individual culture that is expressed through the art displayed here.

Something unites us, therefore, to the Maya and their long pilgrimage, because, despite their mass
emigration, they retained much of their original identity.

Once again Palazzo Grassi invites the public to admire the aesthetic marvels of one of the world's
peoples, but particularly to meditate on this glimpse of the past, and reflect on what it signifies
for the present. Through this exhibition we are introduced to this ancient American civilization,
and are brought closer to its present heirs, whom we must thank for their commitment
to the exhibition, first and foremost the government of Mexico, which was enthusiastic
about the exhibition, and those of Guatemala, Honduras, Belize, Costa Rica, and El Salvador.
A vital contribution has come from museums across the United States, Germany, Great Britain,
and the Netherlands, with loans of pieces of irreplaceable value.

Palazzo Grassi would like to express its thanks to the National Council for Culture and Arts,
and the council's president Rafael Tovar; and to the general director of the Mexican National
Institute of Anthropology and History, María Teresa Franco, without whose concerted
contribution this exhibition would never have been possible.

Feliciano Benvenuti

GULF OF MEXICO

Dzibilchaltún   Izamal   Ekbalam

Mayapán   Chichén Itzá

Ikil

Uxmal
Kabah   Labná
Sayil

Isla de Jaina

Calkiní

Tahcok

Edzná   Xtampak

Nohcacab

Dzibilnocac

Hochob

El Resbalón

Balamkú   Becán   Dzibanch

Hormiguero   Xpuhil   Kohunlich   Sta.

Chicanná

Río Bec   Río Hondo

Nohmul

Comalcalco

Río Grijalva

Río Usumacinta

Calakmul   Cuello

Río Azul   Al

MEXICO

Lamanai

Mirador
Uaxactún

BELIZE

Palenque   Pomoná

El Perú

Piedras Negras

Tikal   Cahal Pech

Yaxhá   Xunantunich

Toniná

Yaxchilán
Bonampak

Caracol

Altar de Sacrificios

Ceibal

Dos Pilas   Lubaantún   Nimli punit

Chinkultic

Aguateca

Machaquilá

Arriaga

Cancuen

Tzutzuculi

Pijijiapan

El Pajón   Zaculeu

GUATEMALA   Quiriguá

Izapa

Río Motagua

Iximche   Mixco Viejo

Copán

Níspe

Abaj Takalik

Kaminaljuyú

PACIFIC OCEAN

Cehuatán

Tazumal   Cerén

San Andrés

EL SALVADO

Ecab

El Meco

El Rey

Xcaret

Aguada Grande
San Gervasio

Cobá

Xelhá
Tulum

Muyil

CARIBBEAN SEA

N

Corozal

GULF OF HONDURAS

HONDURAS

Salitrón

Scale:

0   100   200   300 Km

0   100   200 Mi

The exhibition has been organized
with the National Council
for Culture and Arts
of Mexico

Special thanks to:

Rafael Tovar
President of the National Council for Culture and Arts

Teresa Franco
*General Director of the Instituto Nacional
de Antropología e Historia*

Alejandra de la Paz
Coordinator for International Affairs

Miguel Angel Fernández
*National Coordinator
of Museums and Exhibits
INAH*

Adriana Konzevik
*National Coordinator for Promotion
INAH*

Mesoamerica is considered one of the few truly original civilizations in history. It was not an heir to earlier civilizations, nor did it maintain contacts with others contemporaneous with it. Historically and geographically isolated, it was the exclusive achievement of the family of peoples and cultures that established themselves within a vast territory that forms part of what is today Mexico and Central America.

The Maya were undoubtedly one of the most noteworthy and amazing members of this civilization. Their great architectonic accomplishments, their artistic genius, their writing and literature, their scientific knowledge, their high degree of social organization, their cosmovision and their history, in sum, have garnered the admiration of the world for centuries. Maya culture is one of the most studied in Mesoamerica, yet its heritage still surprises us because its extent and richness remains largely unknown and hidden. At the same time it is deeply alive in todayís Maya peoples, in the strong identity they preserve, in their millenary traditions, in their vast ethnic and cultural diversity.

For these reasons, celebrating the image of the Maya and expanding our knowledge of their legacy is both timely and appropriate. It is a great honor for Mexico that one of the most notable endeavors aimed at this reevaluation takes the form of a great exhibition in one of the most important galleries in the world, the Palazzo Grassi in the city of Venice.

This exhibition is the most comprehensive and meticulous presentation of Maya culture that has been organized to date. It assembles about six hundred of the most superb pieces, several of them discovered only recently and exhibited for the first time, offering a synthesis and an integrated panorama of this culture: from its architecture, art, religion, and science to its social organization, daily life, and history. The whole represents the techniques and languages that served as a means of expression: painting, sculpture, codices, metallurgy, ceramics, and jewelry.

This exceptional exhibition, outstanding both for the number and for the quality of its works, was made possible by the contribution of museums and collections in Mexico, as well as in six countries in the Americas and five in Europe. Of particular importance was the generous contribution of the governments and cultural institutions of Guatemala, Honduras, El Salvador, and Costa Rica, as well as that of the United States and the European Community. The holdings from major Mexican museums, among them the National Museum of Anthropology, the most important collection of Mesoamerican civilization in the world, was thus enriched to form a unique assembly of testimonies of the great Maya past.

This effort occurs at a stage of strengthening cooperation initiated by Italy and Mexico in recent years. We are deeply grateful for the collaboration of the Palazzo Grassi and the Italian Embassy in Mexico, as well as for the sponsorship of the Fiat Group, which made it possible for the joint effort of the Secretariat of Foreign Affairs, the Embassy of Mexico in Italy, and the National Council for Culture and Arts in Mexico, through the National Institute of Anthropology and History, to bear fruit in the form of this exhibition.

It is a profound honor for us that the Palazzo Grassi continues its brilliant trajectory in the milieu of the presentation of international exhibitions with an exhibition such as that of Maya, which places the cultural legacy of Mexico once again in the discourse of universal traditions.

Rafael Tovar
President of the National Council for Culture and Arts, Mexico

The end of the millennium is a propitious moment in which to reflect on one of humanity's great civilizations: the Maya. It is a fitting tribute, particularly since this century discovered the vigor of that ancient culture. We have been witnesses: thanks to archaeology, the enigma of the Maya past has been resolved in art, in a history that is read, integrated, and that has persisted until this very day. The Maya of today, Cakchiquels, Chols, Chontals, Chortis, Itzas, Lacandons, Mams, Pocomans, Poconchis, Quekchis, Quiches, Tzeltals, Tzotzils, and others, are heirs to this great culture. Only recently has it been possible to move with certainty through fascinating cosmogonies, cities held as axes of the universe, deciphered writings, and precise calendars.

To speak of the Maya is to speak of the jungle, of the true men who built temples and lived the marvels of a cosmos in equilibrium. Although they made war, they also knew how to impose an aesthetic quality that the passage of centuries has not erased. The Mayas persistently interrogated the stars, wrote poems on their brief transit on earth, left their knowledge and even their fears recorded on stone and on strips of paper. Today we know of this from the resurrection promised by archaeology, the development of which has been exceptional during the last five years in Mexico. As a result, we have reached remarkable settlements, some urban, some paradisiacal, lost for a while and found again.

One of the ways of interpreting the greatness of Maya civilization requires confronting its relics. This exhibition fulfills this assignment: to show ritual and domestic sides of Maya life, details and the whole picture, to reconstruct reality based on fragments.

To achieve this, however, has been no small task. Ancient Maya geography now requires very complex efforts in many areas ranging from museum installation, technical work, and even diplomatic relations. Archaeologists, restorers, architects, curators and innumerable professional staff have pooled their talents to make this exceptional exhibition possible, and special recognition should be given to the labors of Miguel Angel Fern·ndez.

Diminutive Jaina figurines to monumental stelae and altars weave a sequenced history portraying the faces of generations that have disappeared more than a thousand years ago. Hundreds of pieces from many sources are gathered in these exhibition halls to form a mosaic of quetzals and orchids, jaguars and feathered serpents, strange bestiaries, and men on the level of their gods. The National Council for Culture and the Arts, by way of the National Institute of Anthropology and History, in collaboration with the government of Italy, and the sponsorship of the Fiat Group have made it possible for the splendid Palazzo Grassi in Venice to be the temporary keeper of this treasure from the Americas. The participation of the governments and museums of Guatemala, Honduras, El Salvador, Belize, and Costa Rica is of equal importance, as well as that of museums in the United States and Europe.

We all agree that in order to preserve this heritage for another millennium, it is essential to reveal the character of this great civilization, based on the conviction that this is the best way to guarantee its survival.

María Teresa Franco
General Director of the Instituto Nacional de Antropología e Historia, Mexico

Tabula gratulatoria

The following people and institutions
contributed to the realization of this exhibition:

FOR GUATEMALA
Augusto Vela Mena
Minister of Culture and Sports of Guatemala

Carlos Enrique Zea-Flores
Vice Minister of Culture and Sports of Guatemala

Juan Antonio Valdés
General Director of Cultural and Natural Heritage

Technical Committee
Dora Guerra de González
*Director of the National Museum of Archaeology
and Ethnology of Guatemala*

Rodolfo Yaquián
National Museum of Archaeology and Ethnology of Guatemala

Estuardo Mata
Chairman of the Board of the Popol Vuh Museum

FOR HONDURAS
Herman Allan Padget
Minister of Culture, Arts and Sports

Olga Marina Joya Sierra
*Director of the Honduran Institute
of Anthropology and History*

Technical Committee
Carmen Julia Fajardo Cardona
Head of Department of Anthropological Research

Leonel González
Portable Objects Registrar at the Protection Department

Omar Talavera
Portable Objects Registrar at the Protection Department

FOR BELIZE
Henry Young
Minister of Tourism and Environment

John Morris
Commissioner of the Department of Archaeology of Belize

FOR COSTA RICA
Astrid Fischel
Minister of Culture, Youth and Sports

Melania Ortiz Volio
General Director of the National Museum of Costa Rica

Marlin Calvo
Head of the Department of Cultural Heritage Protection

Leidy Bonilla
Department of Cultural Heritage Protection

Cristóbal Zawadzki
Executive President of the National Insurance Institute

Zulay Soto
Director of the Jade Museum "Lic. Fidel Tristán"

FOR SALVADOR
Roberto Antonio Galicia
President of the National Council for the Culture and the Art

María Isaura Aráuz
National Director of Cultural Heritage

Ana Mercedes Salazar
Director of Inventory and Registry of the Cultural Heritage

Grateful acknowlegements

Carlos Roberto Flores
Constitutional President of the Honduras Republic

Mario Moya Palencia
Mexican Ambassador in Italy

Ismael Penedo Sole
Guatemalan Ambassador in Italy

Oscar Cassaty
Honduran Ambassador in Italy

Bruno Cabras
Italian Ambassador in Mexico

Alessandro Serafini
Italian Ambassador in Guatemala

Pier Franco Valle
Italian Ambassador in Honduras

Juan José Serra Castillo
Guatemalan Ambassador in Mexico

José Servando Chávez
Mexican Ambassador in Honduras

Enrique Hubbard Urrea
Mexican Ambassador in Belize

Paz Cervantes
Director of Mexico-Belize Cooperation and Culture Institute

Giancarlo Ligabue

New Holland-Mexico

Claudio Landucci
for his linkage in Mexico
on behalf of Palazzo Grassi and the publishers

Lenders

MUSEUMS IN MEXICO

Balancán, Museo "José Gómez Panaco"
Campeche, Museo de las Estelas "Román Piña Chán"
    Baluarte de la Soledad
Campeche, Museo Histórico Fuerte
    de San Miguel, Baluarte de San Miguel
Campeche, Centro INAH Campeche
Chetumal. Centro INAH Quintana Roo
Cancún, Museo Arqueológico de Cancún
Chichén Itzá, Museo de Sitio de Chichén Itzá
Chichén Itzá, Bodega del Laboratorio
    de Arqueología
Comitán, Museo Arqueológico de Comitán
Comalcalco, Museo de Sitio de Comalcalco
Dzibilchaltún, Museo del Pueblo Maya
Jonuta, Museo "Omar Huerta Escalante"
Mérida, Museo Regional de Yucatán
    "Palacio Cantón"
Mexico City, Museo Nacional
    de Antropología
Yucatán, Bodega del Sitio Arqueológico de Kabah
Palenque, Museo de Sitio "Alberto Ruz Lhuillier"
Pomoná, Museo de Sitio de Pomoná
Puebla, Fundación Amparo-Museo Amparo
San Cristóbal de las Casas , Museo del Ex Convento
    de Santo Domingo
San Cristóbal de las Casas, Centro Cultural
    de los Altos de Chiapas
San Cristóbal de las Casas, Centro Cultural
    Ná Bolom
Toniná, Sitio Arqueológico de Toniná
Tuxtla Gutiérrez, Museo Regional de Chiapas
Uxmal, Museo de Sitio de Uxmal
Valladolid, Centro Coordinador del INI
Villahermosa, Museo Regional de Antropología
    "Carlos Pellicer"

MUSEUMS IN GUATEMALA

Guatemala, Museo Nacional de Arqueología
    y Etnología
Guatemala, Museo Popol Vuh,
    Universidad Francisco Marroquín

MUSEUMS IN HONDURAS

Copán, Parque Arqueológico Ruinas de Copán
Copán, Centro Regional de Investigaciones Arqueológicas
Copán. Museo Regional de Arqueología
San Pedro Sula, Cortés, Museo de Antropología e Historia
Tegucigalpa, Bodegas Centrales del Instituto Hondureño
    de Antropología e Historia

MUSEUMS IN BELIZE

Belmopán, Bodegas del Departamento de Arqueología

MUSEUMS IN COSTA RICA

San José, Museo Nacional de Costa Rica
San José, Museo del Jade Lic. Fidel Tristán
    Instituto Nacional de Seguros

MUSEUMS IN EL SALVADOR

El Salvador, Museo Nacional de Antropología
    "Dr. David J. Guzmán"

MUSEUMS IN GERMANY

Berlin, Museum für Völkerkunde
Cologne, Rautenstrauch-Joest-Museum

MUSEUMS IN GREAT BRITAIN

London, The British Museum

MUSEUMS IN THE NETHERLANDS

Leyden, Rijksmuseum voor Volkenkunde

MUSEUMS IN THE UNITED STATES OF AMERICA

New York, The Metropolitan Museum of Art
Washington D.C.
    Dumbarton Oaks, Research Library Collections

Exhibition

FOR MEXICO

Carlos Córdova
*Director of International
Exhibits
INAH*

Peter Schmidt
Academic Curator

Rocío González
Academic Counsellor

Mercedes de la Garza
Academic Counsellor

Elvira Báez
Organization

Felipe Solis
Academic Counsellor

Sonia Peña
Operations Counsellor

FOR ITALY

Installation design
Agata Torricella Crespi
of Studio
Caruso &Torricella
collaborators
Margherita Cugini
Simone Fumagalli

Graphic design
Italo Lupi
with the collaboration of
Silvia Kihlgren

Lighting
Matteo Fiore

Coordination secretary
Michela Craveri

Press relations
Vladimiro Dan

Catalogue

FOR MEXICO

Publishing coordinator
Adriana Konzevik

Photography
Michel Zabé

Academic consultants
Antonio Benavides
Rocío González
Tomás Pérez

Editorial Staff
Rosa María Curiel
Leonor Lara
Sol Levin
Raúl Luna
Laura Rivera

Technical revision
Liwy Grazioso
Martha Cuevas
Hernando Gómez Rueda
Tomás Pérez

Epigraphic revision
Alfonso Arellano
Guillermo Bernal
Tomás Pérez

FOR ITALY

Editorial Director
Mario Andreose

Graphic design
Flavio Guberti
Realization
Break Point

Coordinating Editor
Simonetta Rasponi

Editorial Staff
Valentina Del Pizzol
Gianmarco Milesi
Patrizia Rizzo
Valérie Viscardi

*Translations
of texts from Spanish*
Debra Nagao
of texts from Italian
Andrew Ellis
David Lowry
of entries from Spanish
Debra Nagao
of entries from German
Jonathan Hunt

Programming
Milena Bongi

Production Staff
Eriberto Aricó
Sergio Daniotti
Carmen Garini
Valerio Gatti
Daniele Marchesi
Stefano Premoli
Enrico Vida

Secretary
Marcella Cipolla
Luisa Gandolfi

Contents

19 The rediscovery of a civilization
Mercedes de la Garza

28 A Brief History of Archaeological
Exploration
Ian Graham

38 Vegetation of the Maya Region
Arturo Gómez-Pompa

52 Ancient Maya Civilization in Space
and Time
Jeremy A. Sabloff

72 The Maya and Their Olmec
Neighbors
Tomás Pérez Suárez

84 Maya Frontiers
Giuseppe Orefici

102 The Maya City
Enrique Nalda

130 Maya Architecture
Antonio Benavides C.

158 Maya Daily Labors:
A History in Lower Case
Mario Humberto Ruz

178 Maya Writing
Maricela Ayala Falcón

192 Calendrical Cycles and Astronomy
Victoria R. Bricker
Harvey M. Bricker

206 The Maya Codices
Thomas A. Lee Whiting

216 Maya Cosmogony
Enrique Florescano

234 Maya Gods
Mercedes de la Garza

248 Portable Objects
Clemency Chase Coggins

270 Classic Maya Painted
Ceramics and the Stories
They Tell
Dorie Reents-Budet

296 Sculpture and Murals
of the Usumacinta Region
Merle Greene Robertson

308 The Highlands of Guatemala
and Chiapas
Zoila Rodríguez Girón
J. Héctor Paredes G.

320 Dynastic History and Politics
of the Classic Maya
David Stuart

336 Copán: Art, Science, and Dynasty
Ricardo Agurcia Fasquelle

356 Archaeology of the Central
Lowland Mayas: Tikal
Héctor L. Escobedo
Juan Antonio Valdés

372 The Metropolis of Calakmul
Campeche
Ramón Carrasco V.

386 Jaina: Its Funerary Art
Román Piña Chán

400 Uxmal and the Puuc Zone:
Monumental Architecture
Sculpture Facades and Political
Power in the Terminal
Classic Period
Jeff Karl Kowalski

426 Contacts with Central Mexico
and the Transition to the Postclassic:
Chichén Itzá in Central Yucatán
Peter J. Schmidt

450 Navigation and Trade
on the Eastern Coast
of the Yucatán Peninsula
Rocío González de la Mata
Anthony P. Andrews

468 Political Organization of the Yucatán
Mayas During the Eleventh
to Sixteenth Centuries
Sergio Quezada

482 The Conquest of the Mayas
of Yucatán and Maya Resistance
During the Spanish Colonial Period
Grant D. Jones

494 The Mayas in Modern Times
Jan de Vos

507 Works in exhibit

651 Timeline

661 Glossary

671 Maya Gods

672 Entries References

683 Index of the names

The appearance of the Mayas in western history

When the Spanish conquerors arrived in the lands inhabited by the Mayas in the sixteenth century, the monumental vestiges of an original and splendid civilization, as well as their unknown creators, became known to western culture with an impact that continues to be felt today. The ruins of great cities, abandoned several centuries earlier in the warm peninsula of Yucatán, were seen by the Spaniards, at the same time that they confronted the Maya Indians and the difficult, often merciless task of Christianization. Thus, the subjugation and alienation of Mesoamerican man began.

Far from there, among the volcanoes and coniferous forests of the highlands of Guatemala and the mountains of Chiapas, the Quiches, Cakchiquels, Tzutuhils, Tzeltals, Tzotzils and other ethnic groups were subjected by the Spaniards a few years after the conquest of Tenochtitlan.

Between these two regions extends a thick, humid tropical jungle, occupied at the time of the conquest by the Itzas, a Yucatecan Maya lineage that remained free until the end of the seventeenth century, becoming perhaps the last Mesoamerican natives subjugated by the Spaniards, as well as those of the Lacandon jungle. Until that time, no one had made a connection between these natives because they were located in very distant places, they had different customs and spoke different languages. It was known only that the Yucatecan Maya were the descendants of the builders of the abandoned cities of the north of the peninsula. Some explorers had found vestiges of human occupation in the jungles of the central region, but these did not spark major interest until the middle of the eighteenth century, two centuries after the arrival of the Spaniards, when a strange, spectacular city in ruins was discovered in the Chiapanecan jungle. No one knew anything about it and very few associated it with the Chol Indians of the region, who perhaps knew of it, but their link with the past had been broken considerable earlier.

That great city, whose original name in Maya is unknown to us, was called Palenque, because of its proximity to the town of the same name founded in the sixteenth century. It awakened the interest and astonishment of the western world because of its magnificence and its site. There have been many different interpretive hypotheses, which scientific research has ultimately rejected such as that of the supposed European or Asian origin of Maya cultural creations. However, there were also those who associated Palenque with other abandoned cities, such as Copán in Honduras and with the ruins known in the peninsula. In this way, beginning in the eighteenth century, the different indigenous groups began to be interrelated and identified with the material remains of a remote past, silent vestiges of their great ancestors. At the same time, by fate or due to the interest of a handful of scholars, valuable documents related to native groups were discovered in archives in America and Spain, documents written by Spaniards from the sixteenth century, as well as books written by Mayas in their own languages, but in the Latin alphabet, at the beginning of the colonial period. These texts began to be studied and translated becaming, beside the ruins of these ancient cities, the main sources of knowledge about the ancient Maya. The Spanish documents contain valuable information on the native pre-Hispanic past, because many of their authors were aided by native informants. Furthermore, they witnessed the manifestation of a culture that was so alien to them, at the same time that they invalidated and destroyed it. Most remaikable among these native texts are the *Popol Vuh* of the Quiches, the *Memorial de Sololá* of the Cakchiquels, and the *Books of Chilam Balam* of the Yucatecan Maya. Although they were written in the colonial period, they are copies of ancient codices and they gathered oral traditions that accompanied them; that is to say, their primary content is of pre-Hispanic origin, since their basic purpose was to preserve the ancient traditions.

In addition to those mentioned, a large number of these books and native documents constitute the corpus that we might call Maya literature; their they are the only books that we can read, because hieroglyphic writing has not yet been completely deciphered. Their content is highly diverse, but they contain the essential symbols and myths of Maya religion, as well as multiple rituals. Furthermore, they record lineages the protagonists of Postclassic Maya history. Although the documents written by Spaniards are also of great value, the indigenous texts have the added merit of being the vision the Mayas of themselves, their history and their religion.

Since the eighteenth century, a lengthy and extended research on the Mayas has developed. Science has cleared up mysteries about this great civilization, one of the most notable of antiquity, and today we know much more about these people. But this does not mean that we have the absolute truth and that the twenty-first century will not reject many of our interpretations, just as we have discarded those of the eighteenth and nineteenth centuries.

The Mayas, their space, and their history
The current scientific view, from many different disciplines, presents us with the Mayas not as a homogeneous group, but rather as an ethnic complex of different languages, customs, and historical trajectories. Nonetheless, all of them share certain characteristics that allow us to consider them as a single culture. At the same time, this civilization is integrated into another great cultural whole called Mesoamerica, which in the pre-Hispanic period was located in the central and southern part of Mexico, as well as northern Central America.
Although the origins of this culture are still a problem for science, the groups that created it seem to have developed free from influences from other continents and based on the domestication of maize and the resulting settlements of the population. Archaeological vestiges reveal to us that the Mesoamerican people always had close tie between themselves and even with other peoples in America.
As for Mayan-speaking groups, they settled in a continuous territory covering the modern-day Mexican states of Yucatán, Campeche, Quintana Roo and parts of Tabasco and Chiapas, as well as the Central American countries of Guatemala and Belize, and western portions of Honduras and El Salvador. The Maya territory extended over almost 400,000 square kilometers. One of the groups, the Huaxtecs, separated in remote times from the common trunk and established itself outside of this territory, finally developing a distinct culture, although its language forms part of the Mayan family. The remaining twenty-eight ethnic groups, based on their language which are: Yucatecan Maya, Itzá, Lacandon, Mopán, Chortí, Chontal, Chol, Cholti (Historical Lacandon), Tzotzil, Tzeltal, Coxoh, Tojolabal, Chuj, Jacaltec, Kanhobal, Mochó, Tuzantec, Mam, Aguacateca, Ixil, Quiche, Tzutuhil, Cakchiquel, Uspantec, Achi, Pocomam, Pocomchi, and Kekchi. Mayan languages are a linguistic group with a common origin. They are not dialects, as they are sometimes called (generally in a derogatory sense), but rather languages with their own grammatical structure.
The overall Maya area possesses extraordinary geographic variety and wealth. There are hot, humid climates with jungles filled with immense trees, high rainfall and extensive swampy regions; there are also cold climates, mountain chains of volcanic origin with altitudes of up to 13.200 foot meters, great lakes and dense forests. Fast flowing rivers, such as the Grijalva and the Usumacinta, cross the area, although flat regions almost entirely lack rivers and rain, and possess poor vegetation. Nevertheless innumerable subterranean currents and deposits of water, which the Mayas called *dzonot* (*cenote*), were the main sources of water for the inhabitants.
The variety of animals in the area is also surprising. There are large cats, among which the jaguar is of particular note, different species of monkeys, deer, wild boars, tapirs, and other mammals. The jungles are inhabited by innumerable species of insects, reptiles and birds, among which the remarkable quetzal, is considered to be the most beautiful bird, and the imposing tropical rattlesnake, creatures that were symbols par excellence of the sacred.
Maya culture cannot be understood outside of the extraordinary natural environment in which it was created because animal and plant symbols populate the religion and the artistic creations of these men. Nature and natural forces inspired cosmogonic and cosmological conceptions, as well as the creation of sacred spaces in the heart of their great cities. All this reveals to us an exceptional awareness of the man-nature continuum, of cosmic unity, that was and continues to be at the core of Maya culture.
The pre-Hispanic historical development of the Mayas spans approximately from the eighteenth century B.C. to the sixteenth century A.D., that is to say, around 3,400 years. After the Spanish conquest, its history underwent a radical change, but 500 years after that fateful moment for the Mayas, the majority of the ethnic groups still inhabit their territories, speaking their languages and conserving some of the beliefs and their daily customs, albeit modified, by violent imposition of another culture.

Preclassic period

In the most ancient period, called the Preclassic (ca. 1800 B.C. to 250 A.D.) in scientific research, the traits that would give the Maya culture its distinctive character were structured, with different influences from other Mesoamerican groups, such as the Olmecs of the Gulf Coast of Mexico and the creators of the Izapa culture in the southern portion of the Maya area itself. In this period, the first villages were established, generally alongside rivers, and agriculture was the economic base. At that time some forms of irrigation were used, although crops primarily depended mainly on fall rains. The main products were corn, beans, squash and chili.

With the rise of agriculture, population increased and ceremonial centers were created, that is to say, specific constructions for religious cults. Society began to be stratified into a hierarchy as activities going beyond mere immediate material necessity began to develop. These included writing, visual arts, and the cultivation of "sciences."

Classic period

During the third century A.D., the period of the maximum development in all orders, called the Classic period, for this reason began reaching its people in the ninth century. Initially, there was a great development of agriculture, with systems of irrigation and commercial crops, such as cocoa and cotton. Relations with other peoples in Mesoamerica increased, such as with those of the metropolis of Teotihuacan. There was an increase in technology, although still not highly developed, and political organization was consolidated closely connected to religion, which by this time displays a high degree of complexity.

In the Classic period, numerous settlements and large ceremonial and political centers were constructed that may properly be called cities. In addition to buildings clearly intended for cult activities, there were constructions that seem to have served non-religious purposes–residences, markets, plazas and others, which reveal a very well-organized civil and religious power structure. Among the many sites that flourished in this period, we might highlight Kaminaljuyú, Tikal, Uaxactún, Palenque, Yaxchilán, Piedras Negras, Bonampak, Chinkultic, Copán, Quiriguá, Ceibal, Calakmul, Edzná, Uxmal, Kabah, Sayil, and Classic period Chichén Itzá.

This was a time of profound spiritual creativity is produced fundamentally in the central region. The Mayas have reached a very distinguished place in the history of humanity are their many achievements: writing, mathematics, astronomy and chronology flourished. We could call such knowledge "scientific," from a western point of view, but for them, this was a way of knowing and managing the sacred energies that emanated mainly from the stars, which were conceived of as divine beings or epiphanies of the sacred forces. This knowledge was exercised in the field of religion.

To put it briefly, the Maya writing system is the most advanced to have developed in America. They invented, for the first time in history, (more or less a thousand years before the Hindus) the positional value of mathematical signs and the use of zero, conceived of as an empty position. They measured the solar cycle with noteworthy precision (with an error of only 17.28 seconds), as well as those of the Moon and Venus, among others, and they could also predict eclipses. They created a complex system of dates based on different cycles, which include the solar, lunar, and ritual calendar, the latter of which was the basis of ritual life which is still used by many Maya groups. They also employed other cycles, utilizing a "era date," which corresponds in our calendar to August 13, 3114 B.C. and seems to record the beginning of the current cosmic era (according to their ideas on the origin of the universe).

In the Classic period, the visual art and architecture flourished as seen their cities. At the same time, there was considerable awareness of man and of his position in the world, expressing itself in the form of unique humanism in sculpture, and the appearance of historiography: their texts recording the history of the great ruling dynasties. The discovery of this historiography is the result of epigraphic research under taken by the German scholar Heinrich Berlin and the American Tatiana Proskouriakoff beginning 1958. Although today epigraphic readings are still interpretative, they have revealed to us a considerable amount of information about the power groups of several cities and about the social and economic life Mayas of the Classic period.

In turn written sources of the colonial-period tell of the existence of many historiographic codices that were destroyed in the evangelical zeal of the Spanish friars. The content of these lost documents was preserved, in part, in texts that the Mayas themselves wrote after learning the Latin alphabet. These texts reveal to us not only the history of some lineages, but also the obvious fact they were recording their history to avoid losing political power. Their other primary concern was the essential purpose of Maya historiography, which was to record accomplishments so as to know what would happen in the future, because according to their cyclical concept of time, the acts of men would be repeated the same as the natural cycles, when the same conjunction of divine influences returned to unfold over the world.

Thus, both science as well as historiography were framed in a context of religion, and reveal not only an attempt to know the energies of the gods, but also to manage them for the good of man. The Maya believed that the future was predetermined, but they did not submit themselves passively to the gods. Rather, they attempted to know them so as to model their lives by way of ritual, which was the complex of practices to communicate with the gods, feed them, turn bad influences into good, and to thus maintain the life of the cosmos intact. Because of this unique conception of the world and of life, where man is the axis of the universe in that he is the sustainer of the gods, ritual was the primary activity of Maya society.

The ancient Maya had multiple ritual practices and the written sources tell us of a complex priestly hierarchy. But in the Classic period, the central religious responsibility seems to have been in the hands of the ruler, who is represented in multiple visual arts as an *axis mundi* and as the controller of cosmic forces. One of the best examples is the tomb of the Temple of the Inscriptions at Palenque, where the great ruler Pacal was buried with a jade sphere in one hand and a cube in the other, the two fundamental cosmological symbols of the sky and the earth, of time and space. On the slab covering his sarcophagus, Pacal is represented at the center of the universe, on the terrestrial level, between the sky and underworld; above him rises a cross, the axis of the universe and symbol of the four cosmic sectors, in the form of a dragon.

The main symbol of the ruler is, in effect, the dragon, which represents the supreme god Itzamna, who grants him the power to govern. Rulers bear images of the dragon on all their accouterments, on their thrones, on objects of power that they carry in their hands (such as ceremonial bars and manikin scepters). At the same time, they bear *axis mundi* crosses, which reveal their situation in the cosmos.

But this granting of divine status to rulers was not based solely on their illustrious lineages; they had to pass through a strict initiation ritual, surely to have access to the throne. Furthermore, they carried out constant ascetic practices, as revealed in several lintels from Yaxchilán, where we see the ruler beside objects for self-sacrifice at the last moment of his initiation, when he emerges from the jaws of a great serpent. This image coincides with initiation rites practiced by some Maya groups to this very day, in which the initiate must be swallowed by a great serpent to re-emerge transformed into a shaman. Thus, Maya rulers, just like many Maya medicine men and diviners to this day, were also shamans. Visual images from the Classic period can be corroborated by colonial indigenous texts, such as the *Popol Vuh* and the *Título de Totonicapán*, where leaders are described as portentous men capable of transforming themselves into animals and natural forces, that is to say, as shamans.

One of the rites practiced by Classic period rulers, which was important in Maya religion throughout all periods, was the ball game. In many Classic period cities, we find ballcourts to play the ball game located in ceremonial centers.

The symbolic-religious significance of the game is the struggle of cosmic opposites that makes existence itself possible. At times it symbolized the conflict between the Sun and the Moon; day against night; at others, the struggle of the gods of the underworld, representing death, against the celestial gods of life. But, the game is always related to the stars and sacred warfare, due to its meaning embedding the opposition of contrary forces. The game was accompanied by processions and decapitation ceremonies, though it is difficult to believe that it resulted in the sacrifice of the players. The decapitated head symbolized the stars, balls and in fertility ceremonies, ears of maize.

The ball game rite took on a meaning of sympathetic magic, that is to say, by carrying it out, one magically propitiated the movement of the stars. But it was also an initiation rite, as expressed in the myth of the origin of the Sun and Moon in the *Popol Vuh*, where by way of the ball game in the underworld against the gods of death, two heroes achieve their apotheosis as the Sun and Moon.

In the Classic period, different gods and rulers are represented as playing ball; in the Postclassic period, the rite became secularized and there are references to professional players and bets. Some of the Classic period reliefs, which in general are ball court markers, describe the initiation episode of the emergence of the Sun and Moon; other depict rulers playing the game, which shows that for them, playing the game was an initiation rite. Thus, in the same way that star gods are created through the game, rulers carried out part of their initiation as shamans by practicing the rite.

The Maya collapse

Around the ninth century, after the remarkable cultural florescence in the Classic period, a historical process that has been called the "Maya collapse" unfolds. This is expressed mainly in the fact that political and cultural activities cease in great cities in the central area; many cities were abandoned and disappeared beneath the thick jungle. There are several hypotheses on the causes of this phenomenon, including agricultural crisis, a rupture in the ecological equilibrium, and famines, which could have led to serious political conflicts within the cities or the states themselves and between them. Unlike what occurred in the central area, where Maya culture never flourishes again, in the regions to the north and south (north of the Yucatan peninsula and the Guatemala and Chiapas highlands, respectively), there were profound changes influenced by the arrival of different groups from other regions of Mesoamerica.

Postclassic period

The period from 900 A.D. to 1524 A.D., the time of the fall of Gumarcah the capital of the Quiche empire, after which the rest of the Maya were gradually conquered until the fall of Ta Itza in 1697, is known as the Postclassic. The main events of this period were recovered in indigenous and Spanish texts written in the early years of the colonial period, which is why we know more about this phase of Maya history.

In general, we can say that in the Postclassic period there was a great cultural change in the northern Yucatan peninsula, caused by the arrival of highly diversified groups from the Gulf Coast of Mexico (the region of the Chontalpa around Laguna de Términos) who conquered some sites, such as Chichén Itzá (a city apparently founded by the Itza lineage) and Mayapán (governed by the Cocoms). Another famous lineage of the time was that of the Xius, foreigners who established themselves at Uxmal.

During the Postclassic period, contacts with different peoples intensified, trade occupies a central role in Maya life, and commercial emporiums were created, such as that of the Chontals or Putuns from the Gulf Coast of Mexico. At the same time, many activities become secularized, due perhaps to the predominance of militarism and to pragmatic interests. In this way, new gods and cults were introduced; the cultivation of science diminishe; new artistic styles arose and gave rise to a blossoming reflected mainly in the city of Chichén Itzá, where the sacred cenote was one of the great pilgrimage centers visited by groups from throughout the Maya area.

After various power struggles, around the year 1200, A.D., Chichén Itzá and other important cities are conquered by Mayapán, a center that dominate the region until its fall in 1441. Concurring with archaeological data, texts record that the city was set on fire and the Cocom lineage was annihilated, except for one member who at that time was in Honduras. After this event, the major cities were abandoned and new settlements were founded, which constituted the "provinces" found by the Spaniards.

The conquest of the northern Yucatán peninsula did not take on the appearance of the great epic poem of the conquest of Tenochtitlán in Mexico and that of Gumarcah in Guatemala. Constant wars had led to cultural decadence, and between 1527 and 1546, the region fell into the hands of Francisco de Montejo, his son and nephew, both of the same name.

As for the Postclassic history of the highlands, in the south of the Maya area, the arrival of different groups of foreigners who modified historical process is also recorded. The Quiches, who narrated their history in different texts after the Spanish conquest (mainly in the *Popol Vuh*) created a powerful military state that subjugated other ethnic groups, such as the Cakchiquels and the Tzutuhils. They had strong contacts with the Mexicas of the central highlands, to whom they paid tribute, and at the time of the arrival of the Spaniards, under the command of Pedro de Alvarado, their city met with a violent end, such as that of the Mexicas themselves, only three years after the conquest of Tenochtitlan.

Maya society

It is evident, as exemplified in all cultures of the world, that great cultural creations were not conceived of nor carried out by the entire Maya population, but rather by a social group. Sources tell us of a social organization with clearly differentiated groups. In the different regions, these groups are known by different names and there are some variants. Here we will highlight some traits of the social organization of the Yucatecan Mayas of the Postclassic period. At the head of society were the almehenoob (noblemen), individuals of illustrious lineage, destined by divine decree to govern others, whether by way of political control, religious power, or the force of arms. Rulers, called halach uinicoob, "True Men," priests (ahau can, "Lord Serpent" and ah kinoob, "Those of the Sun," among others), war chiefs (Nacoms), and perhaps merchants belonged to this privileged class. Under them were the ah chembal uinicoob, "Lower Men," the commoners, the men without nobility, who were devoted to working the land, to building, producing crafts and other essential work for group survival. These constituted the materially productive class, who allowed nobles to carry out high intellectual and artistic creations. Therefore, we can say that, in the imposing cities, in the original sculptural works, in the hundreds of hieroglyphic texts, and in the other material vestiges preserved of Maya culture, there lies the silent labor of the commoners, who are also eternalized there. The cultural achievements, which give the Maya their unique identity and universal worth, are not solely the product of the social elite, rather, they belong to all Mayas.

On the current state of Maya research

The current scientific vision of the ancient Maya (which runs parallel to that of legendary and popular viewpoints) is the result of new methodological approaches in archaeology, epigraphy, iconography, history, history of religions, history of art, physical anthropology, and linguistics, which have been integrated into interdisciplinary projects along with other scientific fields, such as those of biology and astronomy.

But it is only fair to recognize that these new approaches have their roots in those of the great Mayanists from the beginning of the century, including Sylvanus Morley, Eric Thompson, Ralph Roys, Herbert Spinden, Yuri Knorosov, Alberto Ruz, and many others. In the sciences, each new interpretation nourishes the others, although they differ from them, because science is not improvisation, but rather a revitalizing assimilation of the past. In the history of science, we might recall what George Santayana said about the history of man: "He who does not know the past, is condemned to repeat it." New ideas will never be new if they do not take the past into consideration.

In the first half of this century, an idealized vision of the Maya as men sui generis was promoted by the English archaeologist Eric Thompson. The Maya were believed to be extraordinarily spiritual, knowledgeable priests unconcerned with prosaic and material matters in life–without wars, without bloody sacrifice; a people of philosophers and astronomers, "pure" scientists, with their eyes glued to the sky, confined to sidereal space. But even then some of his contemporaries, such as Alberto Ruz, did not share this vision; Ruz went beyond his teachers, Morley and Thompson. On the one hand, he refuted Morley's theory of the Old and New Maya Empires, and on the other, he contributed to demythifying Maya culture, revealing a people who shared the same miseries and the same magnificence as other Mesoamerican groups. Without overlooking their great artistic and scientific achievements, he was concerned with profane and mundane aspects of Maya culture and was one of the Mayanists who enthusiastically accepted the discoveries of

Heinrich Berlin and Tatiana Proskouriakoff on the historical content of Maya inscriptions, which is the starting point of current epigraphy. Even Thompson himself, faced with the discoveries of Berlin and Proskouriakoff, admitted his error with respect to the Mayas' lack of interests in their own history.

Alongside these developments in epigraphy, which have shown what the Mayas recorded of their history and much of their political and social life, and even the mundane interests of those singular men, archaeology has also taken a new turn. Now the focus is on the search for forms of everyday life, customs of the common people, settlement patterns, food, and political, social and economic relations between different Maya cities, based on important interdisciplinary projects.

On the other hand, some historians have begun to study Maya religion for itself, as a independent cultural phenomenon and not as a "reflection" of political or other interests, based on methodological perspectives from the science of religions, leaving behind interpretations of religions that had been employed in archaeology and other disciplines. Furthermore, Maya astronomy and mathematics have begun to be studied from the perspective of astronomy and mathematics as a science, and not solely from the viewpoint of archaeology. Thus, in a little more than three decades, the reigning idealized and partial image of Maya culture has been substantially modified.

Nevertheless, in some cases the antithesis has occurred. That is to say, the balance of archaeological research and Maya epigraphic studies has leaned heavily toward the political and economic life of the people, often overlooking the religious and scientific interests of the Mayas. Today some see the Maya merely as men guided by a zeal for political power and aggrandizement of their lineage; solely concerned with writing their own history; solely as warriors and merchants. In light of these interpretations, the same Maya cities, codices, symbols, myths, astronomical records, and inscriptions clearly demonstrate that this position is just as partial as the other one, which considered them lofty, spiritual beings. Both notions of the Maya are clearly reductionist.

The very same epigraphic research has shown us that the major subjects about which the Maya wrote, in addition to their own history, were their basic myths and astronomical knowledge, which were all intimately interrelated. The fact that myths and astronomy were always linked to the history of man is corroborated by advances in other disciplines. Thus it may be said that the Maya based their entire culture on a religious conception of the world and of life; that they were great politicians, warriors and merchants, at the same time that they were wise astronomers and mathematicians; and that all this knowledge, in addition to their cosmogonic and cosmological conceptions, guided the construction of their cities.

All this evidence confirms that the Maya were a profoundly religious people of exceptional spirituality and great artistic sensitivity, not with standing their wars, their economic concerns, the zeal for domination and the egolatry of their rulers. They possessed an original humanism that is the foundation of all their creations. To achieve a true understanding of the Maya and all aspects of their culture, it is necessary to begin with the fundamental principle that they created a conception of the cosmos as a unity in which the gods, world and man were not separate spheres, but rather profoundly connected.

The Mayas in Europe at the end of the twentieth century

The great exhibition on the art of the ancient Maya presented by the Palazzo Grassi is the first time extraordinary works of the ancient Maya from all periods and all regions of the culture area have been assembled together under the same roof. Exceptional works have been gathered from museums in Mexico, Guatemala, Belize, Honduras, El Salvador, the United States, Germany, Holland and England, which will offer one of the most comprehensive images that the western world has ever had of the great cultural legacy of the Mayas.

Among the nearly six hundred pieces in the exhibition, there are outstanding works in stone, such as monumental lintels, stelae, sculptures, and thrones. Smaller-scale works include minor sculptures, modeled stucco, clay figurines of an exceptional caliber such as those from the island of Jaina, exquisite jades and items worked in shell and bone with naturalistic and symbolic motifs, metal objects, a wide variety of ceramics, textiles, and the noble stucco found beneath the sarcophagus of one of Pacal of Palenque.

It must be emphasized that these extraordinary objects were not created as a luxury or as a decoration for temples and palaces. Nor should Maya art be considered a mere reflection of religious, social and political ideas, since art was essentially imbued with religious significance, and often even served a practical end. Many works were recipients of divine energy because it was believed that the gods and the ancestors who had acquired a sacred nature upon death were embodied in these images during rituals. Gods and ancestors received the food essential for their existence through these images.

Works of art were also intended to show people the power of the gods and of men in whom they had deposited a portion of their sacredness, giving them the right to govern others; they sought to represent the grandeur of their illustrious lineages to guarantee their positions of power. Therefore, rulers always represented themselves accompanied by the gods, whose images appear on their accoutrements and attributes of power.

Thus, although Maya art has an obvious political character reinforced by accompanying inscriptions, it is primarily religious in all periods and throughout the Maya area, as evidenced by the predominance of religious symbols (including those that express political power because almost all of them are figures of gods). It may be said that the majority of forms, images, and allegories of Maya art are symbolic. However, at some sites, such as Palenque, the body, expression, and poses of man are naturalistically represented. The image of man is charged with a significance that goes beyond his appearance and is manifested in the accoutrements and objects that are held in the symbolic context in which they appear. These symbols are mainly religious; they seek to express the inexpressible, the coded message, what cannot be apprehended by the senses.

In this way, the central purpose of Maya art seems to be extra-artistic and the meaning that it has for the community is not to evoke an aesthetic response, but rather a religious feeling and a fear and veneration for powerful men. Nevertheless, this does not mean the art lacked historical and political significance or aesthetic value. We cannot ignore the creative freedom in Maya works that shaped the aesthetic joy of the artist—the fantasy and new modes of expression. The Maya artist always sought new forms (including written signs), and this is precisely the aesthetic element that makes these material works of the Maya more than mere documents of the society that created them; they are works of art with an intrinsic value. The mysterious amalgamation that is produced between the aesthetic and the mystical was characteristic not only of Maya art, but rather of all artistic creations of ancient cultures.

The essays in this catalogue reflects the multiple paths taken by current research on Maya culture, both in subjects, and in approaches and perspectives. The articles are written by renowned Mayanists from different countries, including archaeologists, anthropologists, epigraphers and historians. Thus, the catalogue gives us a complete overview of Maya culture and history, a general panorama of the creations of this great civilization and of the ideas on which it was based.

The twenty-eight essays cover very different subjects: Ian Graham presents a general survey of archaeological exploration in the Maya area from the arrival of the Spaniards to the Yucatán peninsula in 1511 until the twentieth century. Among these general works is an essay by Arturo Gómez Pompa, who offers a specialized study of vegetation in the Maya region as well as knowledge of its geographic characteristics, while Jeremy Sabloff discusses pre-Hispanic Maya history, from its origins to the Spanish conquest. Tomás Pérez deals with the relations between the Mayas and other Mesoamerican groups, notably the Olmecs.

Giuseppe Orefici describes Maya frontiers, and Enrique Nalda analyzes the Maya city, underscoring its great variety. After describing different cities, such as Tikal, Lamanai, El Mirador, Calakmul, Copán, Sayil, Kohunlich, Dzibanché, Chichén Itzá and Mayapán, he proposes abandoning the traditional definition of the city, to celebrate the diversity of Maya culture. Antonio Benavides, in turn, deals with establishing what an architectonic style is, and he defines the different styles that developed in the Maya region.

These are followed by an essay by Mario Ruz on the current trend to shed light on the daily life of the Mayas. He discusses the activities of the lower strata of Maya society: peasants, farmers and fishermen, presenting "a brief overview of the subsistence activities" of Maya society in general.

Among the most notable cultural creations of the ancient Mayas covered in the catalogue are writing, religion, historiography, astronomy, calendars, and visual arts–sculpture, painting, ceramics. All of these articles provide valuable background information.

Maricela Ayala offers a general vision of Maya writing and the history of its decipherment. Then Victoria and Harvey Bricker develops the outstanding theme of calendrical cycles and astronomy, emphasizing the fundamental fact that this was not an isolated activity, but rather one directly related to religion, the government, warfare, and historical records.

Thomas Lee Whiting surveys Maya codices, and Enrique Florescano and Mercedes de la Garza present two fundamental aspects of Maya religion that display the conception of the world and the life that sustained the entire Maya creation: the cosmogony and the gods.

Clemency Chase Coggins speaks of Maya art in general, although she emphasizes the importance of small-scale objects and interprets their symbolism.

Dorie Reents-Budet analyzes the functions and importance of the extraordinary painted Maya ceramics from the Classic period, in which there are religious, social and historical themes, which convert this body of work into a historical document of primary importance, beyond its obvious aesthetic value.

Merle Greene Robertson also covers the subject of Maya art, focusing on sculpture and murals of the Usumacinta region.

Other works refer to aspects of a single region of the Maya area. Zoila Rodríguez Girón and Héctor Paredes describe the geography and the first inhabitants and offer a synthesis of the history of the highlands of Guatemala and Chiapas. David Stuart, after mentioning the beginning of the historical focus in Maya epigraphy, presents the dynastic and political history of the Classic period Maya, based on current advances in this science, to reveal new insight into Maya politics. He identifies Maya inscriptions primarily as historical and political documents. Héctor Escobedo and Juan Antonio Valdés deal with the history of the central lowlands (Belize and the Petén), based on archaeological discoveries. Several articles also focus on a single city, such as Copán, discussed by Ricardo Agurcia Fasquelle; Calakmul by Ramón Carrasco; Jaina by Román Piña Chán; Uxmal by Jeff Kowalski; and Chichén Itzá by Peter Schmidt. These articles exemplify the variety and richness of the Mayas in the creation of their cities.

Other articles focus mainly on the Postclassic period. Rocío González de la Mata and Anthony Andrews discuss navigation and trade in the Yucatán peninsula, and Sergio Quezada describes the political organization of the Yucatecan Maya of the eleventh to sixteenth centuries. These are followed by an article by Grant Jones on the Spanish conquest of the Mayas of Yucatán, and the catalogue ends with a work by Jan de Vos on contemporary Maya-speaking groups in Chiapas and Guatemala.

The great exhibition on the visual arts of the ancient Maya in Venice will present in Europe one of the most brilliant and creative cultures of antiquity, one that has awaken the interest and admiration not only of specialists, but also of all those who seek to know more about the life and creations of men of the past.

A Brief History of Archaeological Exploration

The first Europeans to make contact with the Maya were survivors of a Spanish caravel, shipwrecked near Jamaica in the year 1511. Of the few who reached the east coast of Yucatán, two managed to gain acceptance by the Maya; the others perished. Of those two, one would later be summoned by Hernán Cortés to serve as interpreter, but it was the other, Gonzalo de Guerrero, who must have had the more interesting tales to tell, since he had integrated himself fully into Maya village life.

It is history's loss that when emissaries of the titular Governor of Yucatán, Francisco de Montejo, made contact with him nine years later, his new loyalties prevented him from rejoining the Spaniards. If only he had been willing to tell of his experiences as an acculturated Maya! He is still remembered, though, for in Chetumal, close to where he settled, he is the central figure of an enormous public monument celebrating *mestizaje*–racial mixture.

In 1518, Juan de Grijalva, sailing along the same coast, perceived with wonder "a city or town so large, that Seville would not have seemed more considerable or better; one saw there a very large tower . . . [and] the same day we came to a beach near which was the highest tower we had seen." This may have been Tulum, which has once again become a populous place–although now a carefully preserved ancient city within a defensive wall, surrounded by a pullulating tourist town. But if Grijalva's comparison with Seville was exaggerated, it may well be ascribed to his wonder that an assemblage of stone buildings of any kind should exist in that land. If this surprised him, then he would have been truly astonished by an ancient city extending over about 9 square kilometers that can be found 40 kilometers inland from Tulum–just too far for its immensely tall pyramids to be discerned from the sea. The American traveler John Lloyd Stephens heard of and wanted to visit these ruins in 1840, but feared that his shoe leather would not survive the long walk. As it was, this city, Cobá, would not be described in any detail until the 1920s, largely because the Maya uprising known as the War of the Castes discouraged travelers from penetrating into that part of the peninsula.

The Maya built no really large Maya city, in fact, on the east coast of Yucatán, in spite of their active coastal trading before the Conquest; perhaps they avoided doing so out of fear of seeing Venus as morning star arising out of the sea–it was a sight that sent anyone unlucky enough to witness it running for shelter.

In 1531, only a few years after Grijalva's visit, the Spaniards for the first time came upon a vast, abandoned ancient city; this was Chichén Itzá. Francisco de Montejo, son of the provincial governor of the same name, occupied it, established a garrison there, and bestowed on it a grandiose name, Ciudad Real. But soon the initial, if reluctant, cooperation of the Cupul ruler ended in attempted murder of Montejo. The Royal City was besieged by the Maya, and the Spaniards only succeeded in escaping thanks to a ruse involving a hungry dog tied just out of reach of food by a cord attached to the clapper of a bell. The constant ringing of the bell was interpreted by the Maya as a sign of preparations for an attack on them; instead, the Spaniards were stealing away under cover of darkness.

Spanish attempts to subdue Yucatán ended in complete withdrawal from the peninsula in 1534; but in 1540 Montejo the younger returned and within six years the conquest was brought to a successful conclusion. Twenty years later a Spanish bishop, Diego de Landa, was at work preparing his *Relación de las cosas de Yucatán*, an ethnography of the Yucatec Maya, now regarded as a work of the highest importance.

Even before Yucatán had at last been subdued, the Spaniards had Chiapas, Guatemala, and Honduras under their control. Columbus himself had landed in Honduras in 1502, and permanent Spanish settlement in that province began there twenty years later, although not without provoking native uprisings for many years. Today, the single justly celebrated ruined city in Honduras is Copán, and it happens that the earliest surviving description of this site is also more accurate than any other of Maya ruins that would be written for over two hundred years. This was a report addressed to King Philip II in 1576 by Diego García de Palacio, chief judge of the Audiencia Real of Guatemala. "On the road [from Guatemala] to the city of San Pedro," he wrote, "in the first town within the province of Honduras, called Copán, are certain ruins and vestiges of a great population, and of superb edifices, of such skill and splendor that it appears they could never have been built by the natives of that province. They are found on the banks of a beautiful river in an extensive and well-chosen plain . . . On arriving . . . we come to ruins, and among them, stones sculptured with great skill; also a great statue,

Sylvanus G. Morley at Copán
Honduras, 1912

View of the Palace at Palenque
drawing by Antonio Bernasconi

more than four yards in height, which resembles a bishop in his pontifical robes with a well-wrought mitre and rings on his fingers. Near this is a well-built plaza or square with steps . . . In some places there are eighty steps, in part at least of fine stone, finished and laid with much skill. "In this square are six great statues, three representing men, covered with mosaic work and with garters round their legs, their weapons covered with ornaments; two of the others are of women with long robes and headdress in the Roman style. The remaining statue is of a bishop, who appears to hold in his hand a box or small coffer. They seem to have been idols, for in front of each of them is a large stone with a small basin and a channel cut in it, where they executed the victim and the blood flowed off." He then describes the acropolis, mentioning that "on one side of this structure is a tower or terrace, very high, and overhanging the river which flows at its base. Here a large piece of the wall has fallen, exposing the entrance of two caves or passages extending under the structure, very long and narrow, and well built . . ." This description holds good today, except that the river has now been diverted.

A third great ruined city, Uxmal, was also ably described in the sixteenth century by the writer Antonio de Ciudad Real, secretary to the Franciscan Padre Alonso Ponce, who visited ruins together with him in 1588. His description, while shorter, is at least as detailed as that of García de Palacio's of Copán, for he describes corbel-vaulted roofs, and even cord-holders in doorjambs for securing curtains across them. He and the Padre also visited Chichén Itzá, inspecting the *cenote*, or Well of Sacrifice.

From then until the end of the eighteenth century, there is scarcely a mention to be found in print or manuscript of the great ruins of antiquity. For this silence, perhaps the Inquisition and the fearful narrow-mindedness it engendered may be held responsible.

With the accession to the Spanish throne of Carlos III in 1759, more liberal attitudes began to prevail, and officials in New Spain were even encouraged to examine and report on pre-Conquest remains. So it came about that in 1770 Ramón Ordoñez y Aguiar, a canon of the cathedral of Ciudad Real (now San Cristóbal de las Casas), whose great-uncle had told him of ruins in the jungle about fifty years earlier, persuaded the mayor and other officials to look for the ruins; and finally a report reached Guatemala (Chiapas then being part of Guatemala). As a result, Antonio Bernasconi, an Italian architect living in Guatemala, was sent in 1784 to examine this city, which we now call Palenque. His drawings, while neatly executed, are quite naive, as is the accompanying report. Over the next forty-odd years there followed other travelers with widely varying abilities, such as Almendáriz, del Río, Castañeda, Dupaix, Waldeck, and Caddy. We notice at once a change here: two names that suggest non-Spanish origins. The independence achieved by Mexico and Central America had of course opened their borders to all comers. (Earlier, there had been one great exception, Alexander von Humboldt,

Las Ventanas, Copán, Honduras
watercolor by Juan Galindo
This image shows the acropolis
a section of which had fallen
undermined by the river at its foot
Two ancient passage ways appeared
as *ventanas*

Colonel Juan Galindo

whose friendship with the Spanish prime minister enabled him to explore South America and Mexico between 1799 and 1804. His great 1810 book, *Vue des cordillères et monuments des peuples indigènes de l'Amérique*, even contains a drawing of a Palenque relief that he had been given, although wrongly described as coming from Oaxaca.)

In Europe, at the beginning of the nineteenth century, the public's interest in archaeology, and of course that of scholars, too, was greatly stimulated by the French expedition to Egypt led by Denon, and the discovery of the Rosetta Stone. So with peace re-established after the Battle of Waterloo in 1815, and railways and steamships beginning to make travel so much easier and more dependable, the growing middle classes began to visit distant lands and their ruins as never before. Responding to this burgeoning of interest in foreign countries and exotic ruins, the Société de Géographie de Paris was founded in 1821, and nine years later, the Royal Geographical Society.

A notice that the Société was offering medals for exploration reached a dashing if somewhat erratic Englishman with a Spanish grandfather, John Galindo. In 1827, when aged 25, he settled in Guatemala (thereafter calling himself Juan), and only four years later was appointed governor of Petén, Guatemala's northern province. The interest in archaeology that he soon displayed may have owed something to hopes of a medal, for he lost no time in visiting Palenque and a much smaller site in Petén, Topoxté, and promptly sent reports on them to Paris. Then when the man originally commissioned by the government of Central America to report on Copán resigned from the task for fear of "the Asiatic *cholera morbus*," Galindo eagerly stepped in, and spent four weeks at the ruins. His site plan and drawings, some of them quite creditable, were the first ever made of the site. Full of hope, and anxious to achieve fame, he sent copies of these to the Société, which printed his text, although inexplicably not the drawings. Nevertheless, he was awarded a silver medal.

Then in 1838 the Société offered a gold medal for the best work on Palenque. Unfortunately Galindo was no longer free to revisit the ruins, but a second silver medal, awarded him for contributions to geography, may have assuaged his frustration. He was then recalled for military duty when the Central American Federation collapsed, and lost his life in the campaign. Because Galindo's contributions to knowledge were so long neglected, he had little impact on Maya studies, but he should be remembered for having been perhaps the first to comment on the close similarity in physiognomy between contemporary Mayas and the sculptured or modeled heads at Palenque; and for his opinion that hieroglyphic writing was a uniquely Maya achievement.

Then at last, in 1840, came John Lloyd Stephens, the travel writer and diplomat, and his collaborating artist, Frederick Catherwood–two immortals in the history of Maya studies. The

View of the Ruins of Uxmal, Yucatán
Lithograph
by Frederick Catherwood, 1844

first site they explored was Copán (which possibly they knew of from Galindo's briefer reports that were published in London and New York), and from Copán they progressed in a great semicircle, passing through Chiapas and ending in Yucatán.

Stephens was a lawyer, presumably well versed in the rules of evidence, and skeptical about mythical histories concerning the Maya. His wide experience of life and of travel, combined with a sense of humor, allowed him to write a far more sensible, interesting, and sprightly narrative than any predecessor–or, for that matter, successor!

Catherwood for his part contributed drawings of unprecedented accuracy, and in their later lithographic form, great beauty. As an architect, he had acquired professional skill at free-hand drawing and at rendering landscapes and figures. In addition, however, he was equipped with a recent invention, the *camera lucida*–a little prism mounted on an adjustable arm attached to the drawing board. Applying his eye to this, Catherwood could see a reflection of the scene he was drawing superimposed upon the drawing board, and so could trace its outlines accurately. Stephens produced two books incorporating Catherwood's numerous illustrations: *Incidents of Travel in Central America, Chiapas and Yucatán* (1841), and two years later, after further explorations in the peninsula, *Incidents of Travel in Yucatán*. Besides describing and illustrating many ruined cities far better than ever before, these books were the first to present previously unknown ruins, among them Kabah. Both works were translated into other languages, enjoyed huge success, and had immense influence in raising interest in the Maya, something that had scarcely existed before.

From then on, the progress of exploration and discovery was to some extent determined by conflicting influences: on the one hand, a protoarchaeological enthusiasm was growing in Europe and North America, and to some extent in Mexico, while on the other, independence in both Mexico and Guatemala was bringing in its wake episodes of armed conflict, which even in some remote Maya regions could deter or impede travel. Thus, the War of the Castes in Yucatán in 1847 made it dangerous to venture into the central and eastern portions of the peninsula until the end of the century.

In spite of this, the photographer and writer Désiré Charnay, commissioned by the French government, courageously visited Chichén Itzá in 1861, complete with giant camera and darkroom tent; as did the picturesque and eccentric Augustus Le Plongeon, who used his much smaller camera to good effect, excavated the largest and finest *Chac Mool* sculpture (successfully concealing its exact provenance), and became a fertile source of fantastical in-

Palacio n. 1 at Tikal, Guatemala
drawing by Eusebio Lara, 1848
London, courtesy of The Society
of Antiquaries

The Tower of Palenque
photographed
by Alfred Maudslay after clearing
the Western Court in 1891
London, courtesy
of The Museum of Mankind

terpretations of Chichén Itzá's past. Life in Guatemala was not always peaceful, either; strife broke out several times in the nineteenth century. But the area referred to as the central Maya lowlands, the heartland where in the Classic period art and architecture reached its zenith, remained unaffected, simply because it was sparsely occupied and of no political importance. Most of this area lay within the Guatemalan district (now department) of Petén, the central portion of which, surrounding Lake Petén Itzá, was only brought under Spanish dominion in 1697. The old Itzá stronghold on an island in that lake, now Flores, was then used mainly as a prison for criminals and political exiles until Guatemala gained its independence in 1821. The remainder of the district was populated by scattered settlements of Itzá, Lacandon, and Mopan Maya, while the only link between Flores and Guatemala City was a muddy track, which under good conditions took ten to fifteenth days to traverse.

It was one of Galindo's successors as governor, Ambrosio Tut (or perhaps Tutz), an Itzá Maya from the lakeside village of San Andrés, who followed up rumors of great ruins lying to the north of Flores, at a distance of two or three days' walk. That he ever heard about those distant ruins was apparently owing to the fact that, not long before, a few families of Itzá (or perhaps Lacandon) Maya had settled near the ruins, though after a time they were obliged to abandon the place because the pond had dried up.

After a brief visit of inspection, the Governor enlisted the help of Modesto Méndez, the *corregidor* (or mayor) for a second expedition, and they engaged Eusebio Lara, who can charitably be described as the expedition's artist. The report written by Méndez and illustrated with Lara's drawings was eventually published in a German geographical journal. More than thirty years would pass, however, before that report would inspire a more competent person to set out for Tikal and examine the ruins more thoroughly. Photography is an important tool in the preliminary exploration of archaeological sites. On their second visit to Yucatán, Stephens and Catherwood were quick to employ the newly invented Daguerreotype, albeit with limited success.

From about 1855 until 1880 expeditionary photographers used the collodion wet plate, despite the appalling difficulty of coating and sensitizing the plates in a dark tent immediately before taking the photograph; the even greater inconvenience of this procedure in a tropical jungle can well be imagined. So the introduction in the late 1870s of dry plates, close cousins of modern photographic film, came as a great boon.

It was by a fortunate series of events, then, that the new dry plates became available just as

Alfred Maudslay at Chichén Itzá
Yucatán, 1889, detail from
a photograph by Henry N. Sweet

two extremely able and determined individuals entered the field just at a time when Guatemala and Mexico (still excepting the east coast of Yucatán) were experiencing tranquility. Another fortunate development was the patronage eventually extended to one of them by a university museum.

The two men were Alfred Maudslay and Teobert Maler. Maudslay, born in 1850, was eight years younger than Maler, but he entered the field of Maya research first. One of five sons of a very prosperous marine engine manufacturer, he graduated from Cambridge University with a degree in natural science. At the age of 30, having gained experience of administration in the South Pacific, he decided to visit Central America to see the ruins of Copán and Quiriguá, having been recommended to do so by a well-traveled British naturalist. Maudslay's epiphany came when, having pulled a mat of moss from a fallen stela at Quiriguá, an intricate hieroglyphic inscription came to light.

Almost certainly, Maudslay already had archaeological exploration in mind before he left for Guatemala, and therefore paid close attention when a fellow passenger on the Atlantic crossing told him about ruins lately found north of Flores. So on leaving Quiriguá, he greatly expanded his original itinerary, and set out on the long ride up to Flores, where local men were recruited to help him at Tikal. On arrival, the men set to work with axes, felling the heavy growth of forest trees so that Maudslay could survey the principal structures and take photographs. These he developed in the vaulted Maya chamber he had chosen for his sleeping quarters, since he could not gamble on the plates having received the proper exposure. On succeeding expeditions Maudslay sometimes brought with him from England a professional plaster worker, whose job was to make plaster or papier-maché molds of the sculpture. On return to London, casts would be taken, and artists were engaged to make drawings of them for publication.

Maudslay mounted expeditions to many of the most famous sites: Copán, Quiriguá, Tikal, Yaxchilán, Palenque, and Chichén Itzá, and a century after their publication, the large volumes of photographs, plans, and drawings that resulted from his expeditions remain an essential reference work for Mayanists. As the first scientifically trained explorer of the Maya area, he is honored alike for the quality of his work and for his refusal to elaborate grand historical scenarios at a time when reliable data were few.

Teobert Maler, born in Rome to parents from Baden, Germany, received some training in architecture, but rather than follow that career he chose to join an Austrian corps of volunteers for service in Mexico in support of Emperor Maximilian. After the emperor's execution, he lingered in Mexico for eleven years, traveling widely. During a visit to Palenque in 1877 he thought he had discovered the Temple of the Foliated Cross; in fact, an unpublished drawing of it had been made ninety years earlier, but the illusion of discovery may have helped sway him toward a career of archaeological exploration.

After his father's death, Maler returned to Germany in an attempt to disentangle his inheritance. A few years later, in 1885, he returned to Mexico, but this time to Yucatán, where he spent the rest of his life. For the next 10 years he was occupied in exploring the Peninsula for ruins, recording them both photographically and in measured plans. Cobá he visited briefly, and then in 1895 embarked on a grueling journey through the jungle as far as Flores, Petén. From there he went on to Sayaxché to visit the almost unknown ruins of Ceibal, then headed for home by canoe down the Río de la Pasión and the Usumacinta as far as the rapids permit; then overland to catch a steamer back to Yucatán.

In the course of this 1,500 kilometer journey he discovered the ruins of Motul de San José, near Lake Petén, took the first photographs of the splendid stelae at Ceibal, and discovered a site of the greatest importance, Piedras Negras. The university museum cited above was the Peabody Museum of Harvard University. In the 1890s, Frederick W. Putnam, its director, suspected, or at least hoped, that the isolated and unconverted Lacandon Maya living in the lowland forests of eastern Chiapas might retain some knowledge of Maya hieroglyphic writing. After an unsuccessful attempt to persuade a linguist to make contact with them, it was decided that a graduate student, Alfred Tozzer, should be trained for the task.

Tozzer was to spend the first years of this century among the Lacandons, producing a valuable ethnographic study on their culture (now virtually lost), and a comparison of it with Landa's account of sixteenth-century Yucatec Mayas. But Maler, who had evidently been

Captain Teobert Maler, about 1866

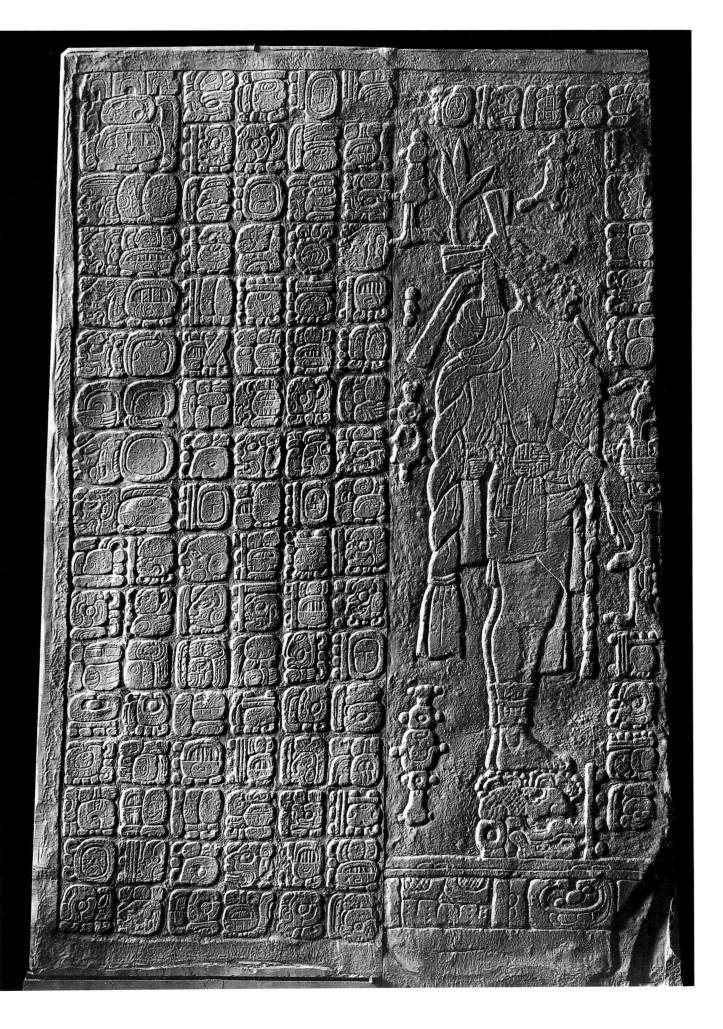

Leader of a Lacandon group
in ceremonial bark-cloth robe
photograph
taken by Alfred Tozzer in 1903

considered unsuitable for that mission, was engaged by the museum to search for ruins on the Chiapas side of the Usumacinta. He did find some of minor importance, but the really valuable work he did was in photographing those sculptures at Yaxchilán that Maudslay had missed, the splendid stelae of Piedras Negras and Ceibal, and those of three important sites in eastern Petén–Yaxhá, Naranjo, and Tikal.

Maler's work for the Peabody Museum inaugurated a period of institutional backing for exploration. Similar work involving small teams would soon be resumed under the aegis of a different patron, the Carnegie Institution of Washington. Through the skillful petitioning of Sylvanus Morley, the Carnegie provided a large annual budget to Maya research until 1958, much of it, certainly, for excavation and consolidation of already-discovered ruins, but many expeditions in search of new ruins were mounted between 1914 and 1934. The majority of these were confined to the northeastern quandrant of Petén, where many sites, among them Uaxactún, were found, but the very last expedition focused on southern Quintana Roo–the War of the Castes having ended before World War I.

Led by Karl Ruppert, this was notable for the several discoveries, including that of one of the largest of all Maya cities, Calakmul, and for the precision with which it and other sites were located. Traditional celestial navigation was used, with one important refinement: in order to obtain accuracy in longitude a shortwave radio was brought for picking up time signals from Washington.

In 1946, a *chiclero* who had found ruins in the Lacandon forest led two young Americans to the site, where they found a splendid stela. Hearing of their discovery, Giles Healey, a photographer keenly interested in archaeology, soon followed them, and it was he who first saw the building containing three chambers embellished with mural paintings–or more accurately, he was the first outsider to see it, because of course the Lacandons had long known it. With INAH's permission, the Carnegie Institution quickly mounted an expedition to record the murals, bringing in the Guatemalan artist Antonio Tejeda to make watercolor copies of them, and to record the site itself, now known as Bonampak.

After the Carnegie ended its patronage of Maya research, further archaeological exploration of Petén was carried out on a small scale by the author, who found several important sites in areas not entered by the Carnegie expeditions, that is, in northwestern and southern Petén. Undoubtedly others remain to be discovered.

References

CATHERWOOD, FREDERICK
1844
Views of ancient monuments in Central America, Chiapas and Yucatan. London

CHAMBERLAIN S., ROBERT
1948
The conquest and colonization of Yucatan. Publication 582. Washington, D.C.: Carnegie Institution of Washington

CHARNAY, CLAUDE-JOSEPH-DÉSIRÉ
1863
Cités et ruines américaines. Paris

GRAHAM, IAN
1967
Archaeological explorations in the Department of Petén, Guatemala. Middle American Research Institute. Publication 33. New Orleans: Tulane University
1977
"Alfred Maudslay and the discovery of the Maya." In *Collectors and collections*. London: The British Museum Yearbook 2
1997
"Teobert Maler–eine Lebensskizze." In *Peninsula Yucatan von Teobert Maler*. Ed. by H.J. Prem. Monumenta Americana 5. Berlin: Gebr. Mann Verlag

HUMBOLDT, ALEXANDER VON
1810
Vue des cordillères et monuments des peuples indigènes de l'Amérique. Paris

LANDA, DIEGO DE
1941
Relación de las cosas de Yucatán. With notes by A.M. Tozzer. Cambridge, Mass.: Peabody Museum Papers 28

MALER, TEOBERT
1901–10
Various titles in Memoirs of the Peabody Museum of Archaeology and Ethnology. Vols. 2 and 4, Cambridge, Mass.

MAUDSLAY, ALFRED P.
1889–1902
Biologia Centrali–Americana: Archaeology. 5 Vols., London

MORLEY, SYLVANUS G.
1920
Inscriptions at Copán. Publication 219. Washington, D.C.: Carnegie Institution of Washington
1946
The Ancient Maya. California: Stanford University Press

Relación
1872
"Relación de las cosas que sucedieron al Padre Fray Alonso Ponce." In *Colección de documentos inéditos para la historia de España*. Vols. 57–58, Madrid

RITTER, C.
1853
"Über neue Entdeckungen und Beobachtungen in Guatemala und Yucatan." In *Zeitschrift für Allgemeine Erdkunde*. Berlin, 161–93

RUPPERT, KARL, JOHN H. DENISON
1943
Archaelogical Reconnaissance in Campeche, Quintana Roo and Peten. Publication 543. Washington, D.C.: Carnegie Institution of Washington

RUPPERT, KARL, J.E.S. THOMPSON, AND TATIANA PROSKOURIAKOFF
1955
Bonampak, Chiapas, Mexico. Publication 602. Washington, D.C.: Carnegie Institution of Washington

STEPHENS, JOHN LLOYD
1996
Incidents of Travel in Yucatan. Washington, D.C.: Smithsonian Institution Press

TOZZER, ALFRED M.
1907
A Comparative Study of the Mayas and the Lacandones. New York

Vegetation of the Maya Region

Anthropomorphic figurine
emerging
from a flower showing
a large bract of *Philodendrum* sp.
Classic period
Mexico City
Museo Nacional de Antropología
cat. 300

The Maya have occupied and continue to occupy an area of Mesoamerica spanning the peninsula of Yucatán, the states of Campeche, Tabasco, and Chiapas in Mexico, the entire territory of Belize and Guatemala, and the western portions of Honduras and El Salvador. In this territorial extension we find great biological and ecological diversity, the product of different geological, climatic, edaphic, evolutionary, biogeochemical, and cultural processes. These ecological processes, interacting among themselves and through time, have molded the different environments and types of vegetation that characterize the region.

In the Maya zone we can identify two main geographic areas: the hot lowlands and the temperate or cold mountainous zones of Chiapas, Guatemala, and Honduras. The lowlands are characterized by a hot climate, with average temperatures above 18°C in the coldest month. In these areas, the environmental factors that have the greatest influence on the distribution of vegetation are rainfall and soil. In those areas with long periods of drought–the northwest of the Yucatán peninsula and the Chiapanec central depression–vegetation types with abundant xerophyllic species may be seen. In contrast, in the low zones with high rainfall and without a dry season, we find exuberant evergreen forests.

In the highest altitudes, in addition to variations in the quantity and distribution of rainfall during the year, we have different gradients in temperature. Thus, we find a gradient ranging from semicold climates at the highest mountains of the region (Tacaná volcano at an altitude of 4,030 meters), with average temperatures between 5 and 12°C, to semihot climates, with average temperatures above 18°C and the coldest month less than 18°C, bordering the hot lowlands.

Soil is a fundamental factor in the presence and abundance of different species that form distinctive types of vegetation. Edaphic characteristics explain many of the local patterns of species distribution within a given type of vegetation or even the presence of different types in the same climate. Soil in turn is influenced by topography, type of bedrock, and land use. The ecological mosaics so common in the different landscapes of the Maya zone are mainly caused by edaphic mosaics.

Two major types of soils are important in defining different types of vegetation: soils that are subject to inundation and those that are not. Soils not subject to inundation may be permanent or seasonal. The seasonality of flooding is a fundamental factor for many species, the presence or absence of which is linked to time of year in which they are flooded or even to the frequency of floods throughout the years. This variable gives us different types of vegetation in zones subject to inundation in different climates and in different soils.

There are other climatic factors important to an understanding of the ecological diversity of the Maya zone. One of the most notable yet little appreciated factors has been hurricanes. We know that these atmospheric phenomena periodically lash the Caribbean coasts and often have a spectacular effect on vegetation. The presence and frequency of hurricanes has had a lot to do with ecological dynamics (regeneration following the hurricane) and biological structure (species or ecotypes present) of vegetation in the east of the Maya region.

The Maya zone also has great geological diversity. The following groups of rocks have

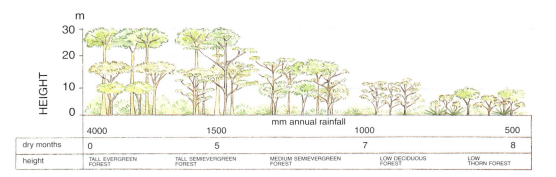

	4000	1500		1000	500
dry months	0	5		7	8
height	TALL EVERGREEN FOREST	TALL SEMIEVERGREEN FOREST	MEDIUM SEMIEVERGREEN FOREST	LOW DECIDUOUS FOREST	LOW THORN FOREST

Types of vegetation in the Maya zone

Cenote

been reported in the region – limestone, igneous, metamorphic, and sedimentary. Limestones are notable in the Yucatán peninsula, where they form a single flat platform, virtually without elevation except for the so-called Ticul Hills, which reach some 275 meters in altitude to the north. To the south of the Maya zone we find large areas in the low zones of Chiapas and Guatemala with limestone rock where geological thrusts (mountain ranges) reach considerable heights.

An important area of this zone is covered by rocks of igneous origin in the central part of Chiapas, Guatemala, Honduras, and El Salvador. These rocks originated from ancient and recent volcanic activity. The so-called Sierra Maya of Belize is composed of a mountainous mass (up to 1,200 meters in altitude) of very ancient metamorphic rocks not found in any other zone of the peninsula. To the south of Chiapas, there are also important outcrops of metamorphic rocks. Sedimentary rocks of recent origin are found in a large portion of the state of Tabasco and in the coastal zones of the north of the Yucatán peninsula and the coasts of Chiapas and Guatemala.

A very important factor in the constitution of vegetation in the Maya zone has been human activity. The zone has been inhabited since little more than 10,000 years ago and came to be densely populated for several centuries during the so-called Classic period (A.D. 300–900). This continuous occupation through time has had a major impact on vegetation, given that it has been necessary to obtain the food to feed millions of inhabitants for several centuries. The main activities that had an impact on vegetation were agriculture and silviculture through which large areas of forest were transformed into cultivated fields and habitational zones.

The use of fire to clear and prepare soils for cultivation must have had a great influence on the evolution of many species and on the floristic composition of the natural vegetation (though this is difficult to prove because in this process many species of organisms

have become extinct). What we do know is that many surviving species are well adapted to the processes of disturbance and fire.

Natural ecosystems that we want to protect today from a new wave of human disturbances are, perhaps, precisely the product of disturbances of the recent or remote past. Ancient Maya silviculture has been an enigma; nevertheless research indicates that the trees of the ancient rain forests were the object of care, protection, and cultivation by the ancient Maya.

From them they obtained food, wood, medicine, and other products. These anthropogenic forests were the "protected areas" of antiquity and in them biological diversity was conserved. This means that the great biological diversity that exists in today's rain forests has been possible thanks to the protection and management of forests by the ancient Maya.

In this physical and cultural environment, complex diversity in types of vegetation developed, each one composed of innumerable combinations of species responding to different complexes of environmental gradients.

Forests

Forests are characterized by having few dominant tree species and few lianas. In the Maya zone, two main types of forest are known: pine-oak forests and deciduous forests of oak and sweetgum.

Pine-Oak Forests (Bosques de pino-encino) have been found with two different climatic zones: temperate, cold mountainous Guatemala and Chiapas and areas with poor soils or deficient drainage in the Maya lowlands. Temperate pine-oak forests are found in mountainous zones generally between 750 to 3,000 meters in altitude in Chiapas, Guatemala, and Honduras. These forests are dominated by *Pinus* and/or *Quercus* (pine

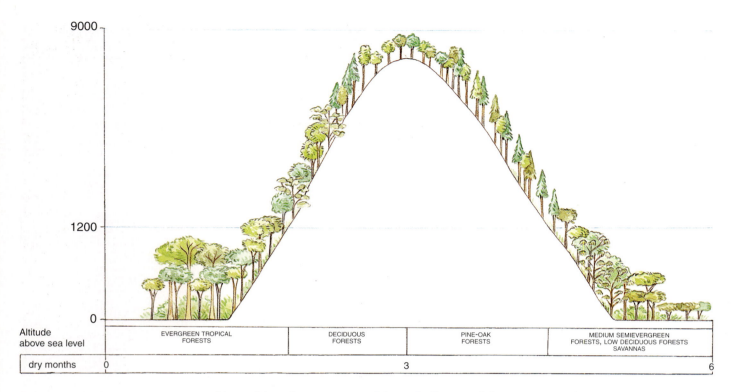

9000			
1200			
0			

Altitude above sea level	EVERGREEN TROPICAL FORESTS	DECIDUOUS FORESTS	PINE-OAK FORESTS	MEDIUM SEMIEVERGREEN FORESTS, LOW DECIDUOUS FORESTS SAVANNAS
dry months	0		3	6

Altitudinal gradient in the Maya zone

and/or oak) and accompanied by rich flora and fauna. For each altitudinal zone there are combinations of characteristic species: in the lowest parts (300 meters or less) in soils with poor drainage, pine stands of *Pinus oocarpa* with *Quercus oleoides* have been found.

At altitudes of 700 to 2,800 meters, forests are dominated by different species of pines (*Pinus strobus, Pinus pseudostrobus, Pinus tenuifolia, Pinus ayacahuite, Pinus teocote*) mixed with different species of oak (*Quercus*) and other temperate-climate genera. In the same areas we find forests dominated by oaks (*Quercus acatenanguensis, Quercus insignis, Quercus peduncularis*). In humid zones some oaks (*Quercus skinneri*) are mixed with sweetgum (*Liquidambar styraciflua*), forming large stands. In the highest parts above 2,800 meters, *Pinus hartwegii* and *Pinus rudis* dominate, frequently accompanied by *Abies guatemalensis* in humid escarpments.

In the coastal areas of Belize, *Pinus caribaea* woodlands are found occasionally mixed with oak woodlands and savanna. These forests occur in sandy soils with very little organic matter. In the south of Quintana Roo, a single large patch of this pine has been found. At somewhat higher altitudes in Belize (above 300 meters), pines of the species *Pinus caribaea* are often found in poor soils derived from metamorphic rocks. These form dense forested masses constituting a very interesting ecological mosaic with the tall tropical forests that live on limestone outcrops.

These low altitude pine stands are probable remnants of colder climates from the geological past, and from that time there are also other genera typical of temperate zones, such as *Quercus, Myrica, Ternstroemia*, and *Clethra* mixed with tropical genera such as *Byrsonima, Crescentia, Miconia*, and *Clusia*.

Oak stands in the Maya zone share an ecological parallel with pine forests, not only because they form part of them, but also because they constitute forests dominated by different species of *Quercus*. Generally oak stands occupy moist, humid sites and those with the best soils. They are found from sea level up to 3,000 meters in altitude in the highlands of Chiapas, Guatemala, and Honduras.

In the lower mountainous zones, between the high tropical and the temperate forests (between 700 and 1,200 meters above sea level) we can find cloud forests—sites often shrouded in mist. These are majestic forests that reach 40 meters in height and are characterized as deciduous because several of the dominant species lose their

The cloud forest

leaves in winter (*Liquidambar, Ulmus, Quercus*). They are very rich in species, both tropical as well as temperate ones and are noteworthy because about 60 percent of species are endemic, unique to the area. Some authors have considered these forests to be a relic of ancient flora that occupied large tracts of North America in the geological past.

Among the most notable genera, we can cite *Liquidambar, Persea, Quercus, Nyssa, Cornus, Carpinus, Clethra, Magnolia, Myrica, Ulmus,* and *Platanus*. This type of vegetation is found on the moist mountainous slopes of Chiapas and Guatemala, forming dense forests with an abundance of epiphytes and tree ferns that give the region a physiognomy of unequaled beauty.

On the peaks and slopes of humid mountains of eastern and northern Chiapas (at altitudes of 900 to 3,200 meters) is a forest with a large quantity of epiphytes, which has been called an evergreen cloud forest. This forest may be stunted on the peak and reach considerable sizes on the slopes. Among the notable genera that constitute this forest are *Abies, Ardisia, Brunellia, Chiranthodendron, Clethra, Clusia, Drimys, Magnolia, Meliosma, Oreopanax, Persea, Quercus, Turpinia, Weinmannia,* and *Wimmeria*.

Tropical Forests

This category includes a group of distinct vegetation types that share several common characteristics: warm climate, dominated by trees with abundant branching, high species numbers, and many vines and epiphytes.

The Tropical Evergreen Forests (Selvas Altas Perennifolias) are found in the best soils not subject to inundation of hot-humid zones. They are majestic communities of 30 or more meters in height, rich in vines, epiphytes, and with several shrub and tree strata. Just as in other tropical zones of the world, this type of vegetation is the richest in species in the Maya zone. In only one hectare of this forest in Chiapas, 267 different species of plants have been found.

This vegetation is found in the most humid region of the Maya zone, with average annual rainfall greater than 1,500 millimeters (even reaching 4 meters or more per year), and with no dry season at all or else a very brief one. On the Gulf slope it is found southwest of Campeche, Tabasco, north of Chiapas in Mexico, and in the Petén region of Guatemala. On the Pacific slope there is a strip between Mexico and Guatemala in the low parts of the mountainous region (the Sierra Madre of Chiapas, Tacaná volcano, and other mountainous zones of Guatemala), and on the Caribbean slope it is found in the south of Belize and north of Honduras.

There are several tree species that are common to almost all these forests. Among the most notable are: the *chicozapote* (*Manilkara achras*) tree is valued for its delicious fruit, its latex (the original chicle now largely displaced by synthetic products) and for its hardwood used by the ancient Maya for temple construction; the *ramón* (*Brosimum alicastrum*) produces seeds believed to be the ancient Maya's alternative to maize in times of scarcity. It must have been cultivated and protected in the past. Today the Maya continue protecting and planting this species in their orchards and in their fields left to fallow; the *canshán* or *sombrerete* (*Terminalia amazonia*) is one of the dominant species of the forests on the Gulf coast side of the Maya zone; on the Pacific slope of the Maya zone, it is replaced by *Terminalia oblonga*; the *guapaque* (*Dialium guianense*) is another species dominating the upper strata of these forests; the cacao (*Theobroma cacao*) is perhaps the most famous tree of the lower strata of these forests. The Maya and their predecessors appreciated the tasty pulp of its fruit and they discovered how to make chocolate from its seeds. They selected the best varieties among wild trees, and they achieved full domestication of this notable species.

Other important tree species include the *palo de agua* (*Vochysia guatemalensis*) with its beautiful yellow color in the flowering season; the *ceiba* or silk-cotton tree (*Ceiba pentandra*), the imposing sacred tree of the Mayas; the *caoba* (*Swietenia macrophylla*), widely appreciated for its beautiful wood; the majestic *sapote mamey* (*Pouteria sapota*) with its delectable edible fruit; the *amate, higueras* and *matapalos* (*Ficus* spp.) abundant in these forests; the *barí* (*Calophyllum brasiliense*) with its yellow latex; the *palo mulato*

Ceiba pentandra, a sacred tree of the Maya

height (m)

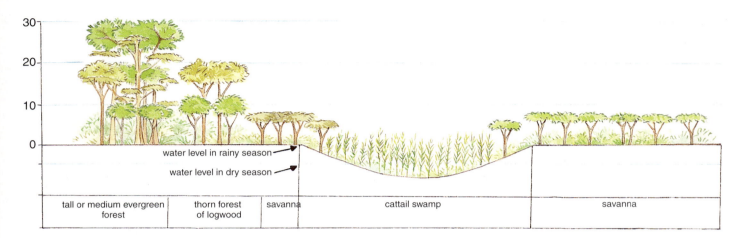

| water level in rainy season → | | | |
| water level in dry season → | | | |

| tall or medium evergreen forest | thorn forest of logwood | savanna | cattail swamp | savanna |

Vegetation on a soil moisture gradient

(*Bursera simaruba*) with its typical bright red bark; and several genera of Moraceae (*Pseudolmedia*, *Ficus*). In the lower strata of the humid forest, in addition to cacao, it is worth mentioning allspice (*Pimenta dioica*), with its smooth, yellowish trunk that produces *pimienta gorda*. Many other species abound, including palms (*Chamaedorea* spp.), Rubiaceae, Piperaceae, Myrtaceae, ferns, and grasses.

This type of forest is not found in drier regions, with the exception of very humid habitats known as *rejolladas* and *cenotes* (natural sink holes) to the north of the Yucatán peninsula.

Climbers are without doubt the most characteristic plants of these forests. Among them is the water vine (*Vitis* spp.), which carries crystal clear water from the roots to the foliage at the tops of tall trees; its stems are often cut by the explorers of these forests to quench their thirst. Also notable are the climbing species of the Bignoniaceae family, whose flowers give beautiful colors to the tops of trees on which they grow.

Epiphytes living on the branches of trees and shrubs are abundant. Among them are many species of Araceae (*Anthurium* spp., *Philodendrum* spp.), orchids (of many genera and species), bromeliads (*Aechmea*, *Tillandsia* spp.), cacti, ferns, Piperaceae, and even a rare species of *Yucca* (*Yucca lacandonica*).

Unfortunately, the flat, deep soils of these forests are the preferred sites for livestock raising and agriculture. Most of these forests in the Maya zone were converted to these uses in recent years, and many are now covered by secondary vegetation of different ages. The failure of commercial agriculture in these soils has been extensively studied. It is known to be the result of the rapid decomposition of organic matter after the forest is felled, caused by the rise of soil temperatures due to the removal of shade provided by the forest and the rapid accumulation of weeds and pests.

Apparently the ancient Maya managed to exploit these forests in three ways: transforming them into artificial forests rich in useful forest species; practicing agriculture imitating the structure of forests, as was the case of cacao plantations with shade trees; and imitating the natural process of forest regeneration, cultivating maize, beans, and squash mixed with many other useful species in totally exposed, deforested soils.

All ecosystems on earth have been and are being continually disturbed by environmental factors, both natural and man-made. Mature forests may be lashed by hurricanes, fires, or simply the death and decay of old trees. These disturbances set off natural processes of recovery or regeneration that consist of the rapid growth of a series of species (called secondary species), which were present but in latent form in the soil seed-bank of the forest.

These species constitute what is called secondary vegetation. The germination of seeds or propagules is stimulated by the increase in light and temperature. They grow rapidly, and soon they cover the soil, creating conditions propitious for other original species (called primary species) from seeds or propagules of undisturbed adjacent sites to grow and heal the ecological wound. This complex process has been studied and has been the key to understanding the regeneration of these forests.

Secondary species participating in this process are numerous, contributing to the enormous diversity of flora in these regions. Among them we find genera, domesticated by ancient ethnic groups of tropical America, that have played a very important role in the cultural development of the region, such as *Piper* (*acuyo*), *Cnidosculus* (*chaya mansa*), *Manihot* (*yuca* or *mandioca*), *Carica* (*papaya*), *Cordia* (*ciricote*), *Spondias* (*ciruelo*), *Cedrela* (*cedro rojo*), *Pithecellobium* (*huamuchil*). Other examples of secondary genera notable in the regeneration of tall forests are *Cecropia*, *Croton*, *Ochroma*, *Luehea*, *Acacia*, *Guazuma*, *Leucaena*, *Schizolobium*, *Casearia*, *Conostegia*, and many others.

The Tall or Medium Semievergreen Forests (Tropical Deciduous Forest, Semievergreen Tropical Forest–Selvas Altas o Medianas Subperennifolias) are found at sites with precipitation of more than 1,000 millimeters per year, but unlike tropical evergreen forests, they can survive with a dry season of three to five months. These forests are also found in the most humid zones, but in rocky soils (mainly limestone) with rapid drainage, or on hills. The distribution of these forests is very widespread. They are the dominant forests in the states of Quintana Roo and Campeche. They are found to the south of the state of Yucatán, in the north of Belize, and on the Pacific coast to the south of Chiapas, Guatemala, and El Salvador, bordering tall evergreen forests.

This type of vegetation is very similar to that of tall evergreen forests in its physiognomy, its biotic wealth, and its composition of flora and fauna. The dry season apparently limits the presence of some species; nevertheless many of the dominant species of tall evergreen forests continue to be the same in this type of forest, although they are often smaller in size, which is the case of the *chicozapote* or *ramón*, *caoba* (mahogany), and *palo mulato*. Nevertheless, in these forests other species may enter as dominant. Several of these species lose all or part of their foliage in the dry season, giving it the deciduous appearance characteristic of these forests.

In the Yucatán peninsula and Belize, we may mention as dominant the following: *Alseis yucatanensis*, *Brosimum alicastrum*, *Bucida buceras*, *Bursera simaruba*, *Enterolobium cyclocarpum*, *Lysiloma latisiliqua*, *Manilkara achras*, *Swietenia macrophylla*, *Tabebuia rosea*, *Talisia olivaeformis*, *Vitex glummer*, and *Zuelania guidonia*. On the Pacific slope of Chiapas and Guatemala, there are forests dominated by another group of species: *Bumelia persimilis*, *Ginoria nudiflora*, *Hura polyandra*, *Hymenaea courbaril*, *Mirandaceltis monoica*, *Poepigia procera*, and *Platymiscium dimorphandrum*.

These forests have been strongly modified by agricultural, livestock and forestry activities for more than 100 years.

A notable physiognomic variant of the forests is the so-called *palmares* (palm stands), which are communities dominated by palm species. Generally they are in moister soils and in frequently flooded areas along rivers. Nevertheless, their flora is similar to that of neighboring forests.

The must notable palm stands linked to tall and medium forests are those formed by the so-called *corozos* (*Scheelea liebmannii*, *Orbignya guacuyule*)–in the forests of the Petén region of Guatemala, the Lacandon forest of Chiapas, the southern part of the Yucatán peninsula, and northern Belize–and the palm stands formed by *Scheelea preusii* in the Soconusco region of Chiapas. Several authors have noted that these palm groves are of ancient anthropogenic origin.

In the north of Quintana Roo a palm stand mixed with a low forest has been reported on the coastal dunes and formed by the genera *Pseudophoenix* and *Thrinax*.

The Low Deciduous Forests (Tropical Deciduous Forest, Tropical Dry Forests–Selvas Bajas Caducifolias) are found frequently bordering and intermixed with palm stands. They are characterized by the smaller size (less than 10 meters) of the dominant trees and the abundance of deciduous species.

They are found in the driest climates of the Maya zone with annual precipitation of less than 1,200 millimeters and with a very pronounced dry season of up to 8 months long.

Tree ferns are common in deciduous temperate forests

Heliconia
is a beautiful genus from the tropical
evergreen forests

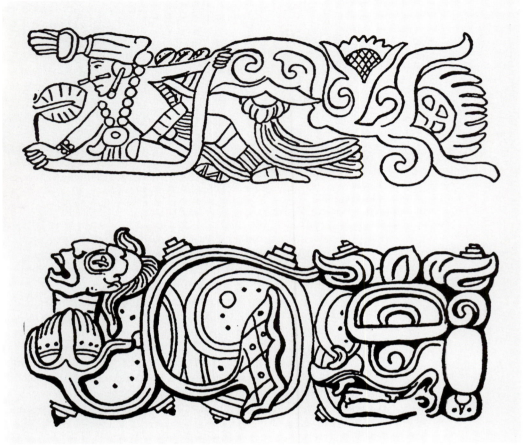

Plant motives
from Chichén Itzá
and Palenque

Several of the most xerophilous species of the semievergreen medium forests form part of these forests, just as many species that are secondary in these forests become dominant in this type of vegetation.

This type of vegetation is known from the northwest of the Yucatán peninsula and in the central depression of Chiapas. In these two zones there has been considerable disturbance for a long time, because in these forests were established the capitals of Yucatán (Mérida) and Chiapas (Tuxtla Gutiérrez), which had a great impact on the vegetation of neighboring areas.

Some common tree genera are: *Acacia, Agave, Alvaradoa, Bursera, Caesalpinia, Leucaena, Lonchocarpus, Lysiloma,* and *Piscidia.*

In parts of these dry forests (400–800 millimeters of rain) are also thick-stemmed cactus species (*Cephalocereus, Lemaireocereus,* and *Pterocereus* in Yucatán and *Acanthocereus, Melocactus,* and *Nopalea* in Chiapas) and Agavaceae (*Agave* in Yucatán and Chiapas and *Beaucarnea* in Yucatán). A variant of this vegetation constitutes the so-called low thorn forest, dominated by thorny tree and shrub genera of the Leguminosae family (*Acacia, Prosopis, Pithecellobium*). Deciduous forests are very susceptible to forest fires, and this factor surely has influenced the evolution of species that form this vegetation.

The Coastal Dune Vegetation is located in all sandy littorals of the Maya zone. It is characterized by a series of pioneer halophyte genera such as *Cakile, Ipomoea, Portulaca, Sesuvium,* and *Suaeda* followed by different shrub communities formed by other characteristic genera: *Agave, Capparis, Coccoloba, Chrysobalanus, Hippocratea, Jacquinia, Maytenus,* and *Opuntia,* among others.

Throughout the Maya zone there are large expanses of soil that remain flooded for part of the year. Perhaps the most notable state in this sense is Tabasco. Nevertheless, a large part of the coast of the Yucatán peninsula and Belize is also subject to these floods.

Palm stands are common in the Maya lowlands

Red mangrove is the most common species in mangrove swamps

Among the main types of forests recognized there are the Logwood Forests (*Tintales*) that are forests of some 10 meters in height dominated by logwood (*Haematoxylon campechianum*), which lives in soils subject to inundation (called in Maya *ak'alche*) in the rainy season. Logwood forests have been described in Tabasco, northern Chiapas, the center and south of Campeche, Quintana Roo, Belize, and in the northern Petén in Guatemala. Logwood forests border and combine with tall and medium semievergreen forests, savannas, and mangrove woodlands.

Other notable species that abound and often dominate in these logwood stands are the *chechem negro* (*Metopium brownei*), the *canacoite* (*Bravaisia integerrima*) and the willow (*Salix chilensis*).

The Savanna (*Sabanas*) is found in soils subject to inundation in the rainy season. It is found in shallower soils than in those of logwood forests. It is characterized by the dominance of a herbaceous stratum dominated by Cyperaceae and Gramineae species and by the scattered presence of trees with umbrella-like tops. Tree species typical of the savannas are the same as those throughout the Maya zone, and all of these may be dominant: *Acoelorraphe wrightii* (*tasiste*), *Byrsonima crassifolia*, *Byrsonima bucidaefolia* (*nanche*), *Crescentia cujete*, *Crescentia alata* (gourd tree), and *Curatella americana*.

Phytomorphic shells used
as ornaments by Maya kings
and notables from Copán
Classic period
Copán, Centro Regional
de Investigaciones Arqueológicas
cat. 158

Natural edaphic savannas of the Maya zone are closely related to tropical pine and oak woodlands. Nevertheless, the trees that define these communities (*Pinus oocarpa* and *Quercus oleoides*) have a more limited distribution than the tree species of the savanna. The savannas have been considered as ecosystems influenced by fire, because they have been subject to periodic fires since antiquity; nevertheless their edaphic origin is undoubted. What has caused this confusion is that the presence of periodic fires in other types of vegetation not subject to inundation (low deciduous forests and medium semievergreen forests) also produce secondary vegetation that is physiognomically very similar to natural savannas; even the same species of natural savannas may be the dominant.

Natural savannas have been found in the Maya zone of Tabasco, north of Chiapas, Campeche, north of Quintana Roo, and Belize.

Different mangroves may be found throughout almost the entire coast of the Maya zone: along the banks of bays; on estuaries, coastal peninsular or half-open lagoons; and at the mouths of rivers. There is a relationship between the species of mangrove, salinity, and degree of flooding.

The red mangrove (*Rhizophora mangle*) is found in the most saline and submerged soils, followed by the white mangrove (*Laguncularia racemosa*), the dark mangrove (*Avicenia nitida*), and the little buttonwood (*Conocarpus erectus*). This last species lives in soils with lower salinity that remains emerged for part of the year.

Other vegetation types have been described from different types of soils subject to inundation in the Maya zone. Stretches of cattail (*Typha dominguensis*) are widespread in lowlands; they are found in large extensions or in small swamps (called *aguadas* or *bajos*). In less humid soils we find, mixed with the stretches of cattail, other notable grassy communities dominated by *Cladium jamaicense*, *Phragmites australis*, *Scirpus lacustris*, *Eleocharis cellulosa*, and others. In Tabasco stands of *popales* (called *popoay*, *Thalia geniculata*) are found at sites with 1 meter or more of inundation and *mucal* swamps (formed by *Dalbergia brownei*).

All these wetlands border different types of vegetation–savannas, palm stands, logwood forests, and mangrove woodlands–forming ecological mosaics along the water-level gradient. In the Maya zone, there are several other types of vegetation that have been recognized by different authors that would require a more extensive discussion beyond the scope of this chapter.

What has been described is a theoretical reconstruction of the potential vegetation of the Maya zone. Most of today's vegetation is a mosaic of areas strongly disturbed by human action. Fortunately, still conserved are floristic remnants of mature communities that have allowed us to identify the types of vegetation that represent the main climatic and edaphic environments of this impressive zone of the American neotropics.

Miniature vessel
with a phytomorphic decoration
Early Classic period
Mexico City, Bodega
del Museo Nacional de Antropología
cat. 211

Plant Vessel
Early Preclassic period
from San Isidro, Chiapas
Mexico City, Bodega
del Museo Nacional de Antropología
cat. 178

References

BREEDLOVE, D. E.
1973
"Phytogeography and Vegetation of Chiapas." In A. Graham. *Vegetation and Vegetational History of Northern Latin America*. Elsevier Scientific Publication 149–65

FLORES, J. S., AND ESPEJEL CARVAJAL I.
1994
"Tipos de vegetación de la Penísula de Yucatán." In *Etnoflora Yucatánensis* 3, 1–135

GÓMEZ POMPA, ARTURO
1965
"La vegetación de Mexico." *Boletín de la Sociedad Botánica de México*, 29, 76–120

GÓMEZ POMPA, ARTURO, AND R. DIRZO
1995
Las reservas de la biosfera y otras áreas naturales protegidas de México. Publicación de la Secretaría de Medio Ambiente, Recursos Naturales y Pesca. Mexico City: Instituto de Ecología e di CONABIO, 159

HOLDRIDGE, L. R.
1969
Mapa ecológico de America Central. Unidad de Recursos Naturales. Unión Panamericana
1971
Forest Environments in Tropical Life Zones: A Pilot Study. Oxford and New York: Pergamon Press, 747

LUNDELL, C. L.
1937
The Vegetation of Petén. Publication 478. Washington, D.C.: Carnegie Institution of Washington, 1–244
1940
The 1936 Michigan–Carnegie Botanical Expedition to British Honduras. Publication 522. Washington, D.C.: Carnegie Institution of Washington, 1–57

MIRANDA, F.
1958
"Estudios acerca de la vegetación." In *Los recursos naturales del sureste y su aprovechamiento*. Ed. by E. Betrán. Ediciones Instituto Mexicano de Recursos Naturales Renovables, 215–71
1975
La vegetación de Chiapas. 2nd edition. Tuxtla Gutiérrez: Ediciones del Gobierno de Chiapas

MIRANDA, F., AND X.E. HERNÁNDEZ
1963
"Los tipos de vegetación de México y su clasificación." *Boletín de la Sociedad Botánica de México*, 28, 29–179.

PENNINGTON, T. D., AND J. SARUKHÁN
1968
Arboles tropicales de México. Instituto Nacional de Investigaciones Forestales and FAO, 413

RAMAMOORTHY, T. P., R. BYE, A. LOT, AND J. FA
1993
Biological Diversity of Mexico: Origins and Distribution. New York: Oxford University Press, 812

Duck sculpture decorating one of the walls of the Great Acropolis
Late Classic period
Comalcalco
Museo de Sitio de Comalcalco
cat. 22

Effigy vessel
from La Lagunita, Quiché
Terminal Classic period
Guatemala, Museo Nacional de Arqueología y Etnología
cat. 11

opposite
Brick with the representation of a crocodile
from Comalcalco, Tabasco
Terminal Classic period
Comalcalco
Museo de Sitio de Comalcalco
cat. 13

Ancient Maya civilization flourished for more than 2,000 years, from the middle of the first millennium B.C. until the Spanish Conquest of the sixteenth century A.D. Its cultural heirs, who number in the millions today, continue to thrive in modern-day Mexico and northern Central America. The ancient Maya are renowned for their achievements in art, architecture, writing, science, and urban planning in the varied and challenging environment of the greater Yucatán peninsula and neighboring areas. In recent years, pathbreaking archaeological, epigraphical, and ethnohistorical research has transformed scholarly understanding of this important Pre-Columbian civilization and has provided significant new insights into the development and accomplishments of the ancient Maya. Scholars now understand, as well, that the Maya area was an integral part of a wider cultural area known as Mesoamerica, which includes the Maya area and most of Mexico to the north, and that the ancient Maya had numerous economic, political, and ideological interactions with peoples in such parts of Mexico as the Gulf Coast lowlands, the Valley of Oaxaca, and the Basin of Mexico.

Space
The Maya area covers over 300,000 square kilometers, which encompasses a territory that today includes southern Mexico (the states of Campeche, Chiapas, Tabasco, Quintana Roo, and Yucatán), Guatemala, Belize, and parts of Honduras and El Salvador. To the north, the Maya area is roughly bounded by the Isthmus of Tehuantepec, while to the south its boundary is marked by the Lempa and Ulúa Rivers in western El Salvador and western Honduras, respectively. This area can be divided into three principal zones: the lowlands, the highlands, and Pacific coastal plain and piedmont. The lowland and highland zones can further be subdivided into southern and northern zones. A wide variety of environments, which do not significantly differ from those of more than 2,000 years ago, can be found in these zones. The Maya successfully exploited these differing and challenging environments but also had to cope with their fragility and the impacts of short-term changes such as drought, and natural disasters such as volcanic eruptions. Ancient Maya civilization reached its zenith in the lowlands, especially in the south, but all of the geographic zones played key roles in the growth and flowering of this fascinating, complex Pre-Columbian culture.
The Northern Lowland Zone. The lowlands were heavily forested in the past as are many parts even to this day. The southern part with its higher annual rainfall supported a tropical forest covering, while the northern part had more of a scrub forest. The lowlands sit on an underlying limestone shelf that is tilted toward the north. Thus, the northern half of the Yucatán has shallow soils with the porous limestone right below. Rain water is absorbed rapidly, and standing water sources are relatively scarce. Water conservation was thus a key concern to the ancient Maya in this zone. The northern lowlands have little relief, with low hills in the Puuc region the only major exception to this flat topography. Extensive cultivation apparently was the norm, although a variety of techniques, such as terracing in the Puuc region, allowed the ancient Maya to intensify their agricultural production. Salt was collected along the coastlines and specialized produce such as honey was widely traded.
The Southern Lowland Zone. The southern part of the Yucatán peninsula has high rainfall, especially in its southern parts where average annual rain can exceed 300 centimeters. The

N

GULF OF MEXICO

NORTHERN LOWLANDS

MEXICO

CARIBBEAN SEA

Río Grijalva

SOUTHERN LOWLANDS

Río Hondo

GUATEMALA

Río Usumacinta

Río de la Pasión

BELIZE

NORTHERN
HIGHLANDS

GULF
OF HONDURAS

Río Chixoy

Río Motagua

HONDURAS

PACIFIC
OCEAN

SOUTHERN
HIGHLANDS

COASTAL PLAIN

EL SALVADOR

Scale:

0   100   200 Km

0   100   200 Mi

opposite
Cultural Maya area

Ruins at Las Palomas
Uxmal, Mexico

tropical rainforest in this part of the lowlands has highly fertile but fragile soils that—with careful controls as to length of cultivation and fallow cycles—were able to support large populations. Both extensive and intensive forms of cultivation were practiced. Reclamation of swamp areas also provided very fertile agricultural lands on which intensive cultivation could be undertaken.

On the eastern side of the southern lowlands, the Maya mountains were the source of a variety of materials including hard stone for grinding tools. A series of significant rivers, including the Usumacinta, Río de la Pasión, Candelaria, Nuevo, Hondo, and Río Belize, can be found on the western, southern, and eastern sides of the southern lowlands. The rivers offered important transportation routes, provided useful food resources, and, with some modifications like terracing, allowed intensive agricultural exploitation of their banks and flood plains. In addition to maize, crops such as cacao (which was used as currency as well as the basis for a prized chocolate drink) and cotton were grown in riverine locales.

The Highland Zone. This rugged and varied zone contains a series of large mountains, with some of the highest peaks reaching over 4,000 meters. The southern highlands include a number of active volcanos, which have wrought havoc and destruction on the lives of both the ancient and modern Maya alike. It also is an earthquake zone. The highlands are essentially temperate in climate with some parts, particularly in the north, nearly tropical. The northern highlands are relatively wetter than the southern highlands with some parts approaching the southern lowlands in annual rainfall; but both zones have great agricultural potential, especially in the numerous valleys that cut through the mountains. A number of important rivers, including the Grijalva, as well as the headwaters of the Usumacinta and the Motagua, flow out of the highlands. The highlands also yield a number of important mineral resources such as hard stone for grinding tools, jade (which was a highly desired elite trade good), and the important volcanic glass, obsidian, which has several key sources in the southern highlands and was traded widely throughout the Maya area.

The Pacific Coastal Plain and Piedmont Zone. This productive zone, which runs along the entire southern margin of the Maya area, has relatively high rainfall and a variety of fertile agricultural regions. It includes the actual coastline, which provides direct access to a host of marine resources and from which salt can be gathered. Parts of the coastline also contain lagoons, which are rich in animal and plant life. The coastal plain is cross-cut by a large number of small rivers that flow south from the adjacent highlands and provide large areas of productive agricultural land. The shoreline and widespread rivers offered numerous trade routes, which the ancient Maya exploited throughout their history. The low foothills of the highlands to the north featured a rich piedmont zone that also supported intensive cultivation of such key crops as cacao. Through time, the demographic, economic, and political focus of ancient Maya civilization shifted across the landscape of the vast and varied homeland area. The beginnings of complexity emerged in the Pacific coastal and piedmont zone. Shortly thereafter, both the highlands and lowlands began to develop rapidly with writing first flourishing in the former and large monumental architecture in the latter. The lowlands ultimately emerged as the center of Maya civilization, first in the south and later in the north, although the highland and Pacific coastal and piedmont zones also witnessed important

Ancient Maya civilization chronology

YEARS	2000 B.C.	900 B.C.	300 B.C.	250 A.C.	
TRADITIONAL PERIODS	Dart point Cuello, Belize	Simojovel celt Chiapas	Miniature vessel Altar de Sacrificios, Guatemala / Structure XXIII Becán, Campeche	Bowl with human figure Becán, Campeche	
	EARLY PRECLASSIC	MIDDLE PRECLASSIC	LATE PRECLASSIC	EARLY CLASSIC	
PHASES	EARLY			MIDDLE	

developments throughout the later history of Maya civilization. The end of the ancient civilization came with the arrival of Europeans. The whole area was conquered by the Spanish, beginning in the early sixteenth century A.D., although the timing and intensity of the Conquest differed significantly within and among the zones.

Time

The Maya area was initially occupied soon after the close of the last Ice Age, more than ten thousand years ago. Over the following millennia, small groups of nomadic hunters and gatherers utilized the area's varied animal and plant resources, leaving occasional traces of their short-term occupations in the form of stone tool fragments. The beginnings of the domestication of the crucially important maize plant currently can be traced as early as the middle of the fourth millennium B.C., with settled village life that was based on the productivity and storage of cultivated plants emerging by the second millennium. It is at this time that the roots of ancient Maya civilization can be found.

The chronology of ancient Maya civilization has traditionally been divided into three parts, Preclassic, Classic, and Postclassic, with their own subdivisions. These chronological periods were originally formulated to mark significant changes in Maya history, especially what was seen as the peak of Maya civilization: namely, the Classic period in the southern lowlands. Recent research has shown that the hallmarks of the Classic period, such as writing, monumental art and architecture, the corbeled vault, and polychrome pottery, were all in use during Preclassic times. It also has shown that the Postclassic period was not a time of Maya decline after the end of the Classic and that other zones besides the southern lowlands witnessed significant cultural developments, as well. Nevertheless, the traditional periodization of Maya history remains well entrenched in both scholarly and popular usage, and to avoid confusion, we will continue to use it in this volume. However, as I wrote more than

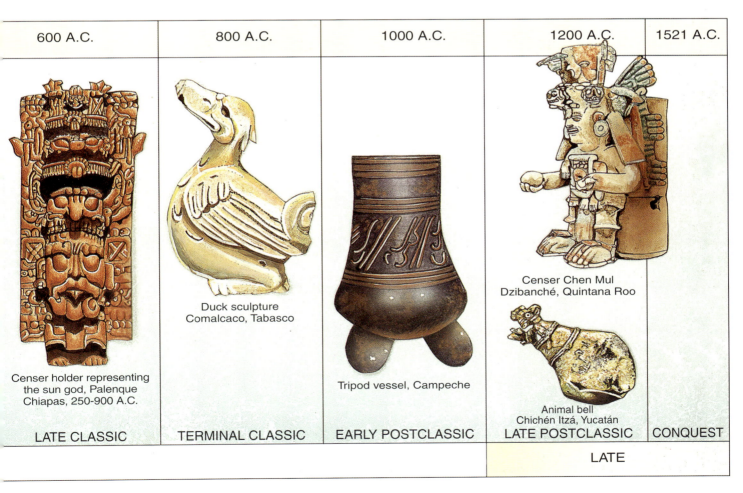

600 A.C.	800 A.C.	1000 A.C.	1200 A.C.	1521 A.C.
Censer holder representing the sun god, Palenque Chiapas, 250-900 A.C.	Duck sculpture Comalcaco, Tabasco	Tripod vessel, Campeche	Censer Chen Mul Dzibanché, Quintana Roo — Animal bell Chichén Itzá, Yucatán	
LATE CLASSIC	TERMINAL CLASSIC	EARLY POSTCLASSIC	LATE POSTCLASSIC	CONQUEST
			LATE	

opposite
Stela 50 of Izapa in Chiapas
Late Preclassic period
Mexico City
Museo Nacional de Antropología

Feminine figurine
found on the Guatemalan
Pacific coast
Middle Preclassic period
Guatemala
Museo Popol Vuh
cat. 239

a decade ago, it is useful to group these traditional periods into three longer phases: *Early* (2000 to 300 B.C.), *Middle* (300 B.C. to A.D. 1200), and *Late* (A.D. 1200 to the 1540s), which better correspond to the general developmental trends in the ancient Maya world than do the traditional period scheme and which use more neutral terms. The Early Phase includes the Early and Middle Preclassic periods; the Middle Phase includes the Late Preclassic, the Classic, the Terminal Classic, and Early Postclassic periods; and the Late Phase corresponds to the Late Postclassic period and the Spanish Conquest. The discussion that follows will be organized by these larger phases and the periods within them.

The Early Phase (2000–300 B.C.). Scholars can trace the beginnings of Maya civilization to the Early Phase when settled agricultural villages, which cultivated a number of productive crops including maize, were fully established throughout the Maya area. The rise of complex technological, economic, political, artistic, and religious developments also can be traced to this time. The fertility of the Pacific coastal and piedmont zone and the ready availability of a wide variety of food resources around the shoreline lagoons led to the rise of the first villages in this zone and to its early prominence in cultural developments in the Maya area, although the highlands and southern lowlands soon followed suit. In the centuries that followed, growing populations throughout the Maya area moved into previously unoccupied

Polychromatic box
found on the Guatemaltecan
Pacific coast
Classic period
Guatemala, Museo Nacional
de Arqueología y Etnología
cat. 252

opposite
Effigy vessel
Late Classic period
Mexico City
Museo Nacional de Antropología
cat. 301

following pages
Figurine on a throne
Late Classic period
Palenque, Museo de Sitio
"Alberto Ruz Lhuillier"
cat. 319

Sculpture, probably a throneback
Classic period
Puebla
Fundación Amparo/Museo Amparo
cat. 292

Jar, Late Preclassic period
Pomoná, Museo de Sitio de Pomoná
cat. 213

Globular jar, Late Preclassic period
Cancún, Museo Arqueológico
cat. 206

zones and the sizes of individual farming villages expanded. Between 1000 and 500 B.C., increasing population together with decreasing land available for settlement and agricultural production led to larger population aggregations with all the consequent administrative developments, more intensive forms of agriculture to support the growing populations, and ultimately the emergence of competition and conflict over scarcer lands and resources.

The first highly visible signs of change began to appear by 500 B.C., if not earlier, as several population centers began to increase relatively rapidly in size, and large public buildings burst upon the scene at population centers such as Nakbé, El Mirador, and Tikal in the southern lowlands, and Kaminaljuyú and El Portón in the highlands. Monumental carved stones with depictions of local rulers also first appeared in the highland and coastal zones during the Early Phase. It is evident that rulers were now able to mobilize considerable labor forces to construct large public buildings and use monumental sculpture to glorify and consolidate their economic, political, and religious powers.

Moreover, even in these early times, the Maya already were interacting with groups in neighboring areas, such as the Olmecs from the Gulf Coast, Mixe-Zoquean peoples from the adjacent highlands and coast, and Zapotecs from Oaxaca. These interactions led to trade, as well as the introduction of new ideas and ideologies. For example, the use of hieroglyphic writing and calendrics were invented to the north of the Maya area in places such as the Valley of Oaxaca. These ideas spread to the Maya area, where the Maya built on these early innovations to produce their own sophisticated writing system before the end of the Early Phase. Clearly, what archaeologists generally call "chiefdoms" emerged at this time, as many Maya settlements grew in cultural complexity, and the roots of Maya cities and states were planted.

The Middle Phase (300 B.C.–A.D. 1200). It is during this epoch that Maya civilization is widely perceived to have reached its height.

Its cities reached their largest size, its rulers had their greatest powers, and its artistic, architectural, and scientific achievements were extraordinary.

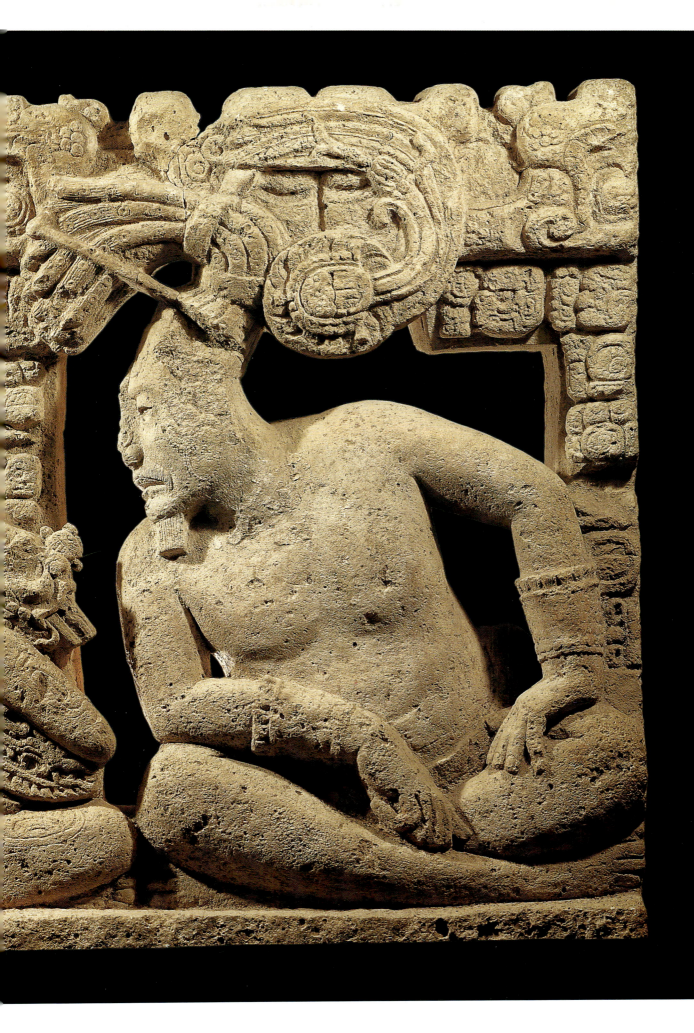

opposite
Head of a figurine
Late Classic period
San Cristóbal de las Casas
Centro Cultural
de los Altos de Chiapas
cat. 290

Onyx vessel
Late Classic period
Washington, D.C.
Dumbarton Oaks
Research Library Collections
cat. 439a

While the southern lowlands were the heartland of these cultural accomplishments, all the other geographic zones also witnessed significant developments in this key era. Scholars now understand that many of the hallmarks of "Classic" Maya civilization were present by the Late Preclassic period, if not earlier. In particular, the growth of urban centers, political states, and dynastic rulership can be traced to this time in both the highlands and lowlands. Hieroglyphic inscriptions with calendric and historical information became more widespread in the highland and Pacific coastal and piedmont zones and soon spread into the lowlands. These inscriptions, which were carved on stone monuments, were associated with depictions of rulers in the former two zones. By the middle of Late Preclassic times they had also begun to utilize the uniquely Maya calendric system, the Long Count, which was based on a linear calendar that reckoned time from a start date of 3114 B.C. Such associations and use of Long Count dating did not become common in the lowlands until Classic times.

The locus of widespread cultural developments during the first period of the Middle Phase was in the highlands and Pacific coastal and piedmont zones and most particularly in the southern highlands. The principal Maya center of the time was Kaminaljuyú, which is located within the borders of the urban zone of the modern capital of Guatemala, namely Guatemala City. Kaminaljuyú controlled a key obsidian source near the city and also was able to control major trade routes to and from the Pacific coast and the lowlands. Meanwhile, in the latter zone, sites such as El Mirador and Tikal rose to prominence. Rulers at the former site constructed some of the largest structures that were ever built in the Maya area, with immense stone platforms supporting huge elite buildings. Toward the end of the Late Preclassic period, the highland and Pacific coastal centers suffered a major decline, as did some of the lowland ones such as El Mirador. One of the factors in this decline may have directly or indirectly been the eruption of the Ilopango volcano near the eastern border of the southern highlands around A.D. 250. This eruption caused vast destruction, stymied agricultural production, and severely harmed trade. Lowland centers such as El Mirador, which had close ties to the highlands, may also have been adversely affected and declined, as well. Other Late Preclassic centers, however, began a major new flourishing in the third century A.D. The idea of dynastic rule, which had been present in the highlands, took root in the lowlands and both older sites like Tikal and relatively newer ones like Copán near the southern frontier of the lowlands grew in size and importance under dynastic political leadership. It is at this time that the political and economic locus of Maya civilization shifted from the highlands to the lowlands. Although Kaminaljuyú and other highland sites recovered from their declines at the close of the Late Preclassic period, they lost their preeminence to the lowlands.

During the Classic period, Maya civilization burgeoned in all geographic zones. Populations at older centers increased, while many new cities were founded as the landscape was filled in by the growing numbers of peoples. The northern lowlands prospered and regions such as the Río Bec on the northern border of the southern lowlands rose to prominence later in the

Polychrome vessel
Late Classic period
Campeche, Museo Histórico Fuerte
de San Miguel
Baluarte de San Miguel

opposite
Circular altar that was probably
used for sacrifices
Early Postclassic period
Chichén Itzá
Museo de Sitio de Chichén Itzá

Animal sculpture
Terminal Classic-Early
Postclassic period
Chichén Itzá
Museo de Sitio de Chichén Itzá
cat. 59

period. Although there is great scholarly debate about the figures, by the beginning of the Late Classic period, the overall lowland population alone may have exceeded five million and the larger cities such as Tikal had populations in the many tens of thousands. The arts and architecture thrived; significant achievements in astronomy and mathematics were made; and an intricate ideological system involving numerous deities with multiple personae evolved. Social divisions became exacerbated with a small elite class growing in wealth and power and a large peasant class supplying the food and labor that supported the expanding cities. There is considerable scholarly debate about whether the nonelite class was further divided into a series of subclasses, as well. Recent dramatic advances in the decipherment of Maya hiero-glyphic texts now allow scholars to appreciate the very complicated political landscape dur-ing Classic times in the lowlands and the waxing and waning of political fortunes of individ-ual cities and ruling dynasties. Important archaeological research at the great urban centers of Tikal and Calakmul, for instance, along with new historical understandings from the texts, have illuminated the rivalries between these two cities, with Calakmul and then Tikal gaining the upper hand with either direct or indirect influence over a number of other lowland cen-ters. In addition, significant ongoing research at Copán has been able to tie together dynastic rule, architectural growth, urban and rural settlement, and the ecology of the Copán Valley in a highly edifying picture of the city's rise and fall throughout the Classic period.

The Maya area also was an important player in the larger Mesoamerican cultural system dur-ing this period. Cities such as Tikal and Kaminaljuyú had ties with Teotihuacan, the great city in the Basin of Mexico, and elite goods and peoples moved over relatively large distances.

Toward the close of the eighth century A.D., after a lengthy flourishing, many of the princi-pal cities in the southern lowlands declined rapidly in population and power. From this time on, this zone remained relatively lightly populated and drastically less important both polit-ically and economically. The causes of this demise were systemic and multiple with demo-graphic stress, a possible drought, trade disruptions, and intercity conflicts all implicated in this downturn. Scholars used to believe that Maya civilization collapsed in the ninth century A.D., but recent research indicates that this was not the case. First, some southern lowland cities, especially those located near water trade routes and rich cacao and cotton growing

Mural
Mayapán, Mexico

areas, continued to thrive while other cities were declining. Second, cities in the northern lowlands, especially Chichén Itzá and the Puuc region cities including Uxmal, Kabah, Sayil, and Labná, began to thrive just as many southern cities were collapsing. Third, a mercantile, water-oriented Maya group from the Gulf Coast lowlands of Tabasco and Campeche, known as the Chontal or Putun, who had close economic contacts with many areas of ancient Mesoamerica, began to spread their influence at this time in both the highlands and lowlands, ultimately focusing their attention on the northern lowlands. Thus, just as the demographic, political, and economic focus of Maya civilization had shifted from the southern highlands to the southern lowlands in the first part of the Middle Phase, so did the focus shift again in the later part of the phase, from the southern to the northern lowlands. Maya civilization did not collapse but continued to prosper in a different and more restricted area.

During the Terminal Classic period, some southern lowland cities, several new centers in the northern highlands, and Chichén Itzá, the Puuc cities, and other northern lowland places bloomed, with Chichén Itzá ultimately emerging as the preeminent Maya city of the time. New research at this great site and elsewhere in the north at such places as Isla Cerritos on the northern coast is beginning to shed new light on this hitherto enigmatic city and indicates that it had widespread political (including military conquest) and economic influence throughout the northern lowlands during the Terminal Classic and into the Early Postclassic period. It probably played a key role in the rapid demise of the Puuc cities in the tenth century A.D. It also had tremendous religious importance, and its sacred well, or *cenote* was a key pilgrimage destination. Its rulers, perhaps Chontal Maya, had close relations with groups elsewhere in Mesoamerica, especially Central Mexico. Most scholars now believe that this major political capital was not conquered by the Toltecs of Central Mexico and that the similarities between Toltec Tula and Maya Chichén Itzá resulted from common cultural ties. Sometime toward the close of the Early Postclassic period, Chichén Itzá declined for reasons that are still not fully understood, and the northern lowlands split into a number of small political polities.

The Late Phase (A.D. 1200–1540s). This phase witnessed some important cultural shifts in ancient Maya civilization, including new emphasis on mercantile activities; changing urban designs; significantly diminished investments by the ruling elite in large, labor-intensive architectural projects to glorify themselves and their cities, and innovative forms of political control. The latter is best illustrated by the emergence of an extensive political confederacy led by the northern lowland center of Mayapán, which was a walled city with a dense population of about 12,000 people within its boundaries. Long-distance, water-borne trade around the Yucatán peninsula gained greater importance with several trading centers, including the island of

Anthropomorphic urn
Mixco Viejo, Chimaltenango
Postclassic period
Guatemala, Museo Nacional
de Arqueología y Etnología

Capilla de Indios
(Indios Chapel)
sixteenth century
Dzibilchaltún, Mexico

Cozumel off the east coast, becoming key nodes in the exchange of bulk goods such as cotton, honey, and salt. In the highlands a series of regional centers that had first emerged toward the end of the Middle Phase, including Utatlán (the capital of the Quiche Maya) and Iximche (the capital of the Cakchiquel Maya), gained additional power and prominence. These cities were still thriving at the time of the sixteenth-century Spanish Conquest. However, Mayapán had declined by the middle of the fifteenth century and the political scene throughout the lowlands when the Spanish arrived was one of small, decentralized polities. The Spanish Conquest of the Maya area, which began with the early voyages of Hernández de Córdoba, Grijalva, and Cortés in 1517 to 1519, was essentially completed by the 1540s, although parts of the area were not conquered until the next century and some Maya remained resistant to Spanish and then Mexican control up to modern times. The Spanish Conquest destroyed much of the Maya elite and their cultural practices, and it decimated a significant part of its population through diseases it introduced, such as measles and smallpox. Taken together, the varied results of the Spanish Conquest effectively brought an end to Maya civilization after more than two thousand years.

Acknowledgment
I wish to thank Professor Wendy Ashmore for her helpful comments on this chapter.

References

MARCUS, JOYCE
1995
"Where is Lowland Maya Archaeology Headed?" *Journal of Archaeological Research* 3, 1, 3–53

MARTIN, SIMON, AND NIKOLAI GRUBE
1995
"Maya Superstates." *Archaeology* 48, 6, 41–47

POHL, MARY D., *ET AL.*
1996
"Early Agriculture in the Maya Lowlands." *Latin American Antiquity* 7, 4, 355–72

SABLOFF, JEREMY A.
1985
"Ancient Maya Civilization." In *Maya: Treasures of an Ancient Civilization.* Ed. by C. Gallenkamp and R. E. Johnson. New York: Harry N. Abrams, 34–46
1990
The New Archaeology and the Ancient Maya. New York: W. H. Freeman

SCHELE, LINDA, AND DAVID FREIDEL
1990
A Forest of Kings. The Untold Story of the Ancient Maya. New York: William Morrow and Co.

SHARER, ROBERT J.
1994
The Ancient Maya. Fifth edition. Stanford: Stanford University Press

The Maya and Their Olmec Neighbors

Celt from Simojovel
Chiapas, detail
Middle Preclassic period
Mexico City
Museo Nacional de Antropología
cat. 237

The geographic and cultural space that we call the Maya area extends northward to the Atlantic Ocean, thus separating the Gulf of Mexico from the Caribbean Sea. In the south, the Pacific Ocean marks the limit of this territory. The eastern boundary, occupied by non-Maya speakers such as the Jicaque, Lenca, Xinca, and Pipil, is difficult and imprecise, given that this frontier is established by an imaginary line crossing Honduras and El Salvador. This line runs from north to south, from the mouth of the Ulúa River in the Caribbean Sea, to the mouth of the Lempa River in the Pacific Ocean. In turn, the Isthmus of Tehuantepec, occupied mainly by Mixe-Zoque-speaking groups and the location of the Olmec heartland, is considered the western limit of the Maya area.

We can then say that the Maya area encompasses the totality of the Mexican states of Campeche, Quintana Roo, Yucatán, a part of Tabasco and Chiapas, as well as the Central American countries of Belize, Guatemala, and the western portion of Honduras and El Salvador. The Pacific coast, which runs from Chiapas to El Salvador, is considered part of this area, but strictly speaking it is not because there are no Maya speakers there. Rather, this zone has functioned as an important multi-ethnic cultural corridor.

This demarcation of Maya space has been established through the presence of certain cultural patterns and a number of archaeological materials that coincide stylistically with the current distribution of the various languages constituting the Mayance family. Huastec is excluded, although it is a member of this linguistic family, because its geographic space does not form part of the Maya area. Linguistically we can say that no Mesoamerican region is as homogenous as the Maya territory, since the more than twenty-five languages that are spoken here pertain to a single family.

Nevertheless, we should not envision an isolated Maya area. Its occupants, just as other Mesoamerican cultures, were involved in a series of relations that changed in nature, orientation, and intensity depending on the different cultures with which they came into contact over the course of the years. This essay offers an overview of Olmec influence on the Mayas, a process that occurred between 1200 and 300 B.C.

Archaeological Evidence

A little more than four thousand years ago, the first sedentary communities arose in Mesoamerica. We know almost nothing of this shift, which is associated with the beginning of agriculture. Nevertheless, the appearance and presence of ceramics has been viewed as a good indicator of this sedentarism, which evolved in a number of Mesoamerican civilizations. Among these, Olmec civilization stands out for its precocity and monumentality, to the extent that it has been considered a "mother culture."

It is believed that the ethnic antecedents of this culture may perhaps be located in village communities that were established in the coastal region of Soconusco, near the border with Guatemala. This hypothesis is based on the results of excavations that recovered ceramic materials from several archaeological sites in the municipality of Mazatán, Chiapas, that date to between 1900 and 1800 B.C. (Lowe 1973).

Despite their antiquity, since they stand out as the earliest in the Mesoamerican southeast, Barra phase vessels display great technical quality, are attractive in form and have varied designs in their decoration. Some scholars believe that during the next two hundred years (1800 to 1600 B.C.), Mixe-Zoque speakers, bearing this ceramic tradition, moved from Soconusco to the Gulf Coast of Mexico, to the region that would become the home of the rise of the first great Mesoamerican civilization: the Olmecs (Clark and Blake 1989).

Results of excavations at sites in the Olmec heartland, such as Tres Zapotes, La Venta, Manatí, and San Lorenzo, tell us that it was close to 1200 B.C. when society shifted from village to urban life, from tribe to state (Coe and Diehl 1980). We then see how the ideology of this people, whose name in reality we do not know, began to manifest itself in the plan of their cities, ceramics, in monumental sculpture and in innumerable objects with a distinctive stamp attributable to this culture. It is not certain that they were the absolute creators of this ideology that characterizes the Mesoamerican being, but they were the first to represent it graphically.

Communication and contact are human nature, but above all it was the need for raw materials (jade, obsidian, flint, ilmenite, hematite, cinnabar, amber, feathers, shells, cacao, salt,

N

GULF OF MEXICO

Dzibilchaltún

Chichén Itzá

Cozumel

Yucatán

Chacsikin

Edzná

Quintana Roo

MEXICO

Becán

Campeche

Calakmul

Río Hondo

Cuello

Tres Zapotes

Veracruz

La Venta

Tabasco

Balancán

Mirador

San Lorenzo

Río Grijalva

E. Zapata

Tenosique

Uaxactún

Tikal

BELIZE

San Isidro

Simojovel

Xoc

Río Usumacinta

Lago Petén Itzá

Oaxaca

Ocozocuautla

Chiapa de Corzo

Ceibal

GULF OF HONDURAS

Laguna Zope

Mirador

Tutzuculi

Chiapas

Altar de Sacrificios

Río de la Pasión

PACIFIC OCEAN

Pijijiapan

Río Chixoy

GUATEMALA

JICAQUE LANGUAGE

Pampa El Pajón

La Lagunita

Río Motagua

Izapa

Salamá

HONDURAS

Mazatán

El Sitio

Kaminaljuyú

Copán

LENCA LANGUAGE

Abaj Takalik

Salinas La Blanca

XINCA LANGUAGE

Tiquisate

Monte Alto

PIPIL LANGUAGE

Chalchuapa

EL SALVADOR

CARIBBEAN SEA

Legend:
- ● Maya sites
- ● Olmec sites
- Olmec metropolitan area
- Olmec influence orientation
- MAYA LANGUAGE
- MIXE-ZOQUE LANGUAGE
- CHIAPANECA LANGUAGE

Scale:
0 — 100 — 200 Km
0 — 100 — 200 Mi

Distribution of Maya and Olmec sites and the languages spoken

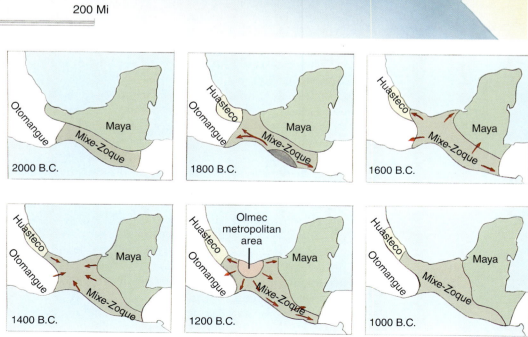

Migrations of Mixe-Zoque

2000 B.C. — Otomangue, Maya, Mixe-Zoque

1800 B.C. — Huasteco, Otomangue, Maya, Mixe-Zoque

1600 B.C. — Huasteco, Maya, Mixe-Zoque

1400 B.C. — Huasteco, Otomangue, Maya, Mixe-Zoque

1200 B.C. — Huasteco, Otomangue, Olmec metropolitan area, Maya, Mixe-Zoque

1000 B.C. — Huasteco, Otomangue, Maya, Mixe-Zoque

Ceramic vessels
from the Barra phase
painted by Ajax Moreno

and so forth) unavailable in their surroundings that led to the interaction of the Olmecs with different peoples and cultural areas of Mesoamerica including the Maya.

It seems that much of the most ancient pottery traditions of the central lowlands of the Maya area originated in this region of the Gulf Coast, known as the Olmec heartland. This is the case of the site of Cuello in Belize (Hammond *et al.* 1991, 62), where the earliest ceramic materials date between 1200 and 900 B.C.

In the basin of the Pasión River, in the Guatemalan Petén region, the first ceramic complexes of Altar de Sacrificios and Ceibal also display a strong affiliation with materials from the Olmec zone (Sabloff 1975). An offering, found on the central plaza of Ceibal and arranged in a cruciform shape, contained five ceramic vessels, six jadeite celts, and an awl similar to those recovered in excavations at La Venta and Cerro de las Mesas (Willey 1978, 86–89, 97; Smith 1982, 117–18).

The region of the Motagua River basin has been a source of jade since Mesoamerican times. It is in this zone where the fertile valleys of the Copán River, are located at the eastern limit of the Maya area. Recently the Copán Project, working in the residential group known as Las Sepulturas, excavated several burial sites from the Middle Preclassic period (W. Fash 1985, 138). One of them contained a rich offering consisting of vessels with different designs showing the so-called Olmec dragon, jade celts, and several jade beads.

Massive offerings of green stone celts, which symbolize kernels of maize, are abundant at La Venta and fairly frequent at several Olmec sites, so that we might think that this practice reached the Maya area from the heartland (Pérez Suárez 1997). Routes of passage were numerous and varied, following natural land routes or using the coasts and numerous rivers furrowing Maya territory.

For example, along the Usumacinta basin, which was the main riverine route of communication between the Gulf of Mexico and Maya lands, there is clear evidence of Olmec-Maya relations. It may be observed in the region of the municipalities of Emiliano Zapata, Balancán, and Tenosique in Tabasco, from where we know of several Olmec clay figurines from sites such as Tierra Blanca, Trinidad, Pomoca, and Pocvicuc. But it has also been found upriver, at sites located in the basin of the Pasión and Chixoy Rivers, tributaries forming the Usumacinta. In the basin of the Pasión River, which originates in the Maya mountains of the southeast of the Petén, was the offering at Ceibal. On the other hand, in the basin of the Chixoy River, which originates and drains the highlands of northern Guatemala, a sculpture with Olmec traits has been reported at the site of La Lagunita (Ichon 1977, 34) and ceramics from 1200 to 900 B.C. in the region of Salamá (Sharer and Sedat 1987).

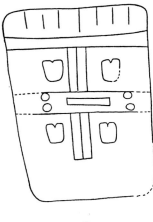

Motifs engraved on Celts
from Emiliano Zapata
Tabasco

opposite
Simojovel Celt
Middle Preclassic period
Mexico City
Museo Nacional de Antropología
cat. 237

Downriver, again in the plains of the Gulf and on the outskirts of the city of Emiliano Zapata, Tabasco, more than thirty celts were found in a massive offering located under a mound that was destroyed to obtain fill material (Ochoa 1982; 1983). Two of these celts display incised Olmec motifs.

The Museum of the City of Balancán exhibits a unique votive celt, found when the movie theater was built in the city. We know one Olmec stela carved in limestone that comes from Mirador, an archaeological site located in the basin of the San Pedro Mártir River, a tributary straight from the Usumacinta, in the same municipality of Balancán (Hernández Ayala 1981). From the *ejido* (communal lands) of Emiliano Zapata, located in the municipality of Tenosique, comes an Olmec relief bearing the image of an acrobat, a frequent subject in several Olmec monuments and figurines (García Moll 1979).

Near Toniná, in the municipality of Ocosingo, Chiapas, and in the basin of the Jataté River, another of the many tributaries of the Usumacinta that irrigates the Lacandon jungle, there was another interesting monument: "The Olmec Relief of Xoc." Today this monument is only known from photographic references because before 1972, it was brutally destroyed in an act of vandalism (Ekholm-Miller 1973).

Also in the state of Chiapas, but in the municipality of Simojovel, comes an engraved celt with Olmec traits. Colonial documents and codices, as well as extensive archaeological evidence, suggest that amber was an important product in Mesoamerican trade networks. The presence of objects of this material in offerings excavated at La Venta shows that it was prized and possessed symbolic value at an early date. It seems that the region of Simojovel in the state of Chiapas, which now is occupied by Tzotzil-speaking Mayas, was and still is the main source of amber in Mesoamerica. Undoubtedly, some relationship must exist between the presence of amber in the offerings of La Venta and the magnificent engraved celt of Simojovel.

Going back to the Grijalva River, which after some twists and turns changes name and is called the Mezcalapa or Río Grande de Chiapas, the Olmecs established contacts with different peoples settled along its course or its tributaries. It should be mentioned that the central depression of Chiapas, through which this river runs, has served as a natural border between Maya speakers and those of the Mixe-Zoque family. It is for this reason that archaeological sites located in the southwestern portion of the state of Chiapas are not recognized as Maya, since they formed part of an extension of the Olmec area (Lee 1989; Lowe 1994). This is the case of San Isidro, now buried under the waters of the Malpaso dam, where excavations unearthed Olmec ceramic materials and the characteristic offerings of celts (Lowe 1981).

Strong Olmec presence in this region of the state of Chiapas has also been recognized in Ocozocuatla, Chiapa de Corzo, Padre Piedra, and above all at Mirador and Plumajillo. These last two archaeological sites, in the municipality of Jiquipilas, were occupied by a small Olmec group that came from the heartland in order to control deposits of the mineral iron and to establish a permanent center in this region to supply hematite and ilmenite (Agrinier 1989, 34).

These iron minerals were used as raw materials in the manufacture of mirrors and in the production of objects of more or less cubic shape, the sides of which measure 2 to 3 centimeters and at least four of them display a perforation. We know of more than two thousand of these ilmenite cubes recovered in a workshop in Plumajillo, Chiapas, and more than two tons of them in an offering at San Lorenzo, Veracruz; nevertheless, the use and function of these small objects remains obscure.

During the Middle Preclassic period (1200–500 B.C.), the coastal strip of the Pacific, from Laguna Zope, a site near Juchitán, Oaxaca, to Chalchuapa, in El Salvador, functioned as an important Olmec cultural corridor.

Evidence of Olmec presence occurs in the form of monumental sculpture, ceramics and a variety of easily transportable objects and products that also indicate the existence of complex networks of commercial exchange.

Moving from west to east, in the state of Chiapas, we can mention the reliefs of Tzutzuculi, a site located on the outskirts of Tonalá (Mc Donald 1983). In the municipality of Pijijiapan we have magnificent reliefs of Olmec manufacture (Navarrete 1969). A skull with pear-

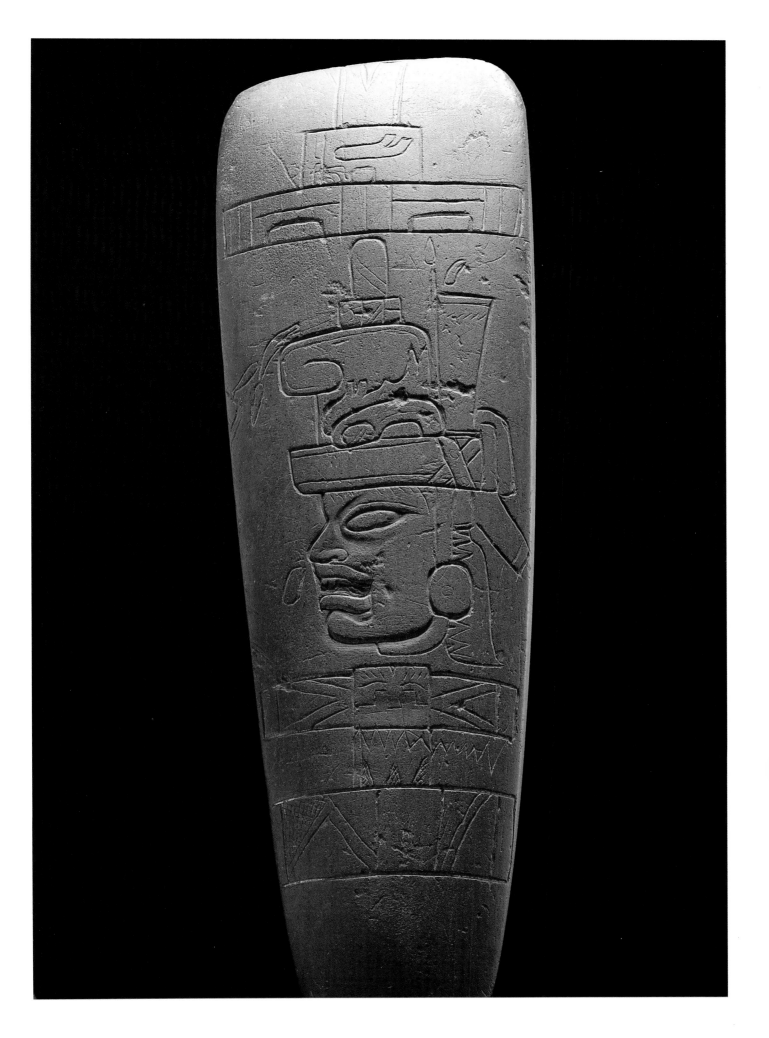

Olmec figurine
from Ocozocuatla
Tuxtla Gutiérrez, Museo Regional
de Chiapas

opposite
Colossal Olmec head
Villahermosa, Tabasco
Parque Museo La Venta

shaped deformation similar to that seen in Olmec figurines was excavated at the site of Pampa El Pajón (Paillés 1980). In the Soconusco region, evidence of Olmec presence may be found in several sites in the municipality of Mazatán. In addition to clear ceramic evidence, we have a three-dimensional sculpture now tenoned into cement in the Alvaro Obregón Park and another from the site of Ojo de Agua exhibited in the Regional Museum of Soconusco in Tapachula (Navarrete 1971).

After passing through Izapa, we enter Guatemalan territory. Here, Olmec presence may be seen in the celt from El Sitio (Navarrete 1971), in the ceramics of Salinas La Blanca (Coe and Flannery 1967), in the sculptures of Sin Cabeza, a site near Tiquisate (Shook 1950), as well as in the beautiful Olmec relief of unknown provenance that displays the frontal and side view of an acrobat. The site of Abaj Takalik, located in the Department of Retalhuleu, deserves special mention. At least a dozen monuments that may be considered to be in Olmec style come from this site.

On the same Pacific coast, we leave behind Monte Alto, Guatemala, and we arrive at Chalchuapa, in El Salvador, where early occupation has been detected that may be dated between 1200 and 900 B.C. (Sharer 1978). Here, in this Salvadoran region, we find the Olmec reliefs of Las Victorias. Following this coastal strip, we arrive at the Nicoya peninsula, in Costa Rica, a zone considered to be the southeastern frontier of Mesoamerica and where objects with characteristic traits of the Olmec style have also been reported (Pohorilenko 1981).

In the Yucatán peninsula, although we lack early ceramics (predating 700 B.C.) and monumental Olmec sculpture, there are numerous jade objects attributable to the Olmec tradition. We might mention some little spoons that were found when the *cenote* of Chichén Itzá was dredged (Proskouriakoff 1974), the jade pectoral excavated in a tomb in Cozumel (Rathje 1973), and the almost twenty jade objects that were recovered by chance in Chacsinkin, a site near the town of Peto, Yucatán (Andrews 1986).

Some of these Olmec pieces were re-used, since they appear in later contexts. Others of unknown provenance but reportedly found in the Yucatán peninsula display images and glyphs contrasting with the Olmec style. This is the case of the pectoral in the Dumbarton Oaks collection in Washington, D.C. (Coe 1966).

It is feasible that Olmec expansion toward the northern Yucatán peninsula may in part be attributed to the need to obtain salt, a resource abundant in this region that subsequently also attracted other Mesoamerican peoples.

Final Comments

The dividing line between the Mayas and Olmecs was not fixed, but rather it fluctuated and changed in nature throughout the years. During the Middle Preclassic period (1200–500 B.C.), a large part of the western portion of the territory that we now consider to be Maya was Olmec.

In those times, in addition to the simple exchange of raw materials, Olmec influence is expressed in a style that seems to move from west to east, that is to say from the Olmec region to the Maya one.

The certainty of this Olmec presence may be seen in sculpture, in various ritual objects, and above all in the earliest ceramic materials that have been recovered from archaeological excavations at Maya sites.

These ceramic traditions seem to have had precursors in cultural expressions produced in the Olmec heartland during the San Lorenzo phase (1150–900 B.C.), so that the time

Handmade iron objects
Mexico City, Instituto Nacional
de Antropología e Historia

opposite
Olmec sculpture
from Uaxactún, Petén
Late Preclassic period
Guatemala, Museo Nacional
de Arqueología y Etnología
cat. 240

Jade pectoral
from Cozumel, Quintana Roo
Merida, Museo Regional
de Yucatán "Palacio Cantón"
cat. 236

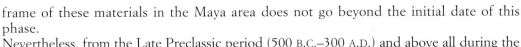

Olmec sculpture
from Ojo de Agua
Tapachula
Chiapas Museo del Soconusco

Olmec relief
found on the Guatemalan
Pacific coast

frame of these materials in the Maya area does not go beyond the initial date of this phase.

Nevertheless, from the Late Preclassic period (500 B.C.–300 A.D.) and above all during the Classic (300–1000 A.D.), influences were from the Maya area toward the west, displacing and thus Mayanizing, the Mixe-Zoque population that occupied part of Tabasco and Chiapas. To conclude, we might suggest that not only the Mayas were enriched by Olmec influences, but rather that a large part of Mesoamerica displays this presence in contexts and archaeological materials. There are numerous patterns and cultural guidelines that the Olmecs contributed to the formation of this cultural macro-area. This may be found both on a material level, as well as on a spiritual one, since the religious symbols and images that we see in visual representations of the so-called archaeological Olmecs, played a decisive role in the process of formation of late mythologies and traditions of Mesoamerican peoples.

The small advances that have been made in knowledge of Olmec cultures show us the importance of this people to the origins of Maya civilization. But also the data, of which we now know about pre-Hispanic Maya society, can provide us with information to understand this cultural phenomenon that we call Olmec. Of its presence in the Maya area, we have only archaeological evidence in the form of some of the examples presented in this essay.

Realistic drawings of engraved figures
found on the Guatemalan
Pacific coast

Phytomorphic vessels
from Cuyamel, Trujillo Colón
Early and Middle Preclassic period
Tegucigalpa, Bodegas Centrales
del Instituto Hondureño
de Antropología e Historia
cat. 179–180

References

AGRINIER, PIERRE
1989
"Mirador-Plumajillo, Chiapas, y sus relaciones con cuatro sitios del horizonte olmeca en Veracruz, Chiapas y la costa de Guatemala." *Arqueología*, no. 2, 19–36. Mexico: Instituto Nacional de Antropología e Historia.

ANDREWS, E. WYLLYS V (ED.)
1986
"Olmec Jades from Chacsinkin, Yucatan, and Maya Ceramics from La Venta, Tabasco." In *Research and Reflections in Archaeology and History*. Publication 57. New Orleans: Tulane University. Middle American Research Institute, 11–47

BOGGS, STANLEY
1950
"Olmec Pictographs in the Las Victorias Group, Chalchuapa Archaeological Zone, El Salvador." In *Notes on Middle American Archaeology and Ethnology*. Vol. 4 (99). Washington, D.C.: Carnegie Institution of Washington, 85–92

CLARK, JOHN E. (ED.)
1984
"Antecedentes de la cultura olmeca." In *Los olmecas en Mesoamérica*. Mexico: Ediciones del Equilibrista, 34–44

CLARK, JOHN E. AND MICHAEL BLAKE
1989
"El origen de la civilización en Mesoamérica: los olmecas y mokayas del Soconusco de Chiapas." In *El Preclásico o Formativo: avances y perspectivas*. Ed. by M. Carmona. Mexico: Instituto Nacional de Antropología e Historia, 385–405

COE, MICHAEL D.
1966
An Early Stone Pectoral from Southeastern Mexico. Studies in Precolumbian Art and Archaeology 1. Washington, D.C.: Dumbarton Oaks

COE, MICHAEL D., AND KENT FLANNERY
1967
Early Cultures and Human Ecology in South Coastal Guatemala. Contribution to Anthropology, 3. Washington, D.C.: Smithsonian Institution Press

COE, MICHAEL D., AND RICHARD A. DIEHL
1980
In the Land of the Olmec. Austin: University of Texas Press

EKHOLM-MILLER, SUSAN
1973
The Olmec Rock Carving at Xoc, Chiapas, Mexico. Papers of the New World Archaeological Foundation, no. 32. Provo: Brigham Young University

FASH, WILLIAM L.
1985
"La secuencia de ocupación del Grupo 9N-8." In *Yaxkín*. Vol. VIII (1–2). Tegucigalpa: Instituto Hondureño de Antropología e Historia, 135–50

GARCÍA MOLL, ROBERTO
1979
"Un relieve olmeca en Tenosique, Tabasco." In *Estudios de Cultura Maya*. Vol. XII. Mexico: Universidad Nacional Autónoma de México, 53–59

HAMMOND, NORMAN
1982
Ancient Maya Civilization. The State University of New Jersey: New Brunswick, Rutgers

HAMMOND, NORMAN, ET AL.
1991
"Stratigraphy and Chronology in the Reconstruction of Preclassic Development at Cuello." In *Cuello, An Early Maya Community in Belize*. Ed. by N. Hammond. Cambridge, Mass.: Cambridge University Press, 23–69

HERNÁNDEZ AYALA, AND MARTHA IVON
1981
"Una estela olmeca en el área del Usumacinta." In *Boletín*, II (17). Mexico, 25–28

ICHON, ALAIN
1977
Les Sculptures de La Lagunita, El Quiché, Guatemala. Guatemala: Editorial Piedra Santa.

LEE, THOMAS A.
1989
"Chiapas and the Olmec." In *Regional Perspectives on the Olmec*. Ed. by R. Sharer and D. Grove. Cambridge, Mass.: Cambridge University Press, 198–226

LOWE, GARETH W.
1973
The Early Preclassic Barra Phase of Altamira, Chiapas. Papers of the New World Archaeological Foundation, no. 38. Provo: Brigham Young University
1981
"Olmec Horizons Defined in Mound 20, San Isidro." In *The Olmec and Their Neighbors*. Ed.

by E. Benson. Washington, D.C.: Dumbarton Oaks, 231–55

1994

"Comunidades de Chiapas relacionadas con los olmecas." In *Los olmecas en Mesoamérica*. Ed. by J. Clark. Mexico: Ediciones El Equilibrista, 113–19

MCDONALD, ANDREW J.
1983

Tzutzuculi: A Middle Preclassic Site on the Pacific Coast of Chiapas, Mexico. Papers of the New World Archaeological Foundation, no. 47. Provo: Brigham Young University

NAVARRETE, CARLOS
1969

"Los relieves olmecas de Pijijiapan, Chiapas." In *Anales de Antropología*. Vol. 6. Mexico: Universidad Nacional Autónoma de México, 183–95

1971

"Algunas piezas olmecas de Chiapas y Guatemala." In *Anales de Antropología*. Vol. 8. Mexico: Universidad Nacional Autónoma de México, 69–82

OCHOA, LORENZO
1982

"Hachas olmecas y otras piezas arqueológicas del medio Usumacinta." *Revista Mexicana de Estudios Antropológicos*, tomo XXVIII. Mexico: Sociedad Mexicana de Antropología, 109–22

1983

"El medio Usumacinta: un eslabón en los antecedentes olmecas de los mayas." In *Antropología e historia de los mixe-zoques y mayas*. Ed. by L. Ochoa and T. Lee. Mexico: Universidad Nacional Autónoma de México-Brigham Young University, 145–74

ORREGO CORZO, MIGUEL
1990

Investigaciones arqueológicas en Abaj Takalik, El Asintal, Retalhuleu, año 1988. Reporte no. 1. Guatemala: Instituto de Antropología e Historia de Guatemala

PAILLÉS H., MARICRUZ
1980

Pampa El Pajón, An Early Middle Preclassic Site on the Coast of Chiapas, México. Papers of the New World Archaeological Foundation, no. 44. Provo: Brigham Young University

PÉREZ SUÁREZ, TOMÁS
1997

"Los olmecas y los dioses del maíz en Mesoamérica." In *De hombres y dioses*. Coord. by X. Noguez and A. López Austin. Mexico: El Colegio de Michoacán-El Colegio Mexiquense, A.C., 17–58

POHORILENKO, ANATOLE
1981

"The Olmec Style and Costa Rica Archaeology." In *The Olmec and Their Neighbors*. Ed. by E. Benson. Washington, D.C.: Dumbarton Oaks, 309–27

PROSKOURIAKOFF, TATIANA
1974

Jades from the Cenote of Sacrifice, Chichén Itzá,

Yucatan. Memoirs of the Peabody Museum of Archaeology and Ethnology. Vol. 10(2). Cambridge, Mass.: Harvard University

RATHJE, WILLIAM L.
1973

"El descubrimiento de un jade olmeca en la isla de Cozumel, Quintana Roo, México." In *Estudios de Cultura Maya*. Vol. IX. Mexico: Universidad Nacional Autónoma de México, 85–91

SABLOFF, JEREMY
1975

"The Ceramics." In *Excavations at Ceibal, Department of Petén, Guatemala*. Ed. G.R. Willey. Memoirs of the Peabody Museum of Archaeology and Ethnology. Vol. 13(2). Cambridge, Mass.: Harvard University

SHARER, ROBERT J.
1978

The Prehistory of Chalchuapa, El Salvador. University Museum Monograph 36. Philadelphia: University of Pennsylvania Press

SHARER, ROBERT J., AND DAVID W. SEDAT
1987

Archaeological Investigations in the Northern Maya Highlands, Guatemala: Interaction and the Development of Maya Civilization. University Museum Monograph 59. Philadelphia: University of Pennsylvania Press

SHOOK, EDWIN M.
1950

"Tiquisate Users Scoop Archaeological World, Find Ruined City on Farm." *Unifruitco*, August. New York: United Fruit Company, 62–63

SHOOK, EDWIN M., AND ROBERT F. HEIZER
1976

"An Olmec Sculpture from the South Pacific Coast of Guatemala." In *Journal of New World Archaeology*. Vol. I (3). Los Angeles: University of California, 1–18

SMITH, A. LEDYARD
1982

"Major Architecture and Caches." In *Excavations at Ceibal, Department of Petén, Guatemala*. Ed. by G.R. Willey. Memoirs of the Peabody Museum of Archaeology and Ethnology. Vol. 15 (1 and 2). Cambridge, Mass.: Harvard University

VIEL, RENÉ
1993

Evolución de la cerámica de Copán, Honduras. Tegucigalpa: Instituto Hondureño de Antropología e Historia-Centro de Estudios Mexicanos y Centroamericanos

WILLEY, GORDON R.
1978

"Artifacts." In *Excavations at Ceibal, Department of Petén, Guatemala*. Ed. by G.R. Willey. Memoirs of the Peabody Museum of Archaeology and Ethnology. Vol. 14 (1, 2, and 3). Cambridge, Mass.: Harvard University

Maya Frontiers

Female figurine
from Kaminaljuyú, Preclassic period
Guatemala, Museo Nacional
de Arqueología y Etnología
cat. 312

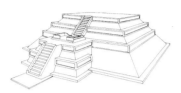

Plan of a Teotihuacan-style structure
at Kaminaljuyú, Guatemala

The Maya settled in a territory of around 400,000 square kilometers now occupied by the Mexican states of Yucatán, Quintana Roo, Campeche, Tabasco, and Eastern Chiapas, and by Belize, Guatemala, western Honduras, and El Salvador. This area, which displays an extreme variety of geographical features, divides orographically into highlands and lowlands, which, for various geographical, environmental, and cultural reasons, are further subdivided into a northern, a central, and a southern area.

From the very earliest Maya times, the exchange of artifacts and influences from neighboring populations played a decisive role in local cultural evolution. The first trading routes and the invention of a calendar and methods of writing can be attributed with certainty to the Olmec people, who as early as the Preclassic period established the main channels through which the most sought-after goods were distributed. In the southern Maya area, Olmec elements combined syncretically with local traditions to generate what is known as Izapan Culture between the Middle Preclassic Olmec and the Early Classic Maya. A major center that grew up within Maya territory on the basis of external traditions and expressions was Kaminaljuyú. At the end of the Early Classic period, this important ceremonial complex, which ranks as one of the main focal points of Maya political and cultural interests in the southern area, slowly fell into decline. Around 400 B.C. the highlands were ruled by Teotihuacan and a group belonging to this cultural area of Central Mexico moved to Kaminaljuyú and it built a scaled-down version of the capital of their home territories.

In this way, new social classes were established on the basis of the political situation that had developed, with a privileged elite holding sway over a population of Mayan origin. This political arrangement eventually led to a hybridization of customs and cultural developments, and an intermingling of Maya traditions and influences from Central Mexico, even outside the highland territory, as can be seen in the Classic period architecture and sculpture in Tikal. Teotihuacan influences can also be seen in one of the buildings at Dzibilchaltún, in Yucatán, in which the characteristic *talud-tablero* is found. Yucatán traditions underwent substantial changes in the Postclassic period as a result of the Toltec invasion, which introduced new religious and stylistic elements that are documented in architecture, sculpture, and pottery. The Itzá people, who invaded in the thirteenth century, took possession of the center of Chichén, establishing their presence in the peninsula and giving their name to the city originally conquered by the Toltecs.

However, irrespective of external influences and contributions to Maya civilization from populations that settled directly in their territory, two distinct frontiers can be drawn to the east and to the west. The first runs from the Atlantic Ocean to the Pacific through present-day El Salvador and Honduras; the second, which in part follows the course of the Río Grijalva, includes eastern Chiapas and Tabasco.

The populations of both adjoining areas, with whom the Maya often traded and enjoyed friendly relations, were heavily influenced by their powerful neighbors. So dependent were these populations, in fact, that they suffered largely the same socio-political and economic collapse when the Classic period came to an end.

The Eastern Frontier

Prior to the establishment of the Maya civilization, a long evolutionary process took place in the territories along the eastern frontier, as attested by the presence of some extremely ancient archaeological sites. Local cultural phenomena are the result of millennia of gradual evolution and contacts between ethnically and socially diverse populations: the Mesoamerican populations were influenced from the north and those of the Central Area from the south. The oldest known settlements, dating back some 5,000 years, were established by bands of hunters and gatherers who camped in caves or on open sites. The main vestiges of this occupation can be seen in mineral fields with rock carvings, where evidence of stone tool working has come to light. During the Archaic period, the Sula Valley was used by populations governed by semi-sedentary systems and a complex social organization, as finds at Río Pelo near El Progreso demonstrate. Independent cultures developed between 4000 and 2000 B.C. The societies that grew up in the Formative period gradually acquired technological know-how that led to a more rational use of the land. They began to occupy the most fertile valleys bordering on the area where the Maya groups later settled, which eventually

Dzibilchaltún, Yucatán
group of structures
referred to as Siete Muñecas

gave rise to the development of the center at Copán. Specialized farming techniques were used and pottery produced from as early as 2000 B.C. The social structure closely resembled that adopted by the Maya population; both were based on a rigid hierarchy and the supremacy of a priestly elite exercising centralized power over small territorial areas. Around 1000 B.C. more stable, settled communities grew up. The Yarumela site in the Comayagua Valley confirms that these took the form of farming villages organized around monumental religious buildings. Permanent villages also grew up in the Copán area, such as Las Sepolturas and El Bosque, which were inhabited by farmers known to have made pottery and adopted funerary practices that included burial beneath the floors of the deceased's own dwelling. Between 900 and 400 B.C. a dense network of relations between the Pacific coast and the highlands developed, although this did not alter the traditional local autonomy of style in sites in which Maya civilization developed. The Preclassic period, when products were transported by merchants across the western territories towards the Valley of Mexico, saw the spread of ceramic styles typical of the people of Honduras and El Salvador, a phenomenon which coincided with the introduction of Teotihuacan elements from the north. These territories were, however, heavily influenced by the central area, through which traditional elements of South American culture were imported.

Linguistic studies in the Salvadoran area suggest that the earliest settlements were probably made by Zoque-speaking and not Maya peoples. The oldest evidence of this is the center located near the Hacienda El Carmen in the valley of Río Cara Sucia, active from 1400 B.C. to 250 A.D. The remains of two important complexes were discovered at Chalchuapa, one on the north coast of the Laguna Cuzcachapa, the other near the El Trapiche source. The

presence of pottery belonging to the Tok complex, notably in the form of the *tecomate* or globular, neckless jar and the *cajete*, a dish with flared sides, clearly traces its origins back to the Pacific coast of Guatemala and Chiapas. Materials unearthed at El Carmen corroborate the theory that the populations which settled in western El Salvador belonged to the Zoque ethnic group. Between 900 and 800 B.C. the most important Preclassic settlement in Salvadoran territory was undoubtedly Chalchuapa, part of a group of political and economic power centers of Locona-Ocós cultural descent, whose influence extended from Oaxaca to present-day El Salvador. The most important centers were Chalcatzingo (Morelos), San José Mogote (Oaxaca), La Blanca, El Mesak, Abaj Takalik (Guatemala), and Chalchuapa itself (El Salvador). These centers were linked by trading networks that continued to be used by the Maya right up to the Classic period and were also centers for the distribution of ceramic materials belonging to the territory's southern cultural area. Society was predominantly Olmec, from the Mexican Gulf Coast. In addition to the rapid proliferation of planned centers with typically monumental public architecture, this age also saw a phase of intense cultural interaction that favored the exchange of cultural innovations. How much actual influence the Olmecs had on even quite distant areas is still a matter of controversy and open to various interpretations, although there is evidence of the spread of religious concepts, ceremonial practices, and many different kinds of artifacts. Luxury items such as cocoa, obsidian, jade, animal skins, and tropical bird feathers were traded from the Pacific area. At the end of the Middle Preclassic period, Chalchuapa became the main ceremonial center of the south-easternmost part of Mesoamerica. In the Late Preclassic period, it was a major cultural center and maintained a position that was anything but marginal to the Maya

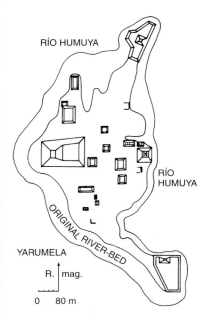

RÍO HUMUYA

RÍO HUMUYA

YARUMELA

ORIGINAL RIVER-BED

R. | mag.

0   80 m

Yarumela, Honduras
layout of the main structures

area. Hieroglyphic writing and calendar systems had already been developed in Chalchua-pa: the stela with glyphs found at El Trapiche suggest that this was probably one of the Maya areas where the tradition of chronicling events in graphic form began. For a long time Chalchuapa had close ties with the lowlands. In terms of artifact production, Usulután-type pottery was, in the region under Chalchuapan control, one of the most widely traded wares of the whole Maya area. The obsidian production center at Ixtepeque and trading of this choice material in the lowlands may well also have been under Chalchuapan control.

Other important centers during the Preclassic period have been identified in the region of El Cerrón Grande. Unfortunately, however, the majority of sites from this period are hidden by a thick layer of volcanic ash. The most important among those recorded is El Perical, the site of a settlement dating back to 1000–900 B.C. whose pottery is very similar to that of Chalchuapa. An interactive cultural network characterized by the presence of Uapala pottery flourished in both eastern El Salvador and western Honduras in the Late Preclassic period. One of the most important centers in which this ware was found is Quelepa, which developed between 200 B.C. and 200 A.D. and had links with such sites as Copán, Yarumela, Los Naranjos, and Santa Rita, to the west of Honduran territory. The population was probably Lenca, a Maya-speaking group that separated from its more powerful relatives in the Preclassic period.

The development of society in western and central El Salvador was abruptly interrupted by the violent eruption of the Ilopango volcano around 260 A.D., which covered an area of some 10,000 square kilometers and destroyed the preceding settlements. There is no evidence that any major migrations ensued, although the area was devastated and the population had to reorganize itself in new centers.

In Honduras, complex societies were established between the Late Preclassic and Early Classic periods. Centers like Los Naranjos and Lo de Vaca grew up at about the same time as Kaminaljuyú and Chalchuapa, whereas the Copán Valley did not feel the effects of the cultural ferment in neighboring areas, for reasons which remain unknown. Up to the sixth century A.D., Maya influence seems to have been negligible throughout northwest Central America, with the exception of Tazumal (Chalchuapa, El Salvador). In the lowlands, monumental centers like Uaxactún, Mirador, Tikal, and Cerros flourished.

In the Río Motagua Valley, Maya history is closely bound up with the presence of two main centers, Copán and Quiriguá, which began their development as hubs of regional life from the Preclassic period.

Copán reached the peak of its urban growth between 400 and 900 A.D., thanks to the establishment of an institutional dynastic Maya power that introduced hieroglyphic writing and new aesthetic parameters. The historic records of some of the sovereigns quote two dates–159 A.D. and 160 A.D.–in reference to the beginning of the dynasty's rule (Stela 1). However, the most ancient hieroglyphic inscriptions associated with the reign of Yax K'uk Mo', whose qualities earned him the title of founder of the dynasty, date back to 426 A.D. (Stela 15). Until 737 A.D. Copán dominated the territory and the smaller centers, including Quiriguá itself, controlling the obsidian trade to the Guatemalan highlands and the jadeite deposits of Guaytán. Midway through the eighth century, following the defeat by Cauac Sky of the thirteenth governor of Copán, 18 Rabbit, after which this important urban center came under the control of Quiriguá, a new equilibrium was achieved. The old satellite center benefited in particular from this situation, replacing Copán as the controller of trade, the resources of Lake Izabal, and the port of Nito on the Río Dulce, an access point of coastal routes towards the Caribbean area. The urban development that took place in Quiriguá in subsequent decades demonstrates the economic advantages gained by the Sky (Ka'an) dynastic elite. In Copán, the confusion following defeat lasted three decades, but when reorganization eventually came, it ushered in a new period of splendor, marked by the creation of architectural complexes.

This new situation had consequences on the economy, technology, and progress of native populations. Maya power, in all its various expressions, had the effect on the one hand of influencing and halting the development of existing cultures, and on the other of increasing trade and the spread of a property culture throughout Mesoamerican territory, thanks to the presence of Copán and Quiriguá, which both enjoyed the benefits of its already consolidated trading system. The customs and socio-political system of the populations of western

Usulután-type vessel
from Chiapa de Corzo, Chiapas
Protoclassic period
Mexico City
Museo Nacional de Antropología
cat. 216

Honduras were modified by the influx of new models from the Guatemalan area. Religion, architectural expression, the introduction of writing and the calendar, and the hierarchical social class system brought about a radical change in local traditions. Maya influence led to the use of polychrome decoration in pottery, which incorporated cultural innovations while developing its own particular style. The layout of the settlements also changed: building complexes were organized around rectangular patios, and there was a more widespread use of ball game pitches and raised platforms used as a base for building. Writing was not adopted by populations outside the Maya world as a means of conveying information: the use of glyphs on the pottery made by inhabitants of the valleys of central Honduras and El Salvador was purely decorative with no semantic meaning.

The precise reasons for the radical changes that took place in the Classic period are not fully understood. The centuries between 500 and 850 A.D. saw a population increase and a period of marked economic prosperity, which in archaeological terms corresponds to the presence of the Polychrome Ulúa phase in the Late Classic period. One further indication of the cultural complexity of this age is the rapid rise and expansion of settlements over-

opposite
Effigy vessel
from Uaxactún, Petén
Early Classic period
Guatemala, Museo Nacional
de Arqueología y Etnología
cat. 480

Ball court
Copán, Honduras

looking strategic points on the main communication routes to the confluence between the Chamelecón and the Ulúa and to the Valley of Comayagua (Cerro Palenque).

The relationship between the native populations and the Maya in this period also remains something of a mystery. Ulúa-type stone and pottery artifacts unearthed in Maya-occupied sites, especially in the domestic sectors of Copán, would seem to attest the existence of trading activities involving obsidian and ceramic. However, the possibility of enclaves of foreign elites in the main centers cannot be ruled out. Certain building and architectural models in the Sula Valley, such as sphaeristeria and decorated public temples, and the presence of stela and iconographical elements in pottery design raise doubts as to whether this was a question of direct Maya influence or of local Maya-inspired variants.

During the Classic period, Chalchuapa (in the area that is now El Salvador) was not abandoned after the eruption of the Ilopango volcano, although the quantity of pottery from this period does suggest a fall in the population. Relations with Kaminaljuyú were probably also severed and monumental building work interrupted.

In the Zapotitán Valley there are thought to have been more than 280 settlements in the Late Classic period, with a population somewhere between 40,000 and 100,000. The main administrative and ceremonial center was unquestionably San Andrés, at the confluence of the Río Sucio and Agua Caliente. This was the capital of a powerful regional state that played a leading role in the distribution of obsidian from Ixtepeque and jade towards the Valley of Motagua. One of the centers under the rule of San Andrés was Joya de Cerén, a farming community reused after the eruption of the Ilopango volcano. This site, which was hastily abandoned by its people when catastrophe struck, has yielded invaluable archaeological information. All the everyday objects used by the people who lived there were covered by ash, providing a highly detailed picture of local lifestyles, farming techniques and animals.

Chalchuapa retained its importance as a regional state. In the Classic period it had ties with San Andrés and the center at Copán, concentrating its activities towards the Maya area when contacts with Kaminaljuyú were broken off. Tazumal, located at the extreme south of the Chalchuapa archaeological area, was, however, the main center during the Classic period. Between 550 and 850 A.D. it reached the peak of its architectural development in the form of a 24-meter pyramid with vertical terraces. The exquisite material discovered in its tombs suggests links with Teotihuacan and has prompted theories that the local social elite were descended from a dynasty instated by the Teotihuacans, although the influence is perhaps more likely to have come from centers like Copán or Kaminaljuyú, which in turn had a

Ruler lid
from Copán, Honduras
Late Classic period
Copán Ruinas
Museo Regional de Arqueología
cat. 138

strong Teotihuacan ancestry (Fowler 1995, 117–24). Objects in Copador style, which testify to the close links with Copán, are among the most significant finds from the Tazumal excavation site. Similarly, the presence of Salúa (or Ulúa-Yojoa) pottery suggests strong ties with the Maya area.

According to the theory expounded by Sheets, colonization of the area by Chorti Maya groups may have been coordinated from Copán, although this idea now seems fairly improbable. The pre-existence of these centers and their independent development suggests, rather, that the political elite of Tazumal and San Andrés chose to emulate the privileged castes of Copán to assert their own political power, which did, however, develop independently of the Copán sphere of influence and was not produced by outside invaders. Between 700 and 950 A.D., which also saw a period of crisis in the Maya social system, the

Effigy vessel
from Uaxactún, Petén
Early Classic period
Guatemala, Museo Nacional
de Arqueología y Etnología
cat. 481

center at Cara Sucia (Ahuachapán Dept.) became a territorial extension of the culture of Cotzumalguapa, whose distribution center was in the Escuintla area on Guatemala's southeast Pacific coast. This enabled the Cotzumalguapans to take over production of cocoa, salt, and cotton. Between 800 and 900–1000 A.D., when the Classic period came to an end, populations which had contact with the fringes of Maya territory found themselves in a similar situation to that which had led to the collapse of the political and social system of their better-organized neighbors. Many flourishing centers were abandoned, although Cerro Palenque, in present-day Honduras, retained its importance as a center of power until the end of the first millennium. Mexican influences in this period favored cultural development to the south, in El Salvador, Nicaragua, and Costa Rica. The area now occupied by Honduras, on the other hand, underwent a general decline, which can be explained by its closer ties with the Maya world and economy. Its collapse had inevitable repercussions on populations that had concentrated on the specialized production of goods marketed within the Maya trading network. The Postclassic period (900–1500 A.D.) was characterized by increased tension between indigenous peoples and by contact with the Mexicanized Maya of the Yucatán peninsula. In the Sula Valley, links were established with cultural traditions originating in the Valley of Mexico; the cities of Comayagua and Tenampuá were transformed into defensive strongholds as a result of mounting tension and the socio-political effects of the instability brought about by the break-up of the Maya system. The collapse at the end of the Classic period had a profound effect on Mesoamerican life, as Mexican power expanded and entire regions were quickly subjugated, creating tension and instability. After the abandonment of Copán and Quiriguá, the effects of the Maya downfall on the frontier territories were not immediate, but the collapse of the trading system between the various city states had drastic consequences for the economies of native peoples, and unbalanced the organizational and administrative systems.

Traditional values were replaced by those created by new cultural stimuli, and economic systems changed as a result. One of the most evident cases is that of Naco, in the valley of the same name, which in the Postclassic period had achieved a considerable degree of development since it was one of the main trading hubs on which the Toltec-Maya and Mexican-Maya merchants converged.

By contrast, central and southern Honduras were affected by the presence of other groups such as the Pipiles and Chorotegas, who transported their tradable goods in caravans under military escort. New metalworking techniques were introduced from the central area, with the growing influence of populations living in what is now Costa Rica, Nicaragua, and Panama.

The Western Frontier

The Río Grijalva basin is the demarcation line that separates the Maya-controlled territories to the west from the Mesoamerican area in the area of the Isthmus of Tehuantepec. The adjoining regions were part of Tabasco and Chiapas and ran from the Atlantic to the Pacific coast. Our understanding of the cultural past of the peoples who settled in these lands, relations with their Maya neighbors, and possibly even their own origins comes mainly through linguistic studies, which show migrations, contacts, and similarities in the tongues used, in addition to the regional dissemination of archaeological materials. When the Spanish embarked upon the conquest of Chiapas in 1523, the native groups spoke at least three languages in the Mayan family: Tzeltal, Tzotzil, and Tojolabal. Inhabitants of the eastern highlands spoke Coxoh, although whether this should more accurately be considered a dialect form of Tzeltal or of Tojolabal is still under debate. The cultural context in that period in the eastern Chiapas regions was therefore Maya, although what form it took prior to this is still uncertain. As they completed their conquest of the territory, the Spanish documented the existence of another tongue, Zoque, spoken throughout western Chiapas as far as the borders with Oaxaca and with the Gulf Coast territories, Tabasco and Veracruz. Archaeological finds and glottochronological studies point to a marked cultural heterogeneity in all the neighboring territories from as early as the Preclassic period.

The Pacific coastal plain from Chiapas to El Salvador was occupied from ancient times by people who established pioneering pottery traditions, as seen in Barra in the Chiapas and Ocós and Cuadros along the south coast of Guatemala. The second of these in particular spread rapidly and is well documented archaeologically. Ocós pottery can be said to have introduced and popularized, from 1500 B.C. onwards, most of the typological and decorative elements found in southern Mesoamerica, with the exception of necked jugs: one representative stylistic derivation is that of the Ojochi ceramic complex, which corresponds to the early occupation of San Lorenzo in Veracruz several centuries before it became one of the main Olmec centers. The most frequently found forms are bowls with effigies, the bases and bodies of *tecomates*, tripod receptacles, dishes with vertical sides, incense burners on pedestals and countless fragments that testify to an impressive array of decorative techniques. Sites coming under the Ocós sphere of influence are strangely absent from the central Chiapas depression, possibly having been destroyed by erosion because of their precarious nature and limited size. They do, however, appear in the upper reaches of the Río

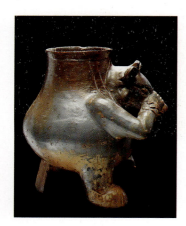

top and front page
Effigy vessel of Tohil
Plumbate ware
Terminal Classic–Early
Postclassic period
Merida, Museo Regional
de Yucatán "Palacio Cantón"
cat. 26

Jade pectoral pendant
from the Hieroglyphic Stairway
at Copán
Copán, Museo Regional
de Arqueología
cat. 394

Grijalva and the Guatemalan highlands in Verapaz. The migratory route taken by the bringers of this tradition to the northeast is still unclear, whereas there is abundant evidence to show that it spread northwards through the isthmus to southern Veracruz and Tabasco on the Gulf Coast. According to Lowe, the archaic Barra-Ocós tradition, which extended throughout the isthmus region and later generated the Ojochi, Bajío, and Chicharras pottery phases on the Gulf Coast and the Cuadros phase on the Pacific coast, was propagated and possibly even invented by Zoque people.

Linguistic studies have identified a large family, the Zoque-Mixe-Popoluca, which occupied the whole isthmus. Scholars believe that around 1600 B.C. one language was spoken and that it did not begin to branch off in different directions and reach its final form until around 600 B.C. An exception to this was Tapachulteco, which became distinct from Zoque later, around 1000 B.C. From an archaeological viewpoint, little is known about the sites that can be associated with these populations in the Early Preclassic period, if ancient Ocós occupations are excluded. More can be gleaned from sites belonging to the Middle Preclassic period, which saw the development and consolidation of Olmec society and the spread of its stylistic and ideological elements over a vast area, leading to the rise of a dense network of trading routes. In the Late Preclassic period (500–300 B.C.), a transformation in Olmec society can be inferred from the growing power of numerous regional centers, such as Chiapa de Corzo, San Isidro, Mirador, and Izapa, characterized by the use of finely polished pottery, a growing tendency to plan the sites on which buildings were erected, and the use of complex funerary practices involving lavish offerings.

The end of this phase saw the first signs of the beginnings of Maya civilization and early forms of hieroglyphic writing. The two events appear to be unrelated, since records relating to older inscriptions date back to as early as 1100 B.C. in the Olmec area and the process continued in Oaxaca and Izapa in Chiapas, on the basis of tongues in use at the time and probably spreading in the manner of the Zoque-Mixe-Popoluca. According to some authors, the writing was introduced by Maya of the Mixe group in Izapa. During this Early Classic period, the Maya conquered the central Chiapas depression, its highlands and the upper reaches of the Río Grijalva, establishing the basis of an ethnic frontier that survives to this day. To the north and to the west the centers at Veracruz, Tabasco and Oaxaca took on increasing importance. Throughout the Early Classic period the major non-Maya regional centers extending from one coast of the isthmus to the other developed their own characteristics and disseminated a style of black pottery with white edging that was the most frequently used offering in the rites celebrated in the many karst caves in Chiapas territory.

This was followed by a period of heavy Teotihuacan influence, as can be seen in numerous sites such as Mirador, Izapa, and San Isidro. The cultural ferment found in the centuries of the Late Classic period was fired mainly by the Izapa, which spread San Juan plumbate ware and by San Isidro, again black pottery with white edging, which continued to be used as an offering in caves, at least up to 900 A.D. In the Postclassic period the Chiapas area was heavily influenced by central Mexican cultures, especially by the Toltecs, whose own iconographical motifs were extensively assimilated by local cultures to the point of becoming part of traditional Tohil plumbate ceramic. Finds have been documented as far south as Panama and in northwest Mexico and can be considered a "fossil-guide" ranking on a par with Usulután pottery. The cultural situation at the end of the Postclassic period during Mexican rule is still not fully understood, although Spanish chroniclers' records confirm that Pacific coast settlers were largely Mixe-speaking, while inland populations spoke the Zoque tongue. The region extending from Ocozocuatla to the artificial basin of Malpaso is one of the archaeologically less well-documented areas. The most important sites to have been studied or documented are Lopez Mateos, El Cafetal, Varejonal, la Cueva de la Media Luna, and Piedra Parada. A tributary of the Grijalva, the Río La Venta, flows through this area. This river forms a steep canyon rising as high as 500 meters, with caves that show signs of occupation. To the east, the dense Ocote Forest still extends intact over 12,000 square kilometers.

Recent archaeological research in the area has revealed a uniform kind of architecture consisting of large temple complexes built on earthworks, and fenced-off areas for the ritual ball game. Although little is known about the cultural evolution of these centers in the Early and Middle Postclassic periods, it is certain that they are evidence of a well-estab-

Human head
Late Classic period
Comalcalco
Museo de Sitio de Comalcalco
cat. 70

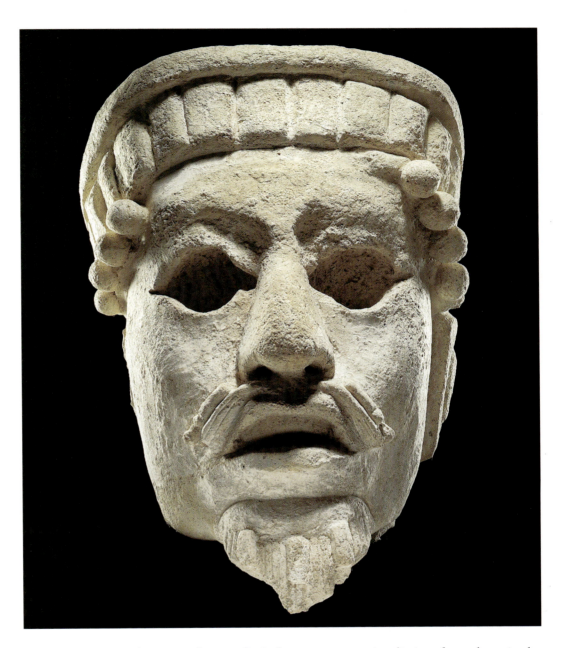

lished tradition in the area, whose stylistic features were quite distinct from those in the Maya sphere of influence.

The buildings, erected on rectangular bases, were constructed using rectangular limestone blocks. The main body was clad in horizontal rows of stone slabs interrupted by vertical elements, creating a panel-like effect. The doorway led into the interior spaces whose walls were embellished with niches, sometimes used as tombs. Some sites grew to considerable proportions: the site at Kang, recently uncovered in the Ocote Forest spreads, over more than 11 hectares. The construction of these complexes implies a sizable population and well-developed social organization, elements that denote a consolidated regional culture. There is still little information about the socio-economical life of these populations, but much has been learned about the rituals celebrated in the inaccessible Río La Venta caves. The most important concern funerary rites for children (Cueva del Lazo), or ones relating to offerings found in caves at 350 meters above the river (Endless Walk). It is impossible to know what relations these people had with their Maya neighbors, but it is certain that they maintained their own linguistic and cultural identity, probably thanks to the model of solid political cohesion they engineered.

References

ADAMS, RICHARD E.W.
1977
The Origins of Maya Civilization. Albuquerque: University of New Mexico Press

AGRINIER, PIERRE
1969
"Reconocimiento de Varejonal, Chiapas, México." *Anales 1967-1968*, México, INAH, 69–93

ANDREWS, E. WYLLYS V.
1970
"Excavations at Quelepa, Eastern El Salvador." *Cerámica de Cultura Maya*, 6, 21–40
1986
La arqueología de Quelepa, El Salvador. San Salvador: Dirección de Publicaciones e Impresos. Viceministerio de Comunicaciones

ÁNGEL ESCALONA DEL, ANDRÉS, AND CARLOS SERRANO SÁNCHEZ
1995
"La relación coxoh-tzeltal-tojolabas desde una perspectiva biológica. " In *Memorias del Segundo Congreso Internacional de Mayistas*. México: UNAM, 643–61

ARMAS MOLINA, MIGUEL
1976
La Cultura Pipil de Centro America. San Salvador: Ministerio de Educación

Arqueología Doméstica
1991
Arqueología Doméstica en Joya de Cerén. San Salvador: Ministerio de Educación

BAUDEZ, CLAUDE-FRANÇOIS, AND PIERRE BECQUELIN
1968
"Recherches Archéologiques dans la région du Lac Yojoa, Honduras." *Journal de la Société des Américanistes*. Vol. LVII. Paris, 135–38
1969
"La séquence céramique de Los Naranjos, Honduras." In *Akten des 38 Internationalen Amerikanistenkongresses (1968)*. Vol. I. Stuttgart-München, 221–28
1985
I Maya. Milan: Rizzoli–Serie L'America Precolombiana

BENAVIDES CASTILLO, ANTONIO
1995
"El sur y el centro de la zona maya en el Clásico." In *Historia Antigua de México-El horizonte Clásico*, Vol. II. Ed. by L. Manzanilla and L. López Luján. México: INAH, UNAM, Miguel Àngel Porrúa, 65–99

BERNAL, IGNACIO
1970
"The Olmec Region." In *Observations on the Emergence of Civilizations in Mesoamerica*. Berkeley: University of California Press

BRYANT, DOUGLAS, AND JOHN E. CLARK
1983
"Los primeros mayas precolombinos de la cuenca superior del río Grijalva." In *Antropología e historia de los mixe-zoques y mayas: Homenaje a Frans Blom*. Ed. by T. A. Lee, Jr. and L. Ochoa. México: UNAM-Brigham Young University 223–39

CAMPBELL, LYLE
1988
The Linguistics of Southeast Chiapas, Mexico, Papers of the New World Archaeological Foundation, no. 50. Provo: Brigham Young University

CIUDAD REAL, ANTONIO DE
1976
Tratado curioso y docto de las grandezas de la Nueva España. Ed. by J. García Quintana and V.M. Castillo Farreras. 2 Vols., México: Instituto de Investigaciones Históricas, UNAM

COE, MICHAEL D.
1986 [1966; 1980]
Los Mayas-Incógnitas y realidades. México: Editorial Diana
1989
"Olmecas y Mayas: estudio de relaciones." In *Los orígenes de la civilización Maya*. Ed. by Richard E. W. Adams. México: Fondo de Cultura Económica, 205–18

CREAMER, WINIFRED
1979
"Sistemas de Intercambio en el Golfo de Nicoya. Costa Rica, 1200–1550 D.C." In *Vínculos-Revista de Antropología del Museo Nacional de Costa Rica*. Vol. 8, nos. 1-2, San José: Museo Nacional de Costa Rica, 13–38

CULBERT PATRICK (ED.)
1973
The Classic Maya Collapse. Albuquerque: University of New Mexico Press

DIXON, BOYD
1989
"Estudio Preliminar Sobre el Patrón de Asentamiento del Valle de Comayagua: Corredor Cultural Prehistórico." In *Yaxkin*. Vol. XII, no. 1, Tegucigalpa: Instituto Hondureño de Antropología e Historia, 40–76

FASH, WILLIAM L.
1983
"Deducing Social Organization from Classic Maya Settlement Patterns: A Case Study from the Copán Valley." In *Civilization in the Ancient Americas*. Albuquerque: University of New Mexico Press
1984
"Historia y Características del Patrón de Asentamiento en el Valle de Copán y Algunas Comparaciones con Quiriguá." In *Yaxkin*. Vol. XI, no. 1, Tegucigalpa: Instituto Hondureño de Antropología e Historia, 1–20
1991
Scribes, Warriors and Kings. London: Thames and Hudson Ltd.

FASH, WILLIAM, RICARDO AGURCIA FASQUELLE ET AL.
1996
Visión del Pasado Maya. Asociación Copán, no. 2. Ed. by W. Fash and R.A. Fasquelle. San Pedro de Sula

opposite
Censer base
from Tapijulapa, Tabasco
Late classic period
Villahermosa
Museo Regional de Antropología
"Carlos Pellicer"
cat. 374

FERRERO A., LUIS
1987
Costa Rica Precolombina. San José: Editorial Costa Rica

FOWLER, WILLIAM R. JR.
1995
El Salvador-Antiguas Civilizaciones. San Salvador: Banco Agrícola Comercial de El Salvador

GARCÍA-BÁRCENA JOAQUÍN, AND DIANA SANTAMARÍA
1992-93
"El Cafetal, Ocozocoautla, Chiapas." *Revista de Difusión Científica, Tecnológica y Humanística*, Vol. II, no. 5, Tuxtla Gutiérrez: Consejo Estatal de Fomento a la Investigación y Difusión de la Cultura, 65–72

HASEMANN, GEORGE
1987
"El Patrón de Asentamiento a lo largo del Río Sulaco durante el Clásico Tardío." In *Yaxkin*. Vol. X, no. 1. Tegucigalpa: Instituto Hondureño de Antropología e Historia, 58–77

HIRTH, KENNETH, GLORIA LARA PINTO, AND GEORGE HASEMANN
1989
Investigaciones Arqueológicas en La Región de El Cajón. Vol. I, Pittsburgh-Tegucigalpa: University of Pittsburgh, Department of Anthropology-Instituto Hondureño de Antropología e Historia

JOESINK-MANDEVILLE, L.R.V.
1986
"Proyecto Arqueológico Valle de Comayagua: Investigaciones en Yarumela-Chilcal." In *Yaxkin*. Vol. IX, no. 2, Tegucigalpa: Instituto Hondureño de Antropología e Historia, 17–41

JOYCE, ROSEMARY A.
1985
"Resultados Preliminares de las Investigaciones en Cerro Palenque, Valle de Ulúa." In *Yaxkin*, Vol. VIII, nos. 1-2. Tegucigalpa: Instituto Hondureño de Antropología e Historia, 175–89

KAUFMAN, TERRENCE
1974
"Areal linguistics and Middle America." In *Current Trends in Linguistics*. Ed. by T. Sebeok. Vol. 10. The Hague, 445–83
1974
"Idiomas de Mesoamérica." In *Seminario de Integración Social Guatemalteca*, no. 33, Guatemala C.A.
1976
"Archaeological and linguistic correlations in Maya-land and associated areas of Mesoamerica." *World Archaeology*. Vol. 8, no. 1. London, 101–18

LEE, THOMAS A. JR.
1980
"Algunos aspectos antropológicos del pueblo coxoh." In *Rutas de intercambio en Mesoamérica y el norte de México*, XVI Mesa Redonda de la SMA, no. 2. México: Saltillo, 415–18

1985
"Cuevas secas del Río La Venta, Chiapas Informe Preliminar." Revista de la UNACH, Tuxtla Gutiérrez: Universidad Autónoma de Chiapas, 30–42
1986
"La lingüistica histórica y la arqueología de los zoque-mixe-popolucas." In *Memorias de la 1.ra Reunión de Investigadores del Area Zoque, Centro de Estudios Indígenas*. Tecpatán, Chiapas, 7–36
1989
"La arqueología de los Altos de Chiapas." In *Mesoamérica*. Pubblicazione semestrale del Plumsock Mesoamerican Studies e Centro de Investigaciones Regionales de Mesoamérica, 10, no. 18, Antigua, Guatemala and South Woodstock, Vermont, December, 257–93
1994
"Fronteras arqueológicas y realidades étnicas en Chiapas." *XXII Mesa de Antropología - Memorias*. Tuxtla Gutiérrez: Gobierno del Estado de Chiapas, Instituto Chiapaneco de Cultura, 41–53

LORENZO, CARMEN
1995
"La circulación." In *Historia Antigua de México-El horizonte Postclásico y algunos aspectos intelectuales de las culturas mesoamericanas*. Vol. III. Ed. by L. Manzanilla and L. López Luján, México: INAH, UNAM, Miguel Ángel Porrúa, 355–81

Los Orígenes
1989 [1997]
Los orígines de la civilización Maya. Ed. by R.E.W. Adams. Mexico: Fondo de Cultura Económica

LOWE, GARETH W.
1959
The Chiapas Project, 1955-1958, report of the Field Director. (Papers 1). Orinda, California: New World Archaeological Foundation
1989
"Los Mixe-Zoque como vecinos rivales de los Mayas en las Tierras Bajas primitivas." In *Los orígenes de la civilización Maya*. Ed. by R.E. W. Adams. México: Fondo de Cultura Económica, 219–74
1995
"Presencia maya en la cerámica del Preclásico Tardío en Chiapa de Corzo." In *Memorias del Segundo Congreso Internacional de Mayistas*. México: UNAM, 321–41

MATOS MOCTEZUMA, EDUARDO
1990
Teotihuacan. Milan: Jaca Book

MONTMOLLIN, OLIVIER DE
1992
"Patrones fronterizos de los reinos mayas del Clásico en los altos tributarios del río Grijalva." *Arqueología*, no. 7, January-June. Mexico: INAH, 57–67

OREFICI, GIUSEPPE
1992
"Architettura teocratica e struttura urbana." In *Centroamerica*. Milan: Fabbri, 45–66
1997
"Le culture preispaniche dell'Honduras." In *I Maya di Copán: l'Atene del Centroamerica*. Milan: Skira, 23–34

PIÑA CHAN, ROMAN, AND CARLOS NAVARRETE
1967
Archaeological Research in the Lower Grijalva River Region, Tabasco and Chiapas. Papers of the New World Archaeological Foundation, no. 22. Provo: Brigham Young University

REYES MAZZONI, ROBERTO
1976
Introducción a la Arqueología de Honduras. Tegucigalpa: Editorial Nuevo Continente

ROBINSON, EUGENIA J.
1985
"Los Pueblos del Clásico Tardío del Valle de Sula." In *Yaxkin*. Vol. VIII, nos. 1-2. Tegucigalpa: Instituto Hondureño de Antropología e Historia, 161–74

RUSSEL, S. ROBERT
1954
"A new type of archaic ruins in Chiapas, Mexico." *American Antiquity*, Vol. XX, no. 1. Salt Lake City, 62–64

SANDERS, WILLIAM T.
1990
Excavaciones en el área urbana de Copán. Vols. 1, 2, 3. Tegucigalpa: Instituto Hondureño de Antropología e Historia

SANDERS, WILLIAM T., AND BARBARA J. PRICE
1968
Mesoamerica: The Evolution of a Civilization. New York: Random House

SCHELE, LINDA
1989
"Apuntes sobre Copán n° 8 - Los fundadores del Linaje de Copán y otros sitios Mayas." In *Yaxkin*. Vol. XII, no. 2, Tegucigalpa: Instituto Hondureño de Antropología e Historia, 107–38

SCHELE, LINDA, AND DAVID FRIEDEL
1990
A Forest of Kings: The Untold Story of the Ancient Maya. New York: William Morrow and Co.

SHARER, ROBERT J.
1990
Quirigua. *A Classic Maya Center and Its Sculptures*. Durham: Carolina Academic Press

SHARER, ROBERT J., AND J. C. GIFFORD
1970
"Preclassic Ceramics from Chalchuapa, El Salvador, and Their Relationship with the Maya Lowlands." *American Antiquity*, Vol. 35, no. 4. Salt Lake City

SHEETS, PAYSON D.
1978
"Artifacts." In *The Prehistory of Chalchuapa, El Salvador*. Ed. by R.J. Sharer. Vol. 2. Philadelphia: University of Pennsylvania Press, 1–131
1984
"The Prehistory of El Salvador: An Interpretative Summary." In *The Archaeology of Lower Central America*. Ed. by F.W. Lange and D.Z. Stone. Albuquerque: University of New Mexico Press, 85–112

SNARSKIS, MICHAEL J.
1981
"The Archaeology of Costa Rica." In *Precolumbian Art of Costa Rica*. New York: Harry N. Abrams, Inc., 15–84

STONE, DORIS
1941
Archaeology of the North Coast of Honduras. Memoirs of the Peabody Museum of Archaeology and Ethnology. Vol. IX, no. 1. Cambridge, Mass.: Hardvard University

STUART, DAVID, AND LINDA SCHELE
1989
"Apuntes sobre Copán N° 6 - Yax-K'uk'-Mo': Fundador del Linaje de Copán." In *Yaxkin*. Vol. XII, no. 1. Tegucigalpa: Instituto Hondureño de Antropología e Historia, 143–50

THOMAS, NORMAN D.
1974
The Linguistic, Geographic and Demographic Position of the Zoque of Southern Mexico. Papers of the New World Archaeological Foundation, no. 36. Provo: Brigham Young University

THOMPSON, J. ERIC S.
1963
Maya Archaeologist. Norman: University of Oklaoma Press

VARGAS PACHECO, ERNESTO
1994
"La frontera meridional de Mesoamérica." In *Historia Antigua de México-El México antiguo, sus área culturales, los orígenes y el horizonte Preclásico*. Ed. by L. Manzanilla and L. López Luján. Vol. I. México: Miguel Angel Porrúa, INAH, UNAM, 145–74

WILLEY, GORDON R., RICHARD M. LEVENTHAL, AND WILLIAM FASH
1978
"Maya Settlement in the Copan Valley." *Archaeology*, 31 (4), 32–43

The Maya City

Beyond the close linguistic relationship of those who inhabited and continue to live in southeastern Mexico and western Central America, and contrary to what is often said, the "Maya," as a cultural phenomenon, is a very heterogeneous reality. It is found in radically different environments: in very different landscapes, climates, biota and hydrospheres; it is therefore often represented in equally varied subsistence and settlement patterns.

The diversity attributed to Maya culture is not only the product of the great environmental variability in which it developed. It is also a historical product: it was transformed profoundly with time, and it was expressed in very peculiar forms, depending on the political atmosphere within its different communities at that time and on the particular characteristics of their own history.

The variability that typifies the Maya also applies to its cities. The concrete form in which it is manifested cannot be understood, and therefore is less important than conditioning factors and specific needs that the architecture tried to resolve. Discourse on the Maya city thus imposes the need to detach oneself from definitions applicable to other cultures. The first definition that must be examined is precisely that of the "city."

From the perspective of the Old World–and from even closer places, such as Teotihuacan or Tenochtitlan in Central Mexico–a city is, above all, an urban center, understood as a planned, ordered, regulated complex equipped with public services, sheltering a large, highly concentrated population of diverse origins, roles, and occupations. It is, in sum, the antithesis of what is rural; it is the focal point of concurrence, the center of services of exchange, and the seat of power. From the perspective of some of these characteristics, Maya cities are not cities. With few exceptions, the population density of the most well-known settlements are far below those found in other cultures; none has a grid plan that serves as the basis for the organization of residential compounds of Teotihuacan, nor the sophistication of the drainage system found at that same site.

From the perspective of function, Maya cities are, nevertheless, equally effective responses to similar problems. If the goal is ordered and productive co-existence of a large center of population, then–as will be seen below–Maya cities have been perhaps the most effective in Mesoamerica. Nevertheless, the same effect may be achieved in different ways. If what is understood by "city" is the human response characterized by monumental architecture; by the presence of structures of public function (civic-religious, in other words); by a relatively high population level and a certain functionality independent of the character of the population sharing the settlement, then the Maya city, as such, exists. In fact, it makes its appearance in very early times.

The most notable example of an early Maya city is El Mirador. Located at the northern limit of the tropical rain forest of Guatemala, El Mirador flourished during the Late Preclassic period between 150 B.C. and A.D. 150, the date when it was then abandoned. In the Late Classic period it was reoccupied, although on a much smaller scale, and around A.D. 900 it was abandoned again, this time definitively. According to Ray T. Matheny, one of the archaeologists who studied the site, the settlement covers an extension of 16 square kilometers and it must have had a population of several tens of thousands of inhabitants. The greatest architectural achievement, covering roughly 4 square kilometers in area, consisted of two architectonic groups situated two kilometers apart from each other. The western group had a central plaza around which are aligned the Tiger Complex and the Central Acropolis.

Three additional complexes were at the outer limits of the group: El Cascabel (the Rattle), the acropolis known as the Complejo de los Monos (Complex of the Monkeys), and the Tres Micos (Three Long-Tailed Monkeys), the latter attached to a wall where there were several accesses to the architectonic complex. Here, according to Matheny, the most exclusive rites must have taken place. What stands out from the group is the Pyramid of the Tiger: an acropolis type platform of close to 50 meters in height, topped by three temples with roofs of perishable materials. A small attached structure, known as the Temple of the Tiger, was decorated with large stucco masks; one of them, flanking its western side, was a mask with feline traits, decorated with earplugs and ties equivalent to the *ahau* glyph or symbol of "lord."

Frontal view of Temple I
at Tikal

Urban plan of El Mirador, Guatemala

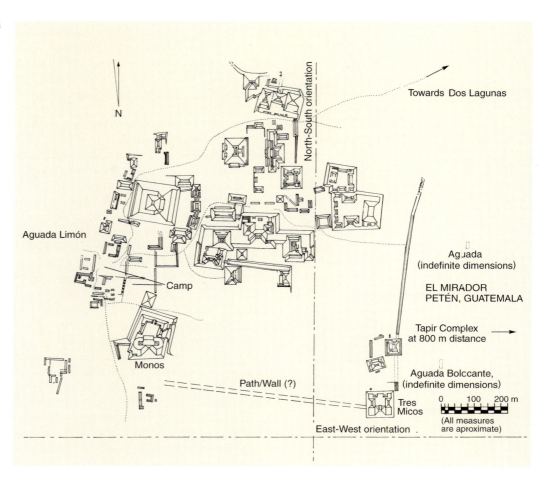

The eastern group of El Mirador contained the Tapir Complex, which was a great acropolis constructed on a hill, marked by the Tapir Pyramid, which was almost as tall as that of the Tiger. If one counts the platforms of the structures and the hill from which the entire complex rose, the total height of the complex was 45 meters higher than that of the Pyramid of the Tiger. It is known, however, that such imposing monuments were not surmounted by relatively elaborate or impressive temples: just like the rest of the buildings of El Mirador, none of the temples of the Tapir Complex had vaulted rooms.

One of the most distinctive traits of the Maya settlements throughout several periods and regions is found at El Mirador: *sacbeoob* that join architectonic complexes. They seem to be constructions directed at proving or reinforcing the dependency and hierarchical organization of intentionally or fortuitously separate components. In the case of El Mirador, there is a *sacbe* connecting the Tapir Complex with the so-called Sacred Precinct; others communicate El Mirador with neighboring centers, occasionally over depressions: Nakbé (pioneer in the region in the construction of monumental public buildings from 600 to 400 B.C.) and Tintal. The size of the population, the monumentality of its constructions and the materials found at the site–pooled with the functional interpretation of *sacbeoob* as roads to facilitate trade–have led Forsyth to postulate the existence at El Mirador of a primitive city-state. This form of organization was not believed to have existed in the Maya area at such an early date as the first or second century B.C., the time assigned to El Mirador's splendor.

El Mirador shares with other contemporary sites in the Maya area and Central Mexico an emphasis on the volume of its public buildings. The height of the Pyramid of the Tiger at El Mirador was similar to that of great platform number N 10-43 at Lamanai in Belize, which was 33 meters above the level of the plaza. It was also decorated with stucco masks on the first level of the platform on both sides of the central stairway. Such

Plan of Becán, Campeche

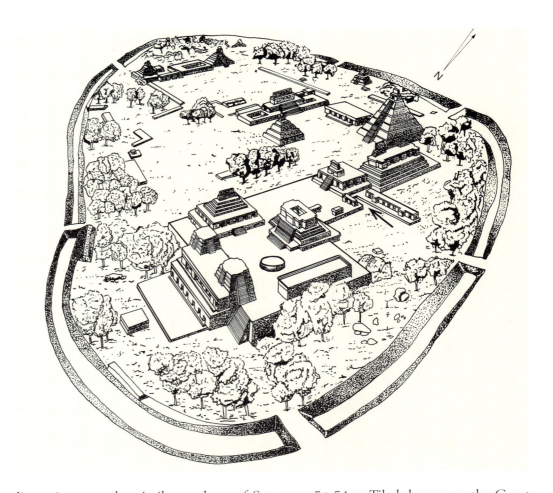

dimensions are also similar to those of Structure 5C-54 at Tikal, known as the Great Pyramid of the Mundo Perdido Complex, with its platform slightly more than 30 meters in height. It was designed with stairways on four sides and great masks flanking them, but without any temple on top of its platform (or, if there was one, it would have been made from perishable materials). Both buildings, at Lamanai and at Tikal, were constructed in the Late Preclassic period. Around that time, approximately the second century, the great platform known as the Pyramid of the Sun was built at Teotihuacan, which surely must have been topped by a modest temple.

All of these buildings were apparently constructed in relatively short time spans; in addition, all of them were built on a foundation faced with thick layers of stucco that hid imperfections on the surface of the worked or selected stones. Clearly the interest in monumentality surpassed the concern for a finished surface and the presence of decorative elements. It would not be the first time that the height of buildings was a sign of privilege, but it is particularly noteworthy given the relatively small size of the population in these respective regions at that time. Millon (1973) has estimated a population of between twenty-five and thirty thousand inhabitants for Teotihuacan in the Tzacualli phase, similar to that of El Mirador, except significantly more concentrated.

There must be a reason for this interest in overwhelming the spectator with massive constructions. It is interesting to note that the Late Preclassic period in the Maya area was a period of strong demographic expansion–as it also was in the Basin of Mexico. The emphasis on monumentality must have been an effective strategy for the integration of a growing population, particularly in a generalized climate of competition, in which emerging communities, undergoing accelerated development, sought to achieve hegemony in their respective regions. The tensions that must have arisen in this environment of competition could have lead to armed confrontations of a frequency and intensity that would have justified the construction of more or less formal defenses.

An example of a response of this type, although slightly later in date, may be seen at Becán, in southern Campeche. The site contained a nucleus of monumental architecture surrounded by a pit, the construction of which has been dated by Webster (1976) to between the second and fourth centuries A.D. With an average width of 10 meters and a longitude of close to 2 kilometers, this pit constituted a formidable obstacle to external attack. In addition to the average depth of the pit, which was 6 meters, the parapet formed by the earth and limestone extracted to excavate it and accumulated on its internal edge was 5 meters high.

The pit can be crossed by way of seven narrow accesses; once these control points are passed, one reaches three later on. These Río Bec-Chenes architectonic complexes formed the civic-religious center of a much larger settlement that extended in a dispersed pattern to the other side of the pit. Basically grouped around three plazas, the buildings that may be seen today are, in their vast majority, "palaces," structures different from the typical platform topped by temples. At Becán, in fact, an architectonic plan predominates combining the two basic forms: temples and "palaces." However, it is not for this reason that it loses its character as a "civic–ceremonial center" with the majority of its residential structures located beyond the nucleus surrounded by the pit. The defensive system of Becán is not unique in the Maya area. Of the same type, although without a towering parapet that the enemy would have to overcome, were two linear pits at Tikal: one of them, 4.5 kilometers to the north of the center of the site, was close to 10 kilometers in length and had an average width of 12 meters. It was possibly constructed during the Early Classic period, and according to Puleston and Callender (1967), it could have operated as an obstacle to possible aggression from Uaxactún.

This type of construction could have been accompanied by palisades, which were very popular, at least in the Late Postclassic period. There are multiple reports from the time of the Spanish conquest in Maya territory, which mention this type of ephemeral barrier, frequently built to prevent the free reign of the cavalry. From the same period, equally well known, are the stone walls surrounding not only civic-religious centers, but also entire settlements. Examples of the first type include the great wall of Tulum and the almost totally destroyed wall of Ichpaatún, both on the Mexican Caribbean, as well as the less impressive fortifications offering partial coverage at Xelhá, also on the coast of Quintana Roo and Chacchob, surely from the Late Classic period. The wall of Mayapán belongs to the second type, for it is much more modest with regard to its significance as an obstacle, although it is very long, measuring a little more than 9 kilometers.

The plan of El Mirador says little about the character and function of the site as a whole. It is the plan of a "ceremonial" center of a much larger settlement, surely constituted by a relatively high number of surrounding towns. It is the common type of plan for a Maya site covered for the most part by dense vegetation. It widely exposes the spaces dedicated to cult and administration, and the areas reserved for the elite, but it says almost nothing about how the common Maya lived, how the population was distributed, or how the countryside had been conditioned. Mapping surveys covering both public and residential areas are very scarce.

One of the first mapping projects of this type–the first of a large Maya center–was conducted at Tikal; it was by Carr and Hazard and published in 1961. Covering a total of 16 square kilometers, it permitted appreciation of the site in all its complexity, with its multiple palatial complexes and large pyramidal platforms, connected by wide causeways. Beyond this core was an enormous quantity of residential units constructed mainly of perishable materials and distributed in a landscape of hills surrounded by depressions and reservoirs, which ensured the continuous supply of water to the settlement, some of them, including the largest sources, very close to the central plaza or the Great Plaza.

Among the most outstanding architectonic complexes at Tikal are the arrangement of buildings around the Great Plaza, where Temples I and II are located, constructed around A.D. 700; the enormous complex of "palaces" apparently of residential and administrative function known as the Central Acropolis–a tangle of rooms around six

Plan of Tikal, Guatemala
courtesy: University
of Pennsylvania
Museum of Archaeology
and Anthropology

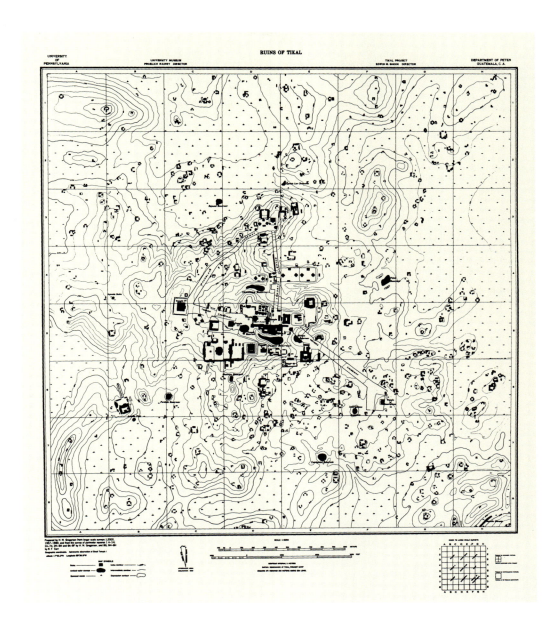

patios interconnected by corridors and stairways; and the North Acropolis. The constructive sequence of the latter took off in the Middle Preclassic period and ended, just as that of the Central Acropolis, in the Late Classic period, which is the date of the majority of buildings visible today at Tikal. This architectonic complex operated as a center of activity at the site.

The system of causeways radiated out from it, to the west leading to Temple IV, the largest ceremonial structure at Tikal with a height of 65 meters; to the north to Group H which may also be reached by following a causeway that goes from Temple IV and that contains, among other buildings, a Twin Pyramid Complex. This was one of the seven complexes of this type built at Tikal between A.D. 633 and 790, apparently as buildings commemorating the end of the *katun*. To the southwest, another causeway leads to the Temple of the Inscriptions.

The diversity of residential constructions mapped at Tikal constitutes a clear indicator of the diversity of roles and positions that existed in greater Tikal. On the other hand, it is this variability expressed in an uninterrupted space, in an urban-rural continuum, as an integrated whole; in its time it definitively broke with the idea that large Maya sites had been simple ceremonial centers.

following pages
Panoramic view of the Great Plaza
Tikal, Guatemala

It also showed an intensity of occupation far from insignificant: the area under the immediate control of Tikal had been, according to calculations made by Culbert (1990), around 120 square kilometers, and its population of sixty thousand inhabitants during its climax between A.D. 550 and 900. Materials recovered in excavations conducted at this same time confirmed that a major amount of work was invested by craftsmen in the production of prestige items for consumption that went beyond the need for basics, such as food.

Tikal then emerged as a center with a high level of population and occupation density, as well as a planned, regulated, complex, diversified center of uncommon monumentality. Nevertheless, its internal order had been retained despite its long occupational sequence from 800 B.C. to the close of the Late Classic period.

Another equally useful map for understanding the relationship between countryside and "urban center" is that of the site of Calakmul, one of the most important regional centers of the Classic period. The mapped area of Calakmul extends over 25 square kilometers. Like that of Tikal, it displays a core of large-scale architecture, clearly differentiated from the dispersion of relatively modest buildings found in its surroundings; this distinction in scale becomes greater as buildings get further away from the nucleus of the monumental area. The similarities in settlement pattern between Calakmul and Tikal would seem to be based at least partially on the fact that they share a similar environment: well-drained lands surrounded by depressions that were subject to agricultural exploitation. The position of the civic-ceremonial center of Calakmul, near the extensive low area located to the west in an eminence of land a little more than 20 meters above the level of seasonal flooding, suggests an inclination toward cultivation in sunken areas, perhaps because, if manipulated correctly, they could be highly productive. The pattern based on a nucleated center with monumental architecture, surrounded by dispersed residential units in an extensive territory is a constant of Classic period Maya settlements. The dispersion could be greater or lesser as a result of resources available in the area, land and water in particular. It could also be affected by irregularities in the terrain—for example the existence of depressions or of large, rapid rivers—or of the very history of the site's development. However, that dichotomy between nucleated and dispersed will always be seen between public and private, sacred and secular.

The same pattern is also equally evident at Tikal, Calakmul, and Copán: at the first two, residential dispersion occurred between low or sunken areas, producing a space interrupted by areas of annual flooding; at Copán, dispersion was produced linearly, along the river of the same name. At Tikal and Calakmul, located in a region lacking surface rivers, natural water sources were used and reservoirs were conditioned to guarantee the availability of water year round. This produced a distinctive image at sites of this particular hydrological region based on large water sources near civic-ceremonial centers (which surely mark the location of the first settlement) and minor reservoirs distributed throughout the landscape, together with innumerable *chultuns* (cistern like artificial water storage facilities) of different functions. For obvious reasons, this situation was not found at Copán, or at other sites near rivers, such as Yaxchilán for example, sites that, nevertheless, retain the dual pattern of nucleated center and dispersed periphery.

Of all the plans offering an image beyond the so-called "ceremonial" center, the most complex and interesting due to its interpretative possibilities is that of Sayil, a Puuc site in northern Yucatán, occupied in the so-called Terminal Classic period. The work carried out there by Sabloff and Tourtellot (Tulane University, 1991) ended in 1985 as the first phase of a larger project encompassing excavations, as well as environmental, ethnographic, and local historical studies.

The area covered by the mapping survey was approximately 5 square kilometers. Recorded in this survey were the remains of stone buildings; rows of stones from houses constructed with perishable materials (wooden posts, cane and mud walls, and palm roofs); platforms of structures of all types, including those that operated as areas to catch water for *chultuns*; and isolated elements, such as earthen walls, *chul-*

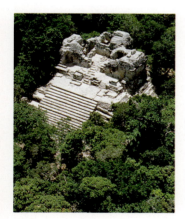

Aerial photo of Structure III
Calakmul, Campeche

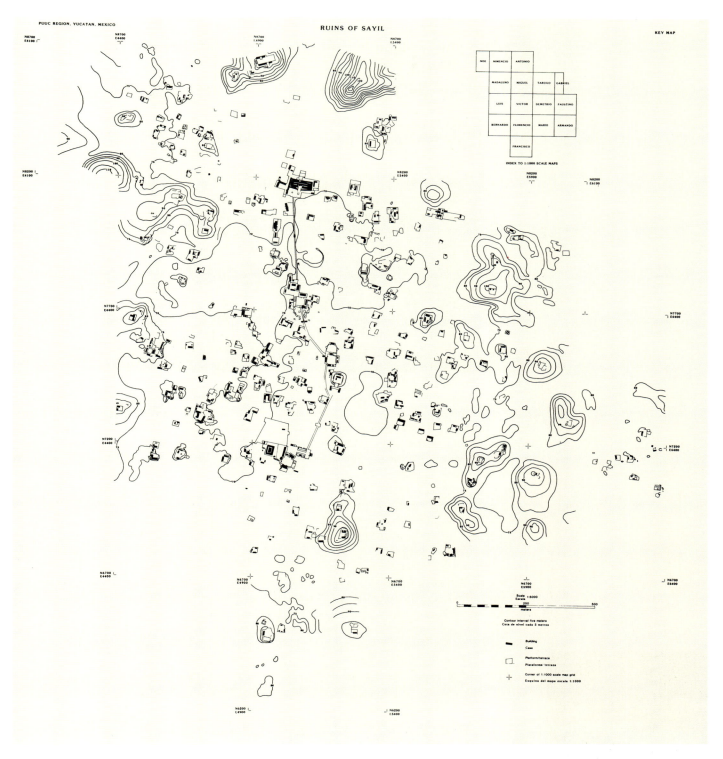

Plan of Sayil, Yucatán
courtesy Sayil Project

tuns, sculptures, grinding stones, and mounds of stone–the function of which is still not understood.

The panorama that emerges from the mapping work at Sayil is that of a typical Maya city in the Classic period. The nucleus consists of monumental architecture, in which its main buildings are connected by *sacbeoob*, with a certain dispersion of residential units around that nucleus. Its population has been estimated to be ten thousand inhabitants at the core of the settlement, and seven thousand in the "suburbs."

Sayil has, nevertheless, certain peculiarities. It has relatively definable limits–somewhat

The Great Palace of Sayil
Yucatán

difficult to find at settlements such as Tikal or Calakmul, where the residential continuum seems endless, a situation that reinforces the idea of Sayil as a city. On the other hand, in contrast with Classic period arrangements in the Petén, but in no way different from what is found in other Puuc sites, or Becán itself in the Río Bec period, the most well-known buildings in the nucleus of Sayil are multiple room structures. At the site, there are only three pyramidal platforms—one of them, according to Sabloff and Tourtellot, presides over the space that could have been the market. All are relatively small and none in positions of particular significance within the basic plan of the site. What also attracts attention is the proliferation of *chultuns*—hundreds of them—although it should be stated that perhaps the high number recorded is more a product of intense prospecting.

Equally notable is the apparent lack of water sources, natural or conditioned, at the site. Finally, the great number of stone buildings at Sayil is noteworthy. If one considers that many of the structures constructed with perishable materials were really part of residential complexes, with the main structures made of stone, then counting complete compounds—or domestic units—not isolated structures, what predominated were stone houses. If in addition one assumes that the remains of rows of stone that usually supported cane and mud walls were in fact much later structures, then it could be concluded that the common house at Sayil was mostly made of stone. This would not be important if it were not for the very well-accepted preconception among Mayanists that houses for the common people in the Maya area were constructed from perishable materials; stone houses and particularly those with the Maya vault, would be reserved, according to this way of thinking, for the elite.

Of course, it is not our intention to dismiss the idea that there were a greater or lesser number of houses of perishable materials in the Maya area. But the peculiarities noted at Sayil are not exclusive to this site. Our own work at Kohunlich, which includes extensive excavations in three residential complexes forming a kind of transection beginning in the main plaza and reaching the periphery of the site more than a kilometer away, have revealed identical situations.

The Kohunlich that is known today is fundamentally a Late Classic and Terminal Classic site. Its surface area is similar to that of Sayil; nevertheless, it must have had only a little more than half that site's population.

Typical house
in northern Yucatán

following pages
outside
View of Tulum
inside
Buildings at Chichén Itzá

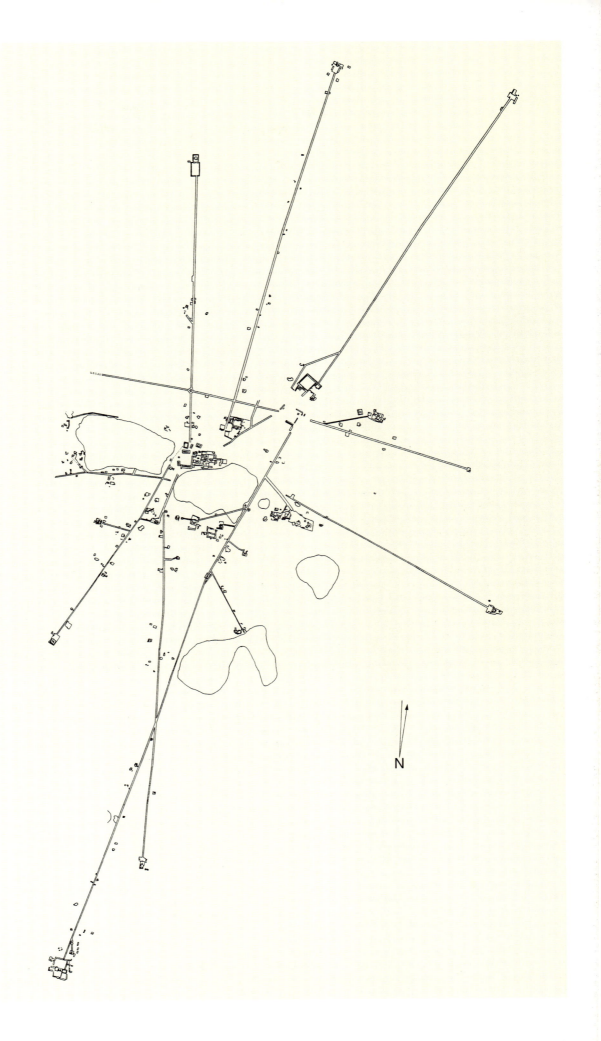

Plan of Cobá
Quintana Roo, showing
the *sacbeoob*

N

View of Tulum, Quintana Roo

With the exception of the Temple of the Masks—constructed in the Petén style in the Early Classic period—all the structures at Kohunlich were built between A.D. 700 and 1000. At this site there is only one pyramidal platform of appreciable size topped by a Late Classic temple, and it borders the west side of the main plaza of the site.

All the others are multiple-room structures supported on more or less tall platforms, some of them clearly civic-ceremonial in function; the vast majority are, however, simple residential units. Discarding the possibility that in the main plaza at Kohunlich there might have been remains of cane and mud structures overlooked by those who worked this area, in none of the areas that we excavated have constructions similar to modern Maya houses in northern Yucatán been found, that is to say, houses oval or rectangular in plan, with cane and mud walls and palm roofs.

All the residential units at Kohunlich were made of stone; in fact, with rare exceptions, all of them were covered with the false Maya arch. More than a kilometer must be crossed in any direction from the main plaza of the site to find structures without a vault. These houses are spacious houses with 50 to 75 meters between them, certainly inhabited by farmers—to judge from the absence of remains that indicate some specialization—and even in this remote position, which was clearly rural in nature, the houses were still made of stone.

The situation admits only two possible interpretations: the entire site of Kohunlich was an elite settlement, including its immediate periphery, or simply that the Mayas in this

region and at that time, made their houses or at least their rooms of stone. At Dzibanché, 35 kilometers to the northeast of Kohunlich, a similar situation has been found. Late and Terminal Classic period houses were made of stone, the majority of them vaulted with a false Maya arch, even those relatively separated from the core of monumental architecture. Houses of perishable materials, indicated by the existence of alignments of stone that served to retain cane and mud walls, have only been found in abandoned plazas and over ruins of structures of earlier periods; ceramics dating to the Terminal Classic period and the initial part of the Early Postclassic period associated with these constructions have been found.

The proliferation of *sacbeoob*, fortifications and earthen walls delimiting agricultural fields, plots, special resources, and in some cases, possessions of groups transcending the family level, is a characteristic of late periods in the Maya area. Chichén and Cobá are two sites that strongly express the formalization of special relations based on *sacbeoob*. The central area of Chichén–which Kilmartin and O'Neal mapped in the 1920s for the Carnegie Institution–focused on a large walled platform, bordering the main plaza of the site and serving as a base for the well-known buildings of the Temple of the Warriors and the Great Ballcourt.

In central position was the Castillo; to the east, forming part of the same platform was the Group of the Thousand Columns with the Mercado. Several *sacbeoob* radiated out from the plaza of the Castillo, for example no. 1 connected the plaza with the Cenote of

opposite
The Pyramid at Cobá, Quintana Roo

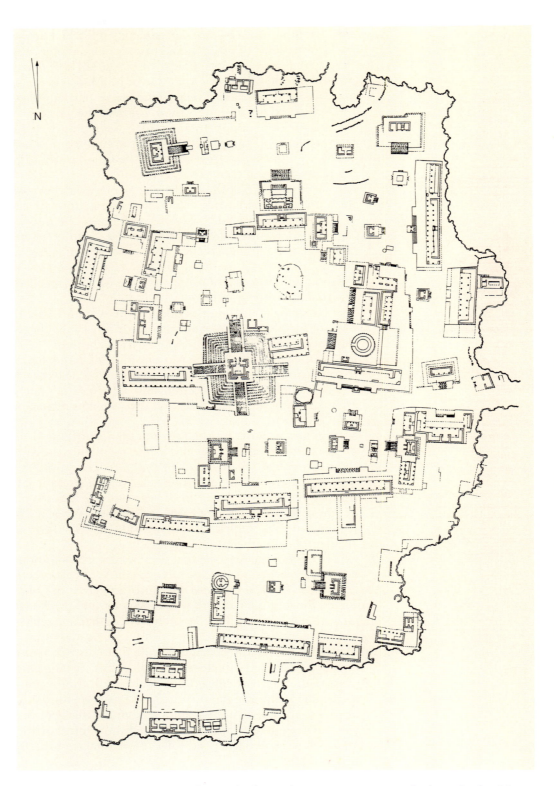

Plan of Mayapán, Yucatán

Sacrifice; no. 5 communicated it with the architectonic group including the buildings known as the Caracol and the Nunnery; and two more causeways lead to the Osario: a pyramidal structure located in a walled space, again connected by way of another *sacbe* with the *cenote* of Oxtoloc.

More than twenty additional causeways, some several kilometers in length, joined larger architectonic complexes, and linked these with minor groups and isolated structures and even with areas of few resources, such as *sascaberas* (open air stone quarries where

exposed limestone or *sahcab* is extracted and which is used as an aggregate in cements, wall finishes and floors). The main plaza at Chichén operated in effect as a center of radiation, not only geographically but also for social activity and political power. The general layout, function and design of buildings on the great platform on which it was located could have a mythical significance, particularly to the myth of the Creation, if the Mayas did in fact reflect their vision of the world in the plan of their cities and the architecture of monuments. Freidel, Schele and Parker (1993) have put forth an interpretation of the planning of this architectonic space. According to the proposal of these authors, the great plaza of the Castillo would be the Primordial Sea of Creation, the body of water that, according to the *Popol Vuh*, was emptied by the gods for the emergence of the earth. The Venus Platform, opposite the northern access of the Castillo, would symbolize precisely the "four divisions made by the gods at the beginning of the world" (id.: 156), separating the sky, the sea, the earth and the Maya kingdom. The nine-tiered pyramid of the Castillo, which has corners oriented toward sunrise at the summer solstice and sunset at the winter solstice, with its four stairways and its feathered serpents at the base of the balustrades on the north side, would be the mountain where Xmucane, the First Mother, molded the first human beings of the fourth and last creation from maize dough.

The Great Ballcourt, on the other hand, would be the place of the celebration of the myth of the Hero Twins, who, also according to the *Popol Vuh*, lived in the world of the third creation. Their father, decapitated by the gods of *Xibalba* as a punishment for having disturbed them while he was playing ball with his brother, impregnated the daughter of one of the lords of the underworld. The twins to whom she gave birth, Hunahpu and Xbalanque, rescued the remains of their father and uncle, buried in the ballcourt after defeating the gods of the underworld, thus managing to expel the gods of *Xibalba* from the world of humans (id.: 110).

Seen in its entire extension, the internal network of *sacbeoob* at Chichén forms a complex scheme of circulation and urban regulation. Beyond the concern for formalizing the hierarchical organization of the parts composing the main civic-religious buildings—a concern that as mentioned earlier, was present since early times—at Chichén the profusion of *sacbeoob* within the site and the heterogeneity of their origin and destination marks a difference from earlier sites. What it allows us to see at Chichén is a true urban plan, which although it does not conform to any sort of grid, except by accident, is nonetheless functional.

Chichén is not the only site that displays this proliferation of internal causeways. In fact, it is not even the most impressive example of this type; perhaps the most spectacular example is Cobá, a site near the Caribbean coast of Quintana Roo.

There, the internal network was enormous, and the external one surprising: the longest *sacbe* that is known, 100 kilometers in length, connected Cobá with the site of Yaxuná, close to Chichén.

Mayapán, heir to the hegemonic role that Chichén had until the middle of the eighth century, developed a nucleated pattern, a new arrangement in the Maya area. The mapping of the site was carried out by Jones at the beginning of the 1950s, also for the Carnegie Institution; the survey shows structures and other standing elements in detail, as well as the topography resulting from the decay of buildings. It is a relatively disorganized conglomeration of residential units, often with walls delimiting garden plots and civic-religious spaces, as well as more than twenty *cenotes*, all within a huge wall that had twelve openings.

Its population, estimated to be approximately twelve thousand inhabitants, was concentrated in an area of barely 4.2 square kilometers, which represents a density five times greater than that of the resedential areas of Tikal that are closest to the nucleus of monumental architecture.

Mayapán's apparent concern with possible outside aggression seems to have been shared by other contemporaneous sites in the same general region. Tulum, as we already mentioned, also had a wall; in fact, its particular position, directly on the shore of the coast, made an attack on the site doubly difficult. Nevertheless the area within the wall

View of the *cenote* of Mayapán
Yucatán

was relatively reduced and it was not planned for house residents who were not members of the elite. At Tulum, population was dispersed outside the city wall. Walls surround residential units at Mayapán, while at Tulum residential units were often outside the defensive wall: they were long squat alignments of stone, surrounding houses, simple plots and *cenotes*.

They were marks of individual or community possession that seemed to reflect a generalized situation of confrontation between pairs. This interpretation is compatible with the vision of the Maya area at the moment of the arrival of the Spaniards, which is that of a politically fragmented area, composed of independent chiefdoms that came to be allied only ephemerally, maintaining their autonomy and occasionally entering into conflict with each other.

Maya *sacbeoob* were used in multiple ways: their contours suggest their use as a processional walkway; as a form of claiming and controlling resources; and as a route of communication; in synthesis and as mentioned earlier, as a formalization of subjugation and loyalty. There is, nonetheless, another possible reason for their existence; at Dzibanché they seem to function as an element reinforcing the union of intentionally dispersed groups.

At the beginning it was believed that the site of Dzibanché, with its occupation throughout the Classic period, was restricted to the area where the greatest group of monuments was found; however, after prospecting and excavation carried out over the last ten years at this site, it has been concluded that this architectonic conglomerate is only part of a greater settlement including Kinichná, a little more than 2.5 kilometers to the north (which is no more than a great acropolis rising from a plaza in which other much smaller buildings are found, and beyond that, the rural landscape of dispersed residential units), and Tutil, at approximately the same distance to the west (which is an architectonic center of great monumentality with a proliferation of minor compounds, each one presided over by a pyramidal platform of average size). It is not possible for the moment to establish the function of each one of these groups; what we do know is that the three sites have very different internal configurations (in fact, some have what others lack), although all subscribe at some time to the same architectonic style, and therefore they must be contemporaneous at least in part of the sequence of occupation.

All these details support the hypothesis that it is a situation of complementary sites, that each one of the groups is nothing more than a segment of the totality that we now call the settlement system of Dzibanché. Time has proven us correct; years after having proposed the hypothesis, we found fragments of *sacbeoob* joining Kinichná with Tutil and the "old" Dzibanché with Kinichná; it was, in this case, a matter of formalizing relations between parts.

Today we believe that the dispersion of major architectonic groups at Dzibanché was not a fortuitous result, but rather a response to the need to achieve social cohesion and political control in a situation of generalized dispersion of those who resided in the locality. The final product of "dismemberment of the public totality" of Dzibanché was an important reduction of the distance between fundamental resources–basically land and water–and the settlement itself. On this matter, it should be kept in mind that Dzibanché and Kinichná are located practically on the edge of depressions that were exploited in their time. Compared with Teotihuacan, this scheme, which brings the most distant inhabitants closer to specific segments of the system and that enormously increases the total surface–domestic units and the majority of cultivated land–under direct control, is more efficient: it achieves a better level of integration through time that makes the very existence of this integration visible.

It would be, in this way, a very well-planned alternative that does not preserve a relationship with supposed environmental restrictions and specific forms of land exploitation discussed extensively in the literature on the Mayas. In this context, there is no doubt that abandoning the traditional definition of city allows us to appreciate–and enjoy–Maya cultural variability and the ingenuity with which they resolved fundamental problems of their political and social life.

Bibliography

BULLARD, WILLIAM R. JR.
1953
Property Walls at Mayapan. Publication 52. Washington, D.C.: Carnegie Institution of Washington, 258–64

CULBERT, PATRICK T., LAURA J. KOSAKOWSKY, ROBERT E. FRY, AND WILLIAM A. HAVILAND
1990
"The Population of Tikal, Guatemala." In *Precolumbian Population History in the Maya Lowlands*. Ed. by T.P. Culbert and D.S. Rice Albuquerque: University of New Mexico Press 103–21

FREIDEL, DAVID, LINDA SCHELE, AND JOY PARKER
1993
Maya Cosmos: Three Thousand Years on the Shaman's Path. New York: William Morrow and Co.

KILMARTIN, J.O.
1924
Report of Mr. J.O. Kilmartin on the Survey and Base-Map at Chichén Itzá, México. Publication 23. Washington, D.C.: Carnegie Institution of Washington, 213–17

MATHENY, RAY T.
1986
"Investigations at El Mirador, Peten, Guatemala." In *National Geographic Research*. Vol. 2, 332–53

MILLON, RENÉ
1973
Urbanization at Teotihuacán, Mexico. University of Texas Press

POLLOCK, HARRY E.D., RALPH L. ROYS, TATIANA PROSKOURIAKOFF, AND T., AND A. LEDYARD SMITH
1962
Mayapán, Yucatán, México. Publication 619. Washington, D.C.: Carnegie Institution of Washington

PULESTON, DENNIS E., AND D.W CALLENDER JR.
1967
"Defensive Earthworks at Tikal." In *Expedition* 9, 46–48

SABLOFF, JEREMY A. AND GAIR TOURTELLOT
1991
The Ancient Maya City of Sayil: The Mapping of a Puuc Region Center. Middle American Research Institute Publication 60. New Orleans: Tulane University

TOURTELLOT, GAIR, AND JEREMY A. SABLOFF
1994
"Community Structure at Sayil: A Case Study of Puuc Settlement. An Hidden Among the Hills: Maya Archaeology of the Northwest Yucatan Peninsula." In H.J. Prem *Acta mesoamericana*, 7. Möckmühl: Verlag Von Flemming, 71–92

WEBSTER, DAVID L.
1976
Defensive Earthworks at Becan, Campeche, Mexico: Implications for Maya Warfare. Middle American Research Institute Publication 41. New Orleans: Tulane University

Detail of the western façade
of the Codz Pop at Kabah, Yucatán

When we visit an archaeological site what most captivates our attention are its buildings. We are drawn by the colossal dimensions, forms so different from what we are accustomed to seeing, the decoration, and distribution of spaces. Architectural complexes spark our imagination so that we ask how such well-cut blocks were shaped, how they were placed, what activities were carried out there, what were these rooms used for, and so forth.

In fact, for centuries Maya buildings have attracted both locals and foreigners. For rural people, these vestiges of an ancient culture are often clear points of reference associated with the presence of water, fertile lands, curious objects, or dwellings of supernatural beings, or they are sources of interesting legends. But for the urban visitor, Maya buildings generate a good number of questions, they stimulate an interest in Pre-Columbian culture, and they offer the opportunity for a bit of healthy relaxation among the ancient stones and tropical vegetation.

A quick look at Maya architecture allows us to point out that not all buildings share the same characteristics. Some are extremely elevated; horizontal volumes predominate in other structures; still others are encased in profuse and apparently inexplicable decoration.

The stone that covers some structures is very well worked; at other times they are only roughly hewn blocks, while on other occasions we encounter an almost incredible mastery of cut stone assembled into sculptures or geometric mosaics. Nevertheless, in all these cases we are only seeing the shell of the structure, that is to say that the entire stone surface of the building was covered with a layer of stucco painted with several colors, particularly red.

The distribution of buildings, plazas, patios, and different levels, complexes resembling acropolises, and a variety of roofed spaces also differ from one region to the next. But there are certain common elements that have allowed the classification of Maya architecture into several specific styles.

But what is an architectural style? Many times styles have been considered as decorative additions, as preconceived elements added to provide a certain value. Nevertheless, an architectonic style implies interrelated characteristics that identify the work with the society that created it. Style is the result of a logical application of a constructive system with appropriate materials in a given period. In this way, style becomes an aesthetic value (from here arises the difficulty and futility of discussing which is the best or worst) and it is closely linked with the culture to which it belongs. An architectonic style is, in addition, a product of its time. Therefore, if today we construct a gothic or baroque building, in reality it will be neither style, but rather something similar to it.

Returning to the subject that concerns us, we see that Maya constructions may be grouped regionally in time and space. A quick synthesis of the vast Maya world allows us to enumerate the following styles:

Early Petén. The Early Petén style is characterized by the presence of large modeled stucco masks decorating both sides of the stairways of main, pyramidal platforms. The best-known cases are the Structure E-VII-sub at Uaxactún, Structure 34 of the Tiger Complex at El Mirador, Structure 5D-33-3 at Tikal, and Structure 5C-2nd at Cerros, Belize.

The masonry is crude, that is to say that the blocks are roughly cut, joined with plaster and a regular use of quoins or spalls. A thick layer of stucco evened out the exterior surface of the work. Spaces were roofed with corbeled arch vaults built on the basis of stepped slabs.

Architectonic forms include pyramid bases, platforms, temples, palaces, and residences. The approximate time span of this style would be from the second century B.C. to the fourth century A.D., if we consider examples from the Early Classic period such as those of Structure 5D-22 of Tikal, the substructure called the Rosalila of Copán, the Pyramid of the Masks of Kohunlich, Quintana Roo, or the substructure of the main building at Balamkú, Campeche.

Stucco mask panel representing
the Solar deity at Kohunlich
Quintana Roo

It might be thought that the heart of this style is found in the north of Guatemala in the Department of the Petén. However, in multiple locations in the Yucatán peninsula, including its northern area, there are buildings displaying characteristics of the Early Petén. A good example is Acanceh in Yucatán and another is Cobá in Quintana Roo.

Late Petén. The Late Petén style is derived from that of the Early Petén. Constructions are larger and tend to be grouped in enormous architectonic masses called acropolises. Some buildings enhance their verticality through the addition of roof combs, ornamental walls erected on the roofs of temples and principal structures. As for stuccoed decoration, it tends to represent human figures, plant motifs, and cartouches with hieroglyphs, among other elements.

Profusely carved stelae and altars predominated. These monuments were generally placed at the foot of facades of main buildings. This is an architectonic complement, the origins of which go back to the "stela-altar complex" of the Preclassic period, as seen at Izapa, Chiapas.

Late Petén architecture is visible at places like Tikal, Calakmul, Edzná, Dzibanché, Cobá, Ekbalam, and Acanceh. What is most evident are the compact mounds made of roughly cut blocks. A common element that relates architectonic complexes in the space of some dozens of meters or else over several kilometers of longitude are stone walkways (*sacbeoob* in Maya). These roads are not exclusive to the north of Guatemala. We also find them in other regions of the Maya world, such as Tzum, Campeche; Uxmal-Nojpat-Kabah; Izamal-Aké or else the network within Chichén Itzá. Nevertheless, the largest and most complex system of stone roads reported to date is that of Cobá (including Yaxuná and Ixil), in the northeastern part of the peninsula.

The time frame assigned to constructions of this architectonic style correspond basically to the Late Classic, the years A.D. 600–900.

Usumacinta. The Usumacinta style, a variant of the Petén, is found in large cities of the valley of the abundant Usumacinta River, which forms part of the border of Mexico and Guatemala. Typical examples of this style are the cities of Yaxchilán, Palenque, and Piedras Negras, although we may also include here other settlements such as Bonampak, Pomoná, and Comalcalco.

Among the most distinctive characteristics of buildings constructed in the region of the Usumacinta are the outward inclination of the upper parameter or roof of constructions; the use of openwork roof combs with geometric designs; and the decoration of piers, of some interior walls, and of the upper parameter (roof) panels with modeled stucco motifs that include fantastic masks and human figures.

It is worth mentioning here the finely worked *tableros*, or rectangular panels, lintels, and stelae that reproduce scenes relevant to the life of leaders. They tell of dates, specific individuals, and events at the same time that they decorate palaces and temples of urban centers.

The skillful use of modeled stucco at Palenque has led some authors to propose the existence of a style specific to Palenque. Nevertheless, evidence indicates the presence of a regional phenomenon not centered at a single site. This area-wide phenomenon chronologically locates the Usumacinta style between the sixth and ninth centuries A.D.

Motagua. Also deeply rooted in the Petén tradition, the ancient cities of Copán, Quiriguá, La Entrada, Los Higos, and El Puente, among others, rise from the basin of the Motagua River of Honduras. The relatively marginal location of these sites at the southeastern end of the Maya area perhaps facilitated their differentiation from the neighboring Petén region. It has been estimated that these sites peaked between the years A.D. 600 and 800.

Many constructive and decorative elements recall the above-mentioned styles, but technical progress is evident in the better workmanship of cut blocks covering the rubble-

The pyramid at Edzná, Campeche

work. In addition, there is greater refinement in sculptures and panels on the facades, as well as in hieroglyphs, stelae (which are almost freestanding at Copán), and in zoomorphic altars.

Megalithic. Another variant of Petén architecture, the Megalithic style has a broad peninsular distribution, but it is more evident in the northern part of Yucatán. It is characterized by the use of very well cut stone blocks and it surely developed between the years A.D. 300 and 600, during the Early Classic period. One of the best examples is the pyramid of Kinick Kakmo, a gigantic structure today incorporated into the city of Izamal. Other nearby towns with similar architectonic elements are Aké and Cansahcab. Nucuchtunich, a small site located to the south of the Puuc Hills and joined by a stone causeway to Yaxhoom, also displays only megalithic pieces in its construction. It is worth recalling here the monumental stairways constructed with enormous blocks at other sites such as Edzná, San Miguel Pakchén (or Xpulyaxché, according to Maler), Dzibiltún, and Nadzcaan in Campeche; or the megalithic structures of El Naranjal, Tres Lagunas, and Cobá in northern Quintana Roo.

Río Bec. This name was coined at the beginning of the twentieth century by the French explorer Maurice de Perigny. The characteristic elements of the style are elevated towers at the ends (and occasionally in the middle) of long constructions housing chambers arranged in groups of two. The towers have false stairways with steps that simulate a real stairway but whose treads are too narrow to climb. At the top there are also simulated temples, which cannot be entered.

Main Structure of the archaeological
area of Aké, Yucatán

Reconstruction drawing
of the Three Towers Structure
at Xpuhil, Campeche
by Tatiana Proskouriakoff, 1963

opposite
Stela C at Copán, Honduras
foreground

The corners of the towers and platforms do not form straight angles but rather are
rounded, and all the stones are perfectly cut and fitted. There is an insistence on the representation of large fantastic masks at the entrance to main buildings and also stone
mosaic masks or stylized renditions are placed in central locations or areas evidently of
public domain.

The most representative sites of the Río Bec style are found in the region of Becán, at
the base and center of the Yucatán peninsula. Its principal political and economic
development occurred between the years A.D. 600 and 800. In addition to this important hegemonic city, we might mention several sites with the Río Bec cast, such as
Xpuhil, Chicanná, Hormiguero, Manos Rojas, or a score of architectural groups also
known as Río Bec and designated alphabetically or with Roman numerals.

Chenes. Classic period Maya architecture also reached extremes in terms of the abundance of decorative elements. This is the case of Chenes buildings, the facades of which
display huge zoomorphic masks. The entrance of the building is surrounded by maws,
including teeth and fangs. The squinted or crossed eyes and prominent nose are found
above the lintel. Large earplugs, ornaments, and various symbols complement the impressive facade.

One of the principal creatures represented this way is Itzamna, the sacred earth monster, mythological entity of origins, associated with a fantastic reptile (an iguana in some
regions, a crocodile in others) in the indigenous mind. Those powerful ancient images
were created in intricate stone mosaics covering virtually the entire structure. The
majesty of these constructions is generally enhanced by the use of openwork roof
combs, as occurs at Hochob, Tabasqueño, and Santa Rosa Xtampak, to cite the best-
known examples.

The name Chenes is derived from a Yucatecan Maya word that means "well, cistern, or
cave with water," because this region of northeastern Campeche and southern Yucatán
is where water is obtained only in cavities of this kind. The architectural style has been
dated between the years A.D. 600 and 900.

Puuc. Puuc is the Yucatecan Maya name for the range of low hills of northern
Campeche and southern Yucatán. In this region there are several buildings dressed

Western façade of the Codz Pop
Structure at Kabah, Yucatán

with very well worked stone and organized in precisely oriented, harmoniously balanced complexes. The lower portion of construction almost always offers a pleasant rhythm of light sections alternating with dark ones (walls versus openings). At the same time, the upper part of the building is richly ornamented with stone mosaics forming geometric motifs, colonnades, or long, hook-nosed anthropomorphic masks, as well as human, zoomorphic, and/or fantastic representations, among other elements.

The most well-known Puuc sites are Uxmal, Kabah, Sayil, and Labná, but there are also others open to the public, such as Chacmultún, Oxkintok, and Xcalumkin. In fact, they are found in the center of the stylistic region, but the Puuc cast is also found at Dzibilchaltún (to the north of Mérida), at Chichén Itzá and Culubá (in the eastern Yucatán peninsula), and in the central and western portions of Campeche. Some examples in the latter region are Kayal, Edzná, Villa Madero, Ley Federal de Reforma Agraria, Yohaltún, and Xkanacol.

In Puuc constructions, development may be divided into six phases, Early Oxkintok (which we believe is equivalent to Early Petén), Proto-Puuc (A.D. 550–650), Early Puuc (650–750), Junquillo (750–850), Mosaic (850–1000), and Late Uxmal (1000–1050). In this way, from the fourth to eleventh century A.D. there was a wide region of the Puuc where a gradual change occurred that led to wider-roofed spaces and improved construction systems and stonework. It also resulted in the creation of different geometric and symbolic mosaics, masks, and even articulated sculptures for assembly.

Maya-Mexican. As its name indicates, this architectonic tradition fuses Yucatecan forms with others apparently arriving from the Gulf Coast and Central Mexico. This style flourished between the years A.D. 1000 and 1250, so that it is not at all related to the Mexica (or Aztec) culture, which would develop later.

The key site is Chichén Itzá, although we also find similar elements in other settlements, such as Uxmal, Kabah, and Edzná. Buildings display an inclined wall or slope on the lower part of the lower wall and on platforms.

following pages
outside
Ball court at Cobá, Quintana Roo
inside
Panoramic view of Palenque
Chiapas

Main Structure of Hochob
Campeche

The stone blocks are well cut, similar to the Puuc style. Stairways are flanked by *alfardas* and topped by pedestals or with serpentine motifs.

Sculpture associated with architectonic decoration is abundant and adds motifs that seem to be related with the Totonac region (recall El Tajín in Veracruz), as well as with the Mexican highlands (Xochicalco and Tula).

Other elements very common at Chichén Itzá are the representations of men in a posture of offering (the so-called *Chac Mool*) and anthropomorphic standard bearers, as well as felines (such as pumas and jaguars), atlantean (or supporting figures), and feathered serpents.

This Maya-Mexican style corresponds exclusively to the Early Postclassic period (A.D. 900–1200) and it seems to be present, at least sculpturally, in other sites near Chichén Itzá's sphere of influence, such as Xtelhú (several stelae exhibited in Yaxcabá come from this site) and Yulá (where several lintels have been recorded).

Eastern Coast. The term "Eastern Coast style" was used for the first time in the 1920s by American archaeologist Samuel K. Lothrop to refer to Maya constructions of the northern coast of Quintana Roo. Buildings are constructed of roughly worked blocks joined with plaster and with quoins of different sizes. The entire structure was covered with a thick layer of stucco that hid the angular cuts and/or imperfections of the stone.

In the upper part of the main facade some structures have niches containing modeled stucco motifs (once polychromed), among which the representation of an anthropomorphic deity in the act of descending is a common motif. Entrances to large and small buildings have a recessed lintel.

Small cubical sanctuaries measuring a maximum of 40 by 40 by 40 inches (1 cubic meter) are common. Also the erection of small quadrangular altars occupying less than 1600 square inches (1 square meter) in area by 8 to 16 inches (20–40 centimeters) in height are frequent.

following pages
The Labná Arch, Yucatán

Chichén Itzá, Yucatán
on the left the Temple
of the Warriors on the right the Castillo

148

following pages
Panoramic view of Tulum
Quintana Roo

A typical example is Tulum, but these Maya works of the Late Postclassic (A.D. 1250–1500) are also found at El Meco, Cancún, Xcaret, Playa del Carmen, Xelhá, Akumal, Tancah, and Muyil (Chunyaxché), among many other coastal sites in Quintana Roo.

The Eastern Coast style is also present at inland sites. Therefore we see it in the temple crowning the enormous pyramidal platform called Nohoch Mul or the Compound of the Paintings, both at Cobá. In the eastern Yucatán peninsula, at Ekbalam, structures have also been reported with these characteristics. Continuing this imaginary journey toward the west, we might stop at Mayapán and again find buildings in the eastern peninsular architectonic tradition.

The preceding reminds us of the futility of rigidly labeling an architectonic style and linking it with a given geographic region.

Another important element that we find at Tulum, Xcaret, Ekbalam, and Mayapán is the presence of a thick defensive wall protecting the nucleus of the settlement.

Guatemalan Highlands. The southern Maya area saw the flowering of settlements located on elevated, easily defensible areas, such as Mixco Viejo, Zaculeu, Utatlán, and Iximche, during the Late Postclassic period.

Buildings were erected with well-cut blocks and covered with stucco, with forms recalling Mexican buildings but with less decoration. Stairways with balustrades topped by square stone blocks were common, as well as tall, spacious temples with a sloped base, which were constructed on multitiered pyramidal platforms. The distribution of structures, patios, and plazas display some irregularities due to the spatial limitations of elevated locations.

The coexistence of different buildings or the combination of architectonic elements visible today in the same archaeological zone is no more than the result of this sum of constructions that occurred with the passage of time. As an example, we recall the small temples with recessed lintel, characteristic of the Eastern Coast style, which are found between the imposing Petén constructions of Cobá; the Puuc masks decorating the Postclassic monuments of Mayapán; and the amalgamation of Petén, Chenes, Puuc, and Maya-Mexican structures present at Edzná.

In addition there is a trend in recent research that promises more precise results in the study of pre-Hispanic architecture. It deals with analysis of spatial relations and basic

Illustrated glossary
of some architectural elements
of Maya architecture

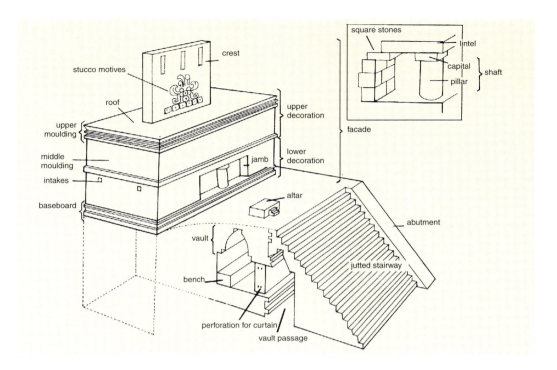

forms of buildings. Included here is the notion of the political predominance of some cities. Every human community tends to evolve socially and economically, so that it acquires a greater or lesser position in the hierarchy with respect to its neighbors.

In the case of Pre-Columbian settlements, we observe marked differences between the volume and quantity of buildings at a site and others in the same region. This fact has led to propose the possible existence of regional capitals with specific and distinctive styles of construction.

Continuing this chain of thought, what remains to be explained is the reason why structures of one style or another exist so far away from their center of origin. It is worth mentioning the possibility that foreign enclaves may have existed, given the communication and interrelations between contemporary political units.

Based on a general overview, the architectural development of the Pre-Columbian Mayas originated in the first centuries of our era. At that time, so-called Petén-style architecture was common throughout the Yucatán peninsula, as well as in central and northern parts of Guatemala, Belize, and the Motagua River basin. Thus, with the Petén tradition, the development of Maya civilization begins.

The growth of settlements and their social diversification became generalized so that populations began to adopt norms of planning and administration that permitted greater development and improved capacity to function.

Maya urbanism flourished in Late Petén cities and prospered in the centuries to come. Note that we speak of an urbanism distinct from what we are accustomed to discussing in Western culture. Different regions were organized and constructed on the basis of local needs.

Sharing the same basic culture, the Maya differentiated among themselves politically and regionally, conveying these differences in the architectural sphere. The region of the Usumacinta and Motagua basins and the north-central part of Yucatán invented new forms of construction techniques, which characterized their works during the fourth to seventh centuries. In the central axis of the Yucatán peninsula, from south to north and during the Late Classic period (A.D. 600–900), there also seems to have been regional political units that distinguished between themselves architecturally: Río Bec, Chenes, and Puuc. The latter style also had its own evolution in which the role played by the Chontal Maya of southwestern Campeche and northeastern Tabasco remains to be clarified. Later, during the five centuries prior to contact with the Old World, the Maya area

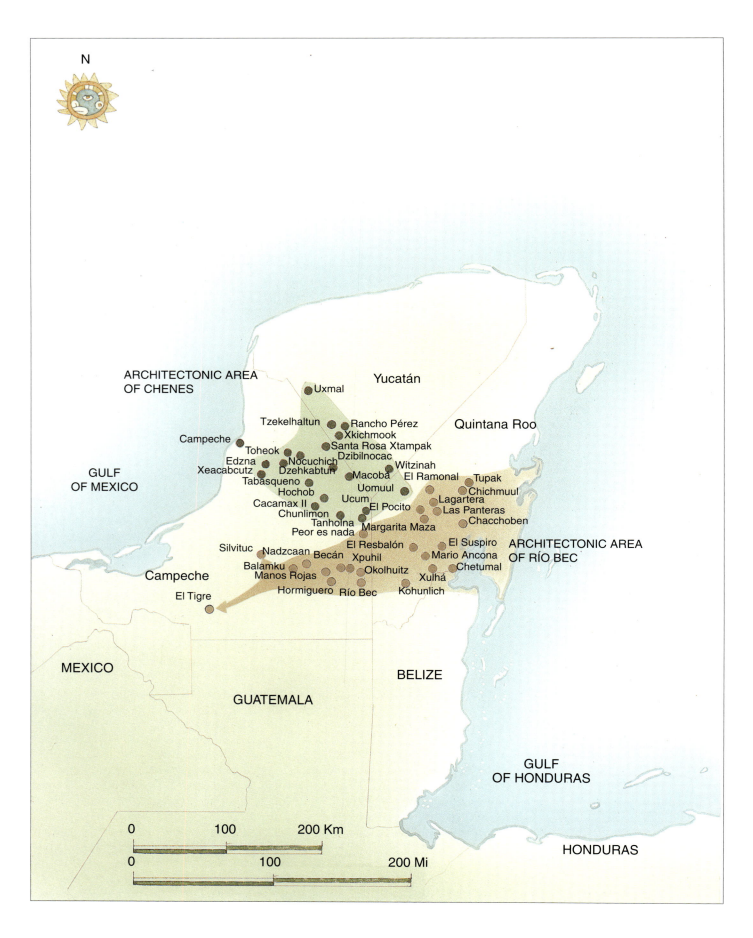

N

ARCHITECTONIC AREA
OF CHENES

Yucatán

Uxmal

Tzekelhaltun   Rancho Pérez   Quintana Roo
                                Xkichmook
Campeche   Santa Rosa Xtampak
        Toheok   Dzibilnocac
    Edzna   Nocuchich   Witzinah
Xeacabcutz   Dzehkabtun   Macoba   El Ramonal   Tupak
    Tabasqueno   Chichmuul
        Hochob   Uomuul   Lagartera
    Cacamax II   Ucum   Las Panteras
GULF   Chunlimon   El Pocito   Chacchoben
OF MEXICO   Tanholna   Margarita Maza
                    Peor es nada
        Silvituc   El Resbalón   El Suspiro   ARCHITECTONIC AREA
            Nadzcaan   Becán   Xpuhil   Mario Ancona   OF RÍO BEC
        Balamku   Okolhuitz   Chetumal
Campeche   Manos Rojas   Xulhá
        El Tigre   Hormiguero   Río Bec   Kohunlich

MEXICO   BELIZE

        GUATEMALA

GULF
OF HONDURAS

HONDURAS

0   100   200 Km

0   100   200 Mi

opposite
Map of Río Bec
and Chenes architectural styles

Brick with the representation
of a temple from Comalcalco
Terminal Classic period
Comalcalco
Museo de Sitio de Comalcalco
cat. 65

Miniature vessel
from Dzibilnocac
Campeche
Classic period
Campeche, Museo Histórico Fuerte
de San Miguel
Baluarte de San Miguel
cat. 66

was related to a large extent with other Mesoamerican peoples and in regional terms other architectural styles predominated in which Maya elements were fused with others belonging to the Gulf Coast and the central highlands. We are then talking about architectonic styles as indicators of political entities, a subject that in the future will shed more light on the ancient history of the Maya.

References

ANDREWS, GEORGE F.
1975
    Maya Cities. Placemaking and Urbanization. Norman: University of Oklahoma Press
1986
    Los estilos arquitectónicos del Puuc. Una nueva apreciación. INAH *Colección Científica* 150. Mexico City: Instituto Nacional de Antropología e Historia

BENAVIDES C., ANTONIO
1995
    "Becán y su región." *Journal de la société des Americanistes*, 81. Paris, 259–66

1996
    "Petén: región, estilo y tradición cultural." In *Investigadores de la Cultura Maya*. Vol. 3, no. 2, Campeche: Universidad Autónoma de Campeche, 407–47

BENAVIDES C., ANTONIO, AND RENÉE L. ZAPATA
In press
    "¿Qué tan extensa en la región del Puuc?" In *Antropológicas*. Mexico: UNAM

GENDROP, PAUL
1983
    Los estilos Río Bec, Chenes y Puuc en la arquitec-

tura Maya. Mexico City: Universidad Nacional Autónoma de México (UNAM)

HOHMANN, HASSO
1995
Die Architektur der Sepulturas-region von Copán in Honduras. Graz, Austria: Academic Publishers

LOTHROP, SAMUEL K.
1924
Tulum: An Archaeological Study of the East Coast of Yucatán. Publication 335. Washington, D.C.: Carnegie Institution of Washington

MALER, TEOBERT
1997
Península Yucatán. Berlin: Gebruder Mann Verlag

MARQUINA, IGNACIO
1964
Arquitectura prehispánica. Mexico City: INAH

MORLEY, SYLVANUS G., G. W. BRAINERD, AND R. J. SHARER
1983
The Ancient Maya. Stanford: Stanford University Press
MORRIS, E. H., J. CHARLOT, AND A. A. MORRIS
1931
The Temple of the Warriors at Chichen Itzá, Yucatán. Publication 406. Washington, D.C.: Carnegie Institution of Washington

POLLOCK, HARRY E. D.
1970
Architectural notes on some Chenes ruins. Papers of the Peabody Museum. Vol. 61. Cambridge, Mass.: Harvard University

POLLOCK, HARRY E. D., R. L. ROYS, T. PROSKOURIAKOFF, AND A. L. SMITH
1962
Mayapán, Yucatán, Mexico. Publication 619. Washington, D.C.: Carnegie Institution of Washington
1980
The Puuc. An Architectural Survey of the Hill Country of Yucatán and Northern Campeche, Mexico. Memoirs of the Peabody Museum of Archaeology and Ethmology. Vol. 19. Cambridge, Mass.: Harvard University

POTTER, DAVID F.
1977
Maya Architecture of the Central Yucatán Peninsula, Mexico. Middle American Research Institute. Publication 44. New Orleans: Tulane University

PROSKOURIAKOFF, TATIANA
1963
Album de arquitectura maya. Mexico City: Fondo de Cultura Económica. Published in English as *An Album of Maya Architecture* (Norman: University of Oklahoma Press, 1963)

ROYS, LAWRENCE, AND EDWIN M. SHOOK
1966
Preliminary Report on the Ruins of Aké, Yucatán. Memoirs of the Society for American Archaeology. no. 20. Salt Lake City: Society for American Archaeology

SMITH, A. L.
1965
"Architecture of the Maya Highlands." In *Handbook of Middle American Indians*. Vol. 2. Ed. by G. R. Willey. Austin: University of Texas Press, 76–94

The weaver figurine
Jaina Island, Campeche
Late Classic period
Mexico City
Museo Nacional de Antropología
cat. 182

The primary image of the Maya as renown astronomers who gave life to a series of exact and complicated calendars, as architects of splendid cities that impress us today, as inventors of a precise numerical system which incorporated the number zero before that of the Hindus, as creators of a writing system that combined versatility with precision and grace, or as consummate artists of stone, clay, and stucco, has very often blinded us to a good part of their humanity. Bombarded by pseudoscientific, even vulgar publications, we have become accustomed to idealizing their democracy, wisdom, and holiness, even endowing them with extraterrestrial characteristics. From this we gain a prestigious cast of heroes or demi-gods for the American pantheon, and, in exchange, we lose out on the chance to link their achievements and failings with the rest of humanity and thus, the opportunity to relate to them. Thanks to the work of epigraphers, today we undoubtedly know a little more regarding who ruled the people, but in the heroic narrative of their feats–as biased and partial as the accounts of any dominant group–only rarely may the Maya farmer, hunter, or fisherman be glimpsed. Although the dedication date of this or that building is noted, practically nothing is said about the actual builders of these structures. We know how long a certain noble and his relatives lived and their names, but nothing is mentioned of the people who sustained them. It is not strange that in epic tales of yore, rarely do those individuals appear who make history, not by writing it, but rather by living it. To approach the experiences and day to day labors of the "common" Maya, the people, is not an easy task. The fascination with the great intellectual and material achievements of the Maya on the part of chroniclers of other periods, as well as contemporary ones, has until recently largely overlooked the most simple aspects of their daily life. We possess only a few facts about the daily life of the Maya and available information is often very fragmentary. In fact, to put together an ethnographic sketch of the ancient Maya people, we have only references from certain chroniclers and early indigenous testimony, material evidence studied by archaeologists, information from the few codices that survived the religious zeal of friars, as well as some dictionaries from the early colonial period. Joining such sparse threads, and falling back on analogous comparisons with contemporary Maya villages, it is possible to contrive the fabric of the daily life of the ancient Maya, although the results in any light are crude when one imagines the magnificent brocade which must have dressed this civilization, considered by many to be the most enlightened of America.

Because this work includes essays on the geography, social organization, trade, specialized knowledge, and religious aspects of this ancient civilization, I will limit myself to a brief overview of Maya subsistence activities, understood not only economically, but also culturally. The majority of studies on the topic are devoted to agricultural work, particularly cultivation techniques, while the daily subsistence of the ancient Maya covers a much broader area, depending on the different ecological niches where they settled (rain forest, tall mountains, coasts and wilderness, lake and swamp zones, cloud forests and extensive plains). Added to this diversity are the communal and personal choices of the thirty or so groups which compose the Maya linguistic family; choices which influenced their manner of conceiving and representing the environment, both in terms of ways in which the Maya interacted with their sphere, as well as the changes which occurred over the course of centuries during which its culture developed. Although the following notes attempt to offer a general panorama, because of space limitations they fail to cover the complexity and diversity of the subsistence activities developed by the various Maya groups. There were, as can be expected of groups which came from a common cultural matrix, shared knowledge and techniques. Hunting, for example, was from ancient times one of the most frequent activities; there is material evidence of this practice from the time man arrived in America over 40,000 years ago. The immense variety of ecological niches occupied by the Maya explains the diversity of hunted species, for which different methods were developed, some of enormous sophistication. The catch was destined for self-consumption or barter, while some parts of the prey were used for the production of utensils or utilitarian, commercial, therapeutic, magical, and ritual products. Skins and feathers could also be employed in exchange, as if currency.

It is impossible to list all the prey, which ranged from large jaguars to diminutive hummingbirds, and included pheasants, pumas, ducks, wild boars, tapirs, squirrels, toucans, eagles, rabbits, turkeys, snow leopards, foxes, macaws, partridges, hares, gophers, and so forth. Three animals stand out for the frequency with which they are mentioned–deer, iguanas, and

Madrid Codex, page 37
Madrid, Museo de América

The typical Ocellated Turkey
of the Maya area

quetzals, species which provided delicious meat and precious skins, and feathers. The methods used to capture them varied–nets, ropes, small stones, slings, blowguns, bows and arrows (beginning in the Postclassic period), traps hidden in the soil, and flint-tipped lances or pointed sticks, among others. On occasion, above all when hunting deer, they organized expeditions to flush out game in which fifty to one hundred individuals would come together, not only to keep an eye out for their prey, but also to attract them with special whistles, spreading out nets or traps and pushing the animals toward them or toward the hunters positioned in the dirt. They also conducted rituals prior to hunting, to request permission and protection from the deities who were guardians of mountains and animals, and later to thank them for the capture obtained. Thus, these were privileged moments of confluence and social collaboration, in addition to an opportune time to recreate the ritual ties that bound the people. Since the purpose of bird hunting was often to get feathers, hunting techniques were designed to catch the bird without damaging its plumage. To achieve this goal, the Maya used fine nets, baskets, torches for night birds, manual capture in nests (particularly macaw, duck, and parrot chicks for domestication), and above all, viscous substances placed on branches where birds perched. The Maya plucked the necessary feathers and then allowed the birds to grow new feathers. The feathers from certain birds were so valuable that in some areas, sons inherited the birds from their fathers as property, and in other places, such as the Verapaz region, where quetzals were abundant, the trees where the birds nested were passed down from generation to generation, and even the watering spots the birds frequented. Among some groups, according to the chroniclers, anyone who killed a quetzal was subject to capital punishment. In addition to the immense economic importance of birds, whose "clothing" was traded with dwellers of the central highlands of Mexico or paid in tribute to local lords, it is not strange that the sumptuary universe of the Maya was to a good measure a feathered universe. Feathers were incorporated into embroidered designs on luxurious *huipiles* (loose-fitting upper body garments worn by women) of the upper classes; braided into their headdresses or earrings; adorning their hats and crests; balancing themselves in the litters of the gods or waving in fans, insignia, and banners (the famous Bonampak murals are an excellent example of this practice) and accompanying the mortal remains of lords as an offering in their tombs. Feathers also appeared as an ornamental motif on ceramics, lapidary stone pieces, modeled stucco, codices, and even on architectural structures, as seen at Kaminaljuyú. Feathers even appeared in the judicial sphere, where it was not unusual that fines for certain crimes were paid for with feathers and even live birds. The area occupied by the ancient Maya included coastal lands; lands furrowed by abundant rivers or innumerable streams; lands splashed with lakes, lagoons, marshes, swamps, and tidelands; frozen wilderness in the Cuchumatanes highlands; and enormous rocky extensions lacking surface water currents, as in the Yucatán peninsula, where, according to Fray Diego de Landa, "nature worked . . . so differently . . . that the rivers and sources that run all over the world, all join together here from their secret meatus underneath the earth." Considering this ecological range, it seems quite appropriate that the Maya displayed their inventiveness for preparing fish and seafood in such different ways.

To adapt oneself to the changing environment in order to benefit from it, it is obvious that one must have a profound knowledge of nature. That the Maya did possess such knowledge is clearly evident in early linguistic documents, in which a multitude of terms, even poetic, refer to nature, showing how the culture domesticated space by naming its variations, as well as how men adjusted to these variations. The high sea, calm, vast, agitated, blown by winds or driven by storms; rising or tranquil rivers; roaring streams during the rainy season and the sound of water "which runs without making noise;" sandbanks, gulfs, creeks, islands, capes, reefs, ocean seas, marshes, salt tidelands–a thousand and one terms for geographic irregularities that a good fisherman should have at his fingertips, and upon which oarsmen or rowers made their journey in large boats or small canoes, prepared with straw or flexible branches to protect fragile cargo, to facilitate the voyage of passengers or the patient waiting of fishermen. The grouping of aquatic animals (the *taxa* of biologists) in Western culture does not always coincide with the method employed by Maya peoples, since local classifications alluded to characteristics at times distinct from those we use (i.e., the form or color of animals, the fact that the animals moved near to the water, on water or within water). The novelty of many American species which forced the chroniclers to limit themselves to indicating, on occasion, that the animals

opposite
Masculine head from Palenque
Chiapas
Late Classic period
Mexico City
Museo Nacional de Antropología
cat. 472

Painted plate
Late Classic period
Mexico City
Museo Nacional de Antropología

"resembled . . . " or in the best of cases, to describing them superficially, at times made the animal's precise identification problematical, but there is no doubt of the existence of a large variety of freshwater and saltwater fish, crabs, crayfish, oysters, turtles, shrimp, snails, lizards, baby eels, and so forth. For example, Colonial Yucatec dictionaries, rather than assigning a generic word for the fish called *cay*–susceptible to modification with such adjectives as large, small, fresh or salted (an important commercial product)–recorded specific names, the literal translation of which gives one a good idea of the peculiarities in form that attracted the attention of the Maya. We have, among others, catfish or "peel" fish, needlefish or "interwoven," sea bass or "rod," banana fish or "skinny," barracuda or "mouth," sardine or "little bone," *huh cay* or "iguana fish," *ib* or "bean," grouper or "leaf," *och* or "fox," flying fish or "dragonfly," or *zib cay* "flowing fish", river fish or "soaked," *mex* or "spiderfish," *p'u* "a fish which inflates with air," *gata marina* or "knot," saurel or "ferocious," *corbina* or "sweet potato," and the poetic *buluc luch*, "submerged gourd," which was a whale. Similar are the terms for lobster, octopus ("monkey fish" or "beard"), shrimp ("sperm fish"), eel, oyster (*booc*: smell), crab (*bab*: foot), crayfish, lizard ("the scaly one"), and different types of freshwater and saltwater turtles. To obtain such prey, the Maya employed their knowledge of the environment and the habits of the animals, thus the Cakchiquel language uses different terms to designate a river full of fish and a "river or lagoon that had no fish." But, it was not enough to know that there were fish, one also had to know the sites where the fish "ran," "teemed," or laid their eggs; where the turtles, lizards, or crabs were located; and even where the fishbait earthworms called *xilom* swarmed. Once the site was found, and depending on the animal, multiple tools could be employed in their capture; tools such as arrows (perhaps harpoonlike ones such as those still used by the Lacadons today), wood harpoons (sometimes attached to ropes and buoys to follow the trail of wounded fish), and bag nets made of twigs, straw, or grasses. Crabs hidden under the river's rocks could be picked up by hand. Sometimes the Maya placed small fish among the reeds as bait. They would even drug the fish facilitating their capture, by pouring into the water some type of substance obtained from roots or herbs. Once the waters were poisoned or "mucking"; the prey was trapped using partitions or dams which diverted the river's current. In addition to their flesh, some aquatic animals provided the Maya with other products. The Tzeltals used mollusks for dying fabric, the Yucatecs exploited the eggs of certain turtle and fish varieties. Shark teeth, known as *xooc*, were used to make arrowheads, and the little "saws" from fish known as *ba*, "very pretty because they have a strange white bone . . . , which cuts like a knife," were used as instruments for autosacrifice, "and it was the job of priests to have them, and they had many," states Landa. The Pocomchis knew about pearls and something called *amizcle* of lizard, the use of which we do not know. While the Chontals copied the forms of shells and turtles to make necklaces and pendants, the Cakchiquels made little metal turtles

Polychrome bowl
from Tabasco
Classic period
Balancán
Museo "José Gómez Panaco"
cat. 28

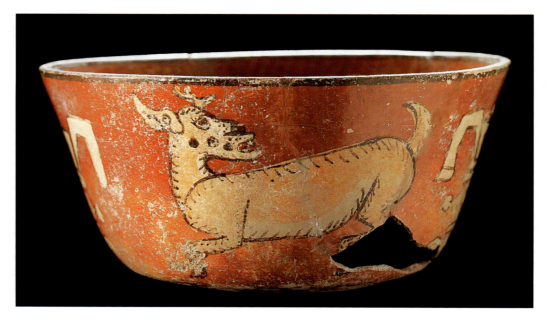

Tetrapod plate
from Tabasco
Protoclassic period
Mexico City
Museo Nacional de Antropología
cat. 6

which were hung around the neck, and according to Thomas de Coto "to safeguard chickens, from kite [*milano*], or other birds of prey, instruments were made with little bones and crab shells, and even with eggshells and leaves, which made noise with the breeze, and they were called *xibibal*, i.e., instruments to inspire fear." Seashells (*Strombus gigas*) used as horns and drums made with the carapace of a small, reddish turtles were employed by many peoples for festivals and rituals. We know that to clean fish, they were soaked, scraped with sharp instruments to remove the scales, and hung on wooden hangers. Fish were either salted or cooked in leaves, grilled on wood grills, or steamed, fried, roasted, or even prepared in *empanadas* (small filled breads or dumplings). Fresh or prepared, the fish was offered in markets, and once salted, transported long distances–as Yucatec and Tzutuhil merchants were accustomed to doing–and they were even left on doorsteps by humble traveling salesmen.

In equal measure to hunting rituals, fishermen threw their nets toward the sacred. The aquatic deities also demanded recognition. Whoever displayed reverence before them could obtain a good catch and even good fortune or health, given that in some groups it was believed that spirits would appear next to rivers, fountains, pools, and other water sources, to communicate with certain specialists to help their devotees. The Cakchiquels similarly believed that monstrous fish, members of the *lab* category, referred to omens or "bad things," and it was also said that frogs, shrimps, and certain little fish sometimes fell from the sky in strong rains, accompanied by thunder and lightning. These were not the only aquatic presences in the heavens; one of the Cakchiquel names for the Milky Way was *Ru bey palam*: the path of the sea turtle, referring to the tracks left by animals on the sand. The diversity of hunting and fishing products pales in comparison with the huge variety of products obtained from gathering, which in addition to serving as food or for seasoning (e.g., salt, a widely traded product), also included an enormous range of materials for housing, work tools, therapeutic purposes, rituals, and even adornment. To enumerate all the uses would require a volume. We can barely mention a few examples, such as the enormous importance of honey and wax obtained from wild and domesticated bees, or the appetite for different classes of worms, such as those collected to make the ointment known as *axi*, another type of worm from which a kind of silk was obtained, those used to calm toothaches, and even, among the Cakchiquels, a species of "attractive green worms" which were hung from hats as adornment. The enormous variety of trees and shrubs growing in the zone were used not only for their edible fruit and firewood, but also for constructing homes, bridges, and canoes, and of course, a multitude of utensils for daily life: from handles for farming equipment, plates, and spoons, to shields, hoisting tackle for pulley systems, and locks and keys. Branches were used to make brooms, resistant bark (like reeds) served for cords or rope, while other trees were fermented for alcoholic beverages. Flowers, symbols of happiness (in Cakchiquel, for example, "to be happy and content" was literally said "to have a flowering heart") were used to decorate wreaths, hats, homes, and tombs, while other more fragrant flowers were mixed into food and drinks, including the famous beverage chocolate. Some leaves, seeds, and roots were consumed during lean times, so that certain dried fruits were very coveted, as *cascabeles* (little bells). Resins were used as dye, incense, mordent, or glues, and there was never a shortage of thorns which were utilized as needles, nails, fishhooks, pins, and even as instruments in minor surgery. Gourds and calabash cups (*Crescentia* sp.) were–and continue to be–particularly valuable for assisting in daily activities. They were used to transport water, honey, liquors, tortillas, or even seeds for planting in the maize fields. Filled with small grains and pebbles, and provided with a stalk-like stick, they served as percussion instruments in dances or were used as rattles to "hush small babies." Divided in half, these gourds and cups were employed as spoons, and pierced with many holes to be used as colanders. Medium-sized half gourds were used to rinse out the mouth, while larger gourds were sometimes used as plates, and the smallest ones served as bases on scales to measure salt, *chian* (sage), and other tiny seeds. Gourds were even used as chamberpots! By the way, the Tzeltals employed hay for toilet paper.

While canes and other grasses were used to build fences and walls (sometimes, mixed with clay); to make mats, beds (hammocks, in contrast, were made with thin rope or cord), baskets, hats, and sandals; and even to stuff pillows, palms were used for their fruit and above all their leaves. Palm leaves were used to weave fans, sandals, rain capes, mats, basketry, and padded rings for carrying cargo on the head, and to manufacture roofs. Other leaves, in contrast, served to cover salt, to wrap or transport food products, or to cook food while suffusing it with the flavor of the leaves. At the same time, other leaves were also used to make dyes for blankets, gourds, hair, or skin–and not only for ornamentation, but also to intimidate one's enemy in battle, to protect oneself from certain insects, or to be used in rituals. For example, the

Seashell used as a ceremonial instrument (trumpet) from Uaxactún, Guatemala
Classic period
Guatemala, Museo Nacional Arqueología y Etnología
cat. 345

Madrid Codex, page 17
Madrid, Museo de América

Cakchiquels covered the lords they took office with a tarlike substance, while the Yucatecs painted victims of arrow sacrifice with indigo. Copal, obtained from different resins, was primarily used in rituals, although it also had therapeutic purposes (chewed or diluted in water), as had different types of tobacco, which could be smoked or chewed. "Inebriating substances" referred to some mushrooms, the fruit of the tree called *uqa* in Cakchiquel (a species of strawberry tree), and the liquor obtained from the bark of the tree known as *balche* in the Yucatán peninsula, or in other places, the liquor obtained from the fermentation of maguey juice. Regarding earth, minerals, and metals, records indicate their usage as colorings, clays, and for removing grease for ceramic production and construction purposes, as lapidary and agricultural tools, knives for multiple purposes (shaving, hunting fish, and cutting food, in war, and for bloodletting), and even to make children's toys, such as clay dolls in the western Guatemalan style, which could be made of wood, rags, and even, "little animal or bird skins filled with straw," according to the notes of Fray Thomas de Coto. Metal jewelry was even more elaborate; when made of gold, it was an exclusive luxury for the lords. Metal was used for making necklaces, earrings, bracelets, rings, nose plugs (nose pendants), and lip plugs (lip ornaments). Given the scarcity of metals in the zone, it was more common that jewelry was made of stones the Maya regarded as precious. However, the most general use for stone material was to manufacture cutting implements, different types of grinders, and even mirrors. Considering the uses described above, it is easy to imagine a rich therapeutic arsenal based not only on animals, but also on plants and minerals; texts record analgesics, substances to induce abortions, and even aphrodisiacs. For example, while the Tzeltals valued a snail (*Aplexa*) as an aphrodisiac, the Dominican friar Varea reports the Guatemalan belief that the leaves of the herb *xulu queh çaqul*, given to a man to drink or to put under his bed, "gives him a good heart with his women so that he does not quarrel nor get angry with them . . . it takes on the metaphor of the leaf, as it shrinks, it is said that the heart of whoever drinks it will shrink." Much more common–and important from the economic point of view–than devising amatory techniques was undoubtedly obtaining daily food, an activity which from at least 2500 B.C. was based primarily on agriculture, once the domestication of different plants was achieved, or grains and plantules from other regions of Mesoamerica were obtained. When they interfered in the biological reproduction of certain plants, the Maya were capable of radically transforming their subsistence patterns, and with that, the rest of their cultural patterns, given that sedentary life gave rise to changes not only in the material sphere, but also in social and religious organization. Since these topics are covered in other chapters of this volume, we limit ourselves now to mentioning that since that time a good part of community life revolved around the cultivation of what is known as the "Mesoamerican triad": beans, squash, and maize. Maya agricultural patterns were primarily qualified as migrant or itinerant agriculture; farmers felled large trees and cut down weeds, leaving the remains to dry out and later, to burn, allowing the ash to fertilize the earth. Later, they planted the seeds using a planting stick, calculating the rainy season so that the small germinated plants benefited just in time from the rains. Then came the continual clearing of the land to prevent weeds from overwhelming the plants or robbing them of nutrients; the occasional fertilizing of the

Zoomorphic pipe
from Chichén Itzá, Yucatán
Early Postclassic period
Merida, Museo Regional
de Antropología "Palacio Cantón"

top and opposite
Necklace made of shells
and green stones
from Chichén Itzá
Terminal Classic-Early Postclassic
period
Merida, Museo Regional
de Antropología "Palacio Cantón"
cat. 148

land with animal manure or vegetable products; making dirt ridges to facilitate the passage of water; arranging dirt around the stalk to hold it up; the continual struggle against natural predators; irrigation by hand when rains were scarce . . . After several cycles of planting-harvesting, the duration of which varied according to the type of earth, the land was allowed to rest and the operation was moved to another spot, preferably the adjacent land.

In this way, the matter strikes one as simple and even dull, but nothing could be further from reality. In the pre-Hispanic era, iron instruments were not used, so one can imagine the time and effort needed to fell the exuberant tropical trees with only stone axes. In Mesoamerica there were no teams of draft animals nor beasts of burden. As a result, activities such as hauling, turning the soil over, and plowing all relied on human strength, subjected to the occasional whim of nature, which proved to be fairly fickle in a region frequented by cyclones and hurricanes, when not jolted by earthquakes. On the other hand, it was not enough to produce food for family consumption; the sedentary lifestyle accelerated the development of cities and the institutionalization of a dominant, burdensome system that included civil, religious, and craft specialists. Although of primary importance, this type of agriculture was not the only source of support for the sophisticated, vast, and complex dominant group. Although we do not possess very much information on the matter, what can be assumed is the importance of the agricultural practice of developing domesticated gardens, where a good part of the fruit and vegetables were cultivated. In any case, ever since the period known as the Middle Pre-classic, there is evidence of improved cultivation techniques, such as irrigation systems (drainage fields, canals, irrigation ditches, dams, aqueducts); terraces for leveling lands with excessive gradients; platforms to avoid excessive humidity; and even *chinampas*, artificially built-up plots of land like islets anchored in areas of abundant water. All of this allowed for larger surpluses which would lead to the portentous Maya development in the Classic period. The centralization of power arose at that time, resulting in the consolidation of state societies and sparking a more specialized workforce, which included masons, painters, scribes, merchants, and full-time warriors (including mercenaries), together with a growing number of stone, wood, bone, clay, or textile artists. Since the Maya region was an outstanding producer of textiles in Mesoamerica, it is worth examining this product for a moment. We know that there were people responsible for removing the seeds from cotton, unraveling and combing the fibers, spinning them with spindles (of different thickness depending on the kind of cloth one planned to weave), and winding the fibers onto skeins, which the weavers could use on their backstrap looms to make warps and for weaving. The fabrics obtained from the process displayed brocades, needle embroidery, stamping, tying, and hemstitching, and they included featherwork, depending on the fashion, local uses, and of course the economic position of whoever acquired the textile or embroidered it for personal use.

The use of feathers, although the most exotic feathers without doubt were not inexpensive, was among the most highly esteemed and widespread practices in the Maya region. It has been shown, for example, that Huaxtec women braided their hair with feathers of different colors; that the famous tubular nose plugs–the use of which was limited to chiefs and lords–consisted of gold tubes "crossed by a colorful feather." These lords were presented in war adorned with visible touches of feathers, ornamenting themselves on the back and the ears. Another observation of a Dominican chronicler on the Yucatán and Campeche Mayas: "All that they wear and dress themselves with . . . is embroidered handsomely with various colors of feathers and with red and yellow cotton." In contrast to the simple clothes of the common man, which were often limited to a cotton loincloth and sleeveless shirts, the Yucatec lords of Sinanché, according to the famous *Relaciones histórico-geográficas* (a sort of census commissioned by the king of Spain) of the sixteenth century, wore "mantles with many feathers." Meanwhile, the Muchuppipp and people from the province of Cochuah adorned themselves with "cotton and feather vests woven into the shape of a jacket with two flaps of many colors" and loincloths which had "many feathers" on the tips. Yucatec merchants distinguished themselves by carrying beautiful palm or feather fans together with walking sticks and net bags for transporting currency. Warriors went to battle "unclothed, adorned only with feathers and smeared with red body paint." The Pocomams of Guatemala not only used hummingbird and quetzal feathers for dances or duck breast feathers "for interweaving in the garments of women", but quetzal, parrot, macaw, and other precious bird feathers were deposited in the tombs of great lords

Brick representing a character
drinking
from Comalcalco, Tabasco
Terminal Classic period
Comalcalco
Museo de Sitio de Comalcalco
cat. 460

Eccentric considered
by Mayas as a cult object
Campeche
Centro INAH Campeche
cat. 353

top and opposite
Censer lid
from the south coast of Guatemala
Classic period
Guatemala
Museo Nacional de Arqueología
y Etnología
cat. 173

together with other offerings, and feathers figured as part of the dowry which subjects gave when their lord's daughter married. Tzutuhil lords demanded the delivery of quetzals from their subjects. Equally varied were the uses the Cakchiquels made of feathers, both in daily life as well as in special events: from tribute to ritual paraphernalia. They were also employed in flyswatters or fans, crowns, small tubes for writing; and for putting "on the *guaipil*'s chest" or in hats. Feathers were particularly coveted for self-adornment in dances; they were displayed in bracelets, in "plumage" used on the head or arm, or as single quetzal feathers "large and green, for dancing." There were even verbs for denoting the movement of feathers in the dance: "to wave the crests or feathers of those dancing, as if sowing wheat, shaking the feather with the air." According to philologist Thomas de Coto, feathers which shone brightly during the dance were compared to the golden bellies of fish under water, fire, fireflies, sand, stars, the "clear, shining" moon and the sun "when the rays touch the mountain peaks."

The information we have about Maya-speaking peoples in the area that is now Chiapas at the time of contact with the Spaniards refers mainly to the Tzeltals of Copanaguastla and to the Tzotzils of Zinacantán, but the information helps in developing a sense of what occurred in the rest of the region. The Tzeltals, inhabitants of the town known as "mother of cotton," were famous for their works in that fiber. They were particularly renowned for the variety of their large cloths: thin, thick, woven, embroidered, spun, worked, hemstitched, embroidered only on the edge; white, black, red, painted with Brazilwood, striped, or vermilion-colored. Clothes for work, parties, weddings, mourning, and war were made from this material, as were shrouds, swaddling clothes, canopies, curtains, shields (also made of leather), handkerchiefs, bandages, colanders, sheets, mattresses, and even girdles for alleviating inguinal hernias. Yet, cotton clothing was not the only type employed; dictionaries speak also of garments made of "maguey linen" (also used to make bandages) and of those–such as wedding clothes–in which feathers were interwoven throughout, with green feathers being the most prized, since they came from quetzals and parrots. The Copanaguastleca women, covered with *naguas* (underskirts) and *huipiles* (loose-fitting upper garments), were accustomed to braiding their hair, adorning themselves with ribbons, plucking their eyebrows, and painting their faces with iron oxide. They liked necklaces, strands of beads, bands of bells, and they shared with men a fondness for amber lip plugs and nose pendants and crowns of flowers, feathers, and even metal. Men favored loincloths, shirts with sleeves, and cloaks made from cotton blankets. They wore their hair long, sometimes covered with hats adorned with feathers, or *panaches*. At the other end of the body, woven maguey or *ixtle* fiber, deerskin, or palm sandals were worn, on occasion with soles of thick cotton. The outfits of the Zinacantán Tzotzils appear to have been considerably more modest: they used headdresses, woven-palm rain capes, handkerchiefs dyed with cochineal, gloves, rabbit hair clothing, turbans, "garlands or crowns" for

Vessel from Chamá
roll out depicting merchants
and Ek Chuah God
the protector
Late Classic period
Boston, The Museum of Fine Arts

dances, and the use of "perfumes" is mentioned, too. Yet, to think that very elaborate clothing was the privilege of everyone would be incorrect; rich feather *panaches* or amber nose pendants were used by a very few; going barefoot and barely covered with a loincloth was the only possibility for the immense majority. Tomás de la Torre, speaking of Zinacantán in approximately 1545, noted: "They go about naked, and when it becomes cold or a festival requires them to don clothing, they put a blanket on their shoulders with two knots on the right side." Since possessing feathers or cloths with feathers interwoven denoted wealth (feathers and woven materials could be rented for dances), it is not difficult to imagine that in the pre-Hispanic period "feather officials" formed part of the groups of craftsmen in service to lords, and they benefited from the tribute of the common people, sometimes contracting cheap labor. We know, for example, that among the Cakchiquels and the Copanaguastlecs there were women who wove for a living, hiring themselves out to work and embroider cloth in exchange for a little maize, and as a result, it is hard to believe that these same women could wear the fine clothing that they themselves created. References are made to darned *huaraches* (sandals) and patched clothing, which was known as *loltic*, the same word that designated a wounded man. These threads help us reconstruct a view of the social fabric.

The primary agents involved in the making and selling of these garments and paraphernalia were merchants, who appear to have played a major role throughout the Maya region. Dictionaries enumerate merchants who sold at open-air markets and fairs, door to door, in stores, on roads, and on the doorsteps of their own homes, while distinguishing between those who sold wholesale, retail, on credit, and for barter (e.g., maize, chile, cacao) and even those who allowed for bargaining and those who cheated on prices. They either worked alone or managed a group of burden bearers–contracted or slaves–on streets, stone causeways, wide roads, trails, short cuts, and even rivers, with the assistance of leather bands with ropes, padded rings for the head, and saddlebags covered with leather. In accordance with this variety of merchants, buyers appear to have been able to acquire products "at a discount," "by bulk" (wholesale), or in small amounts; the latter were "purchases of the poor or orphaned," to use a Tzeltal expression.

Another indication of the importance of textiles and other finery is the frequent mention of dyes (annatto tree, indigo, Brazilwood and Campeche wood, cochineal, and certain mollusks), obtained by merchants not only in the Maya region, but also in Oaxaca, the Zoque region, and on the Soconusco coast. Copper needles, which were appealing since they lasted longer than those made of maguey, bone, or wood, and even counterweights of gold for spindles belonging to the most important ladies, came from Guatemala and central Mexico. A good part of the rabbit skin and the maguey linen, whether in the form of fibers or already

opposite
Female figurine
from Jaina Island
Late Classic period
Campeche
Centro INAH Campeche
cat. 106

Quetzal, the typical bird
of the Maya area

woven, came from the highlands. What were the valuable items for barter? Copper hatchets, feathers, mantles or blankets, and cacao. But, one also had to be careful. There was a fair share of deceitful merchants who sometimes filled cacao almonds with maize dough, or avocado pits. Perhaps Aztec merchants did the same (as well as cooking the almonds so that they would look bigger, riper, and plumper), against whose tricks the Franciscan Molina warned, no less than in a confessional! Thieves–who also existed in Maya society–appear to have been even more dangerous, particularly those who robbed *tamemes* ("carriers") of their coveted burdens. *Tamemes* often worked as employees for merchants.

Just as today, there were also individuals who made a living entertaining others. Musicians, dancers, and clowns were the source of entertainment at that time. From documents describing these members of society, among other sources, one of the pre-Hispanic songs from Dzitbalché was known as "The Dimming of the Ancient on the Mountain," a metaphor for the new fire ceremonies held to celebrate the *katun*, a new period of time. In this ceremony, together with the erection of the stela, which tells of the event, the gods venerated are mentioned, as well as the musical instruments, the song and dance school (*popolna*), their professors, and some of the actors who participated in the representations:

"The sun sets in the folds of the sky in the west
The *tunkul*, the shell, and the *zacatán* dream and the singing gourd blows
Everyone has chosen . . . they have come.
Later, jumping, they will arrive at the *popolna*, where the Ahau Can is . . .
The singing musicians, farce actors, contortionists, jumpers, and the hunchbacks
  and the spectators have arrived.
All the people have come . . . to the entertainment which will take place in the middle
  of the plaza of our town.
When the sun peeks above the folds of the sky
it is time to begin . . . "

The text, as we can see, alludes to the trickster "necromancers" or "farce actors," who were like Western minstrels traveling from village to village presenting amusing and even obscene comedies, imitating bird sounds, telling and singing old stories or creating new ones satirizing the government. "They are great with jokes and with nicknames they give to their mayors and judges: if they are harsh, if they are weak, if they are ambitious, and thus with much fluidity and in one word . . . ," noted Sánchez de Aguilar in roughly 1615. They also could interpret different types of fortune, which without doubt was the delight of the village. Thus, they burned a handkerchief and later showed the same handkerchief as whole; they squeezed water from the handle of a knife; they hit themselves in the chest and other parts of the body with big rocks without showing any sign of pain or injury; they broke eggs and put them together again, ate fire without burning themselves, and cut the trunks of thick trees and put them back together. According to the chroniclers, there were some who were so talented that they could pretend to form "a sea, a river, and a fountain or very deep well in the plazas or fields." The famous Bernardino de Sahagún described the performance of this type of illusionistic game among the Maya-Huaxtecs during very early periods. In addition to singers and dancers,

they were "friends of deception, tricking the people, making them believe what was false was true, such as making people believe they burned houses which were not burned, and making a fountain of fish appear. It was nothing more than an illusion of the eyes. And that they killed themselves, making slices and pieces of their flesh, and other things which were apparent and not true." Although descriptions of these acts come from the colonial period, without doubt, necromancy was a long-standing tradition with deep pre-Hispanic roots. The *Popol Vuh* speaks of how the Hero Twins, with their special powers to defeat the lords of the underworld, allowed themselves to be burned in a bonfire, their bones ground and their ashes thrown into the waters of a river, later to reappear as fish. Furthermore, they burned houses and returned them to their previous state, even killing each other and bringing themselves back to life. Just like their eighteenth-century descendants, Hunahpu and Xbalanque interwove their magic acts with a dance such as the *ixtzul*, a particularly violent dance which included among its steps, putting "sticks down one's throat and bones in the nose" and hitting oneself "on the chest with a big stone." No more, no less than the necromancers described centuries later. Irrefutable masters of time management, the Maya also created spaces and individuals to help them enjoy their leisure. Professional musicians and dancers, song and dance teachers, prostitutes, and barbers, among many other occupations, appeared in large urban centers, as well as in small rural villages, providing entertainment and relaxation to the governing elite or lending their services to the humble people, when not entertaining both together, just as popular comedians did on the occasion of public festivals, so that according to the testimony of Landa, they delighted the town of Chichén Itzá from the high stage of "hewn stone theaters." A

Clay vessel and roll out
depicting a codex painter
from Central Petén
Classic period
Private collection

few years after the Spanish conquest, Juan Farfán attended one of the last festivals of the "new year" in Yucatán and he was surprised by the diversity of dances ("which were of more than a thousand types") and of the number of people attending: " . . . more than fifteen thousand Indians gathered together and had come from more than thirty leagues to see it, because as I said, they had the festival for a very big event," he noted in the *Relaciones histórico-geográficas*. With greater or lesser splendor, festivals undoubtedly were held throughout the Maya region. Carpenters, lapidary carvers, scribes, farmers, gatherers, burden bearers, messengers, midwives, nannies, prayer leaders, curers, gravediggers, diviners, rowers, hunters, weavers, and fishermen—all the representatives of the enormous range of available occupations found in a civilization as refined as that of the Maya—occasionally would gather in ceremonial centers to exchange news, products, techniques, and experiences, when not to forge alliances. For others, it was the appropriate time for recreating social ties and rituals which brought the community together. Considering that the subsistence of men, throughout the universe, depended on maintaining the gods, they would make offerings to them, while invoking their protection with words perhaps similar to those recorded in the *Popol Vuh*: "Oh You, Tzacol, Bitol! Look at us, listen to us! Do not leave us, do not desert us! Oh God in the sky and on earth, Heart of the Sky, Heart of the Earth! Give us our ancestry, our succession, while the Sun marches on and there is clarity! Let the sun rise, let daybreak come! Give us many good paths, flat paths! Let people have peace, much peace, and let them be happy. And give us a good life and useful existence! Oh You, Hunahpu, Tepeu, Gucumatz, Alom, Qaholom, Xpiyacoc, Xmucane, grandmother of the sun, grandmother of light! Let the sun rise, let daybreak come!"

Whistle with human figures
from Copán, Honduras
Late Classic period
Tegucigalpa, Bodegas Centrales
del Instituto Hondureño
de Antropología e Historia
cat. 368

Male figurine
from Nebaj, Quiché
Late Classic period
Guatemala, Museo Nacional
de Arqueología y Etnología
cat. 340

References

ACUÑA, RENÉ (ED.)
1978
Farsas y representaciones escénicas de los mayas antiguos. Mexico City: Universidad Nacional Autónoma de México (UNAM), Instituto de Investigaciones Filológicas (IIF), Centro de Estudios Mayas (CEM)
1991
Arte breve y vocabularios de la lengua pok'om. Basado en los manuscritos de fray Pedro Morán y fray Dionisio de Zúñiga. Mexico City: UNAM, IIF, CEM

ALVAREZ, M. CRISTINA
1984
Diccionario etnolingüístico del idioma maya yucateco colonial. 2 Vols. Mexico City: UNAM, IIF, CEM

ARA, DOMINGO DE
1986
Vocabulario de lengua tzendal según el orden de Copanabastla. Edited by M.U. Ruz. Mexico City: UNAM, IIF, CEM

Cantares
1965
Cantares de Dzitbalché. Translated, with introduction and notes by A. Barrera V. Mexico City: Instituto Nacional de Antropología e Historia (INAH)

CARDÓS DE MENDEZ, AMALIA
1959
El comercio de los mayas antiguos. Mexico City: Escuela Nacional de Antropología e Historia (ENAH), Sociedad de Alumnos

CHASE, ARLEN F., AND PRUDENCE M. RICE (EDS.)
1985
The Lowland Maya Postclassic. Austin: University of Texas Press

COTO, THOMAS DE
1983
Thesaurus verborum. Vocabulario de la lengua cakchiquel vel guatemalteca, nuevamente hecho y recopilado con summo estudio, trabajo y erudición. Edited, with introduction and notes by R. Acuña. Mexico City: UNAM

FLANNERY, KENT V. (ED.)
1982
Maya Subsistence. Studies in Memory of Dennis E. Puleston. New York and London: Academic Press

HUDSON, JEAN
1990
"Spatial Analysis of Faunal Remains in Hunter-Gatherer Camps." In *Etnoarqueología. Primer coloquio Bosch-Gimpera*. Ed. by Y. Sugiura and M. C. Serra P. Mexico City: UNAM, IIA, 219–40

HUNN, EUGENE S.
1977
Tzeltal Folk Zoology. The Classification of Discontinuities in Nature. New York and London: Academic Press

LANDA, DIEGO DE
1994
Relación de las cosas de Yucatán. Edited and with a study by Ma. del Carmen León. Mexico City: Consejo Nacional para la Cultura y las Artes (CNCA)

LAUGHLIN, ROBERT M., AND JOHN B. HAVILLAND (EDS.)
1988
The Great Tzotzil Dictionary of Santo Domingo Zinacantan. With Grammatical Analysis and Historical Commentary. 3 Vols. Washington, D.C.: Smithsonian Institution Press

Libro de Chilam Balam
1973
Libro de Chilam Balam de Chumayel. Translated by A. Mediz Bolio. Mexico City: UNAM

MILES, SUZANNE W.
1983
Los pokomames del siglo XVI. Translated by F. Rojas Lima. Guatemala: Seminario de Integración Social Guatemalteca (SISG)

MORÁN, FRANCISCO
1935
Arte y diccionario en lengua Choltí. A manuscript copied from the *Libro Grande of . . . of about 1625.* Facsimile edition of W. Gates. Baltimore: Maya Society

OCHOA, LORENZO
1979
Historia prehispánica de la Huaxteca. Mexico City: UNAM, IIA

PÉREZ SUÁREZ, TOMÁS
1996
"De los orígenes a las primeras aldeas." In *Los mayas. Su tiempo antiguo.* Ed. by G. Bustos and A. L. Izquierdo. Mexico City: UNAM, IIF, CEM, 85–100

Popol Vuh
1980
Popol Vuh. Las antiguas historias del Quiché. Translated and with notes by A. Recinos, in M. de la Garza. *Literatura Maya.* Caracas: Editorial Galaxis (Bibl. Ayacucho, 57)

Relaciones
1982
Relaciones geográficas de Guatemala. Siglo XVI. Ed. by R. Acuña, Mexico City: UNAM, IIA

1983
Relaciones histórico-geográficas de la Gobernación de Yucatán. Ed. by M. de la Garza *et al.*, Paleography by M. del Carmen León, 2 Vols. (Fuentes para el estudio de la cultura maya: 1 and 2). Mexico City: UNAM

RIVERA, ROBERTO
1980
Los instrumentos musicales de los mayas. Mexico City: SEP-INAH

ROJAS RABIELA, TERESA
1979
La tecnología agrícola y los instrumentos de cultivo en Mesoamérica. Paper presented at the XLIIIth International Congress of Americanists (Vancouver, 1977). Manuscript. Mexico City: Centro de Investigaciones Superiores del INAH (CISINAH)

RUZ, MARIO HUMBERTO
1992
Copanaguastla en un espejo. Un pueblo tzeltal en el Virreinato. 2nd edition. Mexico City: Instituto Nacional Indigenista (INI-CNCA)
1997
Gestos cotidianos. Acercamientos etnológicos a los mayas de la época colonial. Campeche: Instituto de Cultura, universidades autónomas del Carmen y de Campeche e Instituto Campechano

SAHAGÚN, BERNARDINO DE
1981
Historia general de las cosas de Nueva España. Ed. by A. M. Garibay. 4th edition. Mexico City: Porrúa

SÁNCHEZ DE AGUILAR, PEDRO
1987
"Informe contra Idolorum cultores del obispado de Yucatán (1639)." In *El alma encantada. Anales del Museo Nacional de México.* Presented by F. Benítez. Mexico City: Fondo de Cultura Económica (FCE), 17–122

TAPIA ZENTENO, CARLOS DE
1985
Paradigma Apologético y noticia de la lengua huasteca. Study and notes by R. Montejano y Aguiñaga. Ed. by R. Acuña. Mexico City: UNAM, IIF

THOMPSON, J. ERIC. Q.S.
1979
Historia y religión de los mayas. Mexico City: Siglo XXI Editores

XIMÉNEZ, FRANCISCO
1971–75
Historia de la provincia de San Vicente de Chiapas y Guatemala, de la Orden de Predicadores. 7 Vols. Guatemala: Sociedad de Geografía e Historia.

Dupaix slab
from Palenque, Chiapas
Late Classic period
Mexico City
Museo Nacional de Antropología
cat. 415

Among the cultures that succeeded in creating a writing system, Maya groups have had relatively little luck, given that despite the evidence, Maya writing is still often viewed in a negative light by specialists. Reactions range from "No, they didn't have writing because they were primitive, barbaric people" to "No, it will never be deciphered," followed by "No, these readings are incorrect, my system is the correct one."

These opinions have been expressed in different periods and moments. Nonetheless, almost all those interested today concede one point: it is a type of writing from a past that we all wish to rescue, since it is yet another fragment of the history of humanity.

Since the arrival of the Spaniards in the New World, there was news on the existence of writing, books, and repositories for these tomes. In fact, some friars made use of the knowledge that these people had of writing to communicate the new religion. At the same time, priests also used writing to comprehend the significance of native religion in their attempts to destroy it and thus annihilate that past and its ethnic awareness.

Therefore, Maya peoples lost their own system of writing, first for their own historical reasons and later due to Spanish colonization. Nevertheless, they did not lose their desire to preserve their history, or their ethnicity, culture, and writing.

It is obvious that we cannot speak of the Mayas without speaking of Mesoamerica and the commercial, economic, social, and political relations that existed within this area. It is precisely because of these connections that another type of approach arose: cultural.

Geographically, the Maya zone is located next to two areas crucial in early Mesoamerica, the Olmec zone and Oaxaca. The Olmecs were the first traders, artists, and rulers, while the first Mesoamerican calendrical system recorded in monuments was created in the zone of Oaxaca, which implied the development of the first writing system in the region. At least this is what is demonstrated by archaeological evidence from Monte Albán.

How writing in Mesoamerica evolved still cannot be explained, and perhaps it will never be possible to do so, due to the absence of archaeological evidence. What we do know is that around 500 B.C. a tradition already existed at Monte Albán to conserve the historical past which was situated in time by way of a calendar. This calendar was transmitted throughout Mesoamerica and in some regions has come down to us today.

This is composed of two cycles, based on the combination of the numbers 13 and 20. The first cycle consists of the combination of 20 gods-days with 13 gods-numbers, creating a year of 260 days (13 x 20 = 260). Its name in Nahuatl was Tonalpohualli and the books or codices in which record of these years was kept were the Tonalámatl. We do not know what they were called in Maya, but it could be, according to one colonial document, *tzolkin* (*Ch'olk'Ih*), "day count."

It is the most commonly used and commented upon cycle, because any date corresponds to a numeral-day. Since its creation, it was the same throughout Mesoamerica and it was never altered; thus, the day of the arrival of the Spaniards was recorded exactly in the same way throughout Mesoamerica. The 20 days formed in turn the *veintenas* or "months," of which there were 18 plus a small month of 5 days, with which there is a total of 365 days (18 x 20 + 5 = 365). It is the second cycle of the basic Mesoamerican calendar and its name in Mayan is *haab* or *tun*. The *veintenas* also carried associated numbers that went from 1 to 20, or as the Maya recorded it, from 1 to "zero," or "completion."

Both cycles began at the same time and the dates were recorded by four components: numeral and day and numeral and month. For a specific date to repeat itself, it was necessary for 18,980 days to pass; that is to say, 52 years of 365 days and 73 of 260 days. We do not know why, but as time passed, the months ceased to be recorded in Mesoamerica, with one exception: the Maya zone.

The Mayas adopted the Oaxacan calendar with their numeral system in which the dot signifies 1 and the bar is 5, but the Mayas went beyond that with the creation of "zero," or the sign for completion. This allowed them to invent a system in which cycles that were recorded increased their value 20 times, according to the position that they occupied.

Glyphs of the 20 Maya days *tzolkin*, the sacred year was split in 260 days indicated by placing glyphs to numbers from 1 to 13

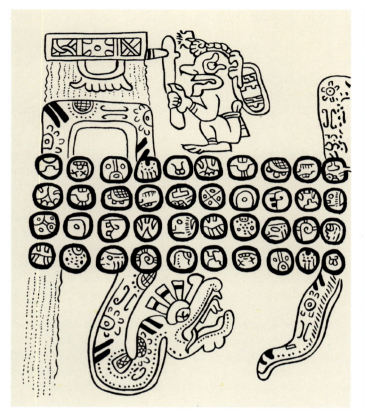

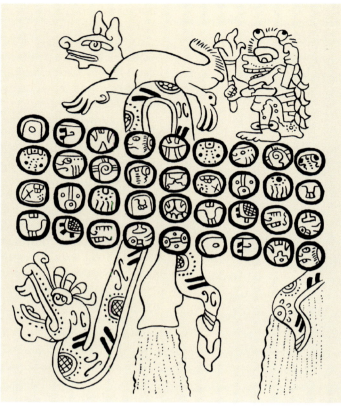

Reconstruction drawing
Madrid Codex
pages 14 and 15, section B

All Maya numerical notations that we know are calendrical and they record dates in the so-called Long Count system, and its later variants. For its creation, it was necessary to have a starting point, a "Creation Date," which corresponds to August 13, 3114 B.C., and that in the Maya system was written as 13.0.0.0.0 4 *ahau* (day) 8 *kumku* (*veintena*), and indicates that the following period of time had transpired:

13 *baktun* (of 144,000 days each)
0 *katun* (of 7,200 days each)
0 *tun* (of 360 days each)
0 *uinal* (of 20 days each)
0 *kin* (of 1 day).

The numeral-day was 4 *ahau* and the numeral-month was 8 *kumku*.

This date, recorded on Maya monuments and codices, has several implications. First, it deals with a mythical date invented by the authors of the Maya calendar; it does not mean that they had begun writing since that time. The system is so exact that this date will not repeat itself in millions of years.

The next 13.0.0.0.0 will occur in A.D. 2012, but the numeral-day and the numeral-month will not be the same. Second, it implies that they believed in the existence of an earlier time inhabited by the gods. Third, it implies that any numerical amount could be written with three signs, as may be seen in Stela 1 of Cobá which records the date: 13.13.13.13.13.13.13.13.13.13.13.13.13.13.13.13.13.13.13.0.0.0.0 4 *ahau* 8 *kumku*.

Although there are doubts with respect to who they were, at the end of the Preclassic period, the occupants of the site of Chiapa de Corzo, Mexico, carved a monument with

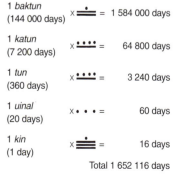

1 *baktun* (144 000 days)   x = 1 584 000 days
1 *katun* (7 200 days)   x = 64 800 days
1 *tun* (360 days)   x = 3 240 days
1 *uinal* (20 days)   x = 60 days
1 *kin* (1 day)   x = 16 days
Total 1 652 116 days

Examples of numbers of bars
dots and completion
Reading of number 1,652,116

on the right
Glyphs of the number 0
and of the numbers from 1 to 19

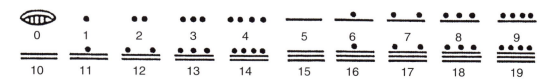

The Maya calendar or *haab* it was split in 19 months: 18 months of 20 days and 1 month of 5 days

a date. This is the earliest known inscription in the long count system. Although fragmentary, the inscription from Chiapa de Corzo Stela 2 bears the date 7.16.3.2.13 6 *ben* (December 9, 36 B.C.), which must be when the Maya began to write dates, as noted years earlier by archaeologist Sylvanus G. Morley. On this monument is recorded the time that had passed since the mythical creation date until the date commemorated in the inscription. This is the same canon followed by all Maya inscriptions.

The earliest dates (36 B.C.–A.D. 292) of known archaeological provenance and in which the Long Count system is already recorded are located in a geographical area that includes the modern-day Mexican states of Chiapas and Veracruz, and the Guatemalan Pacific coast. The system at the beginning had its variants, but by the Classic period (A.D. 292–909) the same type of recording basically consisted of (a) the god of the corresponding *veintena* within the Introductory Glyph; (b) the time transpired since the creation date with (c) the corresponding numeral-day; (d) the Lord of the Night; (e) the date of the lunar calendar; (f) the numeral-month; (g) the event that occurred on that date; (h) the person who conducted the event; (i) his titles; (j) his place of residence; and, on occasions, (k) his ascendance.

But to reach this point, many years and experiences had to pass. It was necessary to create a system of writing that had its moments of experimentation and adjustment. There were day signs that had to be reformed to avoid confusion since they were used indistinctly as dates and as writing itself.

The hieroglyphs or glyphs of the periods followed the creation of a system of composite writing, basically of two kinds of hieroglyphs: the so-called main signs of larger size and the affixes, minor signs that could be attached to or placed within the main sign to form cartouches.

The union of cartouches forms a sentence and these compose texts that generally display a fixed grammatical order consisting of (a) time marker (date or equivalent grammatical element); (b) verb; (c) subject; and (d) object. But, what makes the task even more difficult is the fact that a single glyph may function in several ways: as a sign for a period, a numeral, a syllable, or a complete word. In addition, they tend to be

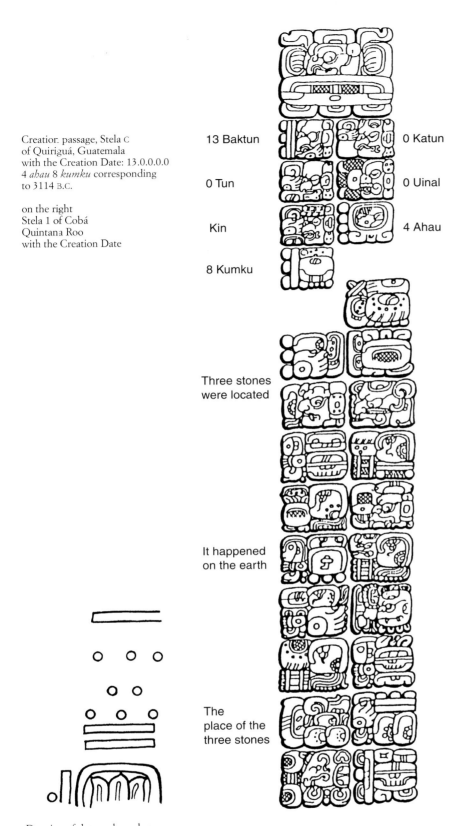

Creation passage, Stela C
of Quiriguá, Guatemala
with the Creation Date: 13.0.0.0.0
4 *ahau* 8 *kumku* corresponding
to 3114 B.C.

on the right
Stela 1 of Cobá
Quintana Roo
with the Creation Date

13 Baktun   0 Katun

0 Tun   0 Uinal

Kin   4 Ahau

8 Kumku

Three stones
were located

It happened
on the earth

The
place of the
three stones

Drawing of dots and numbers
from the Stela 2 of Chiapa de Corzo
the inscription shows
the date 7.16.3.2.13.6 *ben*

opposite
Small glyphic tablet
from the eastern facade
of Temple I, Comalcalco
Terminal Classic or Epiclassic period
Comalcalco
Museo de Sitio de Comalcalco
cat. 413

written in three ways: in normal form, as a head variant, and as a full-body variant. To avoid confusion, phonetic and determinative complements were created, the same ones, as indicated by their names, that serve to clarify the function and reading of glyphs to which they are attached. This was not too much of a problem because only some of the members of the ruling class knew how to read, and the code was part of their cultural heritage.

But many of the inscriptions were destined to occupy sites where the people could see them and thus admire the acts of their ruler. And monuments were complemented by the image of the actor, an image adapted to a conventional register in which the actor never ages and the deities are always present witnessing the acts of the ruler. These depictions of Maya history correspond to what Mircea Eliade called "sacred history."

Stela 11 of Yaxchilán, Mexico
with the date 9.16.1.0.0 11 *ahau* 8 *zec*

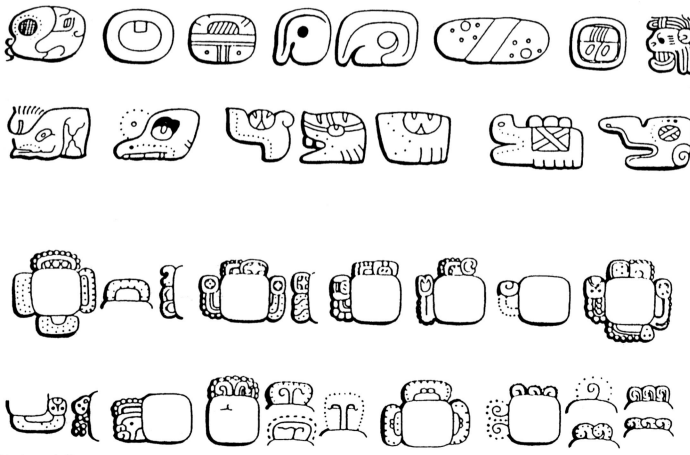

Main signs and affixes

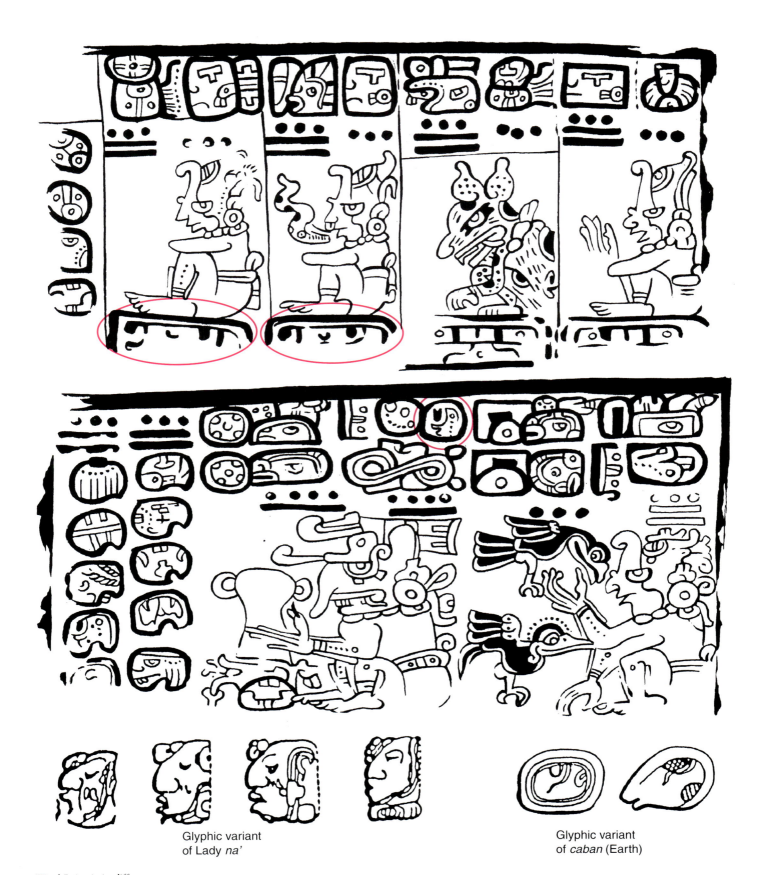

Glyphic variant
of Lady *na'*

Glyphic variant
of *caban* (Earth)

"Earth" sign in its different uses
earth, *caban* day, verb
Lady *na'* and number 1 *na*

Normal

Head variant

Full body variant

Ahau glyphic variants

GI GII GIII

Palenque triad

Sides of the Palenque Sarcophagus
Chiapas, with emblem glyphs
and nominal glyphs

This is a history written by the rulers of each ethnic group in which everyone knew that they were men of corn, who could remember their creators, and therefore who had the obligation to feed the gods who created them, or both worlds would disappear. In this history, ruler-men were in charge of the main responsibility, because it was their task to sustain the cosmos, their gods, and their people. From here arises the symbiotic relationship between Maya gods and men.

Hence, the ruler's need to know in advance the daily passage of the gods of numbers, of days, of *veintenas*, and of cycles. This is because in the end, they are the same gods/rulers/people acting each one under different influences and such knowledge was indispensable to maintain the cosmos in harmonic order. But... man is man and as we now know, the desire for power arose.

Between 1958 and 1964 the history of the decipherment of Maya writing changed radically. The change arose based on the identification that Heinrich Berlin made in 1958 of so-called emblem glyphs, cartouches that identify certain cities. In 1959 the same researcher proved the presence of historical individuals in inscriptions from Palenque. In 1960, first, and then in 1963–64, Tatiana Proskouriakoff proved that Maya inscriptions had historical content and the dates recorded in them, so-called distance numbers, referred to the lives of rulers and associated texts to major events in their lives: birth, designation as heir, enthronement, captures, sacrifices, and death.

Such proposals were initially verified and spread by David Kelley and later by Floyd Lounsbury, Linda Schele, and Peter Mathews. These authors developed a method of deciphering Maya writing that was characterized by the incorporation of prior proposals that had demonstrated their effectiveness. Others were modified in accord with new contributions. What is most important is that they established a method of comparative analysis of clauses, based on the structuralist system, with which it was possible to prove that glyphic substitutions existed, that is to say, that there were interchangeable signs.

It was in this way, thanks to the new epigraphy, the true significance of distance numbers was established. The grammar of texts became known, with which written languages were identified, and they began to identify more and more activities in the lives of rulers.

Discoveries continued and two new currents arose: that of Peter Mathews (1985) reexamining the presence and political implications of emblem glyphs, and that of David Stuart (1987), reanalyzing earlier proposals on the phonetic-syllabic reading of Maya hieroglyphs. The first phonetic-syllabic readings have been followed by many others. The identification of hieroglyphs was substituted by the reading of words, words began to form sentences, and sentences texts.

Maya history speaks to us of a cultural relationship in which each group gradually

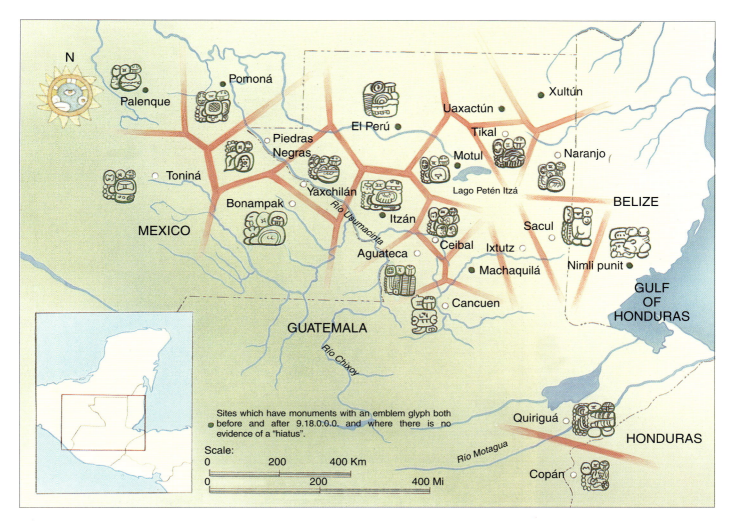

Political map of the Maya
zone based on emblem glyphs

acknowledged its awareness of writing, although this was written in accord with the purposes and circumstances of each "school" of artists.

And the decipherment of writing changed again with the deeper understanding of the character of Maya historical texts. Stuart identified homogeneity in Classic period Maya writing, despite visual differences, and Mathews proposed the existence of political and power spheres based on the emergence and presence of emblem glyphs both at the identified city itself as well as at others.

Their discoveries, pooled with knowledge of the activities of rulers, transformed the long held image of the Maya as a peaceful people dedicated to contemplation and computation of the passage of stars into that of a society much like all others throughout history: aggressive and warlike. However, the purpose of this aggression does not seem to have been solely to dominate another region under the direction of specific rulers that we still do not know, because one of their main objectives was the capture of prisoners who would be sacrificed. Often captives were sacrificed in the ball game, because without their spilled blood, in particular rituals ordered by the ruler-priest–the Mah Kina Ahau Pop or "Great Lord Sun, Lord of the Mat"–the gods would cease to exercise their beneficial influence or humans would not be able to counteract

Comparison of clauses

Glyphic substitutions
of the jaguar glyph

balam

ba-balam

balam-ma

ba-balam-ma

ba-la-m(a)

187

Lintel 2 of Bonampak, Chiapas

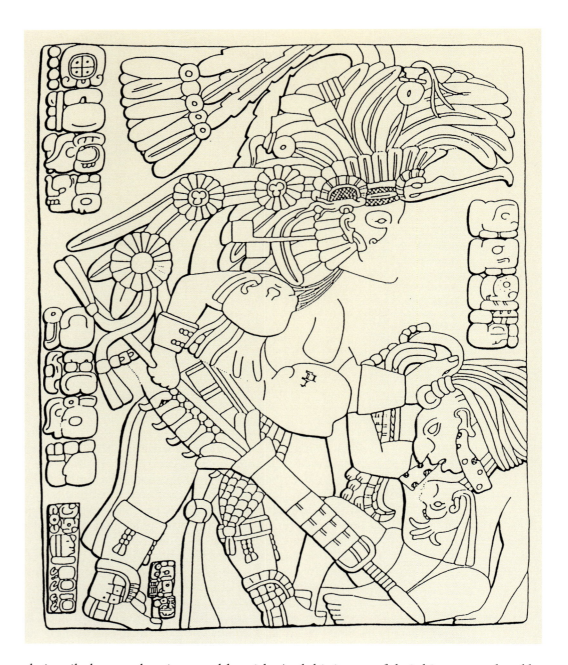

their evil plans, and society would perish. And this is part of their history as related by Maya hieroglyphic texts.

Thus, new epigraphic readings have opened up a world in which rulers speak of alliances, marriages, betrayals, rituals, visits, and exiles–in other words, of their social and political spheres. The most recent discovery is the antagonism between Tikal and Calakmul, cities that in different ways tried to exercise their power over the rest of the area.

Surely there were cultural and political circumstances that brought cities to bellicose conflicts in which we know some of them emerged victorious and on occasions with the help of people from the outside.

Triumph permitted the victor, we imagine, to begin to expand its borders, which happened in the case of the city of Uaxactún, in Guatemala, which when it lost the war against Tikal was governed by Smoking Frog, brother of Jaguar Claw, *ahau* of Tikal, from 8.17.3.1.12, 11 *eb* 15 *mac* (January 16, A.D. 378). This event was recorded on several monuments, such as that of Stela 5 at Uaxactún, Stela 31 at Tikal, Stela 1 at

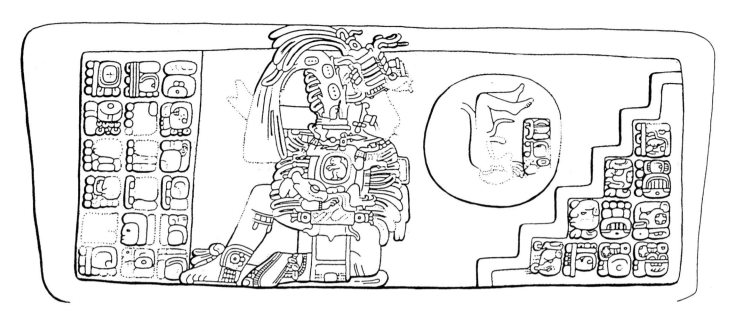

Hieroglyphic Stairway 2, Step VII
Yaxchilán, Chiapas

Uolantun, the "Mundo Perdido marker," the inscription on the "fat man" of Tikal, and Stela 39 of Tikal.

All of these glyphic inscriptions speak of that war between Tikal and Uaxactún. Beginning at this time Tikal tried to continue its conquests and to expand its territory. Nevertheless, from what we know, there was another city, Calakmul, that was also trying to do the same.

But the Maya milieu was not homogenous as certain authors try to indicate. There are cities, such as Toniná, Chiapas, with an iconography that deviates from established canons. History barely begins. Each reading has to be tested in its different contexts, for a number of the proposals might not correspond to reality, a reality that must be supported by the archaeology of the site and of the area. This reality must be tested, in turn, by the history and culture that still survives in the region.

It is true that five hundred years have passed since the arrival of the Spaniards. It is true that one thousand years have passed since the so-called Maya Collapse, but it is also true that we have a large quantity of written documents by the same Maya people in their own language, in the Latin alphabet, and by the same evangelical friars who on warning their colleagues of "the tricks used by the Indians of these lands" to continue with their pagan activities, provided a great amount of information that we can use.

Take for example the case of the Zinacantecans, an ethnic group that continues to live today in Chiapas. Fray Francisco Ximénez, citing Fray Tomás de la Torre, who knew the Zinacantecans in the middle of the sixteenth century, tells us two interesting things. The first refers to their activities: "They were dedicated to the salt trade and they had wars with their neighbors for possession of these salt mines."

The second, cited more widely by the same Francisco Ximénez, says that the Tzotzils took their name (bat people) "because when they arrived at the site they found a stone in the shape of a bat." Ximénez himself states: "They used some painted mantles made into a twist as if Moorish and placed on the head."

All this would sound anecdotal, but at Toniná, Chiapas, two monuments have been located that mention the capture of people whose origins could be established based on their headdress, because they have hair twisted with a cloth and forming a spiral, and they have a glyph on the leg: a bat. Thus, I was able to establish that these captives were probably from Zinacantán, that is to say, they were Tzotzils.

The decipherment of Maya hieroglyphic texts is still not complete. Of the possible readings, what must be incorporated at each site is archaeological information if it exists, as well as linguistic, anthropological, ethnographic, and historical data.

And when the decipherment of historical texts has been achieved, another task remains. We still do not fully understand the significance of the codices with their dates, gram-

Lintel 24 of Yaxchilán
with the self-sacrifice of Lady Xoc

matical form, images of gods, astronomical tables related to Venus, eclipses, and the Maya zodiac–namely, all that is associated with these religious books. Although they may be read to a large extent, we still do not know why they do not contain history. Everything indicates that the three codices that were saved, all three from the Early Postclassic period (A.D. 1000–1500)–the *Dresden Codex*, the *Madrid Codex*, and the *Paris Codex*–are religious texts containing prayers and magic formulas, as well as rituals conducted for different groups: hunters, farmers, fishermen, merchants, weavers, and beekeepers. These also deal with rites carried out during the last five days of the year and to begin the next.

We do not have any maps, although we know that they existed. Nor do we have inscriptions on monuments from that period. The closest information is what is written in Colonial period indigenous books: the *Popol Vuh, Anales de los Cakchiqueles, Memorial de Sololá, Título de Totonicapán, Ritual de los Bacabes*, and the so-called *Libros de Chilam Balam*, to mention only a few. But this will be another part of history.

Stela 39 of Tikal, Guatemala

References

AYALA FALCÓN, MARICELA
1983
    "El origen de la escritura jeroglífica maya." In *Antropología e historia de los mixe-zoques y mayas*. Mexico: Universidad Nacional Autónoma de México-Brigham Young University
1987
    "La estela 39 de Tikal." In *Memorial del Primer Coloquio Internacional de Mayistas*. Mexico City: Universidad Nacional Autónoma de México

BECQUELIN, PIERRE, AND CLAUDE-FRANÇOIS BAUDEZ
1982
    Tonina, une cité maya du Chiapas. Vol. III. Collection Etudes Mesoaméricaines no. 6–3. Paris and Mexico City: Mission-Archéologique et Ethnologique Française au Mexique

FREIDEL, DAVID, LINDA SCHELE, AND JOY PARKER
1994
    Maya Cosmos. Three Thousand Years on the Shaman's Path. New York: William Morrow and Co.

MATHEWS, PETER
1985
    "Maya Early Classic Monuments and Inscriptions." In *A Consideration of the Early Classic Period in the Maya Lowlands*. Publication no. 10. Institute for Mesoamerican Studies. New York: State University of New York at Albany
1997
    La Escultura de Yaxchilan. New Haven: Yale University, México, INAH

MORLEY, SYLVANUS G.
1961
    La civilización maya. 4th edition. Mexico: Fondo de Cultura Económica

STUART, DAVID
1987
    Ten Phonetic Syllables. Research Reports on Ancient Maya Writing, 14. Washington, D.C.: Center for Maya Research

THOMPSON, J. ERIC S.
1962
    A Catalog of Maya Hieroglyphs. Norman: University of Oklahoma Press

The ancient Maya kept track of the passage of time in terms of several different calendrical cycles, grouping days into longer periods based on astronomical and other considerations. Placement within such cycles was recorded for historical events, like the birth or accession of a ruler, and the scheduling of ritual practices may have been determined, in part, by such cycles as well. Because the Maya kept track of different kinds of cycles, producing periods of very different lengths, there was a demonstrated concern for understanding how different cycles fitted with each other–for example, how a cyclic pattern of eclipses fitted with solstices and equinoxes or with the 260 day sequence of named days. This concern with *commensuration*, the interaction of cycles of different lengths, is central to understanding ancient Maya astronomical knowledge and the uses to which it is put.

At the heart of the Maya calendar is a vigesimal number system that was used for structuring many of its cycles. For numbers below 20, the Pre-Columbian Maya used a quinary notation based on three symbols: a shell or flower for zero, a dot for 1, and a bar for 5. The numbers, 2, 3, and 4, were represented by two dots, three dots, and four dots, respectively. Numbers from 6 through 19 were formed by combining dots and bars, e.g., one dot plus one bar for 6, two dots plus one bar for 7, two bars for 10, two bars plus three dots for 13, three bars for 15, and three bars plus four dots for 19. A special glyph for 20 was sometimes combined with bars and dots to represent the numbers from 21 through 39. However, for most purposes, the Maya used a positional notation for numbers above 19 that was essentially vigesimal. There were also head variants of the numbers from 0 to 20.

In the positional notation, all the positions except the second increased in value by a factor of 20, moving from bottom to top. As will be explained below when we discuss the Era calendar, it was necessary to change the maximum value of the second position from the bottom from 20 to 18 in order to define a vigesimally based civil year that was closer to the length of the solar year (360 days versus 400 days). Thus 20 was represented by a shell (for zero) in the units position and one dot (for 20) in the twenties position. Two dots in the twenties position and a shell in the units position signified 40. One bar in the units position and three bars in the twenties position equalled 65 ($3 \times 20 + 5$). The largest number that could be expressed with only two positions, 359, was composed of three bars and four dots in the units position and three bars and two dots in the twenties position ($17 \times 20 + 19$). The addition of 1 to that number, equalling 360, placed one dot in the third position from the bottom and shells in the two positions below it. The next highest position had a value of 7,200 (20×360) and the one above it 144,000 ($20 \times 7,200$). The system could be continued indefinitely, but it usually stopped with the fifth position because the solar era was defined in terms of five places.

Our description of Maya positional notation is based on its application to the calendar because there are no examples of its use in other contexts. It is, of course, possible that they employed a fully vigesimal notational system, with 400 as the factor in the third position, for counting chocolate beans, feathers, and other objects. Unfortunately, the only records we have of the enumeration of non-calendrical items involve numbers below 40, which do not help to resolve the question of whether the factor in the third position was 360 or 400.

The Maya calendrical cycle that was most similar to the Western Gregorian calendar was the *haab* of 365 days. It was divided into eighteen named months of 20 days each (*pop, uo, zip, zotz, zec, xul, yaxkin, mol, chen, yax, zac, ceh, mac, kankin, muan, pax, kayab,* and *kumku*) plus a short, intercalary month of only five days (*uayeb*), which was also known as the

193

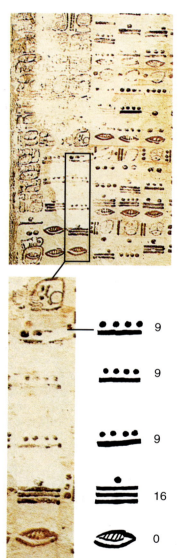

Positional notation
Dresden Codex, page 24B

"nameless days" (*Xma Kaba Kin*) or the "lost days" (*chay kin*) in several Mayan languages. The days in the 20 day months were numbered in terms of elapsed time from 0 to 19. The first day of the month was referred to metaphorically as "the seating" of the month. For example, New Year's day, 0 *pop*, was called "seated Pop," the second day of the month was 1 *pop*, the third day was 2 *pop*, and so forth. The first day of *uayeb* was "seated *uayeb*," and the rest of the days were 1 *uayeb*, 2 *uayeb*, 3 *uayeb*, and 4 *uayeb*.

The *haab*, with its length of 365 days, is a close approximation to what is called the tropical year, the year of the seasons–the period of about 365 1/4 days from one spring equinox to the next. Unlike our Gregorian year, the *haab* made no leap-year correction to deal with the quarter-day-per-year inaccuracy. Its New Year's day drifted backward through the seasons–for example, from the spring equinox around A.D. 560 to the winter solstice around A.D. 930 to the fall equinox around A.D. 1300.

Architecture of the Classic period shows that the Maya were concerned with recognizing these stations of the tropical year, the solstices and equinoxes. Because the axis of the Earth's rotation is tilted, the position of the rising Sun on any local eastern horizon varies in a regular fashion during the annual revolution of the Earth around the Sun (the same is true for the setting Sun on the western horizon). Sunrise on the day of summer solstice defines a (latitude-dependent) extreme position north of due east, whereas the winter solstice sunrise is at the corresponding southern extreme. Twice a year, at both equinoxes, sunrise occurs at the midpoint of the range, at due east (if the horizon is flat). At Uaxactún and several other Classic archaeological sites, buildings of so-called E-group structures are aligned so that, from a defined observation point, the Sun rises directly over the midpoint of the structure on the equinoxes and over lateral edges or other architectural features on the solstice days. At El Caracol "observatory" structure of Chichén Itzá, several of the documented architectural alignments are to sunset positions on days of equinox and summer solstice.

Another kind of solar cycle noted by the Maya and other peoples of ancient Mesoamerica is based on solar zenith passage. Between the tropics of Cancer and Capricorn, there are two days a year, one before the summer solstice in the northern hemisphere and one after it, when the Sun at local noon is directly overhead, at the position of zenith. For any given locality, its geographic latitude determines what the two days are and, consequently, the length of time between first and second zenith passage. The closer to the equator, the longer is this period.

At about the latitude of Copán in Honduras, for example, the second zenith passage occurs 105 days after the first, whereas at Mérida, on the northern edge of the Maya area, the corresponding period contains fewer than 60 days. Evidence that the ancient Maya

Pop	Uo	Zip	Zotz	Zec	Xul	Yaxkin	Mol	Chen	Yax

Zac	Ceh	Mac	Kankin	Muan	Pax	Kayab	Kumku	Uayeb

Month glyphs

The Observatory at El Caracol
Chichén Itzá

 baktun

katun

tun

 uinal

 kin

Period glyphs

were concerned with this phenomenon occurs at El Caracol of Chichén Itzá, where there are architectural alignments to the horizon position of the setting Sun on the two days of solar zenith passage at that site.

Although the *haab* was useful for specifying events that took place within a single solar year, it was inadequate for recording historical events that occurred over longer periods of time. For this purpose, the Maya developed an Era calendar, known as the Long Count, that covered a period of 5,125 years and encompassed all of Maya recorded history. The base of this calendar was the 360 day *tun*, a vigesimal unit that was divided into eighteen 20 day *uinal*. Twenty *tun* were grouped into a unit called a *katuns*, and twenty *katuns* formed a unit called a *baktun*.

An Era was composed of 13, not 20, *baktuns*, which was another departure from a strict vigesimal reckoning of time. The current Maya Era began on 11 August 3114 B.C. (Julian day number 584,283 of Western astronomy), and it will end on 21 December A.D. 2012 (which is a day of winter solstice).

The most common method for recording Long Count dates on Classic-period monuments utilized special glyphs for the *baktun*, *katun*, *tun*, *uinal*, and *kin* periods, with coefficients representing the number of instances of each period necessary for expressing the date. In transcribing such dates, epigraphers usually represent the coefficients with Arabic numbers separated by periods, as in 8.14.3.1.12. In this example, 8 *baktuns*, 14 *katuns*, 3 *tuns*, 1 *uinals*, and 12 *kins* have been completed. Here, as in the *haab* count, days and larger periods are reckoned in terms of elapsed rather than current time.

Another calendrical cycle of great importance to the Pre-Columbian Maya and other Mesoamerican peoples was the 260 day ritual or divinatory calendar known to scholars as the *tzolkin* or day count. It was composed of two smaller cycles, a "week" of twenty named days arranged in a fixed order (*imix, ik, akbal, kan, chicchan, cimi, manik, lamat, muluc, oc, chuen, eb, ben, ix, men, cib, caban, etznab, cauac,* and *ahau*) and a sequence of numbers from 1 to 13 that served as coefficients for the days. The permutation of these two cycles, 20 x 13, meant that a given day and its coefficient would not be repeated for 260 days. Thus, beginning with 1 *imix*, the first day in the larger *tzolkin* cycle, the next day would be 2 *ik*, the day after that 3 *akbal*, the thirteenth day would be 13 *ben*, the next day would be 1 *ix*, and so on through the cycle until the last day, 13 *ahau*, is reached.

The glyphs for the 20 days of the Maya week in their normal order, are shown in this book, from *imix* to *ahau*. Their calendrical use is signaled in all cases by a cartouche or frame and, in many cases, a pedestal. In non-calendrical contexts, the same glyphs could have one or more different readings.

Although we do not know why the Maya and other Mesoamerican peoples chose 260 days for their ritual cycle, several interesting suggestions have been offered for its origin. It has been noted that the Quiche Maya of Guatemala highlands regard 262 days as the period for human gestation, which is only two days longer than the *tzolkin*. Perhaps the Maya chose

The Leiden plate, jadeite
from Tikal, Petén
Early Classic period
Leiden, Rijksmuseum
voor Volkenkunde
cat. 428A and B

on the right
Inscription
on the Leiden Plate

8 Baktun

14 Katun

3 Tun

1 Uinal

12 Kin

1 Eb

— seated
— Yaxkin

the 260 day figure because it agreed better with their vigesimal number system. An alternative explanation is related to astronomy. If 260 days are subtracted from 365 days, the length
of the *haab*, the remainder–105 days–represents the length of time it takes the Sun to move
from its first to its second zenith passage at about the latitude of Copán in Honduras. Of
course, this does not explain why the 260 day ritual calendar is found all over Mesoamerica,
nor why the first evidence of it is found in areas where the length of the period between successive solar zenith passages is less than 105 days.

Whatever the origin of the 260 day cycle, it was a felicitous choice because it has some
interesting possibilities for commensuration with astronomical cycles, of which the Pre-
Columbian Maya were undoubtedly aware. Two *tzolkin* cycles of 260 days, or 520 days,
equal three eclipse half-years, and three cycles of 260 days, or 780 days, equal one synodical
revolution of Mars. In this respect, the Maya ritual cycle was superior to any ritual cycle in
the Western calendar, which could not be as easily commensurated with the movements of
astronomical bodies such as the Moon and Mars.

The next cycle of interest to the Pre-Columbian Maya, which scholars refer to as the Calendar Round, resulted from permutating the *haab* of 365 days against the *tzolkin* of 260
days. The least common multiple of these two cycles is 18,980 days, which equals 52 *haab*
and 73 *tzolkin*. Historical dates are almost always expressed in terms of Calendar Round

Imix Ik Akbal Kan Chicchan Cimi Manik

Lamat Muluc Oc Chuen Eb Ben Ix

Men Cib Caban Edznab Cauac Ahau

Day glyphs

196

7 Imix   14 Zec

Star war

Example of a Calendar Round
on Lintel 41, Yaxchilán
London, The British Museum

permutations on Classic period monuments as, for example, 7 *imix* 14 *zec*. The first part
of this expression, 7 *imix*, is a *tzolkin* date; the second part of this expression, 14 *zec*, is a
haab date. This combination of day and coefficient and month and the day in the month
will not recur for 52 years (*haab*).

Calendar Round permutations were frequently paired with Long Count dates in the monumental inscriptions, yielding such lengthy expressions as 8.14.3.1.12 1 *eb* 0 *yaxkin*. This
notation permitted historical or mythological events to be dated uniquely in a cycle much
longer than the 5,125-year Maya Era, extending several hundred thousand years into the
past or future. The Maya were aware of these temporal possibilities and occasionally mentioned hypothetical events taking place before 3114 B.C. and after A.D. 2012.

The changing panoply of the night sky–the Moon, Venus and the other visible planets, the
stars and the Milky Way–provided the basis for other cycles by which the passage of time
was measured. A part of the sky, of particular interest was the band on either side of the
ecliptic, which is the trace, against the background of the stars, of the plane defined by
the Earth's orbit around the Sun.

To a terrestrial observer, this looks like the path through the sky taken by the Sun, and
the visible planets never stray far from the ecliptic either. For the cultures of the West, the
stars of the ecliptic region, grouped into named constellations having mythological significance, comprise the zodiac with its 12 divisions. The stars of this region had special
significance for the ancient Maya, as well. As documented by the so-called zodiacal
almanac of the Paris Codex, one of the four surviving Pre-Columbian Maya books, the
Maya grouped these stars into 13 zodiacal constellations, not 12, and their names or
labels for them (rattlesnake, skeleton, leaf-nosed bat, etc.) were almost totally different
from our own (the one exception is a scorpion, which seems to correspond to Scorpio in
the Western zodiac).

This zodiacal almanac divides the year of the star sequence (technically a sidereal year of
365.2564 days) into 13 units of 28 days each. The resulting period of 364 days, sometimes
called the computing year, was used here and elsewhere for commensurating calendrical and
astronomical cycles because of its divisibility by 13, a factor of the 260 day *tzolkin*.

Additional representations of zodiacal animals (symbolizing constellations) occur among
the paintings of Bonampak and, in sculpted form, on the façade and on a lintel of the Monjas Annex at Chichén Itzá, and in the Throne Inscription of the Palace of the Governor at
Uxmal. The latter serves as a partial sky map, specifying the zodiacal constellations that were
at the "base of the sky" (that is, just above the western and eastern horizons) at the time of

The zodiacal almanac
Paris Codex, pages 23 and 24
Paris, Bibliothèque Nationale

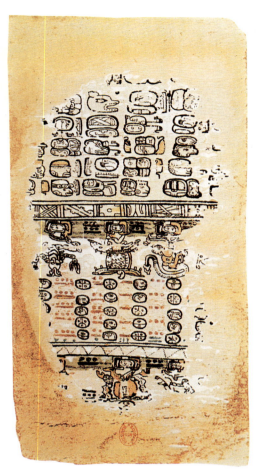

a Venus event important to the function of the Palace (as mentioned further below). Changes in the appearance and location of the Moon provided yet another basis for keeping track of the passage of time. In order to record lunar cycles, the Maya had to depart completely from their vigesimal notation because the length of a lunar month—29.53059 days—does not commensurate easily with the divisions of the *haab*, the *tzolkin*, or the Long Count. The base of these other systems was the 20 day month or week, whereas the base of the lunar cycle was 29 or 30 days.

The Maya avoided any possible confusion here by placing statements about the phases of the Moon after both the Initial Series date and one or both parts of the Calendar Round permutation. In many cases, references to lunar cycles were "bracketed" by the two parts of the Calendar Round, sandwiched between the *tzolkin* and *haab* glyphs and their coefficents, to signal to the reader that the basic unit of time was not the 20 day month or week, but rather the 29 or 30 day lunation.

These lunar records, known as "Lunar Series" among scholars, refer to an eighteen-month calendar divided into three parts, each containing six lunar months. The records tell the reader the age of the Moon on the Long Count date in question, the position of the month in the six-month trimester (expressed in terms of how many months have already been completed), and whether the current month is like to have 29 or 30 days (the closest whole-number approximation to the actual length of the lunar month, because the Maya number system did not handle fractions easily). The alternation of 29 and 30 day months yields an average length of 29.5 days for the lunar period.

This pattern was occasionally interrupted by inserting an extra 30 day month in the sequence, which made it possible to approximate the true mean of a lunation (29.53059 days). It seems that the eighteen-month calendar was the mechanism used for determining when a 29 day month would have to be lengthened by one day.

Lunar series bracketed
by Calendar Round on Stela 3
of Piedras Negras

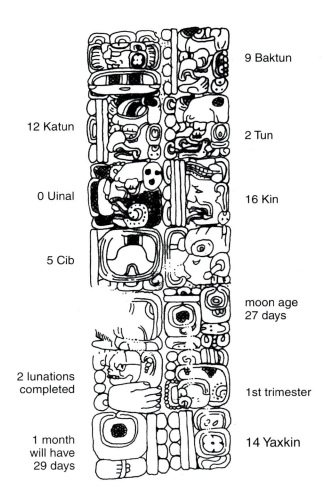

9 Baktun

12 Katun

2 Tun

0 Uinal

16 Kin

5 Cib

moon age
27 days

2 lunations
completed

1st trimester

1 month
will have
29 days

14 Yaxkin

A portion of the eclipse table
Dresden Codex, page 57B
Dresden
Sächsische Landesbibliothek

Another kind of cycle based on lunar periodicities was used by the ancient Maya to predict when solar and lunar eclipses were likely to occur. Eclipses can occur when days of full Moon (for lunar eclipses) or new Moon (for solar eclipses) fall within a few days of what is called lunar nodal passage, the time when the Moon in its orbit around the Earth passes through the plane of the ecliptic (which was explained above). These node days, which define the centers of eclipse seasons during which solar or both solar and lunar eclipses may occur, take place at intervals of about 173.31 days.

This period of time, which is called the eclipse half year, can be commensurated quite precisely with the 260 day *tzolkin* cycle because three eclipse half years (519.93 days) is almost exactly equivalent to two *tzolkin* (520 days). This relationship was used to construct an eclipse warning table, found on pages 51 to 58 of the Dresden Codex (another Pre-Columbian Maya book), that identified the full– or new–Moon dates on which eclipses might occur (anywhere in the world, whether or not they were visible in the Maya area). The table deals with a 33 year or 405-lunar-month span of time in the eighth century A.D., but it gives correction values and other information that seem to indicate that it was intended to serve as an accurate instrument until the eighteenth century A.D. References to eclipses in the carved inscriptions are almost unknown.

What may be an eclipse glyph occurs on a dated eighth-century monument at Poco Uinic, and a hieroglyphic phrase meaning "broken Sun" on a lintel of the Monjas Annex at Chichén Itzá is thought to refer to a solar eclipse in A.D. 877.

One of the most interesting documents of the Pre-Columbian Maya that commensurates calendrical and astronomical cycles is the so-called seasonal table on pages 61 to 69 of the Dresden Codex. This complex, two-part instrument is based on the division of the 364 day computing year into quarters of 91 days each, thereby approximating the lengths of the four quarters of the tropical year. The pictures and hieroglyphic captions that are part of

Reconstruction drawing
Lintel of the door
of the Monjas Annex
Chichén Itzá

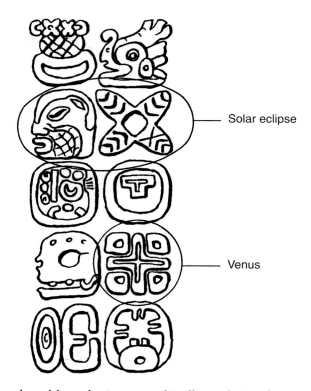

Solar eclipse

Venus

the table make iconographically explicit references to a solstice, an equinox, New Year's day (day 1 of month 1), Half Year's day (day 1 of month 10), and both solar and lunar eclipses. What this does, then, is to commensurate the tropical year, the cycle of eclipse seasons, the *haab*, and, of course, the *tzolkin*–it makes explicit the relationship of each cycle to all the others. Other pictures in the table have to do with rain (certainly a seasonal phenomenon in the Maya area) and, probably, with rituals or ceremonies that we do not understand.

The point of this and other such documents is to relate important and recurring cultural activities to the various cycles by means of which the passage of time was measured. A series of more than a dozen base dates and other data in the table's introduction suggest that an instrument of this general structure was used for a very long time, from the third to the fourteenth centuries A.D.

A concern for cyclic variation in the appearance of Mars is indicated by a table on pages 43 to 45 of the Dresden Codex. From the point of view of an observer on Earth, the movement of Mars through the sky is affected by an optical illusion as Earth, moving faster on its inner orbit around the Sun, first approaches, then catches up with, and finally passes Mars, which is moving more slowly in its outer orbit. From Earth, then, Mars appears to reverse its direction of travel in the sky (as judged by its night-to-night position against the background of the stars) and move "backward" for about two months before resuming its normal "forward" motion for approximately the next two years.

During this time of so-called retrograde motion, Mars sometimes dips down well below the ecliptic as it traces its big retrograde loop. The temporal distance from the middle of one Martian retrograde period to the middle of the next averages about 780 days, and this figure, which is exactly three times the length of the 260 day *tzolkin*, is the length of the Mars table in the Dresden Codex. The iconography of the table, associated by means of a Long Count base date with a Martian retrograde in the early ninth century A.D., may represent Mars, shown here as a beast with an upturned snout, dropping progressively below the ecliptic, shown here as what is called a skyband. Solar and lunar eclipse glyphs in the caption above the third picture indicate that this table is commensurating the Martian cycle with eclipse seasons as well as with the *tzolkin*. Data given in the introduction to the table suggest that it was meant to be recycled repeatedly, with some correction, for use as late as the thirteenth or fourteenth century A.D.

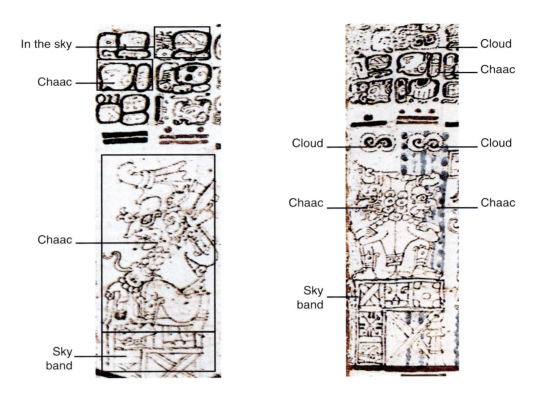

In the sky

Chaac

Chaac

Sky band

Cloud

Chaac

Cloud

Cloud

Chaac

Chaac

Sky band

Picture of summer solstice
showing Chaac sitting
on sky band
Dresden Codex, page 66B
Dresden
Sächsische Landesbibliothek

Picture of vernal equinox showing
Janus-faced rain god Chaac
sitting on sky band with cloud glyph
over each figure
Dresden Codex, page 68A
Dresden
Sächsische Landesbibliothek

Of all the planets, Venus seems to have had the greatest importance for the ancient Maya and other peoples of Mesoamerica. The frequent appearance of Venus in iconography must reflect its central importance in Maya mythology and ritual practice. Several cyclical aspects of the appearance or position of Venus were of concern. As one of the inner planets lying between the Earth and the Sun, Venus becomes invisible to terrestrial observers twice in its orbital journey.

When it is behind the Sun (at what is called superior conjunction), it is invisible for about 50 days; when it is aligned directly between the Earth and the Sun (at inferior conjunction) and therefore lost in the Sun's glare, it is invisible for about 8 days. Between first visibility after inferior conjunction (known as "mfirst" or heliacal rise) and last visibility before superior conjunction ("mlast"), Venus can be seen as the so-called morning star, rising before sunrise and disappearing only in the glare of the new day. Between first visibility after superior conjunction ("efirst") and last visibility before inferior conjunction ("elast"), Venus is visible as an evening star, showing up at dusk as the sky darkens with sunset and setting some time later. These four stations of Venus–mfirst, mlast, efirst, and elast–were of particular interest to the Maya. Another astronomical phenomenon of relevance is what are called Venus extremes.

The plane of Venus's orbit around the Sun is very similar to the Earth's own orbital plane (the ecliptic). This means that when Venus as "morning star" is visible near the eastern horizon (for example), it will be close to the place where the Sun will rise at the end of the night in question. Furthermore, its position north or south of east varies seasonally, as does the Sun's (from equinox to solstice, etc.). However, small differences in the orbits of Venus and Earth mean that Venus can sometimes appear on the eastern horizon (to continue with the "morning star" example) further north than the summer solstitial extreme of the Sun (great southerly extremes are also possible, as are northerly or southerly "evening star" extremes on the western horizon). Such great extremes of Venus were of demonstrated concern to the ancient Maya.

One sort of significance that Venus had for the Maya was as a warrior (in somewhat the same way, one supposes, that Mars was the god of war in Greco-Roman mythology). It has been suggested that events in the Venus cycle may have regulated the scheduling of the "star wars" and military raids that are recorded in the hieroglyphic inscriptions, but, at least for the Maya area, it has not been possible to demonstrate the statistical significance of such

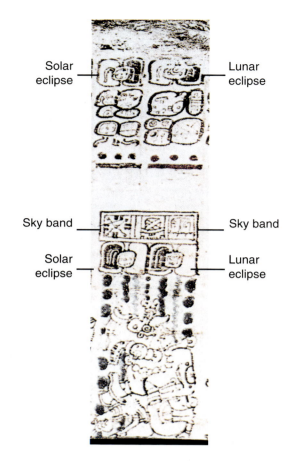

Eclipse glyphs
in the seasonal table
Dresden Codex, page 66A
Dresden
Sächsische Landesbibliothek

Solar eclipse

Lunar eclipse

Sky band

Sky band

Solar eclipse

Lunar eclipse

scheduling. Venus as warrior is depicted explicitly in the Grolier Codex (the most recently discovered Pre-Columbian Maya book) and in the middle series of pictures in the Venus table of the Dresden Codex.

This table, which consists of six pages, is structured around the fact that the 584 day synodical period of Venus (the average time from one inferior conjunction to the next, for example) can be commensurated with the *haab*: five Venus years of 584 days equal eight solar years of 365 days (5 x 584 = 8 x 365 = 2,920). Page 24 is an introduction or preface that contains a base date in Long Count notation and a table of multiples. The other five pages are divided into thirteen rows, each covering a Venus year of 584 days, which are further

The Mars table
Dresden Codex, pages 43B-45B
Dresden
Sächsische Landesbibliothek

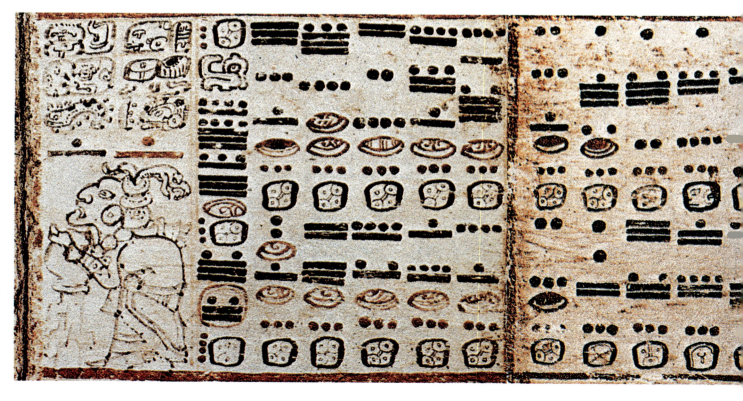

subdivided into intervals of 236, 90, 250, and 8 days. The first three figures are poor approximations of the length of time Venus is visible as a morning star (actually 263 days), invisible at superior conjunction (actually 50 days), and visible as an evening star (actually 263 days), but the last figure is an accurate representation of the mean length of time Venus spends at inferior conjunction.

Summed across the five pages, each row totals 2,920 days, which commensurates five Venus years with eight solar years (the length of time it takes Venus to return to the same position with respect to the seasons). The full length of the table–37,960 days–the result of multiplying each row by 13 ($13 \times 2,920$), is equal to two Calendar Rounds and commensurates three cycles: the Venus year of 584 days, the solar year (*haab*) of 365 days, and the ritual calendar (*tzolkin*) of 260 days.

Another significance that Venus had for the ancient Maya comes from the seasonal distribution of Venus extremes. Great northerly and southerly extremes of Venus coincide closely with the beginning and end, respectively, of the rainy season in large parts of Mesoamerica, and this empiric association of Venus events with rain and the celestial bringers of rain was extended widely in myth and iconography.

Architectural orientations to Venus extremes are known from several Maya sites, most clearly perhaps from Uxmal, where the Palace of the Governor is oriented to create such an alignment. As already mentioned, the glyphic inscription on the façade of the palace includes a representation of the zodiacal constellations at the eastern and western horizons at the time of the Venus extreme.

We should reiterate, in conclusion, that the astronomy of the ancient Maya was not some isolated intellectual pursuit. It had a cultural context in the ritual practices of religion and rulership and in the calendrical frameworks within which such practices were carried out. Astronomy and, specifically, the commensuration of astronomical and other calendrical cycles were applied to the achievement of broader cultural goals.

References

Two standard sources of information on Maya calendrics are Thompson (1960) and Lounsbury (1978); a brief but more technical treatment is given by Closs (1986). Edmonson (1988, 1995) places Maya calendrics in a broader Mesoamerican context and presents evidence for the correlation between

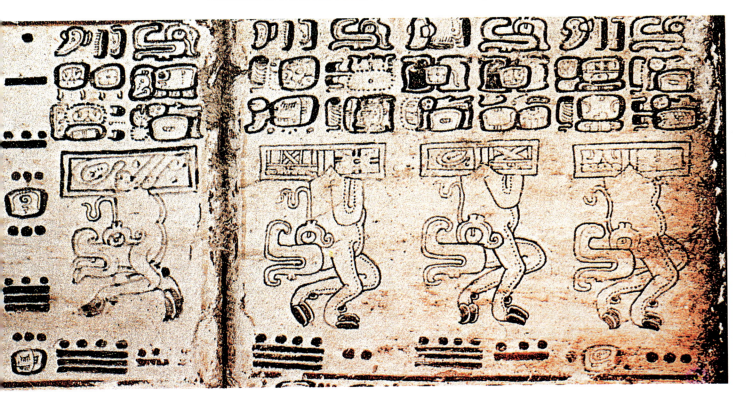

A portion of the Venus Table
Dresden Codex, page 46
Dresden
Sächsische Landesbibliothek

the Maya and the Western calendar. The standard and the only comprehensive source of information on the astronomy of the ancient Maya is Aveni's *Skywatchers of Ancient Mexico* (1980). Some useful updating is given in a survey by Justeson (1989) and in an unfortunately brief popularized treatment by Aveni himself (1997). The astronomical topics covered in this chapter are, of course, dealt with in a number of more specialized works. The classic work on the Lunar Series is that of Teeple (1931), and a necessary update is given by Linden (1986). Fundamental data on astronomically significant architectural alignments at Maya archaeological sites appear in a series of publications by Aveni and Hartung (for example, 1986, 1989, and 1991); the basic study of El Caracol "observatory" at Chichén Itzá is that of Aveni, Gibbs, and Hartung (1975). The question of a Maya zodiac has been reviewed recently by H. Bricker and V. Bricker (1992). For astronomical tables in the Dresden Codex, one may consult Lounsbury (1983) for the Venus table, H. Bricker and V. Bricker (1983) for the eclipse table, V. Bricker and H. Bricker (1986) and H. Bricker and V. Bricker (1997) for the Mars table, and V. Bricker and H. Bricker (1988) for the seasonal table. The question of great extremes of Venus has been thoroughly reviewed recently by Sprajc in both English (1993a, 1993b) and Spanish (1996). The alignment to a Venus extreme at Uxmal and epigraphic evidence bearing on this is treated by H. Bricker and V. Bricker (1996). The "star wars" theme is supported by Schele and Freidel (1990) and Carlson (1993), and it is challenged on statistical grounds by Hotaling (1995).

AVENI, ANTHONY F.
1980
  Skywatchers of Ancient Mexico. Austin: University of Texas Press
1997
  Stairways to the Stars: Skywatching in Three Great Ancient Cultures. New York: John Wiley & Sons

AVENI, ANTHONY F., SHARON L. GIBBS, AND HORST HARTUNG
1975
  "The Caracol Tower at Chichén Itzá: an Ancient Astronomical Observatory?" *Science*, 188, 977–85

AVENI, ANTHONY F., AND HORST HARTUNG
1986
  Maya City Planning and the Calendar. American Philosophical Society. Transactions. Vol. 76, Pt. 7. Philadelphia: American Philosophical Society
1989

"Uaxactun, Guatemala, Group E, and Similar Assemblages: An Archaeoastronomical Reconsideration." In *World Archaeoastronomy: Selected Papers from the 2nd Oxford International Conference on Archaeoastronomy held at Merida, Yucatan, Mexico, 13–17 January 1986.* Ed. by A. Aveni. Cambridge, Mass.: Cambridge University Press, 441–61

1991
"Archaeoastronomy and the Puuc Sites." In *Arqueoastronomía y etnoastronomía en Mesoamérica.* Ed. by J. Broda, S. Iwaniszewski, and L. Maupomé. Instituto de Investigaciones Históricas, Serie de Historia de la Ciencia y la Tecnología, 4. Mexico City: UNAM, 65–95

BRICKER, HARVEY M., AND VICTORIA R. BRICKER
1983
"Classic Maya Prediction of Solar Eclipses." *Current Anthropology,* 24, 1–23
1992
"Zodiacal References in the Maya Codices." In *The Sky in Mayan Literature.* Ed. by A. Aveni. New York: Oxford University Press, 148–83
1996
"Astronomical References in the Throne Inscription of the Palace of the Governor at Uxmal." *Cambridge Archaeological Journal,* 6, 191–229
[In press]
"More on the Mars Table in the Dresden Codex." *Latin American Antiquity,* 8

BRICKER, VICTORIA R., AND HARVEY M. BRICKER
1986
"The Mars Table in the Dresden Codex." In *Research and Reflections in Archaeology and History: Essays in Honor of Doris Stone.* Ed. by E. W. Andrews V. Middle American Research Institute. Publications, 57. New Orleans: MARI of Tulane University, 51–80
1988
"The Seasonal Table in the Dresden Codex and Related Almanacs." *Archaeoastronomy,* 12 (*Journal for the History of Astronomy,* 19), 1–62

CARLSON, JOHN B.
1993
"Venus-regulated Warfare and Ritual Sacrifice in Mesoamerica." In *Astronomies and Cultures.* Ed. by C. Ruggles and N. Saunders. Niwot: University Press of Colorado, 202–52

CLOSS, MICHAEL P.
1986
"The Mathematical Notation of the Ancient Maya." In *Native American Mathematics.* Ed. by M. Closs. Austin: University of Texas Press, 291–369

EDMONSON, MUNRO S.
1988
The Book of the Year: Middle American Calendrical Systems. Salt Lake City: University of Utah Press
1995
Sistemas calendáricos mesoamericanos: el libro del año solar. Translated by P. García Cisneros. Mexico City: Universidad Nacional Autónoma de México

JUSTESON, JOHN S.
1989
"Ancient Maya Ethnoastronomy: an Overview of Hieroglyphic Sources." In *World Archaeoastronomy: Selected Papers from the 2nd Oxford International Conference on Archaeoastronomy held at Merida, Yucatan, Mexico, 13–17 January 1986.* Ed. by A. Aveni. Cambridge, Mass.: Cambridge University Press, 76–129

LINDEN, JOHN H.
1986
"Glyph X of the Maya Lunar Series: An Eighteen-month Lunar Synodic Calendar." *American Antiquity,* 51, 122–36

LOUNSBURY, FLOYD G.
1978
"Maya Numeration, Computation, and Calendrical Astronomy." In *Dictionary of Scientific Biography.* Ed. by C. Gillispie. Vol. XV. New York: Scribner's, 759–818
1983
"The Base of the Venus Table in the Dresden Codex, and Its Significance for the Calendar–correlation Problem." In *Calendars in Mesoamerica and Peru: Native American Computations of Time.* Ed. by A. Aveni and G. Brotherston. Oxford: BAR International Series, 174, 1–26

SCHELE, LINDA, AND DAVID FREIDEL
1990
A Forest of Kings: The Untold Story of the Ancient Maya. New York: William Morrow and Co.

SPRAJC, IVAN
1993a
"The Venus-rain-maize Complex in the Mesoamerican World View: Part I." *Journal for the History of Astronomy,* 24, 17–70
1993b
"The Venus–rain–maize Complex in the Mesoamerican World View: Part II." *Archaeoastronomy,* 18 (*Journal for the History of Astronomy,* 24), 27–53
1996
Venus, lluvia y maiz: simbolismo y astronomía en la cosmovisión mesoamericana. Mexico City: Instituto Nacional de Antropología e Historia

TEEPLE, JOHN E.
1931
Maya Astronomy. Carnegie Institution of Washington, Publication 403, and Contributions to American Archaeology. Vol. I, no. 2. Washington, D.C.: Carnegie Institution of Washington, 29–116

THOMPSON, J. ERIC S.
1960
Maya Hieroglyphic Writing: An Introduction. Norman: University of Oklahoma Press

Dresden Codex, pages 47 and 60
Dresden
Sächsische Landesbibliothek

Perhaps only hidden treasures of gold, silver, and precious gems excite the imagination of the general public more than ancient writing and codices or rare books. For the learned scholar, historian, or archaeologist, however, the allure of the written word, ancient communication beyond the pale of death, has an incalculable historical and humanistic value far more important than material wealth. Down through the ages the search for ancient documents, old books, or writing in any form has been the goal behind many long and arduous expeditions to all corners of the world; be they to the great torrid and arid deserts, or to the hot and humid tropical forests. The possibility of finding an ancient record of communication, no matter how small, recording whatever the ancient scribe wished to preserve, but written in his own words, has fired the imagination of explorers, scholars, and collectors almost since writing began. For this very reason we know of the cuneiform writing on small clay tablets recording agricultural production and commercial contracts among the ancient Sumerians; the hieroglyphic religious transcriptions of the Egyptians carved in stone for public display; and the oracle texts on animal bones among the ancient Chinese–to mention only three of the most widely known writing systems of the Old World.

Writing is also known to have existed among several ethnic groups in different regions of the New World, if more restricted and slightly less developed than its Old World counterparts. In Mesoamerica, the cultural area of the Maya, writing was the most highly developed of any region in both continents of North and South America. There is little disagreement among specialists that the Maya occupied the pinnacle of this brilliant intellectual accomplishment. Several writing systems developed in Mesoamerica, initiated by the Zapotecs in the first millennium B.C., but soon the Zoque, Olmecs, Mixtecs, Totonacs, and Aztecs, as well as other peoples of Mesoamerica had also written, in one form or another, long before the arrival of the Spanish conquerors in the sixteenth century.

For example, among the Zoque, immediate western neighbors of the Maya in Tabasco and Chiapas and unrelated linguistically to this latter group, two ancient codices were recovered as part of the mortuary offerings accompanying two elite male burials at the site of Mirador, in the municipality of Jiquipilas in Chiapas and dating to the Early Classic period, around A.D. 450. A most disturbing fact is that these two ancient books have been so badly preserved that they cannot be opened. One was apparently made on bark paper, the inner bark of the wild fig tree called *amate* locally, while the other may have been painted on deerskin. Both were sized with a white lime background. The organic portions of the books have decomposed and the lime sizing has recrystallized in such a way that the individual crystals cross between the layers of fan-folded pages and literally nail them all together. In spite of numerous attempts to separate the pages and study them, none has been successful. The oldest Maya codices known also date to the pre-Hispanic period and have been found by archaeologists as mortuary offerings with burials in excavations in

Madrid Codex
facsimilar reproduction
Madrid, Museo de América

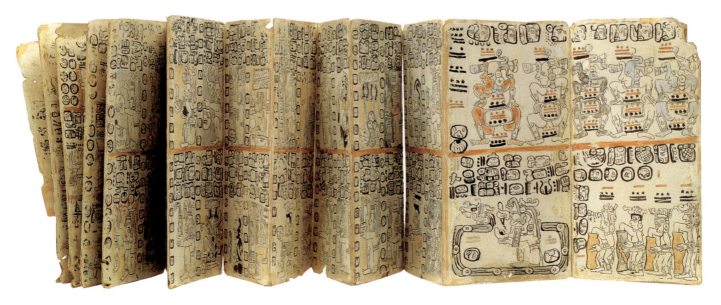

Uaxactún, San Agustín Acasaguastlán, and Nebaj in Guatemala; at Altun Ha in Belize; and at Copán in Honduras. The six examples of Maya books discovered in excavations date to the Early Classic (Uaxactún and Altun Ha), Late Classic (Nebaj, Copán), and Early Postclassic (San Agustín Acasaguastlán) periods and, unfortunately, all have been changed by the pressure and humidity in the ground during their many years in the ground, eliminating the organic backing and reducing all into unopenable masses or collections of very small flakes and bits of the original lime sizing and multicolor painting. The result being, unfortunately, more old books which will probably never be read.

The Spanish priests who arrived with the conquerors knew the value of the codices to the Maya for the preservation of their culture and precisely because of their fervent desire to effectively implant a new religion, Christianity, the priests burned thousands of these ancient books in great public orgies of religious zeal, claiming that they were the works of the Devil. They were, of course, religious books of ancient indigenous cosmological doctrine with specific cultic rituals dedicated to the Maya's traditional gods. Written on strips of bark paper or animal skins folded like a fan, the codices contained the complex ritual formulas–linked to astronomical cycles, the seasonal year, and real time–that guided the Maya priests and their people along the path of harmony and spiritual well being throughout the year as set down by their forefathers. Organic, old, and very dry, the codices burned with a fury in the fires of the zealous Spanish priests. Like life itself, the written word is vital, delicate and irreplaceable. The elimination of an enormous religious corpus of Maya doctrine was fundamental in the Maya's swift conversion to Catholicism and was as effective as it was disastrous.

Only four of these ancient books of the Maya are currently known. They are the Dresden, Grolier, Madrid, and Paris codex. Only the Grolier is not named after the city where it presently resides. The Grolier is named after the antiquarian book club that organized the exposition of Maya writing in New York where it was first displayed in 1971, and it is the only codex that is still the property of Mexico, where, unfortunately, it has never been on public display.

The codex served the Maya priest as an ultimate guidebook and source for the correct ritual practices necessary to preserve the harmony and balance of the Mayas throughout their daily lives. Yurij Knorosov, the Russian epigrapher who discovered the phonetic basis of Maya writing and translated the three better-known codices, states that every priest had a book and that there were libraries of them in their cities.

To understand the codices one must remember that the native calendars, a 260 day sacred system (*tzolkin*) and the 365 (*haab*) vague year, were astronomically exact and a knowledgeable priest could, with the aid of his codex, predict the movement of several planets in our solar system, including Venus, Mars, the Sun, and the Moon, and forecast major astronomical events such as eclipses and equinoxes. Since the days, months, and years were governed by different patron gods, each required the attention of the priests with different cultic practices of food and blood offerings–both human and animal–incense, prayers, song, and dance.

The books were indispensable for knowing what god was to be venerated on what days and what were the exact ceremonial procedures that were necessary for carrying this out in the correct manner. Priests were searched out before all major undertakings of daily life to learn of the ritual obligations required to carry this out with an optimum of good will on the parts of the gods. When to plant, when to hunt, when to marry, when to bury, and the auguries and name of a newborn child were just a few of the consultations made of the priests, who in turn used their ancient books to ascertain the best day to begin an undertaking and learn the predisposition of the god involved, good, bad, or indifferent.

Undoubtedly any one of the four authentic Maya codices was just one of several books any one priest had for personal reference and there probably never was just one single book of doctrine which outlined all Maya cosmology and astronomy. We know little about how these ancient books were cared for and handled, the rites and traditions directed specifically to them as containers of religious truth and mystically accurate astronomical formulas.

The most detailed knowledge about the ancient Maya books and the traditions of their care and use, as well as the sacred, almost mystical way in which they were held in ancient

Maya society comes from the hand of precisely one of the Spanish priests who burned so many of them in the sixteenth century, Fray Diego de Landa. Landa described the *analtes* or "books of science" as the most important of the noble possessions, apparently controlled not by sacred authority but by the very highest secular official. However, these archives of traditional lore were written, cared for (with rites, including periodic cleansing), read, and interpreted by the priests. And it was with the bodies of priests that the books were buried. Landa writes: "during the month Uo the priests, the physicians and sorcerers, who are all the same thing, began to prepare by fasts and other things for the celebration of another festival . . . First the priests celebrated theirs, which they called *Pocam*. Having assembled, clothed in their ornaments (a feathered jacket, a pointed cap with ribbons hanging down, like tails under the jacket), at the house of the lord, first they drove away the evil spirits as usual; then they took out their books and spread them out on the fresh boughs which they had for this purpose, and invoking with prayers and devotions an idol named Kinich Ahau Itzamna (supreme god and inventor of hieroglyphic writing), who they say was the first priest, they offered him gifts and presents and burned before him their balls of incense with the new fire. Meanwhile they dissolved in a vessel a little of their verdigris with virgin water, which they said had been brought from woods where a woman had never penetrated. With this they anointed the boards (wooden cover plates) of their books so as to purify them. This having been done, the most learned of the priests opened a book and looked at the prognostics of that year, and he manifested them to those who were present . . . "

In spite of the unrelenting search for and persecution of the native priests and their religion, deep in the jungle of the Petén of Guatemala, more then 170 years after the Spanish Conquest, the Maya were still making, reading, and using the ancient codices. In Chiapas, almost at the same moment, the local bishop, Don Francisco Nuñez de la Vega documented, in two separate reports, one in which he enclosed "calendar and notebook" (sent first to the president of the Consejo de Indias in Spain, and second, to the Vatican), that he had gathered up more than two hundred calendars of "superstitions and divining" books of the Indians in his diocese, which he destroyed. Most of these came from the Tzeltal community of Oxchuc in the Chiapas highlands, and the Zoque-Mixe town of Huehuetán on the Pacific coast.

With this very brief introduction to the nature of the ancient Maya books we will turn now to the few which still remain. Since each codex is quite different in thematic content and since there are so few, what follows is a brief physical description of each along with what little historical information has been ascertained for each, as well as a summary of its ritual content and recent interpretations. It must be stressed at the outset, however, not one of the four has been completely studied and understood. Much remains to be accomplished in this regard.

Dresden Codex

The Dresden Codex is presently located in the Sächsische Landesbibliothek in the city of Dresden, Germany, where it has been since its purchase in 1739 by Johann Christian Gozte, then director of the Royal Library in Saxony. He purchased it in Vienna from an unknown source, but there has been considerable reasoned speculation as to the possibility of it having been sent as part of the New World gifts, perhaps by Francisco de Montejo, to the Emperor Charles V, who lived much of the time in Vienna and named Montejo as governor of the province of Yucatán. The codex could have passed along with other notable Pre-Columbian items that still are found in different museums of that city. Perhaps the best known of these objects is the so-called headdress of Moctezuma.

This codex is considered to be the finest of the Maya codices in terms of its penmanship and content, but now it is badly damaged from water after the severe bombing of Dresden during the Second World War.

It is composed of a single strip of *amate* paper 3.52 meters long and 9 centimeters high, fan-folded into 39 leaves sized with white lime and painted on both sides, all except for three and one-half blank leaves. The principal colors used are red and black, but include blue-green, two tones of yellow, and brown or red in some of the details and the background. The style of the painting is carried out with a narrow brush and the leaves are normally divided

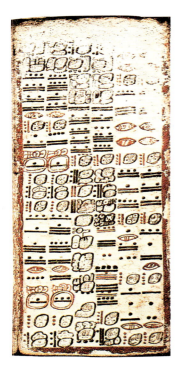

Dresden Codex, page 70
Dresden
Sächsische Landesbibliothek

into three horizontal divisions, outlined with a narrow brown line, each containing three undivided horizontal sections, a glyphic text above, a line of bar and dot numbers below and then two or, more often, three figures across the bottom of the section. The codex is probably the work of a single artist, but at least as many as eight individuals were involved in bringing it to completion. The renowned Mayanist Sir J. Eric S. Thompson of England thought the codex was produced in Chichén Itzá around the end of this great center's prime. More recent research, however, suggests that it was surely painted during the Late Postclassic period (A.D. 1250–1500) following an earlier model, perhaps with information dating as early as the Late Classic. Since this codex contains obvious iconographic, glyphic, and ceramic vessel similarities with the Late Postclassic period in contemporaneous sites in a wider area in central Yucatán, the region of the Chenes and Puuc styles, and the east coast of Quintana Roo and Belize, the exact place of elaboration is unknown. Most certainly the Dresden Codex was from this general area.

The figures most often represented in the Dresden Codex are of the seated gods, sometimes in pairs, but also include human and animal combinations, animals, birds, snakes, and fish alone, and anthropomorphized animals. Inanimate drawings include rain, trails, and crossroads, ball courts, pyramids, thrones or seats, temples, *coas* or digging sticks, ceramic vessels, canoes, paddles, ladders, food offerings, incense burners, incense pouches, spears, spear throwers, shields, axes, ropes, musical instruments (pottery drum, flute, and rattle), torches, and ceremonial staves. These figures are intimately related to the adjacent glyphic texts and calendrical notations; in fact they help explain visually what is being considered.

The Dresden Codex has been studied more than any other of the four extant Maya books, but there is still much to do. No definitive work of this codex exists. The major divisions of the codex are known and generally agreed on, the glyphs and numbers related to the calendrics are fairly well understood, though there is plenty of debate on some issues, the Mars tables for example.

What has yet to be studied in detail are the glyphic texts that explain and complement the figures. This is the work of not only an epigrapher or specialist in ancient Maya writing, but one who has been trained in the last two decades since the discovery of the phonetic nature of the Maya writing system has been recognized. To this date no analysis of all the glyphic texts of the codex has been carried out and published.

In the seventies, Thompson, following on the work of Gates, divided the Dresden Codex into fourteen general divisions or chapters of different lengths. These are, in order of appearance, Miscellaneous Almanacs: Series 1; The Moon Goddess; Miscellaneous Almanacs: Series 2; The Planet Venus; Lunar Tables; Multiples of 78; *katun* Prophecies; Serpent Numbers and the 7 x 260 day Almanacs; A Torrential Downpour; New Year Ceremonies (*uayeb* rites); Farmer's Almanacs; The Chaac; Multiplication Table and the Sky Beast; and Multiples of 364.

The more recent published research on the Dresden has focused on the iconographic and glyphic identification of the area and date of its manufacture and use, internal cross-dating, the "proof" and descent of the recognition of the planet Mars tables, noun and astronomical syntax, types of clothing, faunal and food offerings, New Year ceremony, and discourse structure of the glyphic texts as well as several more-limited works which deal with the nature of specific ceremonies, glyphs, and gods.

Grolier Codex

The Grolier Codex is located in the Biblioteca Nacional de Antropología e Historia in Mexico City, where it remains locked away from the public because its authenticity is still doubted by local authorities. Part of this problem stems from its sudden appearance less than thirty years ago in the Grolier Club exposition on ancient Maya writing in New York. The codex was, perhaps still is, part of the personal collection of Josué Sáenz of Mexico City, who purchased it along with other Late Classic and Postclassic Maya objects (a sacrificial knife with wood handle, wooden box with glyphs, and mosaic mask) north of Yajalón in Chiapas, where it was reportedly found in a dry cave.

Most Maya writing and iconography specialists, as well as a few astronomers who have studied the Grolier believe it is authentic, because of its late style, content (partial Venus table),

Grolier Codex, page 6
Mexico City
Biblioteca Nacional de Antropología
e Historia

Dresden Codex, pages 15 and 16
Dresden
Sächsische Landesbibliothek

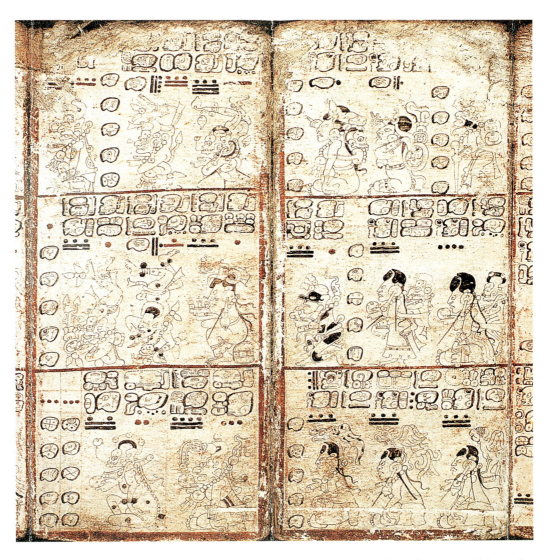

and the fact that it contains concepts about the planet Venus that have been available to the public only after the codex was published.

The Grolier may be the oldest of the Maya codices, as its Maya-Toltec style suggests that it was drafted prior to the Late Postclassic period Dresden Codex, which has Aztec-influenced iconography. It consists of ten separate pages of *amate* fan-fold paper sized with white lime. The pages vary in size slightly from one to another with a maximum length of 19 centimeters and a width of 12.5 centimeters. The graphic and glyphic contents of the codex are painted on only one side in black, red, and light brown, with one small example of blue paint on page 10. A piece of the codex was dated by radiocarbon14 to 1230±130 D.C. which equates very closely to its iconographic placement near the end of the Toltec period (A.D. 900–1200).

The Grolier Codex contains about half of the central portion of a Venus table, which covered the four phases of the planet in 65 cycles. Similar in content to the Venus tables of the Dresden Codex, the Grolier covers the cycle of 584 days (as morning star, 236; not visible, 90; evening star, 250; and not visible, 8) expressed in numbers in circles on each page tied in a bundle. The individual pages portray the gods of different sections of the Venus table, all in menacing attitudes. None of the pages are complete and usually lack the lower third or quarter of each page. Each page has a standing figure or god facing left with fancy headdress and weapons and often restraining a captive. Along the left-hand side of the page are a row of bar-and-dot numbers and day signs of the sacred 260 day calendar (13 numbers and 20 day names), which correlates with the Mesoamerican Vague Year (18 months of 20 days, plus 5 unlucky days, equals 365). There are exactly five elapsed cyclical time periods (synodic) of Venus in eight Mesoamerican Vague Years. Venus, among Mesoamericans in general and especially among the Maya, was considered a malevolent planet and in the Grolier the gods are portrayed with weapons (spears and spear throwers, shields, sacrificial knives, and ropes) and in different despotic acts such as capture of slaves and temples, sacrifice by decapitation of slaves, and domination of slaves.

The Toltec style of the codex originally was used as evidence of its illegitimacy, but now is recognized as part of the general Mexicanization of coastal Maya culture in Tabasco and Campeche, as well as most of the Yucatán peninsula. The Putun Maya of Tabasco became very active in commerce at the onset of the Postclassic period, carrying out trading activities not only along the southeastern coast of Mesoamerica, but penetrating deep inland into the Petén and Lacandon forests, the Central Depression, and the Pacific coast of Chiapas. It should not surprise anyone, therefore, that the Grolier Codex, a Mexicanized Maya document, was found in the north of Chiapas, not far from Tabasco.

Madrid Codex

The Madrid Codex is now in the Museo de América in Madrid. This codex, which appeared during the last half of the past century in that city, is composed of two pieces which were originally thought to be two separate codices, the "Troano" and the "Cortesiano," but were soon proved to be parts of the same document. It is thought that the Troano arrived in Spain with Cortés and was purchased almost three hundred years later from one of his descendants. It would appear that the Cortesiano was separated from it earlier and sold separately.

The codex is thought to date to the fourteenth or fifteenth century and to have come from either the east coast of the Yucatán peninsula or somewhere near the base of that same land form, perhaps near Champotón, Campeche, on the west coast and may well have been collected on Cortés's original trip, which rounded the peninsula before arriving in Veracruz.

The Madrid Codex is the longest of all the ancient Maya books, being some 6.82 meters long divided into 56 pages painted on both sides (and upside down on the back). However, it is not complete, lacking pages at both the beginning and the end. It is made of *amate* paper, fan-folded and sized with lime. The pages vary slightly, averaging 22.6 centimeters high by 12.2 centimeters wide. All pages have painted glyphs and figures in red or reddish brown, black, and blue paint, except page 1 which has only a few smudges left of the base white sizing coat.

The Madrid was obviously made by less experienced or artistic scribes than the Dresden. Not only is the workmanship of this codex inferior to the Dresden, but the spatial arrangement and size of the figures and glyphs is much more varied throughout, ranging from the single page with only one huge figure and three or four big glyphs to the pages divided into four narrow horizontal panels with many tightly grouped hieroglyphic texts closing in around the small illustrative figures. This varied layout may well have been the norm among the ancient Maya books, but our corpus is so small that there is little room for comparison.

The Madrid Codex is another priestly almanac with many different rites dedicated to such mundane activities as beekeeping, hunting, planting, and commerce. Knorosov divides the codex into fifteen sections of unequal length: the movement of the planet of Mars; occupations of the rain god; agricultural divinities; anniversaries; the occupations of the gods of abundance; divinities of thunderstorms and destructive downpours; the 52 and 4 year cycles (*uayeb* years); the hunt; the merchant god; the occupations of the gods (first section); the 32 and 130 day cycles; 260 day cycle and the 13 day period; occupations of the gods (second section), the war god; occupations of the gods (third section); and beekeepers' divinities.

The four pages dedicated to the *uayeb* ceremonies of the New Year are the same rites described in detail by Landa, and his account can be closely followed in the complex scenes of individuals, activities of human sacrifice, planting, burning incense, playing music, the presence of animals and birds, and of food offerings. Unique to the Madrid Codex, on one of these *uayeb* pages, is the seated figure of a Maya astronomer who is lit-

Madrid Codex, page 34
Madrid, Museo de América

erally reaching out with his eye to pull a star from the heavens, demonstrating the intimate relation between the priest-astronomer-scribe, the planets, the codices, and Maya religion and cosmology. More recent research includes new identifications of astronomical constellations in the zodiac almanacs, intercorrelations with the Dresden and Paris codices, and a new book, still in press, of studies by several scholars on the Madrid Codex, which contains articles with the latest thoughts about its content, internal dating, as well as a "calendar round" almanac.

Paris Codex

This codex is in the Bibliothèque Nationale de Paris, where it was acquired by purchase in 1832. It was mentioned soon after by Aubin, but a few years later it was found by León de Rosny, covered with dust in a wastebasket in a corner of the library. The codex was wrapped in a paper which had the name of Pérez written on it, thought to have referred to the nineteenth-century Maya philologist, Juan Pío Pérez, and his name has become a synonym for the codex. Rosny brought the codex to the attention of the few specialists of the Maya in 1864.

Originally students of the codices thought that the Paris Codex came from the Tzeltal region of Chiapas because words in this Maya language were found written in the codex sometime later. Now, because of its style, it is recognized to probably have originated on the east coast of the Yucatán peninsula, perhaps around the ancient Maya cities of Tulum and Mayapán.

Thompson thought that the Paris dated a little later than the Dresden. Currently it is thought to have been made about A.D. 1450 by one student, but that date is hotly contested by others who point out that the codex contains internal solar and lunar eclipse data which sustain a date of the *katun* history as early as A.D. 731–987. To explain this situation–a codex drafted in an obviously late style, but with early astronomical dates–one would have to assume that the basic form and content of the ancient book was worked out in the eighth through tenth centuries and that subsequently the book was copied and recopied at later times, changing its style to that of the moment, until finally it was drafted once again in the style of the fourteenth or fifteenth centuries, a long and complex, but not unreal, possibility.

Paris Codex, page 16
Paris, Bibliothèque Nationale

The codex consists of twenty-four pages of which twenty-two have visible painted hieroglyphs and figures on them, eleven on the front and eleven on the back. Due to the original layout of the content the codex is thought to lack two pages, the front and the back. It is made on *amate* paper in fan-fold form and the individual pages have an average height of 24.8 centimeters and a width of 13 centimeters. The total length is 145 centimeters.

The workmanship is less impressive than the Dresden, though the colors are more varied. Paint occurs in several tones of brown, red, pink, black, blue, and bluish green. The orientation of the figures and glyphic text are the same on the front and the back. The figures and hieroglyphs on every page of the codex are reduced to large oval areas surrounded by highly eroded zones devoid of any painting. Even the white sizing has been worn off in these areas that extend to the edge of each page.

Although it is the second ancient Maya book to have come to light, the Paris Codex has, over the years since its discovery, generally received less attention than the Dresden and Madrid, undoubtedly due to its smaller size and poorer preservation. However, in the last fifteen years three important studies of the Paris Codex have been published, with a final consensus still far from within reach in such important aspects as zodiacal references, internal dating and corrections, planet identification, and solar eclipses, to name only a few.

Each of the first thirteen pages of the codex contain the record of a *katun*, a 20 year division of time which was important to the Mayas at the time of the conquest and many centuries prior to it.

Each page has the figure of the deity which governs the *katun* and it is surrounded by glyphic texts that give the details of the predictions concerning this deity and what can be expected of him for divining purposes. Little advancement has been made in the decipherment of these texts, and they remain the largest stumbling block in truly understanding the codex.

Next in sequence are five pages (the first lost), which according to Knorosov, deal with predictions about nature of the gods of the valley, including the rain god. Then comes a section of two pages with the 52 year and 4 year cycles, followed by a page of the *tzolkin*, 1 *imix*; then a page of serpent periods and finally two pages with the predictions of 13 months (zodiac almanac).

In the last few years, research on the Paris Codex has centered on the internal astronomical count that interrelates the two basic calendar systems of the Maya and Mesoamerica, the *tzolkin* and *haab*, identification of the zodiac animals and their relation to celestial constellations, and the similarities that can be demonstrated between the Paris and the other codices.

Like the "new world" whence they came, these four wonderful old Maya books can lead the intrepid and determined explorer to an equivalent world filled with scientific precision and majesty, poetic beauty and passion, and intellectual discovery and satisfaction.

References

BRICKER, VICTORIA R.
1995
Review of "The Paris Codex: Handbook for a Maya Priest." By Bruce Love. University of Texas Press. In *Latin American Antiquity*. Vol. 6, no. 3. Washington, D.C.: Society for American Archaeology, 283–84

BRICKER, VICTORIA R., AND GABRIELLE VAIL, (EDS.)
[In press]
"Papers on the Madrid Codex"

CARLSON, JOHN B.
1983
"The Grolier Codex: A Preliminary Report of the Content and Authenticity of a Thirteenth-Century Maya Venus Almanac." In *Calendars in Mesoamerica and Peru: Native Computations of Time*. Ed. by A.F. Aveni and G. Brotherson. Oxford: BAR, 27–57
1990
"America's Ancient Skywatchers." *National Geographic*, Vol. 177, no. 3, Washington, D.C., 76–107

COE, MICHAEL D.
1992
Breaking the Maya Code. London: Thames and Hudson Ltd.

GELB, I. J.
1963
A Study of Writing. Chicago: University of Chicago Press

KNOROSOV, YURI
1982
Maya Hieroglyphic Codices. Translated by S.D. Coe. Publication 8. State University of New York at Albany: Institute for Mesoamerican Studies

LEE, THOMAS A., JR.
1985
Los códices mayas. Introduction and bibliography. Color reproductions of the Dresden, Grolier, Madrid, and Paris Codex. Tenth anniversary edition. Mexico City: Universidad Autónoma de Chiapas

LOVE, BRUCE
1994
The Paris Codex: Handbook for a Maya Priest. Austin: University of Texas Press

PAXTON, MERIDETH
1986
Codex Dresden: Stylistic and Iconographic Analysis of a Maya Manuscript. Albuquerque: University of New Mexico, Ph.D. dissertation

SEVERIN, GREGORY M.
1981
The Paris Codex: Decoding an Astronomical Ephemeris

STUART, GEORGE E.
1986
"Los Códices Mayas." A review of *Los códices mayas*. Introduction and bibliography by Thomas A. Lee, Jr., 1985. In *Archaeoastronomy*, Vol. 9, nos. 1–4, 164–75
1992
"Quest for Decipherment: A Historical and Biographical Survey of Maya Hieroglyphic Investigations." In *New Theories on the Ancient Maya*. Ed. by Elin C. Danien and Robert J. Sharer. Philadelphia: University Museum, University of Pennsylvania, 1–63

THOMPSON, J. ERIC S.
1972
A Commentary on the Dresden Codex: A Maya Hieroglyphic Book. Memoirs. Vol. 93. Philadelphia: American Philosophical Society

TOZZER, ALFRED M.
1941
Landa's Relación de las cosas de Yucatán: A Translation. Papers of the Peabody Museum of American Archaeology and Ethnology. Vol. 18. Cambridge, Mass: Harvard University

TREIBER, HANNELORE
1987
"Studien zur Katunserie der Pariser Maya Handschrift." *Acta Mesoamericana*, 2. Berlin: Verlag von Flemming

Maya Cosmogony

The primordial divine couple
Lord I Deer, on the left
and Lady I Deer, on the right
at the moment the creation
of the cosmos began from the *Códice
Vindobonensis Mexicanus* I, page 51

Mesoamerican peoples know of the obsession for origins. Their theogonies and mythologies focus on the mystery of the creation of the world. Who drew the limits of the sky, the earth, and the four corners of the cosmos? How did life arise? Questions on the origins of the world or on the relationship of human beings with the gods and with nature, made an abundant oral literature spring forth, which for generations passed from mouth to ear in the form of chants, rites, and legendary myths. In the different regions of Mesoamerica there is evidence of this tradition. Sometimes we find it frozen in time, carved in stelae and monuments by way of figures or hieroglyphs. We find others coded in the architecture of their ceremonial centers, narrated in codices painted on vegetal fibers and deerskin, or dispersed in the multitudinal oral memory and ritual of their descendants, who continue to incorporate this ancestral code in the most diverse objects, in symbols and rituals that at times escape our comprehension.

Thanks to these varied testimonies we can reconstruct the Maya conception of the cosmos and trace its development through many centuries, since Maya culture has survived until today. I offer here two interpretations of the Maya creation of the cosmos and of human beings. One is based on the version contained in the *Popol Vuh*, the text written in the quiche language, the last version of which was written in Latin characters in the second half of the sixteenth century.

I combine this popular interpretation of the origin of the cosmos with the cult version written by Maya kings and priests in texts and paintings from the Classic period (third to ninth centuries A.D.). Both share the same obsession: to perpetuate the memory of the marvelous act that celebrated the dawn of the civilized world and spread the secrets of its equilibrium and conservation.

The Creator Gods and Their First Undertakings

Myths narrating the creation of the cosmos situate this act in a scenario presided over by the creator gods. In Mesoamerican myths, these gods are present in the form of an omnipotent and omniscient primordial couple. A nahuatl verse calls this couple "Mother of the gods, father of the gods" (Leander 1972, 211). The Vienna Codex contains the Mixtec version of the creation of the cosmos, enriched by the actual representation of the primordial couple (Anders, Jansen and Reyes 1992, 84):

> "Lady I Deer and Lord I Deer,
> the primordial twins.
> They perfumed with copal incense
> and sprinkled ground tobacco
> (cult acts to purify and to give strength).
> They were the Divine Mother and Father,
> who procreated the different beings to follow."

The Mayas of Guatemala summarized their knowledge on the history of human beings in the *Popol Vuh* (translated by D. Tedlock 1993, 65–66), the sacred book where the creation of the current world is recorded:

> "by the Maker, Modeler,
> mother-father of life, of humankind,
> giver of breath, giver of heart,
> bearer, upbringer in the light that lasts
> of those born in the light, begotten in the light;
> worrier, knower of everything, whatever there is . . . "

Seven Macaw represented
on the Blom Plate
Late Classic period
Merida, Museo Regional
de Antropología "Palacio Cantón"
cat. 449

The initial tasks of the creator gods consisted of ending the fruitless chaos, to order the cosmos, and to establish a new era of the world, inhabited by vigorous, intelligent beings. When the gods began their work, the world was a desolate place.

"Not yet one person, one animal, bird, fish, crab
tree, rock, hollow, canyon, meadow, forest.
Only the sky alone is there;
the face of the earth is not clear. Only the sea alone
is pooled under all the sky; there is nothing whatever gathered together.
It is at rest; not a single thing stirs
... only murmurs, ripples,
in the dark, in the night."

Representation of the Hero Twins
in Classic period Maya vessels
on the left Hunahpu
on the right Xbalanque

The *Popol Vuh* (*ibidem* 1993, 66) relates the gods' efforts to establish harmony in the cosmos. Time and again, on three successive occasions, the gods fail in their attempt to create beings capable of infusing life in the world and venerating their progenitors. In their first creation, the gods made animals, which multiplied on the face of the earth. Then the gods asked them to speak and to extol the name of their creators. But the animals only emitted screams, inarticulate sounds, and the gods decided to let their flesh be eaten. In their second attempt the gods wanted to make "obedient, respectful beings who nourish us and feed us." Then they made some beings of mud; but these were soft and they fell apart when they came in contact with water, and they had no understanding. When they saw this, the gods destroyed this creation. Disturbed by these failures, the gods consulted Xpiyacoc and Xmucane, the wise grandfather and grandmother, who were adept at counting time and who had the capacity to see through the ages. The diviners advised them to make a man and woman of wood, and these multiplied and their progeny extended to the four corners of the earth. But they lacked understanding, they did not recognize their creators, and they did not know why they had come to the world. Frustrated, the gods sent a deluge that flooded the surface of the earth and finished off the beings made of wood.

Representation of the fight between
Seven Macaw and the Hero Twins
in a Maya funerary vessel

Stela 25 from Izapa, Chiapas
which shows the battle
between Seven Macaw
and the Hero Twins

The obstacle that prevents the gods from creating beings capable of reproducing themselves, of nourishing and praising their creators is the subject of these three failed creations. In addition to the difficulty in creating beings endowed with these qualities was the uncontrolled action of natural forces that inhabited the different regions of the cosmos. Cosmogonic myths narrate that the initial creations ended in destruction by natural cataclysms. The famous nahuatl account of the appearance and destruction of the cosmogonic suns relates that before today's world was created, there were four suns or ages that disappeared catastrophically, destroyed by jaguars, hurricanes, fiery rain, and a flood. The *Popol Vuh* does not allude to these four cataclysms, but it tells of the destructive action of natural forces at the end of the third creation, when the men of wood were annihilated. The sacred book of the Quiché says that then the gods unleashed a deluge inundating the earth, setting off the collapse of the earth. By narrating this catastrophe, the *Popol Vuh* refers to other disturbances that displaced and endangered the stability of the sky and underworld, the coexistence of which was essential for the continued vitality of the earth. The *Popol Vuh* narrates that the promoters of disorder in the celestial region were three ostentatious individuals. The first was called Seven Macaw, and he boasted of being the sun, moon, and time. He said, "I am their sun and I am light, and I am also their months" (*op. cit.* 1993, 78–79). The other two personages were his sons, Zipacna and Earthquake. The former boasted of being the builder of great mountains; the latter claimed to have the power to remove the tallest mountains. The three claimed the very attributes of the gods, and therefore the creators demanded their destruction.

The Appearance of the Hero Twins and Their Struggle against Seven Macaw, Zipacna, and Earthquake
When coming to the next part of the story, the *Popol Vuh* introduces other actors and concentrates on episodes that apparently suspend the advent of the fourth and decisive creation, that of today's world, which is the point around which the story revolves. Nevertheless, recent

Painting from the Blom Plate
from Río Hondo, Quintana Roo
detail
Late Classic period
Merida, Museo Regional
de Antropología "Palacio Cantón"
cat. 449

discoveries in epigraphy and studies of Maya astronomy, myths, and religious symbols demonstrate that these episodes are directly related to the creation of the cosmos and the appearance of the sun, human beings, and basic sustenance. The *Popol Vuh* narrates these events in the style of great epics, combining the acts of the gods with the feats of heroes. (Coe 1989, 161–84). The first surprise in this part of the *Popol Vuh* is the humiliation of the creator gods as central actors in the narrative, and the rise of a pair of minor gods, Hunahpu or Junajpú and Xbalanque, known as the Hero Twins, who acquire the rank of protagonists in the story. Following a literary convention characteristic of tall tales, the *Popol Vuh* does not explain who these Hero Twins were. It merely states that both were called upon by the creator gods to combat the evil designs of Seven Macaw and his two sons, Zipacna and Earthquake. Thus, turning to the devices of the tall tale, the *Popol Vuh* tells how Hunahpu and Xbalanque courageously decided to confront the proud Seven Macaw. Their adversary's body was covered with brilliant feathers and his face adorned with silver and precious stones, as he shone from the top of a tree.

Hunahpu and Xbalanque discussed attacking Seven Macaw while he was eating in the tree. There they aimed their blowguns at him. Hunahpu's shot hit him right in the jaw and knocked him from the tree. Hunahpu then tried to finish him off, but instead Seven Macaw yanked off his arm and managed to escape. These and other scenes of struggle between the divine Hero Twins and the great bird Seven Macaw are carved on stelae dating to the first years after Christ, and were later reproduced on innumerable vessels and

Scene of the meeting
of the Hero Twins with the lords
of the underworld
Polychrome vessel
from Petén, Guatemala

paintings from the Classic period. The core of this episode is the series of ingenious ruses dreamed up by the Hero Twins to defeat their enemies. One of the most celebrated tells how the Twins, disguised as healer's helpers, arrive at the refuge of Seven Macaw, promise to alleviate him of the pain caused by the mouth wound, and under this pretext, they remove his sparkling ornaments one by one. Once he is stripped of all the trappings that gave him the appearance of greatness, Seven Macaw remained literally empty, and he died. After implanting Hunahpu's arm, the Twins turn to the task of confronting the monstrous forces of Zipacna and Earthquake. This episode is narrated in another series of incredible adventures confirming the talent of the two heroes, who with great subtlety defeat the titans who seem undefeatable.

Once the danger of the false sun and false moon that threatened to destroy order in the celestial region is averted, the story again breaks the narrative sequence and turns to the past, in order to tell the story of the progenitors of the Twins. As will be seen later, the explanation of the origin of the Twins is crucial to understanding their feats and the meaning of the mission with which they had been entrusted.

The Sacrifice of Hun Hunahpu, the First Father, and the Hero Twins' Revenge

The third part of the *Popol Vuh* says that the creator gods' first helpers in constructing the new age of the world were a divine set of twins, Hun Hunahpu (the First Father) and Seven Hunahpu, the father and the uncle, respectively, of the Hero Twins. Before the procreation of the Hero Twins, Hun Hunahpu had two sons, also twins: One Monkey and One Artisan, who "became flautists, singers, and writers; carvers, jewelers, metalworkers as well" (*op. cit.* 1993, 97). Hun Hunahpu and Seven Hunahpu are presented as notable thinkers and wise men, and as able ballgame players. On one occasion when they were practicing their favorite sport, they were heard by the lords of *Xibalba*, who inhabited the interior of the surface of the earth in the underworld. The regents of *Xibalba*, under the pretext that the Twins had made too much noise playing and did not show respect for their investiture, commanded them to descend into the underworld, where they challenge them to play ball.

The descent of the Twins into the depths of the underworld gives rise to describing this unknown region that is depicted as a watery place where darkness and cold reign. It is a region inhabited by fantastic beings and governed by terrible gods, who have the power to unleash fatal diseases. Each one of these gods, headed by their chiefs, One and Seven Death, was assigned a region of *Xibalba* and a type of affliction. On the way to this chilling place, the Twins crossed steep ravines, passed through a place bristling with thorns, and crossed a river of blood. Then they arrived at a crossroads, from which extended four roads: one was red, one black, another white, and the other yellow, the colors of the four directions of the cosmos. The black road spoke and said: "I am the one you are taking . . . This was the Road of *Xibalba*."

Personages of *Xibalba* the Maya underworld

Hunahpu and Xbalanque, on the left greet the lord of the underworld Itzamna, on the right on a Maya vessel from the Classic period

From this moment, the text repeats that the Twins were already defeated by the lords of Xibalba, because unforgivably they fall into one trap after another prepared for them by the underworld lords. Each encounter with the lords of *Xibalba* becomes a loss and a humiliation for the Twins. Later they are locked up in the Dark House to spend the night with a torch and a cigar for illumination and they are given instructions that they are not to use them in order to return them intact at dawn. They fail this test and the lords of *Xibalba* decide to sacrifice them. "They were buried at the Place of Ball Game Sacrifice, as it is called. The head of Hun Hunahpu was cut off; only his body was buried with his younger brother." Then they ordered the head of Hun Hunahpu be placed in a tree that had never before produced fruit, near the ball court. But unexpectedly, "when his head was put in the fork of the tree, the tree bore fruit."

The news of the marvelous tree reached the ears of a maiden of *Xibalba*, called Blood Moon, who driven by curiosity, approached the flowering tree. "What's the fruit of this tree?" she asked. Upon hearing this, Hun Hunahpu's skull, which was hidden among the calabash fruit of the tree, asked if the maiden wanted one of them. When the young girl said yes, the skull cast a spurt of saliva that was to fall on the palm of Blood Moon's hand. The skull then said that through this act, he had given her his spittle and his offspring, and he ordered her to go up to the surface of the earth (*op. cit.* 1993, 104–107).

This miraculous conception in the underworld is the origin of the second pair of twins, the sons of Hun Hunahpu and Blood Moon. According to myth, Blood Moon managed to flee from the region of *Xibalba* and give life to Hunahpu and Xbalanque on the surface of the earth. As is known to readers of the *Popol Vuh*, Hunahpu and Xbalanque were faced with different challenges during their childhood and youth: they suffered from the envy of their older brothers, who finally became monkeys. Then they had to win the confidence of their grandmother and the affection of their mother. Later, they were asked to fight the usurpers Seven Macaw, Zipacna, and Earthquake.

Finally, once they recovered the ball game equipment that their fathers had hidden before leaving on their ill-fated trip to the underworld, they began to enjoy this diversion and they were heard by the regents of *Xibalba*. The lords were annoyed by the noise and they challenged the new Twins to play in the court of *Xibalba*. Accepting this formidable challenge put them face to face with the killers of their father and uncle in the most dramatic episode of the saga. Fortunately for us, the culminating moments of this part are illustrated in abundant paintings from the Classic period, which enrich the episodes narrated by the text. The journey to *Xibalba* by the second pair of twins is the opposite of the trip made by their ancestors. Hunahpu and Xbalanque elude the tricks to which their fathers had fallen prey, and they survive the challenges of spending the night in the Dark House. Taking pride in their intelligence, the Twins anticipate the ruses of the lords of *Xibalba*, and they frustrate and infuriate them. When they challenge them to play ball, the Twins win the first game. Then, when they are lodged successively in Razor House, Cold House, Jaguar House, and Fire House, they escape these dangers. Nevertheless, convinced that the purpose of the lords of *Xibalba* was to kill them, they created the illusion that they were sacrificed in a bonfire to be miraculously reborn later.

In their rebirth, they take on the appearance of two poor men who earn a living dancing and performing wonders to entertain the people of *Xibalba*. What the people of *Xibalba* admired the most was an act in which the Twins killed each other and a moment later they were brought back to life. The news of these astonishing acts reached the lords of *Xibalba*, who called for them to be performed in their presence. Amazed, the lords of *Xibalba* saw the transformist acts of the Twins, the hair-raising moment of their sacrifice, and then their glorious rebirth. With great enthusiasm, they asked the Twins to do the same to them. The Twins proceeded to sacrifice them, but they never brought them back to life. Then they revealed their true identity to the inhabitants of *Xibalba* and proclaimed themselves the avengers of their fathers and uncle, who had been sacrificed by the regents of *Xibalba*. They

Scene in the underworld
before the ball game between
the Twins and the lords of *Xibalba*

went to the place where their fathers and uncle had been buried, but their efforts to resuscitate them were in vain. In exchange, Hunahpu and Xbalanque were promised immortality through the permanent commemoration and continuity of their lineage. These actions demonstrate that the purpose of the journey of the Twins to *Xibalba* was to end the existing disorder in the underworld and to rescue their father and uncle. In this way, by defeating the powers of the *Xibalba*, whose unrestrained appetite consumed living beings, plants, and stars, the Hero Twins put an end to the destructive forces of the underworld. Once these new pacts were established with the powers of the sky and the underworld, the creator gods could initiate the task of giving form to the cosmos and life to human beings.

The Dawn of Life

The fourth and last part of the *Popol Vuh* is devoted to the exultant moment of the creation of the world in which we live today. The book says that when Hunahpu and Xbalanque abandoned *Xibalba*, they went up in apotheosis to the sky, where they were transformed into the Sun and Moon, respectively. Following this event, the gods worked on the task of making human beings. From the inside of the mountain filled with nourishment, they extracted yellow corn and white corn, which were ground nine times, and with this precious flour they made the flesh and body of the first men, the progenitors of the Quiche people.

After this moment, the cosmogonic texts change the subject and characters. The subject that now is imposed on these stories of creation is the appearance of different ethnic groups, the history of their formation, development, and migration under the guidance of their tutelary gods, who lead them to the promised land where they establish powerful kingdoms. In the

opposite, bottom
The cosmic tree called Wakan-Chan
from the Temple of the Cross
Palenque

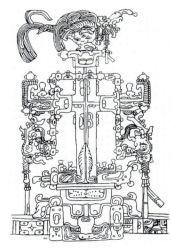

Popol Vuh there is a perfect continuity between the origins of the creation of the cosmos and the history on earth of the groups that emerged from this fundamental genesis. The same may be seen in the texts and codices that narrate the origin of the people of Palenque, and other groups such as the Mixtecs or Nahuas. Throughout, what should be underscored is the link joining the sacred origin of the cosmos with the earthly history of the kingdoms (Florescano 1995, 175–76). What is surprising in the *Popol Vuh* and in other Mesoamerican creation myths is the breadth of the temporal horizon that they encompass. They are texts that explain the origin, order, and equilibrium of the cosmos, as well as the ultimate meaning of human life on earth. The *Popol Vuh* begins "in the darkness, with the world inhabited only by the gods, and it continues from the dawn until the period of the human beings that wrote it" (Tedlock, *op. cit.* 59).

Even when the myth seems to concentrate on the enormous effort of the gods to dominate the forces producing chaos, its story encompasses the complex of supernatural and human affairs that sustain life and give it meaning. The subject of the cosmogonic myth is the description and ordering of the cosmos, the origin and destiny of human beings, the recording of nature surrounding them, and the great events weaving the life of the people and constructing the history of kingdoms.

The need to safeguard, order, and transmit this collective memory is the ultimate purpose of myth. In its oral or written form, the cosmogonic myth is a kind of encyclopedia invented by ancient peoples to preserve their identity and insure their survival. To fulfill this social function, the language of the myth has to satisfy two requirements: on the one hand it must captivate its audience, and on the other it must be a compendium of indispensable knowledge that insures the survival of the group. When a community succeeds in creating this

objective in a story, its maximum ambition is to give the message stability and transmit it perpetually to future generations (see Havelock 1986, 54–77 and 1994, 42-49, 291). This is what the Mayas did with the *Popol Vuh*, a story that began to be told again and again from the dawn of their civilization, in chants and figures carved on slabs, on painted vessels, on the facades of their temples and palaces, and in theatrical ceremonies and rites that commemorated the foundation acts of their history.

The *Popol Vuh* is the popular version of the great encyclopedia of knowledge that the Maya elaborated to survive as a civilized people. It uses a narrative language and concentrates on well-defined characters (creator gods, Hero Twins, lords of *Xibalba*, envious brothers). The plot and resolution of the story express the highest values of the Quiche people, values which are transmitted using tall-tale techniques of theatrical dramatization, forms of communication that continue to be used among their descendants to this very day. As we know, the Spanish translation of the work comes from a Quiche text, which in turn was probably copied from an ancient codex. The Quiche settled in the highlands of Guatemala at the beginning of the thirteenth century, and there they knew the foundations of Maya culture that preceded them. In the era of their splendor, the Mayas of Tikal, Calakmul, Copán, and Palenque had a history of origins of the cosmos very similar to that of the *Popol Vuh*, although more elaborate.

Polychrome Maya vessel
representing the maize god
with two naked women

opposite, bottom
Hun Nal Ye, the Maya maize god
in a sculpture from Temple 22
Copán, Honduras

The decipherment of Maya glyphs and new studies on religion and its symbols has allowed reading the most ancient myth of creation carved in Maya cities from the Classic period.

The myth inscribed on the temples of Palenque says that in the distant year of 3114 B.C., the First Father, who is called Hun Nal Ye, One Maize Revealed, was born. According to this cosmogony, when the sun did not even exist and darkness reigned, Hun Nal Ye created a house in a place called Raised-Up-Sky-Place and he oriented it toward the cardinal directions. Since then, this founding square became the geometric figure par excellence of the Maya world. In the same location, he placed three stones that marked the center of the cosmos and he raised the tree that symbolized the three vertical levels of the world (see Schele and Freidel 1990, 244–61; Freidel, Schele, Parker 1993, 69–72; De la Garza 1987, 15–86).

After these prodigious events, Hun Nal Ye protagonizes the central act of the cosmogony: his resurrection from the underworld in the form of an incredibly handsome youth who transports the precious kernels of maize to the surface of the earth after rescuing them from *Xibalba*.

The marvelous history of the resurrection of the maize god is not narrated in texts, but rather painted on ceramics and on the walls of Classic period monuments. These images

Maya funerary vessel
depicting three episodes
of the journeys of Hun Nal Ye
to the underworld

narrate the history of the first journey to the underworld and show that Hun Nal Ye is actually Hun Hunahpu (the First Father), whose adventures were related in the *Popol Vuh*. The paintings include episodes of this saga of which we were unaware: they describe the meeting of Hun Nal Ye with some beautiful, naked women in the depths of the underworld and of the search for the nourishing kernels inside the mountain of sustenance.

One painted vessel shows the maize god in a canoe and holding a bag of grain clutched to his chest. Other scenes present Hun Nal Ye dancing, as if celebrating his triumph over the lords of *Xibalba*.

Finally, there are scenes describing the climax of this succession of dramatic events: the sprouting of the maize god from the depths of the earth. One vessel shows the paddler gods accompanying Hun Nal Ye to his rebirth. In this scene the maize god (to the left) sprouts from the shell of a turtle (symbol of the earth) with a bag containing the precious

kernels of maize. In another very finely drawn painting, Hun Nal Ye emerges from a cleft in the earth (the carapace of a turtle), and is received by his sons, the Hero Twins, Hunahpu and Xbalanque.

Another painted vessel represents the same jubilant scene with the Twins on either side helping the First Father emerge from the underworld. These scenes show that the apotheosis of Hun Nal Ye is a result of the deeds accomplished by the Hero Twins in *Xibalba*, one of the central subjects of the narrative of the *Popol Vuh*. According to this ancient myth, Hun Nal Ye is the creator of the cosmos, the First Father who inaugurates a new era in the world, the generator of the precious food of human beings, and the tutelary ancestor of the first earthly kingdoms and dynasties.

By comparing the adventures of the Twins narrated in the *Popol Vuh* with texts and paintings of the Classic period, one is left with the impression of having journeyed through a very

Reconstruction drawing
showing Hun Nal Ye
the maize god celebrating
his resurrection from the underworld

Hun Nal Ye, on the left
emerges from the interior of the earth
with the bag containing
the precious kernels of maize

long span of human history and having touched something very profound in that history. Soon we perceive that for more than fifteen centuries, the Mayas related the same history about the origins of the cosmos and the foundations of civilized life.

The cosmogonic story that the Classic Maya carved on their monuments at Copán, Quiriguá, Bonampak, and Palenque indicates that in its origins this was an agricultural myth, a narrative focused on the sprouting of the maize plant from the depths of the earth.

The Maya cosmogony's account of an agricultural birth in which the newly created humanity modeled of maize dough sprouts, reveals that for the most ancient peoples of Mesoamerica, civilization was born with the origins of agriculture and the cultivation of maize (Florescano 1995, 204–19).

Hun Nal Ye is reborn on the interior
of the earth, represented
in this scene by a turtle carapace

The resurrection of Hun Nal Ye painted on a Maya vessel

References

ANDERS, FERDINAND, MAARTIN JANSEN, AND LUÍS REYES GARCÍA (ED.)
1992
Origen e historia de los reyes mixtecos. Libro explicativo del llamado Códice Vindobonensis. Mexico: Fondo de Cultura Económica, 84

COE, MICHAEL D.
1989
"The Hero Twins: Myth and Image." In *The Maya Vase Book.* Ed. by J. Kerr. Vol. I. New York: Kerr Associates, 161–84

FLORESCANO, ENRIQUE
1995
El mito de Quetzalcóatl. Mexico: Fondo de Cultura Económica, 175–76

FREIDEL, DAVID, LINDA SCHELE, AND JOY PARKER
1993
Maya Cosmos. Three Thousand Years on the Shaman's Path. New York: William Morrow and Co., 69–72

GARZA, MERCEDES DE LA
1987
"Los mayas. Antiguas y nuevas palabras sobre el origen." In *Mitos cosmogónicos del México Indígena.* Coord. by J. Monjaras-Ruz. Mexico: INAH, 15–86

HAVELOCK, ERIC A.
1986
The Muse Learns to Write. New Haven: Yale University Press, 54–77
1994
Preface to Plato. Cambridge, Mass.: Harvard University Press, 42–49, 291

LEANDER, BRIGITTA
1972
In Xochitl in Cuicatl. Flor y canto. La poesía de los Aztecas. Mexico: Instituto Nacional Indigenista, 211

Popol Vuh
1985
Popol Vuh: The Definitive Edition of the Maya Book of the Dawn of Life and the Glories of Gods and Kings. Translated from quiche by D. Tedlock

SCHELE, LINDA, AND DAVID FREIDEL
1990
A Forest of Kings: The Untold Story of the Ancient Maya. New York: William Morrow and Co., 244–61

Maya Gods

Maya culture was based on a religious conception of the world and of life, according to which the entire universe began and continues to exist thanks to the action of sacred energies. Manifesting themselves in multiple ways and in different natural beings, these energies determine what comes to pass according to the order of time. For the Mayas, supernatural beings created the cosmos for one express purpose: to insure their own existence by entrusting it to a being differentiated from others by his conscience, in other words man, who thus becomes both motor and axis of the cosmos. Based on this conception of the universe, the Maya people made ritual activity the center of their life.

What may be called gods in Maya religion are visual representations of supernatural beings composed of highly stylized traits of different animals and plants, which sometimes combine with human forms. These beings are also represented in codices and are mentioned in Colonial written sources, both Spanish as well as indigenous, which describe their characteristics and their names. Thus, in order to discuss identification, characterization, significance, and functions of Maya deities, it is essential to conduct comparative analysis of these different sources.

From Colonial written sources we know that gods were not "idols" for the Mayas, as many Spanish sources say, but rather invisible energies capable of manifesting themselves depending on time. These energies could appear in the form of natural phenomena and different animals, as well as in man-made images of them, which functioned in general as incarnations of these sacred energies during rites, to receive man's offerings. Among other authors of the sixteenth century, Fray Diego de Landa (1966, 48) confirms for us the ethereal character of the gods, when he says, "They knew well that the idols were their works, dead and without deity, but they held them in reverence for what they represented."

Maya gods, in spite of their superiority to men and their ability to create, were also conceived of as imperfect beings who are born and die, so that they needed be fed to survive. This idea is manifested in cosmogonic myths, prophecies, and rites (contained in Colonial indigenous books such as the *Popol Vuh*, *Memorial de Sololá* and *Libros de Chilam Balam*), and in hieroglyphic inscriptions dating to the Classic period, such as those of Palenque, where the birth of some of the gods is recorded, according to epigraphic interpretations (Freidel, Schele, Parker 1993).

Each one of the sacred beings has different manifestations and multiple names, in accord with their attributes, and above all, in relation to time. For the Maya, there are no static beings; everything is in constant movement and, therefore, ever changing. Thus the gods, and with them their influences, are different in each period. Therefore, one god may be celestial and terrestrial, benevolent and malevolent, masculine and feminine, the energy of life and the energy of death. In addition, the gods can be one and several at the same time; above all they pluralize themselves into fours, when they span the four directions of the cosmos; into thirteen, the deity of the sky, called in Yucatán Oxlahuntiku, "Thirteen Deity;" and into nine, the deity of the underworld, Bolontiku, "Nine Deity." This results in highly diverse visual representations of each one of the gods, which, pooled with the different artistic styles of each region, makes the study of Maya gods quite difficult. Nevertheless, deities may be identified by some constant symbolic elements, evident in all regions of the Maya area, and all periods.

Synthesizing their fundamental traits, we highlight here the main divine figures of the Mayas, identified by their Yucatec Maya and Quiche names, given to us by written sources. Gods are also identified here by letters they have been assigned, based on the classification made by Paul Schellhas (1904) of gods in the codices (Thompson 1970; Taube 1992).

The Dragon

A divine figure represented during all periods and all regions of the Maya area and that seems to symbolize a supreme sacred energy permeating the entire cosmos is the dragon, composed of different animal traits, especially those of the serpent. In Colonial

Reconstruction drawing
of the central motif from the panel
of the Temple of the Cross
at Palenque representing
the cosmic tree

sources on the Yucatec Maya, the dragon has different names, depending on the level of the cosmos it symbolizes. Itzamna, "the Dragon," is the celestial dragon, which has an anthropomorphic aspect, so-called God D of the codices, and a nocturnal aspect, Chicchan, "Serpent Biter." Itzam Cab Ain, "Terrestrial Crocodile Dragon" or Chac Mumul Ain, "Great Muddy Crocodile," is a symbol of the earth and underworld. Canhel, "Dragon," is the vital principle of the sky in cosmogonic myths and it corresponds to Gucumatz "Quetzal-Serpent," supreme deity and creator in the Quiches' *Popol Vuh*. After the arrival of the Toltecs to the northern Maya area, we find it fused with the figure of Kukulcan, "Quetzal-Serpent."

The dragon is also related to the sun, water, blood, semen, and corn, forces presented as different anthropomorphized deities, who seem to be manifestations of the celestial dragon. This relationship is expressed in multiple symbols, particularly in its serpentine traits: Kinich Ahau (the sun), his eye; Chaac (water), his fertile power; and Bolon Dzacab or Kawil (blood, semen, and corn), his presence among men. There is strong evidence that all these deities, who have traditionally been interpreted as different gods, are aspects of a single, great, supreme god.

The Celestial Dragon: Itzamna, God D

For many people, the celestial god and creator is an "idle god." That is to say, after creating the world, he remained in the last level of the sky without doing anything directly

Sun god represented
on a clay censer holder
from Palenque, Chiapas
Late Classic period
Mexico City
Museo Nacional de Antropología
cat. 329

Man-bird-serpent motif
from the Temple of the Warriors
at Chichén Itzá, Yucatán

affecting the lives of men; so, he is substituted by another figure who becomes the supreme god and who is the one in contact with earth and men. Written sources on the Mayas of Yucatán mention a creator deity who could not be represented, who was called Hunab Ku, "One God;" he could have been the idle creator god, whose substitute was Itzamna, his son, who participated in the creation as a culture hero and became the supreme celestial god of the Maya pantheon in the cult.

The supreme god of the Mayas is essentially celestial, but the basic concept of the Maya religion (and that of Mesoamerica in general) is harmony of opposites, so that this celestial god joins great cosmic opposites, represented by opposing forces of animal symbols par excellence: the bird, personifying the sky, and the serpent, manifesting the earth. Many birds and serpents were sacred among the Mayas, but in the celestial deity one particular bird, the quetzal, is combined with a serpent more powerful than the others, the tropical rattlesnake. The serpent-bird image is enriched by attributes of other sacred animals, such as the jaguar, the lizard and the deer, giving rise to the celestial dragon.

There are multiple ways of representing the celestial dragon known since the Preclassic period: as the bird-serpent (some, such as Taube, 1992 have called the bird-serpent Vucub Caquix, who is the famous false sun of the era prior to our own in the *Popol Vuh*), as bicephalic dragon, as feathered and winged serpent, as bicephalic serpent with starband body, as serpent mask, and as feathered serpent in the form of columns. As examples we could mention: Stela 25 of Izapa, Altars G, O, and 41 of Copán; Lintel 3 of Temple IV of Tikal, Temple of the Cross at Palenque, pages 4b, 5b, and 74 of the Dresden Codex. In Colonial texts, the dragon is identified with the creator gods who acted in the "static time" of cosmic origins. In the *Chilam Balam de Chumayel*, the dragon, with the name of Canhel, appears as the vital principle of the sky which, captured by the gods of death, leads to the destruction of the world.

In the *Popol Vuh* it is stated that Gucumatz, "Quetzal-Serpent," was the common name for all the creator gods, so that their different names seem to refer to different aspects of the same deity. Gucumatz mainly symbolizes water, identified with the vital energy with which the world was formed, and it is, therefore, the impulse that continuously produces life.

In the central highlands, the symbol of the dragon as feathered serpent was the deity called Quetzalcoatl, which fused with the god Ehecatl, which also signified the wind. In the Postclassic period, Quetzalcoatl was also associated with a historical figure called Ce Acatl Topiltzin, thus acquiring an even more complex meaning. With the arrival of Nahua groups to the Maya area, the Quetzalcoatl cult was integrated into Maya religion, which in the Maya world was called Kukulcan and was represented in art as a feathered serpent and as a "man-bird-serpent," taking on a martial character. In the Temple of the Warriors at Chichén Itzá, for example, we see reliefs with the man-bird-serpent motif and columns in the form of feathered serpents. In this way the figure of the Maya celestial dragon, venerated since the Preclassic period, and the Nahua dragon were fused.

The celestial dragon has an anthropomorphic form, called God D, who seems to correspond to the Itzamna mentioned by written sources. He is described as "the dew, or substance of the Sky, and clouds" (Lizana 1893, 4) and represented as an old man with a serpentine eye, that is to say, large, round, or square with rounded corners, which has a curve below; he has a large snubed nose; a toothless mouth or only a single tooth. Sometimes he is drawn with feminine features, that show him as an androgynous deity, similar to Ometeotl, the supreme god of the Nahuas. The image appears painted on many Classic period vessels; sculpted in ceramics; and drawn in codices.

As a culture hero, Itzamna invented agriculture, writing, calendars, and other human creations; he dictated laws and governed through his chosen few. In codices we see him carrying out many activities related to his character as culture hero, for example, in ritual scenes that may be mythical paradigms of priestly functions. We also see him writing, which corroborates his identification with Itzamna, the inventor of scripture, (Sotelo 1997).

God D.
Dresden Codex, page 9B
Dresden
Sächsische Landesbibliothek

God D.
Dresden Codex, page 28C
Dresden
Sächsische Landesbibliothek

Kinich Ahau, God G

The sun was one of the principal deities of the Maya pantheon. Because he is identified as an aspect of Itzamna, he is the supreme deity. The sun was for the Mayas the axis of life, the generator of time, the origin of all happening in general and of the four seasons, as well as of the four-part division of the cosmos. Therefore, he is the patron of the number four and his glyph is a four-petaled flower. His daily cycle gives him an ambivalent character; when he emerges from the underworld to cross the sky, he is light, life, day, order, good; but when he goes into the underworld in the afternoon, he becomes the energy of death transmuted in the jaguar.

The names of the sun god in Yucatán are Kin, "Sun-Day-Time," and Kinich Ahau, "Lord Solar Eye." His identification with Itzamna is expressed, among many ways, in one of the names of the supreme deity: Itzamna Kinich Ahau, "Lord Solar Eye of the Dragon." In visual representations of him dating to the Classic period, the solar god has fairly standard traits. He has large, square, crossed eyes, a filed tooth or protruding tongue, a curved fang in the corners of his mouth, and sometimes a kind of figure eight or cruller on his forehead, which is the body of a serpent.

The anthropomorphic aspect of the solar god in ceramics and in codices is God G. The latter is represented in a way very similar to God D, but with a *kin* (sun) glyph and a band or serpent fangs that emerge from the corners of his mouth.

The solar god is linked to several animals representing aspects of his sacred character, such as the jaguar (dead sun in the underworld), the deer and the hummingbird (sexual energy of the sun) and the eagle (military character of the sun). Other solar animals are those that may be in contact with him and descend to the earth to communicate their sacredness to some men, bring their message, receive human offerings, or simply announce the emergence of the star. These animals are birds: the *chachalaca*, the magpie, and the macaw. The last is called Kinich Kakmo, "Sun-Eye-Fire-Macaw," in Yucatán, and it is said that, incarnated as this bird, the sun descended to receive the offerings of men in Izamal. This city was dedicated to the cult of Itzamna, a fact that corroborates the identification of the two deities.

Chaac, God B

The god called Chaac in Colonial texts, another anthropomorphic deity derived from the dragon, is the most frequently represented supernatural in the three pre-Hispanic Maya codices. In Colonial texts he is mentioned as a deity of cornfields and as a manifestation of both rainwater and lake, river and sea water.

Chaac, God B of the codices, is represented with a long, pendant nose, on which there is an element in the form of a upward-curving volute. He has a serpentine eye, with a pupil in the form of a spiral, and under his lower eyelid he has another volute similar to that of his nose, which is extended over the temple. A curved serpentine canine tooth emerges from the corners of his mouth. In his hand he often carries an axe that symbolizes lightning. Sometimes he carries a torch, symbol of drought, because whether it

opposite
Clay censer holder
representing the sun god
Palenque
Late Classic period
Mexico City
Museo Nacional de Antropología
cat. 329

opposite
God B
Madrid Codex, page 4A
Madrid, Museo de América

God B
Dresden Codex, page 35B
Dresden
Sächsische Landesbibliothek

rained or not depended on him. He also appears in paintings and sculptures.

The deity is clearly derived from the serpent, symbol par excellence of water and vital energy. This is corroborated in images where an undulating serpent with aquatic symbols on the body rising in the middle of water bears the head of God B.

Chaac is one of the four-part deities of the Yucatec Maya, associated with the four colors of the cosmic directions (black, white, red, and yellow). Among other Mayan-related language groups he has equivalents, related above all to lightning.

In Classic period representations in the Yucatán peninsula, made following the Río Bec, Chenes and Puuc styles, Chaac appears with a large geometric mask made of stone mosaic, which decorates a good part of the buildings in these styles. The masks have clear serpentine traits and a long "nose" which may curl upward or downward, adorned sometimes with aquatic circles, and which symbolizes the long upper jaw of the serpent.

The Terrestrial Dragon: Itzam Cab Ain

In his relationship with Earth, the dragon symbolizes both the surface of the earth, as well as the hidden generative power within. This is why he is linked with the god of death who resides there (on the interior of the earth), and with the jaguar, symbol of the dead sun in the underworld and the nocturnal sky. In the Classic period, he is represented as a large mask, sometimes fleshless, which nevertheless bears plant and water symbols, a reason why he is called Earth Monster and Cauac Monster, given the presence of the Cauac glyph, which symbolizes water. (For example, the altars of Stela M and Stela D of Copán).

In many images located in the Maya area, from early representations dating to the time of Izapa up to Colonial period texts, the terrestrial dragon is represented as a large lizard or fantastic crocodile, whose Yucatecan name is Itzam Cab Ain, "Dragon-Earth-Crocodile" and Chac Mumul Ain, "Great Muddy Crocodile." In the *Popol Vuh*, we find the equivalent to this crocodile in the caiman, which is a symbol of the earth, Zipacna, creator of mountains and of the entire earth, son of Vucub Caquix, "Seven Macaw," the imperfect sun of the age preceding the one in which we live.

Bolon Dzacab, God K

One of the serpentine gods that is a manifestation of the celestial dragon in Maya religious thought is so-called God K, which has been identified with the Bolon Dzacab mentioned by written sources and through many coincidences, above all in references from Landa and codices. In addition, Bolon Dzacab means "Nine Generations," which alludes to the illustrious lineages of rulers, to the ancestors that are found in the underworld. His relationship with rulership is very clear in Classic period representations of this god as the "manikin scepter," an anthropomorphic figure with serpentine

Reconstruction drawing
Chaac Mask, Codz Pop Temple
at Kabah, Yucatán

242

Reconstruction drawing
of Altar of Stela M, Copán
Honduras

Reconstruction drawing
of God K. Manikin scepter
on Altar P of Quiriguá

opposite
God B
Madrid Codex, page 12b
Madrid, Museo de América

Reconstruction drawing
of God K
Codex-style cylinder vessel
from Nakbé, Guatemala

traits in the face and one leg converted into a serpent, and that is held in the hands or arms of rulers. In Classic period representations God K appears with a serpentine eye; the *nen* or mirror glyph on the forehead, from which emerge corn leaves (which at times are topped by a corn tassel), flames or an axe; a long bifurcated nose, which is derived from the upper jaw of the ophidian and the curved fang of the serpent at the corners of the mouth, which also appear in other serpentine deities such as Chaac and Kinich Ahau. In addition to having corn leaves emerging from his forehead, he is associated with this plant in many different contexts, so that he clearly personifies it. (For example in the Temple of the Foliated Cross at Palenque, dedicated to the birth of corn, God K is born from a seashell with corn leaves). Taube has called him Ka wil, perhaps because of his association with corn, because the word kawil means "second corn harvest" (Taube 1992. *Diccionario Maya*, 305).

Bolon Dzacab symbolized, at the same time, the offering of human blood to the gods, which was one of the ascetic rites of rulers. The handle of knives used in rituals of autosacrifice often bear the image of this deity, represented in some lintels of Yaxchilán. And as for the scepter, staff, or manikin figure, it symbolized onanist rites of offering semen practiced by Maya rulers (Coggins 1988).

In the *Chilam Balam de Chumayel*, Bolon Dzacab is mentioned participating in a cosmic catastrophe, as the deity that envelops the heart, semen, and seeds and carries them to the sky. He is also identified with Canhel, the Dragon, the vital energy residing in the thirteenth level of the sky, because Canhel is the name of the manikin scepter. In addition, due to the peculiarity of his leg, the scepter is linked with Huracán (Hurricane), "Lightning of a Leg," mentioned in the *Popol Vuh* as celestial deity of rain, who is also called "Heart of the Sky." Thus, he is identified with the supreme celestial god. In multiple visual representations we find this identification of God K and Itzamna. In ceramic pieces, for example, we see God K with a belt with star bands and seated on another band with star signs, which is the body of Itzamna (Stuart and Stuart 1977, 47).

All these coincidences show that God K is an aspect of the celestial dragon, the supreme deity of the Maya pantheon. Because he symbolizes blood, semen, and corn, God K is the presence of the dragon in the human world.

Ah Puch, God A

Death, a necessary complement to life, also had a patron deity, represented as a skull, a skeleton, or as a cadaver in decomposition. In codices, the god of death is drawn with rattles or disembodied eyes on the head, at the ankles, and at the wrists; it is androgynous, since at times it has feminine characteristics. In Colonial Yucatecan texts, it is referred to as Ah Puch, "the Fleshless One," or Kisin, "the Stinking One," Hun

Reconstruction drawing of God A. Stucco panel from Toniná, Chiapas

Death God on Temple XII at Palenque, Chiapas

Ahau, "Lord One," and has been identified with God A of the codices. He has also been called Yum Cimil, "Lord of Death." In the *Popol Vuh*, Quiche deities of death and disease are mentioned, headed by Hun Came, "One Death," and Vucub Came, "Seven Death."

The god of death is associated with night and disease. His place is the lowest level of the underworld, where the spirits of most men who die go. But the interior of the earth is also a place where new life is generated, since it houses the treasures and seeds of humankind. This paradox expresses that death is the dialectic complement to life, so that the god of death is represented with vital traits such as eyes, penis, and anus. Side by side with other gods, God A is drawn in codices as carrying out different activities, some of them ritual, such as smoking lying on his back (ecstasy), self-sacrificing his penis or participating New Year ceremonies, thus showing that death results in the life of the world. As he presides sacrifical ceremonies that favored the life of the gods and the entire universe, he plays a dialectic role.

Maize God, God E

In addition to God K, who as we have said is associated with corn, in codices and visual arts the maize god is represented as an anthropomorphic being without animal features. His head sprouts from an ear of corn, so he has been considered the deity of maize. Sometimes he is represented being born from the Earth Monster, as in Stelae 1 from Bonampak. In codices, he has been identified as God E, and there is no agreement regarding his Mayan name based on Colonial sources. The god of maize is patron of the number eight and his glyph is that of the day *kan*, Corn; often he is associated with the *caban* sign, signifying earth, and with birds that eat corn, such as the crow.

Maize is the human plant par excellence, because it is the staple of the Maya diet. Therefore the Quiche cosmogonic myth says that the body of man was made of maize dough, which explains why that god is drawn as a human figure without animal traits.

There are several myths on a Mesoamerican-wide level on the origins of corn. In the *Chilam Balam de Chumayel* (1985) his birth is narrated at the beginning of time and he is metaphorically referred to as "stone of grace."

Ix Chel

The Postclassic period representations of goddesses in codices, as well as references in written sources, speak to us of the existence of a great mother goddess related to the

God A
Madrid Codex, page 88C
Madrid, Museo de América

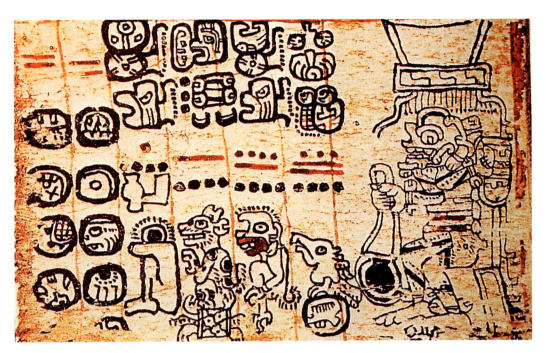

Reconstruction drawing
of God A
Madrid Codex, page 19
Madrid, Museo de América

moon, medicine, birth, and the labors of women, such as weaving. We know several names of goddesses in Colonial texts, but that of Ix Chel stands out, for it seems to correspond to the principal female deities in codices.

It is not specified in texts that Ix Chel was a lunar goddess, but it may be inferred because her name may be translated as "She of White Skin," and in general mother goddesses are related to the moon, which is considered an energy that propitiates fertility, both of the earth and animals, as well as humans. It is a universal belief that the moon regulates the cyclic rhythm of life, tides, and terrestrial water to fertilize the earth.

Therefore, in Maya fertility rites, both of men as well as of women, the moon is petitioned for sexual energy and the ability to procreate. Thus, it is evident that Ix Chel, who is known by several other names, was a lunar goddess. She was also related to the water of lakes and fountains so that she was venerated at aquatic sites, such as the island of Cozumel and the cave of Bolonchén. Moon, water, and fertility always are joined in religious thought.

In codices two goddesses are represented, a young one and an old one. They have been assigned the letters I and O. Thompson (1970, 206–209) interprets Goddess I as Ix Chel, lunar deity, and Goddess O as Ixchebel Yax, the companion of God D. He states that she is the goddess of weaving and painting, because her glyph has a roll of cotton or cloth.

Noemí Cruz (1995, 14), in turn, believes that the young Goddess I is the new moon, while the old Goddess O is the full moon, considering them as two aspects of the same deity, whose principal name was Ix Chel. The moon goddess thus unites several meanings: as a young goddess, she represents medicine and childbirth, and as an old goddess, the earth, vegetation, and weaving. Ix Chel seems to symbolize, in synthesis, the moon and the earth, which in the majority of ancient cultures have been associated with what is feminine.

This interpretation is corroborated by Classic period images, where we see her represented as a young woman seated on the growing moon carrying a rabbit (Schele and Miller 1986, 55), an animal whose shape can be seen in the full moon.

There are many other deities and many other manifestations of the main gods, but here we have limited ourselves to highlighting the essential characteristics of the deities of the great cosmic spheres and those related to those of fertility, one of the fundamental concerns of the Mayas.

from left
God E
Madrid Codex, page 24D
Madrid, Museo de América

God E
Madrid Codex, page 20C
Madrid, Museo de América

Goddess I
Dresden Codex, page 22B
Dresden
Sächsische Landesbibliothek

Goddess O
Dresden Codex, page 74
Dresden
Sächsische Landesbibliothek

Maize god
Sculpture from Copán

References

Reconstruction drawing
of the lunar goddess

BARRERA, VÁSQUEZ, ALFREDO (ED.)
1992
Diccionario maya Cordemex. Mérida: Ediciones Cordemex

Códices Mayas
1985
Códices Mayas. Facsimile. Introduction and bibliography by Thomas A. Lee, Jr., Tuxtla Gutiérrez: Universidad Autónoma de Chiapas-Brigham Young University

COGGINS, CLEMENCY CHASE
1988
"The Manikin Scepter: Emblem of Lineage." *Estudios de Cultura Maya*. Vol. 17. Mexico City: Centro de Estudios Mayas, Universidad Nacional Autónoma de México, 123–57

CRUZ CORTÉS, NOEMÍ
1995
Ixchel, diosa madre entre los mayas yucatecos. Bachelor's (licentiate) thesis in History. Mexico City: Universidad Nacional Autónoma de México

El libro de Chilam Balam
1985
El libro de Chilam Balam de Chumayel. Trans. by A. Médiz Bolio. Mexico City: Secretaría de Educación Pública (Serie Cien de México)

FREIDEL, DAVID, LINDA SCHELE, AND JOY PARKER
1993
Maya Cosmos. Three Thousand Years on the Shaman's Path. New York: William Morrow and Co.

GARZA, MERCEDES DE LA
1980
Literatura Maya. Compilación y prólogo, Venezuela, Biblioteca Ayacucho, 57. Barcelona: Editorial Galaxis
"Memorial de Solalá. Anales de los cakchiqueles." In *Literatura Maya*. Venezuela: Biblioteca Ayacucho, 57. Barcelona: Editorial Galaxis
"Popol Vuh." In *Literatura Maya*. Venezuela, Biblioteca Ayacucho, 57. Barcelona: Editorial Galaxis
1997
"Las Fuerzas Sagradas del Universo Maya." In *Los mayas clásicos*. Jaca Book
In press
"Las fuerzas sagradas del universo Maya. Periodo Posclásico." Jaca Book

LANDA, DIEGO DE
1966
Relación de las cosas de Yucatán. 9th ed. Mexico City: Editorial Porrúa

LIZANA, BERNARDO DE
1893
Historia de Yucatán. Devocionario de Nuestra Señora de Izamal y conquista espiritual. Mexico City: Imprenta del Museo Nacional

REENTS-BUDET, DORIE
1994
Painting the Maya Universe: Royal Ceramics of the Classic Period. Durham, N.C., and London: Duke University Press

SCHELE, LINDA, AND MARY ELLEN MILLER
1986
The Blood of Kings, Dynasty and Ritual in Maya Art. Fort Worth, New York: Kimbell Art Museum

SCHELLHAS, PAUL
1904
Representation of Deities of the Maya Manuscripts. Papers of the Peabody Museum of American Archaeology and Ethnology. Vol. 4, no. 1. Cambridge, Mass.: Harvard University

SOTELO, LAURA ELENA
1997
Los dioses antropomorfos en el Códice Madrid. Doctoral dissertation in Mesoamerican Studies. Mexico City: Universidad Nacional Autónoma de México, unpublished

STUART, GEORGE E., AND GENE S. STUART
1977
The Mysterious Maya. Washington, D.C.: National Geographic Society

TAUBE, KARL ANDREAS
1992
The Major Gods of Ancient Yucatán. Studies in Pre-Columbian Art and Archaeology no. 32. Washington, D.C.: Dumbarton Oaks, Research Library and Collection

THOMPSON, J. ERIC S.
1975
Historia y religión de los mayas. Mexico City: Siglo Veintiuno Editores

YADEUN, JUAN
1992
Toniná. El laberinto del inframundo. Mexico, Gobierno del Estado de Chiapas

Gold mask: eyerings and mouthpiece
from Cenote of Sacrifice
Chichén Itzá
Terminal Classic period
Harvard University
Peabody Museum of Archaeology
and Ethnology

Only grand monumental art and a variety of small portable objects, "minor arts," remain as testimony to the artistic skills of ancient civilizations, and usually the creators of such masterpieces, whether large or small, were anonymous. Unlike most modern works of art, ancient arts were the fruits of millennial craft traditions, developed to technological and expressive excellence in response to the needs of rulers and empowered religious leaders. Monumental art generally portrayed such patrons, whereas small objects were often the personal tools and possessions that would accompany these individuals into the tomb. Sometimes generically described as funerary furnishings, such talismanic adornments and emblems of identity may symbolize and express the unique character, the role, the lineage, and the world view—religious, political, and economic—of the defunct.

Maya rulers commissioned life-size portraits in stone (stelae) and wall paintings which often depicted these same precious possessions encountered in royal burials. But it is rare that connections can be made between a monumental portrait and a burial, because few important burials have been excavated compared to the untold thousands that have been sacked and destroyed. As a consequence, the possessions and ritual paraphernalia of the rulers of many Maya sites can be known only as "beautiful examples of Maya art" that probably once belonged to somebody. Such "lost" objects can tell us little about their origin, their patron, or their personal and local significance—and thus very little about their place in an artistic milieu, or about their singularity.

Monumental Maya art is impressive by virtue of its size and, in most cases, its pictorial grandeur. Completely sculptural, three-dimensional Maya monuments are confined to a few sites where the modeling techniques were perfected in stucco and transferred to soft stone, as at Copán, Honduras. Otherwise, Maya art is preeminently drawing. In Mayan languages drawing and painting and writing are all the same word, a word that probably signified "art" to the Maya—if they ever had such a concept at all. The Monkey God, Ah Chuen, was the supreme craftsmen, artist, and scribe, patron of the "fine arts." Indeed written or drawn figural designs on flat surfaces were the realm of the Monkey God, and they are characteristically Maya at every scale, but a greater variety of form, content, and technique is encountered in the many smaller, portable objects that may exemplify a particular Maya lineage and its local matrix—usually without any written or drawn signs. These objects might be made of jade, shell, bone, chert, or wood. But first among these was jade.

Jade

From Middle Preclassic times until the Spanish Conquest jade was the most valuable, symbolically potent, and thus the most desirable material in all Mesoamerica. Jade was difficult to acquire—probably all jadeite came from a single source in the Motagua River Valley in the southeastern corner of the southern Maya lowlands—and jadeite is very hard to work.

Only the most powerful could obtain it and support craftsmen skilled enough to shape and decorate it. Varying in color from white through several greens to blue-green, jadeite is dense, tough, and so hard it can only be worked by a harder abrasive like quartz. While jadeite epitomized the ideal "precious jade," other hard green stones might substitute for it and carry the same symbolism; these are described as "cultural jade" since they served the same social purpose.

The supernatural significance and supreme value of jade were first defined by the Olmecs, who imported it to their Gulf Coast sites at the beginning of the first millennium B.C. They worked it into small three-dimensional sculptures, life-size masks, and into celts (long knifelike forms) which they engraved with pictographic figures and signs. Later Mesoamerican peoples treasured jade equally, but it became increasingly scarce, and throughout the Classic period the Maya, closest to the source, used it most abundantly.

One large green quartzite "jade" Olmec pectoral portrays a high-relief Olmec mask flanked by perforated flanges with crossed bands (face of pectoral; Coe 1966). Probably from the Yucatán peninsula, where Olmec jades were encountered by the Maya

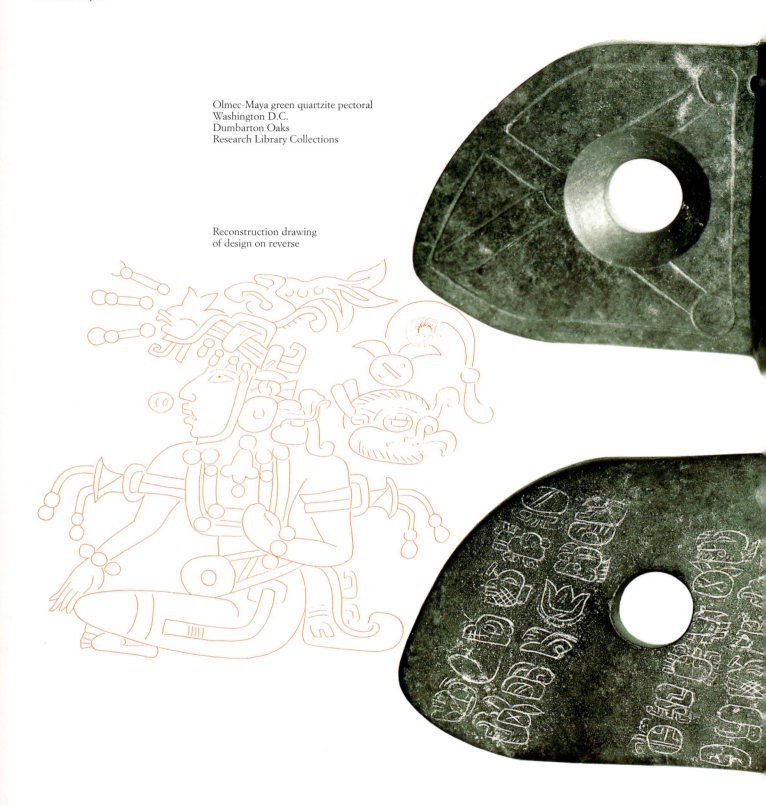

Olmec-Maya green quartzite pectoral
Washington D.C.
Dumbarton Oaks
Research Library Collections

Reconstruction drawing
of design on reverse

six or seven centuries later, this pendant typifies the Maya adoption of Olmec values, both lapidary and royal, since it was reused by a Maya lord who may have traced his ancestry back to the Olmecs. The figure of a seated Maya was engraved on the smooth reverse of the pectoral, accompanied by an inscription that names him and describes his "seating."

In contrast to the more sculptural Olmec mask on the front, this captioned image of a much later Maya "enthronement" exemplifies the flowing lines and didactic mode of Maya calligraphy, which details each essential element of regalia–beads, earflare, and headdress–displaying them arrayed around the profile head, and upon the turned frontal upper body and profile waist and folded legs.

following pages
Jadeite plaque
from Nebaj, Quiché
Classic period
Guatemala, Museo Nacional
de Arqueología y Etnología
cat. 280

Perhaps six hundred years later another jade plaque displaying an enthroned Maya lord was placed in a jade-rich cache at Nebaj in the southwestern Maya highlands (Smith and Kidder 1951, 35). Here the ruler scowls and gestures as he leans toward a withdrawn seated dwarf, both enframed by supernatural heads, bordered scrolls, and vegetation in a dynamic style which was never associated with inscriptions. Unlike many incised and more calligraphic versions of this important enthronement motif, such late examples from the western Maya country emphasize the outlines of the low relief with vigorous curvilinear forms which are segments of the diameters of hollow drills of varying size. Throughout the history of Maya art, in many media, unusual stylistic diversity is found in jades which reflect schools of workmanship, patronage, and iconography.

Jadeite head
Cenote of Sacrifice
Chichén Itzá
Late Classic period
Harvard University
Peabody Museum of Archaeology
and Ethnology

Small flat emblematic masks and incised celts in the Olmec tradition were common motifs for Maya jades, but there was also more sculptural work. One such, originally a big chunk of jade, is a Late Classic head that was an offering to the Cenote of Sacrifice at Chichén Itzá at the northern end of the Yucatán peninsula, although an inscription on the back indicates this sensitive portrait originally came from Piedras Negras on the Usumacinta River to the southwest (Proskouriakoff 1974, 154). A head of this type, flattened at the back, would have been worn at the center of the belt or collar of a Maya lord, whereas another type of jade portrait, the full-size mask, was probably worn only in the tomb.

Jade portrait masks were usually mosaic, employing shell and obsidian elements for the eyes and mouth in addition to numerous jade pieces of varying size. Sometimes large jade elements were carved as the contours of the face, as in the famous excavated examples from the sarcophagus of Pacal at Palenque, and recently from the tomb in Structure VII at Calakmul. More often, however, as jade may have become scarcer, small pieces of jade were used, perhaps scraps from a jade workshop, as in one extreme example from Calakmul. Only at Altun Ha, Belize (200 kilometers north of the Motagua River Valley by sea), where there was an abundance of worked jade, was a very large, round jade cobble devoted to the creation of a single massive head of the Sun God, who was deity of the eastern horizon and of Altun Ha at the edge of the eastern sea (Pendergast 1969).

Most Maya jade was used for beads, however. Tens of thousands of jade beads of all sizes and shapes were offered to the Cenote of Sacrifice, at Chichén Itzá (Proskouriakoff 1974), and jade beads are found in countless burials as the principal funerary furnishing. The round jade bead is the essential Maya form and symbol for jade. Maya rulers are often shown with a bead levitating in the air before their nose; this is their precious royal breath, symbol of life. Jade denotes life, what is green and living, and it conferred immortality on those who possessed it. Perhaps the most perfect illustration of the significance of the Maya jade bead was excavated from a cache at Copán, Honduras where a large jade bead in a bed of brilliant red cinnabar was enclosed within the two valves of a *spondylus* shell (Gordon 1896, 21). Such a bead specifically denoted life and rebirth, hidden, as it was, within this womblike shell which was symbolic of women and of motherhood.

Shell and Bone

Small shell beads, usually imported from a distant coast, are found in Preclassic Maya burials. Much of the value and desirability of shells apparently derived from their remote origins as well as from the particular significance of the sea. Much of Maya territory was surrounded by sea, and Postclassic origin myths, as in the *Popol Vuh*, describe the creation of the world out of a primordial ocean. Seashells evoke the encircling water and its generative character. The most valuable shell, the bivalve *spondylus* or thorny oyster, with its "thorns" intact was obtainable only by diving below ten fathoms. *Spondylus* shells were worn by male Maya rulers, as insignia comparable to jade pectorals (at Tikal, for instance), whereas the few ruling Maya women on monuments usually wear an open *spondylus* shell like an apron over the womb that the shells signify. The *spondylus* was also especially valued for its coral red inner layer which was used to make beads and mosaic elements.

Other valued shells–conches (*strombus*) used as trumpets, olivas as belt ornaments, and many others–were worked into beads and small pendants, and occasionally larger pendants decorated with inscriptions and scenes of enthronement. But in addition to its role as a trumpet, when cut in half lengthwise a conch shell was used as the scribe's paint pot and thus came to signify the artist's work.

Bones, like many shells, signified themselves (their original form) first. However, the choice of human, jaguar, tapir, or peccary bones was a large part of their symbolism, and additionally the bones were modified or decorated. For instance, the decorated pairs of femurs in a Tikal tomb were both human and jaguar. Many bore incised hieroglyphic

Jadeite, cinnabar, *spondylus* shell cache from Copán
Late Classic period
Harvard University
Peabody Museum of Archaeology and Ethnology

Carved bone
Late Classic period
from Xcalakdzonot
Valladolid
Centro Coordinador del INI
cat. 429

following pages
Flint eccentric
Classic period
Mexico City
Museo Nacional de Antropología
cat. 350

Jadeite mosaic mask
from Calakmul
Late Classic period
Campeche
Centro INAH Campeche

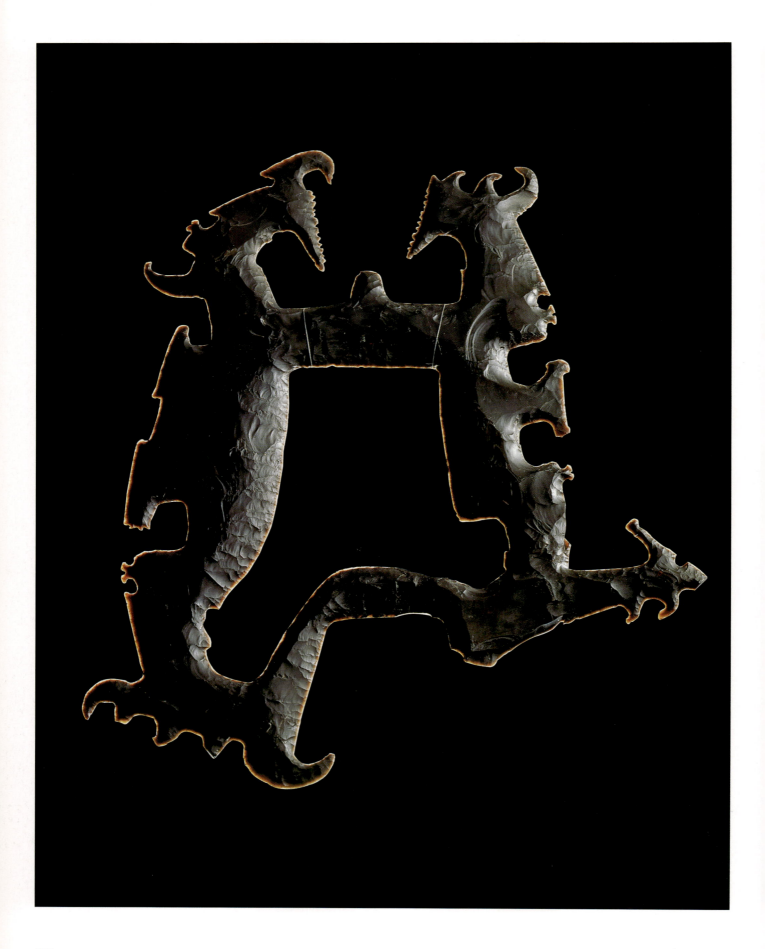

opposite
Wooden sculpture of seated man
Late Classic period
New York
The Metropolitan Museum of Art
the Michael C. Rockefeller
Memorial Collection, bequest
of Nelson A. Rockefeller

writing and other manuscript conventions to record bits of lineage history, portray prisoners, and illustrate scenes from the afterlife–all emblematic of death (Trik 1963). Indeed, the Yucatecan Maya word for bone, *bak*, was employed here as a characteristic pun in this depiction of a condemned captive, since the closely homophonous word *bak'* signifies captive–both meanings clearly implied on this mortuary bone.

Chert

Like bone and shell, chert (flint), signified its origin, in this case as stone from beneath the ground. This was apparently not true of jade. Probably no one knew where jade came from or realized that it was "just" stone. The whole Yucatán peninsula is a limestone shelf. Stone for most Maya was everywhere present as the limestone beneath their feet, and it was used for all their masonry buildings, commemorative stelae, and tools.

This white stone was understood to be the bones, or skeleton, of the earth, and in some places siliceous nodules formed within this sedimentary limestone yielded deposits of a much harder stone–chert–which was used for tools and spear points. Working this stone was perhaps the most ancient, specialized Mesoamerican industry; in the east where the best chert was found, master craftsmen created technically spectacular scepters and ritual weapons out of the vitreous stone.

These visually complex silhouette scepters, many recently found at Copán, usually depicted enthroned Maya lords wearing elaborate headdresses and backdresses, and because of the idiosyncrasies of the stone and skills of the knapper, each was unique (Fash 1991, 53–57). Unlike jade, chert embodied the stony significance of the bones of the earth–with connotations of structural permanence in addition to the bony reminder of death. As scepters, however, they also embodied their elite role as cutting weapons and sacrificial knives–symbolic of the martial pursuits of most Late Classic Maya rulers.

Wood

Wood was probably the commonest material used to make small sculptured objects and the components of royal regalia, although virtually none of it remains. As a rule, the preservation of wood requires a dry climate, as in the few high caves where such organic artifacts have survived in Mesoamerica, or a wet anaerobic environment where the wood has been submerged and waterlogged in a swamp or lake. Striking evidence of the craft of Maya three-dimensional wooden sculpture is found in a small, but monumental, Late Classic portrait of a kneeling man (Ekholm 1964). Except that it is said to come from somewhere near the Tabasco, Mexico-Petén, Guatemala, border, its cultural origin and functional context are completely unknown, as is the means of the figure's preservation.

The hot, flat riverine lands of the reported provenance would seem to preclude dry preservation, while the worshiping position of the priestly figure may recall paintings in Maya caves, although men were seldom shown in this position. The carved head worn as a pectoral is Maya in style, but the dangling ear disks are more a southern Maya trait, as is the curling mustache, while the small nose and bulging forehead are unusual–and quite the opposite of the Maya ideal. This commanding sculpture is loaded with tantalizing cultural information, which is of little use without any concrete idea of the sculpture's original context. Instead, we must confine ourselves to admiring this exceedingly rare wooden image as a homeless work of art.

The principal source of ancient Maya wood is the Cenote of Sacrifice at Chichén Itzá, Yucatán. Between about A.D. 700 and 1500 many kinds of worked wooden objects were offered to this sacred well, which is a limestone sinkhole filled with water (Coggins 1984). Among the best preserved works of art is a group of wooden scepters, each with a small carved human figure at the top and a serpent head at the base of the handle (Coggins and Ladd 1992, 269–83).

These Postclassic scepters served the same purpose as the "manikin scepters" held by Maya rulers on the monuments of the Classic period. The anthropomorphic finials are

Symbolic bone
from Copán
Late Classic period
Copán Ruinas
Museo Regional de Arqueología
cat. 348

small lively sculptures that embodied the inherited right to rule, their faces covered with gold or mosaic; whereas the serpentine handle combined that most ancient Mesoamerican symbolism in which the serpent evoked lightning, the ruler's axe, and thus his military and sexual potency.

Ceramic Figurines

Ceramic figurines occupy an anomalous position in a consideration of small-scale Maya art; it is likely they belonged to a different sphere of Maya craftsmanship from all those we have considered. This separateness would have derived, principally, from the fact that the ceramic industries, not quite as ancient as the working of stone tools, were basically confined to the production of containers from a shapeless plastic earth medium. This is in contrast to the other crafts we have considered which involved the reduction of an existing form into a finished object. Furthermore stones, shells, bone, and wood were materials with symbolic associations that were different from clay which, like dirt, connoted earth and fertility–female symbols.

Indeed, in Preclassic times throughout Mesoamerica figurines usually represented naked women and babies–suggesting the underlying significance of the clay itself, as well as the personification of prayers for agricultural and familial fecundity. In the Maya regions there followed a hiatus of three to five centuries in which relatively few figurines were made, then in Late Classic times figurines, often whistles, were made–usually in molds, suggesting the standardized manufacture that was always to some degree present in ceramics production. Early in Late Classic times in the Maya central lowlands and highlands, a more monumental figurine craft was developed for the creation of *incensarios*, or incense burners, and lids, but it was in the west, at Late Classic Palenque, Chiapas, that this genre was carried to a spectacular level of artistic achievement. Recent excavations at Palenque have encountered new arrays of the well-known tall flanged cylinders that were used to support *incensarios*. These are embellished with a profusion of supernatural images and natural forms that combine to create the defining headdress of the deity or ancestor to whom the censer and its burning *copal* incense were dedicated.

Although limited in time and area extent, the Late Classic figurines known from the cemeteries of Jaina Island, Campeche, are probably the best-known examples of Maya art. While figurines of this type fill private collections and museums around the world (as do a great many fakes), scientific Mexican excavations on Jaina Island encountered many of the finest figurines in burials, with all of their cultural and personal associations, including carved bone, shell, and jade (Piña Chán 1968). The earlier, hand-modeled figurines embody the explicitly naturalistic and sculptural qualities of the genre and provide a fund of information about the lives and culture of the Maya of this coastal region.

They say little, however, about the craftsmen who developed this singular modeled clay tradition, about its relationship to other sculptured media, or even about its role in local ceramic production.

Gold

It must be emphasized that Mesoamerican cultures developed and flourished without the use of metal, although a metallurgy of extraordinary sophistication was developed in Andean America in the second millennium B.C. But even there metal was used primarily for sumptuary and religious purposes. When, about the ninth century A.D., copper metallurgy was introduced into western Mesoamerica, it had relatively little cultural impact. The Maya probably never worked gold, except at the simplest level, and even when they used it for ceremonial purposes, it never took the place of jade as the supreme material.

Many gold objects were offered to the Cenote of Sacrifice at Chichén Itzá, but most had been worked elsewhere, like, for instance, the numerous cast gold-alloy animals and figurines from lower Central America, or the countless cast copper-alloy bells from Veracruz and West Mexico.

Ceramic support
for a censer base
from Palenque, Chiapas
Late Classic period
Palenque, Museo de Sitio
"Alberto Ruz Lhuillier"

The only local Maya gold working involved the cutting and repoussé impression of designs into imported sheet gold.

These objects tended to reflect the infusion of Mexican culture into Yucatán at the new northern capital of Chichén Itzá beginning in the eighth century A.D. An elegant example of this bicultural symbolism is a gold "mask" consisting of mouth and eye elements cut from sheet gold and fashioned to display the celestial Mexican feathered serpent above the eyes with terrestrial Maya serpentine emblems at either side of the mouth (Coggins 1984, 55). Despite a limited Postclassic elite use, the exotic gold was never as valuable as jade, to the disbelief of the gold-hungry Spaniards–nor could it be analogous in meaning.

Textiles
Textiles represented another major Mesoamerican industry, and three kinds of evidence testify to their great artistic importance for the Classic period Maya. First, magnificent

opposite
Censer base
from Palenque, Chiapas
Late Classic period
Palenque, Museo de Sitio
"Alberto Ruz Lhuillier"
cat. 330

opposite
Ballplayer
Jaina Island, Campeche
Late Classic period
Mexico City
Museo Nacional de Antropología
cat. 362

Necklace
from Iximche, Chimaltenango
Late Postclassic period
Guatemala, Museo Nacional
de Arqueología y Etnología
cat. 153

textiles are represented in monumental art–particularly on the lintels of Yaxchilán. Second, quantities of textiles were offered to the Cenote of Sacrifice at Chichén Itzá, although only blackened fragments survived the long immersion and subsequent dredging from the sacred well (Lothrop 1992). Third, the weaving of textiles is still a brilliant living tradition in both the Mexican and Guatemalan highlands. Otherwise we know sadly little about ancient Maya weaving.

Manuscripts
Even though they are portable, and involved an ancient craft tradition which was the proper sphere of Ah Chuen, the Monkey God, manuscripts probably should not be included in a consideration of "minor arts." They were the principal, enduring source of elite Maya knowledge and "art," but their permanence was perpetually endangered by the lowland Maya climate and finally betrayed by the religious zeal of the Spanish friars.
The three or four extant Postclassic examples are concerned with the calendric and astronomical formulae and rituals necessary for agriculture, hunting, and the maintenance of daily religion. The holy words, divination rituals, scriptual stories, and the lineage and calendric histories of the Maya were all surely once preserved in these screen-fold bark paper documents where the records were painted upon smooth stuccoed surfaces. Manuscripts may have been the principal repository of the images of Maya rulership, as well as the ultimate source of all hieroglyphic inscriptions.
They were, thus, the historical resource for most Maya monumental sculpture and painting. The calligrapher-artists who created manuscripts were part of the educated elite-scribes and painters who inhabited a completely different cultural sphere from the stone-workers, wood carvers, and figurine modelers. They would, however, have served as necessary consultants to the jade, shell, and bone carvers whose individualized works gained much of their power and value from esoteric decoration. Thus, at every period, the creation of small, portable works of Maya art involved ancient craft traditions in the service of Ah Chuen, the Monkey God, whose patronage served to define what we now call Maya civilization.

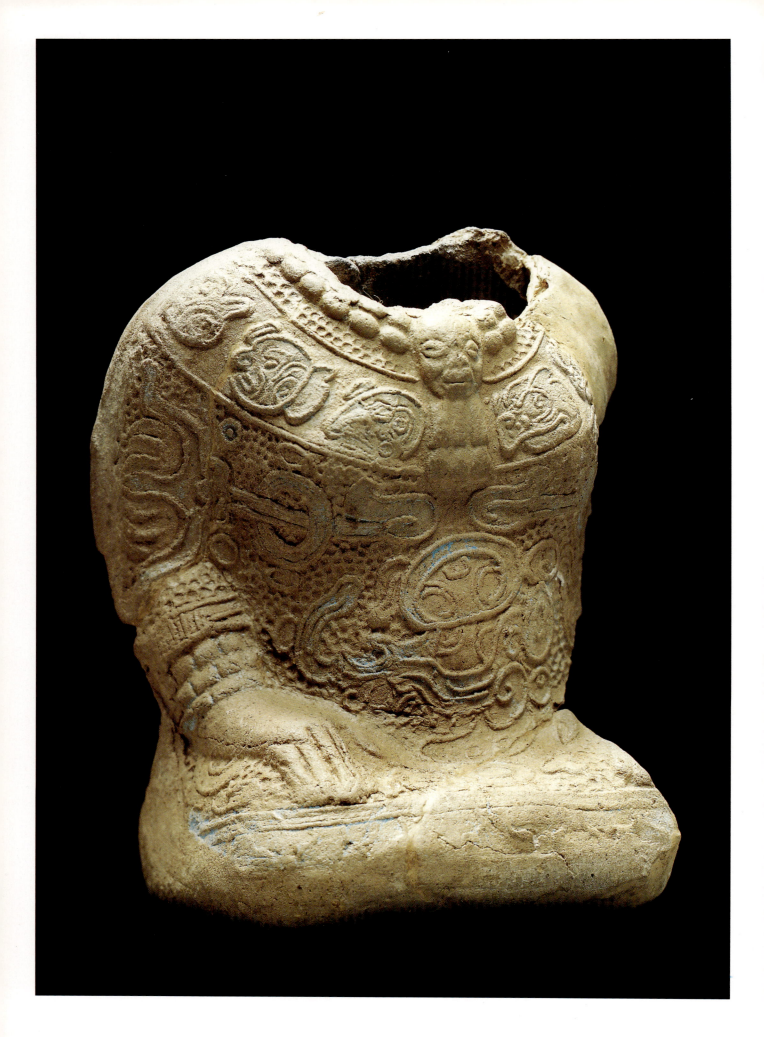

opposite
Anthropomorphic figurine
from Lagartero, La Trinitaria
Late Classic period
Tuxtla Gutiérrez
Museo Regional de Chiapas

Female figurine
Jaina Island
Campeche
Late Classic period
Mexico City
Museo Nacional de Antropología
cat. 119

Detail from the motif
of a polychrome textile
from Cueva de la Garrafa
Siltepec municipality, Chiapas
Postclassic period
Tuxtla Gutiérrez
Museo Regional de Chiapas
cat. 183

References

COE, MICHAEL D.
1966
"An Early Stone Pectoral from Southeastern Mexico." In *Studies in Pre-Columbian Art and Archaeology*, no. 1. Washington, D.C.: Dumbarton Oaks

COGGINS, CLEMENCY CHASE
1984
"Catalogue." In *Cenote of Sacrifice: Maya Treasures from the Sacred Well at Chichén Itzá*. Ed. by C. Coggins Chase and O.C. Shane III. Austin. University of Texas Press

COGGINS, CLEMENCY CHASE, AND JOHN M. LADD
1992
"Wooden Artifacts." In *Artifacts from the Cenote of Sacrifice, Chichén Itzá, Yucatán*. Ed. by C.C. Coggins. Memoirs of the Peabody Museum of Archaeology and Ethnology. Vol. 10, 3. Cambridge, Mass.: Harvard University

EKHOLM, GORDON F.
1964
"A Maya Sculpture in Wood."In *The Museum of Primitive Art: Studies Number 4*. New York: Museum of Primitive Art

FASH, WILLIAM L.
1991
Scribes, Warriors, and Kings: The City of Copán and the Ancient Maya. New York: Thames and Hudson

GORDON, GEORGE BYRON
1896
"Prehistoric Ruins of Copán, Honduras. 1896: A preliminary Report on Explorations 1891–1895".

Memoirs of the Peabody Museum of Archaeology and Ethnology. Vol. II. Cambridge, Mass.: Harvard University

LOTHROP, JOY MAHLER
1992
"Textiles." In *Artifacts from the Cenote of Sacrifice, Chichén Itzá, Yucatán*. Ed. by C. Coggins Chase. Memoirs of the Peabody Museum of Archaeology and Ethnology. Vol. 10. Cambridge, Mass.: Harvard University

PENDERGAST, DAVID M.
1969
Altun Ha, British Honduras (Belize): The Sun God's Tomb. Occasional Paper, no. 19. Toronto: Royal Ontario Museum

PIÑA CHÁN, ROMAN
1968
Jaina. La Casa en el Agua. Mexico: Instituto Nacional de Antropología e Historia

PROSKOURIAKOFF, TATIANA
1974
Jades from the Cenote of Sacrifice, Chichén Itzá, Yucatán. Memoirs of the Peabody Museum of Archaeology and Ethnology. Vol. 10. Cambridge, Mass.: Harvard University

SMITH, A. V., AND A. V. KIDDER
1951
Excavations at Nebaj, Guatemala. Publication 594. Washington, D.C.: Carnegie Institution of Washington

TRIK, AUBREY S.
1963
"The Splendid Tomb of Temple I at Tikal, Guatemala." *Expedition*, 6, 1, 2–18

opposite
Figurine representing
a woman scribe
Jaina Island, Campeche
Late Classic period
Mexico City
Museo Nacional de Antropología
cat. 456

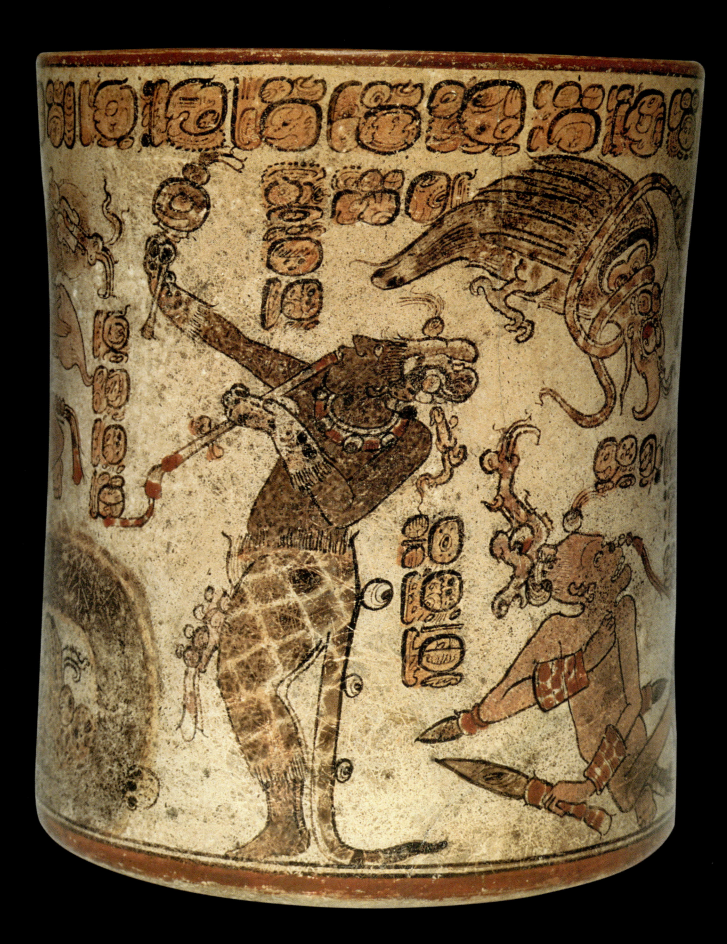

Classic Maya Painted Ceramics and the Stories They Tell

Vessel identified as the creation of a master painter known as the 'Altar Master' Princeton, The Art Museum

The painted pottery of the Classic Maya is one of the world's outstanding ceramic art traditions. These painted vessels often are compared to classical Greek pottery because they share artistic features. For example, both traditions focus on realistic pictorial representations of human and divine figures engaged in historical and mythological activities. Both traditions are renowned for their elegant representations and aesthetic refinement, and their being the works of highly trained and talented artists. Further, both Greek and Maya vessels were special objects used among the elite during important social rites. In spite of these shared features, a closer examination reveals Classic Maya painted pottery to be a unique polychromatic tradition, unlike the generally bichromatic Greek paintings on ceramic. Even more striking is the scraffito origin of Greek pottery painting, which is based on scratching fine lines into the clay surface with a stylus. The resulting pictorial forms are filled in with a flat field of color (usually a brown-black). In contrast, Maya painted pottery is based on the brush, with brushstrokes being an integral part of the tradition's aesthetic. Maya pottery painters also excelled in fully exploiting the multiplicity of hues and values inherent to the medium of polychrome painting.

Classic Maya Painted Pottery

The extraordinary and often detailed pictorial expressions painted on these vessels open a window onto Maya culture. The scenes preserve unique pieces of Classic period social history, religious mythology, and cosmology. When excavated by professional archaeologists and analyzed from a variety of humanistic perspectives, these painted artworks reveal crucial sociohistorical information not retrievable through traditional, single-focus methods of historical inquiry. Insights can be gained from the pottery by studying its many facets, including the vessels' forms, the painted imagery and hieroglyphic texts, the painting styles, and the chemical composition of the ceramic bodies (pastes). Classic Maya painted pottery is remarkable for its technical sophistication, which characterizes the work of full-time specialists fully trained in their craft. These vessels were built by hand without the use of the wheel, the potter adding coils of clay to a tortilla-shaped bottom. Using this simple method, Maya potters constructed vessels with well-balanced and symmetrical forms, many having exceptionally thin walls similar to those of the best porcelains from China. The painted imagery is created with clay-based paints known as slip paint or *terra sigillata*. Although slip paints have been used by many cultures, such as the ancient Greeks, none has surpassed Maya pottery's highly glossy surface, wide range of colors, and exquisite watercolor effects. For example, the artist who painted the vase was a master of subtle hues and values, here seen especially in the brown skin of the figures and the delicate pink wash embellishing the hieroglyphs. After being painted, the vessels were fired at low temperatures (about 800 °C) in a highly controlled oxidation atmosphere. Although there is archaeological evidence for kilns being used by various Mesoamerican cultures in Mexico, their general absence among the Maya suggests they did not use them extensively (see Abascal 1975; Payne 1982). Perfectly fired pots can be achieved in an open pit firing if the ceramicist has mastered all technical aspects of the firing process. These include the correct stacking of the vessels in the pit, devising ways to protect the vessels' surfaces from fire and ash, using specific types of wood fuel, stacking the fuel around the vessels to ensure a proper firing, and knowing when and how much fuel to add during the firing process.

Vessel depicting an enthroned lord from the Río Azul Private collection

following pages
Roll out
from the vessel

The exceptional knowledge and skills of these ancient artists is also seen in the pottery's pictorial images and hieroglyphic texts. These feature Maya history, especially the rituals of sociopolitical power, and religious mythology, which was the ideological foundation of Maya rulership and culture. Many of these scenes are complicated pictorial narratives that, when photographed as a "roll-out" image, are equal in compositional sophistication to the best paintings of Europe and Asia. Maya pottery paintings may actually have been more difficult to produce, however, because the artists painted on the curved surface of cylindrical vessels.

Only a small portion of the composition could be seen at one time, requiring exceptional painting skill because there is no room for error. Once slip paint is applied, it can-

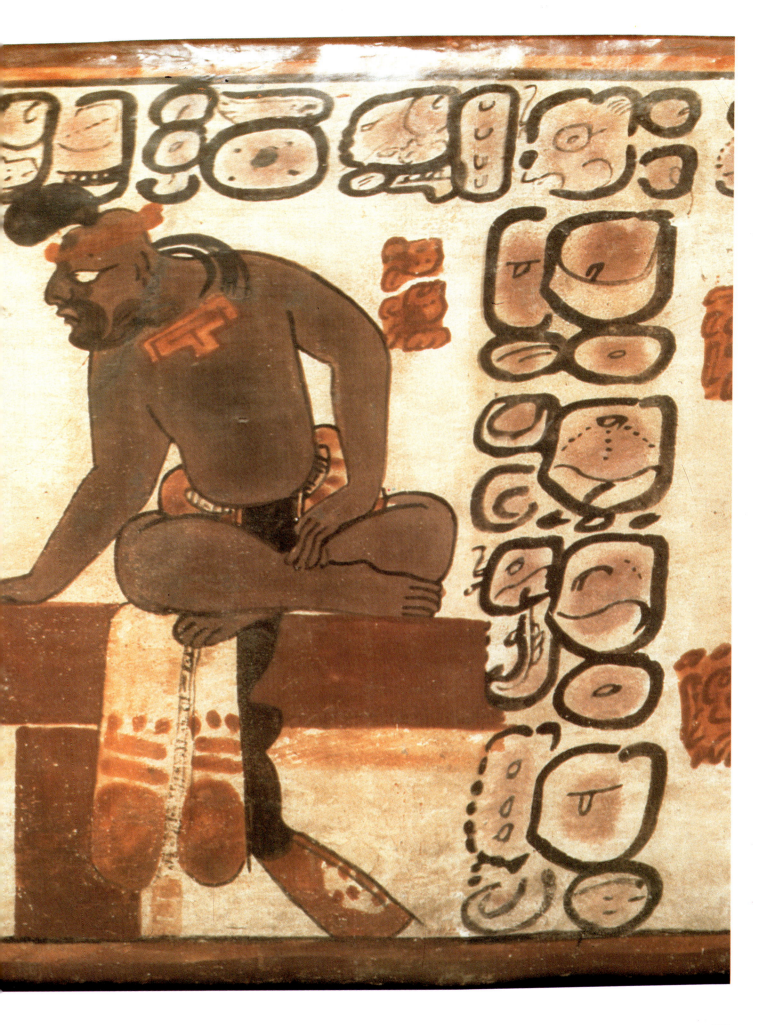

Roll out of the vessel identified as the creation of a master painter known as the 'Altar Master' Princeton, The Art Museum

not be removed without damaging the vessel's surface and being visible forever. Thus, Classic Maya pottery painters had to master the technical difficulties of hand-built, low-fired, slip-painted pottery, and the creation of beautiful and complicated pictorial and hieroglyphic narratives on a cylindrical surface. Who were these artists? What were the social processes behind the creation of these unique masterpieces? To answer these questions, we first must explore the Classic period functions of these pots.

Functions of Classic Maya Pottery

One of the primary archaeological contexts in which the painted pottery is found is in graves and tombs, which has led to their interpretation as funerary offerings (Coe 1973; 1978). In addition, however, painted vessels were used to serve food during important gatherings among the Maya nobility (Reents-Budet *et al.* 1994, 72–105). This function is well illustrated on many painted vessels whose scenes depict these social events, and include representations of painted vessels filled with food and drink.

A third function of the pottery is that of "social currency," wherein beautifully painted vessels were used as gifts exchanged among the nobility. Some of these vessels are commissioned works of art whose patrons were members of the ruling nobility. A selected vessel would be given by its patron-owner to a member of the local elite or to a "foreign" noble from another site as part of the process of securing and maintaining that person's

allegiance. For example, the famous Blom Plate was discovered in a mound near modern-day Chetumal, in Quintana Roo, Mexico. However, its painting style and the chemical composition of its ceramic paste indicate it was made in northern Belize, perhaps at the large center of Altun Ha. This plate, then, is material evidence of Classic period elite interaction, perhaps its being a gift between the two regions' respective ruling nobility.

Identity of the Artists

Who were the artists who created these painted vessels which honored the divine dead as well as the elite living? Clearly, they were full-time specialists who had practiced their art for many years. They were well educated in Maya history and religion, and were master calligraphers in total control of the visual and linguistic poetic potentials inherent to Maya hieroglyphic writing. Their social importance is suggested by the fact that, in some instances, their names and/or personal titles, that is, their "signatures," were painted on the vessels. Their social and intellectual positions are further defined by titles found in these nominal phrases, including *ahau* (lord), *itsat* (artist), *chehen* (maker), and *miyats* (savant) (see Reents-Budet *et al.* 1994, 36–71; Stuart 1987). In addition to highlighting these artists' status as members of the Maya elite, these titles also imply that the artists were perceived as having relationship to the gods of Creation (Coe 1977; Reents-Budet 1997). This may be why the artists' renditions of themselves often include supernatural attributes.

Roll out of a vessel depicting
a lord sitting on a bench-trone inside
a palace like building
Private collection

The Painted Scenes
The pictorial scenes painted on these vessels reveal many details of Maya culture, of both its historical events and religious cosmological beliefs. These unique visual expressions preserve specific ideals of history and religion that have not survived in any other form. For example, the vase preserves, pictorially and hieroglyphically, a meeting between the lords of Tikal and Topoxté, a nearby site. This tribute-paying event takes place inside a wide room with white curtains tied open along its ceiling (lintel) line, the lintel being supported by pillars. This type of building is found at most Maya sites, often being interpreted by archaeologists as a palace or meetinghouse. Such renderings provide unique details of how these now ruined buildings were decorated and used by the Classic Maya. Interestingly, on this vase, the building's ceiling line and pillars are suggested by the horizontal and vertical rows of hieroglyphs.

A variety of these so-called peak events are pictured on the pottery. In addition to banquets and tribute payment, other vessels depict warriors, the sacrifice of prisoners, the ritual ball game, and socioreligious dances complete with the attending orchestra. Marriage negotiations also are rendered on a few vessels. These latter representations hint at the importance of marriage among the Maya nobility as a powerful sociopolitical mechanism during the Classic period.

Religious mythology and beliefs concerning the creation of the cosmos are featured on some painted vessels. Michael Coe (1973) was the first to connect these representations with the tales recounted in the sixteenth-century Maya epic *Popol Vuh* (Tedlock 1996). For example, a plate in the Boston Museum of Fine Arts depicts the resurrection from the underworld of First Father, who was saved from the lords of death by his sons the Hero Twins, whose sixteenth-century names are Hunahpu and Xbalanque.

Blom Plate
found in a burial outside
Río Hondo, Quintana Roo
Late Classic period
Merida, Museo Regional
de Antropología "Palacio Cantón"
cat. 449

On this plate, their Classic period names are painted in front of them (here Hun Ahau and Yax Balam). In this scene, the Hero Twins pour sacred liquid (water/blood) from a jar into the crack in the earth, here rendered in its symbolic form as a turtle shell. By this action, First Father escapes from death and the underworld, and emerges into the world of the living. At his resurrection, First Father takes on the attributes of the young corn god (Taube 1985). These features suggest that, for the Classic Maya, the natural cycle of corn functioned as a metaphor for resurrection of the human soul after death.

In addition to renderings of *Popol Vuh* vignettes, Classic period painted vessels depict many other mythological and cosmological scenes. These remain some of the most challenging images awaiting future scholarly interpretation and understanding. Although we know these images preserve details of Maya religious mythology, we have no surviving sixteenth-century or modern Maya religious texts to assist in their interpretation. Ongoing research by art historians and archaeologists is focused on discovering the meanings of these cryptic images.

One group of vessels bridges the gap between the mythological and the historical. These so-called Dynastic Sequence Vases are painted with a list of kings whose emblem glyph is that of the so-called Snake Head Polity (Coe 1978, 28; Kerr and Kerr 1981; Martin 1997; Robicsek and Hales 1981, 151–60). This polity is now generally accepted to have had its center at the site of Calakmul, Campeche, Mexico (Marcus 1973; Martin 1996a; Martin and Grube 1995; Mathews 1979). Simon Martin recently has interpreted the hieroglyphic texts painted on these vessels as a list of kings pertaining to mythological time (Martin 1997, 862). This king list also served as the source for the names of Classic period rulers at Calakmul. Martin suggests one of the reasons behind this choice may be the establishment of an ancient heritage for the Calakmul rulers, tying them to the mythological and the sacred (Reents-Budet, Martin, Hansen, and Bishop 1997). Such an origin would lend special power and prestige to the ruling dynasty of the site.

The Hieroglyphic Texts

Two types of hieroglyphic texts are painted on Classic period vessels. One refers to the vessel itself and the other to the painted scene. The most prevalent is the one which refers to the vessel itself, and was termed the "Primary Standard Sequence" or PSS by Michael Coe (1973). Coe was the first to identify this text and its importance to our understanding of Classic Maya polychrome pottery. The PSS is repeated on many painted and carved Classic period vessels, although each rendering exhibits idiosyncratic variations of syntax, glyphic forms, and/or affix patterns. These variations represent the painters' exercising their artistic license to create individualistic expressions.

Through the years, many epigraphers have contributed to the decipherment of the PSS, dividing the text into five main sections (see MacLeod in Reents-Budet *et al.* 1994, 106–63). The text opens with a phrase which dedicates the pottery vessel itself. We might think of this phrase as something akin to making the vessel socioreligiously proper (or "kosher") for its intended life among the living as well as among the honored dead. This is followed by the surface treatment section, which indicates whether the vessel was painted or carved (Stuart 1987). The exact syntactical referent of this second part remains somewhat enigmatic, prompting the suggestion that perhaps the act of painting was part of the process by which the vessel was made "proper" (Reents-Budet *et al.* 1994, 111–13, 125). The third part of the PSS is the vessel type section. This specifies the form class to which the vessel belongs (drinking vessel, plate, etc.) (Houston, Stuart, and Taube 1989). Correlated with the form class is the subsequent contents section. Here is recorded what food or other substance was contained in the vessel. Not surprisingly, tall cylindrically shaped vessels were used to hold liquids, specifically one of the many chocolate-based drinks pioneered by the ancient Maya. Dish forms held semisolid foods such as *atole* (corn gruel), called *ul* in Mayan languages and in the Classic period hieroglyphic texts. And the most common food served on plates was *wah* (corn *tamal*).

The fifth and last part of the Primary Standard Sequence is the closure section. This final section names the owner and/or patron of the vessel, listing his (sometimes her)

Plate depicting the artist himself
Boston, The Museum of Fine Arts
gift of London T. Clay

elite titles and occasionally a personal name (Houston and Taube 1987). The titles are most likely religious and political epithets. On rare occasions, the nominal section of the PSS ends with the name/titles of the artist who created the vessel.

Interestingly, the PSS is completely independent of the pictorial image on the vase. These two narratives (the PSS and the pictorial image) are independent conceptual units with separate semantic and informational domains. Their separation is clearly indicated by the fact that the vast majority of PSS texts and pictorial compositions have different "starting points," each proceeding around the vessel as an independent rotation.

The second type of hieroglyphic text painted on the Classic period pottery is that which pertains to the pictorial image. These usually comprise short texts, and are painted within the scene. Often these texts name the participants as well as give glyphic narrative details concerning the event. The short nominal phrases include elite titles of office and/or relationship not found in the inscriptions on stelae and other public stone monuments. Although the majority of these titles either await decipherment and understanding as to their sociocultural meanings, they promise to be important to our reconstruction of Classic Maya sociopolitical structures.

Painting Style and Social Interaction

The area of cultural reconstruction in which Classic period painted pottery has most recently become important is that of social interaction among the ruling families of individual sites and polities. Because pieces of pottery played a role as gifts exchanged among the elite, it was necessary for the Maya to imbue these vessels with "additives of prestige." These additives include such features as being painted with the name/titles of the vessel's patron/owner and being a finely painted artwork. The most important additive, however, is painting style, which allowed a vessel to be an outward sign of social identity and political connections when used in a social context.

Given the political complexity of the Classic period, it is not surprising that the Maya developed myriad pottery painting styles. Each is the unique expression of a group of socially related artists, their patrons, and other consumers of the pottery style. Although a painting style is easily recognizable, the attribution of the style to a particular area or archaeological site has been made possible only recently with the advent of chemical compositional analysis through instrumental neutron activation. This is the work of the Maya Polychrome Ceramics Project (MPCP), Conservation Analytical Laboratory (CAL), Smithsonian Institution (project archaeologist is Ronald L. Bishop, chief research scientist at CAL). With the active participation of many INAH archaeologists (especially those at the Centro INAH Yucatán and Centro INAH Campeche, as well as the support of Alejandro Martínez, national coordinator of archaeology, INAH) and colleagues in Belize, Guatemala, Honduras, and El Salvador, the MPCP project has chemically sampled thousands of archaeologically excavated potsherds and hundreds of looted whole vessels (identified by their chemical sample number, e.g. MS 1688). By combining stylistic analyses of these vessels with the chemical composition of their ceramic pastes, it is possible to connect a painting style with a specific area or site.

Applying stylistic and chemical data to excavated pottery, it is possible to recognize "foreign" vessels in the archaeological record. These are the material remains of sociopolitical interaction between sites, and even between historical individuals, during the Classic period. The painted pottery, then, encompasses a unique source of sociopolitical information not necessarily recoverable in any other manner, revealing details about specific moments and actions that occurred twelve hundred years in the past.

For the pottery vessels to tell us their stories, however, we must know where they were found. That is, the vessel or shard must be excavated by trained archaeologists, not ripped from the ground by looters to be sold on the international art market. Looting destroys all information about context, including the site and the specific location (tomb, palace midden, etc.) where the ceramic object was found. Without this kind of contextual data, the pottery can only recount the barest of facts. And the world loses forever the rich details of Maya history embodied within these painted wares.

Ongoing collaborative research with archaeologists working at Calakmul, Mexico, demonstrates the contributions to be made by the painted pottery to our reconstruction of Maya history. These excavations by archaeologists William Folan (with ceramic analyses by María del R. Domínguez Carrasco, both of the Centro de Investigaciones Históricas y Sociales de la Universidad Autónoma de Campeche) and Ramón Carrasco V. (with ceramic analyses by Sylviane Boucher, both of the Centro INAH Yucatán) are discovering the major role played by Calakmul during the Classic period (Carrasco V. 1996; Folan 1988; Marcus 1973; Martin 1996b). As part of their ongoing projects, pottery excavated at Calakmul is being analyzed chemically and stylistically in conjunction with traditional forms of ceramic analysis. Below is a brief discussion of just one of the discoveries resulting from this interdisciplinary approach to archaeological ceramics.

Calakmul and Its Ceramics

Calakmul created its own local tradition of painted pottery. These local wares reflect general Campeche-region aesthetics and ceramic types, although the Calakmul pottery artists distinguished their products with specific stylistic features. The chemical analyses of these samples reveal them to be made from mixtures of local clays and tempering materials. Armed with an understanding of the typological, stylistic, and chemical characteristics of Calakmul-produced pottery, it is possible to identify "foreign" vessels in the corpus of excavated ceramics from Calakmul. Some were made in the vicinity of Becán, others near Río Azul, Guatemala. The most surprising finds, however, are the vessels painted in codex style.

Codex-style pottery is unique in its highly restricted distribution in the Mirador Basin of northern Guatemala where this pottery was made (Hansen 1991; Reents and Bishop 1987; Reents-Budet, Martin, Hansen, and Bishop 1997). Generally speaking, codex-style pottery seems not to have functioned as "social currency" in the realm of ritual gift giving among sites and polities. Instead, it seemingly served specific ritual functions pertaining to the Classic period ideology of the Mirador Basin as a sacred place of origin.

Roll out of a vessel depicting
a meeting between
the lords of Tikal and Topoxté
Private collection

Vessel representing
a group of warriors standing guard
over their prisoner
Private collection

Roll out of a vessel depicting
a ball game
Private collection

Interestingly, unlike other styles of painted pottery, codex-style vessels are painted almost exclusively with mythological scenes, some of which probably make reference to the ideological myths associated with the Mirador Basin. Given the highly restricted distribution of codex-style pottery within the Mirador Basin, the excavation of a number of codex-style vessels at Calakmul is especially meaningful. All have been found in tombs located in the site's main pyramids, which suggests these are the burials of members of the site's ruling family or families. The paste chemistry of the sampled codex-style vessels indicates they were made at the site of Nakbé in the Mirador Basin. Two of these codex–style vessels include in their hieroglyphic texts the names of two Late Classic period Calakmul kings (R. Carrasco V. 1996; S. Martin 1997: personal communica-

tion). Interestingly, among the locally produced pottery from Calakmul are a few whose painting recalls codex-style pottery. These suggest that some Calakmul pottery artisans were creating imitation codex-style vessels in response to the important roles it played on the sociopolitical stage of this authoritative polity.

The codex-style pottery excavated at Calakmul, the presence of the snake head emblem glyph on other codex-style vessels, and the codex-style "Dynastic Sequence" vases combine to suggest a Classic period link between the Mirador Basin and Calakmul. The hieroglyphic texts painted on the Dynastic Sequence vases represent a very ancient king list that shares the emblem glyph and personal names with some of the Classic period rulers of Calakmul.

Roll out of a vessel depicting
a dancer
Private collection

Roll out of a vessel depicting
a scene interpreted as rendering
a marriage negotiation
Private collection

Codex-type 'Dynastic Sequence' vessel from Calakmul
Private collection

These create a bridge between a mythological or legendary dynastic past associated with the Mirador Basin and the historical Late Classic dynastic present at Calakmul. Together, these data imply that the Classic period divine *ahau* of Calakmul were laying claim to the Mirador Basin and its mythological power. By so doing, the Calakmul rulers were augmenting their own power through a perceived connection with the ancient and mythological traditions of the Mirador Basin (Reents-Budet, Martin, Hansen, and Bishop 1997). Classic Maya painted pottery comprises an incredibly rich source of cultural information. These painted works inform us about the artists who made them, their social positions and personal identities, and even about the artists' mythological connotations. The Primary Standard Sequence hieroglyphic texts painted on many vessels convey singular information about vessel function and contents, the identity of the patrons-owners of these objects, and the nature of Classic period artistic production. The vessels' pictorial images record unique historical events, the accompanying glyphic texts identifying the many participants whose names are found nowhere else in the archaeological record. These painted images also depict religious scenes, revealing specific aspects of the mythological and ideological beliefs underlying Maya culture. When properly excavated and recorded by archaeologists and art

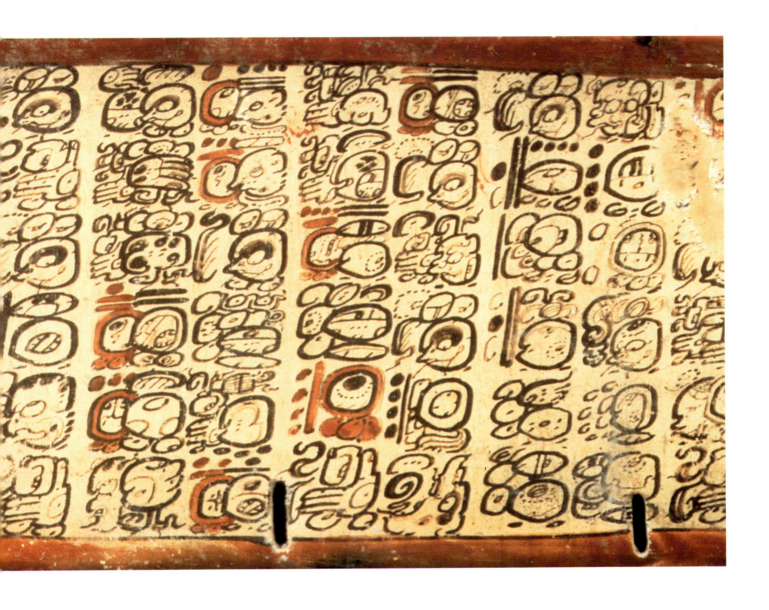

historians, and when analyzed from many different perspectives, these painted ceramic vessels have much to recount concerning their Classic Maya creators and consumers. These painted vessels are witnesses of the ebb and flow of power relationships among the ruling elite of the Classic Maya. They live on as the surviving shadows of long-past human aesthetics, ideology, and history.

References

CARRASCO V., RAMÓN
1996
    Calakmul: Proyecto Arqueológico de la Biosfera de Calakmul. Subproyectos y estudios especiales. Vol. II. Mérida, Centro Regional de Yucatán, INAH

COE, MICHAEL
1973
    The Maya Scribe and His World. New York: Grolier Club
1977
    "Supernatural Patrons of Maya Scribes and Artists." In *Social Process in Maya Prehistory: Studies in Honour of Sir Eric Thompson.* Ed. by N. Hammond. London: Academic Press, 327–47
1978
    Lords of the Underworld: Masterpieces of Classic Maya Ceramics. Princeton, N.J.: The Art Museum, Princeton University Press

FOLAN, WILLIAM
1988
    "Calakmul, Campeche: el nacimiento de la tradi-

Codex-type cylindrical vessel
Calakmul, Campeche
Late Classic period, Mexico City
Museo Nacional de Antropología
cat. 448

ción clásica en Mesoamérica." *Información*, 13. Campeche, 122–90

HANSEN, RICHARD
1991
"Resultados preliminares de las investigaciones arqueológicas en el sitio Nakbé, Petén, Guatemala." In II *Simposio sobre Investigaciones Arqueológicas de Guatemala*. Ed. by S. Villagrán de Brady, H. Escobedo, H. Guerra de González, J.P. Laporte, J.A. Valdés. Guatemala: Museo Nacional de Arqueología y Etnología, 160–74
1993
"Investigaciones de sitio arqueológico Nakbé: temporada 1989."In III *Simposio sobre Investigaciones Arqueológicas de Guatemala*. Ed. by J.P. Laporte, H. Escobedo, and S. Villagrán de Brady. Guatemala: Museo Nacional de Arqueología y Etnología, 57–77

HOUSTON, STEPHEN, AND KARL A. TAUBE
1987
"Name-Tagging in Classic Mayan Script." *Mexicon* 9, 2. Berlin

HOUSTON, STEPHEN, DAVID STUART, AND KARL A. TAUBE
1989
"Folk Classification of Classic Maya Pottery." *American Anthropologist*, 91, 3. Washington, D.C., 720–26

KERR, JUSTIN
1997
The Maya Vase Book. Vol. 5. New York: Kerr Associates

KERR, BARBARA, AND JUSTIN KERR
1981
"Some Observations on Maya Vase Painters." Paper presented at the Conference on Maya Funerary Ceramics. Princeton, N.J.: The Art Museum, Princeton University

MARCUS, JOYCE
1973
"Territorial Organization of the Lowland Classic Maya." *Science*, 180, 911–16

MARTIN, SIMON
1996a
"Calakmul y el enigma del glifo Cabeza de Serpiente." *Arqueología Mexicana*, 3, 18. Mexico: INAH, 42–45
1996b
"Calakmul en el Registro Epigráfico." In *Calakmul: Proyecto Arqueológico de la Biosfera de Calakmul. Subproyectos y estudios especiales*. Vol. II. Ed. by R. Carrasco V. *et. al.* Mérida: Centro INAH, 63–113
1997
"The Painted King List: A Commentary on Codex-style Dynastic Vases." In *The Maya Vase Book*. Vol. 5. Ed. by J. Kerr. New York: Kerr Associates, 846–67

MARTIN, SIMON, AND NIKOLAI GRUBE
1995
"Maya Superstates." *Archaeology*, 48, 6, 41–46

MATHEWS, PETER
1979
"Notes on the Inscriptions of Site Q. Manuscript on file." Department of Anthropology. Alberta, Canada: University of Calgary

REENTS, DORIE, AND RONALD L. BISHOP
1987
"The Late Classic Codex Style Polychrome Pottery" In *Memorias del Primer Coloquio Internacional de Mayistas*. Mexico City: UNAM, 775–90

REENTS-BUDET, DORIE
[In press]
"Elite Maya Pottery and Artisans as Social Indicators." In *Craft and Social Identity*. Ed. by C. Lynne Costin and R.P. Wright. Washington, D.C.: Archaeological Papers of the American Anthropological Association

REENTS-BUDET, DORIE, JOSEPH W. BALL, RONALD L. BISHOP, VIRGINIA M. FIELDS, AND BARBARA MACLEOD
1994
Painting the Maya Universe: Royal Ceramics of the Classic Period. Durham, N.C., and London: Duke University Press

REENTS-BUDET, DORIE, SIMON MARTIN, RICHARD HANSEN, AND RONALD L. BISHOP
[In press]
"Codex-style Pottery: Recovering Context and Meaning." Paper presented at the 21st Annual Maya Hieroglyphic Workshop. Austin: University of Texas

ROBICSEK, FRANCIS, AND DONALD HALES
1981
The Maya Book of the Dead: The Ceramic Codex. Charlottesville, Va: University of Virginia Art Museum

STUART, DAVID
1987
"Ten Phonetic Syllables." *Research Reports on Ancient Maya Writing*, 14. Washington, D.C.: Center for Maya Research

TAUBE, KARL ANDREAS
1985
"The Classic Maya Maize God: A Reappraisal." In *Fifth Palenque Round Table, 1983*. Ed. by V. Fields. San Francisco: Pre-Columbian Research Institute, 171–82

TEDLOCK, DENNIS
1996
Popol Vuh. The Definitive Edition of the Mayan Book of the Dawn of Life and the Glories of Gods and Kings. Second edition. New York: Simon and Schuster

Detail of the Bonampak murals

Realism in ancient Mesoamerican sculpture and murals appears at its finest in the Usumacinta drainage region of Chiapas, Mexico. Excellence in stucco sculpture at Palenque can be favorably compared to any old-world sculpture of its type, and the murals of Bonampak are the finest in all of Mesoamerica. During the seventh and eighth century, known of as the Late Classic, the Usumacinta cities, namely Palenque, Yaxchilán, and Piedras Negras were at their peak of importance in the Maya realm. They not only traded wares, but exchanged marriage partners between cities a great distance away.

Palenque was ruled by one king, Pacal the Great and his sons Chan Bahlum and Kan Xul Hok, all of the seventh century and into the eighth. The role of kingship was bestowed upon Pacal in A.D. 615, when he was twelve years old by his mother Lady Zac Kuk, and he was to rule until A.D. 683, when he has then reached the almost unprecedented age, for those days, of 80 years. His son Chan Bahlum, who probably should be credited with much of the building and sculptural activity of the city, ruled for eighteen years after him. Then for nine years his younger brother Kan Xul Hok continued with the Palenque building program until he was captured by warriors of the nearby city of Toniná in A.D. 711. Pacal's mother was not the first woman ruler of the city.

Lady Kanal Ikal, of the same lineage ruled the dynasty for twenty-one years. She must have been a powerful personage indeed to have been able to govern a kingdom successfully for such an extensive period of time, a time immediately preceding the decline of the Maya in the Petén, Guatemala. Lady Kanal Ikal and Pacal's mother, Lady Zac Kuk, became queens because they were the daughters of kings when there were no eligible males. When Lady Zac Kuk turned the rule over to her son, the ruling lineage changed from that of the Ikal lineage to the dynasty of Pacal.

House E, the first structure built on the upper terrace of what was to become the Palace at Palenque, was built by Lady Kanal Ikal, thus the Ik glyph-alike openings appear in the walls of this building, as well as all later buildings at Palenque. In the western corridor of this building, there is a dais which served as the accession throne of Pacal as well as all other kings following him.

A stone plaque, known as the Oval Palace Tablet, depicts the accession of the young king Pacal seated lotus fashion on a double-headed jaguar throne, giving the hand-raised-in-front-of-the-chest gesture, a gesture of acknowledgment. He is simply attired in a short kilt, beaded belt and loincloth, and jade wristlets and anklets. His mother, elaborately attired in beaded cape and a skirt of long and short beads, the "Maize Goddess" costume, hereby assumes the role of this goddess. She hands over the "drum major" headdress of rulership to the newly installed king, thereby performing the unprecedented act of bestowing the power of kingship by a living monarch. The art on the western face of this early structure is unlike anything in the Maya realm. Painted white and embellished with rows of four-petal flowers and small stylized insects, birds, and animals, this wall must have been commissioned to a codex (bark paper book) artist. It is not a mural, but more a wall painting. Even at this early date, realism of flowers was adhered to, just as realism in portraiture was to follow shortly. Although the Maya did not know that the stamen were "male" and the stigma were "female" elements of the flower, they did attribute duality to all living things. The paired extensions of the four-petal flowers on this wall are all shown,

The Temple of the Inscriptions at Palenque, Chiapas, Mexico

Reconstruction drawing
of the Oval Palace Tablet
Palenque

and these artists would have known that these go into the heart of the flower (the ovary). This building has a very special function involving the underworld, as indicated by its iconography. It is the entrance to the underworld. Deer are known to have played an important role in the underworld and in sacrifices. They are shown both on the exterior painted wall and sculptured in the vault of the subterranean passage. Giant underwater fish take up an entire wall space, and in the same room a giant serpent head mural frames the northern doorway. This serpent-framed entrance to the underworld is the most often repeated theme at Palenque, not only in mural painting, but in stone sculpture and stone bas-relief sculpture, as on the sarcophagus cover in the crypt of the Temple of the Inscriptions.

The Temple of the Inscriptions was built by Pacal as his own memorial. The 4 x 9 meter cross-vaulted crypt, the most spectacular ever uncovered in all of Mesoamerica, was built first. A monolithic slab of limestone 374 x 220 centimeters, quarried from the mountain behind the temple, serves as the sarcophagus cover. The temple was then constructed on top of the crypt, incorporating a complicated engineering system of corbel-vaulting for a stairway going all the way to the temple floor above. Nine Maya lords dressed in splendid attire are modeled in stucco against the sides of the crypt. These magnificent figures, once painted in reds, blue-greens, and yellows, stand out almost in three-dimensional form, an accomplishment that would have demanded the most exacting ability of stucco sculpture, taking into account the space in which they were sculptured.

Reconstruction drawing
of the western wall of House E
was covered with floral motifs
Palenque

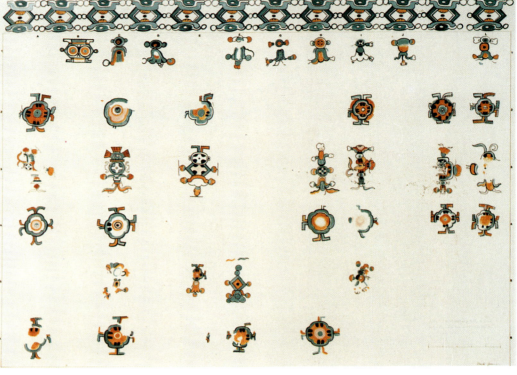

Realistic and botanical parts
of flowers were well-known
to the Maya
from the murals of Palenque

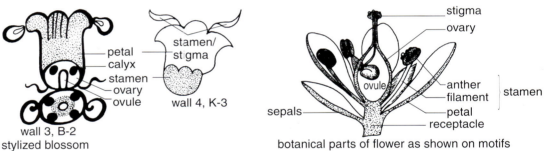

The Maya belief system of "three worlds," the underworld, the living world, and the Heavens is spelled out in bas-relief carving on the sarcophagus cover. Pacal is shown in reclining position, falling into the other world between the wide-open jaws of a serpent, the same event that is happening in House E of the Palace. He here assumes the role of God K, a principal god of rulership at Palenque, as indicated by his hairstyle of pompadour cut with the flair issuing from his forehead. He also wears the beaded skirt of the Maize God, thereby assuring that, at death, he becomes both God K and the Maize God. The World Tree, the *ceiba* (sacred tree of the Maya), rises behind him to the heavens above, where the celestial bird is perched. A double-headed undulating serpent with wide-open jaws wraps itself around the tree, forming a cross.

The open jaws on the left (west) contain the head of God K, while the jaws of the serpent head on the right (east) display the jester god, another principal god of Palenque. The sarcophagus itself has beautifully carved portraits of seven ancestors of Pacal, two each of his mother and father, and two of his great grandmother, the famous Lady Kanal Ikal, the dynamic woman who held power over a dynasty of men. As no one had entered the ancient tomb until Alberto Ruz, the Mexican archaeologist who discovered it in 1952, the original red and black cursive cartoons, indicating where carving was to be made, can still be seen in areas where the sculptor did not accurately follow the directive lines. The stucco sculptured piers flanking the front of this temple, depicting royal personages holding a child (Chan Bahlum) in their arms, are formed almost in the round. Armatures of narrow flat stones act-

Lady Zac Kuk, mother of Pacal
from a relief at Palenque

on the right
The piers of the Temple
of Inscriptions have sculptured
figures holding Chan Bahlum
as the serpent-footed God K

opposite
The sarcophagus lid
in the Temple of the Inscriptions
crypt at Palenque

ed as bones for the limbs, while thin larger slabs were used on chest and stomach areas. Wet plaster was formed on top of these armatures, resulting in very realistic portraits of well developed, sturdy individuals. These figures were all painted in reds, blues, and yellows. In applying color, every change of color required a change of plane. Palenque sculpture is linear in style, even when it acquires a three-dimensional quality. The outline requires the eye to follow the form, and cannot be detached from it.

George Kubler points out that "iconography is spatial and visual," and that "it conveys conventional or agreed meanings." Palenque's iconographic sculpture was the visual content of the spoken word. Color, through the medium of stucco sculpture, developed into an iconographic language. Painted stucco sculpture was not just a work of art, but it was a speaking work of art, one bound by a rigid framework of specifications.

Background areas of piers, buildings, both inside and out, bodies of humans, including their hair and major portions of their clothing, and human like parts of serpent bodies were all painted red, albeit different shades. Red was the color of the living world. Blue was designated the color of things divine, motifs pertaining to the rights of kings, to things precious, such as jade and quetzal feathers, divine beings, such as serpent-footed babies (God K), and dwarfs. Yellow was reserved for motifs pertaining to the underworld such as jaguar tails, crosshatched areas, underwater plants, and the portions of serpents (dead scales). Sculpture on the piers of House D of the palace was even more three-dimensional than on the Temple of the Inscriptions. Pacal's portrait on Pier D is a fine example. Every detail of his face stands out beautifully modeled. The "personified tree" in his hair ornament holds a completely three-dimensional flower. His belt and buckle function the same as do our belts today.

His powerful chest is exactly what would be expected for a person with a debilitating club foot, a deformity well documented for Pacal on his sarcophagus cover, as well as on other stucco and stone sculpture. Pier B, of this same building portrays the First Pacal, with an even more severe form of club foot than that of Pacal the Great. The measurements of the leg and foot on both of these depictions are typical of the wasting of a limb of restricted use. Portraits appear indicating other physical deformities in the ruling lineage of Palenque as well. Chan Bahlum, son of Pacal, and ruler after him, is shown more than once with poly-

Pacal's portrait of the Palace
Palenque

Chan Bahlum has six fingers
on his right hand
Palenque

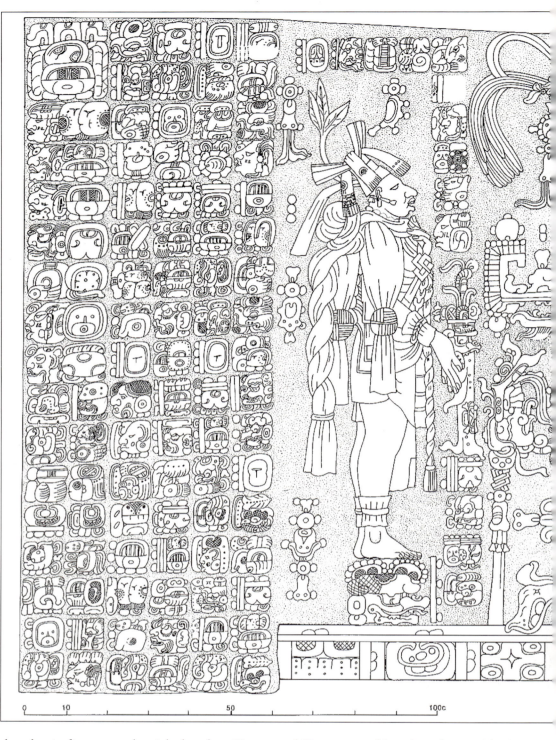

dactyly, six fingers on the right hand on Pier D, and House A, and in other places with six toes on one foot, notably on the figures of children held in arms on the piers of the Temple of the Inscriptions. Pacal's mother apparently had acromegaly (a rare clinical syndrome in which a tumorous enlargement of the pituitary gland at the base of the brain causes an abnormally enlarged and elongated jaw, the mouth to hang open, a broad nose, puffy eyes, and bulbous fingers). The progression of this disease can be traced on the Oval Palace Tablet, to her portrait on House A of the palace, and to her death portrait in the sarcophagus of her son Pacal. Dwarfism and hunchback shows up on the sculpture of House E, both in stucco sculpture and mural painting.

The low relief carved stone tablets in the sanctuaries of the Cross Group temples, the Temple of the Cross, the Temple of the Sun, and the Temple of the Foliated Cross, built by Chan Bahlum when he was forty-nine years old, are unique as to size and the complicated hieroglyphic information concerning the purpose of each temple, as well as the roll of the three Palenque Triad Gods GI, GII, and GIII, and the dynastic history of the kings and their legitimate right to rulership. Unlike any other group of buildings in the entire Maya realm, these three temples play the role of a Maya codex (bark paper book) in three

Reconstruction drawing
of the sanctuary tablet
from the Temple of the Cross

parts. History, both real and mythical, is recorded, and it unfolds like the pages of a book from temple to temple. Taking into account the order in which the gods were born, the first built temple would have been the Temple of the Cross, whose patron god is GI, then the Temple of the Sun, whose patron is GIII, and finally the Temple of the Foliated Cross with GII its patron god. The story of the Triad Gods, or more accurately, two of them, GI and GIII, the Hero Twins, plays an important role in the sacred book of the Quiche Maya, the *Popol Vuh*.

Sculpture and mural painting were designed for both public space and for private space. The stucco sculptured piers on all of the buildings were designed for public space, where all could see them and be let known that they must bear allegiance to the king. These brilliantly painted sculptures, set against red painted buildings, would certainly have been arresting to the eye of the beholder. To be sure that the whole figure was visible at a great distance, as well as close up, the figures were elevated on a platform consisting of either a huge mask or an underwater band at the bottom.

Likewise, vividly painted roofs and roof combs displaying giant masks on early buildings and seated rulers on thrones on later buildings would have impressed, as well as amazed,

Temple 33 at Yaxchilán, Chiapas

emissaries and merchants coming from foreign cities. Splendid and overpowering public art not only was a reminder to everyone that the king was to be obeyed and honored, but that he was to be recognized as a living god. It also served a political purpose by displaying the splendor of a city whose powerful reigning lord was able to command the finest artists and sculptors known to build a capital unprecedented in beauty, a political boast, in other words.

Private space would have been for the elite and designated persons, and would have included the sanctuary tablets within temples, subterranean chambers with their beautiful stucco sculptured figures of realistic animals, as well as gods, the crypt of Pacal with its brilliant painted sculpture on the walls, and the rooms of House E, where only a privileged few would have been allowed to take part in, or even watch, the coronation of a king. Stone, as well as stucco sculpture at the Usumacinta river city of Yaxchilán, is likewise oriented toward both public and private space. The finest carved stone lintels in all the Maya realm are found at Yaxchilán.

Lintels 24, 25, and 26 from Structure 23 (now in the British Museum, London), with their deeply cut background, allowing the magnificently detailed figures to stand out in bold relief, are the most elegant carved lintels known. The delicately carved details of the patterns of the gauze clothing of the women is amazing, knowing that the Maya only had stone tools for carving. It is from these lintels that we know these people were capable of weaving such intricate designs and flowers into thin (probably white), gauze like cloth, if we are to take into account the depictions shown on the Bonampak murals.

Carolyn Tate has been able to show how one can detect the hands of different sculptors on these lintels, especially by noting the differences in cutting and forming hands and nails, as well as the treatment of fabrics and glyphs. These, as well as many other lintels from Yaxchilán, tell us a great deal about their belief system, of the supernatural, of their rituals, and their kings. Autosacrifice is portrayed on many of the lintels, notably Lintels 15, 17, 24, and 25, showing women pulling a thorn-embedded rope through their tongues on Lintels 17 and 25, a male about to perform genital perforation on Lintel 17, and the blood basket, as well as the hallucinogenic trance imagery in serpent form with wide-open jaws on Lintels 15, 17, 24, and 25.

Not actually depicting an act of blood sacrifice, Lintels 1, 5, 7, 32, 53, and 54 show women holding a bundle that contains the self-sacrifice paraphernalia. All of the lintels are carved on the underside of low doorways, openings in the approximately 90 centimeter thick walls. As the small inner rooms of the Yaxchilán structures would have been only open to the elite, this suggests that the lintels were carved for only a privileged few to view, and were not public art. However, in order to see them at all, one must bend over backward or lie on ones back in the doorway. The hypothesis then, is that these lintels were not even carved for human viewing, but were carved to appease or honor the gods. Public art at Yaxchilán is noted by its many stelae, often prominently standing at the base of a high stairway leading to a temple, portraying Yaxchilán's notorious kings Shield Jaguar and

Reconstruction drawing
of the Temple of the Sun at Palenque
by Merle Greene Robertson

on the right
The Temple of the Sun at Palenque

Reconstruction drawing
of the Lintel 25 at Yaxchilán

Bird Jaguar, and hieroglyphic texts telling of the wars won and great accomplishments of the kings of Yaxchilán.

Public art is shown by the many sculptures in the round of rulers or other elite personages seated on thrones in large niches in roofs and roof combs of the buildings, as is also noted at Piedras Negras, further down the Usumacinta River. Although there were murals inside buildings at Yaxchilán, very little of the paint remains. Structure 40, on the South Acropolis, has remnants of polychrome paint on all of the walls and vaults. On one wall there are remains of a beautiful profile of a human head wearing a face mask. Besides this, there are just patches of red, black, yellow, orange, and blue paint, in some places indicating that human figures and floral patterns were once adorning the space. Remnants of a band of red and blue paint run horizontally across the front of this structure about a meter above the ground, suggesting that at least some structures were decorated in more than one color on the exterior. Probably here, as at Palenque, most buildings were painted red on the exterior.

The small but spectacular center of Bonampak is located just 26 kilometers from Yax-

Bonampak murals, Room 2
reconstruction drawing
by Antonio Tejada

chilán. This is the locale of the most splendid of all Maya murals, known worldwide as the Bonampak murals. These murals depict humans in a grand display of three rooms of pageantry taking place at the very end of the eighth century under the leadership of Chaan Muan. All of the rituals, so important in the life of the Maya heir apparent ceremony–war waged and won, sacrifice performed, and celebration event–are displayed on the magnificent Bonampak murals. More than any other Mesoamerican city, the murals contain not just a few individuals, but 126 persons from every walk of life, rulers, elite lords, women, children, nursemaids, dancers, musicians, merchants, scribes, attendants, sorcerers, god impersonaters, and slaves, as well as some probably performing tasks that we do not know existed. The costumes, especially the elegant headdresses worn by the figures in the murals, are the best source for determining what the Maya wore, and the instruments being played in the band procession give us clues to their world of music, and how events were celebrated.

The Bonampak murals are painted in registers, a lower register of processional scenes involving many standing persons: a narrower register at the vault overhang of seated figures (including the sacrificial victims of Room 2); a vault register of approximately the same height as the first, or Bench register (and here the figures are also all standing, except for the throne scene where the young heir is being presented on the west wall of Room 1 and on the east wall of Room 3); and finally, the top vault register of supernatural monster heads and cartouches containing human figures in various seated and gesticulating positions, and others with animals and turtles.

Probably the best known portion of these murals being depicted, is the battle scene of sacrifice and humiliation in Room 2, where at least a hundred figures participate. As described by Mary Ellen Miller, the scene is "rich and sensuous" with both "public sacrifice and private sacrifice of nobility." She also brings to our attention what is probably the most overpowering aspect of the Bonampak murals: its "dramatic rendering of Maya architecture," the way it "wraps around the viewer" and "creates three-dimensional volume on a flat

Detail from the Bonampak murals
Room 2

plane." It is hard to believe that this small structure, where such dramatic paintings completely cover the entire interior, recalling the story of an heir apparency celebration, a battle fought, won, and celebrated, and a celebration of events having taken place, should be only for the elite to enjoy. It seems more likely that this extravagant accomplishment was more likely an "Oscar" won and that Structure 1 was the "movie house," where the entire population, not just the elite, came, a few at a time, to witness, as well as enjoy again and again, this wonderful event that took place in their community.

References

GREENE, MERLE, ROBERT L. RANDS, AND JOHN A. GRAHAM
1972
Maya Sculpture from the Southern Lowlands, Highlands and Pacific Piedmont. Berkeley: Lederer Street & Zeus

KUBLER, GEORGE
1969
Studies in Classic Maya Iconography. Memoirs of the Connecticut Academy of Arts & Sciences, Vol. XVIII. New Haven

MILLER, MARY ELLEN
1986
The Murals of Bonampak. Princeton: Princeton University Press

ROBERTSON, MERLE GREENE
1983
The Sculpture of Palenque. Vol. I: The Temple of the Inscriptions. Princeton: Princeton University Press
1985
The Sculpture of Palenque. Vol. II: The Early Buildings of the Palace and the Wall Paintings; Vol. III: The Late Buildings of the Palace. Princeton: Princeton University Press
1991
The Sculpture of Palenque. Vol. IV: The Cross Group, the North Group, the Olvidado, and Other Pieces. Princeton: Princeton University Press

SCHELE, LINDA, AND MARY ELLEN MILLER
1986
Blood of Kings: Dynasty and Ritual in Maya Art. Fort Worth: Kimbell Art Museum

TATE, CAROLYN
1992
Yaxchilán: The Design of a Maya Ceremonial Center. Austin: The University of Texas Press

Detail from the Bonampak murals
Room 2

plane." It is hard to believe that this small structure, where such dramatic paintings completely cover the entire interior, recalling the story of an heir apparency celebration, a battle fought, won, and celebrated, and a celebration of events having taken place, should be only for the elite to enjoy. It seems more likely that this extravagant accomplishment was more likely an "Oscar" won and that Structure 1 was the "movie house," where the entire population, not just the elite, came, a few at a time, to witness, as well as enjoy again and again, this wonderful event that took place in their community.

References

GREENE, MERLE, ROBERT L. RANDS, AND JOHN A. GRAHAM
1972
Maya Sculpture from the Southern Lowlands, Highlands and Pacific Piedmont. Berkeley: Lederer Street & Zeus

KUBLER, GEORGE
1969
Studies in Classic Maya Iconography. Memoirs of the Connecticut Academy of Arts & Sciences, Vol. XVIII. New Haven

MILLER, MARY ELLEN
1986
The Murals of Bonampak. Princeton: Princeton University Press

ROBERTSON, MERLE GREENE
1983
The Sculpture of Palenque. Vol. I: The Temple of the Inscriptions. Princeton: Princeton University Press
1985
The Sculpture of Palenque. Vol. II: The Early Buildings of the Palace and the Wall Paintings; Vol. III: The Late Buildings of the Palace. Princeton: Princeton University Press
1991
The Sculpture of Palenque. Vol. IV: The Cross Group, the North Group, the Olvidado, and Other Pieces. Princeton: Princeton University Press

SCHELE, LINDA, AND MARY ELLEN MILLER
1986
Blood of Kings: Dynasty and Ritual in Maya Art. Fort Worth: Kimbell Art Museum

TATE, CAROLYN
1992
Yaxchilán: The Design of a Maya Ceremonial Center. Austin: The University of Texas Press

Zoila Rodríguez Girón
J. Héctor Paredes G.

The Highlands of Guatemala and Chiapas

The highlands of Guatemala and Chiapas may be differentiated from the Maya lowlands and coasts by their tremendous environmental diversity displaying dramatic changes and great ecological contrasts. Ranging from volcanic soils to elevated heights, its cones rise to more than 4,000 meters in height.

The mountainous soils of Chiapas and Guatemala constitute part of the Sierra Madre. There, deep valleys with rich forests are watered by abundant rivers, such as the Grijalva, which is born in the Chuchumatán; the Chixoy, which joins up with the Usumacinta in the lowlands; the Polochic, which once it originates in the Verapaz region empties into Lake Izabal and the Motagua River, which in turn drains into the Caribbean, among others.

Already in the sixteenth century, Fray Toribio de Motolinía, when referring to the highlands, said that it was very rugged terrain, with huge ravines, gorges, and many mountains with fine wood. He described fertile valleys and lowlands, where there were plentiful maize harvests. It was a land of abundant and pure waters.

The climate of the highlands is cooler than that of the coasts and the Maya zone. On the other hand, the enormous environmental variety has also produced variation in the inhabitants themselves, their customs, as well as their language.

During the pre-Hispanic era, both highland and Maya lowland regions shared common sociocultural elements with Mesoamerican cultures.

The first evidence of human activity in the highlands dates to the Pleistocene era, 20,000 years before the disappearance of mammoths and American horses. It consists entirely of lithic materials. Some of the most important evidence has been found in Los Tapiales and Chivacavé in Guatemala and in the cave of Santa Marta in central Chiapas. At the same time in the highlands, there was the industry of Amatenango and Chantuto in the tidelands.

The first inhabitants were hunters and gatherers of plants and small animals. Little by little, craft specialization appeared, so that by the year 1600 B.C. many Mesoamerican societies were adopting at the same time a more or less sedentary, agricultural way of life. They also participated in an important exchange network, moving goods over long and short distances.

Formative or Preclassic period (1800 B.C.–A.D. 100)
This period is characterized in Mesoamerica by the presence of sedentary groups familiar with agriculture, as well as lithic and ceramic technology. The first inhabitants settled on the banks of swamps and estuaries, where they subsisted on hunting and fishing combined with agriculture. With rudimentary architecture, they constructed their dwellings on earthen platforms. These early houses were cane and mud huts with palm or straw roofs. Some of them were oval in plan. Barra and Ocós-type ceramics copy plant motifs–gourds, squashes, and other forms–painted in a variety of colors: red, black, white, brown, and combinations thereof. Some of the pigments, such as specular hematite, constitute evidence of long-distance trade.

Between the years 850 and 400 B.C., Olmec culture of the Gulf Coast of Mexico influenced highland groups. This contact may be observed in ceramics made using different firing techniques, the appearance of figurines with baby faces, and other traits. Olmec society, which played a decisive role in the social development of Mesoamerica in general, had an impact on a number of locations in Chiapas. These include sites such as El Vergel, San Isidro, and Finca Acapulco, today under the waters of the Angostura and Chicoasén dams, as well as on the Tzutzuculi coast, Pijijiapan, and Ojo de Agua.

At Kaminaljuyú, located in the valley of Guatemala, high quality painted, grooved, incised ceramics were manufactured. Stone was also carved, and cultural traits were shared with Sacatepéquez, Chimaltenango, and locations in the Valley of San Jerónimo in Baja Verapaz, as well as on the Pacific coast at sites such as Izapa (Chiapas), Abaj Takalik (Guatemala), Chalchuapa in El Salvador, and Yoc in the Jataté, on the way to Lacandon territory.

The inhabitants of these sites lived in simple houses made of perishable materials associated with cultivated fields and with communal kitchen or food preparation areas. They used obsidian from the Motagua Valley and Chimaltenango for their implements. One of the

Urn
from El Quiché
Late Terminal Classic-Early
Postclassic period
opposite, detail
Guatemala, Museo Popol Vuh
cat. 378

Stirrup-type vessel
from Kaminaljuyú, Guatemala
Preclassic period
Guatemala, Museo Nacional
de Arqueología y Etnología
cat. 25

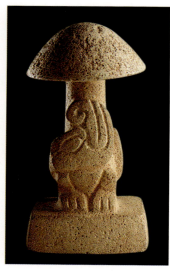

Mushroom
with a stylized animal effigy
from Kaminaljuyú, Guatemala
Preclassic period
Guatemala, Museo Nacional
de Arqueología y Etnología
cat. 305

opposite
Effigy vessel with lid
from Guajilar, Chiapas
Late Classic period
Tuxtla Gutiérrez
Museo Regional de Chiapas
cat. 486

most outstanding traits of this period was the manufacture of modeled clay figurines representing both human beings and animals. These were probably used as propitiatory offerings for abundant harvests and they were associated with religious beliefs.

Perhaps in the beginning they worshiped natural phenomena. The presence of ceremonial centers is evident in the form of small temples built on earthen platforms. On the other hand, the appearance of incense burners and elaborate burials of prominent individuals in the community suggests an already elaborated ceremonialism.

Archaeological research at the site indicates that it functioned as a commercial and cultural nucleus during this period, due to its strategic location. Both ritual as well as domestic objects display a wide variety of styles testifying to this role. The presence of Maya lowland culture is obvious in the form of several sculptural monuments with carved inscriptions.

Architecture also displayed notable development at the end of the Formative period. Civic and ritual monuments were arranged around plazas. Residential zones, causeways, and so forth were also built. There is evidence that agricultural fields of the Valley of Guatemala were artificially irrigated by way of strategically constructed canal systems at the site.

Around the year 100 A.D. there were changes on the level of interregional relations between the highlands and other Mesoamerican areas. Writing in the form of inscriptions on several of the stone monuments of the area did not continue its development, but rather ceased entirely, never to appear again. The custom of making modeled figurines was also abandoned.

Other centers arose in the highlands, such as Zaculeu in Huehuetenango, Zacualpa, La Lagunita and Nebaj in Quiché. In Chiapas, Chinkultic begins and corridors are established across the Chuchumatán and the rivers that flow toward the lowlands of the north.

The Classic period (A.D. 100–900)

The highlands of Chiapas witnessed the entrance of Maya groups from the lowlands. They settled there perhaps between the years A.D. 100 to 300, and they went on to develop their particular culture in the following periods. During this time, Maya groups established themselves in open valleys, close to sources of abundant water, but not in very good agricultural lands. Common housing consisted of low platforms and rooms of perishable materials. Ruling groups built very complex constructions.

Disk from Chinkultic, Chiapas
Late Classic period
opposite, detail
Mexico City
Museo Nacional de Antropología
cat. 364

The governing centers had one or more pyramids dedicated to civic-religious ceremonies. Their leaders were buried on the interior of these pyramids, where they were accompanied by rich offerings, generally ceramic vessels and jade objects brought from the middle Motagua River basin, Quiriguá in neighboring Guatemala, and Copán in Honduras.

For this period, the Guatemalan highlands were densely populated. Adobe was used as a construction material and some of the buildings showed a new type of construction: the *talud* (a sloping base) and *tablero* (a rectangular panel resting on the base) covered with stucco. The latter architectural profile has been related to contact with sites in the Mexican central highlands.

Ceramics and lithics also offer evidence of this relation, with new forms added to those already known, including human effigy urns, *floreros* (vessels shaped like flower vases), *candeleros* (small double-chambered incense burners or lamps resembling candle-holders), the use of molds for small plaques called *adornos* to be applied to incense burners, green obsidian, and so forth. Major deities included Chaac (the rain god) and Ek Chuah (the merchant god), among others.

In the central highlands, patios developed in ball courts. In funerary architecture, rectangular tombs were constructed, roofed with wood, and often were placed intrusively in mounds. The floors of these tombs were covered with woven straw mats. Offerings consisted of sumptuary objects and sacrificial victims or animals.

In Nebaj, Quiché, stone slabs were used to cover mortuary chambers. Later, however, individuals were buried in precious funerary urns. It is believed the latter burials were for individuals of the community due to the lack of offerings and because they have been

Ball Court, Iximche

found outside the ceremonial center. In Chamá, Baja Verapaz, from the Early Classic period recumbent bodies were placed in tombs. Often a jade bead was placed in the mouth of the deceased. As may be seen, the funerary customs of the people varied from region to region. Sometimes the sepulchers were simple, constructed of slabs with one or two niches for offerings.

The years A.D. 700 to 1000 saw a period of expansion and the foundation of new sites. Lapidary art lost the artistic touch of the preceding period. In the southeastern highlands, it became crude and generally represents figures with arms crossed over the chest. There was a collection of more than 70 of these carvings in Chaculá, Huehuetenango. On the coasts of Guatemala and El Salvador, Nahuatl-speaking groups, such as the so-called Pipil, established themselves.

In Chiapas movements of non-Maya groups took place. For example, the Zoque occupied the western highlands, and the Chiapanecs established themselves next to the Grijalva River.

The Postclassic period (A.D. 1000–1200)

One of the characteristics of this period is the abandonment of some of the large ceremonial centers. Defensive sites in valleys and mountains are occupied and they offer their inhabitants safety. There were wars between groups, which brought about militarism and secularization.

Unlike Maya lowland centers, the majority of highland sites did not collapse until A.D. 900. Rather, they displayed continuous occupation until the Postclassic or Protohistoric period. By the year A.D. 1000, a new social system appeared in the highlands of Chiapas. Centers were constructed combining systems of terraces with points in the landscape suggesting a search for a religious answer, in places such as Santo Ton, Hunchavin, and Tenam Puente, among others.

In Guatemala something similar occurred in the Chuchumatán highlands (San Mateo Ixtatán) and the Chamá Sierra. The population becomes concentrated. The construction pattern varies from that of the Classic period; now buildings are made of assembled carved stone. Distribution may be linear or irregular, forming small habitational groups without any apparent order. The burial system varies completely. Cremation is the most common form of mortuary practice with the placement of ashes in urns, accompanied by copper objects (rings) or small sheets of gold.

In Guatemala some sites constituted urban political units that developed in this period and remained occupied until the Spanish conquest.

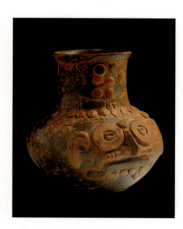

Effigy vessel
representing Tlaloc, the god of rain
from La Lagunita, Quiché
Early Postclassic period
Guatemala, Museo Nacional
de Arqueología y Etnología
cat. 387

Stela 9 from Kaminaljuyú
Middle Preclassic period
Guatemala, Museo Nacional
de Arqueología y Etnología
cat. 309

Tetrapod urn
from Nebaj, Quiché
Late Classic period
Guatemala, Museo Nacional
de Arqueología y Etnología
cat. 48

Cylindrical urn
representing a human face
from Quiché, Guatemala
Late Classic period
opposite, detail
Guatemala, Museo Nacional
de Arqueología y Etnología
cat. 511

These include Zaculeu, Mixco Viejo, Kumarcaaj, Iximche, Chuitinamit, Tzamaneb, and Chuitixtiox. In the highlands of Chiapas, little is known of the period, although sites include Viejo Chamula, Cuajilor, and Las Margaritas, on the border with Guatemala.

The production of salt mines in Chiapas and Guatemala allows for the continuation from centers of the preceding period, such as San Mateo Ixtatán, Sacapulas, and Ixtapa.

Although all these peoples shared a similar ecosystem, they spoke different languages and perhaps also had different ways of seeing the world. This may be seen in indigenous texts, documents preserving the oral history of these people even though they were written years after the conquest.

The best-known of these books is the *Popol Vuh*, written in the middle of the sixteenth century. It was discovered by the Dominican Francisco Ximénes around 1701 in Chichicastenango, Quiché. The history of Cakchiquel speakers consists of *El Memorial de Sololá*, written in Iximche at the end of the sixteenth century. Another valuable work is the dance drama of *Rabinal Achí*, which narrates the shared histories of the Quiche and Rabinal peoples.

The ancestral culture of the highlands of Guatemala and Chiapas, today separated by an imaginary political line, has not ended. It continues to develop day after day, trying to defend its traditions and particular way of seeing and participating in the world.

References

BORHEGYI, STEPHAN DE *ET AL.*
1965
"Archaeological Synthesis of the Guatemalan Highlands." In *Handbook of Middle American Indians*. Ed. G. Willey. Vol. 2. Austin: University of Texas Press, 3–58

BRYANT, DOUGLAS DONNE *ET AL.*
1988
Archaeology, Ethnohistory and Ethnoarchaeology in the Maya Highlands of Chiapas, México. Provo, Utah: New World Archaeological Foundation, Brigham Young University

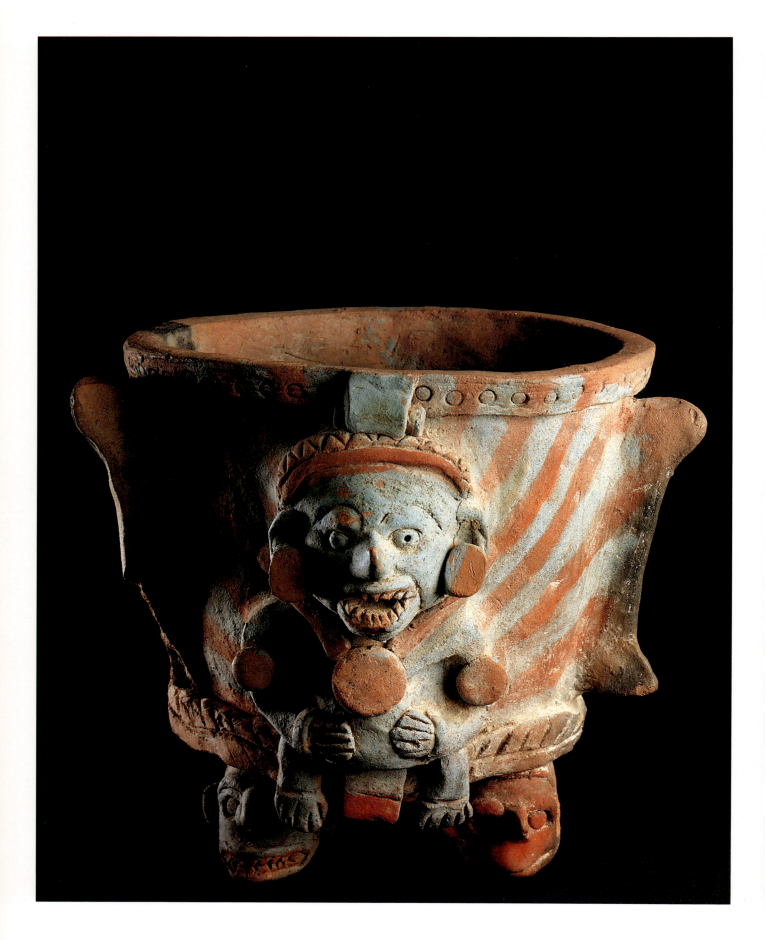

opposite
Bichrome tripod censer
from Nebaj, Quiché
Postclassic period
Guatemala, Museo Nacional
de Arqueología y Etnología
cat. 509

Temple Square of Iximche
Guatemala

CLARK, JOHN E.
1990
"La Fase Lato de la Cuenca Superior del Río Grijalva: indicaciones por el despliegue de la cultura Mokaya." In "Primer Foro de Arqueología de Chiapas." Chiapas: Tuxtla Gutiérrez, 107–10

ESPONDA, VÍCTOR MANUEL
1996
"Santo Ton, una fortaleza del Posclásico Temprano." In "Quinto Foro de Arqueología de Chiapas." Chiapas: Tuxtla Gutiérrez, 233–46

GUSSINYER, JORGE
1976
"Tercera Temporada de Salvamento Arqueológico en la Presa de la Angostura, Chiapas." INAH (Instituto Nacional de Antropología e Historia) *Boletín* época 7, tomo V, 1974–75. Mexico City, 63–84

KANEKO, AKIRA
1996
"Proyecto Hun Chavín, primera temporada, 1994." In "Quinto Foro de Arqueología de Chiapas." Chiapas: Tuxtla Gutiérrez

LALO J., GABRIEL, AND MARÍA DE LA LUZ AGUILAR
1996
"El Posclásico Temprano en Tenam Puente." In "Quinto Foro de Arqueología de Chiapas." Chiapas: Tuxtla Gutiérrez, 23–37

LEE, THOMAS A. (JR.)
1972
Jmetic Lubton: Some Modern and Pre-Hispanic Maya Ceremonial Customs in the Highlands of Chiapas, Mexico. Provo, Utah: New World Archaeological Foundation

LEE, THOMAS A., AND DOUGLAS DONNE BRYANT
1996
"Patrones domésticos del periodo Posclásico Tardío de la Cuenca Superior del Río Grijalva." In "Quinto Foro de Arqueología de Chiapas." Chiapas: Tuxtla Gutiérrez, 53–68

MANZANILLA, LINDA, AND LEONARDO LÓPEZ LUJÁN (EDS.)
1985
Historia Antigua de México. Vol. 3. *El Horizonte Posclásico y algunos aspectos intelectuales de las culturas Mesamericanas.* Mexico City: INAH

NAVARRETE, CARLOS
1979
Las esculturas de Chaculá, Huehuetenango, Guatemala. Mexico City: UNAM
1996
Piezas Maestras Mayas, Patrimonio del Museo Nacional de Arqueología y Etnología de Guatemala. Guatemala: Fundación G & T

PINCEMIN, SOPHIA
1990
"INAH y Prehistoria de Chiapas." In "Primer Foro de Arqueología de Chiapas." Chiapas: Tuxtla Gutiérrez, 21–27

RIVERA, MIGUEL, AND ANDRÉS CIUDAD (EDS.)
1995
Los Mayas de los Tiempos Tardíos. Madrid: Sociedad Española de Estudios Mayas, ICI

TEJADA B., MARIO
1990
"Historia de las investigaciones." In "Primer Foro de Arqueología de Chiapas." Chiapas: Tuxtla Gutiérrez, 51–61

WAUCHOPE, ROBERT
1970
"Protohistoric Pottery of the Highlands of Guatemala." In *Monographs and Papers in Maya Archaeology.* Cambridge, Mass.: Harvard University Press

Lintel 26 of Yaxchilán, Chiapas
detail representing
Lord Shield Jaguar
Late Classic Period
Mexico City, Museo Nacional
de Antropología
cat. 297

The hieroglyphic documents left to us from the Classic period make clear that Maya civilization was in no way "prehistoric"–a label that is still easily but erroneously used by some Mesoamerican scholars. Much to the contrary, the inscriptions that we can now read chronicle events and deeds associated with hundreds of rulers, noblemen, queens, and lesser court members who shaped Maya history over the course of five or more centuries. It is not my purpose in this essay to present an overview of that history, but rather to place the actors and events within its proper political setting. For whereas the Maya records are silent on so many issues about Classic society, it is clear that politics and power relations were central to much of what the Maya had to say and present about themselves.

We have come to a certain detailed understanding of Maya political life through the work of various scholars, but it was not until the late 1950s that the very existence of political history was seriously entertained by specialists in decipherment. Foremost among these was Tatiana Proskouriakoff, who published her groundbreaking studies of inscriptions at Piedras Negras and Yaxchilán between 1960 and 1964 (Proskouriakoff 1960). In these works she forcefully presented the seemingly simple and now obvious view that inscriptions and monumental art related information about historical people and the events of their lives.

In previous decades, most scholars denied that the records contained any such information, diverting their attention instead to the chronological and astronomical themes recognized far earlier in the nineteenth century. Over a stunningly short period Proskouriakoff revolutionized a field of study. In the decades since her publications first saw light, the details of political relations and dynastic histories have continued to be a focus of intensive study (Proskouriakoff 1992). What has emerged thus far is a picture of a political landscape that over the course of several centuries shifted its form, as individual kingdoms rose and fell away, formed alliances with more powerful polities, and engaged in wars of conquest.

In some general respects, the Classic situation is somewhat reminiscent of what the Spanish conquerors encountered during their protracted invasion of Yucatán in the mid-sixteenth century (Marcus 1993). The northern peninsula of that time was occupied by several million Maya peoples (ancestors of modern Yucatec speakers) whose population was divided among seventeen "provinces" of varying size and political and economic power.

Documents left to us by European and native scribes of this time have a good deal to say about the relations among these kingdoms of the contact period, the rulers who oversaw them, and sometimes the intrigues that underlay political relations of the late fifteenth and early sixteenth centuries.

One might be very tempted to look upon these political arrangements as vestiges of a far earlier time (Marcus 1993), but it would be foolhardy to see the state of affairs of Late Postclassic Yucatán as a dim but somehow authentic reflection of the Classic political landscape of many centuries before. Far too much distance exists in time and in place to be comfortable with linking these eras, not to mention the hugely disruptive if little understood events surrounding the "collapse" of Classic kingdoms in the eighth and ninth centuries (Demarest 1992).

There is, in fact, no need to rely on later ethnohistories, as archaeologists and historians so often must, for Classic documents in the Maya hieroglyphic script provide a more complete and wide-ranging body of source materials for the study of more ancient political organizations. With the new decipherments of the last few years, our understanding of Maya kingdoms and their centuries of evolution are now coming much more sharply into focus (Culbert 1991; Houston 1993; Stuart 1992, 1995; Martin and Grube 1995). This essay presents many of these latest finds, and reflects upon our current but ever-changing state of knowledge about Maya politics.

We may introduce the study of Maya politics with a discussion of "emblem glyphs," found throughout the historical inscriptions of the Classic period. In 1958 Heinrich Berlin isolated the existence of these distinctive site "emblems," which varied according to location and seemed therefore to be either place names or family names of some sort (Berlin 1958). Berlin identified emblems for Tikal, Ceibal, Copán, Quiriguá, Naranjo, Palenque, and several other major centers of the Classic political landscape.

Tikal

Palenque

Calakmul

Pomoná

Yaxchilán

Naranjo

Piedras Negras

Motul de
San José

Copán

Ceibal

Toniná

Glyphs of the major sites
of the Classic period

Decades later, it was found that the attached signs which served to mark emblems as a category spelled a certain honorific title, *Kul Ahau*, or "Holy Lord." With the specific emblem sign, the sense conveyed for these glyphs is "the Holy Palenque Lord," or "the Holy Tikal Lord," etc., a reading which agrees with the fact that these glyphs accompany or replace the proper names of high kings. The individual rulers portrayed on stelae and relief sculpture of this time are usually of this supreme and seemingly divine status. Tracing the distribution of emblems throughout the Maya area demonstrates that "Holy Lords" ruled territories throughout the lowland area. We are reasonably able to guess, furthermore, that a site with its own emblem and high ruler possessed a certain degree of autonomy in terms of political and social identity (Mathews 1991).

One might call these "city-states" or "polities," but these terms are either too precise or too general to be of much use. For the present, we can simply refer to these emblematic units simply as "kingdoms." At this writing, between thirty and forty such units have been recognized in the Classic documents. The ways in which these kingdoms vied for control of others, shifted alliance networks, and rose and fell over the centuries forms the backdrop for much of the current work by Mayanists to decipher political relations (Schele and Freidel 1990; W. Fash 1991; Martin and Grube 1995).

The past two decades have seen some lively debates among Mayanists over the nature of the relations among these kingdoms. Were they independent "peer" kingdoms that for centuries sparred among one another for political and economic power with few if any winners among them? Or, in another view, were some urban sites the capitals of large territorial hegemonies, spreading their control through the Maya region by means of outright military conquest and political coercion? Both models, although very simplistic as pictured here, have had their adherents over the past few decades. Rather than see these as exclusive ways of defining Maya politics of the Classic period, I feel it is perhaps more correct to see these categories as existing on two ends of a spectrum, with the "political reality" moving up and down the scale over both time and space.

To illustrate this point, let us look at the kingdoms of the western Maya lowlands, near what is now called the Usumacinta River. Several well-known and important sites existed in this region during the Classic period, chief among them being Palenque, Toniná, Yaxchilán, Piedras Negras, and Pomoná, among several others, no doubt. Records of these sites are extensive and provide for us a picture of several militant elite societies that often fought one another in battle. War captives are displayed throughout the sculpture of Yaxchilán and Toniná, for example, and in some instances we can infer from the histories that one site in fact "conquered" another.

Usually the evidence of a conquest comes in the form of a king or "Holy Lord" shown as a bound prisoner of another kingdom, in the way Kinich Hok Chitam (also known in the literature as Kan Xul) of Palenque appears as a captive in the art of nearby Toniná. This seems a clear indication that Toniná was victorious over Palenque in war, yet the implications of such a "victory" are quite impossible to know from the documents themselves.

In this way archaeological excavations become most important, for in the material record one may be able to witness political changes and disruptions quite easily. More excavations in this entire region are desperately needed, but at present we see little evidence that "conquest" of one site over another was a long-term prospect. Rather, when captives were taken from one kingdom by another, we may see a significant short-term disruption, but one from which the victim site seems to recover within a decade or two.

While surely warlike, I doubt that Maya kings were attempting to expand their territorial control over vast distances, absorbing neighboring kingdoms in their way. Rather, individual polities along the Usumacinta may have been targeted for a sort of "temporary" conquest, with the view toward tribute collection and the acquisition of labor forces for specific purposes, and only for relatively short amounts of time.

I feel this picture generally characterizes the nature of Maya warfare in the Classic period, but some glaring exceptions have recently emerged from the complementary research of Simon Martin and Nikolai Grube, in Europe, and Stephen Houston and the author, in the United States (Martin and Grube 1995; Houston 1993; Stuart 1995). Our

Lintel 3
of Piedras Negras, Petén
with a courtly scene
Late Classic period
Guatemala, Museo Nacional
de Arqueología y Etnología
cat. 294

investigations have centered in some degree on the vast Maya site of Calakmul, proba-bly one of the largest cities to have existed during the Late Classic period. As originally noted by the Mayanist Joyce Marcus some twenty years ago, the emblem of Calakmul is a snake's head, probably read *kan*, "snake," and is cited in the inscriptions of many oth-er sites, many of them quite distant. Martin and Grube have suggested that Calakmul may have been politically controlling these lesser centers, such as Dos Pilas, Cancuen, Naranjo, and El Perú.

Certainly there are indications of hierarchy in the histories recorded in these smaller sites, with the Calakmul king often cited as "overseeing" a certain ritual or even inauguration of a local lord at Cancuen or Naranjo, for example. At the site of Dos Pilas, located near the Río de la Pasión of Guatemala, the founding ruler is called the "lord" of the Calakmul high king, probably in the sense of a vassal or political subordinate of some sort. With this type of evidence, there is much to recommend Martin and Grube's view of Calakmul dominat-ing smaller centers of the central Petén region. The intent of such machinations seems to have been to create a ring of alliances or dominions around Tikal, Calakmul's rival through-out much of the Classic period. The details of these maneuverings elude us, however, lead-ing us to wonder just how the situation of Calakmul reflects a general pattern of Maya geopolitical organization.

Even so, the possible "control" by Calakmul over other centers should be qualified in two important ways. For one, we have no evidence that the secondary sites were "overseen" for any extended period of time. The Calakmul presence in the records of Dos Pilas, for exam-ple, is hardly overt, and lasts for about two generations.

Most important, however, we can see that all of the secondary sites retain their own politi-cal and community identities throughout this time, with monuments celebrating their own local rulers and histories. It presents a picture very different from that of the belligerent kingdoms of the Usumacinta region, who truly seem to have exerted total control over con-quered neighbors.

Even with these differences, we sense that individual kingdoms in the Maya lowlands existed in an unstable setting, with external connections constantly of a tenuous sort (Demarest 1992).

Monument 27 of Toniná, Chiapas
representing a prisoner
Late Classic period
Mexico City
Museo Nacional de Antropología
cat. 86

Whereas large kingdoms such as Calakmul and Tikal exerted considerable power due to sheer size, perhaps, they were like their smaller neighbors in having little long-term institutional structure beyond their own localized frontiers.

Secondary Centers

The nature of relations among Maya polities will no doubt continue to foster debate and discussion as the hieroglyphic evidence becomes carefully assessed and refined, yet another body of data that is of equal importance concerns the nature of political and social relations within polities. Rather than looking at larger political units as the units of analysis, investigations of interpolity organization focus on individuals and the subroyal offices or positions that sometimes associate with them.

Before the mid-1980s, it was largely assumed that rulers and their immediate families were the sole protagonists of the Classic inscriptions. A number of studies have emphasized in recent years that this is not at all the case (Stuart 1993, Houston 1993). Other nobles of varying ranks and functions are named and discussed in the documentary sources of the Classic period, and their relationships to the rulers reveal a number of interesting details about political organization and its apparent variation over time and space.

Perhaps the most important category of nonroyal elites went by the term *cahal* (Stuart 1993). These appear mainly in the records of the western Maya lowlands, at sites in the Usumacinta drainage such as Yaxchilán, Piedras Negras, Pomoná, and Palenque, although some isolated examples appear in the inscriptions of northern Campeche, mainly at Xcalumkin, and at Copán. The distribution is striking, for the regional emphasis of *cahal* reflects differences in how political organization was discussed by the Maya, if not actual differences in the political structures themselves.

In several interesting sculptures, *cahals* appear to be directly identified with *bacab* figures who support the earth and the supreme ruler. At Pomoná and La Pasadita, for example, *cahal* are explicitly named with the *bacab* or *pahuatun* glyph, and wear water blossom headdresses that are the distinctive costume elements of *bacabs* and other watery creatures of the underworld. It is quite likely that this was a cosmological metaphor for showing the hierarchical relationship between the ruler and his subordinates, emphasizing how these military captains and provincial governors were considered the supporters, literally, of the ruler. At the risk of overextending this metaphor, it would be very interesting to know if only four *cahal* could exist at any one time, corresponding to the four *bacabs* of Maya cosmology. Moreover, their own role as governors of satellite sites may have somehow reflected the same internal quadripartite division of polities that existed on a smaller scale among communities in Postclassic Yucatán.

Cahal are "owned" or "possessed" by high rulers, and when named often their superiors are specified. The protagonist of an inscription from Lacanhá, near Bonampak, for example, is named as a *cahal*, then as the *cahal* of the local king, Knot-eye Jaguar. The nature of the relationship between *cahals* and their overlords remains opaque, but their personalized nature is suggested by the fact that *cahal* at provincial sites near Piedras Negras acceded within a few years of the *Kul Ahau*'s own inauguration. Kin relationships between *cahal* and members of the royal family are rare, but it is interesting that at Yaxchilán the mother of a king is called an *ix cahal*. Women often took the *cahal* title, but its precise meaning as a female title is also vague.

Monument 26 of Toniná, Chiapas
representing Ruler 2 Balam Ahau
Late Classic period
Mexico City
Museo Nacional de Antropología
cat. 100

following pages
Stela 2, Machaquilá, Petén
Late Classic period
Guatemala, Museo Nacional
de Arqueología y Etnología

Stela 51, Calakmul
Ruler 7 standing on a captive
Late Classic period
Mexico City
Museo Nacional de Antropología
cat. 2

Polychrome cylindrical vessel
a prisoner is being presented to a lord
from El Señor del Petén
Late Classic period
Chetumal, Centro INAH
Quintana Roo
cat. 133

Dynastic Lines

Thus far we have seen that Maya political units were geographically restricted to some extent, perhaps in the way "city-states" tend to be in ancient cultures worldwide. At the center of these kingdoms were, of course, the kings themselves, the "Holy Lords" who were the focus of monumental art throughout the Classic period. Let us narrow our focus somewhat now to consider the nature of kings and dynasties–that is, the people and offices behind the somewhat vague political structures outlined above.

King lists of varied lengths have now been reconstructed for approximately twenty named polities of the Classic period. As we have seen, some of these kingdoms, such as Tikal and Calakmul, were larger in their territory than other smaller actual city-states. Undoubtedly many more small kingdoms existed, but the surviving records of these sites are either nonexistent or far too fragmentary to allow us to reconstruct their individual royal histories. Some kingdoms, too, were extremely long-lived. One historical text of the major site of Naranjo in northern Guatemala, for example, notes that a ruler of the early seventh century was the "35th" successor of the local dynasty. We can imagine this dynastic line continuing centuries into the past–well into a time when virtually no Maya records exist. Other sites might also have their origins deep in the prehistoric and therefore invisible past.

We easily refer to the king lists of these kingdoms as "dynasties," assuming that succession was passed simply from father to son in a patrilineal system of descent. When we consider king lists of great length, however, we must ask if we are witnessing centuries

Wheel of *katun*

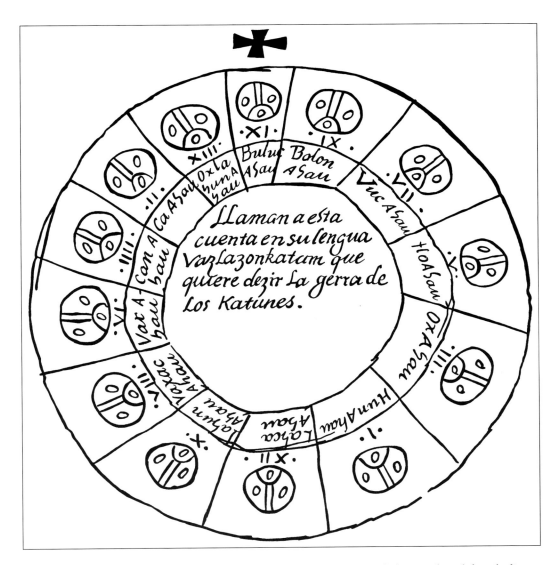

of actual unbroken dynastic descent, or instead groupings of shorter-lived family lines, each connected in some unspecified way to form a greater localized descent group. We know, for example, that the rulers of Palenque generally passed along a patrilineal descent system, with father-to-son descent the norm. However, some major breaks in this pattern are evident, one of the most important coming with the conquest of Palenque by the site of Toniná in the early eighth century. Here, a new ruler, Kinich Akul Anab, takes office.

He is not, it seems, the direct descendant of the great Late Classic ruler Kinich Hanab Pacal (or "Pacal the Great"). The new regent's parents are named in several inscriptions, but appear suddenly in the records, the father not, as far as is known, an earlier king. We may be seeing the introduction of a new family as the ruling line of Palenque, but with the recognition of a true political descent from Kinich Hanab Pacal, who is celebrated throughout the later history of the site. Thus the Palenque "dynasty" may have been composed of several successive family lines, each a sort of dynasty in its own right. The problem often concerns that lack of kinship specifications among the various actors within a local polity (Stuart 1992).

Variation in the Maya Political Landscape
Maya political structure cannot be spoken of in the singular, for as varied lines of evidence, both epigraphic and archaeological, demonstrate, individual political units of the Classic period may well have had their own idiosyncratic structures and patterns of organization.

Stela 6, Piedras Negras, Petén
commemorating
the enthronement of Ruler 3
Late Classic period
Guatemala, Museo Nacional
de Arqueología y Etnología
cat. 3

opposite
Lintel 26 of Yaxchilán, Chiapas
commemorating a marriage alliance
between the sovereign and Lady Xok
Late Classic Period
Mexico City
Museo Nacional de Antropología
cat. 297

Jadeite mask
found in Palenque in the tomb
of the King Pacal
Late Classic Period
Mexico City
Museo Nacional de Antropología
cat. 142

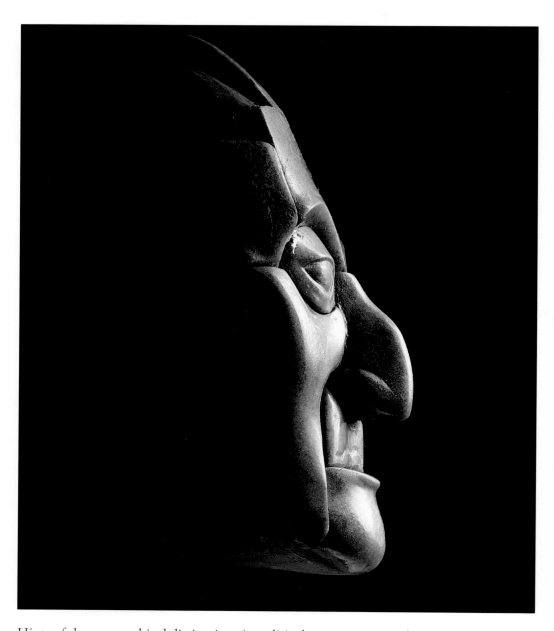

Hints of the geographical distinctions in political structure come, for instance, from patterns in the usage and distribution of specific political titles. *Ahau* and *Kul Ahau*, "Lord" and "Holy Lord," respectively, seem to be ubiquitous in the texts of the lowlands. Rulers come to be seated as *ahau* on a regular basis, from the earliest known texts onward through the Classic period.

However, Tikal's Late Classic inscriptions are unusual in their emphasis on another office called *Kalomte*, to which most if not all of the Late Classic rulers of that site were inaugurated. *Kalomte*, once called the *batab* glyph, is a widespread but little understood title held by rulers of many Maya sites besides Tikal. However, only the Tikal kings claim it as the single position assumed upon inauguration (all other sites state simply that rulers were seated in the *ahau lel*, or "in the rulership").

This distinctive usage at Tikal of the otherwise common *Kalomte* title may have something to do with the unusual relationship that existed during the Late Classic period between Tikal and sites of the Petexbatun region, including Tikal and Aguateca, to the emblem glyph shared between Tikal and sites of the Petexbatun region centered on Dos Pilas and Aguateca. This emblem glyph two Holy Lords seem to have claimed Mutul as their hegemony.

Panel from Xcalumkin, Campeche
Late Classic Period
Campeche, Centro INAH Campeche
cat. 421

Whatever the case may be, the Tikal accession statements are unique in their focus on a different ruling office altogether.

Royal Marriages
Interdynastic marriage or, more precisely, interpolity marriage has received considerable attention in considerations of political and social organization during the Classic period (Marcus 1976). However, only a few marriages are noted in the inscriptions, and it was certainly not a pervasive topic. Indeed, the scattered records of marriages that do exist are largely indirect, and their relationships to political alliances are particularly difficult to discern. Interpolity marriage is often inferred from instances where a "foreign" woman appears in the inscriptions of a certain site. There is, of course, no reason to assume that such references must name a wife of the local ruler, but in most cases the relationship is established through explicit statements of parentage, where a local ruler is named as the son of the preceding ruler and a foreign woman.
Contrary to statements made in a number of sources, there is no known hieroglyph for "marriage." That is to say, no marriage events are explicitly recorded as such in the inscriptions, which may seem somewhat unusual given the importance of royal women in Maya art and

Tablet of the scribes of Pomoná
Late Classic period
Pomoná
Museo de Sitio de Pomoná
cat. 425

writing, as well as the central role of marriage ceremonies in the historical records of Central Mexico and Oaxaca. The only possible exception to this general pattern comes from several texts at Piedras Negras that commemorate an interesting series of rites performed on or by a twelve-year-old girl named "Lady Katun," who later would be named as the wife of Ruler 3 of Piedras Negras. "Marriage" is a meaning often mistakenly assigned to a term of relationship pronounced *yatan*, translatable as "wife of" in Yucatec, but not in Cholan languages. This glyph occurs predominantly in the Postclassic codices, but a handful of examples appear in inscriptions and on pottery.

In the Late Classic inscriptions of Naranjo we find mention of the "arrival" of "Lady 6 Sky" of Dos Pilas, as recorded in several different inscriptions at the site. This may be an indirect statement of marriage to some Naranjo individual, but evidently this was an event of profound importance in Naranjo's local history.

The scarcity of marriage topics in Maya inscriptions is striking, especially given their propensity in other areas of Mesoamerica. Evidently, the precise recording of marriage alliances was never an important priority in the scribal traditions of Maya sites in the Classic period, even though the few hints that exist clearly indicate that interpolity marriages, sometimes over long distances, did in fact take place.

Although highly sophisticated in light of what was known two decades ago, many questions remain unresolved in the current understanding of Maya geopolitical relationships. The size and nature of political and economic coercion by the larger centers such as Tikal and Calakmul, and possibly others, will no doubt garner continued attention. Also, the nature of interpolity organizations will continue to be a focus of both archaeological and epigraphic research.

Given the new paradigms and the questions that arise from them, it is surprising to consider how little remains unknown about this fundamental aspect of Maya research, especially if we assume that Maya inscriptions are historical and political documents for the most part. The hints of political organization that can be gleaned from the inscriptions, mainly in the form of subordinate titles and their distributions, may well represent the deepest insights attainable from epigraphy. Contrary to recent characterizations of the inscriptions, history and political details are not ubiquitous themes in the extant documentary record. Many aspects of Maya political structure may only be discernible through other, more traditional methods in archaeology, especially in areas outside of the Usumacinta zone and the Copán Valley where few inscriptions relate information on internal political structure.

References

BERLIN, HEINRICH
1958
"El glifo 'emblema' en las inscripciones mayas." *Journal de la Société des Americanistes* 47, 111–19

CULBERT, T. PATRICK (ED.)
1991
Classic Maya Political History: Hieroglyphic and Archaeological Evidence. Cambridge, Mass.: Cambridge University Press

DEMAREST, ARTHUR A.
1992
"Ideology in Ancient Maya Cultural Evolution." In *Ideology and Pre-Columbian Civilizations.* Ed. by A.A. Demarest and G.W. Conrad. Santa Fe: School of American Research Press, 135–58

FASH, WILLIAM L.
1991
Scribes, Warriors and Kings: The City of Copán and the Ancient Maya. London-New York: Thames and Hudson

HOUSTON, STEPHEN D.
1993
Hieroglyphs and History at Dos Pilas, Guatemala. Austin: University of Texas Press

MARCUS, JOYCE
1976
Emblem and State in the Classic Maya Lowlands. Washington, D.C.: Dumbarton Oaks
1993
"Ancient Maya Political Organization." In *Late Lowland Maya Civilization in the Eighth Century A.D.* Ed. by J.A. Sabloff and J.S. Henderson. Washington, D.C.: Dumbarton Oaks, 111–84

MARTIN, SIMON, AND NIKOLAI GRUBE
1995
"Maya Superstates." *Archaeology,* 48, 6, 41–46

MATHEWS, PETER
1991
"Classic Maya Emblem Glyphs." In *Classic Maya Political History: Hieroglyphic and Archaeological Evidence.* Ed. by T.P. Culbert. Cambridge, Mass.: Cambridge University Press, 19–29

PROSKOURIAKOFF, TATIANA
1960
"Historical Implications of a Pattern of Dates at Piedras Negras, Guatemala." *American Antiquity,* 25, 454–75
1992
Maya History. Austin: University of Texas Press

SCHELE LINDA, AND DAVID FREIDEL
1990
A Forest of Kings. The Untold Story of the Ancient Maya. New York: William Morrow and Co.

STUART, DAVID
1992
"Hieroglyphs and Archaeology at Copán." *Ancient Mesoamerica,* 3, 1, 169–84
1993
"Historical Inscriptions and the Maya Collapse." In *Late Lowland Maya Civilization of the Eighth Century A.D.* Ed. by J.A. Sabloff and J.S. Henderson. Washington, D.C.: Dumbarton Oaks, 321–54
1995
A Study of Maya Inscriptions. Ph.D. Dissertation, Department of Anthropology, Vanderbilt University. Ann Arbor: University Microfilms International

STUART, DAVID, AND STEPHEN HOUSTON
1994
"Classic Maya Place Names." In *Studies in Pre-Columbian Art and Archaeology,* 33. Washington, D.C.: Dumbarton Oaks

Stela N, Copán
detail representing the 15th ruler

Copán is an enchanting site located in western Honduras, very close to the border with Guatemala, in a small, 24-square-kilometer valley surrounded by pine-and-oak-covered mountains. In the middle of the valley runs the Copán River, on the banks of which the Maya constructed their ancient metropolis. In spite of the fact that Copán is associated with the Maya tropical lowlands, its geography is more characteristic of the highlands, located at 600 meters above sea level. Its climate is cooler than might be expected and an ever-present breeze fills the air with the aroma of clouds and pines descending from the mountains.

A kilometer away from the Main Group of ruins is the town called Copán Ruinas. Here, hidden among straw roofs, adobe walls, and cobbled streets may be found hotels and restaurants of exceptional quality. As throughout the valley, the modern settlement is situated on top of millenary vestiges, an eternal reminder of the cultural heritage of the inhabitants of Copán with whom the simple, hospitable attitude welcoming visitors from very distant lands probably originated.

The traditional, friendly environment of Copán is perhaps also responsible for its long archaeological tradition. Since 1839, the site has been the location of several projects, headed by legendary figures in Maya archaeology such as John L. Stephens, Frederick Catherwood, Alfred P. Maudslay, George B. Gordon, Sylvanus G. Morley, Gustav Stromsvik, and Tatiana Proskouriakoff. Since the beginning, this tradition has played a special leading role in the scientific study of ancient Maya civilization, while attracting the interest of a very wide public throughout the world. Copán is probably the best-known site scientifically. Databanks accumulated over the course of more than a hundred years of research mean that Copán offers the most complete and balanced vision of the ancient Maya world available today.

The modern era of Copán archaeology began in 1975 with a project of archaeological renown headed by Gordon Willey of Harvard University. This was followed by the Proyecto Arqueológico Copán, Primera Fase (PAC I 1977–80) (Copán Archaeological Project, First Phase), directed by Claude F. Baudez of the Centre National de la Recherche Scientifique, France, which completed archaeological knowledge of the urban nucleus of the site and began the systematic exploration of architectonic remains. Then came the Segunda Fase (PAC II 1980–85); the government of Honduras named William T. Sanders of Pennsylvania State University as the head of this project. Based on the preceding foundations, Sanders extended archaeological knowledge to the rural limits of the Copán metropolis to cover a territory of 135 square kilometers.

The Great Plaza, Copán
Plaza de Las Estelas
Parque Arqueológico de Copán

Plan of Main Group at Copán

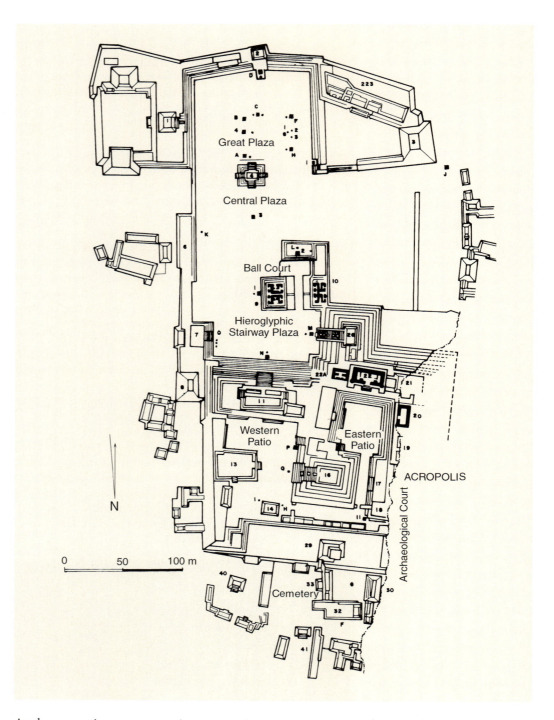

At the same time, an extensive excavation program was implemented to compile a representative sample of all types of residential groups identified during reconnaissance work.

Throughout this process, the spatial, temporal, and architectonic nature of this ancient city was clarified, while at the same time multiple perspectives on its social, political, and economic organization were illuminated. In 1985 William and Barbara Fash of Harvard University, accompanied by Rudy Larios Villalta, began a new era of research with the creation of the Proyecto para el Estudio de la Escultura en Mosaico (Project for the Study of Mosaic Sculpture), the main objective of which was to rescue and interpret Copán's fabulous sculpture. Three years later, these efforts were reinforced and extended with the creation of the Proyecto Arqueológico Acrópolis de Copán (PAAC; the Archaeological Project of the

The bat, Copán
Late Classic period
Copán
Museo Regional de Arqueología
cat. 79

Copán Acropolis), which now involves Robert Sharer (University of Pennsylvania), E. Wyllys Andrews V (Tulane University), and this author, as codirectors. After a decade of research emphasizing settlements dispersed throughout the Copán Valley, attention has returned to the heart of the city and its acropolis.

Site Description
The urban nucleus of Copán is composed of the Main Group, which was the political, civic, and religious center, and a series of residential neighborhoods surrounding it. The modern Archaeological Park includes two of these neighborhoods, which are connected by causeways to the Main Group. One of these is located to the southwest and is called "the Forest" (El Bosque), while the other, to the northeast, is named "the Sepulchers" (Las Sepulturas).
The majestic Main Group, enveloped in a millenary mantle of gigantic trees, is composed of the Great Plaza and the Acropolis. Both may be subdivided into minor architectonic elements, the basic plan of which is that of a rectangular patio surrounded by pyramidal platforms with buildings. Both the Great Plaza and the Acropolis reflect enormous amounts of labor: the former for its great extension of more than three hectares of leveled land that was originally paved, and the second due to its enormous mass elevated to more than 30 meters above the natural level of the land.
The area of the Great Plaza is the site of confluence of the two main causeways of Copán and it consists of large, open spaces. It is evident that it served for public events with a capacity for thousands of people. At the northern end the plaza is framed on three of its sides by enormous tiers or steps that served as seats for the multitudes. In the center of this open-air theater, there are seven stelae and eleven altars forming one of the most beautiful sculpture gardens of Copán, which must have served as the scenario for ritual acts of enormous social importance. At the southern end there is another theater with enormous earthen benches going up to the Acropolis and overlooking the Ball Court, to one side of the Hieroglyphic Stairway.
It is evident that here the focus was on sports, a Mesoamerican tradition with enormous ritual importance even today. In contrast to the Great Plaza, the Acropolis is a private area, with restricted access and reduced spaces. This was the precinct of political and religious power, the lodgings of the ruler and his court.

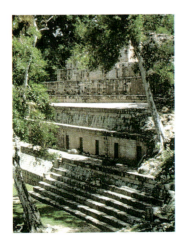

Structure 10L-11
Western Patio of the Acropolis
Copán

Altar Q representing dynasty
of Kinich Yax Kuk Mo
from Copán

Architecturally, the Acropolis is composed of two patios: the Eastern Patio or Patio of the
Jaguars and the Western Patio. Between the two, in the center of the Acropolis itself, is
Temple 16.

The History of a Dynasty
The Preclassic period (1400 B.C.–A.D. 100). Everyone knows that the further one goes back in
time, the more ephemeral the vestiges of man become. The case of Copán is no different in
this sense, because the vestiges of the first inhabitants are scarce. Beginning in 1991 a team
of archaeologists headed by René Viel (Centro de Estudios Mexicanos y Centro-Americanos; Center of Mexican and Central American Studies) and Jay Hall (University of
Queensland) began a project specifically designed to study these remote periods. The initial
results were somewhat discouraging; nevertheless, little by little, they have found greater
quantities of archaeological remains.
The most ancient vestiges are dated to 1400 B.C. and consist of the remains of a dwelling with
rounded corners. The artifacts associated with this humble construction imply relations with
the south and west of Copán and not toward the northern Maya area (W. Fash 1991, 65–66).
Both these archaeological remains and many of those following them in the Preclassic and
Classic periods have given rise to a discussion of the ethnic and cultural affiliation of these
original inhabitants of the Copán Valley (W. Fash and Stuart 1991; Viel 1993). It is possible
that they were not Maya at all and that their cultural tradition has continued at the same time
as Maya culture throughout the site's history. In any case, the peripheral location of Copán
at the southeastern margin of the Maya region is marked from the beginning in the archaeological record of the site, as well as the exchange of goods with cultures from central Honduras and the lower part of Central America.

Altar G1, Copán
Late Classic period
Copán, Plaza de Las Estelas
Parque Arqueológico de Copán
cat. 1

As in so many other border sites, contact between different human groups, far from restraining cultural development, probably served to stimulate it.

For the following stage (Middle Preclassic, 900–300 B.C.), vestiges are a little more abundant and sophisticated. William Fash (1991) found the most extensive evidence of the phase, consisting of construction platforms for multiple dwellings with stone walls. Within these there were numerous, sophisticated burials that implied a more complex cultural development than that of the preceding stage. Ceramic vessels accompanying burials establish links with the Olmec culture that was in full development in southern Mexico in this period.

For the last stage of the Preclassic (300 B.C.–A.D. 100) when the Maya area reaches its first cultural peak, Copán seems to remain a little behind in history. Archaeological remains found to date continue to be scarce. The causes of this phenomenon are the subject of considerable debate, but many believe that it is mainly a sampling problem; that is, remains are scarce because sites of this period are in a different location from the others or because they were destroyed by natural phenomena such as erosion caused by the river.

In any event, the Preclassic at Copán is a captivating mystery for archaeologists. At this time are shaped the origins of a marvelous city in the southeastern periphery of the Maya world. Even with what little we know, the traces of a frontier post may be seen clearly with objects of exchange marking trade routes with very distant sites and the first indications of a society destined for greatness. With progress in the Viel-Hall project, it will be possible to clarify the cultural processes that served as precedents for the great development of the Classic period.

The Protoclassic period (A.D. 100–400) and the Classic (A.D. 400–800). During the Protoclassic period, the archaeological record increases considerably, permitting better inferences on cultural developments. In portable objects, particularly in ceramics, the continued contact

following pages
Sculpture representing
a supernatural
Reviewing stand, Copán

of Copán with areas to the south and east of the site is seen. Nevertheless, strong interaction with the Maya in the Guatemala highlands to the west also arises. As for architecture, numerous constructions appear in the zone that then became the urban nucleus of the city: the Sepulchers, the Main Group, the Forest, and the Modern Town. Constructions are more numerous and the first monumental stucco-covered masonry structures appear. Copán grows and begins to feel the fervor of Classic period splendor.

The Classic period takes off around the year A.D. 400 with vestiges marking a surrender to the imposing Maya tradition that arises with vigor to the east of Copán. It is possible that these traits arrive with the first dynastic ruler of the site, Kinich Yax Kuk Mo.

William Fash (personal communication 1997) has noted that many of the sites in the region of Copán (Cerro de las Mesas, Pueblo Moderno, Cerro Chino, and Los Achiotes) dating to the end of the Protoclassic or the beginning of the Classic are located on elevated and thus defensible lands, unlike the earlier ones which displayed a preference for the lower parts of the valley. At the same time, what has emerged is that perhaps bellicose factors played a preponderant role in the origin of the Copán state. Fash's comments strike me as very accurate and convince me that there was a great deal of political fragmentation in this period in the valley, which probably followed the lines of dominant lineages of the region. A great lord, probably a descendent and representative of the royal power of the great centers to the west, arrives in this setting. A key piece in the story is Altar Q.

Altar Q was commissioned by the sixteenth ruler, Yax Pasah (previously called Yax Pac) in the year A.D. 775. In it are represented all his monarchic predecessors, seated on hieroglyphs with their names. At the head, Yax Pasah, receives the "staff of rulership" from the founder of the dynasty, Kinich Yax Kuk Mo, and by doing so he proclaims his legitimate descendence. In the upper part of the altar, there is a very important hieroglyphic text. The most recent analysis and interpretation of this has been made by Linda Schele and Mathew Looper (1996). The text begins narrating a series of civic-religious acts associated with the arrival of the founder to Copán and the establishment of his dynasty in the year A.D. 426 and ends describing the dedication of the "Yax Kuk Mo altar" by Yax Pasah in A.D. 775.

It is evident from this inscription that the founder was an outsider and his arrival was an act transcending more than three hundred years and fifteen generations of rulers. The question of the origins of this great lord is the subject of considerable disagreement among experts

Reviewing stand, Copán
Structure 10L-11

of Copán with areas to the south and east of the site is seen. Nevertheless, strong interaction with the Maya in the Guatemala highlands to the west also arises. As for architecture, numerous constructions appear in the zone that then became the urban nucleus of the city: the Sepulchers, the Main Group, the Forest, and the Modern Town. Constructions are more numerous and the first monumental stucco-covered masonry structures appear. Copán grows and begins to feel the fervor of Classic period splendor.

The Classic period takes off around the year A.D. 400 with vestiges marking a surrender to the imposing Maya tradition that arises with vigor to the east of Copán. It is possible that these traits arrive with the first dynastic ruler of the site, Kinich Yax Kuk Mo.

William Fash (personal communication 1997) has noted that many of the sites in the region of Copán (Cerro de las Mesas, Pueblo Moderno, Cerro Chino, and Los Achiotes) dating to the end of the Protoclassic or the beginning of the Classic are located on elevated and thus defensible lands, unlike the earlier ones which displayed a preference for the lower parts of the valley. At the same time, what has emerged is that perhaps bellicose factors played a preponderant role in the origin of the Copán state. Fash's comments strike me as very accurate and convince me that there was a great deal of political fragmentation in this period in the valley, which probably followed the lines of dominant lineages of the region. A great lord, probably a descendent and representative of the royal power of the great centers to the west, arrives in this setting. A key piece in the story is Altar Q.

Altar Q was commissioned by the sixteenth ruler, Yax Pasah (previously called Yax Pac) in the year A.D. 775. In it are represented all his monarchic predecessors, seated on hieroglyphs with their names. At the head, Yax Pasah, receives the "staff of rulership" from the founder of the dynasty, Kinich Yax Kuk Mo, and by doing so he proclaims his legitimate descendence. In the upper part of the altar, there is a very important hieroglyphic text. The most recent analysis and interpretation of this has been made by Linda Schele and Mathew Looper (1996). The text begins narrating a series of civic-religious acts associated with the arrival of the founder to Copán and the establishment of his dynasty in the year A.D. 426 and ends describing the dedication of the "Yax Kuk Mo altar" by Yax Pasah in A.D. 775.

It is evident from this inscription that the founder was an outsider and his arrival was an act transcending more than three hundred years and fifteen generations of rulers. The question of the origins of this great lord is the subject of considerable disagreement among experts

Structure 10L-16
on the highest part of the Acropolis

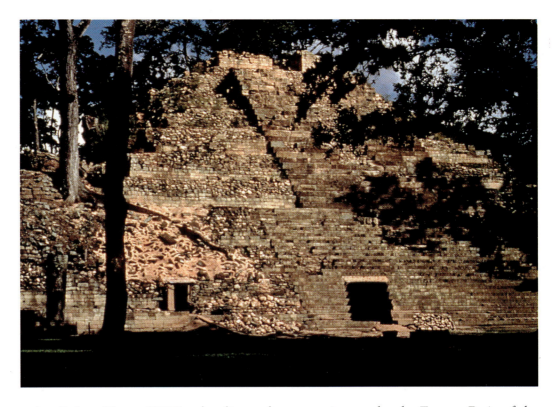

today. Robert Sharer (1997), who directs the excavations under the Eastern Patio of the Acropolis, thinks that he has found the tomb of Kinich Yax Kuk Mo in the oldest levels of the excavations. The sequence of constructions in this location and its iconographic emphasis on the veneration of this ancestor give considerable support to Sharer's thesis (Agurcia Fasquelle *et al.* 1996).

The analysis of the context and content of this tomb brings us important data on the foundation of the city. The construction in which the funerary crypt was placed was built in an architectural style foreign to Copán and one traditionally associated with the great Mexican metropolis of Teotihuacan. It is a platform with a *talud* and *tablero* (a sloped base topped by a framed, rectangular panel). Sharer thinks that the residence of the founder was originally built here, but was destroyed once the great lord died and was buried in the platform. In spite of this, the architecture of the funerary chamber, as well as the style of the burial and the offerings, is typical of the Maya tradition. In summary, Sharer thinks that although there are indications to associate the birth of the Acropolis with Teotihuacan influences, these are not as evident as at other sites in the Maya world in this period, such as Kaminaljuyú and Tikal. Therefore, he thinks that perhaps they arrived here indirectly, filtered through monumental sites in the Maya area such as those mentioned earlier that even geographically are intermediaries. These discoveries are so recent that they still require further analysis and a bit more discussion to achieve the desired degree of scientific maturity. Nonetheless, they do not cease to evoke very intriguing possibilities, and they open up to us as never before a window onto the founding of a great Maya city.

Personally it seems to me very reasonable, although still speculative, that Kinich Yax Kuk Mo arrived at Copán as the representative of a complex society with an advanced state of social and political organization, interested in extending their political and commercial ties to the east. Here he encountered a fragmented, bellicose society in which different leaders or chiefs fought for parcels of land. Located at the edge of Maya territory, Copán offered access to ancestral trade routes with rich, varied resources from central Honduras and the Pacific coast of El Salvador. Here there was cacao, cotton, obsidian, exotic bird feathers, and many other resources. By way of political alliances, including marriage with a very high ranking lady of the locality as Robert Sharer (1997) has suggested, and perhaps with the military backing of a formal state with Teotihuacan ties, Kinich Yax Kuk Mo brought stability, peace,

opposite
Scribe vessel from Copán
Classic period
Tegucigalpa, Bodegas Centrales
del Instituto Hondureño
de Antropología e Historia
cat. 437

Mano and *Metate* (grinding tools)
La Mosquitia, Honduras
Classic-Postclassic period
Tegucigalpa, Bodegas Centrales
del Instituto Hondureño
de Antropología e Historia
cat. 271

and property to the region. His arrival marked the beginning of a royal dynasty that prospered in the short term and came to play a starring role in the Maya world.

Intensive archaeological research of population settlements of the Copán Valley has demonstrated that the growth of Copán was gradual. The incorporation of different families and lineages in a unified society under the rule of a single royal lineage around the year A.D. 400 also coincided with the introduction of hieroglyphic writing and unprecedented development in the construction of monumental buildings charged with complex iconography. The city progressively increased in size and diversity for the following four centuries, forming in the process a state that controlled a vast territory.

Archaeological projects have studied the number, form, and function of ancient settlements that existed within the limits of the small river valley in which Copán is located, such as the ecological capacity and the quality of the site's natural resources. The results of these studies have been tremendously informative. For example, the research of Sanders and his team from Pennsylvania State University on the agricultural use and potential of the valley indicate that in the final decades, Copán was not self-sufficient in its basic food supply and consequently it had to depend on the importation of food from neighboring regions.

The systematic recording of the ruins of all Pre-Columbian residential settlements, represented in detail on maps, confirms a high density of population for the site. In the 24 square kilometers of the plains that surround the Main Group, the remains of 3,450 buildings are located, of which more than one thousand are concentrated in an urban nucleus of 1 square kilometer, around the Acropolis. Extending the systematic reconnaissance of archaeological sites to the area of 135 square kilometers around the Main Site and thus arriving at the natural geographic limits of what was the main area of influence of Copán, Sanders reached a total count of 1,425 archaeological sites with 4,507 buildings. Based on these statistics, it has been estimated that the population of Copán at the moment of greatest occupation in the eighth century came to reach more than 27,500 inhabitants (Webster, Sanders, and van Rossum 1992).

The maps and excavations of residential ruins also helped define numerous aspects of the social structure of ancient Maya society at Copán. This research has spanned the most humble dwelling of a farmer to the imposing palaces of rulers in the urban nucleus. For different analytical purposes, researchers have grouped different residential areas into four types

reflecting an equal number of social classes. In this way, the humblest settlements with cane and mud dwellings are generally located in rural areas and are identified with farmers. The next type covers slightly more formal settlements with some stone constructions and is associated with families of commoners. This is followed by one of the most complex residence types, with stone structures and multiple patios to house a lower nobility, perhaps merchants, craftsmen, or warriors. Finally comes the upper nobility (probably part of the royal court) with its richly decorated palace groups, which are larger and more extensive than the other types of edifices.

In the Barrio of the Sepulchers, to the northeast of the Main Group, eighteen residential compounds have been excavated and restored, representing close to one hundred buildings with more than two hundred rooms. These constitute a complete sample of urban, domestic architecture at Copán.

The architectonic groups chosen as representative of the wealthy class (9N-8), reveals complex and sophisticated architecture, including eleven patios surrounded by close to fifty buildings with almost one hundred rooms. The most outstanding building (9N-82) had facades richly decorated with sculptures and on its interior there was an exquisitely sculpture bench that today is exhibited in the Museum of the Ruins of Copán. This was made in the year A.D. 781 and was dedicated to a noble who formed part of the court of Yax Pasah. In the rooms next to the main one in this palace, the wives and offspring of this individual probably lived. Spanish chroniclers of the sixteenth century noted that polygamy was widely established among Maya nobility. This fact is confirmed by the large numbers of burials in the Sepulchers group (more than 250), in which there is a disproportionate number of women, as we would expect in a polygamous society.

The other residential buildings constructed around smaller rectangular patios contiguous to that of the great lord were probably occupied by the oldest children of the noble, their families and servants. Some constructions had specialized functions. This is the case of one of them that contained accoutrements linked with the ball game. This perhaps served as the place for a team of ballplayers in the service of the chief of the residential compound.

Another of these building groups, located on the periphery of Group 9N-8, indicates that it was inhabited by a different ethnic group, which could be linked based on its architecture, funerary practices, and portable objects to central Honduras. This reemphasizes Copán's frontier location and reminds us of the millenary tradition of the site with non-Maya groups to the south and east. In spite of the fact that this group lived contiguous to the nobles in the most complex and elegant residential group outside of the Main Group of Copán, and they imported products (vessels and whistles from the Sula-Yojoa-Comayagua tradition) of very high quality, its residential area was architectonically restricted in its communication with the other patios and buildings. Therefore, it is possible that they served the nobles in some type of service relationship. The presence of fragments of shell, needles, perforators, and drills on the floors of patios in the buildings implies that the special activity of the group was the manufacture of shell ornaments and the production of textiles, skin articles, and baskets. This group may have been inhabited by a group of artisans attached to the court of a great Maya lord.

Large trash dumps with everyday refuse of the inhabitants have also been found in these residential compounds, such as ceramic pots, pitchers, plates, and pans used for stages of food preparation and service. Other items supporting this identification are grinding stones called *manos* and *metates*, used to process maize and other plant species in the preparation of *tortillas*, *tamales*, and other foods; obsidian blades, used as cutting implements for the processing of food (e.g., the cutting up of animal carcasses); and occasionally the remains of some of these foods (e.g., maize, beans, jute, fish bones, and bones of animals, such as white-tailed deer, *paca* or spotted cavy, the *jabalí* or *chancho del monte*, the *cusuco* or armadillo, and the *chachalaca*).

With the great increase in knowledge of social, political, and economic life of the Maya obtained by work in the Copán Valley, we archaeologists have returned to excavate in the Main Group with a more comprehensive approach than the researchers of yore. Similarly, perhaps even greater has been the concern for safeguarding the most splendid vestiges of the ancient city and its extraordinary sculpture.

Using techniques developed by William and Barbara Fash with Rudy Larios V. in the excavation and restoration of buildings in the Sepulchers group, many of the buildings studied in the nineteenth century and the first half of the twentieth century have been restudied by archaeological expeditions with new insights (W. Fash 1991). Among other things, it has been possible to sort, catalogue, study, and safeguard close to 30,000 fragments of sculpture that had fallen from buildings and had been scattered throughout the site. These now may be assigned to their original constructions, at the same time that their motifs allow us to identify the purpose of structures, as well as the name of the ruler who ordered them built. Barbara Fash has also noted on numerous occasions that the greatest quantity of carved sculpture at Copán is not represented by the stelae and altars that make this city famous, but rather by the facades of buildings. This is evident when one visits the new sculpture museum of Copán, inaugurated in 1996, where the exquisite facades of eight buildings have been reconstructed. In this gigantic museum, the splendor of the ancient city comes alive again.

Work with this mosaic sculpture has allowed us to know that both Temple 10L-26 (of the Hieroglyphic Stairway) as well as 10L-16 (on the highest part of the Acropolis) were dedicated to warfare, death, and the veneration of ancestors (mainly dead kings); Temple 10L-18 is the funerary temple of Yax Pasah, who is exalted as a warrior in sculptures covering its walls; Temple 10L-22 is marked as a "Sacred Mountain," the site of rituals and sacrifices for kings who exercised their prerogatives among the symbols of the entire Maya cosmos; and Structure 10L-22A, the "Popol Na," is the "House of the Community" where the king met with his court and heads of principal lineages to make decisions governing the destiny of the state (B. Fash 1992).

Similarly, by way of tunnels, the interior of pyramids that served as platforms for palaces and temples have been penetrated in an attempt to comprehend the early roots of the city and its historical evolution. The vast majority of buildings and many of the platforms were destroyed by the Maya to cover them with new constructions. Nevertheless, in some cases these were preserved almost to perfection, retaining details as delicate as the sculpture on their facades with plaster and colors still in place.

Perhaps the most extraordinary example of this is the Rosalila Temple, which was buried with its architecture and sculpture intact, under Temple 16 in the center of the Copán Acropolis (Agurcia Fasquelle *et al.* 1996). This building has three superimposed tiers with a total height of almost 13 meters, which is equivalent in modern terms to a four-story building.

The lower floor, which is the main one, has four rooms on its interior with an average size of 2.4 by 11.2 meters each. The two upper levels constitute the decorative crest of the temple. It is probable that the majority of Copán temples had similar crests; however, until now it has not been possible to find a single example.

The rooms of the Rosalila are very well preserved with their cut stone walls and vaults and surfaces plastered with stucco. In addition, red painting decorates the walls, although this does not go higher than the rise of the vaults. From here and above the stucco is unpainted and displays a color between gray and black, the result of smoke produced by the constant smoldering of incense burners within the temple, some of which were found *in situ* in the rooms. Similarly, traces have been found, with decomposed organic remains, of the round wooden beams used to cover the vaults.

The main facade of the temple faces toward the west and it is dominated, on its central axis, by an enormous mask modeled in stucco. The central subject of this decoration is the facade of the sun god, Ah Kin or Kinich Ahau. The representations of this god on the building are numerous and are found repeated both on the first level of Rosalila as well as on the platform that supports it. The main portrait of this solar god has wings on its sides composed of inverted serpent heads with feathers emerging from their jaws. From the plumes sprout a small medallion with a profile head of the same deity, reaffirming the cosmic identity of this solar bird.

Under the molding and at the sides of the door, there are two more representations. Here but on a smaller scale may be distinguished the same composition as above: the face of Kinich Ahau, seen frontally with two enormous, square earplugs on each side. Above his

Reconstruction of Rosalila Temple
Copán
Museo de la Escultura de Copán

face, like a feather crest, is the head of a quetzal (*kuk* in Maya) with the eyes of a macaw (*mo'*), this combination referring to Kinich Yax Kuk Mo, founder of the Copán royal dynasty. It is worth recalling that both on Altar Q as well as in many other texts at Copán, the name of this first king is composed, hieroglyphically, of the head of the quetzal with the eyes of the macaw, as is represented at Rosalila. To the sides of the sun god's face are again wings personified as serpents with feathers in their jaws, under which are distinguished, with all clarity, the talons and claws of the bird.

At the corners of the building there are large serpents with open jaws, from which emerge anthropomorphic figures that could be other representations of Kinich Ahau. Similarly, just around the corners, on the north and south facades, appears a human figure emerging from a niche (probably representing a dead ruler emerging from the underworld). Next to this figure there is another serpent, like those of the main facade; however, under the eye of this serpent appears a new element, a "sacrificial bundle" dominated by a knife. This assemblage of elements reminds us again of human sacrifice in the context of the veneration of the ancestors (and particularly of Kinich Yax Kuk Mo) as in Temples 16 and 26.

The second level of the building is dominated by the mask of a *cauac* or *uits* monster, which marks Rosalila as a sacred mountain, as occurs in Temple 10L-22. In turn, the third level of Rosalila is dominated by a zoomorphic mask with its fleshless lower jaw which seems to represent an incense burner. In this way, the building is also marked as a "house of smoke," a temple. This macabre face is framed by the bodies of two serpents that could symbolize the smoke that emerges from the building as a celestial arc, recalling again the interior portal of Temple 10L-22. In any event, the cosmic and religious message is evident in this building.

The masks of Rosalila are polychromed, mainly in red. Dark green has also been identified (on the face of the quetzal, on some of the feathers of the solar bird, and on the earplugs of the anthropomorphic figures), as well as some traces of yellow and black (on other feathers and feather headdresses of Kinich Ahau).

On the interior of Rosalila, there were many offerings that included flint eccentrics, clay incense burners with carbon remains on their interiors, sculptures carved in the form of cats, and precious objects of shell and jade.

Rosalila rests on a small pyramidal platform. Opposite the platform there is a rectangular plaza, delineated by other buildings. This plaza is 10 meters above the natural level of the land, a difference that may be explained by the presence of an earlier version of the Acrop-

Ball Court at Copán

Copán dynastic sequence

1st ruler
Kinich Yax Kuk Mo
(Quetzal Macaw)
A.D. 426-435
(8.19.10.0.0-9.0.0.0.0)

2nd ruler
Mat Head
A.D. 435- ?
(9.0.0.0.0.0-?)
Monuments:
Stelae 18 and 63
Marker
stone Xukpi

3rd ruler
unknown
A.D. ?-485

4th ruler
Cu Ix
A.D. 485-495
(9.2.10.0.0-9.3.0.0.0)
Monuments:
Stela 34
Structure
10L-26-sub bench
(Parrot)

5th ruler
unknown

6th ruler
unknown

7th ruler
Water Lily Jaguar
A.D. 504-544
(9.3.10.0.0.0-9.5.10.0.0)
Monuments:
Stelae E and 15
Hieroglyphic
Stairway 9 and 55
Rise in font

8th ruler
unknown

9th ruler
unknown
accession A.D. 551
(9.5.17.13.7)
Monuments:
Altar x
Hieroglyphic
Stairway 18

olis that today is being investigated by Sharer's team. By exposing the steps of the Rosalila platform, it was discovered that one of them had a hieroglyphic text carved on its riser, which indicates that the temple was the work of the tenth ruler of Copán, Moon Jaguar, commemorating the year A.D. 571 (9.6.17.3.2). Based on this information it is evident that Rosalila was a sanctuary dedicated to the sun god, patron deity of Copán royalty, and spiritual co-essence of the founder of the dynasty Kinich Yax Kuk Mo, whose name may be translated literally as "Sun Eye Resplendescent Quetzal Macaw."

As one may surmise, this wealth of information obtained in the Acropolis of Copán complements data from the valley to give us an unprecedented overall vision of the rulers and the ruled of ancient Maya society at Copán.

The Collapse and the Postclassic period (A.D. 800–1000). The results of archaeological research indicate that in its last decades, the city and the valley of Copán suffered unparalleled demographic growth. This lead to an intensification of agricultural systems, which in turn accelerated the rhythm of environmental deterioration (Webster, Sanders and van Rossum 1992).

The population embarked on occupying spaces not very apt for agriculture and living, such as the slopes of mountains surrounding the valley. Here they caused greater deforestation, which in itself was already very deteriorated by the demand for wood for construction and firewood for food preparation, illumination of homes, and processing of lime for plaster and stucco floors in constructions. The samples obtained by paleoecologists show dramatic evidence of the disappearance of the forest.

In turn, explorations in the valley have found indications of massive erosion of soils from the slopes. With this occurred drastic climate changes: intensive droughts with rivers and ravines with ever reduced water levels, and floods in winter provoked by the lack of mountainside vegetation to alleviate the rapid runoff of rainwater. The impact of the population increase was equally severe, because specialists in the study of skeletons (physical anthropologists), who have in Copán the largest sample available in the Maya region, see in these many indications of malnutrition, disease, and traumatic growth. In turn, life expectancy is reduced and finally, many children between the ages of five and fifteen years, who are generally the most resistant sector of the population, begin to die (Storey 1992).

10th ruler	11th ruler	12th ruler	13th ruler	14th ruler	15th ruler	16th ruler	17th claimant
Moon Jaguar	Butz' Chan	Smoke Jaguar	18 Rabbit	Smoke Monkey	Smoke Spiral Shell	Yax Pasah	U Cit Tok'
accession	(Smoke Serpent	(Smoke Imix God K)	(Uaxaclahun Ubac C'auil)	accession	(Squirrel	(Yax Pak Dawn)	accession(?)
May 26, A.D. 553	Smoke Sky)	accession	accession	June 11, A.D. 738	Smoke Conch Shell)	accession	February 10, A.D. 822
(9.5.19.3.0)	birth	February 8, A.D. 628	July 9, A.D. 695	(9.15.6.16.5)	accession	February 18, A.D. 763	(9.19.11.14.5)
death	April 30, A.D. 553	(9.9.14.17.5)	(9.13.3.6.8)	death	February 18, A.D. 749	(9.16.12.5.17)	death: unknown
October 26, A.D. 578	(9.6.9.4.6)	death	death	February 4, A.D. 749	(9.15.17.13.10)	death: unknown	Monuments:
(9.7.4.17.4)	accession	June 17, A.D. 695	May 3, A.D. 738	(9.15.17.12.16)	death: unknown	but prior to A.D. 820	Altar L
Monuments:	November 19, A.D. 578	(9.13.3.5.9)	(9.15.6.14.6)	Monuments:	Monuments:	(9.19.10.0.0)	
Stela 9	(9.7.5.0.8)	Monuments:	Monuments:	Structure 22-A	Stelae M and N	Monuments:	
Hieroglyphic	death	Stelae 1,2,3,5,6,10	Stelae A, B, C, D, F, H, J, and 4		Hieroglyphic Stairway	Stelae 8 and 11	
Stairway 9	January 23, A.D. 628	12,13 and 19	Altar S		(Structure 26)	Altars D', F', G1,	
	(9.9.14.16.9)	Altars H',I' and K	Structure 22			G2, G3, O, Q, R,	
	Monuments:	Hieroglyphic	Ball courts II-B and III			T, U, V, W', and Z	
	Stelae P and 7	Stairway 6 and 7				Structures 11, 16	
	Altar Y					18 and 21-A	
	Hieroglyphic						
	Stairway 8						

Main courts at the residential building 9N-8 of the Sepulchers Copán

Following the collapse of the monarchic government, the poverty-stricken population continued inhabiting the vicinity of the Main Group, but gradually they disappear in the framework of an ecologically destroyed valley. Until now the vestiges of the Postclassic were the least known of Copán; nevertheless, in the last two years Kam Manahan, a student of William Fash, has found some constructions from this period in the area called the Forest Barrio, to the southwest of the Acropolis.

Indications are that among the Classic period ruins there was a small Postclassic village whose inhabitants often reutilized the rubble of ancient constructions. In any case, it was a very reduced, poor population. It is possible that up to two centuries passed before the valley became completely depopulated, and the forests began the slow process of recovering the land.

Today Copán flourishes anew as the main tourist center of Honduras and an important pole of growth for the entire western region of the country. After two decades of investment on the part of the government in research and conservation, the recognition of this monument as a World Heritage Site (UNESCO 1980), as well as the construction of infrastructure to support tourists, Copán serves as a model in the Maya region for the sustainable development of an archaeological site. At the same time, it is an inexhaustible source of civic pride for the Honduran people.

References

AGURCIA F., RICARDO, AND WILLIAM L. FASH
1991
"Maya Artistry Unearthed." *National Geographic Magazine*. Vol. 180, 3 (September), 94–105
1992
Historia Escrita en Piedra: Guía al Parque Arqueológico de las Ruinas de Copán. Tegucigalpa: Asociación Copán e Instituto Hondureño de Antropología e Historia

AGURCIA F., RICARDO, AND JUAN ANTONIO VALDÉS
1994
Secretos de Dos Ciudades Mayas: Copán y Tikal. San Pedro de Sula, Honduras: Centro Editorial

AGURCIA F., RICARDO, DONNA K. STONE, AND JORGE RAMOS
1996
"Tierra, tiestos, piedras, estratigrafía y escultura: Investigaciones en la Estructura 10L-16 de Copán." In *Visión del Pasado Maya*. Ed. by W. Fash and R. Agurcia F. Copán: Asociación Copán 185–201

ANDREWS V, WYLLYS, E., AND BARBARA W. FASH
1992
"Continuity and Change in a Royal Maya Residential Complex at Copán." *Ancient Mesoamerica*, Vol. 3, 63–88

BAUDEZ, CLAUDE F., (ED.)
1983
Introducción a la Arqueología de Copán, Honduras. 3 Vols. Tegucigalpa: Instituto Hondureño de Antropología e Historia

FASH, BARBARA
1992
"Late Classic Architectural Sculpture Themes in Copán." *Ancient Mesoamerica*. Vol. 3, 89–104

FASH, BARBARA, WILLIAM FASH, SHEER LANE, CARLOS RUDY LARIOS, LINDA SCHELE, JEFFREY STOMPER, AND DAVID STUART
1992
"Investigations of a Classic Maya Council House at Copán, Honduras." *Journal of Field Archaeology*. Vol. 19, 4, 419–42

FASH, WILLIAM L.
1991
Scribes, Warriors and Kings: The City of Copán and the Ancient Maya. London-New York: Thames and Hudson

FASH, WILLIAM, AND BARBARA FASH
1990
"Scribes, Warriors and Kings: Ancient Lives of the Copán Maya." *Archaeology*. Vol. 43, 26–35

FASH, WILLIAM, AND KURT Z. LONG
1983
"Mapa Arqueológico del Valle de Copán." In *Introducción a la Arqueología de Copán*. Tomo III. Ed. by C.F. Baudez. Tegucigalpa: Instituto Hondureño de Antropología e Historia

FASH, WILLIAM, AND DAVID STUART
1991
"Dynastic History and Cultural Evolution at Copán, Honduras." In *Classic Maya Political History: Hieroglyphic and Archaeological Evidence*. Ed. by T.P. Culbert. Cambridge, Mass.: Cambridge University Press, 147–79

FASH, WILLIAM, RICHARD V. WILLIAMSON, CARLOS RUDY LARIOS AND JOEL PALKA
1992
"The Hieroglyphic Stairway and Its Ancestors: Investigations of Copán Structure 10L-26." *Ancient Mesoamerica*. Vol. 3, 105–15

MAUDSLAY, ALFRED P.
1889
Biología Centrali Americana: Archaeology. Vol. I. London: R.H. Porter and Dulau and Co.

SANDERS, WILLIAM T., (ED.)
1986, 1990
Proyecto Arqueológico Copán, Segunda Fase: Excavaciones en el Area Urbana de Copán. 3 Vols. Tegucigalpa: Instituto Hondureño de Antropología e Historia

SCHELE, LINDA, AND MARY ELLEN MILLER
1986
The Blood of Kings: Dynasty and Ritual in Maya Art. Fort Worth: Kimbell Art Museum

SCHELE, LINDA, AND DAVID FREIDEL
1990
A Forest of Kings. The Untold Story of the Ancient Maya. New York: William Morrow and Co.

SCHELE, LINDA, AND MATHEW LOOPER
1996
Notebook for the XXth Maya Hieroglyphic Forum. Austin: University of Texas

SHARER, ROBERT J.
1997
"The Foundation of the Ruling Dynasty at Copán, Honduras. The Early Acropolis and Mesoamerican Interaction." Paper presented at the symposium "A Tale of Two Cities: Copán and Teotihuacán." Cambridge, Mass.: Harvard University

SHARER, ROBERT J., JULIA C., MILLER, AND LOA P. TRAILER
1992
"Evolution of Classic Period Architecture in the Eastern Acropolis, Copán: A Progress Report." *Ancient Mesoamerica*, Vol. 3, 145–59

STONE, DONNA K., ALFONSO MORALES, AND RICHARD WILLIAMSON
1996
"Sacrificios e iconografía de guerra en el grupo principal de Copán." In *Visión del Pasado Maya.* Ed. by W.L. Fash and R. Agurcia F. Copán: Asociación Copán, 203–13

STOREY, REBECCA
1992
"The Children of Copán: Issues in Paleopathology and Paleodemography." *Ancient Mesoamerica.* Vol. 3, 161–67

STUART, DAVID
1992
"Hieroglyphs and Archaeology at Copán." *Ancient Mesoamerica.* Vol. 3, 169–84

VIEL, RENÉ
1993
Evolución de la cerámica de Copán, Honduras. Tegucigalpa: Instituto Hondureño de Antropología e Historia

WEBSTER, DAVID (ED.)
1989
The House of Bacabs, Copán, Honduras. Washington, D.C.: Dumbarton Oaks

WEBSTER, DAVID, AND ANN C. FRETER
1990
"The Demography of Late Classic Copán." In *Precolumbian Population History in the Maya Lowlands.* Ed. by T.P. Culbert e D.S. Rice. Albuquerque: University of New Mexico Press, 37–61

WEBSTER, DAVID, WILLIAM T. SANDERS, AND PETER VAN ROSSUM
1992
"A Simulation of Copán Population History and Its Implications." *Ancient Mesoamerica.* Vol. 3, 185–97

Cylindrical vessel
made of jadeite mosaic
detail from Tikal, Guatemala
Late Classic period
Guatemala, Museo Nacional
de Arqueclogía y Etnología
cat. 287

The central lowlands are the cradle of Classic Maya civilization. Their territory extends through the majority of the department of Petén in Guatemala, Belize, part of the states of Chiapas and Tabasco, and the south of Campeche and Quintana Roo in Mexico. In this region, archaeologists have discovered abundant evidence demonstrating the significant artistic and intellectual achievements of the ancient Maya, as well as numerous urban centers, the constructions of which have survived the passage of centuries and the ravages of natural phenomena.

The maximum elevation of the central lowlands is less than 2,600 feet (800 meters) above sea level. The environment is characterized by lush tropical forests, savannas, lakes, and shoals or seasonal swamps. The climate is hot and humid because of abundant rainfall. The predominant geological formation corresponds to a layer of limestone of Cenozoic origin that extends throughout the length and breadth of the Yucatán peninsula.

In pre-Hispanic times, access to the central lowlands was relatively easy, since one could arrive by foot or via navigable rivers such as the San Pedro Martir, Río de la Pasión, Usumacinta, Mopán, and Chiquibul. The possibility of transport on these rivers gave some sites, such as Altar de Sacrificios and Ceibal, a strategic role in access, production, and redistribution of important artifacts in the exchange network of the Maya area.

The middle of the central lowlands, where the Petén and Belize are located, offers the earliest Maya centers and therefore it constitutes the original territory from which this civilization spread to the rest of the Maya area. In fact, the Caribbean coasts of Belize seem to have been exploited by bands of hunter-gatherers much earlier than the beginning of sedentary life.

Archaic period

It is thought that the diversity of rich plant and animal resources of the tropical forests of the central lowlands attracted the first populations that emigrated to this territory during the Archaic period (9000–2000 B.C.). Nevertheless, eventually, this zone suffered drastic climatic changes that provoked the extinction of megafauna, which forced the sparse population to change their subsistence habits.

Thus, it is believed that around 3000 B.C. sedentarism began as the result of the domestication of edible plants such as maize, chili, squash, and some tubers. Unfortunately, information on this early period is still fairly limited, because there is very little archaeological evidence.

At sites in Belize such as Ladyville and Colhá, *Clovis*-type projectile points and grains of pollen dating to the Archaic period have been recovered, which indicate the presence of maize and manioc horticulture around 2500 B.C. At the same time, deer, peccaries, dogs, fish, and shellfish provided the necessary protein for subsistence.

Early Preclassic period

Information on the Early Preclassic period (2500–900 B.C.) in the Petén and Belize is also a bit sketchy, although it is believed that some sedentary agricultural villages with a tribal type of organization were present in the central lowlands from this time. Nomadic bands of hunter-gatherers probably occupied that region sporadically from the remotest times.

In any case, it is believed that the population of the region grew gradually due to migrations of farmers from two different areas, which occurred approximately between 1200 and 800 B.C. The first group, Maya speakers, came from the Guatemalan highlands and established themselves in the northeast section at sites such as Cuello and Nakbé.

The second, perhaps Mixe-Zoque speakers, arrived from the Chiapan highlands to settle in the Río de la Pasión valley, at sites such as Altar de Sacrificios and Ceibal. These tribal groups resided in small villages, with less than one hundred inhabitants, and they cultivated maize as their main agricultural product, a fact established by the discovery of maize, pollen, and grinding stones at Cuello in northern Belize.

The centre of El Mirador
Late Preclassic period
reconstruction drawing

In addition, based on the results of excavations at Cuello, it is known that the production of ceramics and the construction of stone buildings began in the last centuries of the Early Preclassic period.

Evidence of the practice of funerary rites also appears for the first time, because under some small habitational platforms from this period, graves have been found accompanied by ceramic vessels as offerings.

Middle Preclassic period

The population grew gradually during the Middle Preclassic period (900–300 B.C.); by 600 B.C. the first agrarian communities expanded toward the inhabited zones of the central lowlands, following the course of the major rivers. Eventually, villages grew slowly in number, extension, and complexity as adaptation to the jungle environment allowed them to prosper. When the size of villages increased, pioneer groups splintered off to establish new tribal communities.

It is believed that social stratification began in the Middle Preclassic, between 1000 and 600 B.C., because at this time relatively substantial ceremonial centers with public architecture, suggesting the existence of chiefdoms, began to emerge. For example, Nakbé, in the northeastern Petén, has provided the best evidence of the beginning of monumental civic-religious constructions found to date in the lowlands. Between 600 and 400 B.C., this site was transformed into a ceremonial center on a monumental scale when two massive basal platforms measuring 105 and 148 feet (32 and 45 meters) in height were constructed in the two main architectural groups of the site, as well as a series of structures with terraces, the height of which ranges from 13 to 59 feet (4 and 18 meters).

The construction of public buildings began to play a preponderant role in architectonic patterns. In particular, this may be observed in the building of the first architectural pattern of ceremonial character in the lowlands, a plaza grouping composed of a long platform placed on the east side facing a pyramid on the west side. Smaller buildings sometimes close the north and south sides of this type of grouping. Examples of this architectural configuration, which has arbitrarily been designated complex E, Astro-

Aerial view of Tikal

nomical Observatory, Astronomical Commemoration Complex, and Ritual Commemoration Complex, may be seen at Uaxactún, Nakbé, Tintal, and Tikal.

The presence of this type of building indicates that religion was increasingly important within the original institutions of Maya society and suggests the emergence of a religious elite with administrative power, who acted as an intermediary between gods and men, especially interceding before those deities that they believed had some relation with agricultural cycles.

The population not only maintained the elite, but also provided the manpower necessary for the construction of monumental buildings in ceremonial centers. Nevertheless, it is believed that the resident population in these complexes was composed mostly of chiefs or hereditary rulers, priests, and servants, plus a small number of craftsmen. The rest of the population perhaps resided in modest wooden huts thatched with palm leaves and located around the epicenters.

Another new trait of the Middle Preclassic is the implementation of long-distance trade around 1000 B.C., as attested to by the discovery of shells from the Caribbean Sea, as well as obsidian and jade from the Guatemalan highlands at sites such as Cuello, Nakbé, Uaxactún, Tikal, Altar de Sacrificios, and Ceibal. Long-distance trade not only fostered access to exotic goods, but also the formation of workshops, specialists, and redistribution systems among early sites–all of which strengthened the privileged social position of chiefs, as administrators responsible for the importation of foreign goods.

Late Preclassic period

The development of Maya populations continued into the Late Preclassic period (300 B.C.–A.D. 250) and seems to have accelerated during the last centuries of the first millennium B.C., when considerable demographic increase occurred. At the same time, the proportion of the population involved in agrarian labors increased. The elites of this period had the ability to mobilize large groups of workers to build enormous temples; they implemented complicated iconographic programs, participated more actively in even more distant exchange networks, and exploited to a maximum their organizational know-how to make their urban centers prosper.

Structure E-VII-sub, Uaxactún
Late Preclassic period
reconstruction drawing

Until now, the most dramatic evidence of the emergence of early state societies in the central lowlands has been provided by centers such as Nakbé, El Mirador, Uaxactún, Tikal, Calakmul, and Lamanai. The monumentality and extension of ritual buildings such as Structure 5C-54 at Tikal, N10-43 at Lamanai, and especially the El Tigre complex at El Mirador, which rises 181 feet (55 meters) above the surface of the land, constitute impressive examples of the organizational complexity of Maya elites during the Late Preclassic period.

In fact, Nakbé, El Mirador, and Lamanai well could have reached urban dimensions in the last centuries of the first millennium before Christ. A little later, at Tikal, the transformation began toward the development of nucleated urban centers, a feature that will characterize Maya sites during the next period.

The large architectonic complexes of the Preclassic period, constructed around plazas, were built with well-cut limestone blocks covered with stucco. Furthermore, the construction of formal masonry tombs also began for the purpose of depositing the remains of rulers.

In Nakbé, El Mirador, and Tintal, uncommon energy was invested in the construction of triadic monumental groups, which consist of an enormous platform sustaining three structures. The largest building of these complexes occupies the central position, while the two smaller structures are found each side of the main edifice. The symbolism of the triadic groups seems related to G-I, G-II, and G-III, three divine beings mentioned in glyphic texts from the Group of the Cross at Palenque. Some researchers identify the figures of this triad with the Hero Twins, Hunahpu and Xbalanque, and their father Hun Hunahpu, protagonists of the *Popol Vuh*, the sacred book of the Quiches.

At Uaxactún, Tikal, Cerros, Nakbé, El Mirador, and Lamanai, monumental pyramids were constructed with stucco facades decorated with enormous masks flanking stairways and representing important deities of the Maya religious pantheon. The participation of the ruler as *axis mundi* in public rituals of autosacrifice carried out on the platform of these buildings demonstrated the close ties between the sovereign and the gods. Therefore, the masks not only represent the beginning of Maya sculptural art but also suggest the crystallization of the concept of the divine origin of Maya dynasties by way of the use of complex religious symbols, the ideology of which legitimates their right to rule over the population.

For the first time, stone monuments were dedicated with carvings representing rulers, as witnessed by the stelae of Nakbé, Tintal, and El Mirador, carvings in the cave of Loltún, stucco sculptures in buildings at Uaxactún, and murals at Tikal. The iconographic style of these examples displays some similarities with contemporary monuments at Kaminaljuyú, Abaj Takalik, El Baúl, and Izapa, sites located in the highlands and on the southern coast of Guatemala and Mexico.

The growing importance of trade is reflected in the emergence of Cerros in northern Belize. Between 50 B.C. and A.D. 200, this center became a prosperous port of trade strategically located on the Caribbean coast of the central lowlands. Cerros could have functioned as a kind of transit station for raw materials from the Guatemalan highlands such as obsidian, jade, basalt, hematite, and quartzite, as well as cacao and cotton; in addition to other exotic products destined for elites, such as quetzal feathers and fine jade and ceramic artifacts.

At the end of the Late Preclassic period, competition for land, population, and resources seems to have led to wars between political entities. For example, it has been argued that the pit and parapet at the site of Becán in Campeche were constructed during this period.

War could have represented a crucial element for the development of sociopolitical complexity, since it forced populations to unify for reasons of safety. The elite perhaps stimulated migration toward major centers in order to increase their labor force and military capacity. At the same time, the largest cities must have needed better planning and organization to be able to produce and distribute food for urban workers, to form a permanent militia, and to build defensive systems.

Painted tomb from Río Azul
Early Classic period

Early Classic period

The most characteristic attributes of Classic Maya civilization are crystallized during the Early Classic period (A.D. 250–600). Tikal and Uaxactún became capitals of state societies considerably before the beginning of this period, while Caracol, Holmul, and Río Azul emerged as new, vigorous political entities. Although it is believed that at the beginning of the Early Classic there was a decline in the population of the central lowlands, the majority of centers of this period include the presence of hundreds of structures with fine masonry, magnificent temples, causeways, large architectural complexes with palaces and administrative buildings, residential units, and lavish tombs.

Tikal in particular was transformed into the center of the predominant political entity in the central lowlands. The advantageous location between two major drainage systems in the central zone probably gave this city a privileged position with respect to east-west exchange networks between the coast of the Caribbean and the Gulf of Mexico.

The prosperity of Tikal also perhaps resided in its close economic ties with Teotihuacan, the great urban center of the Mexican highlands. The presence of "Teotihuacanoid" elements, such as cylindrical tripod vessels with stepped supports, *talud-tablero* architectural profiles, green obsidian, representations of Tlaloc, the Mexican rain god, and other iconographic elements, constitutes evidence of commercial contact, both in utilitarian as well as sumptuary goods, sustained by Early Classic Maya centers with Teotihuacan.

A major achievement was the development of hieroglyphic writing, the most sophisticated writing system in pre-Hispanic America. On stelae, altars, and panels, the Mayas portrayed rulers, nobles, and deities, which testify to the high quality of architectonic and sculptural aptitudes of the ancient Mayas.

Glyphic texts carved on these monuments record several historical aspects of the life of

opposite
Vessel with screw-on top
used to prepare chocolate
Río Azul
Early Classic period

Temple 1 and 2 of Tikal
Late Classic period

rulers and their relatives and supporters, such as births, marriages, deaths, wars, enthronements, political alliances, and public rituals.

Another exceptional development made during this period was knowledge of astronomy, the calendar, and arithmetic. The Mayas had a 365-day civil calendar that was as precise as the Gregorian calendar, much earlier than the development of observation apparatuses adequate to observe the movement of the planets. Priests elaborated tables that recorded the movements of the sun, moon, Venus, and other celestial bodies. In addition, they were capable of predicting solar and lunar eclipses with great precision. These achievements are probably related to the initial need to predict with certainty the proper time of the year to burn agricultural fields, then plant and harvest them.

The development of fine polychrome ceramics constituted one of the most significant advances during the Early Classic. Other less tangible ones were related to the implementation of institutions linked to social, political, economic, and religious organizations.

Near the end of the Early Classic period, between A.D. 534 and 593, in the central lowlands, especially in the Petén, there seems to have been a problematical period of an unclear nature. The majority of centers located there suffered a hiatus or period during which the dedication of sculpted monuments diminished or ceased. Nevertheless, based on archaeological data it is known that the construction of monumental buildings was not suspended.

Late Classic period

The golden age of Maya civilization corresponds to the Late Classic period (A.D. 600–800), a relatively brief period of uncommon expansion and vigor. Apart from the growth in size and complexity of ceremonial centers, several other factors came together so that the Maya consolidated their civilization status, that is, they became a group of societies composed of large populations with complex economic, social, and political organizations that displayed sophisticated intellectual and ideological development.

The political panorama of the Late Classic period consisted of highly competitive states that used emblem glyphs to differentiate among themselves. Nevertheless, there were marked differences between the autonomous political entities of the region with respect to size, influence, and power.

Tikal was transformed during the Late Classic period into one of the most monumental

Panoramic view of Tikal

The "dancers'" vessel
from Altar de Sacrificios
Late Classic period
Guatemala, Museo Nacional
de Arqueología y Etnología

Ceibal, Guatemala
Terminal Classic period

archaeological sites ever constructed by the Mayas. Based on population estimates, it has been determined that this center came to house between 50,000 and 90,000 inhabitants in the sixth century, as indicated by the presence of more than 4,000 structures dispersed over an area of 6.3 square miles (16 km²). Five enormous temples were built in Tikal during the Late Classic; one of them, Temple IV, reaches 230 feet (70 meters) in height. Apart from these constructions, numerous monuments, temples, palaces, ceremonial platforms, residences, a sweatbath, and five causeways attest to the splendor and power of this city.

Although the central zone continued to be dominated by Tikal for a long time, in that period arose other powerful political entities, such as Naranjo, Piedras Negras, Yaxchilán, Palenque, Dos Pilas, Lubaantún, and Xunantunich. At these major centers, enormous pyramids crowned by small temples were constructed, as well as long, low, multiroom range structures that are frequently designated palaces. In addition, a particular architectural style developed, one characterized by the presence of the false or corbeled arch, instead of the true or Roman arch.

Special structures were also built, such as sweatbaths and ball courts. Although the latter originated in the Preclassic, it is during the Late Classic that they were most frequent and numerous. Like other Mesoamerican peoples, the ancient Mayas practiced the ball game, an activity of great religious significance in pre-Hispanic times. It was played with a rubber ball that normally was bounced on the parallel sloped walls of structures separated by a long playing field resembling a corridor or alley.

Classic Maya civilization is perhaps best known for the excellence of its narrative, baroque artistic style, evident particularly in monuments at Usumacinta Basin sites, such as Piedras Negras. Beautiful and complex representations of people, deities, or animals in bas relief may be seen on stone stelae, altars, and thrones, and in stucco masks on the facades of structures, mural paintings, codices, and jade artifacts. An additional achievement was the beautiful polychrome pottery produced by Maya artisans. Polychrome vessels were frequently deposited in tombs of elite individuals, and they depict scenes with political, religious, or mythological connotations. Today it is possible to identify the names of individuals represented, the owners of vases, and the craftsmen who painted them, as well as the liquids that they once contained.

The high degree of cultural development achieved by the Mayas of the central lowlands is even more surprising given that they only possessed a level of technology corresponding to the Neolithic period. Flint deposits were exploited to produce lithic arti-

opposite
Miniature cylindrical vessel
from Tayasal, Petén
Classic period
Guatemala, Museo Nacional
de Arqueología y Etnología
cat. 132

opposite
Mask made of jadeite, Tikal
Classic period
Guatemala, Museo Nacional
de Arqueología y Etnología
cat. 143

Polychrome plate, Tikal
Late Classic period
Guatemala, Museo Nacional
de Arqueología y Etnología
cat. 47

Cylindrical vessel
made of jadeite mosaic, Tikal
Late Classic period
Guatemala, Museo Nacional
de Arqueología y Etnología
cat. 287

facts necessary to cut, perforate, and scrape. In fact, metal was not introduced into the Maya area until after A.D. 900, during the Postclassic period, and it was not used for anything other than fine jewelry. In addition, they had no beasts of burden, nor did they use the wheel for the transport of enormous, heavy stones that they used to construct their major buildings.

As for social organization, there is no doubt that it was of a pyramidal structure, given that the Maya elite enjoyed greater wealth than the rest of the population, judging by the quality and size of their residences, the diversity of artifacts associated with their dwellings, the opulence of their tombs, and the greater access to prestige goods that were exchanged by the Mayas with peoples of adjacent or distant regions. Farmers, who provided the agricultural sustenance and physical labor necessary to maintain and enlarge centers, lived within and around the epicenter, in residential units made of perishable materials that were constructed occasionally on small stone platforms.

The population of Classic Maya settlements varied from several hundred and a few thousand in small towns, to dozens of thousands in cities as large as Tikal. To support this level of population, in addition to the slash and burn system, they developed a series of methods and techniques of intensive agriculture, such as raised fields, the cultivation of *bajos*, and terraced agriculture. They also diversified agriculture by cultivating fruit trees, tubers, fruits, and so forth.

Wars between political entities of the central lowlands occurred more frequently during the last centuries of the Late Classic period. In particular, the rivalry between Tikal and Calakmul, the two preponderant centers of the region, resulted in a series of collateral conflicts between other sites such as Caracol, Naranjo, Yaxhá, Dos Pilas, and Ceibal. In the region of the Río de la Pasión, Dos Pilas established itself for some time as a powerful, expansionistic, militaristic center, whose dynasty proclaimed their genealogical connections with the ruling family of Tikal. These conflicts threatened the prestige and confidence of dynasties, changing forever some of the basic political institutions of Maya society.

Terminal Classic period

The Terminal Classic period (A.D. 800–900) constitutes the final part of the Late Classic, and it consists of the dramatic decline suffered by Maya centers of the central lowlands, culminating in the collapse of the Classic Maya sociopolitical system. This era saw a serious ecological imbalance, overpopulation, invasions, artistic and architectural decline, weakening of the power structure of sociopolitical institutions, migrations, and finally, the abandonment of the majority of principal centers.

Bowl with lid, Tikal
Early Classic period
Guatemala, Museo Nacional
de Arqueología y Etnología
cat. 38

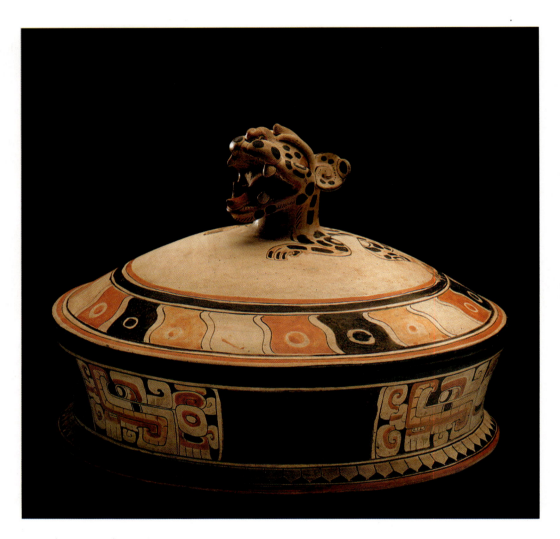

In order to confront this crisis, the Maya elite undertook some structural changes, as suggested by the atypical florescence of Ceibal, a center on the Río de la Pasión. While the majority of political entities of the region collapsed, Ceibal enjoyed a constructive and populational peak during this period. It has been proposed that this situation was provoked by the arrival of groups of invaders called "Putuns," who came from the region called the Chontalpa. This interpretation is based on Terminal Classic stela of Ceibal displaying figures with "non-Classic Maya" features and "Mexican" glyphs; in addition, on the adoption of architectural modes with foreign connotations and the introduction of gray and fine orange paste ceramics, related to a different pottery tradition. Nevertheless, this hypothesis has been refuted in recent times, because the adoption of supposedly foreign sculptural and architectural styles at Ceibal perhaps simply reflects the authority and prestige claimed by local rulers.

In any event, the socioeconomic transformations experienced at Ceibal were unsuccessful, because this center was abandoned around A.D. 950. Thus, in less than a hundred years, Classic Maya civilization collapsed completely, because by the middle of the ninth century, the construction of civic, ritual, and residential structures ceased entirely. In addition, the maximum exploitation of agricultural potential that the Mayas had managed to develop in the central lowlands over the course of two millennia came to an end. Manufacturing, distribution, and exchange of traditional prestige items, such as quetzal feathers and fine ceramic, jade, wood, bone, and shell artifacts also disappeared.

Given the lack of consensus on the most important factor for the collapse, archaeologists have proposed that it was a gradual phenomenon provoked by a series of interrelated factors that, as a whole, caused the weakening of Classic Maya civilization and led to its downfall. Thus, there are different interpretations that arbitrarily take as fundamental factors civil wars, invasions, plagues, natural catastrophes, overpopulation, exhaustion of overexploited resources, or the interruption of extraregional trade networks.

In any case, a few years after the collapse, whatever its nature may have been, the tropical jungle of the region covered the plazas and temples where before the population had gathered to celebrate impressive civic-religious ceremonies. In the search for better horizons, the populations surviving the cataclysm of the central lowlands went northward to the Yucatán peninsula, where they would temporarily enjoy a period of resurgence until the arrival of Spanish invaders in the sixteenth century.

References

ADAMS, RICHARD E. W. (ED.)
1967
The Origins of Maya Civilization. Albuquerque: University of New Mexico Press

ASHMORE, WENDY (ED.)
1981
Lowland Maya Settlement Patterns. Albuquerque: University of New Mexico Press, School of American Research

CHASE, ARLEN F., AND DIANE Z. CHASE (EDS.)
1992
Mesoamerican Elites: An Archaeological Assessment. Norman: University of Oklahoma Press

CULBERT, PATRICK T. (ED.)
1973
The Classic Maya Collapse. Albuquerque: University of New Mexico Press
1991
Classic Maya Political History: Hieroglyphic and Archaeological Evidence. Albuquerque: University of New Mexico Press

CULBERT, PATRICK T., AND DON S. RICE (EDS.)
1990
Precolumbian Population History in the Maya Lowlands. Albuquerque: University of New Mexico Press

SABLOFF, JEREMY A.
1990
The New Archaeology and the Ancient Maya. New York: Scientific American Library

SABLOFF, JEREMY A., AND E. WYLLYS ANDREWS V (EDS.)
1986
Late Lowland Maya Civilization. Classic to Postclassic. Albuquerque: University of New Mexico Press, School of American Research

SABLOFF, JEREMY A., AND HENDERSON JOHN S. (EDS.)
1993
Lowland Maya Civilization in the Eighth Century A.D. Washington, D.C.: Dumbarton Oaks

SCHELE, LINDA, AND MARY ELLEN MILLER
1986
The Blood of Kings: Dynasty and Ritual in Maya Art. Fort Worth: Kimbell Art Museum

SHARER, ROBERT J.
1994
The Ancient Maya. 5th ed., Stanford, Calif.: Stanford University Press

WILLEY, GORDON R., AND PETER MATHEWS (EDS.)
1985
A Consideration of the Early Classic Period in the Maya Lowlands. Publication 10. Institute for Mesoamerican Studies. Albany: State University of New York

The Metropolis of Calakmul, Campeche

The northwest region of the central Maya area, explored in the early 1930s and mid-1940s, received relatively little attention until recent years. Now research has revealed that the urban centers in this region participated actively in the development of Maya culture from its beginnings.

After the discovery of the archaeological site of Calakmul by American biologist Cyrus Lundell in 1931, the Carnegie Institution of Washington sponsored a survey of the region, conducted in 1933 by Karl Ruppert and John Denison. In this study, which was the only one for the area, a series of sites were recorded that are affiliated with the stylistic entities known in the archaeological literature as Río Bec and Petén, Calakmul belongs to the latter.

For a thousand years since its ancient inhabitants abandoned the site and for the sixty-six years after its rediscovery in 1931, Calakmul lay hidden amid the dense vegetation and immensity of the Campechan jungle. Today it awakens, illuminated by the light of knowledge, as a result of several years of exploration, research, restoration, and salvage work to recover its public spaces and sacred precincts. Based on the most recent studies of the epigraphic record, today we know that Calakmul is the most important archaeological zone in southern Campeche because it was one of the superpowers and leading urban centers of the Classic period.

From the time the central Maya area was first settled, its geopolitical history seems to be divided into two camps, marking relations and conflicts that prevailed throughout the entire Classic period. The region of Calakmul and the northern Guatemalan Petén received influences both from the south and from the north due to its location at the heart of the Maya area. Ever since its inception, Calakmul was aligned with a regional sphere integrating the sites of El Mirador, Nakbé, and Uaxactún during the Formative or Preclassic period. During the Middle Preclassic period (700 to 300 B.C.), and corresponding to the earliest evidence for the area, Nakbé emerged as the predominant site, where administrative systems were already well defined by the end of this period. In the Preclassic architecture of Nakbé, platforms and buildings of more than 20 meters in height have been found, showing that in the Maya area, just as in other regions of Mesoamerica, such as Oaxaca and the central Mexican highlands, more enduring masonry architecture had been developed by this time.

During the third century B.C., certain population centers begin to consolidate politically, which allowed them to undertake urban works of major importance. In the southern Maya area, cities of a certain magnitude arose, such as Chiapa de Corzo, Izapa, and Kaminaljuyú; in the northern Yucatán, Dzibilchaltún is the site that marks the beginning of the architectonic tradition of the peninsula.

Mask with earflares
Calakmul, Campeche
Late Classic period
Campeche, Museo Histórico
Fuerte de San Miguel
Baluarte de San Miguel
cat. 141

At this same time, within the tropical jungle, in the geographic center of the Maya world, El Mirador built its imposing triadic complexes and at Calakmul we find the first evidence of public architecture in the building of the largest structures of its entire history.

Years later, Uaxactún and Tikal established their long architectural tradition. In the course of the Early Preclassic period (300 B.C. to 150 A.D.), the sites of Calakmul, El Mirador, and Uaxactún were consolidated into a region at odds with the neighbors to the south, especially Tikal, with which it established a permanently hostile relationship during the two following periods.

Although it is evident from available archaeological evidence that the Maya lowlands were populated around 900 A.D., the focus of cultural traits characterizing the essence of Maya culture arose in the axis that includes Nakbé, El Mirador, Uaxactún, Calakmul, and Tikal. The latter two are the earliest settlements recorded to date, and they also display evidence of an uninterrupted architectonic tradition of more than fourteen centuries from 550 B.C. to 900 A.D. Calakmul and Tikal are also remarkable for the large number of stelae and dated monuments, on which the history of these people is recorded, spanning almost the entire Classic period from the third century until the end of the ninth century A.D.

As for architecture with elements sculpture in stone and modeled in stucco, the most ancient examples known are the stuccoed masks on Building 34 of the El Tigre Complex at El Mirador and the well-known pyramid Structure E-VII-sub at Uaxactún, with its masks flanking the four stairways of the platform. Tikal is also part of this tradition, with stuccoed masks, such as those found in the North Acropolis or on structures at El Mundo Perdido. El Mirador and Uaxactún, as already mentioned, are affiliated with the northern sphere of the southern Maya lowlands in which Calakmul actively participates.

From its inception, public architecture is implicitly burdened with an ideological sense through which power structures represent magic-religious concepts and myths. In the Maya vision of the cosmos, since the Preclassic period, plazas were viewed as the Primordial Sea, and large platforms as Mountains of Creation at the foot of which were erected stelae symbolizing Sacred Trees. The bases of platforms were generally decorated with masks sculpture in stone and modeled in stucco representing cosmic images connecting rulers to the world of the gods.

At the beginning of our era, the construction of corbeled arches, a distinctive trait of Maya architecture, is first seen at the neighboring city of Tikal. These primitive arches are

Map of Calakmul, Campeche
Roman numbers refer
to the numbers which appear
on the structures
of the monumental area

opposite
Tripod vessel displaying
the representation
of the Celestial Bird deity
Tomb 2, Structure IVB
Calakmul, Campeche
Early Classic period
Campeche, Museo Histórico
Fuerte de San Miguel
Baluarte de San Miguel
cat. 256

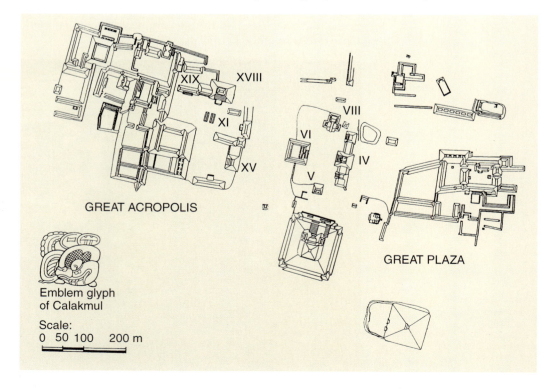

GREAT ACROPOLIS

GREAT PLAZA

Emblem glyph
of Calakmul

Scale:
0 50 100   200 m

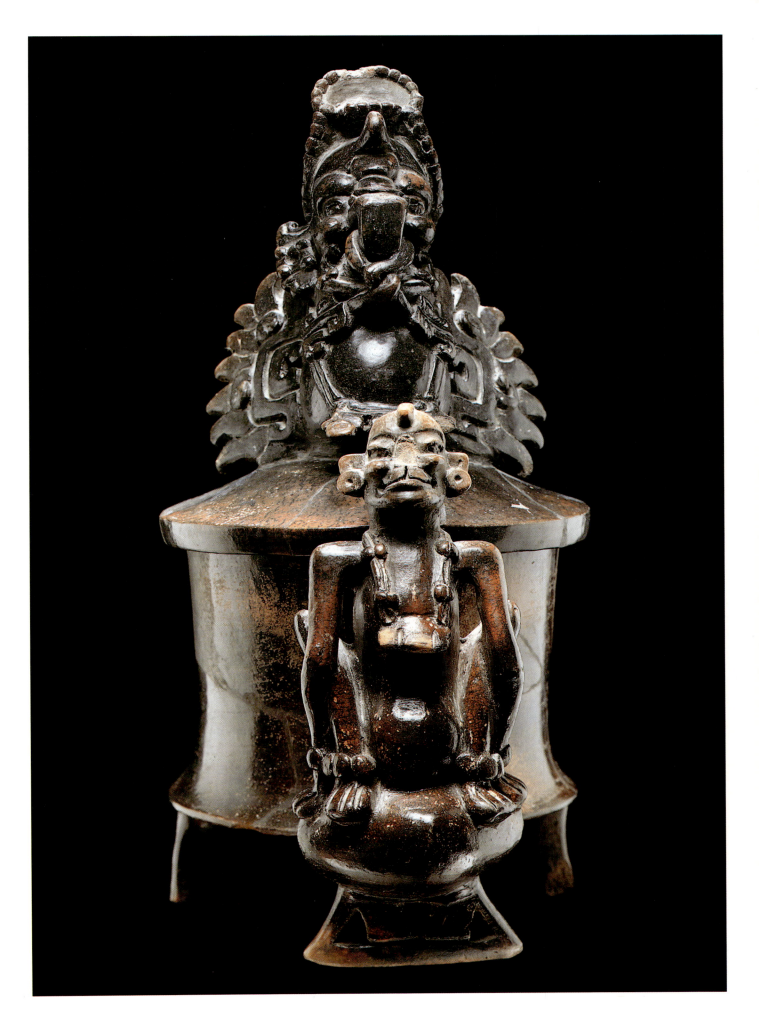

made to cover the tombs of important individuals. Once it was perfected for funerary uses, the arch was then incorporated in monumental architecture, first to cover masonry temples and later on palaces and administrative buildings. Around the middle of the first century A.D., the bases of formal as well as structural elements defining the architectural tradition of the Maya area were established, especially the corbeled arch. The examples known to date are the vaulted palaces of Group H of Uaxactún and those of the North Acropolis of Tikal.

Another element of the pan-Maya tradition is the erection of dated monuments, generally at regular intervals, such as stelae, altars, wood or stone lintels, or texts on the walls of buildings, on ceramics, or on other artifacts. It is in this region that the Long Count system is perfected and that hieroglyphic writing, which tells us the history of these people, reaches the peak of its splendor. The use of the Maya arch, heavy roof-combs crowning the early sanctuaries, and dated monuments together define the beginning of the Classic period at Tikal while in Uaxactún during the second half of the third century A.D.

Commemorating the year 292 A.D., Tikal Stela 29 is, to date, the oldest monument in the Maya lowlands and the earliest of the Classic period. Its "primitive" style establishes a stylistic school that is seen throughout stelae erected at different cities until the first half of the fifth century A.D. During the first centuries of our era, Tikal was the axis around which the politics of the central Petén revolved. Various kingdoms offered tribute to its rulers, who established and consolidated the Sky dynasty. In the following century, the interests of the Tikal royal house began to conflict with those of other states and especially with those of what would become its main rival, its northern neighbor Calakmul.

In what has been identified as the northern sphere of the southern lowlands, after the rise of Nakbé in the Middle Preclassic period and El Mirador in the first half of the Late Preclassic period, these centers had to yield to the growing influence of Uaxactún to the south and Calakmul to the north of their territory.

During the second half of the Early Preclassic, Uaxactún had achieved major development and contributed to establishing the foundations of the pan-Maya tradition. In the Classic period, it became one of the power centers, though reduced by the consolidation of the dynasties of Tikal and Calakmul, which played principal roles in the politics of the Maya lowlands during this period.

From recent interpretations of epigraphic texts, it may be inferred that the kings of the Maya Classic period created political organizations that resulted in a wide network of alliances. These "political units," which have been called "superpowers," were based on a diplomacy that employed several resources, from marriage alliances to vassalage. The two great centers that competed for hegemony over the southern Maya lowlands during the Classic period were Tikal and Calakmul.

From the long process of evolution of Maya culture that began in the ninth century B.C., Tikal emerged as the great center of power in the Early Classic period. In the beginning, its most ancient inscriptions, such as those on Stela 29, refer only to aspects of chronology and genealogy. A few decades later, the relations of vassalage of Bejucal and Motul de San José with Tikal indicate that the kingdoms near this urban center were closely linked. Uaxactún was affiliated with the northern sphere, interacting with Calakmul and El Mirador during the Formative period. In the year 377, it was forced to maintain strong ties with Tikal, its neighbor to the south. By these dates, Smoking Frog, son of Huh Chaan Mah Kina (Tapir) of Tikal, occupied Uaxactún and celebrated a victory ceremony, an important event recorded on Stela 18 of Tikal and Stelae 4 and 5 of Uaxactún. There is clear evidence that in its expansion politics, Tikal extended its influence to kingdoms as distant as Caracol in Belize. The accession of the ruler Yahaw Te Kinich in 533 under the auspices of the ruler Double Bird of Tikal is recorded at this site.

While Tikal was implementing its policy of expansion in the south, the city reached an unequaled peak with the ascent of Ka wil Chaan (Stormy Sky) to the throne in the year 426. At the same time, in the north, the kingdom of Serpent Head (Kul Kan Ahau) became a great political unit or *cuuchcabal* in which Calakmul seems to represent the center where alliances were sanctioned and conflicts settled.

The metropolis of Calakmul was set in one of the largest tropical forest ecological reserves

Tetrapod vessel
Calakmul, Campeche
Early Classic period
Campeche, Museo Histórico
Fuerte de San Miguel
Baluarte de San Miguel

following pages
Tripod vessel
with anthropomorphic supports
Calakmul, Campeche
Early Classic period
Campeche, Museo Histórico
Fuerte de San Miguel
Baluarte de San Miguel
cat. 254

Funerary mask made of ceramic representing Ku Hix
Tomb 2, Structure IVB, Calakmul
Early Classic period
Campeche, Museo Histórico
Fuerte de San Miguel
Baluarte de San Miguel

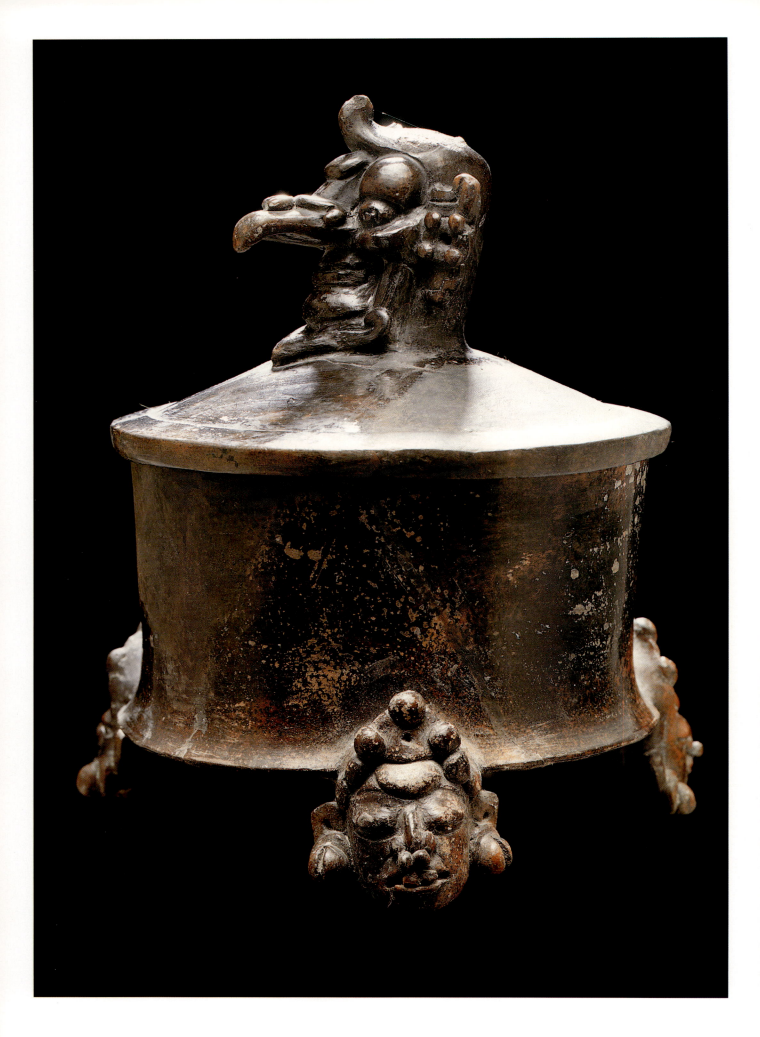

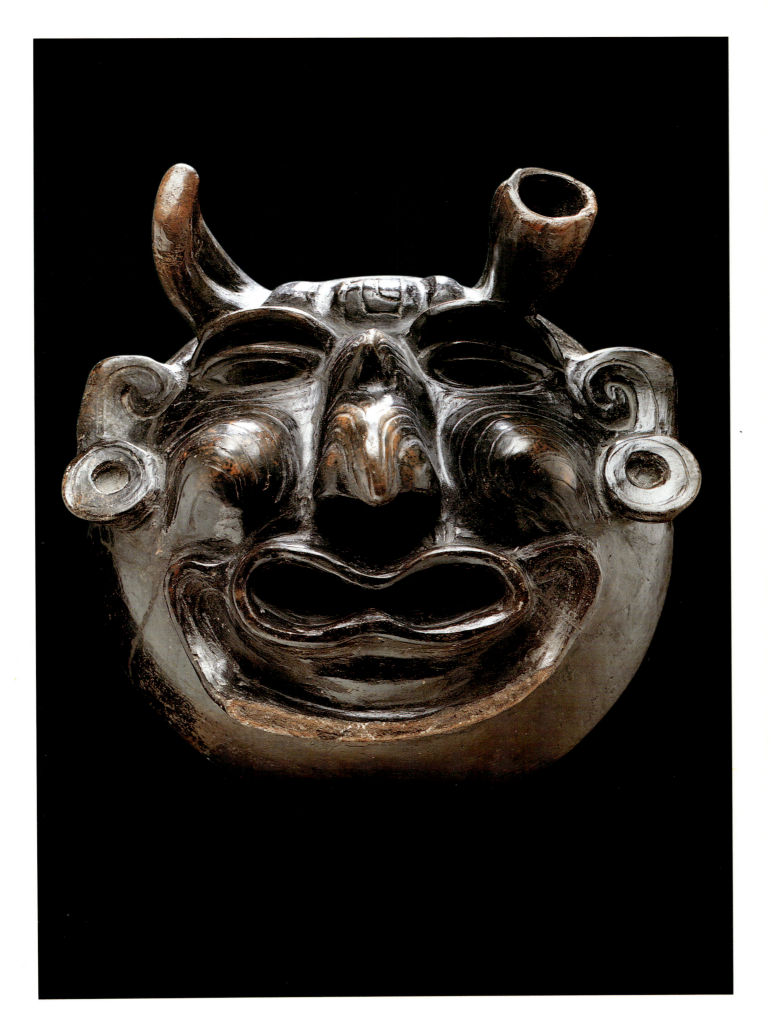

Distribution of the *cuuchcabal* emblem glyph of the kingdom of Serpent

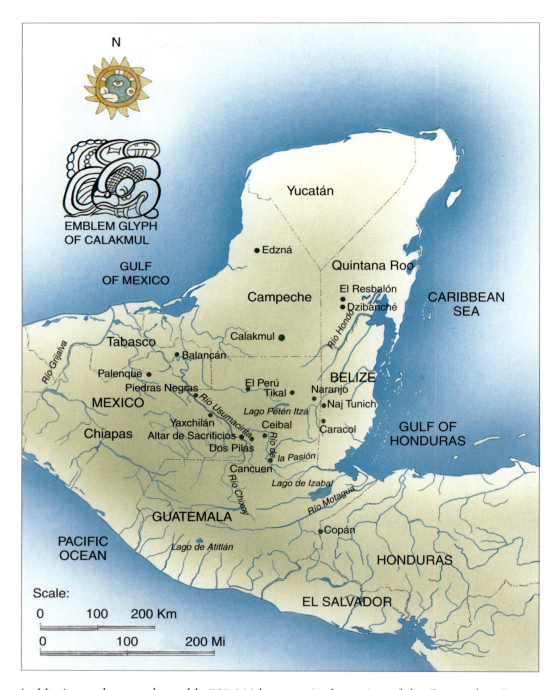

N

EMBLEM GLYPH
OF CALAKMUL

GULF
OF MEXICO

Yucatán

Edzná

Quintana Roo

El Resbalón

Campeche

Dzibanché

CARIBBEAN
SEA

Calakmul

Río Hondo

Tabasco

Balancán

Palenque

Piedras Negras

El Perú

BELIZE

Naranjo

Río Grijalva

Tikal

Naj Tunich

Río Usumacinta

MEXICO

Lago Petén Itzá

Yaxchilán

Ceibal

Caracol

GULF OF
HONDURAS

Chiapas

Altar de Sacrificios

Dos Pilas

Río de la Pasión

Cancuen

Lago de Izabal

Río Chixoy

Río Motagua

GUATEMALA

Copán

PACIFIC
OCEAN

Lago de Atitlán

HONDURAS

Scale:

0   100   200 Km

0   100   200 Mi

EL SALVADOR

in Mexico and covered roughly 723,000 hectares in the region of the Campechan Petén, only a few kilometers from the border between Mexico and Guatemala. This region shares with the Guatemalan Petén not only similar characteristics in flora, fauna, and orography, but also, as we already mentioned, an architectonic style, characterized by buildings constructed on large platforms topped by vaulted precincts with small rooms. The ornamentation of the structures, based on modeled and polychromed stucco, forms a visual unity with the platforms, where the color red predominates. At Calakmul, in the course of the Early and Late Classic period, a large number of sculpture monuments were erected, since it was one of the sites in the Maya area with the largest number of stelae: 120 have been reported to date.

The main nucleus of Pre-Hispanic vestiges in the city of Calakmul was situated on a natural mound of approximately 25 square kilometers. This core was surrounded by watering places and canals constructed to store water, exploiting the areas that flooded easily during

Calakmul, Campeche

the rainy season. Within the territorial space of the mound, settlements are more or less dispersed; the monumental sector occupies the core. In this section, beginning in the Early Preclassic period, two large pyramids were built that dominate the jungle from which the name "Calakmul" is derived and which means "two adjacent mounds." At the same time, palatial complexes resembling large acropolises with buildings around patios and plazas were also constructed.

At Calakmul, ceramics from both the Preclassic and the Early Classic were recovered in all buildings investigated. This marker of site occupation indicates continuity in the use of urban spaces of both a residential and a ceremonial nature. The Early Classic is the period of the greatest production of ceramics, which were found sealed in tombs of Structures IV-B and III. Structure III is the only palace of the typical Petén style that has not been modified in the course of Calakmul's history; it was probably preserved as the heritage of one of the site's most ancient lineages.

In the fifth century, under the direction of members of the Ma Cuch lineage, Tikal completed the ambitious architectonic program begun by Smoking Frog, thus consolidating its prestige as power center.

At Calakmul the ruler who ordered the carving of Stela 114 remodeled the great Preclassic platform of Structure II. The front was covered with enormous zoomorphic masks, measuring more than four meters in height and flanking a monumental stairway, at the foot of which Stela 114 was dedicated in the year 431. Apparently Calakmul then started an extensive renovation project aimed at changing the appearance of the city without modifying the urban plan. In the course of fifth century, the kingdom of Serpent Head begins to consolidate and intensify its foreign politics, just as at Tikal. The first records of probable relations between Calakmul and other power centers are documented at Dzibanché, Quintana Roo in the year 495 A.D., but in the next century, alliances intensified to bring Tikal's hegemony to an end.

Between the middle of the sixth century and the beginning of the eighth, in the agitated political history of the central Maya area, the Serpent Head *cuuchcabal* had consolidated a wide network of strategic alliances, interwoven with lineages of kingdoms as distant as those of the Usumacinta basin or the Petexbatun region.

Around the year 537, a vassal lord of the ruler Ku Hix Kab of Calakmul acted as an emissary of this city in a ritual celebrated by the tenth king of Yaxchilán. In the year 546, Ku Hix sanctioned the accession of Ruler I of Naranjo; in Stela 25 from this site it is recorded that the event took place in the territory of Ku Hix, the *ahau* of Calakmul. With these acts of legitimization of power, the Serpent Head *cuuchcabal* initiated hegemonic policies demonstrating its long-distance influence, which suggests the implementation of a deliberate strategy against Tikal.

Under the rulership of Ku Hix, some renovation projects in the Great Plaza of Calakmul were undertaken, one of which was the remodeling of Structure IV where his remains were buried after his death. The dating of his tomb, based on carbon-14 evidence, yielded results of 560 ± 50, which is consistent with the date of his death. The funerary chamber where his

Mask with earflares
made of large pieces of jadeite
Calakmul, Campeche
Late Classic period
Campeche, Museo Histórico
Fuerte de San Miguel
Baluarte de San Miguel
cat. 146

remains were placed has been profaned in the Late Classic period and part of its contents, specifically the icons of power associated with his investiture, were placed in niches conditioned in the construction fill of Structure IV.

Among the objects in the tomb's offering was a funerary mask made of ceramic representing an individual of advanced age, which seems to portray Ku Hix at the moment of his death. Analysis of the bone remains indicates the advanced age of the dead. In Structure IV, Ku Hix ordered the placement of the only stone lintel reported for this region, though this kind of element was very common in the architecture of the Usumacinta basin; the lintel represents him in a ritual dance of rebirth at the edge of the cosmic cleft.

Double Bird of Tikal broke the alliance that he had established with Caracol since 553, when in the year 556 he defeated and decapitated a noble from this kingdom. Double Bird was then defeated in 562 by Yahaw Te Kinich of Caracol, who established the first strong diplomatic ties with Calakmul. After this defeat, virtually no dated monument was erected at Tikal for a period of 130 years.

Years later, Caracol became the principal ally of Calakmul. Around the beginning of the seventh century, as the visible head of these alliances, the Serpent Head *cuuchcabal* asserted its hegemony in the region, setting itself up as the center of a network of affiliated states and as one of the two superpowers of the Classic period.

Continuing the policy of strengthening of the Serpent Head kingdom, begun by Ku Hix, U ? Kaan la, who ascended to the throne of Calakmul in 564, consolidated the alliance with Caracol in 572. This event is recorded on Caracol Stela 3, commissioned by Kan II, where U ? Kaan la is mentioned as one of the protagonists. This alliance was reaffirmed through the marriage of Lady Batz Ek. Batz Ek married the father of Kan II to secure ties between Calakmul and Caracol after the war against Tikal. U ? Kaan la also established relations with other distant centers; his name is recorded at Palenque in 599.

At the end of the Early Classic period, around 579, U ? Kan ascended to power at Calakmul. He was responsible for one of the first remodeling projects of Structure V, converting it into the most important commemorative building of the site. In the course of a half a century, twelve stelae were erected. Unfortunately, only a few Long Count dates have been preserved, as well as the inscription on Stela 33 where U ? Kan declares that he is the successor of U ? Kaan la. Just as his predecessor, U ? Kan is also mentioned on Stela 4 from Caracol and on the Temple of the Inscriptions at Palenque, which seems to record a confrontation between these two kingdoms in the year 611.

At the beginning of the seventh century Calakmul was the center of the network of the most important alliances in the Maya area. The ascent of the Yukom lineage in this century marks the period in which the diplomatic abilities of their rulers led Calakmul to become a superpower in the southern Maya lowlands. Employing a policy putting into

practice different diplomatic resources ranging from marriage alliance to warfare, they consolidated the Serpent Head *cuuchcabal* to place it at the center of the most extensive network of states of both allies as well as subordinate centers. Starting at this time, references to Calakmul in the inscriptions of other sites multiply and in epigraphic texts; approximately eighty references, including emblem glyphs and place names, allude to the kingdom of the Serpent.

The rulers who ascended the throne of Calakmul undertook private and public urban works in different sectors of the city. In these decades, the building activity increased the palatial complexes of the acropolis, and units dedicated to artistic and specialized craft production were built. Here craftsmen filled commissions for ceramics and other objects of ritual use for their lords.

In the middle of the Late Classic period, in the year 686, one of the most renowned rulers, known in hieroglyphic texts as Yukum Yichak Kak (Great Jaguar Claw), ascended the throne of the Serpent Head kingdom. This controversial figure was involved in a war with Hasaw Chan Kawil, the new *ahau* of Tikal, the kingdom that seems to have been the traditional rival of Calakmul.

There are several accounts of this event, in which the war captains of the *cuuchcabal* of Serpent Head were defeated. On the wooden lintel of Temple I of Tikal, Hasaw Chan Kawil ordered the carving of an inscription declaring that he captured and sacrificed Jaguar Claw on August 5, 695. While this was the official version of events written by members of the Tikal lineage, new archaeological data indicate that Yukum Yichak Kak was probably buried at Calakmul. His remains were found in Tomb 4 of Structure II in January, 1997, which indicates that he probably died after his defeat. The text on a polychrome plate from the offering of Tomb 4 seems to indicate that the remains are those of Jaguar Claw. The inscription, written in elegant calligraphy, records the nominal clause of Yukum Yichak Kak or Great Jaguar Claw surrounding the icon of the head of the Jester God, the tutelary deity of royal lineages. The presence of this deity on some of the vessels of the funerary furnishings seems to reiterate that the royal person of Calakmul, the great *ahau* Jaguar Claw, was buried in this magnificent tomb.

It seems that Great Jaguar Claw himself ordered the construction of the funerary chamber, with its surface finish of painted, stamped, and polychromed mud, for his journey to the underworld. Accompanied by a rich offering, he was buried wrapped in a shroud and dressed with a sumptuous costume, including pectoral and jade mask; he wore a pair of ancient earplugs, inherited from his ancestors, placed on his great headdress.

In Calakmul, as part of the costume of the deceased, it was customary to place a fine jade mosaic or clay mask on the corpses of prominent members of the royal family. These masks represent the faces of historical figures as portraits, perpetuating the image of the deceased beyond death.

At the death of Yukum Yichak Kak, and probably as a result of the defeat suffered by the Serpent Head *cuuchcabal* in the year 695, Calakmul's influence in the central Petén gradually declined as Tikal underwent a resurgence. Several years must have passed before the new political situation of the region to was fully realized. Nevertheless, the Serpent Head *cuuchcabal* continued to preserve diplomatic ties with some of its allies such as Dos Pilas in 702, El Perú in 741 and Yaxchilán, one of its earliest allies, in the same year. When conflicts on a pan-regional level became more serious, within the *cuuchcabal* of Calakmul, ruling families struggled for power, and the death of Yichak Kak was a turning point. With the growing influence of Tikal, rulers who succeeded him redirected the politics of the Serpent Head kingdom toward northern traditions.

At the beginning of the eighth century, To ? ni Uch Kawil ascended to the throne. His name is associated in the records of El Perú as one of the last rulers of Calakmul named in the inscriptions of other states. It was probably during his rule that the relations of Calakmul with its neighbors to the north became closer, especially with the Río Bec area.

With the accession of Yukom ? Tok to the throne of Calakmul, more than a century of hegemony of the Yukom lineage came to an end. This ruler began work in the Great Acropolis where he ordered the erection of Stela 66, which represents a ceremony associated with a ball game event.

Structure II of Calakmul, Campeche

It is probable that the successor of Yukom ? Tok was the ruler who started a program of reforms and public works that changed the image of the city toward the end of the Late Classic period. This ruler carried out the last great remodeling project of Structure II, covering the great masks of the Early Classic with several stepped tiers and elevating the front to a height of 30 meters where Structure II-B is built. The preceding has been inferred from the remains of the Initial Series date, corresponding to the year 751, from one of the graffiti found on the eastern jamb of the substructure where Jaguar Claw was buried. Among the other works of Yukom ? Tok are the remodeling of Structure XIII and the construction of the ball court marking the transition between the first and second half of the Late Classic, as deduced from the date corresponding to the year 731 inscribed on Stela 66, which was broken into four parts and used as construction material at the corners of the ball court.

The Late Classic period (600 to 800 A.D.) corresponds to the time of the culmination of Calakmul, when the majority of the stelae reported to date are erected. The high percentages of ceramic production in this period together with those of the Early Classic indicate that these periods represent those of greatest occupation at the site. As already mentioned, toward the end of the Late Classic, architectural activity in some sectors changes the urban physiognomy.

The latest records of inscriptions at Calakmul are found on stelae associated with Structures IV-B and X, dated to 810. At the distant site of Ceibal the last mention of the Serpent Head kingdom appears around the year 849. At this time, which corresponds to the Terminal Classic, ceramics are one of the principal markers and resources for us to understand changes, given the absence of epigraphic information.

A decline in Petén ceramic traditions may be seen at Calakmul in this same period, as well as the city's integration into the development of ceramic spheres of the north of the Yucatán peninsula, with the introduction of new vessel forms, which perhaps are the result of the acceptance of a new element into the diet or a new way of preparing food. Construction activity is restricted to minor remodeling in the buildings of the Great Plaza and during this time the greatest number of monuments known as "plain stelae" are probably erected.

Like the majority of large centers of the Classic period in the southern Maya lowlands, Calakmul reaches its decline. If with the reorientation of its politics around the middle of the Late Classic period, its rulers managed to integrate themselves into the traditions of the north and share with the sites of this region the peak of the Terminal Classic, in the Postclassic period activity is almost exclusively of ceremonial character. The presence of offerings of effigy censers, among other items, in the buildings at Calakmul testify to human activity in the Campechan Petén region during the Late Postclassic period. But, since no Postclassic utilitarian ceramics have been identified at Calakmul, it is believed that these censers were brought to this region by pilgrims.

References

JONES, CHRISTOPHER
1988
"The Life and Times of Ah Cacau, Ruler of Tikal." In *Primer Simposio Mundial sobre Epigrafía Maya*. 107–20.

JONES, CHRISTOPHER, AND LINTON SATTERTHWAITE
1982
"The Monuments and Inscriptions of Tikal: The Carved Monuments." *Tikal Report* no. 33, Part A, University Museum Monograph 44. Philadelphia: The University Museum, University of Pennsylvania.

MARTIN, SIMON
1996
"Calakmul en el registro epigráfico." In *Informe General del Proyecto Arqueológico de la Reserva de la Biósfera de Calakmul*. By R. Carrasco, *et al.* Manuscript in the INAH, Mexico City: Archivo técnico del Consejo de Arqueología. National Institute of Anthropology and History, Technical Archives of the Archaeology Council

MILLER, JEFFREY H.
1974
"Notes on a Stelae Pair Probably from Calakmul, Campeche, México." In *Primera Mesa Redonda de Palenque*, Part 1. Ed. by M.G. Robertson. Pebble Beach, California: Robert Louis Stevenson School, 149–62

SCHELE, LINDA, AND DAVID FREIDEL
1990
A Forest of Kings. The Untold Story of the Ancient Maya. New York: William Morrow and Co.

Female figurine, detail
Jaina Island, Campeche
Late Classic period
Mexico City
Museo Nacional de Antropología
cat. 120

Before Jaina became a settlement of the ancient Mayas, it was an islet separated from the mainland, and before that it was an extension of the coastal plain (like a peninsula) invaded by the sea. The water level of the Gulf of Mexico was subject to fluctuation, perhaps due to changes in temperature.

Thus, when the sea level went down, this extension of mainland remained an islet, barely separated from the coast. Over years of arduous work, a group of inland Maya carried tons of calcareous earth called *sahcab*, as well as hundreds of stones, to the islet in order to raise the level of its surface and form a platform for the structures of the civic-religious center.

As for its name, in the *Códice de Calkiní* (the name of the capital of the Canuls), it is said that "in those seas of the Canuls had his ships Ah Kin Canul. He had four ships in which his slaves fished." Although it does not mention the name of the place, it could have been Hinal, because when William Dampier writes about pirates in the seventeenth century, he says that "on the hill of Hinal filibusters and pirates took refuge, before or after attacking Campeche."

As Jaina is located some 42 kilometers from Campeche and there is a tall mound on the seashore, it is possible that this is the Hinal mentioned by Dampier. However, the original name must have been Hanal, derived from *Ha* or *Ja*, water; *na*, house, temple; and the particle *i* (I) which indicates an abstraction—all suggesting, "Place of the House" or "Temple in the Water."

Today the vegetation of Jaina is composed of mangroves, sabal or fan palms, wild papaya trees, purslane, blue grama grass and other grasses, and aquatic plants in the clear swamps; while fauna consists of herons or egrets, pelicans, kingfishers, doves, moro crabs, turtles, dogfish or small sharks, *salpanos*, and other fish. In ancient times there were also manatees.

Basically the civic-religious center is composed of a large plaza with a tall pyramidal platform at each end and habitational or administrative platforms at the sides. The platform situated at the east end is called Zacpol (White Head); that of the western end, close to the sea, is called Sayosal. This ceremonial nucleus was surrounded by dwellings of common people, made of wooden trunks, mud, and palm, and this is the area where the most burials have been found.

The inhabitants of the island buried their dead directly in the earth in pits or in large ceramic jars. Adults, youths, and some children were shrouded and deposited in the *sahcab*; infants were placed in jars and covered with a tripod plate. The most common position was with corpse flexed on the right or left side and with arms crossed and holding one or more clay figurines that were placed as an offering. Infants were placed seated and flexed within the jars.

Burials in dorsal and ventral decubitus position are rare. The depth of burials varied

The coast of Campeche
and Jaina Island

following pages
Figurine
Jaina Island, Campeche
Late Classic period
Mexico City
Museo Nacional de Antropología
cat. 123

Male figurine
Jaina Island, Campeche
Late Classic period
Mexico City
Museo Nacional de Antropología
cat. 116

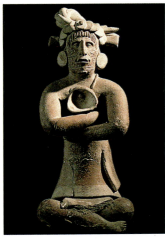

Priest with leather accoutrements
on his face
Mexico City, Instituto Nacional
de Antropología e Historia

Priest with scarification on his face
Mexico City
Instituto Nacional
de Antropología e Historia

opposite
Male figurine
Jaina Island, Campeche
Late Classic period
Mexico City
Museo Nacional de Antropología
cat. 114

following pages
Female figurine
Jaina Island, Campeche
Late Classic period
Mexico City
Museo Nacional de Antropología
cat. 122

Male figurine
Jaina Island, Campeche
Late Classic period
Mexico City
Museo Nacional de Antropología
cat. 104

between 60 centimeters to almost 3 meters, and the deepest appear in water. They were accustomed to depositing an offering with the deceased for the other life in the underworld. Among the objects placed with the deceased are clay figurines, vessels, necklaces, grinding stones (*metates* and *manos*), ornaments and seashell tools, flint points and blades, and other items.

The figurines found in burials at Jaina are the most faithful expression of the fertile imagination and realism achieved by the clay artists of the island. Ceramics reaches the status of true sculpture, where the analytical gives way to the imagination, and where the visual dimension is elevated to the level of mastery.

The clay workers of Jaina used two basic technical procedures to make their figurines: modeling and molds. By way of the former, their able hands formed and shaped the realistic characters of the human model in the clay that convert them into works of art. The second procedure increased the volume of production and perpetuated unique works, perhaps to fill considerable demand.

The physical features of the face, headdress, cranial deformation, scarification, and coiffure are modeled to perfection. The same may be said of the ornaments, costume, postures, rank, and gestures. Some are painted red, white, blue, and yellow, colors perhaps related to the directions of the universe. Because they act as companions to the dead, these objects are also impregnated with cinnabar or red hematite powder that will give them the appearance of life in the underworld.

The figurines may be classified in two groups, solid and hollow. The first are modeled by hand; the second are mold-made. Hollow figurines may be whistles, rattles, and whistle-rattles.

The people who composed the society of the island of Jaina may be seen in the solid and modeled figurines deposited in burials. Many represent the ruling and noble class. There are depictions of important lords seated with dignity on benches or seats; priests with ceremonial costumes and some inside temples; women seated with hands on the knees; warriors; ballplayers with wide waist protectors, knee pads, and arm protectors; dwarfs; one-eyed figures; pregnant women; women weaving on backstrap looms; and many more.

Thus, we see a ruler seated on a circular bench, the symbol of authority. His posture reveals great dignity and his rank is implied by his costume, composed of a large removable headdress, like a helmet with a serpent head edged with precious feathers, related perhaps with the deity Quetzalcoatl or Kukulcan. The figure has a small false beard, circular jade ear ornaments, a ruff with jade beads sewn onto it, and a breastplate hanging from his neck, a skirt with apron, wristlets, leather sandals with heel guards, and a fan in his left hand.

Another figure is seen in a seated position with one hand on his knees and the other half raised. In this case, he wears a headdress like a cap with feather ends. His face is covered by half a leather mask that could be related to the cult to Xipe (god of spring and vegetation), so he is probably a priest serving this deity. Complementing his costume are a skirt with apron, wristlets, and double collar on his neck.

A more general representation of a priest may be seen in another figurine. Here the priest is seated and with his arms crossed over his chest. On his face may be seen scarification and a small false beard. His hair is tied back, leaving bangs on his forehead, and it is tied with a band with attached shell disks. At the same time, he wears a skirt on a loincloth, earplugs, and a shell (mother of pearl) hanging from his neck as a pectoral and symbol of priestly status.

Another magnificent specimen of a solid, hand-modeled figurine is a woman of noble lineage. She is dressed in a large *huipil* (large, loose, woman's upper garment) which covers her breasts and half of her shoulders.

Her hair is parted down the middle with bangs over her forehead. She wears a necklace and earplugs with projecting tubular beads, and she holds in her hands a long staff with a skein of cotton thread, which relates the woman with weaving. She is a spinner.

Among the molded figurines of Jaina, several groups may be distinguished. These

Old blind woman
Jaina Island, Campeche
Late Classic period
Mexico City, Instituto Nacional
de Antropología e Historia

Priest with jaguar disguise
for sacrificial ceremony
Jaina Island, Campeche
Late Classic period
Mexico City, Instituto Nacional
de Antropología e Historia

Female figurine
Jaina Island, Campeche
Late Classic period
Mexico City
Museo Nacional de Antropología
cat. 120

include human beings, animals, temple-deities, and figurines of the central Veracruz type. The group of human beings consists of individuals of different types, such as women wearing hats, ballplayers, dwarfs, old people, blind people, couples with an old man and a young woman, a woman and child, a captive grabbed by the hair, musicians, dancers, and others.

In the group of animals, we have representations of wild turkeys, owls, turtles, monkeys, armadillos, and other species. In the temples-deities group there are images of houses and their associated gods, such as temples dedicated to the feathered serpent, the sun, death, vegetation, and others. Finally, in the group of central-Veracruz-type figures, what predominate are hollow-molded figures, painted white and wearing an embroidered *quechquemitl* (a triangular woman's upper garment) and *huipil*. Sometimes the arms are moveable like puppets. Generally these figurines have one arm upraised.

Exemplifying the first group, the human beings, there is a figurine of a woman whose hair is pulled back and braided with ribbons like a chignon. She has cranial deformation and scarification on her face. Her simple costume consists of a long tunic that covers her breasts and falls over her skirt. Her hands are held close to the waist; one hand grasps a skein of thread to weave, while the other holds a rectangular fan. We can also see a poor blind woman, who is seated with a semiflexed leg and arms raised to chest level. Her hair is pulled back, and she wears only a short skirt tied by a belt. From her neck hangs a thread with a bead.

In the animals group we see an enormous jaguar devouring a person. Because the jaguar is a symbol of the earth, the composition may be interpreted as signifying the earth eating the dead; it might also refer to a priest dressed as a jaguar with a victim

Ballplayer seated on a temple
with two dwarfs
Mexico City, Instituto Nacional
de Antropología e Historia

Woman with *quechquemitl*
such as those from central Veracruz
Mexico City, Instituto Nacional
de Antropología e Historia

for sacrifice. Among the group of temple-deities, we see one of Tlaloc, as the rain god, that is constructed on a platform with masonry walls, a frieze decorated with *chalchihuites* (green stone jewels representing water) and a mask with goggles. The entirety is crowned by a crest of precious feathers.

To the sides of the temple are two jaguar heads (symbolizing the land); at the entrance is a seated ballplayer dressed with typical game accessories: arm protector, waist protector, and knee pad. At his sides, on the platform, are two seated dwarfs, who served as companions both for good luck in the game, and later in the underworld, in the event that he lost. Players passed the night before the game inside the temple. And of the central Veracruz-type, we have an orange clay figurine with remnants of white paint. It represents a woman standing with her right hand raised.

She is dressed in a *quechquemitl* woven with designs related to Tlaloc as the god of war (eyebrows, circular eyes, mustache, and teeth), and a *huipil* with bands of interlaced volutes (signifying water) and symbols of *ik* (T-shaped forms representing wind), all referring to the deity Venus. As we mentioned earlier, within this group there are figurines with moveable arms and legs, connected by thin cords crossing the hollow body. They are also made of orange clay, painted white, and depicted with beautifully woven *huipil*.

The expressive figurines of Jaina reveal numerous aspects of the society of that time. Thus, with regard to the facial features of the people, we see that they had slanted or oblique eyes with the epicanthic fold; an aquiline nose that sometimes blends in with the plane of the forehead due to the cranial deformation that they were accustomed to using; and high cheekbones. They were of short to medium height, and they had straight hair and tooth mutilation in different forms or designs.

Cranial deformation was practiced among both men and women. A few days after birth, flat boards and cloth bands were tied to the forehead and back of the head or at both sides of the head. The result of the first position was an elongated skull flattened toward the back (called oblique tabular deformation), while the second method resulted in a straight up skull (known as tabular erect deformation).

Dental mutilation consisted of the modification of the tooth by techniques including cutting, filing, and encrustation. The cutting technique resulted in teeth cut at an angle at one or both ends and sometimes even ending in a point. Filing produced teeth with one or two grooves. Finally, encrustation involved perforating teeth and then covering them with a small jade or pyrite disk. Occasionally this technique was combined with cutting.

Scarification was practiced among men, priests, and high-ranking women. The designs were more elaborate for men than for women. In figurines a variety of designs may be seen, including two parallel lines separating the corners of the mouth and ending on the cheeks; a series of dots on the chin; dots and undulating lines around the eyes; an undulating parallel line encircling the eye and going down the cheek to the chin; and a T-shaped wind symbol on the cheek.

Another aspect of Jaina life revealed by figurines involves clothing or costumes. In general, men used loincloths or hip cloths, which consisted of a wide cloth that passed between the legs and was rolled up at the waist, leaving one of the ends hanging down the front like an apron, often woven with some design. Another garment was a type of skirt that fell to the ankles, one of the ends of which crossed in front and was held at the waist with a belt. In the same way, they used skirts with attractive designs and at times with shells attached to the ends.

Long skirts that reached halfway down the leg can also be seen. Other garments included shirts or short jackets with long sleeves; different types of tunics or mantles; and short and long capes decorated with feathers. They also wore a type of overall, short pants, and disguises of different animals. Sometimes a type of ruff or gorget is added, at times combined with a breastplate and leather sandals with heel guards. Women dressed in long *huipil*, which were either simple or had edges embroidered with religious motifs.

They also wore long skirts tied with belts; short or long-sleeved shirts; loose blouses that

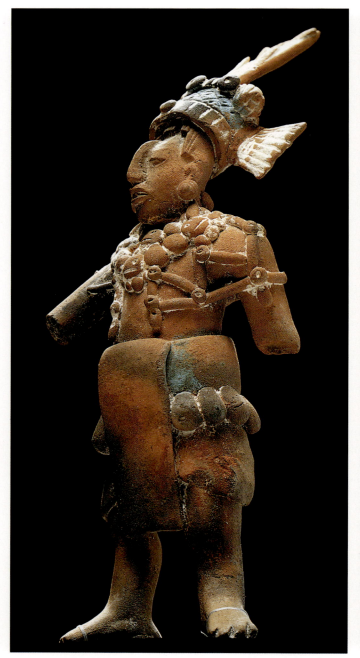 

Male figurine
Jaina Island, Campeche
Classic period
Campeche, Museo Histórico
Fuerte de San Miguel
Baluarte de San Miguel
cat. 127

Male figurine
Jaina Island, Campeche
Late Classic period
Mexico City
Museo Nacional de Antropología
cat. 118

went from the shoulders down to the feet on the back and from the breast to the waist down the front; mantles and *quechquemitl* with rounded or triangular ends, generally with beautiful designs.

In fact, clothing style depended on the social rank of individuals, their occupations, or the role they played within society. In Jaina figurines what are mainly seen are lords, warriors, priests, ballplayers, priestesses, and so forth. There is little that shows us the common people, whose clothing must have been considerably more humble.

The figurines tell us that in general the men had long hair, gathered into a ponytail and tied with cords; this was combined with sumptuous and fantastic headdresses that they used on special occasions, depending on their social rank and occupation. Thus, we might mention a wide variety of helmets made of light materials, such as cane, palm, cloth, wood, and perhaps paper.

These were ornamented with flowers, fringes, tassels, and feathers, and at times came in

Female figurine representing
a mother and her child
Jaina Island, Campeche
Late Classic period
Mexico City
Museo Nacional de Antropología
cat. 101

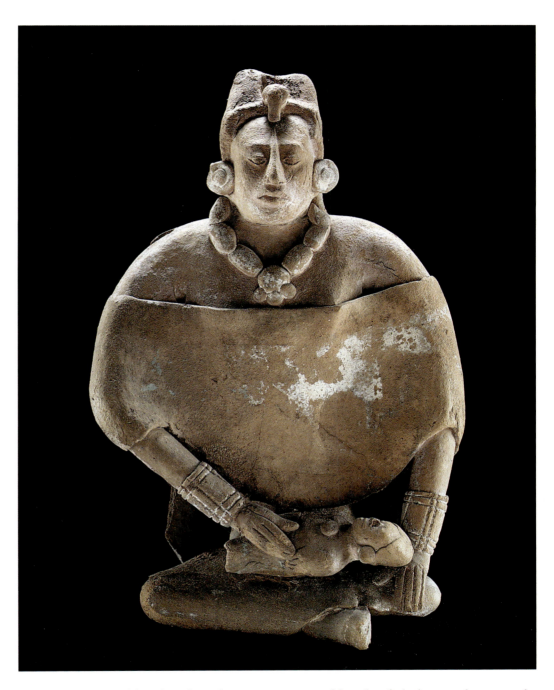

the form of animal heads. They also sometimes used bands of cloth or turbans; masks and helmets with heads of owls and other birds; conical caps; palm hats with wide wings; feather crests that they could put on or take off; circular forms or halos that they placed behind the nape of the neck or on the back; interlaced ribbons and other combinations. In turn, women wore their hair in the form of braids with interlaced ribbons, which could be rolled up on the head like a bow; they also parted their hair in the middle, leaving bangs down the forehead and short hair on the sides. They used turbans decorated with flowers and skeins of colored thread, hats, and so forth. Priestesses generally cut their hair in a stepped form along the front and sides of the face.

As for personal adornment, in figurines we see the use of simple circular earplugs, sometimes with a tubular bead or a feather hanging down from the center of the ear ornament; anklets; bracelets; wristlets; necklaces with one or several strands of beads; pectorals and pendants.

Figurine representing pathologies
Jaina Island, Campeche
Classic period
Mexico City
Museo Nacional de Antropología
cat. 341

Recut stelae indicating the conquest of the site

A wide variety of materials were employed, such as seashells, sharks' teeth, fish vertebrae, jaguar teeth; jade, jadeite, serpentine, pyrite, and other materials. From the chronological point of view Jaina seems to have passed through two periods of occupation. The first, A.D. 500 to 800, is the peak period of solid hand-modeled figurines and the beginning of molded, hollow figurines; the second period, A.D. 800 to 1000, corresponds to the end of molded hollow figurines and the central Veracruz-type. During the first period Jaina was an important center and port of coastal trade. It could have been a trading center for Celestún in the north to Laguna de Términos in the south.

But later, the Putuns (Nonoalco-Zuyuá people) conquered the site, as indicated by a cut stela that shows a captive lord with his arms tied behind his back.

Years later, at the fall of Mayapán around the year A.D. 1441, the Canuls, who were guardians of that place, emigrated toward the west and some reached Calkiní, which they established as their capital. In this way, a Canul could establish a camp at Jaina for fishing.

Today there are only seagulls, herons, and other aquatic birds that nest in the thick swamps of the coast. The ceremonial center remains hidden, and the buildings and cemetery have been covered by vegetation, as if life had been reintegrated to the land, facing a sea that daily is painted with colors of the afternoon.

References

Códice de Calkiní
1957
    Códice de Calkiní. Ed. by A. Barrera Vásquez. Campeche: Gobierno del Estado de Campeche (Biblioteca Campechana)

DAMPIER, WILLIAM
1931
    Voyages and Discoveries. First edition 1699, England: the Argonaut Press

Jeff Karl Kowalski

Uxmal and the Puuc Zone: Monumental Architecture, Sculptured Facades and Political Power in the Terminal Classic period

The Nunnery Quadrangle, Uxmal

Deeply impressed by the overwhelming size and harmonious proportions of the House of the Governor during his first visit to Uxmal in 1840, the writer John Lloyd Stephens enthusiastically praised it as a work of architecture comparable to the great monuments of Egyptian, Greek, and Roman architecture. Since Stephens's time majestic edifices such as the House of the Governor and the Nunnery Quadrangle at Uxmal, the Codz Pop palace at Kabah, or the Great Palace at Sayil frequently have been cited as masterpieces of Maya architecture.

Following Stephens's and Catherwood's earlier efforts to document Puuc ruins in the 1840s, the Austrian explorer Teobert Maler undertook an extensive reconnaissance of the Puuc region from 1886 to 1895, publishing descriptions and photographs of many sites in the German geographic magazine *Globus*. Between 1932 and 1940 Harry Pollock of the Carnegie Institution of Washington conducted an intensive survey of Puuc sites, resulting in a comprehensive publication in 1980.

In the same year, another important source, the *Atlas Arqueológico de Yucatán*, was published (Garza T. and Kurjack 1980). More recent important surveys Puuc settlements and architecture have been conducted by George Andrews and Nicholas Dunning. These imposing structures, along with many other buildings both large and small, embody a distinctive and aesthetically powerful architectural tradition known as the Puuc style. Such Puuc edifices were constructed during a remarkable regional fluorescence of Maya culture that occurred during the Terminal Classic period (c. A.D. 750 to 950/1000) in the hill country of northern Yucatán.

The Puuc, or *sierrita de Ticul*, is the name of the low range of hills that stretches across the northwestern part of the Yucatán peninsula from the Maxcanú southeast toward Lake Chichankanab. South of the Puuc range lie rolling "haystack" limestone hills, known as *uits* (*uitsoob*, plural) to the Maya. Nestled among the *uitsoob* are a host of ancient Maya towns and cities, including better-known centers such as Uxmal, Kabah, Sayil, Labná, Itzimté, and Xcalumkin, as well as scores of smaller ruins.

Archaeological evidence indicates that the largest and most impressive Puuc cities, such as Uxmal, Kabah, or Sayil, were established and began a period of rapid growth toward the end of the eighth century. The diagnostic "slatewares" and other pottery types which constitute the Puuc region's Cehpech ceramic complex began to be manufactured between A.D. 700 and 750 and continued in use until about A.D. 1000.

A long-snouted mask probably representing the Yucatec Maya rain god Chaac on the upper facade of the Main Palace at Labná Yucatán, Mexico

The massive, three-part range structure known as the House of the Governor at Uxmal, Yucatán The structure is adorned with one of the most elaborate sculptured facades in the Puuc region. It was constructed around A.D. 900 during the reign of the Uxmal ruler Lord Chaac

Hieroglyphic dates, many of which were recorded using a regional *tun-ahau* system of dating, tie the late Puuc architecture of Uxmal, Kabah, Labná, as well as the related "Chichén-Maya" architecture of Chichén Itzá, to the late ninth and early tenth centuries (early Cycle 10 in the Maya Long Count calendar).

The latest buildings at Uxmal, such as the Nunnery Quadrangle, the Main Ball Court, or the House of the Governor, as associated with dates between A.D. 895 to 907. At Chichén Itzá, hieroglyphic lintels from the Puuc-related buildings such as the *Monjas*, the Temple of the Three Lintels, the Akab Dzib, and the Temple of the Hieroglyphic Jambs, feature dates between A.D. 832 and 881.

It is clear that during the Terminal Classic period between about A.D. 750 and 950/1000 there was a tremendous burst of architectural and artistic creation in northern Yucatán. During the latter part of this time, the two powerful Maya cities of Uxmal and Chichén Itzá both became capitals of regional states. According to the native historical chronicles of Yucatán, each of these sites was settled by non-local Maya groups, the Xiu in the case of Uxmal, and the Itzá in the case of Chichén Itzá, who after long travels entered northern Yucatán in several migrations or "descents."

The origin place of both the Xiu and the Itzá generally has been placed in the southwestern base of the Yucatán peninsula or in the adjacent Chontalpa region of the Gulf Coast, the area known to the Aztecs as Nonoualco at the time of the Conquest. This location has been questioned, however, since the relative paucity of archaeological remains makes it difficult to see it as the homeland of peoples responsible for the impressive monumental architecture and art at these two northern Maya centers.

More recently, on the basis of inscriptional decipherments, some scholars have suggested that the Itzá may have stemmed from the region controlled by the Classic Maya polity of San José de Motul, Guatemala.

Although the place of origin of either the Xiu or the Itzá remains somewhat hazy, archaeology affirms that both Uxmal and Chichén Itzá experienced rather late and dramatic increases in population and concomitant fluorescences in the creation of monumental architecture and art during the Terminal Classic period, just as many of the southern cities' political regimes were disintegrating.

The well-known eastern Puuc cities began a rapid upsurge in population, settlement size, and architectural construction at about 9.17.0.0.0 to 9.18.0.0.0 in the Long Count (A.D. 770–790), probably as the result of the improvements made in the construction of *chultunes*, artificial cisterns which captured and held rainwater over the dry season. With more secure water supplies, new groups began to exploit the rich agricultural potential of the Puuc region, while others may have immigrated from more distant regions to the south and southwest.

After a time of competition among many autonomous eastern Puuc centers during much of ninth century, the site of Uxmal apparently was able to forge a more effective political military alliance involving the sister cities of Kabah and Nojpat. Uxmal's efforts to expand its influence also may have relied on the assistance of smaller centers like Mulchic, whose vivid battle murals might commemorate a victory in the expansion of this eastern Puuc regional state. There is even some indication that Uxmal utilized Itzá warriors from Chichén Itzá. Throughout the ninth century the growing power of the Puuc polities also exerted an influence (either as a result of local elite emulation or actual intrusions) on more distant sites such as Oxkintok, Dzibilchaltún, and Edzná, where Puuc-style architecture and sculptural formats replaced earlier local traditions.

At its peak during the ninth and early tenth centuries the Puuc architectural style was defined by a specialized construction technique and by a distinctive decorative treatment. In contrast to the block wall and slab vault construction that characterized southern Maya

The North Structure of the Nunnery Quadrangle at Uxmal, Yucatán has an elaborate example of geometric "stone mosaic" sculpture characteristic of Puuc facades The building's sculpture includes stacks of long-snouted masks angular frets, panels of complex serrated lattice-work small huts above several of the doors and a series of human figures

architecture as well as Early Classic period (c. A.D. 250–800) buildings at northern Maya centers such as Oxkintok or Dzibilchaltún, Puuc buildings have a core of lime and rubble concrete faced with finely cut wall and vault stones. The load-bearing concrete core is so strong that facing stones can fall off without causing the building to collapse (and therefore are sometimes referred to as a "veneer masonry"). The thin, well-coursed facing stones are pecked smooth, so that little plaster was needed to cover their surfaces. The latest Puuc buildings, such as the House of the Governor at Uxmal, also have "boot-shaped" vault stones with beveled faces forming the soffit and tapering tenons or "toes" anchored into the vault core.

The lavishly sculptured exteriors of the Puuc buildings differ markedly from earlier Maya architectural facades. They use more complex, multimember medial and cornice moldings, frequently featuring an *atadura* or "binder molding" composed of two sharply cut sloping members separated by a central rectangular course. The upper facades of Puuc buildings are usually vertical, or sometimes lean outward slightly toward the top (in a "negative batter"), as at the House of the Governor or Nunnery Quadrangle at Uxmal. The lower walls are sometimes given a sculptural treatment (often taking the form of groups on inset columns with spools at top, middle, and bottom), but more often architectural sculpture is concentrated on the upper facades to form vivid contrasts between smooth lower walls and elaborately patterned upper zones.

The richly sculptured upper facades represent a high point of Puuc architecture. Masons assembled hundred of precarved separate design elements to create a type of "stone mosaic" which incorporated complex symbolic patterns and motifs. Geometric elements such as step frets, inset columns, banded colonnettes, and X-shaped stones combined to form latticework predominate. In addition, typical long-snouted masks often were placed above the doorways or at the corners of the buildings.

Naturalistic sculptures of stone or stucco also appear on some Puuc buildings, including several at Uxmal, Kabah, and Labná. The multiplanar arrays of sculpture form striking patterns in the strong sunlight of northern Yucatán, harmonizing with the precise, horizontal lines of Puuc architecture.

Several of the architectural forms in Puuc buildings are related to the design of the ordinary Maya pole and thatch hut, or *na*. The contrast between the smooth lower walls and more elaborate upper zone in Puuc structures corresponds to the separation of the lower walls and the thatched roof in a common house. Likewise, the sloping soffits of the stone vaults echo the triangular shape of the thatched roof's interior. The banded columns sometimes seen on the lower walls of stone buildings are based on the bound poles forming the walls of the common house, while the simple lattice pattern resembles a woven mat, which sometimes appears in depictions of houses in the Maya codices. In some cases, as at Uxmal, Chacmultún, or Labná, small models of the *na* are incorporated into the facade sculpture of a stone building, undoubtedly to indicate that it was considered a more permanent and imposing "house".

Many of the sculptural motifs on the Puuc buildings were not purely decorative, but had important religious and cultural significance. The mat-weave lattice patterns apparently indicated that the stone edifices were important elite structures, marking them as buildings worthy of "lords of the mat," a term for high-ranking political leaders in ancient Maya society. More complex lattices, formed of sawtooth or serrated elements framing rosettes or other motifs, were adapted from similar designs which appear on Late Classic Maya textiles. Since Yucatán was an important source of cotton and produced elaborate textiles for interregional trade, these designs allude to one of the principal sources of wealth for the Puuc cities.

Producing such textiles was an important task of the noble women of elite families,

The Mulchic murals, painted in Structure 1, a small early Puuc temple whose walls were later covered by mural paintings

whose patroness was Ix Chel, the goddess of childbirth, medicine, and weaving. The long-snouted masks on Puuc buildings are related to many earlier Maya stone or stucco architectural masks, particularly those which appear slightly earlier in Río Bec or Chenes-style architecture.

The majority of these masks have long been identified as the Yucatec rain god, Chaac. As God B in the Maya codices, Chaac appears with a similar long, pendulous snout. However, some of the masks may represent other Maya deities or supernaturals, such as the *cauac* or *uits* Monster (a spirit associated with the earth, mountains, caves, and rain), the Two-Headed Dragon or Celestial Monster, God K or *kauil* (a deity associated with storms and agricultural fertility, and an important royal patron), and the Principal Bird Deity or Itzam Yeh. By displaying the images of such powerful deities, the Maya elite who lived in and utilized Puuc buildings demonstrated the sacred sources of the political authority.

The architectural traits described above typify late Puuc buildings, but there is also evidence that an early version of Puuc architecture developed between about A.D. 700 and 800. Early Puuc structures are technically less well finished than their late Puuc counterparts. They are faced with thicker and more roughly cut stone blocks, and their vault stones are more slablike and closer to a true corbeled vault. Stylistically, early Puuc buildings tend to be simpler than the more ornate, late Puuc edifices.

Early Puuc buildings normally have simple, rectangular stringcourse moldings, and the medial molding sometimes steps up over the doorways, above which may be small panels of simple geometric sculptural elements. Several early Puuc buildings have projecting stone tenons that originally supported stucco figural sculpture. A regional variant of early Puuc architecture occurs at a number of western Puuc sites located in southwestern Yucatán and Campeche. There, at sites such as Xcalumkin, Xculoc, Xcochá, and others, buildings associated with eighth-century dates display a blend of early and late Puuc traits. Many of these buildings possess finely carved doorway columns, wall panels, jambs, and lintels with figural sculpture and dated inscriptions.

At Xcalumkin the distribution and layout of palace groups, as well as references to several individuals bearing the title of *cahal* (a regional governor or subordinate lord), suggest that the site may have had an early form of conciliar government known as *multepal* ("joint or crowd rule").

Throughout the Puuc region, several centers maintained the Classic Maya tradition of carving and erecting stelae, although with a certain coarsening of sculptural quality and the

South building of the Group
of the Initial Series
Xcalumkin Campeche
The Puuc facade displays columns
made of several drums and a frieze
decorated with polychrome
modeled stucco motifs
On the interior of the north building
a date corresponding
to the year 744 A.D. was found

A cross-section of an arch structure
showing the concrete core
tile-like "veneer" facing stones

introduction of new stylistic elements. At some sites, such as Uxmal and Sayil, stelae were clustered together on a common stela platform rather than standing in front of individual edifices, as at Piedras Negras or Yaxchilán. Many of the Terminal Classic-period stelae at Uxmal, Sayil, Itzimté, and other eastern Puuc cities continue to concentrate visual attention on a principal figure, a composition type known as the "Classic Motif." The prominent individual is often shown holding a manikin scepter, or a spear and shield, and is likely the current *Kul Ahau* ("sacred lineage lord") of the local polity. This traditional compositional format supports the idea that political power at Uxmal, Sayil, Itzimté, and various other sites continued to be vested in a single paramount ruler.

At some sites, however, other Puuc stelae known as "panel-style" monuments feature several figures of roughly equal size (and perhaps rank) interacting in narrative scenes carved in several panels placed one above another.

Not all Puuc sites wielded equal political, economic, or military power. Evidence for a regional political hierarchy has been provided by a settlement survey of the eastern or "Santa Elena" Puuc region conducted by Nicholas Dunning, who mapped and determined the areal extent of settlements, estimated the volume of monumental architecture at site cores, and inventoried the presence or absence of significant political-ideological features such as stelae, glyphic inscriptions, ball courts, and large pyramid-temples. This evidence indicates that at the peak of prosperity in the Puuc region, during the late ninth and early tenth century, Uxmal became the largest and most populous city in the eastern Puuc region. The city covered an area of about eight square kilometers, and its civic-ceremonial core consists of a tightly ordered assemblage of monumental architecture occupying the most massive supporting platforms in the Puuc region.

This settlement pattern data, coupled with iconographic evidence, indicates that Uxmal became the capital of a regional state which coalesced in the eastern Puuc region during this time. Much of this expansion and consolidation appears to have occurred during the reign of a ruler known as Lord Chaac. This king's name glyph and titles appear on the hieroglyphic rings of the Main Ball Court, on a painted capstone from the Nunnery Quadrangle, on Altar 10 (where he bears the *Kul Ahau* or "sacred lineage lord" title), and on Stela 14.

Uxmal Stela 14 is a late monument that features a variation on the traditional "Classic Motif." The visual emphasis is on the centralized ruler, Lord Chaac, who stands in a formalized heel-to-heel pose and wears traditional Maya regalia of royal power; small *ahau* belt masks, oliva shell belt "tinklers," and the Sak Hunal or "Jester God" diadem. The

The so-called Uxmal Queen
a stone-carved mask
from a substructure
of the Wizard Pyramid
Uxmal, Yucatán
Terminal Classic period
Mexico City
Museo Nacional de Antropología
cat. 63

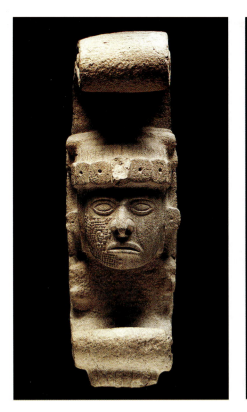

broad-brimmed, feathered headdress worn by this ruler identifies him as a rain god impersonator, carrying on a southern Maya tradition of rulers impersonating the Classic rain god Chac Xib Chac.

This sombrero-like headdress also resembles ones worn by Chaac impersonators on the painted benches in the Temple of the *Chac Mool* at Chichén Itzá. Close correspondences also exist between the warrior figure in the lower right-hand section of Stela 14 and warrior imagery at Chichén Itzá. This supports the idea that Lord Chaac established a military alliance with the Itzá during the Terminal Classic period to facilitate Uxmal's expansionistic state-building in the eastern Puuc region.

Uxmal's close association with Chichén Itzá also is demonstrated by the presence of round temples at both sites. Excavation of Uxmal's round structure in 1992 revealed that the building stood atop a circular platform some 18 meters in diameter. The upper temple had masonry lower walls supporting a conical thatched roof and was likely built during the late ninth or early tenth century, perhaps to emulate the circular Caracol structure at Chichén Itzá.

Caches of effigy vessels of plumbate ware ceramics were placed in the debris of the round building after its destruction by fire, suggesting that individuals with ties to Chichén Itzá may have occupied Uxmal for some time after Uxmal's rulers had lost political control at the site. In addition to depicting Lord Chaac with a possible Itzá warrior, Stela 14 also shows the king standing on a two-headed jaguar throne like that located on a small radial platform in front of the House of the Governor, the grandiose palace building which was probably constructed during the king's reign as a testament to his power and a symbol of his authority.

The upper facade of this massive 99-meter-long palace is covered by a complex array of architectural sculpture, featuring latticework, step frets, and long-snouted Chaac masks. Human figures of different sizes are shown seated along the eastern front of the building, culminating above the central doorway in the depiction of a dominant individual who wears a mat-weave medallion and a towering feather headdress. This was undoubtedly a portrait of Lord Chaac himself, who may have commissioned the House of the Governor as a royal residence and/or as an administrative center.

Reconstruction drawing
of the Uxmal Stela 14 portrays
the local *Kul Ahau*, Lord Chaac
as the dominant central figure
He is accompanied by smaller
figures, including a warrior holding
a circular shield like those depicted
contemporaneously at Chichén Itzá

General view of the Nunnery Quadrangle at Uxmal. The broken remains of a columnar "world tree" monument can be seen near the center of the quadrangular courtyard.

The building may have been a local version of a *Popol Na*, a structure where the ruler met in council with his subordinate lords to discuss affairs of state and plan community festivals. The House of the Governor is also aligned so that its central doorway faces the horizon where Venus rises at its most southern extreme. The spectacle of Venus emerging from the underworld above the jaguar throne in front of the House of the Governor may have been calculated to connect the historical king with cosmic acts of creation.

Another of the most imposing architectural groups at Uxmal is the Nunnery Quadrangle, constructed around A.D. 900–920 during the reign of Lord Chaac. In its plan and architectural sculpture program, the Nunnery Quadrangle embodies fundamental Maya cosmological concepts to convey the idea that Uxmal identified itself as the principal religious center and political capital of the eastern Puuc region. The quadrangular layout and approximate correspondence of the principal buildings to the cardinal points represents an effort to replicate the quadripartite horizontal organization of the Maya cosmos, with east and west associated with the rising and setting sun, and with north and south corresponding to the heavens and underworld.

Further, much of the iconography of the quadrangle can be associated with Maya creation mythology, which served as a divine charter for kingship, and which functioned periodically to ritually renew the bonds between the ruler, the gods, the ancestors, and the living community.

Here we will only mention a few of these cosmological motifs to convey their general significance. The West Structure features the aged turtle-man earth deity, God N. This deity, also known as Bacab or *Pahuatun*, is the Maya "world sustainer," an earth- and sky-bearer who is associated with the "partitioning" of the world and who plays an important role in Maya creation myth.

As a Bacab, he is associated with the great flood that preceded the formation of the present world and with the raising of the Trees of Abundance at the quadrants of the world, and the establishment of a world axis by the raising of the *Yaxcheel Cab*, the "First Tree of the World."

West Building of the Nunnery
Quadrangle

Small miniature Maya huts crowned by reptilian masks and sprouting vegetation scrolls appear above the doorways of the South Structure of the Nunnery. These images recall the maize plant rising from a reptilian earth monster on the Tablet of the Foliated Cross at Palenque, and a related depiction of a leafy maize god emerging from a cleft *uits* monster/turtle carapace on the sculptured pillars of the Lower Temple of the Jaguars at Chichén Itzá.

Other "emergence" or "resurrection" scenes on Late Classic polychrome vases suggest that the young maize god rising from a turtle carapace is a variant of Hun Hunahpu, the "first father" of the Hero Twins in the *Popol Vuh* and a solar-maize deity who is reborn annually in the underworld. The maize-sprouting masks of the South Structure of the Nunnery seem to pertain to this mythic complex, referring to the regeneration of the maize/sun god within the earth.

A massive cylindrical stone column stood at the conceptual center of the Nunnery Quadrangle. This column embodied the *Yaxcheel Cab*, the gigantic *ceiba* tree that formed the central axis of the cosmos. The erection of this tree was the action that separated the sky from the earth at the time of creation, which was associated with the "partitioning" of the world, and which preceded the creation of a new humanity and the subsequent establishment of legitimate political order.

A single-headed jaguar throne originally stood on a low platform near the central stone column/world tree monument. Such jaguar seats function as royal thrones in Classic Maya art, and apparently represent one of the three "throne stones" which were occupied by deities at the time of creation.

At Uxmal the link between the jaguar throne and columnar "world tree" apparently associated the ruler with primordial acts of world creation, and served as a divine charter for kingship. Many of the other sculptural motifs at the Nunnery, such as feathered

serpent sculptures, Tlaloc masks, and captive figures, although not as clearly associated with Maya creation myth, also can be interpreted as symbols of rulership and political authority. Uxmal is connected to two other major Puuc cities, Kabah and Nojpat, by means of an artificial roadway or *sacbe* that extends over some 18 kilometers. Although only portions of Kabah or Nojpat have been adequately mapped, the scale and diversity of their monumental architecture and the presence of many carved monuments indicate their regional political importance.

At Kabah, for example, the massive range-type palace structure known as the Codz Pop features an impressive array of hundreds of stacked Chaac masks covering virtually its entire west facade.

A recent archaeological project at Kabah has revealed that the upper eastern facade of the Codz Pop supported a series of gigantic stone warrior sculptures. Each wears a similar distinctive headdress and has raised facial scarification patterns like those seen on a previously documented Kabah sculpture (known as the "King of Kabah") and seen on dancing warrior figures who appear on the "panel-style" carved jambs of the palace's central doorway. Another impressive structure at Kabah is its monumental freestanding arch that marks the point at which the *sacbe* to Uxmal enters the city.

The most comprehensive mapping project at a Puuc city has been carried out at Sayil, whose areal extent and structural remains were mapped in the 1980s. Although smaller than Uxmal, Sayil also is a major site, where about 10,000 people occupied an urban core covering some 4.5 square kilometers. Some 7,000 additional people lived in a larger surrounding area. They probably provided the city's rulers with a source of tribute in goods and labor.

The Sayil mapping project showed that the site center was organized about a 1.2-kilometer-long north-south internal *sacbe*.

Eastern facade decoration
of the Codz Pop Structure
Kabah, Yucatán

opposite
The so-called King of Kabah
Kabah, Yucatán
Terminal Classic period
Merida Bodega de Sitio
Arqueologíco de Kabah
cat. 62

God N, also known as *Pahuatun*

At the northern end of this causeway was the massive Great Palace (or Three-Story Palace), believed to have been a palatial residence for the site's paramount lineage.

At the southern end of the *sacbe* were more public structures, including a ball court, stela platform, and a multistory palace that probably served as an administrative center. Remains of specialized stall-like structures clustered in the vicinity of the small Mirador Temple may mark the location of a market near the center of the site.

Labná, another Puuc site which has recently been excavated and restored, is an intermediate-size elite center, with a multilevel residential palace connected to a southern pyramid-temple and monumental arch by a short *sacbe*. Even smaller centers, such as Kom or Chacbolay, corresponding to smaller towns, sometimes lack any carved monuments or pyramid-temples, but possess a few groups of elite buildings constructed in typical Puuc "veneer" masonry.

Such regional variations in site size, architectural volume, and associated political symbols implies a corresponding sociopolitical hierarchy among the rulers and leading families of the various centers. The nature of these intersite political relationships is only imperfectly understood, however. Based on our knowledge of political organization in northern Yucatán at the time of the Conquest, it seems likely that many of the smaller centers in the vicinity of a larger city such as Uxmal, Kabah, or Sayil would have been under its control, perhaps administered by subordinate governors who had kinship or other political ties to the ruling family at the principal center.

The spatial distribution and monumental art and architecture at such major sites suggests that they may have been the "head towns" of autonomous polities, although some larger cities probably dominated others at particular times. In this regard, it has been argued that

The Great Palace, or Three-Story
Palace, at Sayil, Yucatán

Kabah and Nojpat were politically independent during the eighth and earlier ninth century,
but that during the later ninth century they were incorporated in a political-military alliance
in which Uxmal was the leading partner. Recent mapping and excavations at the medium-
sized site of Xkipché, located about 10 kilometers southwest of Uxmal, suggest that it may
have become a dependency of the larger center, although the exact nature of the political
relationship remains to be clarified.

At the peak of their occupation and political power during the Terminal Classic period,
Uxmal, Kabah, Sayil, Itzimté, and the myriad other centers in the Puuc region created one
of the most vital expressions of ancient Maya culture. By the late ninth century the great eastern Puuc city of Uxmal apparently became the capital of an expanding regional state,
perhaps as the result of shrewd political alliances between its *Kul Ahau*, Lord Chaac, and
the rulers of the powerful Puuc cities of Kabah and Nojpat, and even with military support
from the Itzá rulers of Chichén Itzá. However, this tremendous Puuc fluorescence apparently did not outlast the tenth century, and the local elite may have lost their ability to
govern at Uxmal by A.D. 950.

The demise of the Puuc tradition may have involved a combination of ecological and human
factors. There is evidence that the Puuc populations were reaching the carrying capacity of
their agricultural system during the tenth century. Such environmental pressures may have
intensified stress and factional competition within local sociopolitical systems. It is probably
that such stress also made Uxmal and other Puuc centers more vulnerable to the growing
military and political power of Chichén Itzá.

Although scholars currently dispute when Chichén Itzá was abandoned, many concur that
Chichén Itzá rose to power concurrently with the Puuc cities and became the capital of an
expansionistic tribute state which eventually defeated the Puuc polities. After the demise of
the Puuc cities, Chichén Itzá may have assimilated some of their nobility into its own *multepal* conciliar government, and then survived as the dominant power in northern Yucatán
and at the eastern capital of an extensive interregional trading network for some 50 to 200
years thereafter.

following pages
outside
Detail of a building of the Nunnery
Quadrangle

inside
Eastern building of the Nunnery
Quadrangle

References

ANDREWS, GEORGE F.
1986
Los estilos arquitectónicos del Puuc: una nueva apreciación. Mexico City: INAH

BRICKER, HARVEY M., AND VICTORIA R. BRICKER
1996
"Astronomical References in the Throne Inscription of the Palace of the Governor at Uxmal." *Cambridge Archaeological Journal*, 6, 2, 191–229

CARRASCO V., RAMÓN, AND EDUARDO PÉREZ DE HEREDIA PUENTE
1996
"Los ultimos Gobernantes de Kabah." In *Palenque Round Table 1993*. Ed. by M. Macri and J. McHargue. Vol. X. San Francisco: Pre-Columbian Art Research Institute, 297–307

DUNNING, NICHOLAS P.
1992
Lords of the Hills: Ancient Maya Settlement in the Puuc Region, Yucatan, Mexico. Madison: Prehistory Press

DUNNING, NICHOLAS P., AND JEFF K. KOWALSKI
1994
"Lords of the Hills: Classic Maya settlement patterns and political iconography in the Puuc region, Mexico." *Ancient Mesoamerica*, 5, 63–95

FREIDEL, DAVID A., LINDA SCHELE, AND JOY PARKER
1993
Maya Cosmos. Three Thousand Years on the Shaman's Path. New York: William Morrow and Co.

GARZA TARRAZONA DE GONZÁLEZ, SYLVIA, AND EDWARD B. KURJACK
1980
Atlas Arqueológico de Yucatán. Mexico City: INAH

GENDROP, PAUL
1983
Los estilos Rio Bec, Chenes y Puuc en la arquitectura Maya. Mexico City: UNAM

GRAHAM, IAN
1992
"Uxmal." In *Corpus of Maya Hieroglyphic Inscriptions. Vol. 4, Part 2*. Cambridge, Mass.: Peabody Museum of Archaeology and Ethnology, Harvard University
1992
"Uxmal, Xcalumkin." In *Corpus of Maya Hieroglyphic Inscriptions. Vol. 4, Part 3*. Cambridge, Mass.: Peabody Museum of Archaeology and Ethnology, Harvard University

KOWALSKI, JEFF KARL
1987
The House of the Governor, a Maya Palace at Uxmal, Yucatan, Mexico. Norman: University of Oklahoma Press

KOWALSKI, JEFF KARL, ALFREDO BARRERA RUBIO, HEBER OJEDA MÁS, AND JOSÉ HUCHIM HERRERA
1996
"Archaeological Excavations of a Round Temple at Uxmal: Summary Discussion and Implications for Northern Maya Culture History." In *Palenque Round Table 1993*. Ed. by M. Macri and J. McHargue. Vol. X. San Francisco: Pre-Columbian Art Research Institute, 281–296

MALER, TEOBERT
1895
"Yukatekische Forschungen." *Globus*. Braunschweig, 68, 247–59, 277–92
1902
"Yukatekische Forschungen." *Globus*. Braunschweig, 82, 197–230

POLLOCK, H. E. D.
1980
The Puuc: An Architectural Survey of the Hill Country of Yucatan and Northern Campeche, Mexico. Memoirs of the Peabody Museum of Archaeology and Ethnology. Publication 19. Cambridge, Mass.: Harvard University

PREM, HANNS J.
1991
"The Xkipche Archaeological Project." *Mexicon*, 12, 62–63

PREM, HANNS J. (ED.)
1994
Hidden among the Hills: Maya Archaeology of the Northwest Yucatan Peninsula. In *Acta Mesoamericana*. Vol. 7. Möckmühl: Verlag von Flemming

PROSKOURIAKOFF, TATIANA
1950
A Study of Classic Maya Sculpture. Publication 593. Washington, D.C.: Carnegie Institution of Washington

RIVERA DORADO, MIGUEL (COORDINATOR)
1991
Oxkintok, Una Ciudad Maya de Yucatan: Excavaciones de la Mision Arqueológica de España en México 1986–1991. Madrid

SABLOFF, JEREMY, AND E. WYLLYS ANDREWS V (EDS.)
1986
Late Lowland Maya Civilization: Classic to Postclassic. Albuquerque: School for American Research, University of New Mexico Press

STEPHENS, JOHN LLOYD
1841
Incidents of Travel in Central America, Chiapas, and Yucatan. 2 Vols. New York: Harper and Brothers
1843
Incidents of Travel in Yucatan. 2 Vols. New York: Harper and Brothers

Peter J. Schmidt

Contacts with Central Mexico and the Transition to the Postclassic: Chichén Itzá in Central Yucatán

Polychrome basin, detail
Chichén Itzá, Yucatán
Terminal Classic period
Merida, Museo Regional de Yucatán
"Palacio Cantón"
cat. 187

The Mayas never lived in isolation. They had strong ties and close relations both with groups of their own culture and language and with their neighbors to the northwest and southeast. We have seen that since the beginnings of village culture, this interaction resulted in the adaptation and diffusion of raw materials such as obsidian and jade. At the same time, ideas and concepts generally traveled by the same routes as material goods and were transmitted by contacts between people who distributed these commodities.

Particularly intense relations occurred with the other cultural subareas of Mesoamerica, by way of the Isthmus of Tehuantepec and along the ancient routes of the Gulf Coast and inland valleys. "Mesoamerica" includes the entire zone of the high cultures or civilizations of Mexico and Central America, where cities, early states, and great art styles derived from a common background of religious cults and scientific advances, involving an exact calendar based on conventional shared periods and systems of writing of different degrees of complexity (Willey 1977; Lee and Navarrete 1978; Miller 1983). Apart from this backdrop of shared culture, what stand out are examples of more direct contacts. These occurred with different intensity, impact, and duration, and with changing focuses and directions, especially during the Classic (c. A.D. 250 to 900) and Postclassic periods (A.D. 900 to 1550 approximately). During the Classic period, the influence of the enormous city of Teotihuacan in the Mexican central highlands is particularly noteworthy. The metropolis extends its contacts both to the north and northwest of Mexico, as well as to the south to the farthest reaches of the Maya zone (Borhegyi 1971; Santley 1983). Its relations functioned in both directions. They are oriented toward the center, for the acquisition and search for raw materials of practical use (for example minerals, foods) or symbolic ones (quetzal feathers, tropical animal skins, a wide variety and great number of mollusks, and so forth) for use in the metropolis. At the same time, they are directed outward, in the distribution and commercial placement of products from the center and in the spread of religious ideas, cults, forms of organization, art, and so forth, in lands distant from the great city.

Leaving the Valley of Teotihuacan and crossing the Puebla-Tlaxcala region toward the Gulf of Mexico, we see, for example, how a great avenue of trade and relations enters Maya territory after crossing the nodes of Matacapan, at the center of the impressive volcanic mountains of the Tuxtlas, cradle of the preceding culture the Olmecs, and the Isthmus of Tehuantepec, still at the moment of the Spanish conquest an obligatory stop for the caravans of Aztec trade (Santley *et al.* 1984; Scholes and Roys 1948). From there the route separates, a branch seeking Yucatán through Xicalanco in Laguna de Términos, the other going toward the south and southeast, crossing the old corridor of Chiapas and reaching Guatemala, El Salvador, and finally the central coast of Central America.

We can find evidence of the scope of these contacts on the one hand in examples of Maya ceramics and a great profusion of tropical products from the southeast at Teotihuacan itself (Rattray 1978), and on the other in forms of Teotihuacan inspiration at centers as distant as Altun Ha in Belize (Pendergast 1971), Xelhá in Quintana Roo, Dzibilchaltún, Ixil, and Oxkintok in Yucatán (Andrews V 1979; Schmidt and Varelta 1989; Fernández M. 1993), and Becán in Campeche (Ball 1974; Matheny 1976), to name just a few. Major centers of distribution such as El Mirador in Chiapas (Agrinier 1975), Tikal in the Petén (W. Coe 1972; Laporte 1987; Rodríguez G. and Rosal Torres 1987), Kaminaljuyú in the highlands (Cheek 1976; Sanders and Michels 1977), Copán in Honduras (Stuart 1997) and the region of Escuintla in the Pacific coast of Guatemala (Hellmuth 1978; Berlo 1984) had, according to some interpretations, even small populations of Teotihuacan origin resident among the dominant Maya. At times it seems that at certain moments in the history of Tikal, these foreign residents came to have a far greater influence than the reduced number that they must have represented, going as far as establishing marriage alliances and dynastic relations (Coggins 1979; Fahsen 1986; Fialko 1988). The military aspect of Teotihuacan presence cannot be excluded, as demonstrated by representations of warriors and gods of war on ceramic vessels and stelae (Greene and Moholy-Nagy 1966; Lee 1996).

One of the basic implantations of the Classic period in Maya lands seems to be the highly characteristic *talud-tablero* architecture of Teotihuacan, perhaps adopted as proof of belonging to the "powers" and advanced forces of the moment, although it is limited to only a few examples at each site (Gendrop 1984; Giddens 1995). Other symbolic forms or

following pages
Panoramic view of El Castillo
Chichén Itzá, Yucatán

Spear and spearthrower
Chichén Itzá, Yucatán
Late Postclassic period
Merida, Museo Regional de Yucatán
"Palacio Cantón"
cat. 94–95

on the right
Stela, Xochicalco
reconstruction drawing

at least forms empowered with important signs are tripod cylinder vases with lids, masks with goggles, the so-called "Mixtec" year sign, and creatures combining man-bird-serpent traits. The roots of the cult of the feathered serpent seem to have extended into this period to contribute one of the most powerful symbols in art and religion in later Mesoamerica. Furthermore, the *atlatl* (spearthrower) is displayed as a weapon of prestige.

At the end of the period, in the Epiclassic or Terminal Classic, an impressive case operating in the opposite direction is the fortified site of Cacaxtla in Tlaxcala. Established in a dominant position in the Puebla-Tlaxcala Valley, it expressed its supremacy and its military exploits in a fully developed and monumental artistic style that is derived from the Maya style of the Late and Terminal Classic period (Abascal *et al.* 1976; Foncerrada 1993). The glyphs of Cacaxtla, however, are not Maya, but they conform to the tradition of the Mexi-

opposite
Plan of Chichén Itzá

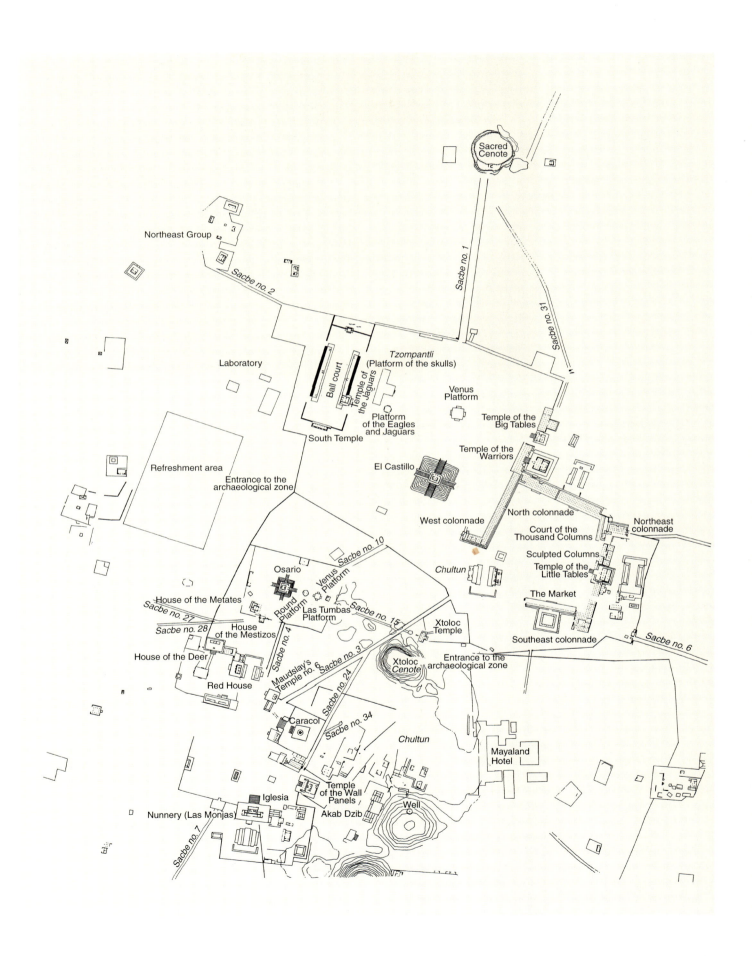

Sacred Cenote

Sacbe no. 1

Sacbe no. 31

Northeast Group

Sacbe no. 2

Laboratory

Tzompantli
(Platform of the skulls)

Ball court

Temple of the Jaguars

Venus Platform

Platform of the Eagles and Jaguars

Temple of the Big Tables

South Temple

Temple of the Warriors

El Castillo

Refreshment area

Entrance to the archaeological zone

West colonnade

North colonnade

Court of the Thousand Columns

Northeast colonnade

Sculpted Columns

Chultun

Temple of the Little Tables

Sacbe no. 10

Osario

Venus Platform

The Market

House of the Metates

Sacbe no. 27

Round Platform

Las Tumbas Platform

Sacbe no. 15

Xtoloc Temple

Southeast colonnade

Sacbe no. 28

House of the Mestizos

Sacbe no. 4

Xtoloc *Cenote*

Entrance to the archaeological zone

Sacbe no. 6

House of the Deer

Red House

Maudslay's Temple no. 6

Sacbe no. 3

Sacbe no. 24

Caracol

Sacbe no. 34

Chultun

Mayaland Hotel

Temple of the Wall Panels

Iglesia

Well

Nunnery (Las Monjas)

Akab Dzib

Sacbe no. 7

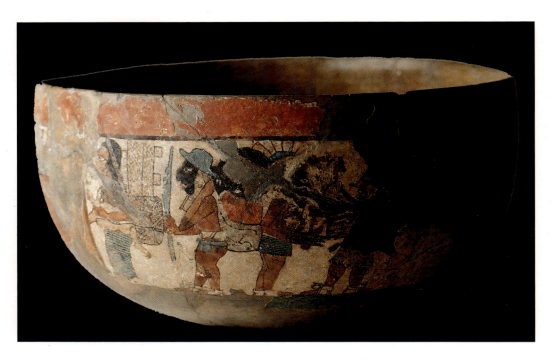

Polychrome basin
Chichén Itzá, Yucatán
Terminal Classic period
Merida, Museo Regional de Yucatán
"Palacio Cantón"
cat. 187

opposite
Round architectural element
Chichén Itzá, Yucatán
Terminal Classic-Early Postclassic
period
Merida, Museo Regional de Yucatán
"Palacio Cantón"

following pages
Chac Mool figure
Chichén Itzá, Yucatán
Early Postclassic period
Merida, Museo Regional de Yucatán
"Palacio Cantón"
cat. 4

can highlands and their closest parallels are at Xochicalco, one of the centers that comes into power after the fall of Teotihuacan. The city of Xochicalco itself displays numerous traits that connect it with the Maya area (Nagao 1989; Fuente *et al.* 1995), among others the representation in public monuments of rulers dressed in Maya style, the erection of stelae and their placement in offerings, and the presence of art objects that seem to come from lands to the southeast (López Luján *et al.* 1995). It is at this moment, after the fall of Teotihuacan, that a substantial change occurs in relations between the Maya area and the center and north of Mesoamerica. One of the main actors is the great city of Chichén Itzá in the north of Yucatán, capital of the powerful Itzá and the man-god Kukulcan, nebulously understood by way of chronicles and legends. Although in ruins since before the Spanish conquest, this city was so sacred that in the beginning there were plans to found the capital of colonial Yucatán there to take advantage of its symbolic value.

In fact, the *Relación de Tekantó y Tepakán*, compiled as part of the official census of 1581, reports: ". . . at one time all this land was under the control of one lord, this being the ancient city of Chichén Itzá, to whom all the lords of this province and even beyond were tributaries . . ." (*Relaciones Histórico-Geográficas*, 1983, 216).

Chichén Itzá, the name of which may be translated as "on the edge of the well of the Itzá," occupies some thirty square kilometers in a zone rich in *cenotes*, subterranean water accesses, and thin, black, but fertile, soil. It is located almost at the center of the northern part of Yucatán, midway between the western and eastern coasts and some one hundred kilometers each from one of the rich salt mines of the north coast and the wide tracts of agricultural lands of the "red hills" of the Puuc region. According to the results of more than a hundred years of archaeological exploration, Chichén Itzá flourished in the Epiclassic or Terminal Classic period (between A.D. 750 and 900) and during a good part of the following Postclassic period (A.D. 900 to 1100/1200). Even afterwards, it was never completely abandoned. In the south central part of the Maya area, construction activity, the erection of stelae, rich burials and–in general–civilized, urban life suffered serious setbacks, so that in popular terms there is talk of a "collapse." Nevertheless, at the same time Chichén Itzá grew together with or immediately after the cities of the Puuc to write a new chapter that is still difficult to understand and causes considerable scientific debate.

The historical sources, friends or enemies of the great city and its rulers, leave no doubt about the dominant role played by Chichén Itzá in "the matters of Yucatán" for a certain time, some centuries before the conquest. On the details of this control, its *raison d'être*, the means by which power was maintained or the causes of its later disappearance, there are

Recostruction drawing
of two Atlantean figures
at Chichén Itzá

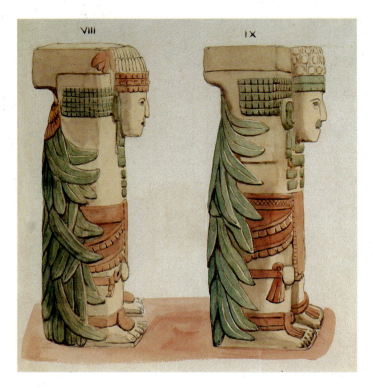

already several different explanations by the time of Bishop Landa (sixteenth century; Landa 1959). Although the importance of a ruler by the name or title of Kukulcan (Feathered Serpent, or Quetzalcoatl in Nahuatl) is generally recognized in the rise of the site, there is little agreement on this absolute or relative chronology. Other rulers who are mentioned are two or three "brothers," perhaps a ceremonial title for regents of the same or similar rank, by virtue of whose union depended the fate of the ancient city and its inhabitants.

A last "king" of Chichén Itzá is also mentioned as Chac Xib Chac, who despite his pompous name, derived from Classic period Maya tradition, played a relatively sad role in an epic history of intrigue. He orchestrated the fall of Chichén Itzá, the dispersal of its inhabitants, and the flight of an important group of them to the region of Petén Itzá in Guatemala, where their descendants saw Cortés pass, but maintained their independent lifestyle until the end of the seventeenth century (Jones in this volume).

The Chichén Itzá that we know archaeologically displays an internal organization typical of northern Yucatán: a wide network of secondary nuclei extends around a central area formed by three great plazas or leveled areas. Many of these secondary nuclei also have monumental architecture, and are intercommunicated with each other and linked with the center by *calzadas* (or *sacbeoob*, artificial causeways). To date, 70 *calzadas* have been identified, between 1.5 and 8 metres in width. Sometimes they are elevated, have low lateral walls, and measure some 30 meters to more than 6 kilometers in length. The longest link the center with the secondary nuclei of Cumtún in the west and Ikil in the east in an underlying scheme, while the longest causeways seem to form a cross oriented some 20 degrees east of north.

In the center of the cross are three main groups of monumental architecture: 1) in a large plaza are arranged the Nunnery Complex, the round tower of the Caracol, also called the Observatory and of supposed astronomical orientation, the Akab Dzib, the Temple of the Panels, and the group of the Red House; 2) and 3) there is an enormous leveled area to the north, surrounded by a wall and a *talud* (sloping base) up to 6 meters high of more than 1.5 kilometers in length, which sustains the plaza of the Castillo and the group of the Thousand Columns, with the tallest pyramid of the site, three ball courts, the *tzompantli*, the Eagle Platform and the Venus Platform, the Temple of the Warriors, wide galleries, and colonnades originally roofed with Maya vaults. The last two are connected by *sacbeoob* with large *cenotes*, areas where the collapse of the superficial layer of limestone has exposed the water level at a depth of 22 meters; the ancient Maya considered such places to be doors to the

opposite
Atlantean figure
Chichén Itzá, Yucatán
Early Postclassic period
Mexico City
Museo Nacional de Antropología
cat. 81

437

438

underworld. It is very possible that the Sacred Cenote, at the north end of the center, had been a decisive point determining the importance of the site of Chichén Itzá. According to Landa, "Into this well they have had, and then had, the custom of throwing men alive as a sacrifice to the gods, in times of drought, and they believed that they did not die though they never saw them again. They also threw into it a great many other things, like precious stones and things which they prized. And so, if this country had possessed gold, it would be this well that would have the greater part of it, so great was the devotion which the Indians showed for it . . ." (Landa 1959, 114). The observation of Bishop Landa was quite accurate. Large quantities of human and animal bones, as well as offerings of ceramics, stone, metal, wood, shell, copal, and textiles have been recovered in explorations of the bottom of the *cenote*. Although broken and charred, these offerings were preserved through lack of oxygen (Coggins and Shane, 1984). Architectural complexes of smaller dimensions are distributed fairly evenly in the zone of the settlement around the center of the site at a distance of between 100 and 700 meters and linked by the above-mentioned *calzadas*. These groups also include domestic architecture with very different degrees of elaboration, from small platforms for isolated straw and *bajareque* (plaited cane and mud houses), to complex agglomerations of rooms, passages, and patios with stairways and columns that resemble modern urban tenements. Notably absent is the apsidal house, so characteristic of today's rural Yucatecan countryside. In the few surviving murals representing houses, we see that the majority, attacked and conquered by warriors from Chichén Itzá, had straw or palm leaf roofs with two or four sloping sides (Morris, Charlot and Axtell Morris 1931; Tozzer 1957). Monumental architecture, on the other hand, was built on solid platforms, often superimposed on earlier constructions. Its thick walls made of compact stone and limestone-mortar fill support roofs in the form of the Maya vault. They were covered with rectangular worked stones with a long tenon, which in most cases functioned as a facing and did not bear weight. Differences in plans, types of buildings, and designs of facades and ornamentation indicate that there were at least two styles of public architecture at Chichén Itzá. These have been called Chichén-Puuc and Chichén-Toltec, and, unfortunately, also simply "Maya" and "Toltec." The first is a local variant of the style common in Yucatán and Campeche in the Terminal Classic period, a local development with its roots in the seventh and eighth century (for example at Oxkintok). The second combines many elements of the same style with forms and concepts from central and northern Mexico as well as from the Gulf Coast and Oaxaca. It is in many ways this very style, derived from different sources but recombined in a perfect amalgam, that characterizes Chichén Itzá.

Puuc constructions are often elevated on tall platforms with rounded corners and with stairways lacking balustrades. Palace-type or range-type structures stand out in plan. Decoration covers the upper half of facades, which extend even further upward by way of roofcombs and "flying facades." The main decorative motifs are stone mosaic masks with different degrees of abstraction and geometric designs that in many cases are also derived from living forms or mythological beings. In addition, lintels are monoliths frequently bearing Maya hieroglyphic inscriptions.

Constructions in the second style, "Maya-Toltec," predominate at Chichén Itzá. Walls rise on platforms often in the shape of a stepped pyramid; they typically have a sloped lower section and rich relief decoration, also largely concentrated on the upper facade. Buildings have wide interior spaces with porticoes flanking the entrance. Semi-open galleries are roofed with enormous vaults, supported by pillars and columns. Characteristic constructions, sometimes of considerable dimensions, are combined patios and galleries, open platforms with stairways on four sides, round structures, sweatbaths, and ball courts with lateral benches and vertical walls. Naturalistic, narrative, and symbolic decoration in polychrome reliefs and paintings cover almost all surfaces of buildings–rectangular panels on platforms, balustrades, facades, jambs, lintels, columns, pillars and benches, in addition to walls and vaults of many interior rooms. Among the most frequent motifs are serpents with or without feathers, rampant or seated jaguars, eagles, coyotes, mythical combinations of man-jaguar-bird-serpent or bird-god, old gods sustaining the sky (*bacab* or *Pauahtun*), trees replete with animals, scenes of warfare, sacrifice or daily life, and endless rows of richly dressed rulers and warriors. The few preserved lintels, usually made of wood, also display

Relief
Chichén Itzá, Yucatán
Terminal Classic-Early Postclassic
period
Chichén Itzá
Museo de Sitio de Chichen Itzá
cat. 68

441

Relief
Chichén Itzá, Yucatán
Terminal Classic-Early Postclassic
period
Chichén Itzá
Museo de Sitio de Chichen Itzá
cat. 68

441

opposite
Battle mural
Chichén Itzá, Yucatán

Disk
Chichén Itzá, Yucatán
Early Postclassic period
Mexico City
Museo Nacional de Antropología
cat. 262

reliefs of rulers in conference and their companions and/or prisoners. Integrated into architectonic space were a series of typical sculptures, which were originally stuccoed and painted in color just as the reliefs. These include semi-reclining figures called *Chac Mool* at the entrances of temples and palaces, figures of small or large atlantids to support altars and lintels, seats or thrones in the form of a jaguar in the center or at the entrance to important rooms, standard bearers, stone braziers on top of balustrades and at the ends of platforms, sacrificial stones in front of altars, human or mythological figures on facades, as well as gigantic serpents converted into balustrades and moldings, projecting friezes, and columns. Pilasters and columns represent an entire army of warriors and dignitaries. Nor is there any lack of masks in Puuc style; although these are generally labeled "Chac masks" after Yucatecan gods of rain, they probably represent supranatural beings related to lineage descent or even to a certain class of supreme gods. Noteworthy is the almost complete

Zoomorphic plaque representing
the Feathered Serpent
Chichén Itzá, Yucatán
Terminal Classic-Early
Postclassic period
Merida, Museo Regional de Yucatán
"Palacio Cantón"
cat. 268

absence of stelae in the old Maya tradition, of which only two have appeared in recent years, one of them without glyphs. At the time of its greatest splendor, Chichén Itzá must have shone with brilliance with its many colors and innumerable details. However, it is difficult to imagine its original appearance when faced with the sober image in green, gray, and white that we have become accustomed to seeing nowadays.

Changes in the earlier tradition and the creative combination of styles that made Chichén Itzá the most splendid city in the Maya zone have led to many attempts to explain it since the late-nineteenth century. What is particularly striking is the extension of city's trade relations and contacts, although they may have been indirect. The offerings from the Sacred Cenote document pieces from as far away as the southwestern United States to northern Colombia (Lothrop 1952; Coggins 1992). In addition to this evidence, there are extensive and surprisingly exact correspondences between Chichén Itzá and the city of Tollan Xicotitlan in Hidalgo, the historical Tula and capital of the Toltecs (Taube 1994), confirming a historical basis for legends and stories (Charnay 1887; Seler 1915). The most widely sustained hypothesis begins with a Toltec invasion and conquest of Yucatán, which would have changed the extant Maya (Puuc) style city into another one more to the taste of the northern conquerors (Tozzer 1930 and 1957). Chichén Itzá would have been a Toltec fortress-garrison in conquered Maya lands; any conflict represented in the art of the city–which are far from a few–was reduced to an ethnic confrontation between Mayas and Toltecs. Nor was the opposing viewpoint lacking; it proposed to investigate whether the correspondences were not the result of Maya impact on Central Mexico (Kubler 1961; Ruz Lhuillier 1962). The answer must be more complex, above all because both in Yucatán as well as in Hidalgo there are important details of absolute and relative chronology remaining to be resolved (Cobean *et al.* 1981; Healan 1989; Mastache F. 1994). The chronology of Chichén Itzá and its relationship with events in the Puuc region are also subject to revision, and advances made in the reading of glyphic texts offer hope for more direct correlations (Kowalski in this volume). Excavations at Isla Cerritos, the supposed port of Chichén Itzá on the north coast, seem to confirm a Puuc-Chichén sequence (Robles C. 1987). Evidence seems to support a long phase of overlapping between the Puuc style and the growth and expansion of Chichén Itzá. In the final instance, Chichén's expansion indeed led to the destruction of Puuc culture (Schmidt 1991 and 1993). Another unresolved question is the mechanism that permitted such detailed correspondences between Tula and Chichén Itzá, given the almost complete lack of evidence for these traits in the considerable stretch between the two sites. The direct control of Tula did not even reach the Puebla Valley (Davies 1980 and 1987). Tenuous indications at Isla de Sacrificios in Veracruz and around the lower Usumacinta perhaps indicate the directions where it is necessary to look. Somewhere beyond the direct path, yet contemporary and in a zone linked to the production of "plumbate" ceramics and to the cultivation of cacao and the ritual ball game, there are iconography and styles of surprising similarity in the Soconusco region of Chiapas and the Pacific coast of Guatemala, especially in the region of El Baul and Cotzumalguapa (Thompson 1948; Parsons 1967-69; Popenoe Hatch 1987). In the northern Maya zone we see the first advances of a new style and new forms of organization in the Late Classic period in the Puuc area itself, where they are still isolated and occur in a cultural environment characterized by considerable communication with the Maya cultures of the southern and central Petén. Typical of this shift are narrative scenes on stelae-panels at Edzná and Oxkintok (Proskouriakoff 1951), the presence of new weapons and pieces of equipment in images in paintings and reliefs, a number of widely distributed ceramic styles produced in the lower Usumacinta area, on the coast of Campeche and Tabasco (Fine Orange), as well as in the already mentioned Soconusco region (Plumbate).

Evidence for sustained contact with Tula and its region on a more practical and mundane level is found in obsidian at Chichén Itzá. More than 60 percent comes from the mines of Ucareo, Michoacán, and Pachuca, Hidalgo, controlled at that time by the Toltec capital.

In recent years, interest has also focused on the question: Who were the Itzá? Attention has been given to Thompson's thesis that they were Putun or Chontal Maya from Tabasco and Campeche who according to their own traditions had constructed a wide commercial "empire," after having "Nahuatlized" many aspects of their culture (Scholes and Roys 1948; Thompson 1970; Peniche R. 1987). Today we know that there were indeed different groups in Itzá society at Chichén Itzá and that they were distinguished by costume, ornaments, equipment such as uniforms, weapons, and much more. However, this distinction is normal at the level of state organization that for centuries had been immersed in trade and dynastic relations, alliances and conflict, just as contemporary societies of central Mexico, where the chronicles also speak to us of two, three, and up to five groups within a single state-society. Furthermore, dominant families and lineages and the groups they controlled must have maintained a certain equilibrium of power. Perhaps in this way the very base of Itzá power was constituted (Wren and Schmidt 1991). After years of research on glyphs and despite the fact that Chichén Itzá is the northern site with the most epigraphic materials, no single dynasty has come to light with elaborate mythico-historical justifications for its authority such as those known for the central and southern Maya area. There are no long series of stelae allowing us to document a hereditary succession of power. On the contrary, almost always whenever we see the armies of Chichén Itzá in action in reliefs or murals, in battles or in formal procession, they are directed by several individuals who seem to have the same or similar rank between them and each one is identified and protected by spirits or gods in the form of the sun or different serpents, with or without feathers. At the same time, ancestral spirits of the peninsular Maya, who probably are presented in the famous long-nosed masks and in the equally elaborate faces of so-called "God K," never lost their importance and occupy prominent places, even in the more "Toltec" buildings of Yucatán.

On the subject of the Maya area's external relations, Chichén Itzá is invested with special importance. It is the first in a series of capitals that, without losing its Maya roots, may be distinguished by its close association with cultures of Central Mexico and the Gulf region, much closer than the ties that Teotihuacan could ever establish.

Chichén Itzá thus may be considered the southern root of the multiple origins that led to the formation of Postclassic Mesoamerican culture, a culture that has been called "international" (Robertson 1970) and whose last representatives were found in all their splendor by the Spanish conquerors in the Aztecs and their contemporaries in Central Mexico. Vaillant coined the unfortunate term "Mixteca-Puebla Complex" to refer to the assemblage of largely ceremonial and artistic traits of this culture, related in his opinion to the major population migrations between northern Mexico and the Pacific coast of Central America, datable more or less to the period in question (Vaillant 1940; Nicholson 1979; Stone 1982). This "Toltec" culture of the south at Chichén Itzá owed a considerable amount to the Maya past, but the new combination and coordination of authority observed there contributed significantly to the cultural formation to which Mayapán and its successor states in Yucatán, and the Cakchiquel and Quiché states in the Guatemala highlands later belonged.

Numerous traits distinguish this formation. These include the appearance of institutionalized warfare with "eagles" and "jaguars" feeding the sun to guarantee the movement of the universe, the identification of Mesoamerican gods known from the time of the conquest, rites of new fire and human sacrifice, sacrificial stones and *tzompantli* (skull racks), emphasis on the feathered serpent and the planet Venus, in addition to a social organization that included multiple rulers, highly codified art styles represented in architectural contexts, artifacts and well-defined styles of calendar, and simple hieroglyphic writing.

As for material culture, art, religion, details of architecture, and so forth, the full participation of Chichén Itzá in this "international" Mesoamerican culture may be seen, but always based on Maya continuity that through the Puuc, Chenes, and Río Bec styles had been heir to the Classic period. It is of little importance in this context whether a specific element originated ultimately between the Mayas of Yucatán or Guatemala and was dispersed northward or whether it originated among the Toltecs and Chichimecs of the north and came to be dispersed toward the south. In any case, it is more probable that both circumstances occurred and played their role in the formation of the culture of the Postclassic period (for Guatemala and Chiapas: Navarrete 1996). What is noteworthy is that throughout the changes and fully integrated into the culture of the Terminal Classic and Postclassic periods, Maya writing and the calendar are preserved to such an extent that the indications of Bishop Landa in the sixteenth century serve us in undertaking the long and difficult path of deciphering and interpreting the entire complicated system throughout the centuries before. Nor should it be forgotten that both in Yucatán as well as in the Guatemalan highlands, at the time of the arrival of the Spaniards, Maya was solidly spoken, even after centuries of close ties with people from the northwest.

Bibliography

ABASCAL, RAFAEL, PATRICIO DÁVILA, PETER J. SCHMIDT, AND DIANA ZARAGOZA DE DÁVILA
1976
La arqueología del Sur-Oeste de Tlaxcala (Primera Parte). *Comunicaciones, Proyecto Puebla-Tlaxcala* Suplemento 2. Puebla: Fundación Alemana para la Investigación Científica

AGRINIER, PIERRE
1975
Mounds 9 and 10 at Mirador, Chiapas, México. New World Archaeological Foundation Papers, 39. Provo, Utah: Brigham Young University

ANDREWS V, E. WYLLYS
1979
"Early Central Mexican Architectural Traits at Dzibilchaltún, Yucatán." In *Actes du XLIIe Congrès International des Américanistes*, Paris 1976, Vol. VIII, Paris, 237–49

BALL, JOSEPH W.
1974
"A Teotihuacán-Style Cache from the Maya Lowlands." *Archaeology*, 27, 1. New York, 2–9

BERLO, JANET
1984
Teotihuacán Art Abroad: Study of Metropolitan Style and Provincial Transformation in Incensario Workshops. Oxford: British Archaeological Reports (BAR), International Series 199

BORHEGYI, STEPHAN F.
1971
"Pre-Columbian Contacts–The Dryland Approach: The Impact and Influence of Teotihuacan Culture on Pre-Columbian Civilizations of Mesoamerica." In *Man across the Sea.* Ed. by C.L. Riley *et al.* Austin: University of Texas Press, 79–105

CHARNAY, DÉSIRÉ
1887
The Ancient Cities of the New World. Being Travels and Explorations in Mexico and Central America from 1875–1882. London: Chapman and Hall

CHEEK, CHARLES D.
1976
"Teotihuacan Influence at Kaminaljuyú." In *XIV Sociedad Mexicana de Antropología, Mesa Redonda. Las Fronteras de Mesoamérica.* Tegucigalpa 1975, Vol. 2. Mexico: 55–71

COBEAN, ROBERT H., ALBA GUADALUPE MASTACHE, ANA MARÍA CRESPO, AND CLARA LUZ DÍAZ
1981
"La cronología de la región de Tula." In *Interacción Cultural en México Central.* Ed. by E.C. Rattray, J. Litvak K., and C.L. Díaz O. Mexico: UNAM, 187–214

COE, WILLIAM R.
1972
"Cultural Contact between the Lowland Maya and Teotihuacan as Seen from Tikal, Peten, Guatemala." In *XI Sociedad Mexicana de Antropología, Mesa Redonda. Teotihuacan.* Vol. 2. Mexico: 257-71

COGGINS, CLEMENCY CHASE
1979
"Teotihuacan at Tikal in the Early Classic Period." In *Actes du XLIIe Congrès International des Américanistes*, Paris 1976, Vol. VIII, Paris, 251–69

COGGINS, CLEMENCY CHASE (ED.)
1992
Artifacts from the Cenote of Sacrifice, Chichen Itza, Yucatán Textiles, Basketry, Stone, Bone, Shell, Ceramics, Wood, Copal, Rubber, Other Organic Materials, and Mammalian Remains. Memoirs of the Peabody Museum of Archaeology and Ethnology, Vol. 10, 3. Cambridge, Mass.: Harvard University

COGGINS, CLEMENCY CHASE, AND ORRIN C. SHANE
1984
Cenote of Sacrifice: Maya Treasures from the Sacred Well at Chichén Itzá. Austin: University of Texas Press

DAVIES, NIGEL
1980
The Toltec Heritage, from the Fall of Tula to the Rise of Tenochtitlan. The Civilization of the American Indian Series, 153. Norman: University of Oklahoma Press
1987
The Toltecs, until the Fall of Tula. 2nd edition. The Civilization of the American Indian Series, 144. Norman: University of Oklahoma Press

DIEHL, RICHARD A.
1983
Tula, The Toltec Capital of Ancient Mexico. New Aspects of Antiquity. London: Thames and Hudson

FAHSEN, FEDERICO
1986
"Algunos aspectos sobre el texto de la estela 31 de Tikal." *Mesoamérica*, 11, Antigua Guatemala, 135–54

FERNÁNDEZ MARQUINEZ, MARÍA YOLANDA
1993
Excavaciones en el Grupo May, Oxkintok, Yucatán. Doctoral dissertation no. 131/93; Universidad Complutense de Madrid, Facultad de Geografía e Historia

FIALKO C., VILMA
1988
"El marcador del juego de pelota de Tikal: nuevas referencias epigráficas para el período clásico temprano." *Mesoamérica*, 15, Antigua Guatemala, 117–35

FONCERRADA DE MOLINA, MARTHA CACAXTLA
1993
La Iconografía de los Olmeca Xicalanca. Instituto de Investigaciones Estéticas. Mexico: UNAM

FOWLER, WILLIAM R.
1983
"La distribución prehistórica e histórica de los pipiles." *Mesoamérica*, 6, Antigua Guatemala, 348–72

FUENTE, BEATRIZ DE LA, AND SILVIA GARZA TARRAZONA
1995
La Acrópolis de Xochicalco. Cuernavaca, Mexico: Instituto de Cultura de Morelos

GALLARETA NEGRÓN, TOMÁS, FERNANDO ROBLES C., ANTHONY P. ANDREWS, ET AL.
1989
"Isla Cerritos: Un puerto maya prehispánico de la costa norte de Yucatán, México." In *Memorias II Coloquio Internacional de Mayistas.* Campeche 1987, Vol. I. Mexico: UNAM, 311–32

GENDROP, PAUL
1984
"El tablero-talud en la arquitectura mesoamericana." *Cuadernos de Arquitectura Mesoamericana*, 2. Mexico, 1–3, 5–27, 47–50

GIDDENS, WENDY LOUISE
1995
Talud-tablero Architecture as a Symbol of Mesoamerican Affiliation and Power. M.A. Thesis in Anthropology. Los Angeles: University of California

GREENE, VIRGINIA, AND HATTULA MOHOLY-NAGY
1966
"A Teotihuacan-Style Vessel from Tikal: A Correction." *American Antiquity* XXXI, 3. Salt Lake City, 432–33

HEALAN, DAN M. (ED.)
1989
Tula of the Toltecs: Excavations and Survey. Iowa City: University of Iowa Press

HELLMUTH, NICHOLAS
1978
"Teotihuacan Art in the Escuintla, Guatemala Region." In *Middle Classic Mesoamerica.* Ed. by E. Pasztory. New York: Columbia University Press, 71–85

KUBLER, GEORGE
1961
"Chichén Itzá y Tula." In *Estudios de Cultura Maya*, I, Mexico: 47–80

LANDA, DIEGO DE
1959 (ed.)
Relación de las cosas de Yucatán. Biblioteca Porrúa 13. Mexico City: Editorial Porrúa

LAPORTE, JUAN PEDRO
1987
"El Talud-Tablero en Tikal, Petén, nuevos datos." In *Un Homenaje a Román Piña Chán.* Mexico: UNAM, 256–316

LEE WHITING, THOMAS A.
1996
"El Soconusco Prehispánico." In *Tapachula, La perla del Soconusco.* Ed. by R. Ramos M. Tuxtla Gutiérrez: Gobierno del Estado de Chiapas, 40–65

LEE WHITING, THOMAS A., AND CARLOS NAVARRETE (EDS.)
1978
Mesoamerican Communication Routes and Cultural Contacts. New World Archaeological Foundation Papers, 40. Provo, Utah: Brigham Young University

LÓPEZ LUJÁN, LEONARDO, ROBERT H. COBEAN, AND ALBA GUADALUPE MASTACHE F.
1995
Xochicalco y Tula. Mexico: CNCA-Jaca Books

LOTHROP, SAMUEL KIRKLAND
1952
Metals from the Cenote of Sacrifice, Chichén Itzá, Yucatán. Memoirs of the Peabody Museum of Archaeology and Ethnology, Vol. 10, 2. Cambridge, Mass.: Harvard University

MASTACHE FLORES, ALBA GUADALUPE
1994
"Tula." In *Arqueología Mexicana*, Vol. II, 7. Mexico, 20–27

MATHENY, RAY
1976
"Teotihuacan Influence in the Chenes and Río Bec Areas of the Yucatán Peninsula, Mexico." In *XIV Sociedad Mexicana de Antropología Mesa Redonda: Las Fronteras de Mesoamérica*. Tegucigalpa 1975, Vol. 2. Mexico: 45–54

MILLER, ARTHUR G. (ED.)
1983
Highland-Lowland Interaction in Mesoamerica: Interdisciplinary Approaches. Washington, D.C.: Dumbarton Oaks Research Library Collections

MORRIS, EARL H., JEAN CHARLOT, AND ANN AXTELL MORRIS
1931
The Temple of the Warriors at Chichen Itza, Yucatán. Publication 406. 2 Vols. Washington, D.C.: Carnegie Institution of Washington

NAGAO, DEBRA
1989
"Public Proclamation in the Art of Cacaxtla and Xochicalco." In *Mesoamerica after the Decline of Teotihuacan A.D. 700-900*. Ed. by R.A. Diehl and J.C. Berlo. Washington, D.C.: Dumbarton Oaks, 83–104

NAVARRETE, CARLOS
1996
"Elementos arqueológicos de mexicanización en las tierras altas mayas." In *Temas Mesoamericanos*. Ed. by S. Lombardo and E. Nalda. Mexico: INAH, 305–52

NICHOLSON, HENRY B.
1979
"Correlating Mesoamerican Historical Traditions with Archaeological Sequence: Some Methodological Considerations." In *Actes du XLIIe Congrès International des Américanistes*, Paris 1976, Vol. IX-B, Paris, 187–98
1982
"The Mixteca-Puebla Concept Revisited." In *The Art and Iconography of Late Post-Classic Central Mexico*. Ed. by E.H. Boone. Washington, D.C.: Dumbarton Oaks, 227–54

PARSONS, LEE A.
1967-69
Bilbao, Guatemala: An Archaeological Study of the Pacific Coast Cotzumalhuapa Region. 2 Vols. Milwaukee: Milwaukee Public Museum, 11–12

PASZTORY, ESTHER (ED.)
1978
Middle Classic Mesoamerica: A.D. 400–700. New York: Columbia University Press

PENDERGAST, DAVID M.
1971
"Evidence of Early Teotihuacan-Lowland Maya Contact at Altun Ha." *American Antiquity*, 36, 4, Washington, D.C., 455–60

PENICHE RIVERO, PIEDAD
1987
"¿Quiénes son los Itzá? Su identidad, sus dinastías y su poder sobre Yucatán." In *Memorias Primer Coloquio International de Mayistas*, 5–10 de agosto de 1985. Mexico: UNAM, 939–52

POPENOE HATCH, MARIO
1987
"Un análisis de las esculturas de Santa Lucía Cotzumalguapa." *Mesoamérica*, 14, Antigua Guatemala, 467–509

PROSKOURIAKOFF, TATIANA
1950
A Study of Classic Maya Sculpture. Publication 593. Washington, D.C.: Carnegie Institution of Washington
1951
"Some Non-Classic Traits in the Sculpture of Yucatán." In *The Civilizations of Ancient America*, Selected Papers of the XXIXth International Congress of Americanists. Ed. Sol Tax. Chicago, University of Chicago Press, 108–18
1970
"On Two Inscriptions at Chichén Itzá." In *Monographs and Papers in Maya Archaeology*. Ed. by W.R. Bullard. Cambridge, Mass: Harvard University Press, 457–67

RATTRAY, EVELYN CHILDS
1978
"Los contactos Teotihuacán-Maya vistos desde el centro de México." *Anales de Antropología*, XV, México: Instituto de Investigaciones Antropológicas, UNAM, 33–52

Relaciones
1985 (ed.)
Relaciones Histórico-Geográficas de la Gobernación de Yucatán. Fuentes para el Estudio de la Cultura Maya 1. Mexico: UNAM

ROBERTSON, DONALD
1970
"The Tulum Murals: The International Style of the late Post-Classic." In *XXXVIII Internationalen Amerikanistenkongresses, Proceedings*, 12 bis 18 August 1968, Vol. II. Stuttgart-München, 77–88

ROBLES CASTELLANOS, FERNANDO
1987
"La secuencia cerámica preliminar de Isla Cerritos, Costa Centro-Norte de Yucatán." In *Maya Ceramics* Pt. I. Ed. by P.M. Rice and R.J. Sharer, Oxford, 99–109

RODRÍGUEZ GIRÓN, ZOILA, AND MARCOS ANTONIO ROSAL TORRES
1987
"La plataforma 5C-53: Un caso de interpretación." In *Memorias Primer Coloquio Internacional de Mayistas*, 5–10 de agosto de 1985 de Mexico: UNAM, 319–30

RUZ LHUILLIER, ALBERTO
1962
"Chichén Itzá y Tula: Comentarios a un ensayo (con réplica del Dr. Kubler)." In *Estudios de Cultura Maya*, II, Mexico, 205–23

SANDERS, WILLIAM T., AND JOSEPH W. MICHELS (EDS.)
1977
Teotihuacan and Kaminaljuyú: A Study in Prehistoric Culture Contact. Pennsylvania State University Monograph Series on Kaminaljuyú. Pennsylvania: Pennsylvania State University Press, University Park

SANTLEY, ROBERT S.
1983
"Obsidian Trade and Teotihuacan Influence in Mesoamerica." In *Highland-Lowland Interaction in Mesoamerica.* Ed. by A.G. Miller. Washington, D.C.: Dumbarton Oaks, 69–124

SANTLEY, ROBERT S., PONCIANO ORTIZ CEBALLOS, ET AL.
1984
Final Field Report of the Matacapan Archaeological Project: The 1982 Season. Research Paper Series, 15, Latin American Institute, Albuquerque: University of New Mexico

SCHMIDT, PETER J.
1991
"Chichén and Prosperity in Yucatán." In *Mexico, Esplendors of Thirty Centuries.* New York: The Metropolitan Museum of Art, 182–211
1993
"Chichén Itzá, Yucatán." In *Arqueología, Memoria e Identidad.* Coord. by Félix-Jorge Azabache, Mexico, 208–29

SCHMIDT, PETER J., AND CARMEN VARELTA T.
1989
"La cerámica del Clásico Medio de Oxkintok y su relación con algunos sitios del norte de Yucatán." Unpublished paper given at the "First International Congress of Mayanistas," San Cristóbal de las Casas

SCHOLES, FRANCE V., AND RALPH L. ROYS
1948
The Maya-Chontal Indians of Acalan Tixchel. A Contribution to the History and Ethnography of the Yucatán Peninsula. Norman: University of Oklahoma Press

SELER, EDUARD
1915
"Die Ruinen von Chichén Itzá in Yucatán." In *Gesammelte Abhandlungen,* V, Ascher, Behrend, Berlin, 197–338

SOLÍS OLGUÍN, FELIPE, AND FEDERICA SODI MIRANDA
1989
"Presencia del Puuc y otros elementos de tradición maya en Tula y Tenochtitlán." In *Memorias II Coloquio Internacional de Mayistas,* Campeche 1987, Vol. II. México: UNAM, 805–22

STONE, DORIS (ED.)
1982
Aspects of the Mixteca-Puebla Style and Mixtec and Central Mexican Culture in Southern Mesoamerica. Middle American Research Institute, Occasional Paper 4. New Orleans: Tulane University

STUART, GEORGE
1997
"The Royal Crypts of Copán." *National Geographic,* 192, 6, December 1997, Washington, D.C., 68–93

TAUBE, KARL
1994
"The Iconography of Toltec Period Chichén Itzá." In *Hidden Among the Hills.* Ed. by H.J. Prem. Möckmühl: Verlag von Flemming, 212–46

THOMPSON, J. ERIC S.
1948
"An Archaeological Reconnaissance in the Cotzumalhuapa Region, Escuintla, Guatemala." In *Contributions of Middle American Archaeology and Ethnology,* Vol. IX, 44, Publication 574. Washington, D.C.: Carnegie Institution of Washington, 1–56
1970
Maya History and Religion. The Civilization of the American Indian Series, 99. Norman: University of Oklahoma Press

TOZZER, ALFRED M.
1930
"Maya and Toltec Figures at Chichen Itza." In *Proceedings of the XXIIIrd Congress International of Americanists,* New York, 1928. New York, 155–64
1941
Landa's Relación de las cosas de Yucatán A Translation. Papers of the Peabody Museum of American Archaeology and Ethnology, Harvard University, Vol. XVIII. Cambridge, Mass.: The Peabody Museum, 179–82
1957
Chichen Itza and its Cenote of Sacrifice: A Comparative Study of Contemporaneous Maya and Toltec (I-II). Memoirs of the Peabody Museum of Archaeology and Ethnology. Vols. XI–XII. Cambridge, Mass.: Harvard University

VAILLANT, GEORGE C.
1940
"Patterns in Middle American Archaeology." In *The Maya and Their Neighbors.* New York-London, 295–305

WILLEY, GORDON R.
1977
"External Influences on the Lowland Maya: 1940 and 1975 Perspectives." In *Social Process in Maya Prehistory.* Ed. by N. Hammond. London-New York: Academic Press, 57–75

WREN, LINNEA H. AND PETER J. SCHMIDT
1991
"Elite Interaction during the Terminal Classic Period: New Evidence from Chichén Itzá." In *Maya Political History.* Ed. by T.P. Culbert. Cambridge and New York: Cambridge University Press, 199–225

Rocío González de la Mata
Anthony P. Andrews

Navigation and Trade on the Eastern Coast of the Yucatán Peninsula

Tulum, Quintana Roo

The eastern coast of the Yucatán peninsula is internationally known for its attractions and beauty. For more than a century and a half, this land has been visited and researched by travelers and archaeologists who located pre-Hispanic ruins along a white sand strip of infinite majesty.

These settlements varied in size, from small isolated shrines to major sites comprising several buildings surrounded by house-habitation platforms, joined by extensive unmortared stone walls. This archaeological evidence indicates the importance and population density of the area during the pre-Hispanic period, especially during the Late Postclassic period of Maya civilization (A.D. 1200–1542). Moreover, sixteenth-century accounts speak of the coastal populations at the time of the arrival of the Spaniards, who found at these beaches a more developed culture than that which had been known in the Caribbean.

They encountered a highly stratified society that lived in urban communities with masonry pyramids and "palaces" decorated with complex stucco-and-carved-stone reliefs. The remains have survived, despite the fragile nature of the limestone with which buildings were constructed, because the coastal zone was one of the areas least affected by the impact of the conquest, because it served as an area of transit for European incursions into inland areas and it remained abandoned for a long time. Many of the major achievements of Maya civilization had been dissipated by the sixteenth century and several centuries would pass before the world became interested again in the importance of this society that flourished in the tropical forest.

Initial Contacts

Although the Postclassic period of Maya civilization has been eclipsed by research on the spectacular vestiges of the Classic period, since the middle of the nineteenth century, there has been increasing interest in knowledge about coastal sites that offered easy access by sea.

The first Spaniards to arrive on the eastern coast were the survivors of the Valdivia expedition, whose ship was wrecked near Jamaica in 1511. In a small boat, they landed on the Mexican coasts and, based on what is stated in the chronicles, only two of them survived captivity. One, Gonzalo de Guerrero, remained with the Mayas the rest of his life, while the other, Jerónimo de Aguilar, years later joined Hernán Cortés as an interpreter in his conquest of Mexico. He was the one who reported the shipwreck.

The first official expedition of Spanish discovery was directed by Francisco Hernández de Córdoba, who arrived on the beaches of Ecab, near Cabo Catoche, in 1517 before setting out into the Gulf of Mexico. A second expedition, under Juan de Grijalva, arrived the next year, and after reaching Cozumel, navigated to the south along the coast to Bahía de la Ascensión.

In the course of its journey, several large towns were observed on the shores, including one that due to its size and grandeur resembled Seville; it is probable that the latter was the contiguous settlement of Zama-Xamanzama, today Tulum-Tancah. In 1519, Cortés arrived at Cozumel en route to Veracruz and his conquest of the Aztec empire.

The exploration of Yucatán began in 1527 when Francisco de Montejo disembarked near Xelhá, where he established the first Spanish camp, which was called Salamanca de Xelhá. From there, Montejo went on several voyages toward the north until he reached a coastal site called Belma–El Meco or Ecab–before venturing into the interior of the peninsula.

Practically nothing is known of the history of the coast during the seventeenth and eighteenth centuries, except for some sporadic reports of military or religious visitors. It is calculated that the population fell some 85 to 95 percent, in part due to diseases contracted from the conquerors, but also because of the reduction in the number of indigenous inhabitants at inland towns.

Once manpower became scarce, Spanish interest in the zone also decreased. From the end of the sixteenth century, the coast began to be frequented by European pirates, and particularly, by English timber dealers, who extracted the famous wood

Panoramic view of the Structure 45 at Tulum, Quintana Roo

known as *palo de tinte* from coastal jungles. These foreigners lived for periods on the coast and nearby islands, together with "pagan" Maya Indians who fled from the Spaniards. In effect, the region of the Caribbean became a forgotten frontier beyond the control of colonial authorities.

Archaeological Explorations
The first archaeological visitors to the coast were the well-known travelers John Lloyd Stephens and Frederick Catherwood, who visited Cancún, Cozumel, and Tulum in 1842.
They published the first news on Maya ruins from these places. With the outbreak of the Caste War–the 1847 Maya rebellion against the Spaniards–the coast remained closed to visitors throughout most of the second half of the nineteenth century. In spite of this, Alice and Augustus Le Plongeon managed briefly to visit the north coast of the region in 1877–1878, leaving descriptions of ruins at Isla Mujeres, Cancún, El Meco, and Cozumel.
Other travelers who ventured to this dangerous coast were Teobert Maler in 1891 and William Holmes in 1895.

They left maps, drawings, and photographs of the ruins they visited. Around 1900, the Mexican government began to have commercial interest in the zone because of the opportunity to exploit *chicle* (gum), *copra* (coconut meat), and precious woods, and it installed military camps in a territory that was still in rebellion.

At the beginning of the 1910s, explorers began to arrive to visit the ruins on the coast of Quintana Roo.

Among these were the members of the Carnegie Institution of Washington, D.C., who in 1916, 1918, and 1922, under the direction of Sylvanus Morley, carried out intensive studies of the ruins of Tulum, Tancah, and Xelhá; they also made maps of the buildings of Chacmool, Canché Balam, Cacakal, Nohku, Cancún, and Playa del Carmen.

For the first time, these studies defined the coast as a cultural entity unlike the rest of the Maya zone and situated its most important development during the Post-classic period. Later, members of the Mason-Spinden expedition (1926) and the Mexican Scientific Expedition (Expedición Científica Mexicana, 1937) reported a large number of additional coastal sites, adding considerable data to what was already known.

Xelhá, Quintana Roo

Subsequently, between 1938 and 1940, Miguel Angel Fernández conducted the first excavations and carried out consolidation work at Tulum. In 1954 and 1955, William Sanders, whose work was also published by the Carnegie Institution, carried out surveys in order to conduct small excavations along the coast. He established a ceramic sequence for the zone and was the first to provide a basic chronology for later studies.

In 1955 and 1956, E. Wyllys Andrews IV of Tulane University began an architectural study of the zone of Xcaret (Polé) and other sites on the central coast, a project that was concluded by Anthony P. Andrews in the 1970s. In 1963 Wyllys Andrews also excavated a shelly deposit on Cancún, which provided important data on the most ancient inhabitants of the coast.

From the 1970s, different explorations have been carried out by the National Institute of Anthropology and History of Mexico (INAH), research that has included surveys, mapping, and in some instances, intensive excavation and architectural consolidation along the coast.

These studies have focused on sites on the islands of Cancún, Isla Mujeres, and Cozumel, as well as at the coastal settlements of Ecab, El Meco, El Altar, Playa del Carmen (Xamanhá), Punta Piedra, Xcaret (Polé), La Iná, Xelhá (Xalá), Tancah (Xamanzama), Tulum (Zama), Muyil (Chunyaxché), Chacmool, Tupak, Punta Pájaros, and several locations in the vicinity of the Bay of Chetumal. Further south in Belize, explorations and excavations have also been conducted of several pre-Hispanic settlements in the keys and along the coast of the mainland. Among these projects are research at the great Preclassic port of Cerros, several sites on Ambergris Cay, and multiple settlements in the zones of Northern River Lagoon, Placencia Lagoon, Wild Cane Cay, and Stingray Lagoon.

Much of this work has been done as part of a race against time to save the history and remains of an important period of Maya culture. The rapid growth of the coast as an international tourist attraction has brought support to carry out more exploration, but at the same time the opening of new highways and the construction of tourist infrastructure has resulted in the systematic destruction of many archaeological vestiges.

San Gervasio, Island of Cozumel
Quintana Roo

The Coast in pre-Hispanic Times

The Maya Caribbean coast has a long history of occupation, which dates back at least to the Late Preclassic period (approximately 300 B.C.–A.D. 300), when small groups of fishermen and farmers lived in coastal villages.

By this time the island of Cozumel was also inhabited, indicating that the inhabitants of the region were able navigators. The largest settlement known from this period was the port of Cerros, on the north coast of Belize; evidently, this site was an important node in sea trade networks that have linked the north and south of the Yucatán peninsula since the Preclassic period.

During the Classic period (approximately A.D. 300–900), several larger towns emerged, such as Muyil, Tancah, Xelhá, and San Gervasio on Cozumel. Unfortunately, we do not know much about these communities, because the remains of later periods have covered much of the evidence of the Classic period. Nevertheless, we know that the towns of the Classic period were fairly extensive and that they participated actively in sea trade between the northern and southern regions of the Maya lowlands. In many cases, coastal settlements served as ports for large inland cities, which was the case of Xelhá with Cobá.

It is possible that Tancah and Muyil also served as ports to the city of Cobá. Classic period trade on the eastern coast involved the exchange of many products between the north and south, including salt, cotton, and honey, which traveled from north to south, while a variety of ceramic, flint, jade, and obsidian artifacts, among other products, traveled from south to north.

Between A.D. 750 and 900, at the end of the Classic period, many cities in the southern lowlands ceased to erect large buildings and sculpted monuments. The population of some cities decreased drastically, while many others suffered total abandonment. This was a complicated, slow process, a consequence of different factors that created strong tensions in the social matrix of the Maya world.

Among them was the exhaustion of agricultural resources to feed a growing population, the struggle between communities for control of the land and other economic resources, the deterioration of the environment, and incursions of foreign groups into the western frontier.

opposite
Bowl with human figurine
Becán, Campeche
Early Classic period
Merida, Museo Regional
de Antropología de Yucatán
"Palacio Cantón"
cat. 253

Necklace
Calakmul, Campeche
Classic period
Campeche, Museo Histórico
Fuerte de San Miguel
Baluarte de San Miguel
cat. 147

The interrelationship of these factors led to the collapse of the economic system, to a major increase in the number and intensity of armed conflicts between many political entities, and to malnutrition, epidemics, and demographic collapse.

While this happened in the south, in the north, Classic culture continued flourishing for one or two more centuries. This was the high point of Puuc cities, such as Uxmal, Kabah, Sayil, and Labná, which undertook monumental constructions while their populations continued growing.

The great city of Chichén Itzá also emerged, and its grandeur perhaps played an important role in the eventual collapse of Maya society in the northern Yucatán. In its time, Chichén Itzá controlled a political and economic sphere as extensive as that of its predecessors of the Classic period.

There is no doubt that the new dynasty that arose at Chichén Itzá brought about a change in almost all aspects of Maya culture. The economy of the Itzas depended to a great extent on the control of coastal resources and access to external trade routes, together with the exploitation of manpower and agriculture inland. The growth of Chichén evidently coincided with the gradual abandonment of other cities of the north–including those of the Puuc–caused by the same processes that led to the ruin of cities of the south.

Eventually, the Yucatecan Maya, reduced and exhausted by processes of the collapse, rebelled against the tribute of the Itzá and destroyed the Itzá capital.

In its place arose the city of Mayapán which joined, through a confederation known as the Mayapán League, the provinces of northern and western Yucatán (Ah Canul, Chakán, Cehpech, Hocabá, Maní, Ah Kin Chel, and Sotuta); these provinces were relatively autonomous, in contrast to the strong central power of the Itzas and of the dynasties of the Classic period.

This fact marked the dividing line between the Classic and Postclassic period for the Yucatán peninsula. Nevertheless, the new monarchs tried to recreate the grandeur of Chichén Itzá even in the architecture of the city, but on a much reduced scale. By the middle of the fifteenth century, due to civil wars and political intrigue, Mayapán fell and Yucatán rapidly was divided into a series of independent provinces.

But while the provinces of the west bled to death in internal strife, the provinces of

N

Legend

- Sea trade routes
- Land trade routes
- Region borders
- ▲ Maya ports
- ● Archaeological areas

PRODUCTS

- salt
- jade
- cacao
- obsidian
- cotton
- feathers
- basalt
- ceramics
- tools
- animal skins
- honey

Cerritos

Isla Contoy

Isla Mujeres

Dzibilchaltún

Playa del Carmen

Xcaret

Isla Cozumel

Mayapán

Chichén Itzá

Cobá

Uxmal

Isla de Jaina

Kabah

Sayil

Muyil

Tulum

Okop

CARIBBEAN SEA

Edzná

GULF OF MEXICO

Xicalanco

Becán

Santa Rita

Comalcalco

Chicanná

Río Bec

Cerros

Nohmul

Ambergris Cay

Calakmul

Cuello

Colhá

Palenque

Mirador

Altun Ha

Río Azul

Kintil

El Perú

Uaxactún

Cayo Moho

Piedras Negras

Tikal

Isla Turneffe

Cayo San Jorge

MEXICO

Yaxchilán

BELIZE

GULF OF HONDURAS

Lacanhá

Bonampak

Caracol

Chinkultic

Naj Tunich

Río de la Pasión

Isla Roatán

Río Chixoy

Wild Cane Cay

Isla Utila

Chantuto

Zaculeu

GUATEMALA

PACIFIC OCEAN

Izapa

Quiriguá

Iximche

Río Motagua

Copán

Abaj Takalik

Kaminaljuyú

HONDURAS

EL SALVADOR

Scale:

0   100   200 Km

0   200   400 Mi

opposite
Map showing the main commercial
routes of the Maya

Eccentric
Palenque, Chiapas
Late Classic period
Museo de Sitio
"Alberto Ruz Lhuillier"
cat. 355

on the right
Obsidian nucleus
El Meco, Quintana Roo
Postclassic period
Cancún, Museo Arqueólogico
de Cancún
cat. 200

the east underwent a rebirth during the Postclassic period. In northeastern Yucatán, along the coast of the Caribbean and on its islands, there was dramatic demographic growth. In this zone, with the highest concentration of Postclassic sites in the Maya area–more than one hundred reported to date–many new communities appeared with administrative and ceremonial centers which included plazas surrounded by pyramids and palaces, and hundreds or thousands of residences.

Among the largest were Conil (Chiquilá), Ecab, and El Meco on the north coast; El Rey and San Miguel on the island of Cancún; San Gervasio and Buena Vista on the island of Cozumel; Playa del Carmen-Xcaret (Xamanhá-Polé), Paamul, Akumal, Xelhá (Xalá), Tancah-Tulum (Zama-Xamanzama), and Muyil (Chunyaxché) on the central coast; and the group of sites of Tamalcab-Ichpaatún near Chetumal, and Santa Rita Corozal in the Bay of Chetumal.

The area of the central coast was the most densely populated: the distribution of the vestiges of constructions is so continuous that it is difficult to determine where one site ends and another begins.

This settlement pattern ran along the coast, without any obstacle; houses were distributed throughout the land, surrounded by a complicated system of unmortared stone or earthen walls that separated plots.

The political organization of the eastern coast at the time of the arrival of the Spaniards is still a mystery that remains to be solved. It is known through historical references that Cozumel and Chetumal were capitals of independent political entities, but we do not have data on the other settlements.

What is most probable is that they had formed a chain of small political entities along the coast, but we have no idea whether these were autonomous provinces, confederacies, or if they had a hierarchical structure. Possible capitals of provinces include Conil (Chiquilá), Ecab, El Meco-Cancún, the zone of Puerto Morelos-Mulchic, Xamanhá-Polé (Playa del Carmen-Xcaret), Xalá (Xelhá), Zama-Xamanzama (Tancah-Tulum), and Muyil (Chunyaxché).

It is probable that the complex of sites around Tamalcab and Ichpaatún represents

Human pendant
Chichén Itzá, Yucatán
Postclassic period
Mexico City
Museo Nacional de Antropología
cat. 263

Animal bell
Chichén Itzá, Yucatán
Postclassic period
Mexico City
Museo Nacional de Antropología
cat. 265

the vestiges of the ancient capital of Chetumal. Farther south, it is possible that Santa Rita had been a subject city of Chetumal, or it may have been the capital of another coastal province.

The Flourishing of Trade and the Coast
On his fourth voyage to America in 1502 and in the vicinity of the islands in the bay of Honduras, Christopher Columbus came across a canoe that was carrying products such as cotton from Yucatán, copper from central Mexico, and cacao seeds, probably from Belize. It is evident that the Mayas did not live in isolation.

Since the beginning of the Preclassic period, communities exchanged products, at times at considerable distances, in order to obtain objects or raw materials that they lacked. By the time of the arrival of the Spaniards in the sixteenth century, the Mayas were promulgators of an extensive trade network that reached frontiers as far away as the north and central part of Mexico, Nito in the Honduras gulf, and Panamá to the south.

As many of the goods traded were perishable materials, it is difficult to archaeologically prove the coming and going of so much merchandise. Therefore, it is necessary to resort to historical accounts to draw analogies and for concrete references on their exchange.

Based on sixteenth-century evidence, we know that cotton was traded from Yucatán to the eastern and western ends of the Maya area. As for cacao, the chronicles also tell us that the zone of Chetumal, on the lower part of the Hondo River, the Ulúa Valley in northwestern Honduras, and some other areas such as Soconusco (the Pacific coast of Chiapas and Guatemala) were the biggest producers of this seed. Salt is another product that certainly was an important object of trade.

There are sites in the north of the Yucatán peninsula where it was produced; from there it was transported to distant destinations.

Honey was cultivated in Chetumal, along the coast to the north and on the island of Cozumel, and implements used for its storage have been found in Belize and other places. Another product that was traded on a large scale was obsidian, a volcanic glass exploited by man since remote times due to its facility for making tools.

It is found abundantly in archaeological sites throughout the Maya area and its sources are located in the central highlands of Mexico and in the lands of the volcanic mountain ranges of Guatemala.

Disk
Tula, Hidalgo
Early Postclassic period
opposite, detail
Mexico City
Museo Nacional de Antropología
cat. 261

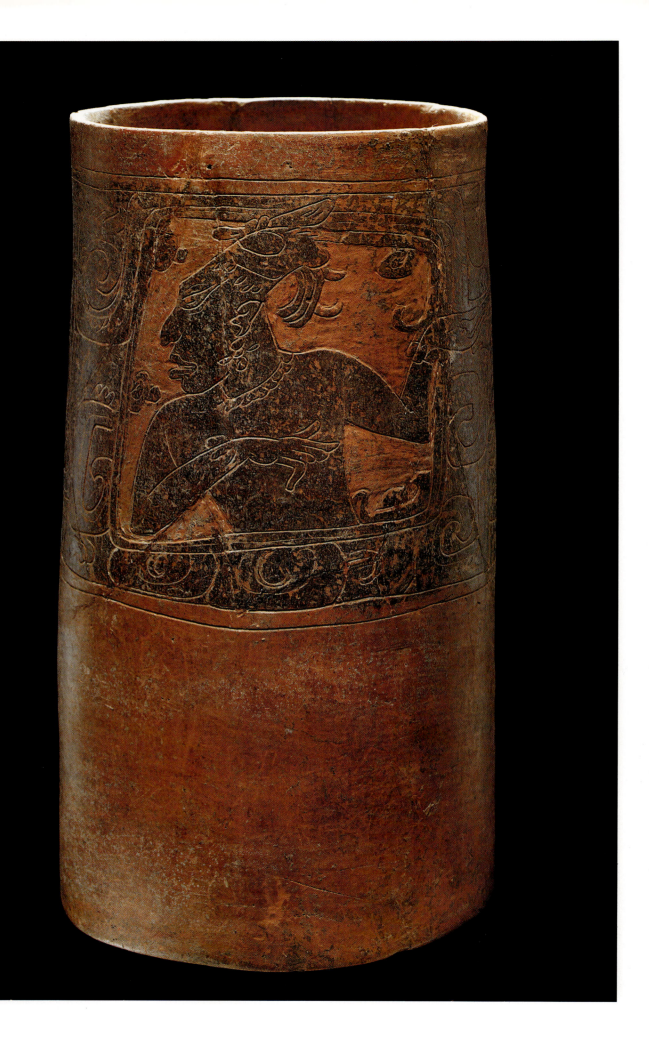

opposite
Vessel
Izamal, Yucatán
Terminal Classic-Postclassic period
Merida, Museo Regional
de Antropología de Yucatán
"Palacio Cantón"

It has been possible to establish the routes of its exchange; one of the main ones was the sea route around the Yucatán peninsula and that was connected with rivers or land routes for inland distribution. The majority of the obsidian that arrived on the eastern coast of Yucatán came from El Chayal, in the Guatemalan highlands.

This obsidian probably was lowered on the Motagua River, and later taken up to ports in Belize and Quintana Roo by coastal trade routes. It is also probable that it passed through Wild Cane Cay, off the southern coast of Belize, an important node of obsidian distribution that branched out from the Motagua River.

Also on the Caribbean coast, some pieces of obsidian from central Mexico have been recovered that were acquired by way of the sea route that originated in Veracruz and went around the peninsula.

One of the luxury products brought to Maya lands was metal, particularly gold and *tumbaga* (tombac), which came from southern Costa Rica and western Panama. On the eastern coast, pieces of gold have been found at Cozumel and Santa Rita Corozal, although it is probable that much of the gold that passed through the coast was en route to cities inland, such as Chichén Itzá.

The links with the Central American isthmus region also include Maya objects that have been found in Costa Rica, such as pyrite mirrors with glyphic inscriptions and plumbate ceramics from southwestern Guatemala.

Objects made of jade, which symbolized vitality and opulence, are found throughout the Maya area, although its origin is located in the rocky mountains of the highlands, in the high basin of the Motagua Valley in Guatemala. Its distribution was as extensive as that of obsidian and it must have been carried out on the same routes, but its use was restricted to the upper classes.

On the Caribbean coast in Quintana Roo and Belize, many pieces of jade, which went up the coast from the mouth of the Motagua River, have been recovered. Furthermore, much of the jade that is found at inland sites in the north of the peninsula undoubtedly entered by way of Caribbean ports.

Clay objects, both of everyday use as well as for shrine purposes, display exchange between different towns, and it is possible, based on studies of style and chemical analysis, to locate their place of origin.

At many sites on the coast, ceramic shards have been analyzed and they indicate clear connections with Cobá, Chichén Itzá, and Mayapán. Furthermore, at several sites on the Caribbean, ceramics such as fine orange, which comes from the coast of Tabasco, have been recovered, as well as plumbate ware, which comes from southwestern Guatemala. Finally, it's worth noting that at several sites in Belize, imported wares from the north of Yucatán have been found and these undoubtedly arrived by Caribbean trade routes.

Here we have barely made some general observations on some of the main trade wares. It is worth noting that the inventory of articles exchanged was much more varied, and the objects about which we have some information add up to more than seventy-five. Among others, there were food products, spices, medicinal plants, feathers, animal skins, leathers, dyes, wax, henequen and agave products, basketry, canoes, stingray spines, amber, wood artifacts, shell, turquoise, flint and basalt, pumice stone, alabaster, iron ore, mercury, objects of copper, silver, and many other things, including slaves.

This evidence demonstrates a high degree of specialization and control in society, which would have been necessary to sustain the trade between the highlands and the lowlands of the north and south, using land and sea routes and with contacts as distant as Costa Rica to the south, and the central Mexican highlands to the north.

The eastern coast played a fundamental role in this trade. All the merchandise passed, was distributed and exchanged through this area.

Therefore, the greatest number of Postclassic sites are concentrated in the northern lowlands. The region's rapid growth seems to be understandable as a result of the constant migration of populations from the interior, attracted by marine resources and coastal trade.

Chocholá-style vessel
Uxmal, Yucatán
Late Classic period
Mexico City
Museo Nacional de Antropología

Map showing the main commercial
products of the Maya

N

Isla Cerritos   Chiquilá   Ecab
San Angel   El Meco
Dzibilchaltún   Mulchic   Isla
Ekbalam   Cancún
Playa del Carmen
Mayapán   Xcaret
Cobá   Isla
Xelhá   Cozumel
Isla de Jaina   Tulum
Muyil   San Miguel
Okop   Chamax
GULF
OF MEXICO   Chacmool
Champotón   Tantaman
Tixchel
Silvituc   Ichpaatún
Xicalango   Santa Rita
MEXICO
Ambergris Cay
El Tigre   CARIBBEAN
SEA
Lamanai
GUATEMALA
BELIZE
Topoxte   Tipú   Punta Colson
Tayasal   Punta Placencia
Wild Cane Cay
GULF OF HONDURAS
Scale:
0   100   200 Km   HONDURAS
0   100   200 Mi   Naco

At the same time, some inland sites were enriched by influences from the Caribbean
through the trade corridor that ran from the north of Belize toward the central Petén.
The Postclassic sites in Belize of Tipuj, Lamanai (on New River), and Santa Rita
Corozal linked the Petén with the Chetumal Bay, a great center of commercial activity by that time.

In the east of the peninsula, important ports also arose during this period, such as
Campeche, Champotón, Tixchel, Isla del Carmen, and Xicalanco, where it is known
that groups from central Mexico gathered. Although archaeological data on this region
are minimal, historical chronicles tell us that they were lands densely populated at the
time of the arrival of the Spaniards.

opposite
Vessel
Campeche, Mexico
Late Classic period
Cologne
Rautenstrauch-Joest-Museum
cat. 442

Bowl
Ocozocoautla, Chiapas
Late Classic period
Tuxtla Gutiérrez
Museo Regional de Chiapas

There are also historical references and archaeological evidence of land trade routes between Campeche and Chetumal. It was only a few years ago that, through research on the eastern coast of Yucatán and Belize, we were able to forge a vision of what came to pass during the last period of Maya civilization, from 1200 to 1500.

Scholars speak of a "decadence" in architecture, sculpture, and even in the production of implements of everyday use, making reference to a past, the Classic period, that could never be equaled. Although from an aesthetic point of view, the preceding statement is true, it is impossible to understand and define the Postclassic Maya only in comparison to the Classic period Maya.

It is another society, with new interests and internal dynamics. Trade–evident from the many objects found in excavations at Postclassic sites such as those already mentioned, and in mural paintings that adorn Postclassic buildings (such as those at Tulum and Santa Rita Corozal)–brought a richness to culture through the contact and influence of new populations.

Unlike its predecessors, Postclassic Maya society based its consumption on the massive production of instruments for daily use and they invested fewer social resources in the construction of temples and sculptures to praise the past. This is also due to the rupture created by a way of government characterized by an autocratic system of royal lineages between several individuals.

The abundance of temples or shrines dispersed between the habitational vestiges along the coast would also come to confirm the decentralization of religious worship and constitute eloquent testimony of the dispersion of economic resources and political power.

The Mayas of the Postclassic period, therefore, were adapting to new forms of life and were in the process of creating a new society when they were violently interrupted by the Spanish conquest.

References

ANDREWS, ANTHONY P.
1985
"The Archaeology and History of Northern Quintana Roo." In *Geology and Hydrogeology of the Yucatán and Quaternary Geology of North-eastern Yucatán Peninsula*. Ed. by W.C. Ward, A.E. Weidie, and W. Back. New Orleans: New Orleans Geological Society, 127–43
1990
"The Role of Ports in Maya Civilization." In *Vision and Revision in Maya Studies*. Ed. by F.S. Clancy and P.D. Harrison. Albuquerque: University of New Mexico Press, 159–67
1993
"Late Postclassic Lowland Maya Archaeology." *Journal of World Prehistory*, Vol. 7, 1, 35–69

ANDREWS IV, E. WYLLYS; ANTHONY P. ANDREWS
1975
A Preliminary Study of the Ruins of Xcaret, Quintana Roo, Mexico. With Notes on Other Archaeological Remains on the East Coast of the Yucatán Peninsula. Middle American Research Institute. Publication 40. New Orleans: Tulane University

GONZÁLEZ DE LA MATA, ROCÍO, *ET AL.*
1988
Guía Oficial: Quintana Roo: Tulum, Xelhá, Cobá, Cancún, San Gervasio. Mexico City: INAH-Salvat Editores de México

LOTHROP, SAMUEL K.
1924
Tulum. An Archaeological Study of the East Coast of Yucatán. Publication 335. Washington, D.C.: Carnegie Institution of Washington

PIÑA CHÁN, ROMÁN
1978
"Commerce in the Yucatec Peninsula: The Conquest and Colonial Period." In *Mesoamerican Communication Routes and Culture Contacts*. Ed. by T.A. Lee Whiting and C. Navarrete. Papers of the New World Archaeological Foundation, 40. Provo, Utah: Brigham Young University, 37–48

ROYS, RALPH L.
1943
The Indian Background of Colonial Yucatán. Publication 548. Washington, D.C.: Carnegie Institution of Washington

THOMPSON, J. ERIC S.
1970
Maya History and Religion. (See chapter 5, "Trade Relations between Maya Highlands and Lowlands.") Norman: University of Oklahoma Press

TREJO ALVARADO, ELIA DEL CARMEN, AND ROCÍO GONZÁLEZ DE LA MATA
1993
"Recapitulación y nuevos enfoques en la arqueología del norte de Quintana Roo." In *II Coloquio Pedro Bosch-Gimpera*. Ed. by M.T. Cabrero G. Mexico City: Instituto de Investigaciones Antropológicas, UNAM, 343–65

Lizard pectoral
Copán, Honduras
Late Classic period
Copán
Museo Regional de Arqueología
cat. 288

Sergio Quezada

Political Organization of the Yucatecan Mayas During the Eleventh to Sixteenth Centuries

The written history of the political organization of the Mayas in Yucatán begins in the tenth century. In particular, this history appears to be associated with important political events that had a lasting effect on the indigenous elite. Although the descriptions are simple, confusing, and contradictory, one can obtain a rough idea of the Maya governmental entities toward the end of the Classic period.

Despite these limitations, historical sources allow us to conclude that at the end of the Classic period, Maya governmental political organization passed through stages of gradual complexity associated with the migration of conquering groups from the Mexican highlands during the second half of the tenth century.

According to the indigenous tradition recorded in the *Chilam Balam*, around A.D. 968–987, the Itzas conquered Chichén Itzá, where they finally settled. Later, between A.D. 987–1007, the Xiu rushed into the peninsula and occupied Uxmal, and finally the Cocom arrived and established settlements in Mayapán. As a consequence of these conquests, in the beginning of the eleventh century these groups brought Maya society under their control and the resulting settlements were to become the ruling political-administrative centers of Yucatecan political life.

Nevertheless, Chichén Itzá began to expand its territory through conquests. Although it is difficult to identify the exact size of its domain, according to historical sources its influence extended into Chiapas and Guatemala. However, recent archaeological research suggests that their area of influence was more limited, since they encountered resistance, and could not dominate the Yaxuná and Cobá region.

In any case, Chichén Itzá's impetus to conquer was dizzying, and by the middle of the eleventh century, it had become a political center of first order over a vast territory and the seat of power for the *ah tepal* or sovereign.

The consolidation of Chichén Itzá as a political center and the appearance of the *ah tepal* meant the creation of a complex political structure to govern their dominions; a type of state organization must have risen in a large portion of the Yucatán peninsula. It is possible that members of the Maya elite were promoted to superior political positions as part of the process of forming this structure. The loyalty of these officials to the conquerors probably played a crucial role in their continued exercise of power, and so the recently promoted could keep their higher ranks.

Miniature figurine
Late Classic period
Mexico City, Museo Nacional
de Antropología
cat. 277

Panoramic view of Mayapán
Yucatán

Furthermore, the accumulation of large volumes of tribute must have created administrative organization and forced on the population a system of officers, capable of keeping tribute, accounts, and organizing the workforce from the population. The leadership position held by Chichén Itzá allowed it to achieve magnificent architectural and sculptural splendor and made it one of the largest, most thriving cities in the Maya area, where it extended almost 25 square kilometers.

Furthermore, the social organization of Chichén Itzá took on a markedly military character as military orders emerged. New gods such as Tezcatlipoca, Tlaloc, and Chicomecoatl, among others, were also imposed on the Yucatecan pantheon, which led to the creation of new rituals in the religious panorama of the peninsula. Without doubt, the most splendid of the religious ceremonies were those for the Kukulcan cult. At the same time, the priesthood system gradually became more complex.

By the middle of the thirteenth century, Chichén Itzá had begun to decline, as a result of the conflict between Chac Xib Chac, their sovereign, and Hunac Ceel, the great lord of Mayapán.

This conflict sparked a period of civil war that brought to the decline of Chichén. By the second half of that century an accelerated process of decline had begun, and Mayapán emerged as the capital of the northern Yucatán peninsula.

The rise of Mayapán as the new capital brought many changes to the religious and political landscape. Its sphere of influence was circumscribed only to the northeastern part of the peninsula, contrary to what had happened in Chichén Itzá. In the religious sphere, the rituals dedicated to Kukulcan continued, but they did not reach the great splendor that had been achieved in the previous century. Architecturally, Mayapán turned out to be only a poor shadow of Chichén Itzá.

At the same time, in contrast with Chichén Itzá which had been the seat of power of the sovereign, Mayapán could represent itself only as the residence of a confederate government. Such a form of organization must have represented a true innovation in Maya political history, since a set of alliances and submissions had to be established among the constituing lords.

This confederation involved the participation of a group of men who can only be identified by the lineages to which they belonged. In Mayapán, the original residence of the Cocom, also settled the Xiu, Chel, Tzeh, Canul, Cupul, and possibly the Luti, Pech, and Cochuah. Apparently, a Cocom lord played a dominant role in this political organization, but without being able to concentrate all the power.

From the second half of the thirteenth century, the political, administrative, and religious destinies of the northern Yucatán peninsula, were defined from Mayapán.

opposite
Ornamental slab representing
the rain deity Tlaloc
Uxmal, Yucatán
Classic period
Uxmal, Museo de Sitio de Uxmal
cat. 54

The Temple of the Warriors
Chichén Itzá
Yucatán

A group of political-administrative innovations were developed to maintain control over the territory that, for example, redefined the zones of influence of the lords in the confederate government.

According to Fray Diego de Landa, the lords "divided the land, giving towns to each one according to the antiquity of their lineage and being." Furthermore, because the governing elite resided in Mayapán, they entrusted the administration of their surplus tribute to an officer named the *caluac*.

In addition, in order to govern each town, Mayapán began to delegate political, judicial, administrative, and even religious responsibilities to the *batab*. Little is known about the connections that existed between this individual and the resident elite in Mayapán, but surely kinship played a decisive role in the designation.

Around the middle of the fifteenth century, as a result of the struggle between the Xiu and Cocom, Mayapán was destroyed and the confederate government disintegrated. A power vacuum was created since the elite was incapable of creating a new central political structure.

Each lord, according to the indigenous tradition recorded by Landa, was "going . . . to their land," and from his capital, each one began to govern with the title of *halach uinic*, or great lord. The Mayas called this new political entity a *cuuchcabal*, the Spaniards, *provincia* (province).

The fall of Mayapán initiated a period of political uncertainty in the Yucatecan Maya world. This situation created an endless number of *bataboob*, or chiefs with their respective towns which remained independent of the indigenous capitals.

The history of the *bataboob* and their domain is unclear, but it is possible that many of them had at one time been dependent of some capital through political or matrimonial alliances.

The less powerful were possibly annexed or simply conquered. One way or another, during the last century of pre-Hispanic life the presence of these autonomous *bataboob* was important in the peninsular territory.

A group of independent *bataboob* settled in the northwestern corner of the Yucatán peninsula, in a region known as *Chakan* (savannah). Another group was found in the north in an area known as *Chikinchel* (East Mountain).

A third group was located in the south of the peninsula, in a territory known as the *Cehache* (Land of the Deer). Finally, the fourth group of independent *bataboob* was located in the margins of the river Dzuluinicoob (New River), to the south of the indigenous province of Chetumal and to the east of the Itzá Maya of the Petén, that is the northern and central part of what is currently Belize.

The structure of the *cuuchcabal* consisted of three levels. The first was the *cuchteel* or *parcialidad*, and it was identified by a toponym or place-name. The *parcialidad* was ntegrated by a group of houses where up to six heads of families lived with their progeny. A description from the middle of the sixteenth century states: "In this land [of

Censer representing the rain deity
Tlaloc
Balancanché, Yucatán
Early Postclassic period
Dzibilchaltún
Museo del Pueblo Maya

Following pages
Chac Mool at Chichén Itzá
Yucatán

El Castillo of Kukulcan
Mayapán, Yucatán

Yucatán] there rarely exists a house which has only one neighbor; rather, each house has two, three, four, six and sometimes more, and among them there is a father of the family, who is the head of the house."

From the *parcialidades*, families went to the maize fields. Although the ownership system for land is not known exactly, it was communal, and family units had the usufructuary right, as a result of belonging to the *cuchteel*.

The Maya native, at the start of the agricultural cycle, chose a parcel of land that had not been previously marked, and he put up some sort of identifying sign to indicate that it had been selected and was therefore occupied.

As Landa wrote, "The lands, for now, are communal and in this way, the first to occupy them is the owner." Once the Maya Indian had selected his land, he measured it. The cultivation of the fields was decided by the head of each family in function of three factors: the household's consumption needs, the capacity of its workforce, and its tributary obligations.

The *parcialidad* was an administrative unit responsible for supplying the workforce and products for the elite. It was also a military unit; it was the system that supported the army during times of war.

Furthermore, it was a political institution since family heads named a person to be *ah*

kul who represented their interests before the rulers. Landa said that the *ah kuloob* were "very much obeyed and esteemed" persons and their word was heeded when the *batab* imparted justice.

The second level was the *batabil* or lordship, which was dominated by the *batab* or cacique. He controlled politically and administratively a group of *parcialidades* and resided in one of them. The *parcialidades* were not necessarily associated within the territory. Generally, they were located a certain distance from where the cacique lived. The *batab*, as central figure of this second level, played the role of uniting its population with the capital it depended from.

He received and used part of the surplus tribute of labor and products, and summoned the population of his *parcialidades* to war and to tutelary festivals and ceremonies. The *batab* organized each of his *parcialidades* in quarters and designated an *ah cuch cab* for each one.

This officer took care that the natives rendered their tribute in products an labor, and gathered them for banquets, feasts and war. Between the *batab* and the population there was a council made up of the *ah kuloob* and the *ah cuch caboob* carrying out political and judicial functions.

The third level was known as the *halach uinic* or great lord, a position determined by

478

Effigy vessel representing
a turtle with human face emerging
from its mouth and seated human
figure on its head
Mayapán, Yucatán
Late Postclassic period
Merida, Museo Regional de Yucatán
"Palacio Cantón"
cat. 303

paternal lineage. The caciques depended on him politically and administratively; he performed religious, military, judicial, and political functions.

The *halach uinic* resided in the capital of the *cuuchcabal* or province. During the first quarter of the sixteenth century, the capitals were Sací, Chichén Itzá, Belma, Chauac ha, Chancenote, Ekbalam, Maní, Sotuta, Hocabá, Dzidzantún, Tihosuco, Chetumal, Popolá, Motul, Calotmul, Calkiní, Cozumel, and Can Pech. In the structure of the *cuuchcabal*, the *batab* and the *halach uinic* dominated and controlled the political and administrative life of this institution.

They belonged to the nobility or *almehenoob* and were organized by lineage. They recognized each other since they made themselves descend directly from a common, famous ancestor.

Some felt in some way connected to the old highland conquerors; others traced the ancestors to the old governing houses of Mayapán.

The ruling lineages used the Zuyuá language to control the access to important offices; in other words, Zuyuá was a mechanism to prevent intruders from rising to positions of power. This language consisted in riddles and puzzles, used to interrogate the successor of the *halach uinic* and the *batab*.

The interrogation was carried out at the beginning of every *katun* (cycle of 7,200 days) and was a well-rooted tradition. This test of legitimacy was transmitted from fathers to sons in noble families. All seems to indicate that there are words associated with political and social ideas in that language's terminology.

The economic prerogative of the *batab* and *halach uinic* was the use of indigenous labor. The *halach uinic* from the province of Hocabá "was so obeyed and feared by his subjects that they did not dare to anger him, rather they served him in senseless wars"; the one from the province of Sotuta had them "so subjugated that without any reward he was served by them."

Map of the early sixteenth century capitals

To the *halach uinic* from the province of Ekbalam: "they recognized and gave tribute by planting his corn and chili, beans and cotton and other things for his sustenance, and they made and repaired his home when it was necessary."

The *halach uinic* and the *batab* also received tribute. The quantities were small and they received them in recognition of their function as lords.

The inhabitants of the town of Dzan, for example, gave their lord "corn, hens, honey and some cotton garments, all very limited and almost voluntarily, it was not more than a recognition of his fief."

When the Europeans began to approach the coasts of Yucatán during the first decade of the sixteenth century, they found a politically divided region. The inhabitants' organization into *cuuchcabaloob* or provinces and *bataboob* or indipendent caciques, made the Spanish conquest a prolonged event, lasting from 1527 to 1547.

References

ADAMS, RICHARD E.W., AND WOODRUFF D. SMITH
1981
"Feudal Models for Classic Maya Civilization." In *Lowland Maya Settlement Patterns*. Ed. by W. Ashmore. Albuquerque: University of New Mexico Press, 335–49

ANDREWS, ANTHONY P.
1990
"The Fall of Chichen Itza: A Preliminary Hypothesis." *Latin American Antiquity*, Vol. 1, 3, 258–67

ARZÁPALO MARÍN, RAMÓN, ET AL.
1995
Calepino de Motul. Diccionario maya-español. 3 Vols. Mexico City: UNAM

BARRERA VÁSQUEZ, ALFREDO; SILVIA RENDÓN
1963
El Libro de los Libros de Chilam Balam. FCE Colección Popular, 42. Mexico City: Fondo de Cultura Económica

BLANTON, RICHARD E., ET AL.
1981
Ancient Mesoamerica. A Comparison of Change in Three Regions. Cambridge, Mass.: Cambridge University Press

BRINTON DANIEL G. (ED.)
1882
The Maya Chronicles. Brinton's Library of Aboriginal Literature, 1. Philadelphia: D.G. Brinton

CHASE, DIANE Z.
1986
"Social and Political Organization in the Land of Cacao and Honey: Correlating the Archaeological and Ethnohistory." In *Late Lowland Maya Civilization. Classic to Postclassic*. Ed. by J.A. Sabloff and E.W. Andrews V. Albuquerque: University of New Mexico Press, 347–77

FREIDEL, DAVID
1983
"Lowland Maya Political Economy: Historical and Archaeological Perspectives in Light of Intensive Agriculture." In *Spaniards and Indians in Southeastern Mesoamerica: Essays on the History of Ethnic Relations*. Ed. by M.J. Macleod and R. Wasserstrom. Lincoln: University of Nebraska Press, 40–63

GARZA, MERCEDES DE LA, ET AL. (EDS.)
1983
Relaciones histórico-geográficas de la gobernación de Yucatán. 2 Vols. Sources for the Study of Maya Culture, 1. Mexico City: UNAM

HAVILAND, WILLIAM A.
1970
"Ancient Lowland Maya Social Organization." *Archaeological Studies in Middle America*, 26. New Orleans: Middle American Research Institute

LANDA, DIEGO DE
1973
Relación de las cosas de Yucatán. 10th ed. Biblioteca Porrúa, 13. Mexico City: Editorial Porrúa

OKOSHI, TSUBASA
1985
"Kokotenki Kokishumatzu no mayahokubute-ichi no ryoikikozo." *Revista Histórica de la Universidad de Gakushuin*, Vol. 23, 26–44

PIÑA CHAN, ROMÁN
1980
Chichén Itzá, la ciudad de los brujos del agua. Mexico City: Fondo de Cultura Económica

PROSKOURIAKOFF, TATIANA
1954
"Mayapan: The Last Stronghold of a Civilization." *Archaeology*, Vol. 7, 2, 96–103

QUEZADA, SERGIO
1993
Pueblos y caciques yucatecos, 1550–1580. Mexico City: El Colegio de México

RIVERA DORADO, MIGUEL
1985
Los Mayas de la antigüedad. Pre-Hispanic America Series, 25. Madrid: Alhambra

ROBLES CASTELLANOS, FERNANDO, AND ANTHONY P. ANDREWS
1986
"A Review and Synthesis of Recent Postclassic Archaeology in Northern Yucatán." In *Late Lowland Maya Civilization. Classic to Postclassic*. Ed. by J.A. Sabloff and E.W. Andrews V. Albuquerque: University of New Mexico Press, 53–98

ROYS, RALPH L.
1933
"Traditions of Caste and Chieftainship among the Maya." In *The Book of Chilam Balam of Chumayel*. Translated by R.L. Roys. Washington, D.C.: Carnegie Institution of Washington, 188–95
1933
"Toltec Military Orders in Yucatán." In *The Book of Chilam Balam of Chumayel*. Translated by R.L. Roys. Washington, D.C.: Carnegie Institution of Washington, 196–200
1943
The Indian Background of Colonial Yucatán. Washington, D.C.: Carnegie Institution of Washington
1957
Political Geography of the Yucatán Maya. Washington, D.C.: Carnegie Institution of Washington
1962
"Literary Source for the History of Mayapan." In *Mayapan, Yucatán, Mexico*. Ed. by H.E. D. Pollock. Washington, D.C.: Carnegie Institution of Washington, 25–86

THOMPSON, J. ERIC S.
1977
Historia y religion de los Mayas. 2nd ed. Colección América nuestra, América antigua, 7. Mexico City: Siglo XXI Editores

WEAVER, MURIEL
1981
The Aztec, Maya and Their Predecessors. 2nd ed. New York: Academic Press

Grant D. Jones

The Conquest of the Mayas of Yucatán and Maya Resistance During the Spanish Colonial Period

Urn representing Itzamna, detail
Mayapán, Yucatán
Late Postclassic period
Mexico City
Museo Nacional de Antropología
cat. 321

Resistance by conquered persons living under colonial rule helps us see these people as subjects of history in their own right, not just as objects of colonial administration or of religious conversion. Throughout world history any form of popular resistance, whether it be seeking refuge from foreign authorities in remote quarters, refusing to work for them, or actually taking up arms against them, deepens our understanding of how people appropriate their own history under conditions of oppression. In examining how the Mayas of the Yucatán peninsula resisted conquest and colonization, we must first emphasize that as in many other areas of the New World these indigenous peoples had created complex, stratified, highly organized societies that posed great difficulties to Spanish conquerors and colonizers. Maya Postclassic civilization was alive and well in 1517, when Yucatán was "discovered" by Francisco Hernández de Córdoba. He and other early visitors found urban temple centers, a well developed system of long-distance trade, a rich literature written in hieroglyphic characters, and a class system of ruling nobles, commoners, and slaves. But although these hundreds of thousands of speakers of Yucatecan and Cholan languages were organized into hierarchical states and chiefdoms, some of great size and territorial extent, they had their own intergroup enemies that prevented them from mounting a unified, peninsula-wide war against the original intruders.

The Conquest of Yucatán

The beginnings of the conquest of Yucatán postdated Hernán Cortés's famous conquest of the Aztec capital of Tenochtitlan between 1519 and 1521 by several years. In 1519 Cortés himself stopped at Cozumel on his way to the Veracruz coast. There he found and took with him a shipwrecked Spanish sailor named Jerónimo de Aguilar, whose life had been spared by his Maya captors and who had learned the Maya language well. It is an irony that Aguilar's language teachers unwittingly facilitated the conquest of central Mexico by enabling him to serve as a translator. Aguilar could speak Maya with the famous doña Marina, Cortés's bilingual Maya- and Nahuatl-speaking interpreter, adviser, and mistress who first met the conqueror in her homeland in Tabasco.

Francisco de Montejo received the royal patent to conquer Yucatán as *adelantado*, and he initiated his project in 1527. Although they were probably already devastated by epidemic diseases introduced by earlier European visitors to a population without natural resistance, the Mayas put up a vicious resistance to Montejo's efforts to conquer the northeastern and southeastern parts of the peninsula. Montejo abandoned his first conquest attempt but

The Labná Arch
by Frederick Caherwood
Private collection

Convent at Izamal, Yucatán

returned again to Yucatán in 1531, when he managed to subdue the populations of Tabasco and to establish a base at the present site of Campeche on the west coast of the peninsula. He sent his lieutenant, Alonso Dávila, to conquer the southeastern part of Yucatán–especially the large trading town of Chaktemal (Chetumal) near the mouth of the Río Hondo. Dávila found Chaktemal abandoned and established a town for the soldiers nearby, which they called Villa Real. Before long, however, the Mayas of the region rose up against the conquerors and laid siege to Villa Real, forcing Dávila and his surviving troops to retreat to Honduras. During 1534 the Spaniards evacuated their forces from Yucatán a second time. Not until 1540 did Montejo's son and nephew begin once more to conquer the Mayas of Yucatán. This time they were better prepared, and the Mayas were probably too worn down and decimated by disease to mount an effective resistance. The Montejos founded Merida in 1542, although the town was soon thereafter attacked, unsuccessfully, by hostile groups from the eastern part of the peninsula. By 1545 the northernmost quarter of the peninsula was in firm Spanish hands, with little resistance having been offered in the west but with intense resistance in the east. To the southeast were the provinces known as Waymil (in present-day Quintana Roo), Chaktemal (on Chetumal and Corozal Bays in Quintana Roo and northernmost Belize), and Tsul Uinicoob (encompassing most of the northern half of Belize). These were subjected to viciously cruel treatment by the conquerors, two cousins named Pacheco, before they finally succumbed. Such treatment, combined with the imposition of tribute by the Spaniards, led in 1546 to widespread open rebellion against the Spaniards around the Spanish *villas* of Salamanca de Bacalar to the southeast and Valladolid in the northeast. It took months for the Spanish to crush this revolt, which left the eastern and southeastern Maya territories in a state of confusion and led to the flight of many native inhabitants to the unconquered interior regions of the peninsula. From then on, throughout most of the colonial period, the principal source of Maya resistance came from these southern interior regions, where a constantly restocked mix of runaways and hardened rebels established independent towns and lured others from the north to join them. To their south were the famed Itzá Mayas on and around Lake Petén Itzá, who remained fully independent from Spanish rule until their conquest in 1697, a century and a half after the establishment of Merida in the north (Jones 1989; Chamberlain 1948; Clendinnen 1987; Farris 1984). The colonial Province of Yucatán was born in violence and armed resistance for which the Spaniards had been ill prepared. The early colonial-period Maya battles waged against Spaniards, although localized, were fierce, characterized by sophisticated strategy, the use of guerilla tactics, and the application of remarkable skills in defensive and offensive warfare. The Mayas were ultimately no match, however, for mounted Spaniards who used firearms–at least not in the more open, drier, and less densely forested areas of the north. There rebellion was forced to go underground in the form of more subtle methods of resistance, but in the rebellious south armed Spaniards found their weapons and horses to be of little value, and it would be many years before they learned how best to confront the enemy in these dense tropical forests.

Maya Resistance in the Colony

Certain circumstances of the European colony in Yucatán fostered a mood of resistance among the Mayas. These conditions varied over the centuries that followed the conquest, but certain similarities remained in place for over two centuries. First were the Spanish methods used to exploit the Maya population. The *encomiendas* were the most famous of these: royal grants to Spanish conquerors and their descendants who would receive the tribute of the native populations. These, despite laws outlawing them elsewhere in the Spanish New World, were retained in Yucatán until the late 1700s. The *encomiendas* extracted coinage, chocolate beans, cotton cloth, honey, maize, incense, and other native products that were then sold by Spaniards on the open market to support their own economic interests. Even more devastating than the *encomiendas*, however, were the *repartimientos*, which in Yucatán took the form not only of forced labor for "public works" (constructing public buildings, churches, and roads) but also of the forced sale to the Mayas of surplus European products (cloth from Flanders, European jewelry, and European finished clothing) in return for native goods. Mayas who failed to fulfill such one-sided contracts were harshly punished. The *repartimiento* was illegal, even in Yucatán, but colonial administrators applied the system

opposite
Effigy vessel
Alta Verapaz, Guatemala
Classic period
Guatemala, Museo Nacional
de Arqueología y Etnología
cat. 170

Tzutuhil woman spinning cotton

knowing that their punishment for doing so would be nothing more than a small fine–a tax, in effect, applied to hefty incomes derived from selling these goods to Mexico and elsewhere. The Spanish priests also applied charges for their services, and a host of small taxes for secular purposes further drained the already strained rural economy. Although slavery was soon outlawed, forms of "personal service" for negligible payment separated Maya families as their members were forced to work in Spanish households or on Spanish ranches and public works for much of the year. The impact of Franciscan and secular missionaries on Maya culture and society were also immense, most vividly expressed during the early *autodafé* carried out against accused Maya "idolaters" in 1562 by Franciscans under the leadership of Fray Diego de Landa (Clendinnen 1987). Other Spanish practices also fostered resentment. Mayas were themselves used to round up runaways from *encomienda* towns, often under the military command of their own nobility who now served Spanish interests. They were thus forced to participate in the punishment of rebels and resistors whose cause they must have admired. Others, resistant to Spanish concepts of theological purity in religion, were punished for participating in even the most benign of rituals that Spaniards considered to be pagan in nature. Those, for example, who were most open in their use of native censers, were assumed by Spaniards to be idolaters and were punished harshly by whippings and imprisonment. Those implicated in rumors of impending military movements against the Spanish risked being executed. Maya society itself enjoyed certain characteristics that made their governance by colonial officials, *encomenderos*, and missionaries particularly difficult and thus "prone" to the spread of anti-Spanish strategies. Despite intense efforts to force the Mayas to stay in one place, in one village, the native population moved around constantly, changing their town affiliations, establishing new villages, and even moving far into the bush beyond any colonial control. Such residential mobility was probably an ancient pattern, and its continuity under Spanish rule made it difficult to maintain a dependable tribute-paying population.

While the Spaniards themselves were largely confined to a few towns, the Mayas were everywhere: in the towns, in the *encomienda* villages, and in the bush. They outnumbered by Spaniards many times over. They had excellent communication with other Mayas all across the peninsula due to extended ties of kinship and long-distance trade networks that continued to flourish throughout the colonial period. These personal and economic networks were fostered by the functional literacy of some Mayas who had learned how to write at the sides of Franciscan priests but who later chose to use their knowledge for other purposes. Some of these literate Mayas became underground leaders with strong religious, charismatic characteristics. Some took on the role of prophets and set up rebel headquarters in the southern forests, presiding as well over well-organized economies that, ironically, received income from Maya peasants in the north who needed these forest products in order to pay excessive tributes that their own labor alone could not fulfill.

Almost all Mayas were exceedingly adept at keeping secrets from Spaniards–not a difficult task given their superior numbers and their collective dislike of the oppressor. They adapted culturally to Europeans' efforts to wring out information from them by honing the ability to remain silent even under the use of torture. Their answers to leading questions about their activities posed by Spanish investigators were brief, spare, and noncommittal.

Even the Maya literature of the colonial period was designed to confuse Spanish readers who might obtain copies of it. The *Books of Chilam Balam*, written in Maya in the Spanish script taught by Spanish priests, contain a great deal of information about divination, religious ritual, ritual language, and prophecy. The poetic language of these books is difficult to translate and may well have been intentionally obfuscated in order to keep Spaniards from discovering their real meaning.

One element of the *Books of Chilam Balam*, however, is fairly well understood: that is, the importance of the sections that address the repetitive cycles of time known as *katunes*. The *katun* cycle was only one element of many in the complex, interlocking system of Maya calendars, but we now know that it was immensely important means by which the Maya could communicate to one another about the importance of timing of events in the past and in the future. Each *katun* lasted a little less than twenty years and was associated with a particular set of characteristic events or qualities that were recorded for the previous occurrences of the *katun*. These events and qualities would, the Mayas believed, characterize the next twen-

opposite
Urn
Mayapán, Yucatán
Late Postclassic period
Mexico City
Museo Nacional de Antropología
cat. 321

Mayas Quiche walking in procession

ty-year period when the same *katun* occurred. Thirteen different *katunes* followed upon one another in a precise order, and at the end of a cycle of thirteen they repeated one after the other all over again. Thus, what happened in *katun* 8 *ahau* between 1441 and 1461 would be a good predictor of what could happen in the same *katun* 256 years later, between 1697 and 1717. This use of history to prophesy the future was a powerful political and ideological tool for Maya resistance against colonialism.

Maya rebel priests who tried to attract followings used such prophecies to predict all sorts of dire events. For example, Spaniards at Bacalar learned about an impending uprising in central Belize in 1638, reporting that villagers told them that local Maya leaders at Tipuj insisted that "They were to give obedience to their king and wished them to abandon their town, saying that if they did not do so all would die and be finished, because at such a time the Itzá would come to kill them and there would be many deaths, and hurricanes would flood the land" (Jones 1989, 207). The year 1638 was the beginning of *katun* 1 *ahau*, when, according to similar language in the *Books of Chilam Balam of Chumayel*, "This shall be the end of its prophecy: there is a great war . . . A parching whirlwind storm is the charge of the *katun*" (Roys 1967, 157). The tactical value of such prophecies for Maya leaders was their general vagueness and openness to interpretation and manipulation.

Spaniards grasped some of these aspects of Maya culture and reacted with some degree of paranoia. Spanish correspondence is filled with statements of fears of attack, even though very few of these fears actually materialized. There was, in particular, an annual period of panic during the processions for Holy Week in the Spanish towns, when rumors of Maya attack would surface. Eventually those who processed took to carrying their weapons. Even in normal times any Maya stranger in town was viewed with suspicion, and the slightest rumor quickly ballooned out of proportion, sending tremors all the way to Merida.

During the colonial period Spaniards applied various measures to prevent such feared attacks from occurring. Every few years the headquarters of runaway Mayas in the southern forests were attacked, their charismatic leaders executed, their so-called idols confiscated and destroyed, and the runaways brought back to be redistributed on the *encomiendas* where they supposedly belonged. Bishops, governors, and lesser officials frequently carried out tours of the *encomienda* towns to root out anti-Spanish criminal activity and idolatry. Although in the early days such *visitas*, as they were called, produced a good number of so-called idols and even hieroglyphic books (all of which were summarily destroyed), in later years the Mayas used sophisticated techniques for concealing information about their underground activities from Spaniards. But even a century after the conquest missionaries and soldiers were able to turn up caches of idols in such out of the way places as Cozumel, where they were ready to be shipped throughout the peninsula. Spaniards also used their own spies to identify suspected rebels in the Maya towns, but the Mayas themselves were usually able to identify these individuals by even more efficient intelligence networks of their own. Spanish officials sent Franciscan missionaries to the most remote frontier zones to apply gentle methods of persuasion through conversion, but few of these missions lasted for more than a few years before their converts would drift away into the bush.

The Itzá: Independence, Conquest, and Rebellion

While in northern Yucatán the Mayas were gradually drawn into the system of Spanish colonial secular and religious institutions, the southern frontiers of Yucatán were dominated not only by rebel runaway Mayas but also by the unconquered Itzá of central Petén. Not until 1697 would the Itzá capital of Nojpetén on Lake Petén Itzá be occupied by Spanish troops from Yucatán, and even during the years that followed the Itzá and their neighbors displayed strong resistance against efforts to Christianize them and to resettle them in Spanish-controlled towns. The Itzá represent one of the most dramatic examples of anti-colonial resistance in the history of Mesoamerica. In a new book, "The Conquest of the Last Maya Kingdom," I examine nearly two centuries of Itzá-Spanish relations. This chronicle begins with Hernán Cortés's dramatic expedition through Itzá territory in 1525, climaxes with the occupation of Nojpetén on March 13, 1697, and ends with accounts of subsequent violent Itzá rebellion, the tragedies of epidemic diseases that swept through the Maya population, and efforts by surviving Itzá elites to reconstitute new "kingdoms" in isolated forest regions (Jones in the press).

Sculpture of sixteenth century
Oxkutzcab, Yucatán
Dzibilchaltún
Museo del Pueblo Maya

The larger picture that emerges from this new examination of the Itzá demonstrates that these people, whose rulers claimed noble descent from Chichén Itzá, pursued a highly effective strategy between 1525 and 1697 whereby they created a wide buffer zone around their territory in order to keep Spanish forces at bay. They accomplished this remarkable feat by punishing those native peoples living along their frontiers who accepted Spaniards in their midst and sometimes by incorporating such groups into a wider alliance by engaging them as rebels against the colonies of Yucatán to their north and Guatemala to their south. As foreign and exotic as the Itzá may have seemed to their ultimate conquerors, these fiercely independent people demonstrated a deep understanding of their would-be conquerors, gathering detailed and extensive information about circumstances in the colonial world beyond their borders. Such knowledge required an intelligence network that certainly penetrated all of these regions and that may well have extended all the way to the colonial capitals.

One particularly well-documented example of Itzá manipulation of their Maya neighbors as allies against potential Spanish aggression concerns their relationship with the people of the town of Tipuj in western Belize. Tipuj was apparently the capital of a pre-conquest Maya province known as Tsul Uinicoob, meaning "foreign people" and probably referring to the geographical remoteness of the region. This province comprised roughly the northern half of present-day Belize. Following the Pachecos' 1543–1544 conquest of the Chaktemal and Waymil provinces, and a portion of Tsul Uinicoob as well, another Spaniard, Juan Garzón, carried out in 1568 his own reconquest of Tsul Uinicoob. As a result, Tipuj became the very last of a string of small Spanish missions extending more than 200 kilometers south from Bacalar. Most of these towns produced cacao that in pre-conquest times was taken down to the coast and then shipped long distances by Maya traders who plied the route between Yucatán and Honduras in large cargo canoes. By the seventeenth century, however, they paid much of their cacao crop as tribute to Spaniards.

Archaeological research on colonial-period Tsul Uinicoob has focused on the site of Tipuj itself and on the site of Lamanai. While my own research has focused on Spanish documents, Elizabeth Graham has directed most of the archaeological study of Tipuj, and David Pendergast has directed the Lamanai excavations. Both are large sites that demonstrate extensive pre-conquest occupations, revealing significant colonial-period architecture and artifacts. At both sites open-air churches, once thatched, and their cemeteries have been excavated along with other colonial-period buildings situated in loosely designed plazas near the churches.

Spanish priests and others introduced to the communities of Tsul Uinicoob a wide variety of European or European-style artifacts, including metal tools; beads made of glass, jet, and amber; silver earrings; and rings made of silver, copper, and brass. Pre-Columbian pottery styles continued to be produced, with minor changes, long after the conquest, little affected by the introduction of European olive jars and majolica wares.

Tipuj became a key player in a long, slow process by which Spanish colonial administrations at Merida hoped to tighten the noose around the Itzá and ultimately to conquer and Christianize them. While the inhabitants of Tipuj were deeply divided over their loyalties to the Spaniards on the one hand and to the Itzá on the other, the Itzá gradually increased their influence over the town. By the mid-1600s Tipuj was controlled by Itzá colonists who were related by marriage to the principal Itzá ruler, Ah Kan Ek. To the Spanish, Tipuj was a fragile buffer between the Christian colony and a vast unconquered hinterland. To the Itzá, however, Tipuj was a potential ally in their efforts to stave off their own conquest.

In 1618 the Franciscans Juan de Orbita and Fray Bartolomé de Fuensalida visited Tipuj, where they found the inhabitants at first to be friendly and welcoming. One told the friars that he was a descendant of the lord of Cozumel who had greeted Cortés when he stopped there in 1519. From Tipuj the friars visited Nojpetén, where they met with Ah Kan Ek, who coolly informed them that the time for them to become Christians had not yet come. When they left a few days later, they were threatened by angry warriors and warned not to return. Tipuan animosity toward the Spaniards surfaced a few months later, when Orbita discovered a "*gran multitud*" of so-called "*ídolos*" hidden in peoples' houses. Orbita threw them into the river, and the priest from Bacalar burned the remaining objects in a bonfire in the plaza, whipped those deemed guilty, and threatened to punish by burning at the stake any Tipuans found in the future to be engaged in such activity. Nevertheless, Fuensalida and Orbita visited Nojpetén again in 1619 but were thrown out again by armed Itzá and warned never to return. In 1622 the Yucatecan Captain Francisco Mirones y Lescano embarked on a venture that he hoped would result in his own military conquest of the Itzá. He, his troops, and a Franciscan friar named Diego Delgado first reached the rebellious territory known as La Pimienta west of Bacalar, where he set up a presidio. He soon moved closer to Petén to a place called Sacalum, from which Fray Diego departed secretly for Tipuj with an escort of Mayas from Yucatán. Delgado then went to Nojpetén with a delegation of Tipuans, but shortly after their arrival in July 1623 the Itzá killed him, his Tipuan escorts, and an escort of Spanish soldiers. While Mirones and his soldiers were at church at Sacalum six months later, a group of armed Mayas attacked the Spaniards, killed them all, set fire to the town and the church, and escaped into the forest. New evidence indicates that the instigators of this massacre were Itzá military leaders.

This spirit of armed anti-Spanish resistance soon spread throughout Tsul Uinicoob. In 1630 Maya inhabitants of villages on the Sibun and Sittee Rivers fled, taking all they had, including the church bells. Over the next several years flight gradually increased, with many of the refugees resettling at Tipuj. In 1638 the Tsul Uinicoob Mayas renewed their flight, and the Spaniards at Bacalar were convinced that the Itzá were behind it. Four years later inhabitants of eight of the rebel towns had relocated to Tipuj, which was by then independent of Spanish control. Recent research indicates that this rebellion was indeed masterminded by the Itzá ruling nobility in order to force the Spanish colonists to retreat from the region.

When Fuensalida returned to Belize in 1642 in hopes of convincing the rebels to return to the Spanish fold, he found Lamanai burned and deserted and the road beyond marked by warning signs. Saksus on the Belize River had also been burned and deserted, the church bells thrown into the underbrush. With the region already in a state of chaos, pirates attacked Bacalar and the Belizean coastline between 1642 and 1684, resulting in the abandonment of Bacalar, which was resettled at the old Maya town of Pachá along the road to Valladolid. Spanish control over Chaktemal and Tsul Uinicoob was virtually lost, and the door was cracked open for the British occupation of Belize and a new era of colonial history.

During the 1690s Martín de Ursúa y Arizmendi, a Basque colonial bureaucrat, initiated plans to conquer the Itzá, an event that climaxed on March 13, 1697, when he and troops from Yucatán attacked and occupied their island capital of Nojpetén. They accomplished this by opening a road, by means of Yucatán Maya labor, from Merida to Lake Petén Itzá, over which they carried heavy artillery and supplies. A brigantine constructed near the shore of the lake was used to launch the attack itself. The events that led to this final occupation and destruction of Nojpetén were complex and involved many Spanish officials, troops, and even missionaries from Guatemala as well as Yucatán. Some Itzá leaders had on occasion displayed willingness to negotiate a peaceful solution, but a series of violent attacks upon Spanish military and religious visitors to the lake during 1695 and 1696 served as the final justification for Ursúa to pursue his military attack.

I regard the conquest of the Itzá to be the critical event that resulted in a subsequent decline in anti-Spanish resistance by the Mayas of Yucatán. It would be several years, however, before Spaniards gained substantial control over the Itzá and their Petén neighbors. In 1704

opposite
Male figure
Jaina Island, Campeche
Classic period
Campeche
Centro INAH Campeche

The church of Chichicastenango
Guatemala

a conspiracy among indigenous leaders led to a major revolt against the Spanish colonists in Petén, resulting in significant loss of Spanish life and the temporary abandonment of newly formed Maya missions on Lake Petén Itzá. The long-term effects of the conquest of the Itzá included massive loss of Maya life due to epidemic disease and continued warfare and the rapid demise of an indigenous political system that had for nearly two centuries served as the center for anti-Spanish resistance throughout the southern regions of the peninsula.

On only one subsequent occasion, in 1761, did an uprising actually go so far as to threaten the colonial regime. In that year, in the Sotuta province where the 1546 rebellion had broken out, a Maya leader named Jacinto Uk de los Santos Canek, reportedly incited a revolt centered at the town of Kisteil, with the stated aim of ridding the peninsula for once and for all of the Spaniards. Supposedly taking his name from the last Itzá ruler, he was crowned with the crown and mantle of the town's patron saint, Our Lady of the Conception–calling himself King Jacinto Uk Canek. His goal, he was quoted as saying in a sermon to those gathered around during a fiesta at Kisteil, was to organize a rebellion that would free the Mayas from Spanish subjugation and allow them to "throw off their yoke of servitude." Drunken Spanish militiamen stirred up the crowd even more by attacking the multitude indiscriminantly, and a few days later reinforcements invaded Kisteil and forced the inciters to flee to the bush. Canek was eventually captured, tortured mercilessly, and executed with a blow to the head; eight other leaders were hanged, drawn and quartered, and their bodies displayed publicly. More than 600 Mayas lost their lives before it was all over. Kisteil's fields were sown with salt, its buildings destroyed, and its population dispersed. It is still not entirely clear whether the Kisteil rebellion was the result of a well-established conspiracy, as some contemporary writers maintained, or whether it was simply the outcome of one leader's momentary delusions of grandeur, blown out of proportion by observers of the time (Bricker 1981; Ruegley 1996, 15). Not until the devastating Caste War broke out during the late 1840s did revolt again become a reality in Yucatán. Whether that rebellion was rooted in colonial patterns of ethnic inequality and resistance or was the result of the changing political economy of Yucatán during the early nineteenth century is a subject of continuing debate (Reed 1964; Bricker 1981; Lapointe 1983; Ruegley 1996). That such a major rebellion must have drawn upon some historical and cultural lessons from the collective Maya experience of the colonial past, however, seems difficult to deny.

References

BRICKER, VICTORIA R.
1981
The Indian Christ, the Indian King: The Historic Substrate of Maya Mith and Ritual. Austin: University of Texas Press

CHAMBERLAIN, ROBERT S.
1948
The Conquest and Colonization of Yucatán, 1517–1550. Publication 582. Washington, D.C.: Carnegie Institution of Washington

CLENDINNEN, INGA
1987
Ambivalent Conquests: Mayas and Spaniards in Yucatan, 1517–1570. Cambridge, Mass.: Cambridge University Press

FARRISS, NANCY M.
1984
Maya Society under Colonial Rule: The Collective Enterprise of Survival. Princeton: Princeton University Press

JONES, GRANT D.
1989
Maya Resistance to Spanish Rule: Time and History on a Colonial Frontier. Albuquerque: University of New Mexico Press
In press
"The Conquest of the Last Maya Kingdom." Stanford: Stanford University Press

LAPOINTE, MARIE
1983
Los Mayas rebeldes de Yucatán. Zamora: Colegio de Michoacán

REED, NELSON
1964
The Caste War of Yucatán. Stanford: Stanford University Press

ROYS, RALPH L.
1967
The Book of Chilam Balam of Chumayel. 2nd ed. Norman: University of Oklahoma Press

RUEGLEY, TERRY
1996
Yucatán's Peasantry and the Origins of the Caste War. Austin: University of Texas Press

opposite
Urn
Mayapán, Yucatán
Late Postclassic period
Mexico City
Museo Nacional de Antropología
cat. 320

The Mayas in Modern Times

History books generally mention 1821 as the beginning of the modern era for Mexico and Central America, since it is the year of the region's independence from the Spanish empire. This periodization was valid only for the small elite Creole community living in cities and on haciendas at that time. The objective of the war of 1821 was emancipation, yet the large impoverished *mestizo* and indigenous masses were not included in this process, as neither subjects nor objects. In reality, the few insurgents that existed in Yucatán, Chiapas, and Guatemala dreamed of shifting positions of authority and benefit from the peninsular Spaniards. They decided to overthrow the yoke of Spanish rule after being assured that Agustin de Iturbide's new imperial plan would guarantee their privileges. And the republican order that was forced on them a short time later did not mean any change in the three new federal states with regard to the social reforms that had been promised. Those who were on top–both liberals and conservatives–were very comfortable living on the backs of those below them in the social ladder and they did not consider renouncing the comfort gained through the ruthless exploitation of the "Indian masses."

The vast majority of the indigenous population was composed of Maya peasants who lived in about 500 colonial towns: some 110 towns in Chiapas, some 130 towns in the Yucatán, and close to 220 towns in Guatemala. Their more than 800,000 inhabitants constituted 80 percent of the total population. For them, independence was a hollow word that concealed the real destiny that time had prepared for them: the extension of their condition as exploited persons, but now by authorities directly identified with local power. This is how the period that we might describe as neocolonial began for the Mayas; it has lasted for almost two centuries given that time has not managed to eliminate completely their centuries of marginalization.

Nevertheless, the year 1821 was not the time when the Mayas first began to suffer profound changes in their way of life. Rather, this process had started half a century earlier with the implementation of the Bourbon reforms. The administrative modernization introduced at that time seriously upset the protective social-cultural system which had been constructed, with great patience and imagination, on top of the wreckage caused by the Spanish invasion during the decade from 1520 to 1530. It was this second conquest, two hundred years after the first, which really marked the introduction to the modern world for the Mayas of Yucatán, Chiapas, and Guatemala, more than the Independence of 1821. According to this other method for measuring time, domination of the Mayas had extended over a period of almost five centuries, beginning around the year 1520 and it still has not ended.

In this brief text, I will present evidence of the life of the Mayas under the neocolonial regime, introduced by the Spanish crown around 1770 and notably intensified by the republican governments beginning in 1821. Three particularly painful experiences should be highlighted: the stripping away of their lands, the proletarianization of their work force, and the fragmentation of their social-cultural world.

I will also describe the different ways in which the Mayas attempted to survive as collective groups in the face of *ladino* (mestizo) aggressions, whether civil or ecclesiastical, rich or poor, with good or bad intentions. The protective strategies which were applied were the same ones that had proven to be efficient in previous centuries: daily passive resistance, long drawn-out negotiations, retreat in cases of emergency, and armed confrontation when all other alternatives had been exhausted.

During the first two centuries of the colonial era, the indigenous towns of the Maya region had enjoyed an appreciable level of real autonomy. The Spanish authorities who resided in the few cities and towns had been accustomed to leaving a good part of the administration of communities in the hands of indigenous governors. These governors had become the true keepers of communal unity thanks to the unconditional respect which their subjects offered them. They were responsible for imparting justice, supervising the collection of tribute and perquisites, controlling the economy of the *cofradías* (associations) and community funds, and ensuring the proper development of festivals.

The "indigenous republics," as the towns were legally known, were not republican in the modern sense of the word. These societies were socially stratified, in which everything was done in a common fashion, but under the mandate of a native aristocracy which monopolized power in its own hands.

Indigenous people harvesting corn
Chiapas

This corporate system, based on a reciprocal relationship of privilege and obedience, had functioned well in the times of the Habsburgs, but in the eyes of the Bourbons it was an unacceptable obstruction in view of much needed fiscal and administrative reform. Furthermore, for the independent governments of the nineteenth century, this system was an offense to the principles of individual liberty and political equality. Traditional communities received the first warning of the changes to come with the introduction, in 1786, of the *intendencias*.

This measure not only meant a new territorial ordering of the old provinces–the subdivision into *intendencias* and *partidos*–but, also, the installation of nonindigenous officials as heads of local administration and the replacement of local indigenous leaders, except in the case of responsibilities directly related to the religious festivals of the community. These responsibilities were more and more difficult to fulfill, given that communities no longer had the personal wealth which they possessed before nor the power to dispose freely of collective income.

The drastic reduction in the authority of native leaders was not the only aggression committed against the indigenous community on the eve of independence. The other outrage was the stripping away of communal lands in favor of the haciendas, which during the same period were transformed from modest cattle-grazing ranches into powerful livestock-producing companies for foreign trade. The large-scale cultivation of cotton, agave (*henequén*), tobacco, sugar cane, and other products demanded not only technological change, but also an increase in the size of workable lands. The new companies did not hesitate to take the land of neighboring and not-so-neighboring indigenous communities. The first step was the appropriation or purchase of the estates of *cofradías*, the second the taking possession of the lands of the community itself.

Indigenous people
in the Soconusco region
Chiapas, 1892

Photo of Yucatec women
by Désiré Charnay

When Yucatán, Chiapas, and Guatemala gained independence from Spain in 1821, the Mayas changed owners but not conditions. Even worse, the Indian Laws, which in some way had protected their rights and property, were no longer enforced. From that point into the future, liberal and conservative governments, which alternated in power, continued to plunder, utilizing legislation which had been written to satisfy the interests of hacienda owners. The mechanism consisted of drastically reducing the extension of legal rural property by declaring excess lands "vacant," a perfect way for the authorities to transfer the lands to individuals with the necessary capital and right political connections to buy the lands. The candidates were interested in indigenous lands because they had already been cleared several times and consequently they could be exploited immediately. In the case of the state of Chiapas, the reports presented by governors throughout the nineteenth century on this procedure were very illustrative in that respect. In 1837 there were only 853 haciendas and ranches; there were 3,159 in 1889; 4,546 in 1896; 4,794 haciendas and ranches in 1903; and 6,862 in 1909.

The new owners did not wait long to also appropriate the labor of displaced indigenous communities. Each person fell in one of two categories: "servants" and "useless." The first were those stripped of their ranches and cornfields when their lands were taken over by a powerful hacienda owner. They had no other choice but to become servants of their new masters. They could remain in their place of origin and cultivate their plot, in exchange for working three up to five days a week for the owner without receiving any remuneration. The second group were forced to abandon their communities for lack of land and other opportunities. These people sold their labor to the haciendas which always had existed or which had been formed, beginning in the second half of the nineteenth century, on land transferred to the church or the nation.

Maya child

The servants, as well as the so-called useless people, ended up bound for life to the hacienda where they had gone to look for work as day laborers. The tactic utilized by the hacienda owners and their foremen was the gradual indebtedness of the worker: they obligated the worker to buy from the company store and when a worker produced below the quota he was fined. Instead of diminishing, debts increased constantly. At the death of the contracted worker, debts were transferred to his children and, when there were none, to the closest relative. In this way, the hacienda was assured of the continuous presence of abundant and cheap labor. All of these Maya laborers, uprooted from their community and bound to the infernal chain of debt, ran the risk of losing their ethnic identity together with their dignity as free men and women.

In contrast to those classified as useless and servants, the indigenous people who were able to maintain ownership of their plots of land enjoyed greater liberty. Nevertheless, their condition as small, independent producers was quickly threatened by the competition of *ladino* agricultural companies and cattle ranchers in the regional market. Humble indigenous ranches, situated on relatively infertile lands increasingly smaller in size, were generally not even able to support the families that inhabited the land. The men began resorting to temporary work on nearby haciendas or going to plantations and hunting grounds of the hotlands, in the case of the Mayas who lived in the highlands of Chiapas and Guatemala. This is how they supplemented the meager earnings which the maize field gave them and the sporadic sale of domestic animals and folk crafts.

Toward the end of the nineteenth century, Maya towns had lost the majority of their land and inhabitants to the haciendas. This caused the appearance of a new type of indigenous settlement, in some way, a duplicate of the traditional community but now not with the church as a physical and social-cultural nucleus. The new agglomeration was concentrated around the home of the hacienda owner, a building much more imposing than the modest hermitage. Always present there was the image of the patron saint chosen by the owner, who also personally took the responsibility of the necessary costs of the festival in the saint's honor. The society formed by these "hacienda Indians" was a sad copy of the original community, since it lacked the elaborate corporate structure which gave the "village Indians" the strength to continue surviving amid aggressions.

There is one additional aggression to mention: the gradual invasion of the communities by mestizos of scarce resources. The mestizos established themselves as ranchers on the outskirts of the town or as shopkeepers and craftsmen in the center of town. The phenomena had already started during the eighteenth century, but increased considerably during the nineteenth century. Many "Indian villages" had thus become "towns" in which a minority of "neighbors" occupied the center and the majority of "natives" lived displaced toward the outskirts. Among these mestizo invaders, manufacturers and merchants of liquor stood out for their perniciousness. The consumption of liquor was an ancient custom among the indigenous population since their libation necessarily accompanied all prayers of petition or curing. Nevertheless, as a result of the deteriorating conditions of the life in the communities, many men began seeking refuge in alcohol. What was in the beginning a religious and festive custom, now became a social vice, fostered by the local saloon keeper.

How did the Mayas manage to survive so many calamities? In the first place, they survived through the patient labor of reconstruction of the community at the level of social life and at the level of their symbolic expressions. In the majority of the cases, this re-creation was revealed as the only viable response to confront the division resulting from the vacancy of nearby haciendas and migratory work in distant plantations. Thanks to this strength, many ethnic groups have survived up to the end of the second millennium; mutilated, yes, but with their identity safeguarded as a result of the alterations which they inevitably suffered in the process. One of the most notable changes was the transformation of the traditional system of *cofradías* or brotherhoods, passed down from the colonial period, into *mayordomías* (stewardships) or socioreligious offices. Due to the chronic absence and premature death of many adult men, brought about by forced labor and unhealthy working conditions in plantations and hunting grounds, *cofradías* lost more and more members and finally they ceased to function. In their place, a series of new practices were introduced, including festivals dedicated to unusual saints, whose celebration was the responsibility of a group of *mayordomos* hand-

Market in Guatemala

Indigenous people of San Cristóbal de las Casas, Chiapas, 1905

S.CRISTOBAL ; Indigenas de 1:Tenejapa , 2:S.Felipe (S.Cristobal) , 3:Amatenango , 4:Rancho de San Felipe ,

5:Chamula , 6:S.Pedro Chanalhò , 7:Cancùc , 8:S.Bartolomè , 9:Zinacantan , 10:S.Andres , 11:Huistan . 1905.

picked for this purpose. In order for these offices to be carried out properly, mayors and governors were accustomed to designating those candidates with a background in a hierarchy of ascending functions. In this way, an elaborate system was born in which the doctrinal priest participated in some fashion but no longer figured as a central person, if at some moment he had indeed enjoyed this privilege. Even more than ever, the Mayas came to control the celebration of their festivals, increasingly adapted to their own tastes and needs. Many rituals which now fascinate cultural anthropologists were elaborated at that time. Still remaining to be studied in depth and in detail is the process of re-creation of these innumerable and complex customs throughout the Maya region. In this sense, the nineteenth century could well reveal itself as equal in inventiveness to the sixteenth century. The subjects of this new creativity saw themselves as restricted by the limits imposed by neocolonial oppression, but they always found enough space to construct and reconstruct their own universe out of autochthonous and foreign elements.

It is important to emphasize that their world was a completely rural one in which the concern for possession and cultivation of the land never ceased to occupy a central position. For this reason, so much devotion and celebration of pre-Hispanic gods persisted, for they were much more identified with the forces of nature than the Christian God and His celestial court of saints and angels. We can postulate the gradual liberation, during the second half of the nineteenth century and the first half of the twentieth century, of many customs that earlier had been inhibited. Springs, caves, mountains, and maize fields had always been privileged sites for prayers and offerings, but in this period they underwent a welcome rebirth. Oral tradition played a more modest, although no less essential, role than ritual in community re-creation. The Mayas seem to have been more imaginative in celebrating than in telling. Nevertheless, the scarcity could be more related to our lack of knowledge than to their supposed lack of myth-making. Many myths, stories, and legends still circulate exclusively among the Maya, locked in a specific language and often restricted to a single community, despite the zealous work of several anthropologists who have begun to discover and collect them. The native oral tradition, if properly rescued, recorded, and distributed, can become the patrimony of all.

The interest of anthropologists and historians in colonial and modern Maya peoples began

Maya housing

Yucatec girl

in the twentieth century and soon revitalized studies of pre-Hispanic culture. The latter had been preceded by the nineteenth century explorers of ruins hidden in the tropical jungle of Yucatán, Chiapas, and Guatemala. During the last hundred years, thousands of books and articles have introduced the Mayans to an ever-growing and demanding reading public. Their authors, so-called Mayanists, are those responsible for the system of linguistic classification which divides the Mayan family into twenty-five different spoken languages, many of which are subdivided into different dialects. This characterization, introduced by academics, has gained such importance that even the indigenous peoples themselves have adopted the custom of identifying themselves ethnically based on their language and no longer according to whether they belong to this or that community.

The linguistic mosaic which is so pronounced in Guatemala and Chiapas strongly contrasts with the situation in the Yucatán peninsula where only one language prevails, Yucatec Maya. This language is so predominant that a good number of mestizos speak it, without mentioning the marked influence that the language exercises on Spanish pronunciation and intonation. But the presence of the Maya in Yucatán is not reduced to the linguistic field, it permeates almost all levels of social life, in contrast to Chiapas and Guatemala where the cultural polarization is much more evident. This is a curious phenomenon, if we take into account that for more than half a century, from 1847 to 1901, native groups and whites in the Yucatán peninsula faced one another in a bloody conflagration, known as the Caste War, which took more than 250,000 lives, more than 30 percent of the population.

The Caste War was, without doubt, the most important Maya rebellion in the last five centuries. It was a combination of two different, but closely related, strategies: an extremely violent armed confrontation, which was relatively short (1847–55), followed by a withdrawal to the forested northeastern part of the peninsula and the transformation of this region into free territory for almost fifty years (1854–1901). The insurrection was born in the indigenous communities of the central region which had organized the greatest resistance to the onslaught of the neocolonial regimen. It was an attempt to preserve the traditional autonomy against the haciendas, which sought to invade new spaces, having concluded their expansion into the northwest. The reaction could only have come from those unyielding towns where the corporate structure had still not been altered. The original leaders of the movement were native governors with the capacity to mobilize and arm the people, thanks to an authority legitimized by custom.

Many Mayas view their body of socioreligious traditions as the most valuable legacy they received from their ancestors and, for this reason, they must protect it at all costs. In the last half century, this heritage has been seriously threatened by different elements from outside the community which wish to convert the Maya to their respective creeds of redemption. Officials from indigenist organizations, Protestant missionaries, Catholic priests, leftist activists, and guerrillas of different tendencies–all arrive with the zeal of promising Maya a more just and dignified way of life, always according to their very particular point of view. Since these groups are antagonistic among themselves, they have converted the Maya world into a theater of ferocious ideological battle with the indigenous cause as their banner.

The confrontation had been particularly tragic in Guatemala, given that the communities were first divided between traditionalists and members belonging to the so-called Catholic Action group or one of the many evangelical denominations. The fascination with the armed option arose later as a possible solution to the apparently hopeless economic and political situation. Soon, the Mayas were trapped in a civil war not their own in which they fell victim to escalating violence which lasted almost thirty years and left more than 30,000 dead and almost a million refugees. Among the refugees were close to 50,000 persons who crossed the Mexican border and obtained protection on the other side as internationally recognized refugees. Some years ago, the difficult return was initiated under the auspices of the United Nations High Commission for Refugees.

Similar events transpired in Chiapas, where the indigenous population also was torn apart by religious and political divisions. This agitation coincided with the colonization of the Lacandon forest by land-hungry farmers who came from the traditional communities of the highlands and from the closest haciendas. The recently founded colonies had a special need to construct a new identity when faced by the uncertainty represented by emigration. In the

Native
of the Yucatán peninsula

501

Girl Tojolabal

beginning, this identity was offered by the personnel of the archdiocese of San Cristóbal de las Casas, through a process of evangelization that was not predicated only on the word of God but included consciousness raising and community organization on social, economic, and political levels. Nevertheless, it soon had to share space with consultants from leftist movements that initially arose in the 1968 movement. Beginning in 1983 a small guerrilla group from the National Liberation Armies came to offer the Mayas once again an armed route as the only solution for their problems.

The unfolding of the Chiapas conflict is known by all. For ten years, guerrillas and peasants took the time to get to know and accept each other mutually in the clandestine setting of the mountains. During this long learning period, the first group abandoned part of its dogmatic rigidity and the second transformed themselves from rebel peasants into insurgents with a program of political change for the entire nation. The result of this symbiosis was the formation of the Zapatista National Liberation Army which broke into the national and international scene on January 1, 1994. Suffice it to say that not all opted for arms. The Guatemalan tragedy, the dissuasive propaganda of government agents, and the lack of support by the archdiocese of San Cristóbal caused many to abandon the Zapatista cause. Nevertheless, the demands of the rebels are shared by many indigenous communities within and beyond Chiapas, despite their opposition to a military solution. Never in Mexican history have the indigenous peoples succeeded in sitting down at the same table with the federal government to explain their needs and to demand justice.

Tzotzil with backstrap loom

Since before the Zapatista National Liberation Army appeared and much beyond its area of influence, the Maya world had just entered a movement announcing a new era to come. The Mayas, in their vast majority, continue to be poor peasants and marginalized citizens, in Mexico as well as in Guatemala. But in the course of recent decades they have had several experiences which have taught them to question their situation and recognize the necessity of joining forces. They have learned that for them, there will be no future if they do not look beyond the limited horizon of their traditional community. They know that only if well organized will they be able to reclaim the place which in all fairness belongs to them within the countries in which they find themselves living. Known as "communities"

opposite
Tzeltal woman making ceramics
Amatenango del Valle, Chiapas

for centuries and as "ethnic groups" for several decades, they have now begun to reevaluate the possibility of their belonging to the same group, the "Maya people." Nevertheless, this new reality has little to do with the "Maya world" of scholars or the "Maya route" of international tourism. It deals with a network of relationships which the Mayas are on the verge of integrating as a fundamental part of an identity in the process of construction. They know that they will need it if they want to get a dignified and just future, beyond the social divisions introduced in the sixteenth century and the political boundaries imposed in the nineteenth.

The Maya people currently consist of less than six million speakers of twenty-five different languages. The overwhelming majority live in Guatemala, where they form more than half of the nation's population, and in Chiapas and Yucatán, where they are an important minority. The remainder are divided between Tabasco, Campeche, Quintana Roo, Veracruz, Honduras, Belize, El Salvador . . . and the United States, a country where they have gone to seek work, as have so many other Mexicans and Guatemalans. With few exceptions, they belong to the social sector qualified in censuses in Mexico and Guatemala as "poverty level" and "extreme poverty level." Further, they suffer the scorn of a good part of the mestizo population, which does not understand why the Mayas want to fight for their cultural, social, and political survival.

As the third millennium approaches, it is hoped that the Mayas finally come to be the subject of their own history. They hope that this will be possible as spaces of democratic participation open up in the countries to which they belong.

They only ask to occupy, within their Mexican and Guatemalan house, the home that they deserve.

References

BRACAMONTE, PEDRO
1995
La Memoria Enclaustrada. Historia Indígena de Yucatán. 1750–1915. Mexico City: Centro de Investigaciones y Estudios Superiores in Antropología Social-Instituto Nacional Indigenista

BRENTON, ALAIN, AND JACQUES ARNAULD
1991
Mayas. La passion des ancêtres, le désir de durer. Paris: Ed. Autrement

DE VOS, JAN
1994
Vivir en frontera. La experiencia de los indios de Chiapas. Mexico City: Centro de Investigaciones y Estudios Superiores en Antropología Social-Instituto Nacional Indigenista

FARRISS, NANCY
1992
La Sociedad Maya Bajo el Dominio Colonial. La Empresa Colectiva de Supervivencia. Madrid: Alianza Editorial

FAVRE, HENRI
1971
Changement et continuité chez les Mayas du Mexique. Contribution á l'étude de la situation coloniale en Amérique Latine. Paris: Anthropos

LE BOT, YVON
1992
La guerre en terre maya. Communauté, Violence et Modernité au Guatemala. Paris: Karthala

LEÓN, CARMEN, MARIO RUZ, AND JOSÉ ALEJOS
1992
Del Katún al Siglo. Tiempos de Colonialismo y Resistencia Entre los Mayas. Mexico City: Consejo Nacional para la Cultura y las Artes

Works on Exhibit

Authors of the entries

AA	Alfonso Arellano
ABC	Antonio Benavides C.
ACM	Amalia Cardós de Méndez
AGC	Arnoldo González Cruz
AK	Adriana Konzevik
APC	Agustín Peña Castillo
AT	Alejandro Tovalín
AV	Adriana Velázquez
CJF	Carmen Julia Fajardo
CLO	Clara Luz Oyarzábal
ECTA	Elia del Carmen Trejo Alvarado
EGL	Ernesto González Licón
ELV	Eliseo Linares Villanueva
EN	Enrique Nalda
FSM	Federica Sodi Miranda
GB	Guillermo Bernal
GLJ	Gabriel Laló Jacinto
GSS	Gabriele Sill-Schmitt
JVGM	Juan Vicente Guerrero Miranda
LCGS	Liwy del Carmen Grazioso Sierra
LFS	Lilia Fernández Souza
LMC	Luis Millet Cámara
MCG	Martha Cuevas García
MCL	Marcia Castro-Leal
MCM	Martha Carmona Macías
MG	Maria Gaida
MJCU	Maria José Con Uribe
MJGG	Miriam Judith Gallegos Gómora
MPC	Mario Pérez Campa
MS	Marla Sullivan
MSB	Mariana Sánchez de Bonifasi
PJS	Peter J. Schmidt
POC	Patricia Ochoa Castillo
RAT	Ricardo Armijo Torres
RCV	Ramón Carrasco V.
RP	Rebeca Perales
SB	Sylviane Boucher
SPA	Sonia Peña A.
TALW	Thomas Arvol Lee Whiting
TPS	Tomás Pérez Suárez
WF	William Fash
YP	Yoly Palomo

Epigraphic reading
Alfonso Arellano

0
Relief map of Tikal
Mundo Perdido, Tikal, Petén
Stone
Height: 10.0 cm; width: 39.0 cm
depth: 25.0 cm
Guatemala, Museo Naciónal
de Arqueología y Etnología

1

1
Altar G1
Late Classic period
Acropolis, Copán, Honduras
Stone
Height: 145.0 cm
width: 45.0 cm
weight: 2,000 lbs
Copán
Plaza las Estelas
Museo Regional
Parque Arqueológico de Copán
Inv. no. CPN-P-37561

A bicephalic feathered serpent is carved on this silhouette-style altar, short panel of hieroglyphs in the center on both sides. These refer to the dedication date of the altar, 9.18.10.0.0 10 *ahaw* 8 *sac*, or A.D. 800, during the reign of the sixteenth ruler, Yax Pasah. The date is followed by the verb *pat*, "to make," and a name for the monument. One serpent head is alive while the other is shown dead. This creature is referred to as the "Bicephalic Monster," and represents the never-ending cycle of life and death. The dead serpent wears a death collar and is characterized by a fleshless jawbone with a snout ending in curling fangs; a solar figure emerges from it covered by serpent markings and the eyelid has the glyph *anek* or star sign. A jaguar face is carved into the upper mouth.   WF

2
Stela 51 of Calakmul
Late Classic period
Calakmul, Campeche
Mexico
Limestone
Height: 312.0 cm
width: 153.0 cm
current thickness: 5.0 cm
Mexico City
Museo Nacional de Antropología
Inv. no. 10-080365

This stela was found at the foot of Structure 1 at Calakmul. It was originally 36 cm in thickness and had inscriptions on three of its

2

sides, but it was extracted with an electric saw by looters, cut up, and reduced to 5 cm in thickness; the lateral reliefs were lost, and only the front side has been preserved. Ruler 7 is represented on the stela, standing on a captive while sustaining a lance in his right hand. Of his finery, his elaborate pectoral and the long cape that falls to his ankles are remarkable. His headdress seems to carry the maw of a fantastic animal, perhaps a serpent, creating the impression that the face of the ruler emerges from the animal.   LCGS

Epigraphic reading by Alfonso Arellano
In (9.12.10.15.0, 9.15.3.10.0, 9.17.16.5.0) 10 *ahaw* 13 *pop* [March 3, 683; February 18, 735; February 5, 787] is *Yaxchil Yaxwana* . . . lord; his name . . . in stone, together with *Mamal Makom*, he of the water lily.
His sculpture of *Zac Muan*, lord . . .
His sculpture of *Zac T'ul*, who invoked . . . sacred.

3
Stela 6 Piedras Negras
Late Classic period
Piedras Negras, Petén

Guatemala
Stone
Height: 265.0 cm
thickness: 85.0 cm
Guatemala, Museo Nacional de Arqueología y Etnología
Inv. no. MNAE 863

The stela commemorates the enthronement of Ruler 3. The ruler is carved in high relief, while the rest of the elements are in low relief. The central figure is seated with his legs crossed on a jaguar pelt cushion. He wears a large headdress with mask and feathers. He has a pectoral with circular beads, bracelets, and loincloth; with his left hand he holds a bag that falls. There are remains of green paint on the headdress, bracelet, and thorax. The niche in which the figure is seated is framed on three sides by celestial bands. On the lower part of the niche there is a band with four footprints, which represent his arrival at the throne. On the left side there is a seated individual with a tall headdress and a column of glyphs; this section is fairly eroded. On the right side there are two columns of eroded glyphs. The stela is dated 9.12.15.0.0. 2 *ahau* 13 *zip* (687 A.D.).   MSB

Epigraphic reading by Alfonso Arellano
It was 9.12.15.0.0. 2 *ahau* 3 *zip*, G9 was lord of the night, the moon was 23 days old, the fourth lunation of the semester had been completed, and it would last 29 days [11-April-687]; the fifth *tun* was seated, the cycle in the hand of . . . Jaguar? [incomplete name] . . . sacred lord of Piedras Negras.

3

He is the son of Lady . . . [name lost] . . .

4
Chac Mool Figure
Early Postclassic period
Chichén Itzá, Yucatán, Mexico
Limestone
Height: 86.0 cm
length: 154.0 cm
Merida
Museo Regional de Yucatán "Palacio Cantón"
Inv. no. 10-251116

One of the most well-known images from Maya culture is that of the sculptural type called *Chac Mool*. It represents a partly

4

dressed figure with bent legs and reclining torso supported on elbows, looking toward one side. The hands are placed on the abdomen, forming a flat surface on which offerings were placed to the gods. The figure is considered an intermediary between man and the gods. The name *Chac Mool*, "red claw," was given to it by the French-American explorer Augustus Le Plongeon, who associated it with a Maya prince of the same name. Twenty-five examples of this sculptural type are known from the Early Postclassic, the majority of which were found at Tula, Hidalgo, and Chichén Itzá, Yucatán. However, there are also examples from Michoacán, Tlaxcala, and Tenochtitlan in the Late Postclassic and from places as far away as El Salvador in Central America. Recently, xamples differing slightly in pose have been found in Yucatán, including one which has a moveable head.   APC

Man and nature

5
Polychrome Plate
Late Classic period
Recovered in a confiscation
Ceramic
Height: 6.4 cm
diameter: 34.5 cm
Cancún
Museo Arqueológico de Cancún
Inv. no. 10-299025

Polychrome plate with a smooth exterior, and a small molding near the rim. The inner walls of the piece are covered by a wide red band, delimited at both ends by a black band. The main design, in the center of the plate, is painted red and black on an orange slip ground. It represents some vegetal elements (in this case, a squash plant) surrounded by geometric designs.   ECTA

5

6

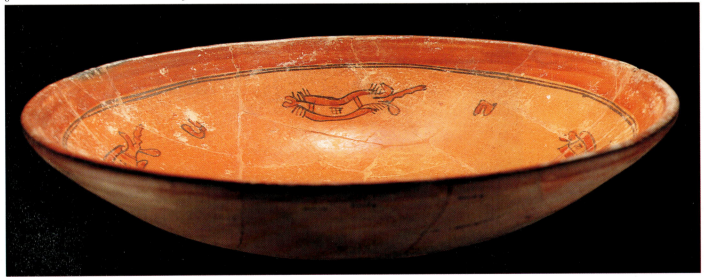

7

6
Tetrapod Plate
Protoclassic period
Tabasco, Mexico
Ceramic
Height: 16.5 cm
diameter: 30.0 cm
Mexico City
Museo Nacional de Antropología
Inv. no. 10-080387

In Protoclassic ceramics, the elements that served as precursors of the Early Classic period make their appearance, including polychrome and "negative" or resist decoration. This plate displays the typical red-on-orange decoration, with a realistically painted fish in a darker tone than that of the background. The silhouette is delineated in black using a double line, while a continuous and a discontinuous line follow the contour of the fish. Fishing was an activity that, just as all daily activities of the ancient Mayas, had a religious connotation. Fishermen had a special god who they invoked and to whom they made special offerings. They used nets, hooks, and harpoons while riding canoes to capture different marine species, including stingrays and sharks.   MCM

7
Polychrome Plate
Middle–Late Classic period
Dzibanché
Quintana Roo, Mexico
Ceramic
Height: 8.5 cm
diameter: 40.5 cm
Chetumal
Centro INAH Quintana Roo
Inv. no. 10-390830
This plate was part of an offering located in an inner chamber of Building 2, Chamber 3, at Dzibanché. It displays five squids, the symbolism of which is associated with the cult of marine animals that would have functioned as a link between men and rain, the sea and fertility.   EN and AV

8
Sculpture
Late Classic period
Dzibilchaltún, Yucatán, Mexico
Stucco
Length: 29.6 cm; width: 21.0 cm
Dzibilchaltún
Museo del Pueblo Maya
Inv. no. 10-290041

This fish formed part of the decoration of the north facade of Structure I-Sub at Dzibilchaltún, one of the oldest buildings in northern Yucatán, filled with profound cosmic symbolism. It had eight great masks of the rain god, Chaac, anticipating the importance that this god would later have in architecture of the peninsula. The masks seem to have associations with numerous signs alluding to the underworld, death, and water. In addition to this fish, researchers found stingray representations which was and possibly that of a crab, motifs expressing its aquatic character. The presence in other sectors of the facade of straight, and interlaced bands with disks and superimposed beads allude to water, which was precious, and to the serpentine character of the decoration.   LMC

8

9
Animal Sculpture
Early Postclassic period
Chichén Itzá, Yucatán, Mexico
Limestone
Height: 22.8 cm
diameter: 16.3 cm
Merida, Museo Regional
de Antropología de Yucatán
"Palacio Cantón"
Inv. no. 10-426357

Among the aquatic animals represented by the pre-Hispanic Maya are frogs, because of their obvious association with precious water. The importance of frogs has endured until the present. In ceremonies petitioning for rain in rural areas of Yucatán, young boys play the role of these amphibians.   APC

10
Effigy Vessel
Preclassic period
Kaminaljuyú, Guatemala
Ceramic
Height: 7.3 cm
diameter: 10.5 cm
Guatemala, Museo Nacional
de Arqueología y Etnología
Inv. no. MNAE 10711

Basin with zoomorphic effigy that represents a frog. The vessel has a small mouth and a flat base. Near the rim is an animal head, with eyes, face, and two front feet that are modeled and appliquéd. The surface is covered with well-polished red slip. This type of ceramic shows the strong relationship between the dai-

9

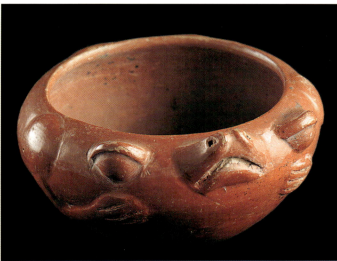

10

13

12
Alligator rattle
Late Classic period
Ceramic, pigment
Length: 18.7 cm
New York
The Metropolitan Museum of Art
The Michael C. Rockefeller
Memorial Collection, Bequest
of Nelson A. Rockefeller, 1979
Inv. no. 1979.206.1143

The island of Jaina off the west coast of the Yucatán peninsula is well known for large numbers of small, mostly mold-made ceramic sculptures deposited by the Maya of the Late Classic period in graves as offerings. While most of the figures depict human beings, often with remarkable handmodeled costume detail, animal sculptures are also known. The majority of Jaina figures are musical instruments such as whistles or rattles, and were probably used during private ceremonial activities before being placed in the tombs. This naturalistically alligator is a rattle and still has much of its original blue pigment on its surface. Crocodiles, alligators, and caimans had earth, water, and underworld associations in ancient Maya mythology.

ly life of the inhabitants of Kaminaljuyú and the aquatic environment that surrounded them. Frog effigy vessels were very common during the Preclassic, perhaps due to the importance of Lake Miraflores today extinct, in the life of the inhabitants. Other scholars believe that this type of vessel, together with "mushroom stones," might be associated with ritual ceremonies for religious purposes in which psychotropic substances were consumed.   MSB

11
Effigy Vessel
Terminal Classic period
La Lagunita, Quiché, Guatemala
Ceramic
Height: 11.0 cm
diameter of the rim: 8.5 cm
Guatemala, Museo Nacional
de Arqueología y Etnología
Inv. no. MNAE 9626

Bowl with a zoomorphic effigy representing a turtle or a frog, based on the features of the face. The head and paws are attached to the body of

the vessel. The surface color resembles the natural pigmentation of both animals, which are both associated with the aquatic environment. In the case of turtles, their carapaces were used as musical instruments (drums) because when they were played with a deer horn or a stick their sound resembled the thunder associated with rain. For the Mayas,

11

turtles were also associated with the earth, so many altars were carved in the form of this animal. Turtle shells have been found as part of funerary offerings. Furthermore, these animals appear in scenes on polychrome ceramics.   MSB

13
Brick with the Image of a Crocodile
(Crocodylus moreletti)
Terminal Classic–Epiclassic period
Comalcalco, Tabasco, Mexico
Ceramic
Length: 28.1 cm
width: 19.3 cm
thickness: 6.4 cm
Comalcalco, Museo de Sitio
de Comalcalco
Inv. no. 10-575756

For the Mayas, the crocodile represented *imix*, the first day of their divinatory calendar, and symbol-

ized water and abundance, associated with the earth monster. In fact, for both Mayas and Nahuatls, the earth was considered to be a crocodile or a lizard. The Maya cosmos was composed of an "animalized space" where an enormous reptile supported all living beings. The crocodile, then was, an important being within the Maya universe. The bones of this animal have been found in funerary contexts or as offerings in important constructions. This piece, nevertheless, displays the interest of the potter who modeled it, in faithfully representing not only the deity, but also the reptile with which he lived daily in the marshy lands, which explains the precision of detail in the treatment of the tail, fangs, and nasal cavities, but especially in the placement of its scales, which permit the clear identification of this species.   MJGG

12

14

15

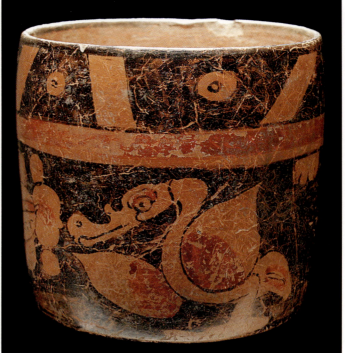

16

17

14
Effigy Vessel
Late Classic period
Jaina Island, Campeche
Mexico
Ceramic
Height: 15.6 cm
diameter: 26.1 cm
Mexico City
Museo Nacional de Antropología
Inv. no. 10-079423

Animal vessel representing a toad. It is made from orange clay with a polished slip. The body has a globular form that is slightly raised at the opening, although it does not form a well-defined neck. It has a smooth rim, concave bottom, flat base, and four small supports that are animal feet. There is no doubt it is a toad due to the parotoid glands and tail that are characteristic of this batrachian. Its body is delineated by black paint and incisions. The texture of the skin was also represented in black in the form of small circles. The toad wears a necklace on his chest, attached behind the neck and topped off with a knot. It probably represents a *Bufo marinus*, a very important species for Mesoamerican cultures because their glands contain bufotenine, a substance with hallucinogenic properties. Toads, represented since the Preclassic period, were used in shamanic and ritual contexts, and perhaps also for curative purposes which are still practiced today. LCGS

15
Animal Sculpture
Late Postclassic period
Mayapán, Yucatán, Mexico
Limestone
Height: 9.5 cm
length: 18 cm
Merida, Museo Regional de Yucatán "Palacio Cantón"
Inv. no. 10-347166

The sculpture of Mayapán, just as ceramics from this site, is poorly finished, but the white bath and blue color give it a certain attractive appearance. This piece must have been used as a receptacle for offerings because it has a hollow in the upper part. The blue color and the turtle itself are related to water. APC

16
Polychrome Cylindrical Vessel
Late Classic period
Usumacinta region, Mexico
Ceramic
Height: 10.8 cm
width: 11.2 cm
depth: 11.2 cm
Villahermosa, Museo Regional de Antropología "Carlos Pellicer"
Inv. no. A-0612

This polychrome vessel depicts an aquatic bird, possibly a cormorant, on a black background. A fish is in front of its beak and in the scene that repeats on the other side of the vessel, the bird is in an erect position and the fish has two additional fins possibly representing a turtle. In Maya cosmogonic thought, animals were associated with the forces of nature, the levels of the universe, and divine forces. Birds active in the daytime are one of the representations of the sky, while aquatic and raptorial birds are representatives of the underworld. Thus, birds of different species are recorded on stelae, mural painting, codices, and ceramics. RP

17
Polychrome Bowl
Early Classic period
Provenance unknown
probably Yucatán
Ceramic
Height: 8.2 cm; diameter: 23.0 cm
Merida, Museo Regional de Yucatán "Palacio Cantón"
Inv. no. 10-425087

The interior decoration of this bowl with basal flange and ring-shaped support of the ware known as Timucuy Naranja Policromo consists of a central motif composed of a stylized, aquatic bird with a long neck, beak, and wing with bristling feathers, outlined in black and contoured in red. Along its beak is a celestial band from which a water lily sprouts, flanked by profile serpent heads with raised nose or possibly closed flowers. The aquatic flower is represented in the same manner as on the large jars from the Gruta de Chac, Yucatán, displaying a medallion with symbols associated with water of the same ceramic tradition and of the same time. The bird with twisted neck, apparently dead, the lily, and possibly the serpent heads refer to the watery underworld. The exterior of the vessel displays geometric red and black decoration. Recently a pair of bowls with the same motifs was found in Tomb 1 of Structure 6F3 at Yaxuná, Yucatán, implying a peninsular production for this type of bowls and a probable funerary function.   SB

18
Polychrome Cylindrical Vessel
Middle Classic period
Dzibanché, Quintana Roo, Mexico
Ceramic
Height: 20.1 cm; diameter: 10.8 cm
Chetumal
Centro INAH *Quintana Roo*
Inv. no. 10-390807

This cylindrical vessel, found in Building 2, Chamber 3 at Dzibanché, formed part of a funerary offering. Vessels such as this one with representations of cormorants, which have been located in royal tombs at different sites in the Maya lowlands, seem to have been used to drink chocolate, a highly prized beverage among the ancient Mayas. These vessels associated the cormorant with the supernatural world, possibly because of their particular habits and their relationship with different natural contexts: they fly, they nest on land, and they live by fishing in the water. Also, throughout the year this bird changes its appearance: during some months its feathers are smooth and dark, while in the mating period it has a beautiful feather crest. Thus, from the viewpoint of Maya religion, where these changing beings who travel through different domains of existence commonly appear, the cormorant seems to be an ideal symbolic representation.   EN and AV

19
Pendant or handle
Late Postclassic period
Xcaret, Quintana Roo, Mexico
Shell
Length: 18.2 cm; diameter: 2.5 cm
Cancún
Museo Arqueológico de Cancún
Inv. no. 10-229005 70/84

Zoomorphic pendant with the image of a bird, possibly a buzzard or a vulture, that was made from the columella of a gastropod. The head of the bird was reproduced in great detail. At the end of the beak, there is a perforation to hang it. The part that represents the body of the animal is stylized and geometric designs were made in it, using the grooving technique. The piece is crowned by a motif in the shape of a

20

19

18

flower. During the pre-Hispanic epoch, it was common to use shells of different kinds. With this raw material, infinite objects were made, from receptacles to tools, but it was in ornamental and ritual pieces that the work of craftsmen showed amazing mastery.   ECTA

20
Bowl
Middle Classic period
Comayagua Valley
Comayagua, Honduras
Ceramic

Height: 13.0 cm; width: 11.7 cm
diameter of base: 23.3 cm
Tegucigalpa, Bodegas Centrales
del Instituto Hondureño
de Antropología e Historia
Inv. no. TGC-C-743

This red, white, and black on orange polychrome tripod bowl has stepped slab feet and is polished inside and out. Its walls have straight divergent ends with a rounded edge and a flat base on the outside. The slip is very fine with a black band on the inner lip of the vessel. Near the outside edge, lined by a white, braided band and on the walls, there is a white figure known as a water bird. It is classified within the Yojoa group. This type of ceramics is characteristic of the Comayagua Valley for the entire Classic period.   CJF

21

21
Plate
Preclassic period
San Isidro, Malpaso, Chiapas, Mexico
Ceramic
Height: 8.0 cm
diameter of mouth: 45.0 cm
diameter of base: 25.5 cm
Mexico City
Museo Nacional de Antropología
Inv. no. 10-128063

In the Central Depression of Chiapas, communities developed in the Early Preclassic period. Later there was an increase in population and tremendous construction activity, causing some agricultural villages to become ceremonial centers. The Malpaso dam was built in the Middle Grijalva, so that many archaeological sites in this region today are covered by water. One of the most important sites in this area is San Isidro. Characteristic of the ceramics of this period are plates with a flat, flaring rim on which different types of animals are represented, such as frogs, fish, or birds, as in this example.   MCG

22
Animal Sculpture
Terminal Classic–Epiclassic period
Comalcalco, Tabasco, Mexico

22

Shell and Ceramic
Height: 51.0 cm; width: 24.0 cm
depth: 51.0 cm
Comalcalco
Museo de Sitio de Comalcalco
Inv. no. 10-575754

This duck of the *Anatidae* species is made with oystershell plaster on a nucleus of brick and fragments of domestic ceramic. The sculpture is modeled in three dimensions and carved out using incisions, appliqué, and plaster-coating. It is only a fragment of a composition that decorated the roofcomb of the funerary building of Temple V on the Great Acropolis of Comalcalco, in which different representations of aquatic birds, such as pelicans, ducks, herons, and seagulls, were found. This suggests a cosmic association with the sky, air, and fire. In the cosmovision of the Mayas, ducks were considered to be the soul of the deceased and messengers of the clouds to the sacred world. It was believed that the spirits and gods assumed their form on journeys between sacred mountains and the sea. They were also considered as bearers of seeds in agricultural fertility rites.   RAT

23
Relief with Animal Figure
Late Classic period
Oxkintok, Yucatán, Mexico

23

Limestone
Length: 31.0 cm; width: 27.5 cm
depth: 26.5 cm
Merida, Museo Regional de Yucatán
"Palacio Cantón"
Inv. no. 10-425348

This piece comes from a building known as the Palacio Chich, dating from the eighth century when buildings at the site were constructed in the architectural style known as Early Puuc. Besides stuccoed figures from that period, there are also magnificent bas-reliefs. The presence of this piece in a place that would usually be coated with stucco and painted with glyphs and the images of gods is unusual. It is common for the capstones of vaults to be painted in red with the image of a god.   APC

24
Effigy Vessel
Early Postclassic period
Acayuca, Hidalgo, Mexico

Ceramic
Height: 17.5 cm
width: 12.0 cm
Mexico City
Museo Nacional de Antropología
Inv. no. 10-047586

Mayas and Toltecs shared a cult of one of the most important gods "the feathered serpent," know as Kukulcan among the Mayas and Quetzalcoatl among the Toltecs. Quetzalcoatl was the creator of humanity under the Fifth Sun, and had a twin brother called Xolotl, who was the divine dog who descended into the underworld every day to bring the sun on his back from the darkness, thus illuminating the world. This numen formed a fundamental part of the creation of humanity, because according to legend, Quetzalcoatl was chosen to rescue the bones of man and woman that were in the power of Mictlantecuhtli, Lord of the Underworld. Transformed into Quetzalcoatl's divine twin, Xolotl managed, after passing a series of tests, to rescue the human bones, stealing them from the underworld and taking them to the heavens where they were ground up by the goddess Cihuacoatl in her mill. Quetzalcoatl let blood from his virile member onto this powder, thus giving life to humanity in the Fifth Era. Xolotl, the divine twin of the feathered serpent, is represented on this plumbate vessel in a seated position, dressed with a braided and knotted necklace, the third support of the piece is his tail.   FSM

24

25
Stirrup-type Vessel
Preclassic period
Kaminaljuyú, Guatemala
Ceramic
Height: 16.0 cm
length: 30.5 cm
Guatemala, Museo Nacional
de Arqueología y Etnología
Inv. no. MNAE 2400

This piece is composed of the figure of a red *coatí* or a possum, and a vessel with a simple shape, joined by a stirrup. The head and paws of the animal are applied onto the surface of the vessel. The face, neck, and right paw are painted red, and the right paw grabs the snout, while the left one is delineated in red. A red volute emerges from the neck. The red *coatí* is a frequently represented animal in Maya art. The simple-shaped vessel has a globular body and a short neck. On the side opposite the stirrup a spout, which indicates that the vessel was used to transport and serve liquids during ceremonies. The vessel is decorated with parallel lines painted red. The entire surface is covered with a polished, cream-colored slip.   MSB

25

26
Effigy Vessel
Terminal Classic–Early Postclassic period
Progreso, Yucatán, Mexico
Ceramic
Height: 19.5 cm; diameter: 8.0 cm
width: 16.0 cm
Merida, Museo Regional de Yucatán "Palacio Cantón"
Inv. no. 10-251139

Among the funerary furnishing of the Maya, it is often possible to find pieces of ceramic, such as this effigy vessel of Tohil Plumbate ware. It represents a red *coatí* or possum, partially kneeling, with certain anthropomorphic traits, such as his pose, the position of his hands, and his necklace and armlet decoration. Plumbate ware is characterized by its dense, fine paste of great hardness; its lustrous surface with metallic iridescence; and colors ranging between olive green, gray, and orange. This ceramic comes from the Soconusco region on the Pacific coast, and its distribution reached a variety of sites, not only in the Maya area, but also in Central Mexico, such as the city of Tula in the modern state of Hidalgo.   LFS

26

27

a deer that, in full flight, turns his head with visible fear. Between both figures, on opposite sides, we see two year symbols in the style of the cultures of the Mexican highlands. This symbol is characteristic of Tlaloc, a deity of Teotihuacán origin that the Mayas adopted as warrior insignia. On the interior we see a ring formed by elements inserted one into the other that resemble the allegory of continuous movement. The deer is related to the earth and the day time sky; also, prisoners destined for sacrifice were often represented with traits of this animal. The jaguar is associated with the nocturnal sky and with the underworld; warriors were identified with the jaguar as predator. The iconography allegorically expresses the continuum of life and death, as well as the struggle that takes place between night and day, the jaguar and his prey, and, in the human milieu, the warrior and his prisoner.   SPA and GB

29
Polychrome Bowl
Late Classic period
Probably Campeche, Mexico
Ceramic
Height: 9.1 cm
diameter: 29.0 cm
San Cristóbal de las Casas
Centro Cultural
de los Altos de Chiapas
Inv. no. 10-168614

This bowl with polychrome decoration bears a combination of geometric designs with animal and hieroglyphic motifs. It is common for this type of fine ceramic to have been used as a funerary offering by the Maya elite. The zoomorphic designs perhaps represent deer.   AGC

27
Effigy Vessel
Terminal Classic–Early Postclassic period
Uxmal, Yucatán, Mexico
Ceramic
Height: 17.5 cm
width: 15.0 cm
Merida, Museo Regional de Yucatán "Palacio Cantón"
Inv. no. 10-426395

This Tohil Plumbate vessel, representing a deer, was found in the Round Structure at Uxmal. This ceramic ware has been the object of considerable research. Its characteristics of hardness, luster, and almost metallic sheen indicate special raw materials and technology, such as firing in a reduced atmosphere. Plumbate ware comes from the plains of the Soconusco region, on the Pacific coast of Chiapas, Mexico, and of Guatemala. Tohil Plumbate employed the techniques of modeling, molds, and incising, and it achieved widespread distribution in the Maya area and beyond.   LFS

Balancán
Museo "José Gómez Panaco"
Inv. no. MB 315

This piece belongs to the ceramic complexes of the Classic, a period characterized by the luster and beauty of its polychrome. This splendid vessel displays a hunting scene: a jaguar is ready to jump on

28

28
Polychrome Bowl
Late Classic period
Tabasco, Mexico
Ceramic
Height: 11.0 cm
diameter of mouth: 22.0 cm
diameter of base: 15.0 cm

29

30
Polychrome Cylindrical Vessel
Late Classic period
El Petén, Guatemala
Ceramic
Height: 15.8 cm; width: 9.4 cm
diameter: 9.4 cm; depth: 15.4 cm
Guatemala, Museo Popol Vuh
Universidad Francisco Marroquín
Inv. no. MPV 0376

This cylindrical vessel, painted black, red, and orange on a light orange ground, features a red band under the rim on a line of glyphs painted in dark orange and outlined in black. The main scene consists of two zoomorphic drawings, one of them perhaps representing a supernatural being. It has the physical traits of several animals, mainly the tapir and anteater. It has a long trunk, elongated oval ear, and a long, thin tail. The chest, and portions of the feet and tail, are painted white; the rest of the body has tones of orange and red. Both figures are shown in profile, standing up on flexed back legs, while the front legs are extended and the body leans forward. MS

31
Polychrome Bowl
Late Classic period
Provenance unknown
probably Campeche, Mexico
Ceramic
Height: 6.3 cm; diameter: 24.7 cm
Campeche, Centro INAH Campeche
Inv. no. 10-566459

This bowl's iconography of seated rodents emerges from the local environment of the Mayas and functions on several levels: as a decoration, as an expression of life, and as symbols of cosmological beliefs. For the ancient Mayas, the roles covered by the animal and plant kingdom are reflected in a large repertory of ceramic forms from the Classic period. Both in ancient as well as modern Maya mythology, animals may be conscious, speaking beings with the ability to exercise judgment and utilize supernatural powers. In the mythical account of the *Popol Vuh*, a sixteenth-century Quiché book, a rat helps the Hero Twins search for the ball and other ball game accoutrements belonging to their ancestors, which are tied to the rafters of the roof, in order to play the sacred ball game. YP

32
Miniature Vessel
Classic period
Provenance unknown
Ceramic
Height: 7.9 cm; width: 9.0 cm
thickness: 3.7 cm
Mexico City
Museo Nacional de Antropología
Inv. no. 10-079005

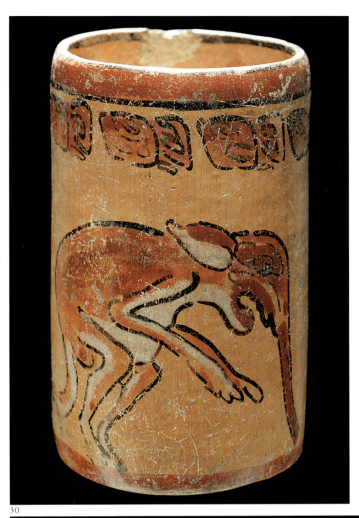

30

This miniature vessel made of polished cream-colored clay has an exceptional form in pre-Hispanic Mexico. On one side is depicted a jaguar and on the other are circles, barely visibile, made with the resist technique. The profile was highlighted with deep incisions creating a series of projecting, symmetrically ordered dots. The jaguar shows front paws raised, the tail erect, and the muzzle half-open with projecting tongue. MC-L

33
Miniature Vessel
Late Classic–Early Postclassic period
Probably Campeche, Mexico
Ceramic
Height: 7.0 cm
width: 8.6 cm
Merida, Museo Regional de Yucatán "Palacio Cantón"
Inv. no. 10-425516

Small flat bottle that has a jaguar on one side and a series of small appliquéd spheres on the edge. It was probably used to store substances used in certain ceremonies. They have been found at Cobá, Quintana Roo; Dzan, Uxmal, and Oxkintok, Yucatán. Very similar forms have been found at Altar de Sacrificios, Uaxactún, and the Motagua Valley, Guatemala; Copan, Honduras; and a flask has been reported from the Ulúa Valley. APC

31

32

33

34

35

time of the site's first occupation, they participated in a Mesoamerican network of economic, social, and ideological exchange. This disk, carved in very fine-grained stone, was discovered by Santiago I. Barberena. JMR

37
Miniature Vessel
Classic period
Provenance unknown
Ceramic
Height: 6.5 cm; width: 4.3 cm
length: 9.0 cm
Mexico City
Museo Nacional de Antropología
Inv. no. 10-076518

36

37

34
Vessel
Late Classic period
Guatemalan lowlands
Ceramic
Height: 21.0 cm; width: 13.0 cm;
diameter: 12.0 cm
depth: 20.2 cm
Guatemala, Museo Popol Vuh
Universidad Francisco Marroquín
Inv. no. MPV 1195

Vessel with curving, converging walls of light brown color features a polished inner surface (without slip, with the exception of a thin, red band), which covers the rim and extends itself on the outer wall. On it are three groups of five glyphs in gray that cannot be deciphered. Below each inscription is a crouching jaguar in profile, whose front feet, with visible claws, are facing forward, while the tail extends toward the back. The fangs and a headdress are also visible. Between each jaguar are orange circles and volutes outlined in black. MS

35
Ulúa Jaguar Vessel
Late Classic period
Las Sepulturas
Copán Ruinas, Honduras
Ceramic
Height: 15.7 cm; width: 11.5 cm
base: 14.5 cm
diameter: 11.3 cm
Tegucigalpa, Bodegas Centrales

del Instituto Hondureño
de Antropología e Historia
Inv. no. CPN-C-742

This handsome vase represents a masterpiece of the Ulúa polychrome tradition. The "speech scrolls" emanating from their mouths let us know they are growling. The stepped fret motif on the lip of the vessel is common on Ulúa polychromes. Beneath the stepped fret is the interwoven mat motif, symbol of rulership and political power for all Mesoamerican cultures. For the Maya, only the ruler had the privilege of sitting on the "jaguar mat," and this pot may have been making reference in some way to that symbol. This vase was found in the grave of the patriarch of Plaza D of Sepulturas Group 9N-8. WF

36
Jaguar Disk
Classic period
Cara Sucia, Department
of Ahuachapán, El Salvador
Stone
Height: 85.0 cm; width: 21.0 cm
El Salvador, Museo Nacional
de Antropología
"Dr. David J. Guzmán"
Inv. no. A2.2-555

This animal sculpture in the form of a disk, known as "The Jaguar Disk," displays the sculpted figure of a jaguar effigy on the main side

and geometric designs in stepped fret form on its rim. It was found at the archaeological site of Cara Sucia, located in the coastal zone of the Department of Ahuachapán. The sculpted motif on the jaguar altar from Quelepa, on which stands out a stylized jaguar, is very similar to the face of the sculpted jaguar on the famous disk found at Cara Sucia. It constitutes evidence of the link between the west and the inhabitants of Quelepa. Since the

This vessel in the form of a jaguar is modeled from light brown clay with a highly polished orange bath. Small, dark-red spots were placed on its eyes, head, eyebrows, cheeks, and around the muzzle, which is half open, thus exposing the animal's teeth, which are made with deep puncture marks. The same technique was used to suggest the claws of the front paws and the openings of the nose. Curious holes pass through the figure at the neck

38

as well as in the tail of the animal, which could have served to suspend it from the wearer's neck.　MCL

38
Bowl with Lid
Early Classic period
Tikal, Petén, Guatemala
Ceramic
Height: 26.5 cm
diameter: 31.0 cm
Guatemala, Museo Nacional
de Arqueología y Etnología
Inv. no. MNAE 11336

This bowl has a basal flange and a ring-shaped base. The former is decorated with triangles and parallel black lines, interpreted as *moan* bird feathers, and a red line around the outside of the entire flange; the exterior is decorated with four stylized serpent designs alternating with black rectangles. The handle of the lid is a jaguar head with open jaws and body painted on the surface. The edge is decorated with a band of curvilinear designs in alternating buff or cream, orange, black because and red colors. Representations of jaguars are very common in funerary contexts is associated this animal with the underworld; the feathers of the *moan* bird reinforce this association with death.　MSB

39
Vessel
Late Classic period
Tabasco, Mexico
Ceramic
Height: 22.5 cm
diameter: 14.5 cm
Mexico City
Museo Nacional de Antropología
Inv. no. 10-001186

This vessel is the best example of realism achieved by Maya ceramic artists, whose ability may be admired in two different ways: first they succeeded in creating a stony appearance, suggesting that the vessel is carved from stone and not from clay. Secondly, they magnificently reproduced the head of this feline, probably a jaguar, with great realism. This animal is very important in Maya art and there are many representations of it, because in addition to forming part of many of their beliefs and religious ideas, there was a jaguar related with the

earth, the underworld, and the sun. Its pelt symbolized the starry night, and as a deity it was the god of the number seven.　ACM

40
Effigy Vessel
Classic period
Yucatán, Mexico
Ceramic
Height: 17.2 cm
diameter: 11.5 cm
Merida
Museo Regional de Yucatán
"Palacio Cantón"
Inv. no. 10-347165

Abstract, naturalistic, conventionalized, and glyphic designs may be found in Maya ceramics. There is a wide variety of pre-Hispanic pieces that represent the fauna of the different regions; fauna in the Maya area was generally an important source of resources, in terms of food, as well as for the imagination of artists. In some cases, the specimens portrayed are stylized animals and in others, they are given certain human characteristics. There are naturalistic examples, as in the case of this zoomorphic vessel made of reddish-ochre clay and representing a spider monkey. The tail projects upward and joins with the head to serve as a spout. The animal's limbs are tucked in and the ears perforated. In the southern Maya area, Guatemala, Honduras, and El Salvador, this type of vessel with an animal effigy, particularly the monkey, is common.　LFS

41
Miniature Jar
Late Classic period
Southeastern corner of Campeche
Mexico
Ceramic

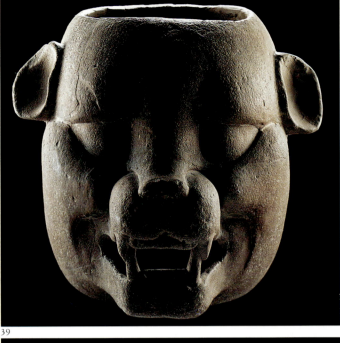

39

41

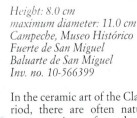

Height: 8.0 cm
maximum diameter: 11.0 cm
Campeche, Museo Histórico
Fuerte de San Miguel
Baluarte de San Miguel
Inv. no. 10-566399

In the ceramic art of the Classic period, there are often naturalistic representations of monkeys. Perhaps these refer to creation myths, when the gods transformed disobedient human-like creatures into monkeys destined to make senseless noises while they swung through the branches of tress. In this case, the extreme realism of the expression on the monkey's face, with his round eyes and open mouth with its reddish tongue, makes us think that we have surprised him in the treetops, where he screams at us. Among the modern Maya, monkeys play an important role in folk tales and in sacred festivities during Carnival.　YP

40

42

43

42
Bowl
Early Classic period
Dzibanché, Quintana Roo, Mexico
Ceramic
Height: 15.4 cm; diameter: 21.1 cm
Mexico City
Museo Nacional de Antropología
Inv. no. 10-571166/2

This vessel with a ring-shaped base
and lid was an offering in the tomb
of a ruler at Dzibanché. Although a
certain Teotihuacán influence may
be perceived in its form, the decoration corresponds to the Maya style
and its symbolism refers to the cosmogonic traditions of that people.
The *Popol Vuh* tells the story of the
older brothers, Hun Chuen and
Hun Batz, who are turned into monkeys for bothering the Hero Twins,
Hunahpu and Xbalanque. The
monkeys on this vessel are shown
with arms raised as if holding something, characteristic of atlantean figures, *bacabs*, or *Pahuatuns*; according to cosmogonic beliefs, these beings sustain the heaven and the
earth. The function of these monkeys sustaining the world is reinforced in this vessel because the figures appear against a background
with a net design that represents a
spider's web, a symbol of one of the
bacabs.   ACM

43
Censer
Late Classic period
Chicanná, Campeche, Mexico
Ceramic
Height: 26.0 cm; diameter: 16.5 cm
Campeche, Centro INAH Campeche
Inv. no. 10-342697 0/2

In different ceremonies, the ancient
Mayas burned aromatic resins such
as copal, although they also inciner-
ated *amate* or bark paper, feathers,
and textiles. For this purpose, they
used receptacles with or without
lids, which were often decorated
with a variety of human, fantastic, or
animal representations. After the
celebration of a ritual, the pieces
were buried, and therefore they have
been preserved until now. Because
of its characteristics, the owl was
considered a bird representative of
the underworld, a type of ambassador of the subterranean deities.
This type of piece is often found at
sites in southern Campeche, such as
Becán, Chicanná, Xpuhil, and Zoh
Laguna.   ABC

44
Figurine
Late Classic period
Jaina Island, Campeche, Mexico
Ceramic

44

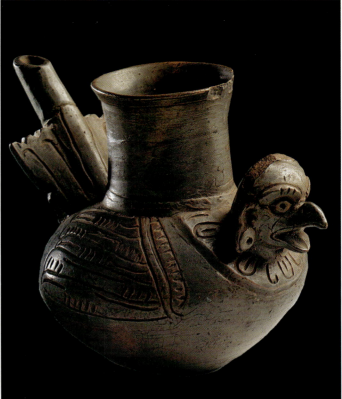

45

46

sistant, with a metallic-looking surface that was highly prized throughout Mesoamerica.　　MSB

46
Polychrome Basin
Classic period
Tikal, Petén, Guatemala
Ceramic
Height: 5.8 cm
diameter of the rim: 12.7 cm
Guatemala, Museo Nacional
de Arqueología y Etnología
Inv. no. MNAE 11304

This vessel has slightly flaring walls and a flat bottom. The interior surface is covered with polished red slip and the exterior with cream slip. A narrow red band surrounds the vessel near the rim. Under this there is a thinner black line. The exterior is decorated with four black coleopterans, fairly common insects in this region during certain times of the year. The piece was found inside of a very similar vessel, as part of a funerary offering in an elite tomb at Tikal.　　MSB

Height: 10.6 cm; width: 6.6 cm
Merida, Museo Regional de Yucatán
"Palacio Cantón"
Inv. no. 10-425388

Among the indigenous fauna of Mesoamerica, the *guajolote* or domesticated turkey (*Meleagris gallopavo, tso* in Yucatec Mayan) was of significant importance to the ancient Maya. Not only was it a nutritious and delicious food, but turkeys were used as offerings in numerous ceremonies. Turkey feathers embellished garments and headgear; long

bones were used as needles, and their image was associated with benevolent deities. For this reason, the turkey was frequently represented. In this case, the turkey form is a whistle. As with other flora and fauna, the turkey is one of the gifts that Mexico has given the world.　　ABC

45
Effigy Vessel
Postclassic period
Asunción Mita, Jutiapa, Guatemala
Ceramic

Height: 15.5 cm
diameter of the rim: 7.6 cm
Guatemala, Museo Nacional
de Arqueología y Etnología
Inv. no. MNAE 4406

Large jar with the representation of a bird in Plumbate ware. The bird has an open beak and wears circular ear ornaments. The head, long tail, and perch of the animal are appliquéd and its details, on the body of the vessel, are incised. The tail is both the handle and spout of the piece. Plumbate ware is hard and re-

47

47
Polychrome Plate
Late Classic period
Tikal, Petén, Guatemala
Ceramic
Height: 8.7 cm; diameter: 27.5 cm
Guatemala, Museo Nacional
de Arqueología y Etnología
Inv. no. MNAE 11141

The surface of this plate, both interior and exterior, is covered with polished white slip. A red band surrounds the vessel near the rim, which extends to the outside and inside of the vessel; underneath appears a very fine black line. Decoration consists of the representation of six black coleopterans on the inside and another six on the outside in white, black, and red. These insects were frequently represented at Tikal because they are common there at a certain time of year. This vessel was found in a tomb to the south of Mundo Perdido in Tikal; it formed part of the funerary offering of a priest and was associated with another basin with similar decoration.   MSB

48

48
Tetrapod Urn
Late Classic period
Nebaj, Quiché, Guatemala
Ceramic
Height: 52.0 cm
length: 70.0 cm
Guatemala
Museo Nacional
de Arqueología y Etnología
Inv. no. MNAE 1180a and 1180b

Tetrapod funerary urn with lid. The base has a fillet with fingerprints on the juncture of the vessel with the base. The supports are zoomorphic. The lid bears the effigy of a reclining jaguar with closed, coffee-bean shaped eyes and an open snout. A fillet surrounds the body of the animal on the lower part. Both the base and the lid show remains of white paint. The jaguar was represented on funerary urns because of its association with the night and the underworld.   MSB

49

50

49
Basin
Late Preclassic period
Kaminaljuyú, Guatemala
Ceramic
Height: 12.5 cm
diameter: 15.0 cm
depth: 11.9 cm
Guatemala, Museo Popol Vuh
Universidad Francisco Marroquín
Inv. no. MPV 0613

This zoomorphic tripod basin with small conical feet is made of a ware known as Kaminaljuyú Brown-Black. It displays a bat with molded eyes, ears, nose, and snout, with a groove in the middle. The extremities have two striations that form the fingers. On the back is a band with seven shallow, wide, vertical incisions. On each side of the vessel there is a rectangular band with an incised design in the form of a woven mat.   MS

50
Effigy Vessel
Late Classic period
Caves to the east of Comitán
Chiapas, Mexico
Ceramic
Height: 10.6 cm
diameter: 15.1 cm
Comitán, Museo Arqueológico
de Comitán
Inv. no. 10-588892

Bowl recovered from a funerary offering in the "El Bailón" cave to the east of Comitán, Chiapas. On the front is an effigy that represents the face of an animal, around which is decoration with wavy motifs resembling clouds. It could represent the face of a bat, in myth with the deities of night and death. Its presence in a cave supports its symbolic value related to funerary rites and the entrance to the underworld.   ELV

The cities

51
Bakná Column
Terminal Classic period
Bakná, Campeche, Mexico
Limestone
Height: 132.0 cm
maximum diameter: 57.0 cm
Mexico City
Museo Nacional de Antropología
Inv. no. 10-080383

This column, with the figure of an old man holding a rattle-staff in his right hand, has been identified as one of the representations of God L, because in his headdress he has *a moan* bird, an animal associated with rain and the underworld. In addition, here he appears carrying God K on his back, a deity closely related to lightning, rain, and fertility, which reinforces his positive, benevolent side. This column is identical to another that is in the Museo de las Estelas "Román Piña Chán," Baluarte de la Soledad, Campeche in which the figure faces the opposite direction.   ACM

52
Column
Classic period
Tunkuyí, Campeche, Mexico
Limestone
Height: 171.0 cm; diameter: 65.0 cm
Campeche
Centro INAH Campeche
Inv. no. 10-342791

Rulers of Maya cities held political, religious, and military power. To commemorate their feats in war or in different official ceremonies, they carried instruments of warfare such as axes and shields, in addition to wearing assorted luxurious costumes reflecting their office. Some of these events were recorded in architectonic elements that would serve to provide permanent public information once they were integrated onto a facade. In this case, five individuals participate: the ruler, seated on his throne and wearing a headdress; a high-ranking warrior; a dwarf, who attended the warrior as an intermediary; and two musicians, each with a trumpet. Dwarfs were considered to possess special powers and were linked with deities. They generally formed part of the court of great dignitaries.   ABC

53
Anthropomorphic Sculpture
Terminal Classic period
Oxkintok, Yucatán, Mexico
Limestone
Height: 171.0 cm; width: 57.0 cm
depth: 80.0 cm
Mexico City
Museo Nacional de Antropología
Inv. no. 10-081344

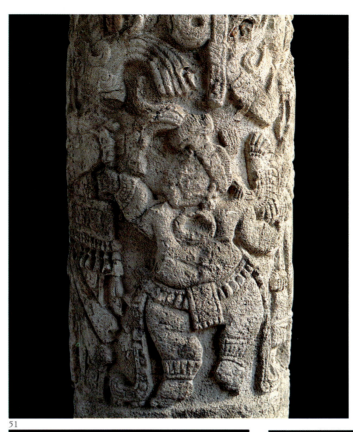

51

The use of columns in doors of buildings is a distinctive trait of the architectonic style of the Puuc region. Sometimes the body of these supports were carved with the image of a ruler or some supernatural being, as in this high relief perhaps depicting the fat god. His entire body is covered with a suit made of feathers and his pectoral ornament displays a hand. To rob and illegally transport this column, looters intentionally mutilated it, leaving only the sculpted part.   TPS

52

53

527

54

55

56a

56b

54
Ornamental Slab
Classic period
Uxmal, Yucatán, Mexico
Stone
Height: 55.5 cm; width: 47.0 cm
depth: 21.5 cm
Uxmal, Museo de Sitio de Uxmal
Inv. no. 10-290133

This ornamental architectural slab from Temple 1 at Uxmal, carved in limestone, represents the rain deity of the central highlands, Tlaloc, with his typical goggles and mustache, framed by three Teotihuacán symbols. This god has appeared since the Early Classic period in the Maya zone, particularly at large cities. He is often related to scenes of autosacrifice involving the nobility in which they extract and offer blood, which is a metaphor for rain. Nevertheless, the Mayas had their own rain deity, Chaac, clearly distinguishable from Tlaloc. In relation to the letting of blood, the deity also appears with war shields, such as that of the figure on the lintel from Cacabbeec, Campeche. MPC

55
Ornamental Panel
Classic period
Uxmal, Yucatán, Mexico
Stone
Height: 54.5 cm; width: 44.0 cm
depth: 33.0 cm
Uxmal
Museo de Sitio de Uxmal
Inv. no. 10-290134

57

This ornamental architectural slab made of limestone from a molding at Temple 1 at Uxmal, Yucatán, displays the face of a deity, probably Tlaloc, who is the god of rain in central Mexico, but among the Mayas he is associated with autosacrifice and the letting of blood as a precious liquid. Characteristics of this god include his goggles and mustache, as well as prominent upper teeth. On the forehead he wears a rectangle with an interlaced triangle, considered to be the Teotihuacán year sign. This deity must

The cities

51
Bakná Column
Terminal Classic period
Bakná, Campeche, Mexico
Limestone
Height: 132.0 cm
maximum diameter: 57.0 cm
Mexico City
Museo Nacional de Antropología
Inv. no. 10-080383

This column, with the figure of an old man holding a rattle-staff in his right hand, has been identified as one of the representations of God L, because in his headdress he has *a moan* bird, an animal associated with rain and the underworld. In addition, here he appears carrying God K on his back, a deity closely related to lightning, rain, and fertility, which reinforces his positive, benevolent side. This column is identical to another that is in the Museo de las Estelas "Román Piña Chán," Baluarte de la Soledad, Campeche in which the figure faces the opposite direction.   ACM

52
Column
Classic period
Tunkuyí, Campeche, Mexico
Limestone
Height: 171.0 cm; diameter: 65.0 cm
Campeche
Centro INAH Campeche
Inv. no. 10-342791

Rulers of Maya cities held political, religious, and military power. To commemorate their feats in war or in different official ceremonies, they carried instruments of warfare such as axes and shields, in addition to wearing assorted luxurious costumes reflecting their office. Some of these events were recorded in architectonic elements that would serve to provide permanent public information once they were integrated onto a facade. In this case, five individuals participate: the ruler, seated on his throne and wearing a headdress; a high-ranking warrior; a dwarf, who attended the warrior as an intermediary; and two musicians, each with a trumpet. Dwarfs were considered to possess special powers and were linked with deities. They generally formed part of the court of great dignitaries.   ABC

53
Anthropomorphic Sculpture
Terminal Classic period
Oxkintok, Yucatán, Mexico
Limestone
Height: 171.0 cm; width: 57.0 cm
depth: 80.0 cm
Mexico City
Museo Nacional de Antropología
Inv. no. 10-081344

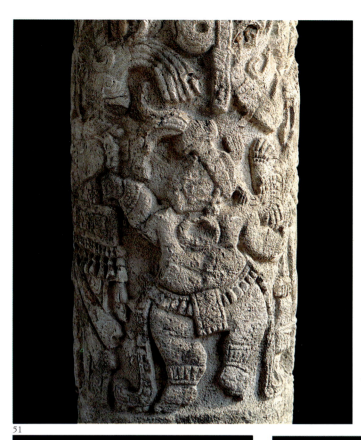

51

The use of columns in doors of buildings is a distinctive trait of the architectonic style of the Puuc region. Sometimes the body of these supports were carved with the image of a ruler or some supernatural being, as in this high relief perhaps depicting the fat god. His entire body is covered with a suit made of feathers and his pectoral ornament displays a hand. To rob and illegally transport this column, looters intentionally mutilated it, leaving only the sculpted part.   TPS

52

53

527

54

55

56a

56b

54
Ornamental Slab
Classic period
Uxmal, Yucatán, Mexico
Stone
Height: 55.5 cm; width: 47.0 cm
depth: 21.5 cm
Uxmal, Museo de Sitio de Uxmal
Inv. no. 10-290133

This ornamental architectural slab from Temple 1 at Uxmal, carved in limestone, represents the rain deity of the central highlands, Tlaloc, with his typical goggles and mustache, framed by three Teotihuacán symbols. This god has appeared since the Early Classic period in the Maya zone, particularly at large cities. He is often related to scenes of autosacrifice involving the nobility in which they extract and offer blood, which is a metaphor for rain. Nevertheless, the Mayas had their own rain deity, Chaac, clearly distinguishable from Tlaloc. In relation to the letting of blood, the deity also appears with war shields, such as that of the figure on the lintel from Cacabbeec, Campeche.   MPC

55
Ornamental Panel
Classic period
Uxmal, Yucatán, Mexico
Stone
Height: 54.5 cm; width: 44.0 cm
depth: 33.0 cm
Uxmal
Museo de Sitio de Uxmal
Inv. no. 10-290134

57

This ornamental architectural slab made of limestone from a molding at Temple 1 at Uxmal, Yucatán, displays the face of a deity, probably Tlaloc, who is the god of rain in central Mexico, but among the Mayas he is associated with autosacrifice and the letting of blood as a precious liquid. Characteristics of this god include his goggles and mustache, as well as prominent upper teeth. On the forehead he wears a rectangle with an interlaced triangle, considered to be the Teotihuacán year sign. This deity must have been introduced by merchants in this community of the central highlands and his presence continued among the Mayas, even after the fall of Teotihuacán. MPC

56a
Atlantean Figure
Late Classic period
Xculoc, Campeche, Mexico
Limestone
Height: 82.0 cm; width: 52.0 cm
depth: 32.0 cm
Campeche
Centro INAH Campeche
Inv. no. 10-342676

This sculpture in the form of an atlantean figure placed in a frieze inside a small niche on each of the three doors of one of the buildings at Xculoc, Campeche. It is an uncommon figure in Maya monuments, perhaps inspired by a model from another region outside the Yucatán peninsula. The figure, with an infantile face and a tight costume, probably made of feathers or a padded fabric, is fairly similar to others represented on columns at Oxkintok, Yucatán, which have their hands on their prominent bellies and have a staff in the form of a star (perhaps Venus), similar to the one carried by the atlantean figures of Chichén Itzá. LMC

56b
Atlantean Figure
Late Classic period
Xculoc, Campeche, Mexico
Limestone
Height: 84.5 cm; width: 50.0 cm
depth: 31.0 cm
Campeche
Centro INAH Campeche
Inv. no. 10-342675

This sculpture in the form of an Atlantean figure placed in a frieze inside a small niche on each of the three doors of one of the buildings at Xculoc, Campeche. It is an uncommon figure in Maya monuments, perhaps inspired by a model from another region outside the Yucatán peninsula. The figure, with an infantile face and a tight costume, probably made of feathers or a padded fabric, is fairly similar to others represented on columns at Oxkintok, Yucatán, which have their hands on their prominent bellies and have a staff in the form of a star (perhaps Venus), similar to the one carried by the Atlantean figures of Chichén Itzá. LMC

57
Sculpture
Classic period
Chunhuhub, Campeche, Mexico
Limestone
Height: 67.0 cm; width: 79.0 cm
thickness: 46.0 cm

Campeche
Museo de las Estelas
"Román Piña Chán"
Baluarte de la Soledad
Inv. no. 10-290666

In northeastern Campeche, there was a populous Maya city today as Chunhuhub. Its buildings were covered with very well cut and assembled stone blocks; its friezes were decorated with seated human figures with their arms in jars. This is how a manifestation of the sun god, Kinich Ahau (Lord of the Solar Face) was represented, an old man with a Roman or aquiline nose and crossed eyes in the art of the Classic period. The feather cape that he wears reveals his daily movement through the sky; among the Mayas historic he was more feared than loved because, without the intervention of the deities of the rain, the sun burned the harvest. This god was associated with the number 4, a numeral of profound symbolic content because it is linked, to the four celestial directions. ABC

58a-b
Sculpture
Late Classic period
Hacienda de San Simón
Yucatán, Mexico
Limestone
Upper part: height: 109 cm
width: 67.0 cm; depth: 55.0 cm
Belt: height: 25.0 cm
diameter: 82.0 cm
Lower part: height: 83.5 cm
width: 57.5 cm
Merida, Museo Regional de Yucatán
"Palacio Cantón" and Dzibilchaltún
Museo del Pueblo Maya
Inv. no. lower part: 10-426255
belt: 10-426256
upper part: 10-290445

This sculpture is one of four pieces decorating a building at the site of X Banqueta-Tunich and belongs to the type of sculpture that employed "nonclassic" elements of the Late Puuc style from the ninth to tenth centuries. The face of the figure is grotesquely swollen and his slender arms are placed in an attitude of supplication or greeting. The figure wears a short cape with geometric designs, a skirt with a merlon border, and a loincloth. A wide belt, decorated with a diamond-shaped design, may indicate the figure is a ball player. His headdress resembles a turban and he wears sandals that tie at the ankles and calves. LMC

58a

58b

59

59
Animal Sculpture
Terminal Classic–Early Postclassic period
Chichén Itzá, Yucatán, Mexico
Stone
Height: 65.0 cm; width: 30.0 cm
length: 122.0 cm
Chichén Itzá
Museo de Sitio de Chichén Itzá
Inv. no. 10-290177

This head was found in the same deposit of dismantled architectural pieces that was found by Augustus Le Plongeon under the Venus Platform (Structure 2D4). Its neck is raised aggressively and it also displays part of the feathered body. There are still extensive remains of polychrome. Photographs taken immediately after its discovery show the two long noseplugs projecting from the tip of the nose, teeth, fangs; a long tongue attached to the lower part; and a flaming element crowning the head between the supraorbital plaques. With all of these details, the heads, placed in their original location on the edge of platforms and benches, such as those of the ball court, must have formed an impressive group, the effect of which was heightened by the smoke of burning copal, fire, and shadows. Despite the movement of these pieces after their discovery, which includes their confinement for several years in the jail at Valladolid, a town near the site, they continue to have a strong impact.   PJS

60
Animal Sculpture
Terminal Classic–Early Postclassic period
Chichén Itzá, Yucatán, Mexico
Stone
Height: 39.0 cm
width: 25.0 cm
length: 89.0 cm
Chichén Itzá
Museo de Sitio de Chichén Itzá
Inv. no. 10-290174

When Augustus Le Plongeon excavated the Venus Platform (Structure 2D4) in the Great Plaza at Chichén Itzá, he found, together with a standard bearer and a large stone vessel, a group of more than 180 stone cones painted red or blue, as well as more than a dozen finely carved serpent heads preserved with all their attachments,

ornaments, and polychrome painting. According to all indications (shape, size, remains of paint and stucco), these heads and part of their bodies were provided with some structure before they were found in a zone where there is evidence of at least three phases of construction. The heads and bodies of the serpents probably pertain to two different friezes that, with impressive polychromy (green, red, yellow, black, etc.), must have adorned the border of a platform or basement. The piece presented here displays a simple open mouth and straight neck.   PJS

61
Sculpture
Classic period
Escuintla, Guatemala

60

61

Stone
Height: 85.0 cm; length: 121.0 m
Guatemala, Museo Nacional de Arqueología y Etnología
Inv. no. MNAE 2013

Tenoned piece representing a naturalistic serpent with open maw and projecting tongue. This type of sculpture was tenoned into the walls of buildings. It was possibly a ballcourt marker. Serpents, jaguars, and parrots were animals with strong symbolic and religious significance in Mesoamerica since ancient times. This reptile may be associated with water, as a conductor of this liquid; and with caves because it opens its mouth toward one. Among the Mayas serpents are associated with certain deities and certain objects of extreme impor-

tance. For example, God K, the manikin scepter, has one leg in the form of a serpent, and the ceremonial bar carried by some rulers has serpent heads at each end.   MSB

62
The King of Kabah
Terminal Classic period
Kabah, Yucatán, Mexico

Limestone
Height: 48.0 cm
width: 33.0 cm
depth: 48.0 cm
Merida, Bodega
de Sitio Arqueológico de Kabah
Inv. no. 10-569619

This head forms part of one of seven sculptures that decorated the central portion of the eastern facade of Structure 2C6 of the Codz Pop in the archaeological zone of Kabah. The head, sculpted from a single block of limestone, is covered with a helmet. There a small figure representing a deity emerges from the beak of a turtle. The face of the main sculpture displays complex scarification surrounding the right eye and going to the cheekbone and chin. Of the group of seven sculptures, six exhibit scarification on the left side, and this is the only one that has it on the right. RCV

62

63
The Queen of Uxmal
Terminal Classic period
Uxmal, Yucatán, Mexico
Limestone
Height: 80.0 cm
maximum length: 99.0 cm
thickness: 99.0 cm
Mexico City
Museo Nacional de Antropología
Inv. no. 10-080380

Serpents in Maya art are ancient and very frequent. A recurrent subject is the head of a deity or of an ancestor emerging from a serpent maw. This sculpture with a tenon formed part of the decoration of the facade of one of the substructures of the Pyramid of the Magician at Uxmal. It represents a serpent from whose open jaws emerges the head of a young man with realistic features. It is possible that it represents a ruler from Uxmal, or perhaps it shows the young maize god. If we consider that the serpent was associated with the earth, it is not difficult to imagine that, just as the corn plant sprouts from the earth, the head of the deity emerges from the open jaws of the serpent. ACM

63

64
Figure in a throne
Late Classic period
Western Campeche, Mexico
Ceramic
Height: 21.0 cm
width: 12.0 cm
thickness: 5.0 cm
Dzibilchaltún
Museo del Pueblo Maya
Inv. no. 10-006276

The government of Maya cities was in the hands of a small group of interrelated individuals who composed a lineage. This ruling

64

family boasted of having links with the gods and supernatural beings, there by maintaining political, economic, and religious control of the community. As a demonstration of their power, they inhabited masonry constructions erected on platforms, sat on stone thrones decorated with cloth and jaguar pelts, and dressed luxuriously, in accord with their elevated status. Maya palaces and temples of the Classic period were typically roofed with a false arch. The exterior was embellished with paintings and symbolic motifs; the upper part displayed human and animal figures that expressed the close relation between rulers and the omnipresent deities. ABC

65

65
Brick with the Image of a Temple
Terminal Classic period
Comalcalco, Tabasco, Mexico
Ceramic
Length: 32.3 cm
width: 17.1 cm
thickness: 22.0 cm
Comalcalco
Museo de Sitio de Comalcalco
Inv. no. 10-575759

In order to copy and reproduce the construction patterns of Palenque, the population of the alluvial planes of the Chontalpa region modeled the abundant local clay into brick walls. At Comalcalco, what stands out is the repetition of a certain temple model composed of two parallel rooms and a wide portico; inside is a precinct that has been identified as a sweatbath. Although brick craftsmen were not participants in the activities that took place inside these spaces, they were familiar with their layout. This example shows an internal chamber of a small sanctuary sheltered in a larger construction. It even records the presence of an ostentatious roofcomb on top of the construction, just as those reported in other graffiti. This feature has not been preserved in any of the structures explored, due to deterioration with the passage of time. MJGG

66
Miniature Vessel
Classic period
Dzibilnocac, Campeche, Mexico
Ceramic
Height: 8.0 cm; length: 9.0 cm
width: 5.5 cm
Campeche, Museo Histórico
Fuerte de San Miguel
Baluarte de San Miguel
Inv. no. 10-339283

Miniature vessels were used to hold pigments or liquids, which the Maya used not only to adorn their face and body, but also objects of daily use. These vessels frequently had small handles that made it possible to carry them suspended from a cord. This interesting piece reproduces a masonry construction that displays the fundamental elements of Chenes architecture, including stepped frets in the frieze, emulating the well-cut ashlar decoration covering the facade of this type of construction.   ABC

66

67
Relief
Terminal Classic–Early Postclassic period
Chichén Itzá, Yucatán, Mexico
Stone
Height: 142.0 cm
width: 131.0 cm
depth: 30.0-56.0 cm
Chichén Itzá
Museo de Sitio de Chichén Itzá
Inv. no. 10-569630 0/18

The relief comes from the upper facade of the Osario and represents a dancer, in this case equipped with what seems to be a two-sectioned hand drum like that of Nabalam. This figure also wears the pendants of the *Pahuatunes*, the bearers of the four corners of the universe, as well as a belt element resembling a double cord. The scepter represents an ideal transition between serpent scepters and those of the foot of the god Bolon Dzacab of the Classic Maya, and the fan with the serpent foot carried by the ancestral lineage of the Xiu in one of the first colonial documents in Yucatán. Among what could be grains, fruit, and jewels, which fill the spaces around the figure and feathers, are clear representations of cacao fruit. Cacao also appears among the mythological birds bearing God K faces that cover the upper levels of the Osario (96 in total).   PJS

67

68
Relief
Terminal Classic–Early Postclassic period
Chichén Itzá, Yucatán, Mexico
Stone and originally stucco
Height: 133.0 cm
depth: 30.0-49.0 cm
Chichén Itzá
Museo de Sitio de Chichén Itzá
Inv. no. 10-569632 0/19

In the structure known as the Osario of Chichén Itzá there are abundant iconographic representations of mythical birds with the head of God K, men dressed as birds, and plants and cacao fruit. The planet Venus appears both in its Maya form, as well as in Mexican form. Unifying the facades are feathered serpents and volutes (clouds), covered with jadeite jewelry and plaques, combined with Puuc-style masks and *Pahuatunes*, among other details. The dedication on one of the pilasters marks the date June 3, 894 B.C. Different panels on the upper facade represent men with bird masks, which seem to be captured at the moment of executing a whirling dance. The body is emphasized in high relief, facing forward, wearing a diadem, a tall tiara which goes up in a spiral and ends in merlons, with a flower in the center. His arms, depicted in low relief, are extended rigidly. He holds a scepter with a serpent head in the right hand and in the left, a musical instrument. On both arms hang "wings" showing feathers in movement. Representations of mouthy appendages typical of *Pahuatuns* stand out from the elaborate skirt. The same are visible in the long feathers on both sides of the head-

dress. A noseplug, necklace with disk pendant, cape, and belt complement the effects.   PJS

69
Jaguar Standard Bearer
Early Postclassic period
Chichén Itzá, Yucatán, Mexico
Limestone
Height: 70.0 cm; width: 34.0 cm
length: 37.0 cm
Mexico City
Museo Nacional de Antropología
Inv. no. 10-176140

During the Early Postclassic period, a series of cultural traits appear in the Yucatán peninsula that confirm the presence of foreign groups who left their influence on several manifestations of Maya culture. Among these expressions are certain types of sculptures known as "standard bearers" because part of their body is positioned or adapted to sustain the shaft or handle of a banner. This sculpture represents a realistic jaguar, an animal often mentioned in myths. Feared and admired for its

68

69

strength and beauty, it was represented frequently; here it is shown in a position of repose, displaying its most distinctive characteristics. On its flank it has a projection with a cylindrical perforation, which must have been intended to hold the base of the standard. The sculpture was found in the Sacred Cenote at Chichén Itzá; however, we do not know if it was left as an offering or whether it fell accidentally when the city was abandoned.   ACM

70
Human Head
Terminal Classic–Epiclassic period
Comalcalco, Tabasco, Mexico
Shell plaster

Height: 54.6 cm; width: 33.2 cm
depth: 65.0 cm
Comalcalco
Museo de Sitio de Comalcalco
Inv. no. 10-575779

Responding to the temporality of this sculptural work, at Comalcalco it is possible to find stucco bas-reliefs that recall the artistic style of Palenque, in which the well-proportioned human figure in several scenes is fundamental. Nevertheless, a local style is clearly distinguishable, consisting of images of dignitaries or important persons from society, who could display rich garb, such as the diadem of thirteen plaques and eight beads worn by this figure, or the mustache and fake beard adorning his face, worked in a heavy, three-dimensional sculpture sustained by a brick core. This type of sculpture was attached to the outer walls of buildings and sometimes to the interior or precincts as part of the vault. The human figure, which came alive when eyes and paint were applied, was associated with

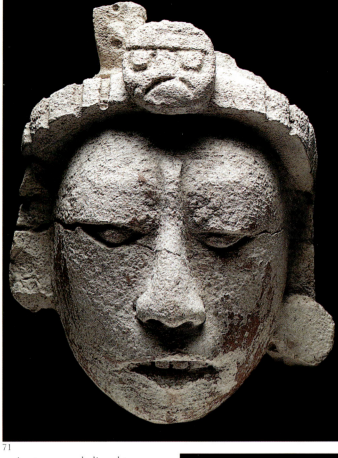

71

representations of deities, Kinich Ahau, Chaac, or God K, and two specific species of animals: crocodiles and aquatic birds, such as ducks and pelicans. MJGG

70

71
Human Head
Late Classic period
Provenance unknown
Stucco
Height: 27.5 cm; width: 21.5 cm
thickness: 17.0 cm
Mexico City
Museo Nacional de Antropología
Inv. no. 10-223509

In Maya art, figures of human beings in stone as well as in painting

or in stucco are believed to represent royal figures, perhaps rulers or members of the nobility, rather than idealized, anonymous men. These three-dimensional heads correspond to their subject with great fidelity. This piece represents an unknown individual. On his head he wears a narrow diadem decorated with grooves simulating plaques; at the center he wears a disk with the schematic traits of a human face, perhaps a insignia of his social status. Covering the natural surface of the stucco, a fine, polished layer of stucco was applied and painted red. MCG

72
Human Head
Terminal Classic–Epiclassic period
Comalcalco, Tabasco, Mexico
Shell plaster
Height: 24.6 cm; width: 14.2 cm
depth: 22.6 cm
Comalcalco
Museo de Sitio de Comalcalco
Inv. no. 10-575780

As evidence of the naturalistic, three-dimensional style developed at Comalcalco, this figure represents an aged individual with his hair tied in a knot at the back of his intentionally deformed skull. The particularities of this sculpture, with respect to the definition of its features, include the proportion of the face,

zigzag dental mutilation of the central, left incisor, and the presentation in profile of its "projecting" teeth. This is an attempt to portray a specific individual rather than reproduce the ideal of the human figure, which is repeated in graffiti drawn on bricks or on figurines molded in the Classic period. This human head was found in the southeast sector of Temple V and it was worked in oyster shell plaster with a fine whitewash on a nucleus of bricks. MJGG

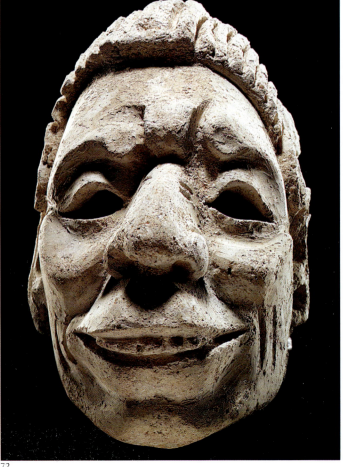

72

73
Human Face
Classic period
Naachtún, Campeche, Mexico
Stucco and paint
Height: 24.0 cm; width: 18.0 cm
thickness: 7.0 cm
Campeche, Museo Histórico
Fuerte de San Miguel
Baluarte de San Miguel
Inv. no. 10-342849

The facades of the most important buildings and roof combs of elevated temples were generally decorated with a large number of hieroglyphic inscriptions and images, both naturalistic as well as fantastic, modeled in stucco. This stucco was made with *sahcab* (a type of limestone sand), lime, and water, elements that combined to produce a mixture with flexibility and hardness similar to that of gesso. The different images were held on cores or stone projections tenoned into the walls. Different colors complemented the work, especially red, which was considered a sacred color because it symbolized the cardinal direction whence the sun is reborn every day. Strabismus, here emphasized by black lines, was a trait of physical beauty for the Maya.   ABC

74
Standard Bearer
Terminal Classic–Early Postclassic period
Chichén Itzá, Yucatán, Mexico
Limestone
Height: 94.0 cm
depth: approximately 62.0 cm
Merida, Museo Regional de Yucatán
"Palacio Cantón"
Inv. no. 10-290459

This stone sculpture was found in the Venus Platform on the Great Plaza of the Castillo at Chichén Itzá. Of considerable dimensions, the figure is seated with legs drawn up and elbows resting on the knees. Noteworthy is the strange twisted position of the right foot and the proportion of the lower part of the body, which give the figure a deformed look. The sculpture emanates movement, unlike the rigidity conveyed by other pieces from Chichén Itzá. There are traces of the original paint, which allow us to see details of the costume: loincloth, anklets, knotted sandals, and a pendant with the Maya symbol *ik*. Remnants of red bands on the head may indicate a cap or hair. The holes in the clenched hands would have held staffs or poles.   LFS

75a-b
Bacabs
Late Classic period
Las Sepulturas, Copán Ruinas
Honduras
Stone

73

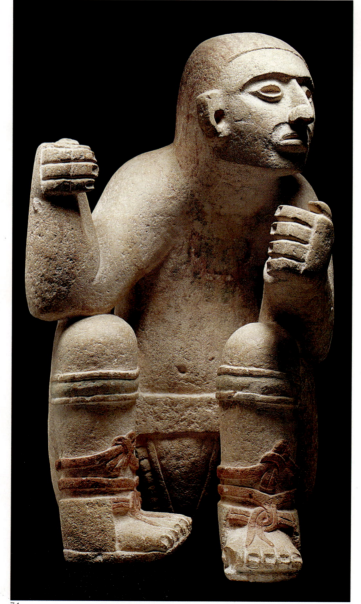

74

75a

75b

Height: 52.0 cm (right)
width: 33.0 cm; depth: 73.00 cm
weight: 263 lbs
Height: 53.5 cm (left)
width 33.0 cm; depth: 75.00 cm
weight: 260 lbs
Copán Ruinas
Museo Regional de Arqueología
Inv. no. CPN-P-4102 (left)
and CPN-P-4101 (right)

According to Maya mythology, *bacabs* lived on the surface of the earth and one of their functions was to uphold the earth. These two *bacabs* are the figures that support the hieroglyphic bench found in the 1980s in Structure 82, in the area of the site called Las Sepulturas. It is believed that the man who lived in this complex and used this bench was a direct relative of the last king. Within the world of Maya cosmology, it has been interpreted that benches are symbols of the validation of a king or of a very close relative.   CJF

76
Human Head
Late Classic period
Palenque, Chiapas, Mexico
Stucco
Height: 40.0 cm; width: 16.4 cm
Palenque, Museo de Sitio
"Alberto Ruz Lhuillier"
Inv. no. 10-458670

Rulers commissioned their portraits both in stone as well as in stucco, perhaps in order to eternally preserve their memory. This

76

77

78

modeled head has been identified as Kan Balam II (Jaguar Serpent II), who acceded to the throne of Palenque in the year A.D. 684 and who is attributed with the construction of the Temples of the Sun, the Cross, and the Foliated Cross, as well as part of the Palace. Clearly this ruler combined a teleological vision with that of the statesman, and it was during his government when the city achieved its greatest influence and splendor. AGC

77
Anthropomorphic Mask
Late Classic period
Temple 22, Acropolis
Copán Ruinas
Honduras
Stone
Height: 64.5 cm
width: 56.0 cm
thickness: 28.0 cm
Copán, Centro Regional
de Investigaciones Arqueológicas
Inv. no. CPN-P-244

Temple 22 had a roof crest as did many carved temples of the Acropolis. This human head with an elaborate headdress once adorned the roof crest of this majestic temple. His large jadeite earspools are surmounted by serpent wings, and the zoomorphic headdress mask sup-

ports a crown with maize iconography. Such masks were joined with a larger-than-life body. Eight of these identical figures sat on cushions, holding lancets like guardians of the sacred mountain that the temple represents. WT

78
Sun God Sculpture
Late Classic period
El Cementerio
Copán Ruinas, Honduras
Stone
Height: 52.0 cm
width: 64.0 cm
Copán Ruinas, Centro Regional
de Investigaciones Arqueológicas
Inv. no. CPN-P-24583

This sculpture represents one of ten robust supernaturals that were carved into the facade of Structure 29, a royal shrine just south of the Acropolis. Only five of the ten are known today, but the solar cartouches they carried upon their shoulders are complete. The head is hairless and the forehead deeply furrowed with a large bead. The figure is related to other solar deities with a mixture of simian and human features. In Maya hieroglyphic texts of the Classic period, the sign for one day, or "one sun," is sometimes rendered as a howler monkey. WF

70

79
Bat Sculpture
Late Classic period
Copán Valley, Honduras
Stone
Height: 58.0 cm
Copán
Museo Regional de Arqueología
Inv. no. CPN-P-4103

This stone sculpture carved to represent a bat was found in the 1930s and is believed to have come from Structure 20 in front of the Acropo-

lis. It has been associated with the underworld and death. Bats were highly venerated animals at Copán and throughout the Maya area. It is for this reason that in the *Popol Vuh* there is a story of the Hero Twins passing a test in which they had to spend a night in the temple of the bats. Throughout Copán, bat heads, which are the emblem glyph of the site, are represented on altars, stelae, and various structures. CJF

80

81

82

80
Atlantean Figure
Early Postclassic period
Chichén Itzá, Yucatán, Mexico
Limestone
Height: 87.0 cm;
width: 49.0 cm
thickness: 29.0 cm
Mexico City
Museo Nacional de Antropología
Inv. no. 10-009795

Supporting figures, together with
standard bearers and sculptures of
semi-reclining figures, called *Chac
Mool*, form part of a series of non-
Maya cultural traits that appear in
Yucatán during the Early Postclassic period. The majority of supporting figures, also referred to as atlantean figures, that have been
found at Chichén Itzá are fundamentally the same, except for certain variations in costume and
adornments. None of them bears
weapons, which is one of the differences with those from Tula, where a
good number of them carry some
type of weapon, which has lead to
their general identification as warriors. This supporting figure is different from others, not only those
from Tula, but also those from
Chichén Itzá itself, due to the fact
that the pectoral displays the image
of a dog attached to a necklace by
several strands. The fact that this
figure uses this type of necklace with
the *xolocozcatl* makes us think that it
represents a "mummy bundle," because the image of the dog on the
necklace was one of the emblems of
the dead warrior among ancient
central Mexicans.   ACM

81
Atlantean Figure
Early Postclassic period
Chichén Itzá, Yucatán, Mexico
Limestone
Height: 86.5 cm; width: 48.5 cm
thickness: 31.0 cm
Mexico City
Museo Nacional de Antropología
Inv. no. 10-080381

During the Late Classic and Early
Postclassic periods, Chichén Itzá
was the most important site in the
Yucatán peninsula. In this sculpture, known as an atlantean figure,
as well as in many other artistic representations from this site, is the
combination of elements from two
cultural traditions: the Mayas and
the Toltecs. It is one of fifteen anthropomorphic support figures
that sustained a bench in the Temple of the Jaguars. These representations have been interpreted as *ba-
caboob (bacabs)*, whose mission was
to keep the skies separated from
the earth.   MCG

82
Atlantean Figure
Early Postclassic period
Chichén Itzá, Yucatán, Mexico
Limestone
Height: 91.5 cm; width: 48.0 cm
thickness: 31.0 cm
Mexico City
Museo Nacional de Antropología
Inv. no. 10-081267

"Atlantean figure" refers to a certain
type of anthropomorphic sculpture
whose main characteristic is that the
arms are extended upward in a pose
of sustaining something; they may
be represented three-dimensionally,
in the form of large columns supporting roofs or lintels, and when
they are smaller, they are tenoned into friezes, decorate temples, or hold
up tables or altars and benches. This
supporting figure is standing on a
smooth, rectangular base; his arms
are extended upward with the
hands not indicated, next to the
head, to form a flat surface. It is believed that it was used as one of the
supports of a table or altar.   ACM

83
Atlantean Figure
Early Postclassic period
Chichén Itzá, Yucatán, Mexico
Limestone
Height: 87.2 cm; width: 50.0 cm
thickness: 32.0 cm
Mexico City
Museo Nacional de Antropología
Inv. no. 10-046608

There are several examples of this
type of anthropomorphic sculpture
with Toltec influence representing a
standing figure with raised arms.
They receive the generic name of atlantes or atlantean figures and they
were used as supports for altars or
slabs integrated into the architecture. For this reason, they terminate
in a flat, smooth surface on the upper part. This figure wears a headdress in the form of a band topped
by three points in the front and
feathers in the back. The nose is
broken, but it may be seen that it
was adorned with a small disk on
each side. He wears large disk-
shaped ear ornaments with small anthropomorphic heads in the center
and he has bracelets composed of
three rows of beads. He wears a
short sleeveless jacket, probably
made of cotton, decorated with
feathers on the edges. On his chest
he wears an enormous pectoral representing a butterfly, similar to those
worn by the atlantes at Tula, Hidalgo, Mexico.   EGL

84
Atlantean Figure
Early Postclassic period
Chichén Itzá, Yucatán, Mexico
Limestone
Height: 87.5 cm; width: 49.5 cm
thickness: 31.0 cm
Mexico City
Museo Nacional de Antropología
Inv. no. 10-041560

The culture of Chichén Itzá shows
great similarities of certain elements
with those of Tula, which expresses
the relations that existed between
these two important centers. One
similarity is in the type of sculptures
known as atlantean figures, which
are characterized by their human
form on a rectangular base of the
same stone. The form's arms are extended upward to the sides, to the
height of the head, forming a flat
surface to support something. This
sculpture comes from the Temple of
the Warriors. It displays a cylindrical headdress with a double forehead band decorated with small
squares, from which rises a feather
crest that falls to cover the entire

83

84

85

back. He wears a nose ornament in the shape of a half moon that covers part of the mouth, while large circular earplugs are decorated with four symmetrically placed flowers. He wears bracelets, a rectangular pectoral, and a hipcloth also decorated with small squares, and there are decorations on his knees and sandals. POC

85
Atlantean Figure
Early Postclassic period
Chichén Itzá, Yucatán, Mexico
Limestone
Height: 86.0 cm; width: 49.5 cm
thickness: 33.0 cm
Mexico City
Museo Nacional de Antropología
Inv. no. 10-001269

Not all atlantes are dressed in the same way, indicating that they could be "portraits in stone" of specific individuals. This figure, which comes from the Temple of the Jaguars, shows traces of red paint. It displays a headdress composed of a wide band; next to the ears is an extension of the headdress, perhaps to se-

cure it to the chin. Although the nose is broken, it may be seen that above the mouth the figure wore a noseplug. Large circular earplugs are decorated with small human faces in the center. At the wrists, bracelets are indicated by five smooth bands. In addition to the characteristic hipcloth or loincloth, he wears a richly embroidered jacket open at the sides; on the lower front is a design based on stepped frets, which generally symbolize water in movement. On the back are several segments with different decorations of volutes and stepped frets; the costume is topped off by a wide necklace formed by six rows of beads. On his thighs and ankles he wears knotted bands in the front that end with fringes; on the outer part of the ankles are disk-shaped decorations. EGL

86
Monument 27 of Toniná
Late Classic period
Toniná, Chiapas, Mexico
Limestone
Length: 96.5 cm
width: 22.0 cm
depth: 5.5 cm
Mexico City
Museo Nacional de Antropología
Inv. no. 10-001258

Bellicose conflicts in the Maya area left physical evidence within sites; such is the case of defensive walls or embankments, as well as information contained in epigraphic texts that appear as the principal motif in innumerable artworks. At Toniná many sculptural monuments represent captives as the central theme. The exceptional quality of this sculpture lies in the way the artist exploited the limits of the stone, intended to serve as a step, to show the figure

87

88

86

in a posture that in itself refers to his condition as captive, perhaps a defeated lord. Other elements allude to the same situation, such as the arms tied behind the figure's back, the use of flexible ear ornaments, possibly made of cloth, and on the neck a cord from which hangs a kind of necktie. The glyphs on the thigh record the name of the captive, while that of the ruler of Toniná, Kinich Baknal Chak, is mentioned in another part of the text.   MCG

86bis
Prisoner
Late Classic
Toniná, Chiapas, Mexico
Limestone
Height: 57 cm
width: 46 cm
thickness: 9 cm
Bodega, Toniná, Chiapas, Mexico

Located in the southwestern zone of the Maya area, a region drained by the Jataté river basin and its tributaries, the city of Toniná expanded its control over vast territories. The feats of its rulers allowed them to dominate sites as far away as those in the Lakanjá and Usumacinta river basins. The images of prisoners captured in these bellicose acts abound in the sculptural inventory of this important city. In this monument we can see an individual whose apprehension must have been of great significance, because there are at least three sculptures with his image. As

is frequent in representations of prisoners, this figure displays cloth ear ornaments and his arms are tied behind his back. On his thigh, an inscription identifies him as Yax Ak "Lord of Anaité," an archaeological zone located on the banks of the Usumacinta, down-river from Yaxchilán.   TPS

87
Polychrome Cylinder Vessel
Late Classic period
Chamá area, Quiché, Guatemala
Ceramic
Height: 16.7 cm
width: 13.7 cm
diameter: 13.7 cm
depth: 16.0 cm
Guatemala, Museo Popol Vuh
Universidad Francisco Marroquín
Inv. no. MPV 0643

This yellowish-white cylindrical vessel, painted red, black, orange and white on a cream-colored base has a red band under the interior rim. On the exterior, there are two richly dressed warriors, painted black and in opposing positions. Both are standing in profile, each one with the left arm on a spear decorated with red feathers. The costume consists of a red loincloth with ribbons, a red fan behind the hip, a red scarf covering the shoulders, and a headdress with short feathers. Wristlets, anklets, and white earplugs adorn the figure. The warriors are separated by two series of four pseudoglyphs.   MS

86bis

88
Painted Vase
Late Classic period
Guatemala
Polychrome pottery
Eigth: 18.5 cm
diameter: 16.8 cm
Washington D.C.
Dumbarton Oaks
Research Library Collections
Inv. no. B-594 MAP

This slightly flaring, cylindrical vase is painted with a scene of fourteen figures preparing for a Maya scaffold sacrifice. At the far left end of the procession are three musicians. In front of the musicians stand four figures with skin skirts, large pectorals, long frontal rattles or banners, conical feathered or animal headdresses, and weapons. Directly in front of the scaffold are two smaller figures, painted white; the first figure stands in front of the scaffold. Within the first level of the scaffold, on the left, sits a dark, skirted profile figure. On the second level, on the right, stands an elaborately garbed frontal figure who balances a vessel in his left hand and holds his right hand to the scaffolding above the victim. The victim on the top has been tied to the poles to stand on all fours, and he wears a white loincloth and cloth ornaments. Finally, two musicians playing huge bottle gourds face the scaffold at the right side; extra bottle gourds indicate more musicians performing "off-stage."

89
Cylindrical Vessel
Late Classic period
Provenance unknown
Ceramic

89

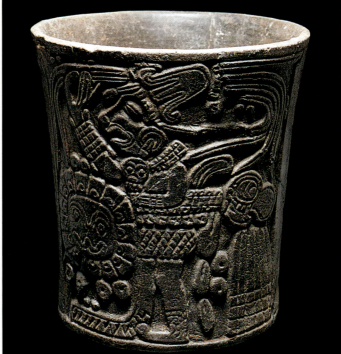

90

91

Height: 16.5 cm
diameter: 13.7 cm
Mexico City
Museo Nacional de Antropología
Inv. no. 10-077413

Frequent decorative motifs in Classic period ceramics are scenes with anthropomorphic figures and symbolic designs, especially those corresponding to hieroglyphic writing, and these appear together or separately. In this blackish vessel, the incised decoration is divided into two panels of different sizes; in the larger panel is a disproportionate human figure with highly elaborate costume and large feather crests that occupy all the space around the main figure. In the narrower panel there are symbolic designs that recall true glyphs, meaning that they may now lack the same significance as the original glyph and their sole function is of a decorative nature; the preceding is not unusual because there are already examples of such imitative motifs.   ACM

90
Vessel
Late Classic period
Possibly Multsubín, Yucatán
Mexico
Ceramic
Height: 16.3 cm
diameter: 15.0 cm
Merida, Museo Regional
de Antropología de Yucatán
"Palacio Cantón"
Inv. no. 10-569276

Vessel with flat bottom and flaring, curved walls. It bears the impression of a standing figure wearing a short skirt, a tubular bead necklace adorned in the front with a large beads with the features of a human face. The headdress resembles the shape of a hat, from which feathers emerge from the upper part. Beside the individual may be seen a circular element, which could be a shield, displaying a central face surrounded by feathers.   APC

91
Cylindrical Vessel
Early Postclassic period
Emiliano Zapata, Tabasco
Mexico
Ceramic
Height: 31.0 cm
diameter: 12.5 cm
Villahermosa
Museo Regional de Antropología
"Carlos Pellicer"
Inv. no. A-0064

A richly dressed figure is represented on this fine orange ceramic vessel. Many of the elements are associated with the Toltec tradition, such as the headdress that seems to end in a central mexican year sign. The figure wears a nose-plug and *buccal* mask. Although the body is shown in frontal position, the upper extremities and head are in profile. There is a pectoral or shield on the chest, which seems to be a crudely represented Tlaloc. Surrounding the figure are elements resembling drops of water, and there is an altar in front of him. The figure is framed by two vertical bands painted black, which could signify water. On the inner part of the pedestal there are traces of striations and fingerprints.   RP

92

92
Vessel
Terminal Classic–Postclassic period
Izamal, Yucatán, Mexico
Ceramic
Height: 23.8 cm
maximum diameter: 15.3 cm
Merida, Museo Regional
de Antropología de Yucatán
"Palacio Cantón"
Inv. no. 10-383156

This fine orange Silhó ware vessel, with straight, sloping walls, has a pedestal base with three vertical perforations and a reinforced rim. Its exterior decoration consists of a standing figure dressed in a strange costume with a cape composed of layered cloths that cover his body down to his ankles. His hands and arms are not visible. In front of the figure is a round shield and a bundle of spears.   APC

93
Polychrome Vessel
Late Classic period
Jaina Island, Campeche, Mexico
Ceramic
Height: 16.5 cm; width: 13.0 cm
Mexico City
Museo Nacional de Antropología
Inv. no. 10-001206

In Maya polychrome ceramics we may distinguish between pictorial styles in which history and cosmogony were expressed, and hieroglyphic texts. On the upper part of this beautiful vase is a band with a repeated design resembling glyphs. As the main motif, there are two human figures painted black and grasping lances. Wearing skirts and feather crests, they could be warriors because, as described by documents and chroniclers, warriors painted their faces and bodies black to appear more fierce. The *Crónica de Tizimin* says that spreading a jaguar pelt in the market was a declaration of war. The army was head-

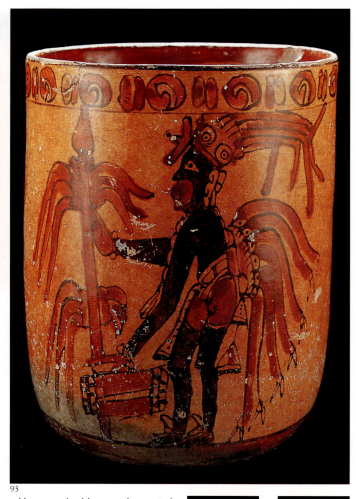

93

ed by a standard-bearer who carried a tall banner; in the middle was the chief (*cacique*) together with two high-ranking nobles in the military: the *nacom* and the *batab*. A great priest on a litter watched over the god Ah Chuy Kak, patron of war; they fought hand-to-hand amidst cries and the sound of drums and conch-shell trumpets. The struggle ended when the *nacom*, who was the military commander and the supreme priest of the army, was dead or captured.   MCM

94
Spear
Late Postclassic period
Chichén Itzá, Yucatán, Mexico
Wood
Length: 100.0 cm
diameter: 4.0 cm
Merida, Museo Regional
de Antropología de Yucatán
"Palacio Cantón"
Inv. no. 10-424802

This rare example of a wooden spear survived because it was preserved in mud and water at the Sacred Cenote at Chichén Itzá. Although its length is considerable, it must have been used with a spearthrower (known as *atlatl* in Nahuatl, and *hulche* in Maya), an artifact used until late periods, when the bow and arrow were introduced

94   95

from the central highlands. There are many images where the use of this weapon may be seen. In Building 2C6 at Kabah, Yucatán, the entrance jambs of Room 21 show warriors fighting each other or at the moment of sacrificing a third figure. In almost all scenes, the spearthrower can be clearly seen in one hand and the spears in the other. In mural paintings depicting bellicose scenes in the Upper Temple of the Jaguars, as drawn by Adela Breton, there are individuals shown using the spearthrower.   APC

95
Spearthrower
Late Postclassic period
Chichén Itzá, Yucatán, Mexico
Wood
Length: 32.7 cm
width: 3.6 cm
Merida, Museo Regional
de Antropología de Yucatán
"Palacio Cantón"
Inv. no. 10-425964

Complementing the spear, is this long object of partially hollowed out wood, the function of which was to considerably augment the force with which the spear could be hurled. In the central highlands, the tool had two lateral perforations where two fingers could be inserted, which also held the spear in place. The absence of such perforations could be compensated, according to Beatriz Repetto, "with a series of thick cords [with which] they could cast it with force and improve the aim."   APC

96
Effigy Vessel
Early Postclassic period
Provenance unknown
Ceramic
Height: 18.5 cm
diameter: 14.5 cm
Mexico City
Museo Nacional de Antropología
Inv. no. 10-081711

A magnificent piece made of plumbate clay, this cylindrical vessel with a ring-shaped base bears an individual with the main attributes of Tlaloc: goggles and a thick upper lip. He is covered with a mantle of feathers transversally covering the body. In his left hand, he carries the symbol for lightning and in the right, he holds a cord from which hangs an object that is difficult to interpret. The representation of the rain god is found in the Maya area, mainly in the zone of Chichén Itzá, on the Temple of the Warriors and on the Platform of the Eagles and Jaguars, where warriors carry staffs of authority and wear ear ornaments characteristic of Chaac (the Maya rain god) or Tlaloc (the Toltec rain deity). Unlike representations rendered by the Maya, images of Tlaloc represented solely with goggles and moustache have been found in these areas, and two slabs with the representation of Chaac have been found at Tula, showing his characteristic hook nose. This distribution supports, together with other observations, the strong relationship between the cultures.   FSM

97
Male Figurine
Late Postclassic
Mayapán, Yucatán, Mexico
Ceramic

96

97

Height: 12.0 cm
width: 7.6 cm
Merida, Museo Regional
de Antropología de Yucatán
"Palacio Cantón"
Inv. no. 10-426104

The figure of a warrior holds a spear and shield and rests on one knee. The body and head are hollow and there is an opening behind the shoulders. The white-slipped figure has a polychrome headdress, earflares, pendants, and necklace; the point of the spear is red, while the shield is orange. APC

98
Statuette
Late Classic period
Jaina Island, Campeche, Mexico
Clay
Height: 29.0 cm

98

Berlin, Museum für Völkerkunde
Jimeno Collection, 1881, SMPK
Inv. no. IV Ca 4938

This freestanding statuette of a warrior is striking for its size and expressiveness and for the luminous blue with which it is painted. The physical posture conveys a sense of dignity and strength. The warrior wears a tunic covered with what are probably strips of leather and adorned with a wide, stiff gorget. The loincloth, which is open at the front, is held up by a belt. The blue color with which the ankle and wrist ornaments, the edge of the loincloth, and the gorget are painted undoubtedly signifies that the warrior is of high rank. The impression of a triumphal attitude is further enhanced by the stern facial expression. In accordance with the Mayan ideal of beauty the man also wears a rubber clip which artificially extends the ridge of the nose. The deformed skull, another feature of this physical ideal, further contributes to this typical figure of a respected warrior of the Classic period in Mayan culture. MG

99
99
Male Figurine
Classic period
Jaina Island, Campeche, Mexico
Ceramic
Height: 12.5 cm; width: 8.6 cm
thickness: 6.0 cm
Campeche, Centro INAH Campeche
Inv. no. 10-339782

In the funerary furnishing of many coastal settlements in Tabasco and Campeche, the presence of human representations of great artistic value is very common. The depiction of a merchant with a fan, shows us one of the ways merchants dressed, with padded garments probably made of cotton and the traditional loincloth. Merchants played a very important role not only in the transportation of objects and products across great distances, but also in the communication of ideas and news. This figurine of an arrogant individual was made from a mold and is hollow so that the piece could be used as a whistle or rattle. These sonorous qualities are frequent in many Maya figurines, which demonstrates an interest in combining musical aspects with mortuary rites. ABC

The social structure

100
Monument 26 of Toniná
Late Classic period
Toniná, Chiapas, Mexico
Limestone
Height: 164.0 m
width: 43.0 cm
thickness: 22.0 cm
Mexico City
Museo Nacional de Antropología
Inv. no. 10-001259

The exact provenance of this piece is unknown, but based on the type of sculpture and its inscriptions, it must be from Toniná. It represents Ruler 2, Balam Ahau, from the Po-o lineage. He wears cloth ear ornaments characteristic of rituals of autosacrifice; in his hands he carries a ceremonial bar with serpent heads on the ends, both with open jaws. On his tall headdress there are three heads, the lower one corresponding to that of a jaguar, the middle one is unclear, and the upper one is of a bird. This type of composition, with several animal or deity heads piled one on top of the other, is very common during the Late Classic period, not only in headdresses, but also in ceramic artifacts such as urns and censers. The interwoven design of a mat, *petate* (pop in Maya), a symbol of nobility, appears in his costume. In the back, on a long cap that falls to the ground, is the inscription, which consists of a double column of glyphs. The date of the erection of the monument is 9.12.0.0.0, which corresponds to July 1 of A.D. 672, 10 *ahau* 8 *yaxkin* in the Calendar Round.   LCGS

101
Female Figurine
Late Classic period
Jaina Island, Campeche, Mexico
Ceramic
Height: 17.5 cm
width: 12.5 cm
thickness: 7.0 cm
Mexico City
Museo Nacional de Antropología
Inv. no. 10-078153

The name Jaina means "Place of the House of Water." The site is famous in art for the discovery of magnificent funerary offerings displaying a great variety of clays, forms, and styles, and constitutes the sole Maya necropolis. In figurines we can see Maya customs of self-beautification such as cranial deformation and facial scarification, which were common practices of deep social and religious value. The Maya also perforated the central part of the nose and the earlobe. They had special appreciation for mutilating the incisors and for inlaying different materials into

100

101

their teeth. Female figurines were modeled to show off clothing and ornaments in accord with their status, in poses appropriate for their gender, such as in this figurine, which represents a mother and her child. Both display cranial deformation achieved with specific apparatuses. It was practiced only on children less than three years of age, and it was the responsibility of midwives and mothers. They both wear earplugs, and the child has a round bead on his chest.   MCM

102
Male Figurine
Classic period
Jaina Island, Campeche, Mexico
Ceramic

102

Height: 22.0 cm
width: 10.5 cm
thickness: 7.5 cm
Campeche, Centro INAH Campeche
Inv. no. 10-342693

Clothing for daily use and corporal beautification occupied an outstanding position in the thought and character of the Pre-Columbian Maya. They liked to dress in style, not only by using facial painting, but also by practicing painful scarification on the face. These modifications of the skin were achieved by way of punctures so that the raised scars were made in a given pattern. Other important elements of personal adornment were jewelry, such as earplugs or necklaces made with pieces of jadeite, shell, or bone. Fi-

nally, there was a great variety of ways of cutting the hair and decorating it with bands, cords, paper, feathers, or other objects.   ABC

103
Figurine
Classic period
Western Campeche, Mexico
Ceramic
Height: 7.5 cm; width: 5.8 cm
Merida, Museo Regional
de Antropología de Yucatán
"Palacio Cantón"
Inv. no. 10-425386

Among the ancient Maya, dwarfs were considered special beings, connected with the "other world" and, by extension, with the gods.

They were members of the courts of important dignitaries, and for this reason it is common to see them richly dressed together with rulers or accompanying elite officials. Dwarfs are also frequently associated with ballplayers and the trade of precious cacao fruit, which in turn links them to possible rituals involving these activities. Besides representation in ceramic figurines and in scenes painted on polychrome vessels, dwarfs appear on several architectural elements of public buildings: lintels, stairways, columns, and a good number of stelae.   ABC

104
Male Figurine
Late Classic period
Jaina Island, Campeche, Mexico
Ceramic
Height: 19.3 cm
maximum width: 11.7 cm
(measured at the extended arm)
Mexico City
Museo Nacional de Antropología
Inv. no. 10-078168

This figurine, made of a fine paste clay, was found in Burial 24 at Jaina. It still shows remains of white, red, and blue paint. It repre-

104

sents a man who has been identified as a speaker. This is probable, given that his pose seems to be that of an individual speaking, reciting, or acting, although what stands out at first sight is the disproportionately large size of his feet in relation to the rest of the figure. He wears a long skirt in back with the end hanging down in front, a band that cinches the waist, and a cap with appliqués that seem to form the head of an animal, possibly of a bird. He wears large earplugs in the form of rings, and on his chest are remains of a pendant. The figure cannot stand by itself and it is highly probable that it had another support, or it originally may have held something in its right arm for this purpose.   LCGS

103

105

105
Male Figurine
Terminal Classic period
Jonuta, Tabasco, Mexico
Ceramic
Height: 17.0 cm; width: 8.0 cm
depth: 5.0 cm
Jonuta
Museo "Omar Huerta Escalante"
Inv. no. MJ-223

Many of the figurines recovered from Jonuta, just as those from other sites, tell us about Maya society. As in the case of this figurine, many refer to individuals of different social levels and reveal a great variety of poses, motifs, and themes. This molded whistle-figurine, representing a person in movement, is dressed with only a loincloth, ornaments below the knees, and a belt crossing the chest area. The arm is flexed, displaying the palm of the hand, similar to many figurines found on the island of Jaina in Campeche. It has traces of red paint and is perhaps the portrait of a warrior.   RP

106
Female Figurine
Classic period
Jaina Island, Campeche, Mexico
Ceramic
Height: 16.0 cm; width: 12.0 cm
thickness: 10.0 cm
Campeche, Centro INAH Campeche
Inv. no. 10-342637

As in many other cultures, the role of women in pre-Hispanic Maya society has not received adequate attention. In addition to her daily work at the heart of the family preparing food, manufacturing textiles, performing housework, carrying wood and water, caring for the domestic sanctuary, overseeing minor crops (condiments, ornamental and medicinal plants), and overseeing domestic animals (bees, birds, and dogs) for household consumption, the Maya woman was a companion, wife, and mother. Occasionally women also filled high ranking positions in public office. Here she is represented with the features of an old woman, possibly evoking the mythical grandmother who raised a son with portentous powers (according to the Yucatec Maya), or the able twins mentioned in the *Popol Vuh* of the Quiche Maya.   ABC

107
Female Figurine
Late Classic period
Xelhá, Quintana Roo, Mexico
Ceramic
Height: 16.6 cm; width: 6.8 cm
thickness: 4.0 cm
Cancún
Museo Arqueológico de Cancún
Inv. no. 10-229042

The anthropomorphic figure of the type known as Jaina, shows a woman of high social rank. Independent of its use as an ornamental or ceremonial object, the piece also had a utilitarian function as a whistle. Its creator had the ability, using different colors, to capture the varied costume elements of the individual with great realism including a long tunic with sleeves, made of a dark cloth decorated with circles of a lighter color (possibly alluding to a feline skin). On the chest and as a trimming on the front opening of the garment, the artist simulated another textile. Under the tunic is a short red *enagua* (skirt) with blue bands. Jaguar skin was imitated to represent what must have been sandals. The ornamentation is complemented by circular earplugs and bracelets, which must have been jadeite, based on the blue color of these areas.   ECTA

108
Female figurine
Late Classic period
Jaina Island, Campeche, Mexico

106

108

107

Ceramic
Height: 16.3 cm; width: 9.0 cm
Mexico City
Museo Nacional de Antropología
Inv. no. 10-006139

Among the most valued and admired ceramic objects of the Maya culture, what stand out are the small figurines modeled in what we call Jaina style. These are remarkable for their beauty and the fidelity with which they portray individuals of all levels of society, all ages and physical conditions. The world around them was a source of inspiration for Maya clay sculptors, as we see in this figurine, which shows an old woman, her face furrowed with angular wrinkles and giving us a blank stare. Her costume includes a smooth skirt which allows us to see her sagging breasts. She wears simple ear ornaments and her hair arranged into a twist. The old woman raises her arm and tucks her fingers into her toothless mouth.   ACM

109
Ocarina
Late Classic period
Guatemalan highlands
Ceramic
Height: 14.0 cm; width: 8.5 cm
length: 12.0 cm
thickness: 7.0 cm
Guatemala, Museo Popol Vuh
Universidad Francisco Marroquín
Inv. no. MPV 0389

The figurine ocarina with three apertures represents an old woman seated with her legs extended out in front of her, where a baby lies face up. The woman has a wrinkled face apparently with scarification on the cheeks and around her mouth. She wears a necklace of circular beads, earplugs, and a dress that covers her breasts down to her ankles. The child clearly displays the cranial deformation practiced on newborns. A wooden board or stick is visible on the forehead, tied with two cords at the sides. The figurine has traces of red and blue paint.   MS

109

110
Statuette of a sitting woman
Late Classical period
Clay
Height: 18.0 cm
Berlin, Museum für Völkerkunde
Jimeno Collection, 1881, SMPK
Inv. no. IV Ca 4969

This figurine represents a noble lady seated in a dignified pose with her legs crossed and her hands on her knees. Her dress is the typical costume of Maya women: a shoulderless mantle, the *huipil*, on which traces of blue paint have been preserved, and a knee-length skirt. She is adorned with wide wristbands, a necklace of large pearls, and big ear-rings. Ornaments of this kind, made of jadeite, have been found in many archaeological excavations of Maya graves. The deformed skull is emphasized by an artistically stepped hairstyle with a part in the middle; it reflects the ideal of physical beauty in Maya society. The statuette is actually a cunningly disguised flute; the mouthpiece is on the right shoulder. Specially shaped musical instruments like this one were presumably used in religious ceremonies. MG

110

111
Male Figurine
Late Classic period
Jaina Island, Campeche, Mexico
Ceramic
Height: 22.0 cm; width: 11.0 cm
Mexico City
Museo Nacional de Antropología
Inv. no. 10-078156

This figurine is made with a fine clay paste, beige clay, with remains of orange paint on the body as if it were painted, while yellow and blue are seen on the clothing and headdress. He displays scarification on the chin and an apparent moustache on the upper lip, which could also be scarification. Both the body paint and scarification were forms of beautification practiced by the Maya. He wears a hipcloth, the dotted band of which indicates a fine weave of great quality. His headdress, in the form of a helmet, has a band attached to the back with a blue tie. The central part of the band displays a bird's

111

head, and to the sides, two circular motifs. He also wears bracelets, earplugs in the form of six-pointed stars, and a necklace of circular beads, all of them rendered in appliqué. LCGS

112
Figurine
Late Classic period
Tiquisate area, Guatemala
Ceramic
Height: 16.0 cm
width: 9.0 cm
thickness: 8.0 cm
Guatemala, Museo Popol Vuh
Universidad Francisco Marroquín
Inv. no. MPV 0300

This hollow figurine represents a women in a seated position with crossed legs. The surface has a well-polished slip. She has hair parted down the middle and two braids, one going behind her and the other forward, with a headband beneath the hair. Her eyes are open; her noseplug is large and completely crosses her nose. Her lower lip sticks out, and two incisors are visible. She has ear ornaments in the form of concentric circles. She is dressed with a necklace, bracelets, and a skirt which covers her belly

112

and legs. Her breasts are uncovered and on her shoulders she has circular decorations that perhaps represent scarification. MS

113
Male Figurine
Classic period
Provenance unknown
Ceramic
Height: 18.0 cm; width: 12.7 cm
Mexico City
Museo Nacional de Antropología
Inv. no. 10-076514

113

This male figurine, a faithful portrait of facial features and costume, represents a barefoot warrior who has a tall coiffure that from behind is divided in two. He wears woven cotton armor at the waist, as well as a small cape, and what perhaps represent feathers extend at the waist toward the sides. He wears a beaded necklace and bracelets, and is barefoot, while in his left hand he holds a rectangular shield. The figure displays traces of blue pigment. Many Maya figurines are rattles or whistles-such as this example. Although they would seem to be associated with music and festivities, they were made mainly for funerary purposes. POC

114

115

116

114
Male Figurine
Late Classic period
Jaina Island, Campeche, Mexico
Ceramic
Height: 19.0 cm
Mexico City
Museo Nacional de Antropología
Inv. no. 10-078159

In the Maya area there are tremendous environmental variations, so that natural resources are diversified. From the most ancient times began the exchange of raw materials and products with which the inhabitants of different regions supplemented what was lacking in their surroundings. With time, this simple exchange became a prosperous, organized activity involving individuals of high status. According to historical sources, at the time of the arrival of the Spaniards, merchants had achieved an important rank in the social scale and it is mentioned that at some sites the custom was to make the richest merchant the local

ruler. This figurine shows us a prosperous merchant, judging by the fan that he holds (a symbol of merchants among the Aztecs and Mayas) and by his costume and adornments.   ACM

115
Male Figurine
Classic period
Jaina Island, Campeche, Mexico
Ceramic
Height: 25.0 cm
width: 9.0 cm
Campeche, Museo Histórico
Fuerte de San Miguel
Baluarte de San Miguel
Inv. no. 10-290659

Clothing for men among the ancient Maya always covered the waist and genitals. Sometimes capes or other garments, necklaces, or pectorals were used on the torso depending on the status of the individual or the occasion or event to be celebrated. Canons of beauty in-

cluded intentional deformation of the skull, a practice conducted during the first months of life, as well as strabismus, scarification, and facial painting. Teeth could also be embellished by filing or by inlaying hard stones. Although the traditional Maya profile displays a broad-based, aquiline nose, the representation of noses with an extended bridge at the forehead is only an artistic convention. There is no osteological evidence of such deformation, nor have archaeological elements been found to indicate the presence of attachments.   ABC

116
Male Figurine
Late Classic period
Jaina Island, Campeche, Mexico
Ceramic
Height: 24.5 cm
width: 9.5 cm
Mexico City
Museo Nacional de Antropología
Inv. no. 10-078161

Among the great variety of objects that the Mayas deposited as offerings to the dead buried on the island of Jaina, modeled clay figurines have come to be considered true documents allowing us to know more about many aspects of this people: their physical characteristics, customs such as cranial deformation and scarification, as well as clothing or specialized costumes of certain professions, or worn by different social classes. An entire world of information is derived from the study of these delicate objects. This example is another display of the rich, elaborate costume worn by important individuals, members of nobles families who held power.   ACM

117
Male Figurine
Late Classic period
Simojovel, Chiapas, Mexico
Ceramic
Height: 30.0 cm
width: 13.0 cm

Mexico City
Museo Nacional de Antropología
Inv. no. 10-002701

In figurines, we may appreciate the physical traits that characterized the ancient Mayas, including the epicanthic fold that makes their eyes seem Asian in cast, the aquiline nose, the high cheek bones, and the straight hair. By way of these pieces, we gain knowledge of the cultural practices applied to the human body, including cranial deformation with boards tied frontally-occipitally, that is at the forehead and back of the head, to obtain a shape elongated toward the back; the custom of perforating the septum of the nose and the earlobes; the mutilation and encrustation of teeth; and the scarification of the face with designs perhaps related to rank. This male figurine, which is shown sitting on his haunches, displays cranial deformation and scarification in the form of lines emerging from the corners of his lips with dots, features that some researchers consider indicators of an important place in society. He wears a great tunic, elaborate bands as a headdress, and a series of cords on his left arm.   POC

118
Male Figurine
Late Classic period
Jaina Island, Campeche, Mexico
Ceramic

118

117

Height: 27.4 cm; width: 11.0 cm
depth: 6.5 cm
Mexico City
Museo Nacional de Antropología
Inv. no. 10-001215

Images of people represented by the ancient Maya are faithful testimonies to the wealth and variety of costume and ornaments that they wore. This appreciation does not refer solely to the diversity of materials utilized in the creation of garments, but also to the wide repertoire of models. An example of this is this Jaina-type figurine, which shows us fairly exclusive accoutrements, beginning with the head, covered with an original headdress in the form of a hat with double wings, and ending with a type of jacket or overcoat worn by the figure. Although the left arm no longer exists, the right is in a pose of holding an object that was also destroyed, although a trace of it remains on the lower part of the coat, which also covers the hipcloth that he must have worn.   ACM

119
Female Figurine
Late Classic period
Jaina Island, Campeche, Mexico
Ceramic
Height: 21.2 cm; width: 10.0 cm
Mexico City
Museo Nacional de Antropología
Inv. no. 10-078160

One of the characteristics that have made famous the figurines deposited as offerings in burials at Jaina is the painstaking care with which the Mayas rendered all details in their creation. There is no doubt that this piece represents a lady of high rank, dressed with an elaborate, wide *huipil* and a fan in her right hand. Her half-open mouth allows us to see that her central upper teeth are artificially deformed; she wears earplugs and a necklace of tubular beads with two pendants.   ACM

120
Female Figurine
Late Classic period
Jaina Island, Campeche, Mexico
Ceramic
Height: 21.2 cm; width: 10.0 cm
Mexico City
Museo Nacional de Antropología
Inv. no. 10-078656

A high percentage of the figurines found at Jaina are musical instruments, which suggests that in addition to their function as funerary offerings, they must have played an important role in ceremonial activities. This figurine represents the image of a woman of lineage, richly dressed and with elaborate facial decoration; she wears a long, wide *huipil* that falls to her feet. On her waist is a rectangular object decorat-

119

120

ed with serpent heads in profile, while her right hand holds a spindle for weaving. Scarification may be seen around her mouth, delineating her lips, as well as on the tip of her chin, and a protuberance is on her forehead. There are still remains of red, white, and blue paint. The mouthpiece of the whistle is on the bottom right.   ACM

121
Female Figurine
Late Classic period
Jaina Island, Campeche, Mexico
Ceramic
Height: 21.4 cm
width: 10.0 cm
Mexico City
Museo Nacional de Antropología
Inv. no. 10-222372

Through new studies and discoveries, the role of Maya women is now recognized to the degree that it is possible to say that the legitimacy of some rulers could have derived through the maternal line. Today we know of the power that some women exercised not only in the role of mothers or consorts of the highest civil leaders, but in their own right. On some monuments women have been identified as having exercised the highest power within their community or city. The woman represented here displays what must have been the costume of women of noble birth: a long skirt; a wide *huipil* with a large, open neckline; and a circular fan, which she holds with her right hand. Completing her costume are facial paint and the intentional mutilation of her upper teeth. There are still traces of blue and red paint, both on her body and on her garb.   ACM

122
Female Figurine
Late Classic period
Jaina Island, Campeche, Mexico
Ceramic
Height: 22.6 cm
width: 10.0 cm
Mexico City
Museo Nacional de Antropología
Inv. no. 10-001197

This figure of a woman has a short, straight garment that descends to her ankles, like a long *huipil*, very similar to the dress worn until recently by Lacandons and known as a *cotón*, and the *huipils* worn by some of the few women represented in stelae. Tabular-oblique cranial deformation may be seen, and a marked protuberance on the bridge of her nose, in accord with Maya canons of beauty. She does not wear a headdress, and her hair, cut in the front, is indicated by fine incisions. The piece is made with a paste of brown-orange clay. She wears a beautiful necklace of spherical beads, circular earplugs, and large, thick bracelets; in her hands she holds a large spiral object that seems to be a twisted textile, based on its texture.   LCGS

123
Figurine
Late Classic period
Jaina Island, Campeche

121

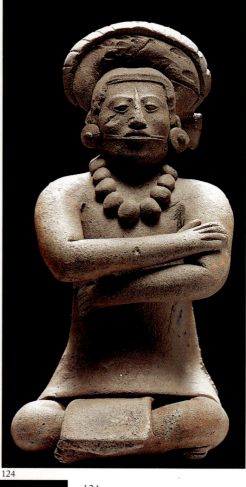

124

122   123

Mexico
Ceramic
Height: 22.0 cm
width: 9.5 cm
Mexico City
Museo Nacional de Antropología
Inv. no. 10-078186

This figurine portrays a great lord or civil leader seated on a round throne; his high status is indicated not only by his elaborate, elegant garb, but also by the dignity conveyed by his overall bearing. On his head he wears a large headdress formed by a serpent maw crowned by long plumes. The figure rests his hands on his knees and in the left hand, he holds a bag for copal. The back part of the body is adorned with a type of aureole, or halo of feathers, similar to those worn by rulers sculpted on stelae, altars, and lintels. These costume details confirm the rank of the individual.   ACM

124
Male Figurine
Classic period
Western Campeche, Mexico
Ceramic
Height: 15.5 cm; width: 7.5 cm
Merida, Museo Regional de Yucatán
"Palacio Cantón"
Inv. no. 10-250989

In contrast to mold-made pieces, hand-modeled figurines exhibit Maya anatomical features, dress, and body adornment with strong realism. The potter creates images of human beings that for all intents and purposes are portraits, which allow for a more accurate assessment of the Maya past. A serious gaze on his face, the man wears a modest beaded necklace, perhaps made of jadeite, that is echoed in his circular earflares. Horizontal scarification on both cheeks intensifies the grave countenance and speaks of his self-sacrifice and concern for enhancing his personal appearance.   ABC

125
Male Figurine
Late Classic period
Possibly the Chixoy Valley
or the Motagua River Valley
Guatemala
Ceramic

125

126

Height: 27.0 cm
width: 9.4 cm
Mexico City
Museo Nacional de Antropología
Inv. no. 10-078652

This bearded man has a pronounced protuberance at the bridge of his nose. He wears disk-shaped ear ornaments, a necklace with what seems to be a mask as a pectoral, and from the position of his hands it is possible that he holds something. For clothing, he wears a sash, called *ex* in Maya. His headdress resembles a turban. On some vessels, there are representations of individuals resembling him. The appearance of this individual is particularly similar to that of the ruler Kan Xib Ahau on a vessel from San Agustín Acasaguastlán, Guatemala; and the individuals on another vessel from the same region, in which Lord Ho Kin Bat and again Kan Xib Ahau appear; it also recalls individuals depicted on the famous Nebaj vessel, and the figure identified as a merchant on the Ratinlinxul vessel from the Chixoy Valley, which could refer to his social status and place of origin. The vessel is made of cream-colored clay, blackened by what seems to be gray clay, while remains of white paint are preserved.   LCGS

126
Male Figurine
Classic period
Western Campeche, Mexico
Ceramic
Height: 15.5 cm; width: 9.8 cm
Merida, Museo Regional
de Antropología de Yucatán
"Palacio Cantón"
Inv. no. 10-425391

Burials at many coastal sites in Campeche and Tabasco were deposited directly in pits dug in the ground. Depth was variable and different treatment was given to the final resting place of the corpse in keeping with the economic status of the family. The body was wrapped in an extended position in cloth or straw matting. This practice was common among many Mesoamerican people and lasted until the second half of the twentieth century in Central Mexico. The tomb of a warrior, as the protective dress of the figure with its avian helmet indicates, could also have included other objects associated with the daily activities of the deceased, such as spears, arrows, a bow, axes, and a shield.   ABC

127
Male Figurine
Classic period
Jaina Island, Campeche, Mexico
Ceramic
Height: 18.0 cm; width: 7.0 cm
thickness: 4.7 cm

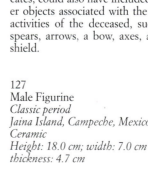

127

Campeche, Museo Histórico
Fuerte de San Miguel
Baluarte de San Miguel
Inv. no. 10-342815

A clear manifestation of political and economic power among the Pre-Hispanic Mayas was access to sumptuary goods, especially those difficult to acquire or those brought from distant regions. Feathers from precious birds, magnificent jadeite-bead necklaces, and shell rattles edging the sober loincloth of this example show the importance of the individual. All these objects were designed with simple tools by specialized craftsmen. Traces of white and blue paint, which added both color and symbolism to the dignitary represented, are still present. Note the great detail on the upper part of the piece, in contrast to the barely delineated feet.   ABC

128
Female Figurine
Late Classic period
Tiquisate area, Guatemala
Ceramic
Height: 19.5 cm; width: 10.0 cm
thickness: 9.0 cm
Guatemala, Museo Popol Vuh
Universidad Francisco Marroquín
Inv. no. MPV 0297

This hollow figurine represents a seated woman with crossed legs and a highly polished slip surface. Her right hand holds a figure that places its hand on the woman's exposed breast. She is adorned with earflares, a noseplug, a necklace, and belt. Her eyes and mouth are open, leaving her two incisors visible. The left arm displays two decorative bands. She has a detailed coiffure, and her hair falls behind her on her back. On top of her hair is an an-

128

129

130

imal-shaped bowl in the form of a bird. She has four circular decorations on her belly, perhaps scarification.   MS

129
Female Figurine
Late Classic period
Lagartero, Chiapas, Mexico
Ceramic
Height: 18.5 cm
width: 8.5 cm
thickness: 6.0 cm
Tuxtla Gutiérrez
Museo Regional de Chiapas
Inv. no. 10-409750

This figurine was found in a huge ceremonial dump at the site of Lagartero. It was associated with large quantities of ceramic material of both domestic and ceremonial types, as well as pendants, animal figurines, and musical instruments. This deposit could contain the remains of ceramics from rituals conducted at the end of a period, ceremonies in which material was destroyed to renew household utensils as well as those of temples. This female figurine is in a seated position with crossed legs. One of its arms is rested on its legs, while the other is bent over the thorax. Details of the clothing are rendered, and on the head there is an elaborate feather headdress decorated with a face.   MCG

130
Female Figurine
Classic period
Western Campeche
Mexico
Ceramic
Height: 14.2 cm
width: 9.0 cm
thickness: 6.0 cm
Merida, Museo Regional
de Antropología
de Yucatán
"Palacio Cantón"
Inv. no. 10-425385

Maya jewelry employed raw materials such as hard stone, different types of shell, bone, horn, and human or animal teeth. Among the most frequently used rocks were jadeite, serpentine, obsidian, quartz, and rock crystal, which were valued for the distance traveled to bring them from their source, the labor invested in their manufacture, and their resistance and permanence. Maya men and women alike decorated themselves with hairstyles, headdresses, ear, nose and lip ornaments, rings, necklaces, bracelets, and pendants. Jadeite was especially prized for its color, symbolic of the center or origin of all that existed in pre-Hispanic mythical thought. Interestingly, the Maya did not distinguish between green and blu, rather they considered them both hues of the same color.   ABC

131

133

Epigraphic reading by Alfonso Arellano
Lady *Nen Te*
Lady Zactun
Xotz, Lord
Is . . . [person]

133
Polychrome Cylindrical Vessel
Late Classic period
El Señor del Petén, Quintana Roo
Mexico
Ceramic
Height: 17.8 cm
diameter: 11.5 cm
Chetumal
Centro INAH *Quintana Roo*
Inv. no. 10-390478

Different vessels made during the Late Classic period display representations of specific historical events, which were usually related to a ritual and acts in which the Maya elite participated. This vessel depicts a palatial scene in which an individual, apparently a prisoner, is being presented to a lord. The act is witnessed by other people, one of them standing with arms crossed and wearing a turban that identifies him as a member of the Classic Maya elite. The artist was concerned with including architectural elements to indicate that the scene took place inside a palace. Thus, we can see the curtains of the room and the bench, complemented by a cushion, on which the lord is seated. He wears the typical costume of an *ahau*, or ruler, including black body paint, headdress, and different jadeite ornaments. In contrast, the man speaking with him has been stripped of his ear ornaments and in their place are strips of paper, a symbol of submission. This object includes a Primary Standard Sequence text, which is comprised of the glyphs in the horizontal band on the upper part of the vessel; in this case, and in many others of the same tradition, it includes the name of the owner and the main activity that is represented on the vessel. It also indicates that it is a vessel used for drinking. AV

131
Human Sculpture
Late Classic period
Palenque, Chiapas, Mexico
Limestone
Height 34.5 cm; width: 24.3 cm
Palenque, Museo de Sitio
"Alberto Ruz Lhuillier"
Inv. no. 10-458700

This sculpture exhibits a form and iconography similar to the ceramic censer holders of superimposed masks from the Cross Group. It includes a glyphic text that begin with the date 8 *chicchan* 13 *zotz*, that in our calendrical system is the equivalent of May 23, A.D. 608. It mentions three enthronements of rulers and a war against Calakmul. The text includes the name of a dignitary called Ah Sikab, whose face was worked as the central motif of the piece. In the lower part is a mask with feline features, in which the characteristic jaguar ear may be seen. The central mask wears a headdress in the form of a feathered drum with two rings in front, insignia associated with the practice of warfare. It was found in Building 1, Group IV at Palenque. AGC

132
Miniature Cylindrical Vessel
Classic period
Tayasal, Petén, Guatemala
Ceramic
Height: 11.2 cm
diameter: 6.0 cm
Guatemala, Museo Nacional
de Arqueología y Etnología
Inv. no. MNAE *9967*

The surface of the miniature vessel is covered with a well-polished cream or buff-colored slip. Surrounding it is a black band right below the rim. Decoration consists of the representation of two women and a man seated in a ceremony. The women are dressed in black tunics and a very simple type of headdress; the man wears a loincloth. Between the man and one of the

132

women is a tripod censer, which suggests that they were conducting a ceremony. Between the women is a vertical band of three glyphs delineated in red that could indicate their names, as was a common practice. MSB

134

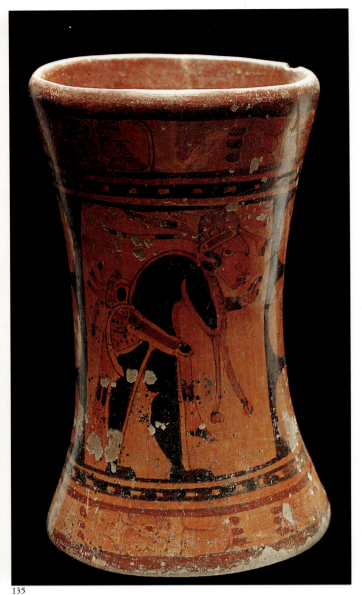

135

134
Polychrome Cylindrical Vessel
Late Classic period
Bonampak, Chiapas, Mexico
Ceramic
Height: 15.2 cm
diameter: 11.0 cm
Mexico City
Museo Nacional de Antropología
Inv. no. 10-342415

The rich Mesoamerican pictorial tradition was captured in Maya polychrome ceramics, where the advanced knowledge and abilities of craftsmen may be seen. The symbolic wealth of the scenes represented on them constitutes an extremely important source of information, mainly with regard to the rituals of the leaders who invested their ideological beliefs in them. This vessel has a repeated scene in which a seated figure communicates some event. Frequently these representations are accompanied by hieroglyphic texts in which the names of the individuals and sometimes the artist are included. 　　　　　　　　MCG

135
Vessel
Late Classic period
Northwestern and central region
of Honduras
Ceramic
Height: 22.8 cm
diameter: 14.0 cm
Guatemala
Museo Popol Vuh
Universidad Francisco Marroquín
Inv. no. MPV 0678

This vessel features converging walls up to the middle of the vessel and diverging walls from the middle to the rim. On the inside it has orange slip and a red band that runs from the inner rim to the outer part. Below the rim and above the base are some decorative bands that consist of the glyphic motif B, common in Copador ceramics, a ware with which this vessel is associated. Below are two panels that consist of human figures separated by two very small panels with square cartouches further divided into four parts, possibly an imitation of the calendrical sign *etznab*. Each figure

has a headdress with feathers and a loincloth tied in the back. The face is painted orange and the body black. 　　　　　　　　　　MS

136
Cylindrical Vessel
Late Classic period
Motagua area, Guatemala
Ceramic
Height: 25.5 cm
diameter: 17.1 cm
Guatemala
Museo Popol Vuh
Universidad Francisco Marroquín
Inv. no. MPV 0662

This cylindrical vessel, with slightly flaring walls and flat bottom, displays remains of red stucco on the interior, near the rim, and on the exterior around the edge and base. There are two decorative panels in relief. The main one shows a seated person in profile, possibly a ruler. As a headdress he wears feathers and the head of God K. From the forehead of the god emerges a maize plant, and possibly some grains or

seeds. The individual is richly dressed. Behind the ruler is a stylized feathered serpent. A plant motif sprouts from his head and beside him is a glyph. The other panel displays three glyphs in vertical position that make up a secondary sequence ending in 7 *kin*. Red specular hematite painting was applied to the reliefs. 　　　　　　　　MS

Epigraphic reading by Alfonso Arellano
Ah . . . yi
Tuc ahau
7 Kints

137
Censer Lid
Late Classic period
Acropolis, Copán Ruinas, Honduras
Ceramic
Height: 61.0 cm; width: 31.0 cm
Copán, Centro Regional
de Investigaciones Arqueológicas
Inv. no. CPN-P-375621

This lid once sat atop a cylindrical base in the offering placed on the

136

137

138

Length: 61.0 cm; width: 31.0 cm
Copán, Museo Regional
de Arqueología
Inv. no. CPN-C-4111

This lid is almost identical to Lid no. 137, the only difference is that the ornaments display variations in form: the earplugs are in the form of flowers and there are fewer beads in the pectoral. They are known as "the Twins." This lid was found with other representations of rulers beneath the Hieroglyphic Stairway.   CJF

south side of the burial chamber of royal tomb XXXVII-4. The pectoral bears a striking resemblance to many of those seen on the ruler portraits on the sides of Altar Q, as does the turban headdress. The turban and the loincloth are painted white; in another case, two figures each have a black turban. The large earflares on this particular figure are identical in form and scale to those worn by the occupant of the tomb.   WF

138
"Ruler" Lid
Late Classic period
Tomb XXXVII, Acropolis, Copán
Honduras
Ceramic

139

141

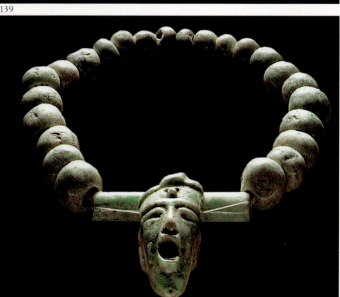

140

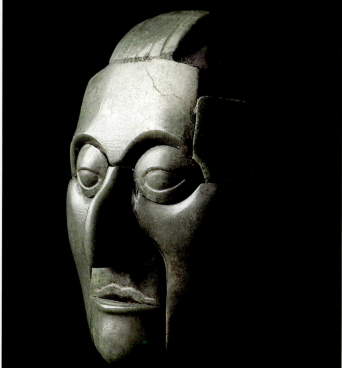

142

139
Strand of Beads
Early Classic period
Dzibanché, Quintana Roo
Mexico
Jadeite
Approximate length: 71.4 cm
Chetumal
Centro INAH Quintana Roo
Inv. no. 10-390947 0/102

Ornamental necklaces made of jadeite or green stone beads are one of the elements most commonly used by the Maya to reinforce the high rank of individuals wearing them. Sometimes these necklaces were accompanied by a plaque or central pectoral and beads that could be strung together in different ways, producing very complex designs. This piece was found as part of the offering corresponding to the tomb of the central chamber of Building 1 of the Kinichná Group.   EN and AV

140
Necklace
Classic period
Provenance unknown
Green stone
Length: 29.0 cm
Mexico City
Museo Nacional de Antropología
Inv. no. 10-000220

In the pre-Hispanic epoch, green stone was widely used to make sumptuary objects destined for the upper classes. So great was its importance and acceptance that, according to historical sources, beads of this material were among the few articles and objects that achieved the status of "money." Among the offerings deposited in tombs, it has been possible to salvage examples of this type. This string is formed by twenty-four spherical beads, one cylindrical one, and a pendant that represents an elongated human face with an expression of astonish-

ment or terror, as seems to be indicated by its exaggerated, open mouth.   ACM

141
Mask with Earflares
Late Classic period
Calakmul, Campeche, Mexico
Jadeite, obsidian, and shell
Length: 18.5 cm; width: 14.8 cm
Campeche, Museo Histórico
Fuerte de San Miguel
Baluarte de San Miguel
Inv. no. 10-566423
earflares: 10-566424 0/2

Funerary mask that accompanied the individual buried in Tomb 1, Structure IID of the archaeological zone of Calakmul. The mask is made of 215 pieces of jadeite, and has a shell noseplug and fangs that give the impression of a deity more than of the face of the person buried in the tomb. Of the urban centers in the central Maya area, Calakmul is

reported to have the greatest number of burials with funerary masks made by the same techniques as this example.   RCV

142
Mask
Late Classic period
Palenque, Chiapas, Mexico
Green stone
Height: 6.0 cm; width: 8.0 cm
Mexico City
Museo Nacional de Antropología
Inv. no. 10-001283

In the Temple of the Inscriptions, thus named for the texts on its walls, located to the south of the great plaza of Palenque, Sun Shield, or Pacal, ordered the construction of what is perhaps the sole funerary monument outside of Egypt that consists of a temple-pyramid with a crypt and sarcophagus. After the death of Pacal, his son Chan

Bahlum finished the construction, buried his father, and sealed the entrance to the tomb, so that the funerary furnishings remained intact. As part of Offering 1, this mask of outstanding beauty was formed by a mosaic of thirteen fragments to represent the face of an elderly man. It was made with pieces of cut jadeite, which display the perfection that the Mayas achieved in working this stone. POC

143
Mask
Classic period
Tikal, Petén, Guatemala
Jadeite and shell
Height: 34.5 cm; width: 25.9 cm
Guatemala, Museo Nacional
de Arqueología y Etnología
Inv. no. MNAE 11082

Life-size funerary mask, made of jadeite, shell, mother of pearl, and pyrite mosaic. It was found in a tomb at Tikal. This type of mask was placed on the face of the deceased. It is believed that it represents of how the individual looked while alive. The headdress is formed of a bird mask with an incised glyph on

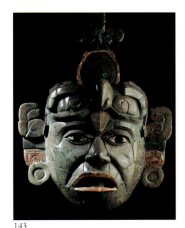

143

145

144

top that was painted red. The circular earplugs are made with a long segment of jadeite and shell. The mouth and eyes are open. The latter are formed of mother of pearl and pyrite inlays. The lips are made of shell. The object can be considered an exotic commodity because its materials were imported from the coast and the highlands. MSB

144
Necklace with Pectoral
Late Classic period
Calakmul, Campeche
Mexico, Jadeite
Width: 116.0 cm; length: 7.0 cm
Campeche, Museo Histórico
Fuerte de San Miguel
Baluarte de San Miguel
Inv. no. 10-290657

Necklace with thirty-six spherical, eight tubular beads and a plaque on which the T-shaped glyph *ik*, signi-

fying "wind" and "vital breath," has been perforated. It was found in Tomb 1 at Calakmul, together with an offering that included a funerary mask made with several jadeite pieces. The tomb pertained to an adult who was dismembered, burned and some of his body parts were ritually consumed. Afterwards, he was wrapped up into a bundle, of which fragments of woven mat have been preserved and several individuals were sacrificed in his honor. LMC

145
Necklace
Early Postclassic period
Chichén Itzá, Yucatán, Mexico
Green stone
Pectoral: Length 10.5 cm
width: 7.3 cm
Merida, Museo Regional de Yucatán
"Palacio Cantón"
Inv. no. 10-425694

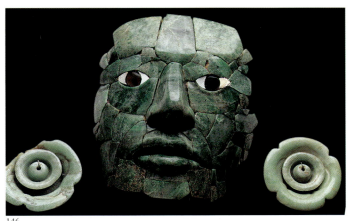

146

147

The central plaque of this necklace, recovered from the Sacred Cenote, is carved on one side with a semicircular line, in the middle of which has been perforated a sign resembling the Greek *tau*. This motif is known among the Maya as *ik* or wind, the name of a day in the calendar. In the widest sense it means life, breath, and, by extension, growth. It is associated with rain gods such as Chac, God B, which may be explained by the close relationship of the wind with the arrival of the rain. It should be recalled that among the Mexicas, it was said that the god Ehecatl blew into the sky to sweep and prepare it for the arrival of the rain. It is highly possible that this pectoral, before being thrown into the *cenote* as an offering, was worn by a priest or ruler. APC

146
Mask with Earflares
Late Classic period
Calakmul, Campeche, Mexico
Jade, obsidian, and mother of pearl
Height: 15.0 cm; length: 13.0 cm
width: 5.0 cm
Campeche, Museo Histórico
Fuerte de San Miguel
Baluarte de San Miguel
Inv. no. 10-290542
earflares 10-290543; 10-290544

An exquisite piece of lapidary work that accompanied the indi-

vidual buried in the mortuary chamber of Structure VII of Calakmul. This life-sized mask, just as others of its type, was fashioned with large pieces of jadeite and with eyes made of obsidian and mother of pearl. One aspect of funerary practices of elite individuals at Calakmul was that the corpse was buried with a mask. The image represented seems to correspond to a portrait of the deceased prior to his demise. RCV

147
Necklace
Classic period
Calakmul, Campeche, Mexico
Jadeite
Length: 33.0 cm
width: 24.0 cm
Campeche, Museo Histórico
Fuerte de San Miguel
Baluarte de San Miguel
Inv. no. 10-342994 0/377

Body ornaments and clothing among the Mayas were extremely diverse, a phenomenon which is illustrated in a wide variety of pieces, among them figurines. Necklaces fashioned of gold, shell, and jadeite, among other materials, were part of the elegant apparel. Jadeite, a highly valued material and the object of trade, was associated with life and fertility due to its green color. It was a symbol of origins and of all that existed. AK

148
Necklace
Terminal Classic–Early Postclassic
period
Chichén Itzá, Yucatán
Mexico
Shell and green stone
Merida
Museo Regional de Yucatán
"Palacio Cantón"
Inv. no. 10-347001 0/814

The conjunction of materials as prized among pre-Hispanic Mesoamerican people as shell and green stone, used together in a single ornament, indicates that its bearer must have been of very high rank. Shell, in addition to its trade value, was used as money in commercial transactions. Similarly, it forms part of the insignia of some supernatural beings, such as the Cosmic Monster, one of the upholders of the sky known as *Pahuatuns*, and of the god Quetzalcoatl himself. On the other hand, green stone, especially jadeite, was highly valued and it

148

150

151

149

symbolized water, among other things.   APC

149
Seashells
Early Postclassic period
Comitán, Chiapas, Mexico
Valve: length: 9.0 cm
width: 9.0 cm
Shell: length: 9.0 cm
width: 8.0 cm
Comitán
Museo Arqueológico de Comitán
Inv. no. 10-588893 0/2

These seashells (*Spondylus*) were part of an offering that included fragments of stingray spines, a pearl, and several jadeite beads. The first of the shells corresponds to a valve, which was deposited inside two juxtaposed vessels. It probably formed part of a necklace or some larger piece, since it has two perforations that could be used for hanging. The second is a complete seashell, composed of two joined valves that were unworked.   GLJ

150
Strand
Early Classic period
Dzibanché, Quintana Roo, Mexico
Shell, pearls
Length of shells
(25 beads): 6.5 cm each
length of pearls
(34 beads): 6.12 cm each
Chetumal
Centro INAH Quintana Roo
Inv. no. 10-390842 0/25
10-390843 0/34

Shells and pearls were widely used by the Mayas for the creation of ornamental objects that complemented the garb of important individuals. At the same time, the shell held an important association with water and continuity of life, although in the other world. Both strands were found as part of the offering of a woman who was deposited in the funerary chamber of Building 1 of Dzibanché. The strand of pearls, and part of the strand of shells, are poorly preserved due to the

fact they were attacked by the corrosion of an object, perhaps made of metal, that was placed over them. The pearls were covered with cinnabar.   EN and AV

151
Necklace
Early Classic period
Calakmul, Campeche
Mexico
Shell
Length: 16.5 cm
Campeche, Museo Histórico
Fuerte de San Miguel
Baluarte de San Miguel
Inv. no. 10-342908 0/34

These small figures in the form of human skulls were made with the tips of *Oliva sayana* shells. The individual features of these small faces were worked using a fine perforator. These figures were part of the central portion of a garment (probably a cape) made of 8,168 small shells, or fragments of them, of different shapes and sizes. This

piece was found in Tomb 1 of Structure III at Calakmul, and a necklace made of shells with the same characteristics was found at Tikal. Representations of skulls alluding to death are an important part of Maya funerary and underworld iconography.   RCV

152
Necklace
Classic period
Tikal, Petén, Guatemala
Shell
Maximum length
of the bead: 2.0 cm
Guatemala, Museo Nacional
de Arqueología y Etnología
Inv. no. MNAE 11528

Necklace composed of twenty-one beads of worked shell cut into skull forms. The use of shell was very common from the Preclassic period. The main artifacts made from shell were ornaments, paint, receptacles and musical instruments. Objects of this type have been found in elite ceremonial and funerary contexts. Shell was widely traded and exchanged, even at sites distant from the coast, because it was considered an exotic commodity and therefore conferred prestige. At Tikal, a site in the lowlands of Guatemala, examples of *Spondylus* shell from both the Pacific and Atlantic Oceans have been found. The shell had mythological importance because often it was associated with God N. In Maya-writing, the shell functioned as a sign of completion and represent red the number 20.   MSB

153
Necklace
Late Postclassic period
Iximche, Chimaltenango
Guatemala
Gold
Length: 27.0 cm
Guatemala
Museo Nacional
de Arqueología y Etnología
Inv. no. MNAE 9097

Necklace of 48 gold beads, composed of ten jaguar heads alternating with 38 small spherical beads. It was found as part of an elite fu-

154

152

nerary offering. Metallurgy was not practiced in Guatemala until the beginning of the Early Post-classic period, perhaps as a result of influence from Mexico and South America. Its use was uncommon and sporadic. As a motif, the jaguar has formed an important part of Mesoamerican belief systems since very early times; together with its respective gods, this animal was associated with the night, caves, and the underworld. Compared with other Mesoamerican groups, the Mayas had a greater number of deities associated with the jaguar; they identified it with the sun; it was represented in art; and its pelt was used on thrones and for the costumes of important individuals.   MSB

154
Pectoral
Late Classic period
Acropolis, Copán, Honduras
Jadeite
Dimensions variable

153

Copán, Museo Regional
de Arqueología
Inv. no. CPN-J-4113 *(main piece)*

Pectoral composed of five pieces: three tubular pieces and two of irregular shape without decoration. Only one has an incision. The elite were accustomed to adorning themselves exclusively with jadeite and they inlaid their teeth with this material. The closest source is the Motagua River in Guatemala, which clearly indicates the ex-

change of raw materials and/or finished objects throughout sites in the Maya area and beyond.   CJF

155

156

157

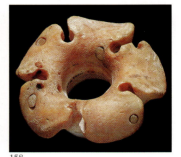

158

155
Earflares
Middle–Late Classic period
Dzibanché, Quintana Roo, Mexico
Jadeite
Height: 5.7 cm; width: 5.3 cm
thickness: 1.8 cm [each]
Chetumal
Centro INAH Quintana Roo
Inv. no. 10-391015 and 10-391016

Jadeite earflares are always a fundamental part of the dress of Maya royal individuals. Their loss and substitution by strips of paper was a symbol of subjugation and defeat, as seen in representations of captives in different monuments of the Classic period. The use of the earflare required that the hole in the ear be gradually enlarged, from infancy, until it could accommodate ear ornaments as large as the ones shown here. This pair of pieces, which possibly had other small pendant ornaments as complements, was part of a funerary mask found in Chamber 3 of Building 2 of Dzibanché.   EN and AV

156
Earflares
Early Classic period
Kinichná Group, Dzibanché
Quintana Roo, Mexico
Jadeite
Height: 5.0 cm; width: 4.8 cm
thickness: 2.3 cm [each]
Covers: diameter: 2.4 cm
thickness: 0.4 mm [each]
Chetumal
Centro INAH Quintana Roo
Inv. no. 10-391014 1/2 and 2/2

The design and complexity of Maya earflares varied depending on the region of their provenance, as well as the importance of the individual for whom they were made. In this case, they include a small cover in the center, which served to hold the piece in the ear. The four small orifices in each piece were for hanging other complementary ornaments, possibly beads of the same material. These early earplugs were associated with the body of a lord who was buried in the main structure of the Kinichná Group.   EN and AV

157
Plaques
Terminal Classic–Early Postclassic
period

159

Chichén Itzá, Yucatán, Mexico
Jadeite
Diameter: 4.5 cm each
Merida, Museo Regional de Yucatán
"Palacio Cantón"
Inv. no. 10-425681 and 10-425652

A large number of jadeite objects recovered from the Sacred Cenote at Chichén Itzá were circular or quadrangular plaques with diameters varying between two to eight centimeters. They have a small perforation in the center, surrounded by one or two concentric circles and four or five petals with a narrow border. Many pieces with this rosette design have been recovered from Late Classic period contexts, although a shell ear ornament from Kaminaljuyú corresponds to the Early Classic period, indicating that it is an older tradition. The flower motif can also be found in sculpture; for example, some figures at Yaxchilán, Calakmul, and

Piedras Negras use the design in their diadems, ear ornaments, or headdresses.   LFS

158
"Trefoil" Earflares
Late Classic period
Copán Valley, Honduras
Shell
Dimensions variable
Copán, Centro Regional
de Investigaciones Arqueológicas
Inv. no. CPN-H-43

These fragile objects were fashioned from *Spondylus* shells to form earflares, the ear accessories preferred by the ancient Maya. Small pieces of jadeite were apparently adhered to the shell flares. Spondylus shell pendants were used by an office-holder in Yucatán at the time of the Spanish conquest. These jadeite earflares of modest size were found complete with the plugs that were

used to stabilize them in the wearer's ear or in more elaborate examples to attach counter-balances on either side of the main assembly. They are finely crafted and polished from high-quality jadeite. They were probably worn by the shaman on important ceremonial occasions during his lifetime, as well as to his grave.   WF

159
Earflares
Late Classic period
Acropolis, Copán, Honduras
Jadeite
Diameter: 5.7-5.6 cm
thickness: 1.7-1.6 cm
weight: 65.8 g
Copán
Museo Regional de Arqueología
Inv. no. CPN-J-4114

Circular, polished jadeite earflares with tube, in an irregular shape

160

161

162

163

angular eyes. His costume is very simple; he wears only a headdress with a tassel projecting forward, and a loincloth (called *ex* in Mayan). Noteworthy is the absence of jewelry such as necklaces or bracelets that might suggest high rank. The back part of the piece is slightly rounded and the details of the anatomy and the dress were not carved on the entire piece.   LFS

163
Bead
Terminal Classic–Early Postclassic period
Chichén Itzá, Yucatán, Mexico
Jadeite
Length: 5.2 cm; diameter: 1.6 cm
Merida, Museo Regional de Yucatán "Palacio Cantón"
Inv. no. 10-424908

This is one of the three beads in the form of a human skull recovered from dredging the Sacred Cenote. These representations are a recurrent theme in sculpted works at Chichén Itzá, as well as in small pieces of different materials. The theme is often associated with sacrifice, as on the *tzompantli*, a structure on which were strung the skulls of decapitated victims. The features on this bead were made by pointed holes representing the eyes and mouth. There are tiny perforations in the septum and the eyebrows, and three more of a biconical type that cross the bead from side to side. The material is jadeite, although not of the best quality, because it is somewhat opaque; it is possible that it could have been subjected to fire at some time.   LFS

simulating a flower. These objects are related to the elite of Copán, possibly in a direct line with the dynasty.   CJF

160
Earflares with Plant Shape
Middle–Late Classic period
Dzibanché, Quintana Roo Mexico
Jadeide
Height: 4.5 cm; width: 4.4 cm thickness: 1.5 cm [each]
Covers: diameter: 2.2 cm thickness: 6 mm [each]
Chetumal
Centro INAH, Quintana Roo
Inv. no. 10-391003 1/4 to 4/4

The symbolic status of ornamental pieces of jadeite worn by members of the Maya elite, especially rulers, depended not only on the quantity and quality of jewelry with which he or she was portrayed or buried, but on the significance the objects themselves implicitly carred. For example, the noble status of the owner of this pair of earflares is reinforced by the floral motif that embellishes them, which surely indicated that he was an *ahau* or ruler. The small pieces accompanying them func-

tioned as covers, and were placed on the back of the ear.   EN and AV

161
Human Pendant
Early Classic period
Kinichná Group, Dzibanché Quintana Roo, Mexico
Jadeide
Height: 6.2 cm; width: 2.5 cm thickness: 1.5 cm
Chetumal
Centro INAH Quintana Roo
Inv. no. 10-390932

Small pendant covered with cinnabar that depicts an individual with flexed legs, hands on the chest, and eyes closed. The nose and mouth are very wide, to the extent that the forehead is broad, probably to accommodate the form of the round pebble that was used as the raw material. It has a number of perforations, perhaps the result of its reuse during different periods. The features of the figure indicate a very early technique, documented at different sites in the Maya area, especially in southern Quintana Roo and northern Belize. This type of pendant was almost always small and was used in combination with other

beads of the same material. Because of the antiquity of these pendants, the Mayas of the Classic period considered them relics and deposited them in funerary offerings, or in important buildings as construction offerings.   EN and AV

162
Human Figurine
Terminal Classic–Early Postclassic period
Chichén Itzá, Yucatán, Mexico
Green stone
Height: 7.0 cm; width: 3.5 cm
Merida, Museo Regional de Yucatán "Palacio Cantón"
Inv. no. 10-425679

This jadeite figurine pertains to a group of pendants that represent dwarves and were recovered in the Sacred Cenote at Chichén Itzá. In general they display a large, rounded belly with exposed navel. Their short legs and the large size of the head in proportion to the rest of their body are evident, the figure holds his arms flexed at his sides, clearly leaving his bulging stomach visible. His jaw is rounded and his facial features are rendered with slightly curved lines, with almost tri-

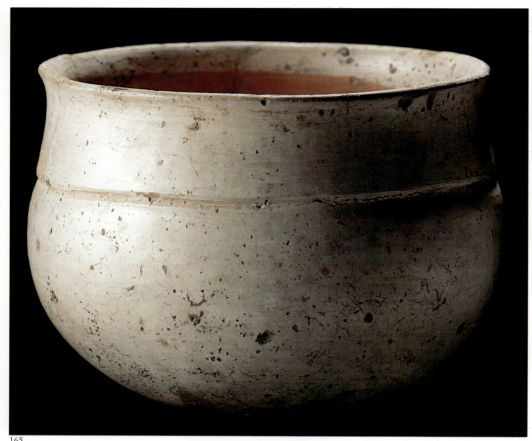

165

166a

166b

166c

on to the orange clay was applied a cream-colored slip. Between the neck and the body there is an incised horizontal line that is the sole decorative element.   POC

164

Jade Heads

Late Preclassic period

Cerros, Corozal District, Belize

Jadeite

35/203-1:54 length: 5.1 cm

width: 2.6 cm; thickness: 1.3 cm

35/203-1:55 length: 4.2 cm

width: 2.5 cm; thickness: 1.2 cm

35/203-1:56 length: 5.7 cm

width: 5.1 cm; thickness: 1.1 cm

35/203-1:52 length: 4.1 cm

width: 2.5 cm; thickness: 1.4 cm

Belmopán, Bodegas

del Departamento de Arqueología

Inv. no. 35/203-1:54, 55, 56, 52

164a

164b

164c

164d

166a-b-c

Three Beads

Early Classic period

Dzibanché, Quintana Roo, Mexico

Jadeite

Height: 2.3 cm; width: 2.0 cm

depth: 9 mm

Chetumal

Centro INAH Quintana Roo

Inv. no. 10-390974 1/2, 2/2

and 10-390973

Breaking the horizontality of the bay of Chetumal, the pyramidal structures of Cerros rise to overlook the blue waters of the Caribbean sea. This site is another one of the early settlements located in northern Belize that in recent years has attracted considerable attention. Its intensive construction activity during the Preclassic period was always accompanied by equally intense ritual activity that is seen in the numerous offerings discovered during its exploration. One of the most important offerings was found among Structures 5C-2 and 6B. It consisted of five small heads made of green stone, which were deposited in the bottom of an urn. Four of them were perhaps attached to a cloth diadem. Small heads and maskettes of this type are common in the Late Preclassic period, although we do not have well-documented contexts that can serve as a basis to explain their true function.   PJS

165

Bowl

Late Classic period

Provenance unknown

probably San Isidro, Chiapas

Mexico

Ceramic

Height: 8.3 cm

diameter: 11.5 cm

Mexico City

Museo Nacional de Antropología

Inv. no. 10-128012

Maya ceramics were used in daily life to cook and serve food, and were made for rituals as well. Such is the case of this simple piece that formed part of the offering from Burial 39 from Mount 20 at San Isidro, Chiapas. This bowl, with curved, converging sides, a flat base, and curved, flaring neck, was identified as the Zuleapa type, which is characterized by its modeling and very fine surface finish;

Three small beads in the form of turtle carapaces. They were covered with a layer of cinnabar, a mineral pigment derived from mercury that was widely used by the Mayas in different ceremonial contexts, especially funerary ones. Two of the beads have small lids on the lower part to cover holes inside them. The Maya traditionally associated turtles with rain and fertility. This animal was seen as a link between the sky and the earth, and it sometimes represented the very surface of the earth. Chaac, the god of rain, and the *bacabs* appear in different representations dressed with a turtle carapace.   EN and AV

Daily life

167
Vessel
Classic period
Jaina Island, Campeche, Mexico
Ceramic
Height: 6.0 cm
width: 9.3 cm
length: 26.3 cm
Campeche, Centro INAH Campeche
Inv. no. 10-342638

Transportation and fishing along the coasts, in rivers, and in other bodies of water were carried out by way of simple but highly practical boats. Among the ancient Maya, the use of large, hollowed-out trunks was common in making vehicles that were not only reported by the first explorers in the Maya world in the sixteenth century, but are also still manufactured today by different communities in Chiapas, Tabasco, and Campeche. The ancient Maya used *ceiba*, cedar, or mahogany trees, among others, to make these vessels. In the Maya cosmovision of the Classic period, canoes were also used by the dead to travel to the underworld accompanied by zoomorphic deities. ABC

168
Polychrome Bowl
Late Classic period
Provenance unknown
probably Campeche, Mexico
Ceramic
Height: 7.5 cm; diameter: 36.8 cm
Merida, Museo Regional de Yucatán "Palacio Cantón"
Inv. no. 10-290413

The curved walls of this bowl flare slightly, displaying an everted rim on the exterior, a somewhat concave bottom, and hollow, hemispherical supports characteristic of the ware known as Cui Naranja Policromo. The painted interior of the vessel shows two hunters with black body paint. Each wears a wide-brimmed hat topped by a large deer head, as well as a necklace, red belt, sandals, and a short skirt layered with palm leaves and/or feathers. Hunters in Maya art are almost always portrayed with a hat and a palm skirt for camouflage. They hold blowguns in their hands with which they are apparently shooting live birds, while dead birds already hang at their hips. It is possible that the two hunters refer to Hunahpu and Xbalanque, the Hero Twins of the Quiche story of the *Popol Vuh*, who are often depicted as hunting birds, one of their favorite pastimes. The placement of the hunters, facing opposite directions, confers a sense of movement to the scene, typical of the painting style of some vessels probably from Campeche. YP

167

169
Polychrome Plate
Late Classic period
Provenance unknown
Ceramic
Height: 10.0 cm; diameter: 31.0 cm
Mexico City
Museo Nacional de Antropología
Inv. no. 10-079006

During the Classic period, the Mayas produced numerous polychrome vessels with scenes recreating mythical passages or activities from daily life. This plate belongs to the latter group, and depicts a deer hunt. The hunters are disguised with the head of the animal, as they try to attract it with a whistle; in the

169

center the hunter carries the catch on his shoulders. This activity appears frequently on vessels and codices, where different types of traps and methods of capture may be seen. It is possible that deer hunting was a ritual activity, rather than a sport or a source of food. ACM

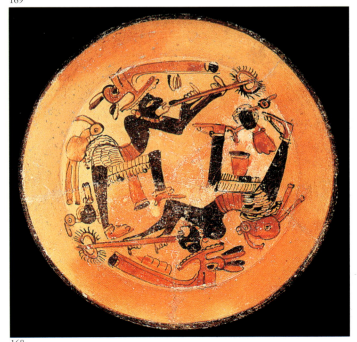

168

170
Male Figurine
Classic period
Alta Verapaz, Guatemala
Ceramic
Height: 23.5 cm
width: 14.5 cm
Guatemala, Museo Nacional
de Arqueología y Etnología
Inv. no. MNAE 5897

Whistle in the shape of a human figure made with a mold. It represents an individual associated with corn. He is standing, perhaps dancing, based on the position of his right foot. He wears circular ear ornaments with a tubular pendant, a pectoral with a human face in the center, bracelets, anklets and a loincloth

170

172

171

tied in the front. With each hand he holds an ear of corn; the right hand is at shoulder level while the left is near his thigh. Maize formed part of the Mayas's, daily sustenance; it was the basic element of their diet. The *Popol Vuh* says that the first human beings were created from yellow and white corn dough. Some Classic period figurines, unlike those of the Preclassic period, are made from a mold. MSB

171
Effigy Vessel
Protoclassic period
Chiapa de Corzo, Chiapas, Mexico
Ceramic
Height: 31.0 cm; width: 34.5 cm
diameter of the base: 14.5 cm
Mexico City
Museo Nacional de Antropología
Inv. no. 10-000134

This vessel was found in Mound 5, which is a residential-type structure composed of different terraces and rooms. It formed part of the most numerous offering found in this building, composed of 212 pieces, many of them imported. This evidence supports the idea that Chiapa de Corzo was the most important site in the central depression of Chiapas; its favorable location next to the Grijalva River permitted communication with different regions.

This piece represents a man carrying a jar on his back while holding the handle spout with his hands, as if it were a staff, or it may be a planting staff. The handle staff is connected with a ring-shaped base on which the figure is standing. MCG

172
Grindstone with mano *and* metate
Terminal Classic–Epiclassic period
Comalcalco, Tabasco, Mexico
Basalt
Dimensions of the metate:
length: 59.9 cm; width: 28.7 cm
thickness: 9.0 cm
Dimensions
of the mano: *length: 45.1 cm*
diameter: 9.3 cm
Comalcalco
Museo de Sitio de Comalcalco
Inv. no. metate: 10-575762
mano: 10-575763

From the pre-Hispanic period to this day, the presence of the *metate*, the grinding stone, and its corresponding *mano*, the long stone grinding tool, is fundamental in the homes of the indigenous population, where the basic staple in their diet continues to be maize. This grain is first cooked in water with lime in order to soften it and release alkalines that permit digestion. Then it is ground on a stone slab to form a soft dough. This dough is

then made into *tamales* (steamed cornmeal cakes nestled in corn or banana leaves), drinks, *tortillas*, and other products. The *metate* has always been a working tool of women, who use it several times a day, from dawn to the end of day to make the last meal; these pieces were found in the south Pit of Temple I of the North Plaza of Comalcalco. MJGG

173
Censer Lid
Classic period
Southern coast, Guatemala
Ceramic
Height: 32.0 cm; diameter: 42.0 cm
Guatemala, Museo Nacional
de Arqueología y Etnología
Inv. no. MNAE 15958

Conical lid with an anthropomorphic figure. The entire lid is covered with elongated applications resembling cacao seeds. The figure is a woman with her torso exposed. Her

hair is cut into bangs, while her eyes and mouth are open. She wears round earplugs with pendants, and a necklace of tubular beads decorated with a pendant in the form of an incised outline resembling a shell. She has circular appliqués around her breasts. Her arm displays appliqués that could also represent cacao. She has wristlets, while her hands flexed at the height of the abotomen support a somewhat deep vessel with two cacao pods on its interior. At the back of her head is a circular perforation to let the smoke escape. The iconography suggests that this censer was used in a ritual context related to cacao. MSB

174
Vessel with Lid
Early Classic period
Copán Ruinas, Honduras
Ceramic
Height: 15.5 cm; base: 11.7 cm
diameter: 12.0 cm
Copán, Centro Regional
de Investigaciones Arqueológicas
Inv. no. CPN-C-156

Cylindrical slab-footed tripod vase, with lid. This vessel has a form that became widely popular throughout Mesoamerica in the Early Classic period, during the heyday of Teotihuacán, where it is ubiquitous. In the case of many vessels in the Maya area, the Teotihuacán vessel form was faithfully copied, but the body and the lid of the vessel, text known as the "Primary Standard se-

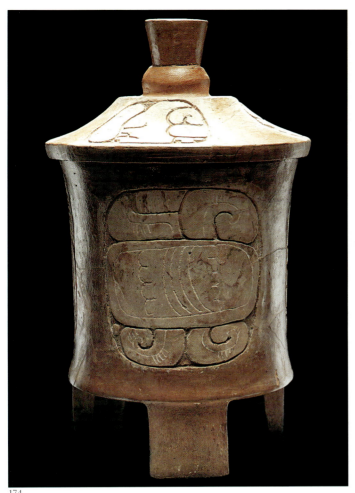

174

176

175

177

178

quence." Decipherment of the longer, more to be "This is the (chocolate) drinking cup of Mr. So-and-so." The owner of this vessel, sadly, is not recorded in its abbreviated inscription. WF

175
Plant Vessel
Late Classic period
Yaxcopoil, Yucatán, Mexico
Ceramic
Height: 9.5 cm; diameter: 16.8 cm
Mérida, Museo Regional de Yucatán
"Palacio Cantón"
Inv. no. 10-489000

This piece is similar to another vessel recovered from Acanceh, Yucatán. Both are typologically identified as a ware known as Policromo Regional, characterized by a lus-

trous, orange slip finish. The example shown here represents the squash *Cucurbita moschata*, popularly known in Mexico as the *calabaza de castilla* or Castilian pumpkin. APC

176
Gourd-shaped Bottle
Preclassic period
Cuencas Cuyamel, Trujillo
Colón, Honduras
Ceramic
Height: 13.5 cm
upper width: 12.0 cm
Tegucigalpa, Bodegas Centrales
del Istituto Hondureño
de Antropología e Historia
Inv. no. TGC-C-745

Monochrome, gourd-shaped vessel, polished on the outside, with a

mouth on the upper part. It is covered with a fine slip, it has grooves made before firing that give it its gourd shape. This piece comes from excavations near caves. The ware type is classified as Higuerito Monochrome of unspecified variety, which has been found in the entire northeast zone of Honduras. CJF

177
Tetrapod Bowl
Early Classic period
From the Usumacinta region, Mexico
Ceramic
Height: 12.5 cm; diameter: 22.0 cm
Villahermosa, Museo Regional
de Antropología "Carlos Pellicer"
Inv. no. A-0601

During the first part of the Early Classic period, vessels supported on four large, hollow feet were common. They are frequently found decorated with motifs fashioned by painting, scratching, incising, and modeling, often all on the same vessel. It is possible to find a combination of all these techniques, as on this excellent piece with a composite silhouette, the form of which resembles a squash, while the supports seem to resemble a wild boar's head. TPS

178
Plant Vessel
Early Preclassic period
San Isidro, Chiapas, Mexico
Ceramic

Height: 14.4 cm; length: 15.8 cm
Mexico City
Museo Nacional de Antropología
Inv. no. 10-128059

Squashes were widely reproduced in the first ceramic forms in Mesoamerica. In the pre-ceramic period, the pericarp of this fruit was used as a receptacle. Depending on the plant species, it could be used as a vessel or as a type of pitcher, the spout of which was plugged with a corncob. In this piece, two species of the gourd family are represented; one gives the shape to the body of the vessel, and the other, popularly called a bottle gourd, integrates the spout. The handle was modeled as a functional element to serve liquid, and was also endowed with a harmony that stylized the form. Once the vessel was highly polished, it acquired the soft, glossy texture of the vegetable itself. The squash is a symbol of abundance and regeneration; it evokes, because of its multiple seeds, the process of gestation and the womb, the place where life is produced. MCM

179

180

182

with fine lines incised on the body of the vessel. Noteworthy are the remains of frescoed decoration applied to the neck of the piece, where a warrior, portrayed with the characteristic Maya sculptural quality, wears a large bird helmet decorated with feathers. This figure formed part of a procession.   FSM

179
Large Bottle
Early Preclassic period
Cuyamel, Trujillo Colón, Honduras
Ceramic
Height: 16.7 cm; width: 14.0 cm
diameter: 10.0 cm
thickness: 3 mm
Tegucigalpa, Bodegas Centrales
del Instituto Hondureño
de Antropología e Historia
Inv. no. TGC-C-322

Large monochrome vessel in natural shades of clay, without slip, and with a composite body shape. The lower section has irregular walls and the upper part has concave walls. The gourd shape is characteristic of this type of bottle. It has been classified as a lemon-type ware of unspecified variety, without slip and without surface polishing, only smoothed on the inside and outside, and with a flat base. The upper walls have linear incisions made prior to firing.   CJF

180
Phytomorphic Bottle
Middle Preclassic period
Cuyamel, Trujillo Colón
Honduras
Ceramic
Height: 15.2 cm; width: 11.2 cm
diameter: 4 cm
Tegucigalpa, Bodegas Centrales
del Instituto Hondureño
de Antropología e Historia
Inv. no. TGC-C-170

Bichrome bottle with composite silhouette, concave vessel walls, a straight rim with rounded edge, and handles near the rim. It has been defined as a non-domestic utensil. The finish is polished on the inside and outside with red decoration and stepped fret designs on the rim and neck, and on the body there are

181

monkeys in the center with separate bands. This ceramic has been classified as Higuerito-type ware.   CJF

181
Effigy Vessel
Early Postclassic period
Acayuca, Hidalgo, Mexico
Ceramic
Height: 17.0 cm; width: 14.0 cm
Mexico City
Museo Nacional de Antropología
Inv. no. 10-047584

Close communication between the Mayas and the Toltecs was based primarily on trade, an activity that in this period resulted in an intense exchange of merchandise. Among the

Maya objects and materials most appreciated by the Toltecs were plumbate clay and the pottery made from it. Both the clay and the ceramics were brought from distant lands to the Central Highlands and were acquired as prized materials. Toltec craftsmen made some objects with this clay, giving their jars and vessels different forms in tribute to their gods or related directed with their religious beliefs. They also acquired pieces made by the Mayas that were endowed with extraordinary realism. This plumbate vessel found in Pitahaya Dam, in which the head of a turkey is represented in appliquéd work, is an example of the close relationship of these groups. The wings were rendered

182
The Weaver Figurine
Late Classic period
Jaina Island, Campeche, Mexico
Ceramic
Height: 17.0 cm; length: 16.0 cm
width: 10.0 cm
Mexico City
Museo Nacional de Antropología
Inv. no. 10-078164

This figurine constitutes a valuable document: it indicates to us that at least 600 years A.D. in the Maya area, the backstrap loom was already in use. This loom received its name because one of its ends is tied to the waist of whoever is using it and the other end is tied to the trunk of a tree where, in this case, the clay artist added a bucolic note with a bird. This type of loom is still used today in many parts of Mesoamerica. It is possible that this young woman, dressed in a skirt and a type of short, closed cape, which is still used by many indigenous women, is not a mere craftsperson but the goddess of the moon, Ix Chel Yax or Ixchel, who is represented in codices with her backstrap loom. This deity is credited with the invention of weaving, and she is also the patroness of fertility, procreation, and birth, and is also the goddess of medicine. Her sanctuary on the island of Cozumel was an important place of worship and pilgrimage.   ACM

183
Polychrome Textile
Postclassic period
Cueva de la Garrafa, Chiapas,
Mexico
Cotton
Length: 112.0 cm; width: 146.0 cm

Tuxtla Gutiérrez
Museo Regional de Chiapas
Inv. no. 10-409936

This textile garment was used as ceremonial garb and it resembles the costumes in the Nuttall Codex. It was probably used in funerary ceremonies or to wrap a mortuary bundle. Among its decorative motifs there are three figures in procession on a yellow band that perhaps represents the surface of the earth. Below this band are zigzag lines with tips that perhaps refer to the jaw of the reptile as the entrance to the interior of the earth. The figures have a shield, noseplugs, and arm protectors, as well as elements that have been interpreted as the representation of the mythical struggle between life and death. This piece was woven in natural, white cotton fiber, on which a base of dark brown color was applied. The decorative motifs were painted in different tones of ochre, green, blue, and yellow, while the figures were outlined in black. The lower part is edged by a woven fringe with strands that are reddish brown in color.   MCG

184
Polychrome Gourd
Postclassic period
Cueva de la Garrafa, Chiapas
Mexico
Gourd
Height: 11.0 cm; diameter: 22.5 cm
thickness: 2.5 cm
Tuxtla Gutiérrez
Museo Regional de Chiapas
Inv. no. 10-204180

The natural conditions of the cave where these perishable objects were deposited, known as the Cueva de la Garrafa, permitted their conservation. There, wood instruments, fragments of *amate* (bark) paper, gourds, ceramics, basketry, and cotton textiles were recovered. The technique of lacquer painting in the production of this piece must have been used throughout Mesoamerica during the pre-Hispanic period, and it continues to be used today in certain parts of the country. Fat mixed with pigments and earth, obtained from boiling a worm called *axe* grown in trees from tropical lands, was applied on gourds. Once the lacquer base dried, a drawing was incised and part of the lacquer ground was removed to inlay lacquer of different colors. The final finish of the piece involved polishing it by applying *chía* (sage) seed oil mixed with *axe* and rubbing it with a piece of cloth.   MCG

185
Spindle Whorl
Late Classic period
Simojovel, Chiapas, Mexico
Ceramic

183

Diameter: 3.2 cm; thickness: 6 mm
San Cristóbal de las Casas
Centro Cultural Ná Bolom
Inv. no. 164 87/255

Spindle whorls take the general form of a disk with a central perforation for the placement of a stick to spin cotton thread by twisting it. The upper part of this example is convex and decorated with a mold-made design painted red. The motif appears to represent a feathered serpent.   TALW

186
Stamps
Late Classic period
Campo Pineda, Sula Valley
Honduras
Ceramic
Dimensions and shapes variable
Tegucigalpa, Bodegas Centrales
del Instituto Hondureño
de Antropología e Historia
Inv. no. SPS-AB-186

Monochrome, solid stamps, all polished on one side, with designs based on incisions and perforations. Two of the stamps represent anthropomorphic figures. These stamps come from a site that was one of the centers for pottery mass-production in the pre-Hispanic period.   CJF

187
Polychrome Basin
Terminal Classic period
Chichén Itzá, Yucatán, Mexico
Ceramic
Height: 11.5 cm; diameter 21.5 cm
Merida, Museo Regional de Yucatán
"Palacio Cantón"
Inv. no. 10-145970

This vessel was recovered from the Sacred Cenote at Chichén Itzá in 1967 by Román Piña Chán. The decoration on this local ceramic type called Pizarra Delgada, or Thin Slateware, seems to represent the scene of a historical event, when the Itzas and another Mayan-speaking group engaged in a confrontation in the northern Yucatán peninsula. Its style is reminiscent of the murals in

184

186

185   187

the Temple of the Warriors, because they both combine scenes of daily life with those of warriors. There are three well-defined sections, and the glyphic panel seems to indicate that the reading goes toward the right. The first scene, limited to the right by a platform and a temple probably symbolizing a settlement, is developed around the town *ahau*, who wears a striped blue skirt, and the military chief of the invaders, with his eye and mouth outlined in black and holding a rectangular shield with geometric emblems. The envoy appears to demand that the town's warriors lay down their weapons. A bare-breasted woman of the town, holding her child, is followed by a burden bearer or a merchant with a staff in the form of a spear; both figures have tumplines. In the second scene, a group of four local warriors, identified by short, striped skirts, are gathered; in their midst, the *ca-hal*, or military chief, stands out with

his jaguar cape. The rest of the pictorial space is occupied by ten warriors who carry standards, rectangular shields, spears, and spearthrowers, as they advance toward the village, defended by four opposing warriors. The number of figures is a metaphor expressing the advancing force of the attackers in contrast to the defenders. Columns of glyphs seem to identify some of the invaders. In the murals at Chichén Itzá, there are no Maya glyphs associated with warriors, implying that the two groups confronting each other belong to the same Mayan language group.   SB

188
Pendants
Late Classic period
Palenque, Chiapas, Mexico
Shell
Shell glyph diameter: 2.6 cm
thickness: 4 mm
interlaced shell length: 5.1 cm
thickness: 2 mm
maximum width: 8.0 cm
Palenque, Museo de Sitio
"Alberto Ruz Lhuillier"
Inv. no. 10-458681 3/42; 4/42

At Palenque, seashells and other shells are commonly manufactured into ornaments, such as pendants, necklaces, and bracelets used mainly in mortuary furnishings. Sometimes it was also common to deposit some marine elements unmodified by artificial means, such as *Spondylus* shells placed on the head of the deceased. Perhaps due to its association with the underworld, these shell objects were deposited in burials.   AGC

189 a-b
Pectorals
Classic period
Jonuta, Tabasco, Mexico
Shell
Zoomorphic piece height: 4.5 cm
width: 10.0 cm; depth: 1.5 cm
Edged piece height: 8.0 cm
width: 11.5 cm; depth: 2.0 cm
Jonuta
Museo "Omar Huerta Escalante"
Inv. no. MJ-137; MJ-138

Profile representation of a crouching animal, possibly an iguana; in the drilled portion of the eye, there may once have been a bead. There are two perforations at the edge of the shell, at the height of the back legs of the animal, where beads or rattles of some perishable material hung. The second pectoral corresponds to a valve cut in the center, while the edge was filed with a stepped contour into the form of *ik,* "wind." For the Maya, shells were some of the most prized objects, used as exclusive ornaments for rulers, which also explains their wide commercial distribution. Symbolically, they are associated with water and the underworld.   RP

190
Pectoral
Late Classic period
Usumacinta region, Mexico
Shell
Height: 4.0 cm; width: 10.0 cm
depth: 4.0 cm
Villahermosa, Museo Regional
de Antropología "Carlos Pellicer"
Inv. no. A-0033

Archaeological excavations in several residential complexes in the Maya area have uncovered the existence of workshops specializing in

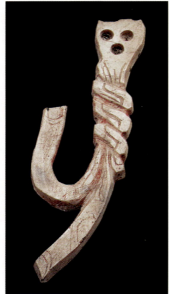

188a

188b

189b

189a

190

different kinds of shell. Proof of the artisans' skill is this marvelous pectoral with the image of an aquatic bird. The bird can be recognized by the beak, head form, and above all, the long curved neck. In the center of the body is a perforation that must have contained an inlay of another material, while on the back, there are four more perforations from which might have hung other decorative elements that made the piece even more beautiful and complex.   TPS

191
Earflares
Classic period
Xicalanco, Campeche, Mexico
Shell

Height: 5.5 cm; width: 3.2 cm
Campeche, Museo Histórico
Fuerte de San Miguel
Baluarte de San Miguel
Inv. no. 10-170206 0/2

Among the ancient Mayas, just as in many societies, personal beauty was achieved with body and facial ornaments. Earlobes, for example, were perforated, both in men and women, to hold pendants of different shapes and materials. The use of beautifully worked shells and their discovery as part of funerary furnishings, for example, speaks to us not only of the ability to transform this hard material from the sea, but also of the interest in beautifying the human body and the hope for life after death. Shellworking was carried

out with limestone tools and generally the motifs have a symbolic character related to the life of the deceased and his relationships with his cult deities. Xicalanco is located in the western sector of Laguna de Términos and it was an important trade enclave where Mayas, Totonacs, and Nahuatls came together throughout the course of several centuries.   ABC

192
Plaque
Middle–Late Classic period
Kinichná Group, Dzibanché
Quintana Roo, Mexico

191

Shell
Height: 2.5 cm; width: 1.0 cm
Chetumal
Centro INAH *Quintana Roo*
Inv. no. 10-390970

This plaque must have formed part of a larger piece, perhaps sewn to the garb of an important individual. It represents God N, or *Pahuatun,* an artist deity who was always represented as an old man, associated with scribes. Quadripartite by nature, God N seems to have had the great responsibility of upholding the sky, so he is related to rain, thunder, and rebirth. This latter avocation is beautifully exemplified in the *Popol Vuh,* when Hunahpu sacrifices God N by pulling him from his protective shell. This sacrifice allows for the defeat of the lords of death, and the Hero Twins' escape from the underworld with the bones of their dead father. This passage is the Maya metaphor for antonomasia, to signify the resurrection of the human soul over death.   EN and AV

193
Miniature Figurine
Classic period
Tikal, Petén, Guatemala
Shell
Height: 7.0 cm
width: 5.0 cm
Guatemala, Museo Nacional
de Arqueología y Etnología
Inv. no. MNAE 11501

192

Carved in shell, this miniature figure represents a standing hunchback dwarf with his left arm on his abdomen and his right arm extended. It has mother of pearl inlays in the eyes and one in the center of the forehead. The details of the face are rendered as fine incisions. Both shoulders, the hands, and the ears display perforations. In Mesoamerica dwarfs generally are associated with hunchbacks; they often appear with mirrors in court scenes next to rulers. Their importance dates back to Olmec times, when they were associated with the sky. They appear Olmec art, often with wings. The Mayas considered them children of the rain gods and tried to attract them. The maize god also appears accompanied by a dwarf.   MSB

194
Pectoral
Late Classic period
Dzibanché, Quintana Roo, Mexico
Shell
Height: 7.0 cm; width: 8.5 cm
thickness: 3.0 cm
Chetumal
Centro INAH, *Quintana Roo*
Inv. no. 10-390837

This is a pectoral made of shell with the image of a fat-cheeked individual wearing an incised headdress. The figures cheeks were defined by exploiting the natural shape of the mollusk. Perhaps the image refers to the fat deities that were widely distributed in the Yucatán peninsula during the eighth to tenth centuries. The perforations on the upper part of the piece must have served to suspend it from a cord or to attach it to the garment of its owner.   EN and AV

195
Funerary Offering
Terminal Classic–Epiclassic period
Comalcalco, Tabasco, Mexico
Mother of pearl, turtle carapace
Average height: 31.0 cm
average width: 2.2 cm
average thickness: 3 mm
Comalcalco
Museo de Sitio de Comalcalco
Inv. no. 10-575781 1/8-7/8

From the partially excavated Temple II of the North Plaza at Comalcalco, these seven figures must have been part of a mortuary offering located on its interior, in which great

194

193

196

ceramic funerary urns have been reported buried within the construction. All display oblique cranial deformation; nevertheless, two show thick lips with a flat nose, alien to physical traits of the Mayas. In all examples, there a trace of a frontal band on the skulls, which lack hair or headdress. Originally they were covered with a reddish mineral, but only some traces remain in the incisions of certain pieces. They lack any indication that they might have been used as pendants, although two of the figures have a small notch around the nape.   MJGG

196
Canine Ornament
Late Classic period
Spondylus *shell*
Height: 9.5 cm
New York
The Metropolitan Museum of Art
The Michael C. Rockefeller
Memorial Collection, Bequest
of Nelson A. Rockefeller, 1979
Inv. no. 1979.206.951

In ancient Maya thought, shells were linked to underworld concepts, probably because of their

a headdress or garment. Depicted is a sitting canine with long tail and raised front paws, its head in profile, with gaping jaws. The Maya, like other ancient Mesoamerican people, kept dogs as pets. They also believed that a canine guide or guardian led the dead through the perils of the underworld.

195

submarine origins, and were included as offerings in burials and caches from the Preclassic period to the time of the conquest. They were also used to create luxury items for the elite, such as ear ornaments and necklaces. This ornament, is carved of *Spondylus* or "thorny oyster" shell, which was a particularly prized shell because of its bright orange color. It may have been a costume element which was attached to

197

199

198

200

197
Vessel
Early Classic period
Dzibanché, Quintana Roo, Mexico
Alabaster
Height: 18.4 cm
diameter: maximum 15.6 cm
Chetumal
Centro INAH Quintana Roo
Inv. no. 10-390824 1/2 and 2/2

This magnificently carved vessel is executed in a style similar to the classic forms of Teotihuacán vessels. Its most notable element is the effigy of the spider monkey (*chuen* in Mayan), which, standing on his four feet, serves as a handle for the lid. The animal's tongue was made with a small shell inlay and he wears a sacrificial cape around his neck, a common characteristic of these animals with supernatural attributes. For the Classic period Maya, monkeys seem to refer to creation myths, especially in the *Popol Vuh*, where the twins Hun Batz and Hun Chuen were transformed into monkeys in punishment for their bad behavior, although they appear as patron deities of art, writing, and calculations. The twins sometimes appear as real monkeys, as represented on this vessel, while on others they appear as humans with monkey attributes.   EN and AV

198
Vessel
Late Classic period
Provenance unknow
probably Oxkutzcab, Yucatán
Mexico
Alabaster
Height: 17.0 cm
diameter of the mouth: 16.0 cm
Merida
Museo Regional de Yucatán
"Palacio Cantón"
Inv. no. 10-426129

In the northern Yucatán peninsula, objects are found made of marble, also known as *tecali*, the name of the area in the central highlands where this stone occurs in abundance. Offerings of this material are known from Uxmal and Chichén Itzá. The raw materials could have come from the Ulúa region in Honduras and could have been traded to Yucatán, but it is also possible that they were imported from the central highlands.   APC

199
Bowl
Late Classic period
Ocozocoautla, Chiapas, Mexico
Alabaster
Height: 14.0 cm

maximum diameter: 20.0 cm
Tuxtla Gutiérrez
Museo Regional de Chiapas
Inv. no. 10-586501

Tripod bowl made from fine, white alabaster. It comes from a hiding place in the cave called El Tapesco del Diablo, located in the canyon of the La Venta River. The grotto belongs to a complex of natural caverns in the cliffs of the canyon, which were used by Zoque inhabitants of eastern Chiapas as housing, funerary precincts, and storerooms. By way of the La Venta River, they moved luxury goods toward the Gulf of Mexico from Maya territory. The caves located along this route must have functioned as temporary depositories. The presence of alabaster objects is evidence of long-distance commercial exchange, because the closest source of the raw material to the south of Mesoamerica is hundreds of kilometers away in Honduras.   ELV

200
Obsidian Nucleus
Postclassic period
El Meco, Quintana Roo, Mexico
Obsidian
Height: 10.9 cm

diameter: 8.5 cm
Cancún
Museo Arqueológico de Cancún
Inv. no. 10-390688

This prismatic nucleus made of black obsidian clearly shows that it was worked, and that blades and flakes were chipped from it. Obsidian is an extrusive rock of igneous origin. It displays a glassy sheen and different tonalities: black, gray, green, brown, and even red. In pre-Hispanic times, the main deposits that were exploited were located in central Mexico and in Guatemala. Its presence at archaeological sites in the Yucatán peninsula (whether in the form of raw materials or as finished objects) is irrefutable proof of the commercial exchange conducted by the peninsular Maya with both regions. ECTA

201
Eccentrics
Late Classic period
Xunantunich, Cayo District, Belize
Flint
27/187-1:71:
27/189-1:32: length: 9.0 cm
width: 4.0 cm
27/189-1:66: diameter: 7.5 cm
thickness: 1.0 cm
27/189-1:71: length: 10.0 cm
width: 5.0 cm
27/189-1:72: length: 8.0 cm
width: 5.5 cm
27/189-1:73: length: 9.5 cm
width: 4.0 cm
27/189-1:78: length: 12 cm
width: 4.0 cm
27/189-1:79: diameter: 8.0 cm
thickness: 1.0 cm
27/189-1:80: diameter: 7 cm
thickness: 1 cm
Belmopán
Departamento de Arqueología
Inv. no. 27/187-1:71, 27/189-1:32
27/189-1:66, 27/189-1:71
27/189-1:72, 27/189-1:73
27/189-1:78, 27/189-1:79
27/189-1:80

The custom of depositing offerings associated with architectural structures and sculptural monuments was a common practice in the Maya area since Preclassic times. Only in this way could a construction be built, dedicated, used, and finally abandoned or destroyed. The nature of materials and the form, as well as the distribution and number of these, determined their efficacy to protect buildings, monuments, and above all the participants in these ceremonies. These nine eccentrics belong to an offering of eighteen pieces of this type that was dedicated under an altar at Xunantunich, Belize, located together with Stela 2 in Structure A 16. PJS

203
Mirror
Late Classic period
Bonampak, Chiapas, Mexico
Pyrite
Diameter: 25.5 cm
thickness: 3.4 mm
Chiapas, Proyecto Arqueológico
de Bonampak, Centro INAH
Inv. no. 10-588889

Circular mirror, made with a mosaic of fifty-nine polygonal pieces of pyrite, originally attached to a base of sandstone with an organic, yellowish adhesive. The surface is totally smooth and the assembly of the polygons is precise. Four perforations on the base allowed the mirror to be carried with two cords. The base was decorated with a fine layer of polychromed stucco. This

203

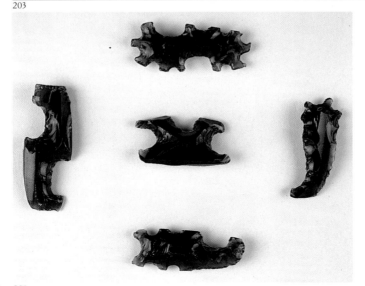

201

object was found as part of a mortuary offering at the feet of an important individual buried in a large tomb at Bonampak. The mirror perhaps pertained to his costume, and its dark surface is associated with the night sun and the underworld, so that it could have had an important magical or divinatory significance. AT

204
Large Jar
Early Classic period
Gruta de Chac, Sayil, Yucatán
Mexico
Ceramic
Height: 40.7 cm
maximum diameter: 35.2 cm
Merida, Museo Regional de Yucatán
"Palacio Cantón"
Inv. no. 10-426356

This three-handled polychrome vessel comes from the Gruta de Chac, near the site of Sayil in the Puuc Hills, where the level of subsurface water is at a depth of about 80 meters. This container would have been used to carry sacred water from the cave. The decoration consists of a medallion with an angular celestial band and a wavy central motif, which is related to water. From this element hang three floral motifs and two volute-rays, which are all common elements. The flowers display a circular pendant hanging from the center, resembling a bell. The central vegetal design has crossed lines in black. In Maya color symbolism, black alludes to the darkening clouds that promise rain.   YP

205
Large Jar
Late Classic period
Gruta de Chac, Sayil, Yucatán
Mexico
Ceramic
Height: 43.5 cm
maximum diameter: 33.5 cm
Merida, Museo Regional de Yucatán
"Palacio Cantón"
Inv. no. 10-348196

Descending into deep grottos or caves to obtain water, particularly in the northern Yucatán peninsula, was necessary for ceremonies or times of drought. For the latter purpose, a special type of container with three handles was made to be carried on the back using a *mecapal* or tumpline, which allowed the weight of the burden to be supported on the forehead and left the hands free to aid in the ascent from the subterranean slopes.   APC

206
Vessel
Late Preclassic period
Punta Piedra, Quintana Roo, Mexico
Ceramic
Height: 29.0 cm; diameter: 34.3 cm
Cancún
Museo Arqueológico de Cancún
Inv. no. 10-389622

This piece, which came from a cave, could have been deposited by the Mayas as part of a propitiatory offering for agricultural activities. It is known that caves were sacred and the presence of water inside them is reason why many of the rituals con-

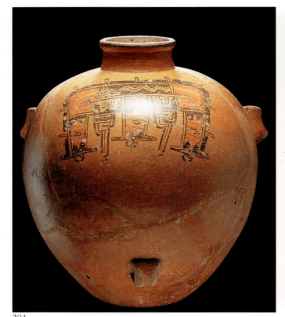

204

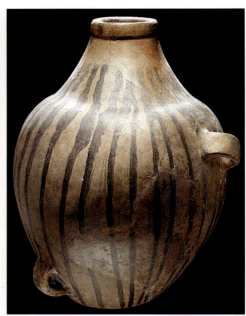

205

207

206

ducted in these places may be related to the cult of the rain deity.

The type of decoration, based on curved lines painted red, as well as the objects associated with this deposit, including censers, may reinforce the ceremonial nature of the offering.   ECTA

207
Large Jar
Postclassic period
Punta Piedra, Quintana Roo, Mexico
Ceramic
Height: 37.0 cm; diameter: 38.0 cm

Cancún
Museo Arqueológico de Cancún
Inv. no. 10-389620

This jar has a cream-colored slip with black decoration. The ornamental designs have two patterns: near the neck, curved lines (like horizontal s-shapes) were painted, forming a band, while the rest of the body has vertical lines. This specimen formed part of a ware called Peto Crema, composed of different vessel types, all of them made for daily use. Large jars were used, just as they are today, to store or transport liquids.   ECTA

208

209

208
Large Jar
Postclassic period
Los Cerritos, Chicaj
Quiché, Guatemala
Ceramic
Height: 17.5 cm
diameter of the mouth: 9.0 cm
Guatemala, Museo Nacional
de Arqueología y Etnología
Inv. no. MNAE 9716

Large jar pertaining to Plumbate ware. This type of ceramic was made in the vicinity of the western coastal inlet of Guatemala near Tajumulco, San Marcos, one of the most important centers of production. This ceramic was made from the Late Classic period until the Early Postclassic periods. During the first period, tall-necked jars and tall cylindrical vessels predominated. During the second period, effigy vessels abounded. This type of vessel was widely traded within Mesoamerica, perhaps because of its appearance and durability; its distribution reached from western Mexico to Panamá. The neck of this piece is tall and resembles a squash. The surface is covered by black cloudy areas and reddish, metallic slip from which the name Plumbate originates, although the chemical analysis of this ware shows that no metallic substances were used in its manufacture.   MSB

209
Basin
Terminal Classic period
Jaina Island, Campeche, Mexico
Ceramic
Height: 8 cm; diameter: 11.5 cm
Mexico City
Museo Nacional de Antropología
Inv. no. 10-534619

Basin with curved, convergent body, with flat base and concave

210

bottom; the rim is slightly rounded, made with clay displaying a very dark and polished orange slip. It belongs to the Silho group of the Fine Orange ceramic ware. Due to its form and surface finish, this vessel seems to have been utilitarian. Ceramics of this type were widely distributed in Mesoamerica during the Late and Terminal Classic periods, and it is associated with an extensive trade network established by the Putuns. The western periphery of the Maya area is possibly the place of manufacture of this ceramic, and specifically the Silho type seems to have had its production center on the coast of Campeche. It is a hard, very resistant ceramic, the paste of which makes it possible to make vessels with very thin walls. The temperate range of this ceramic type is one of the most extensive in the Maya area.   LCGS

210
Bowl
Late Classic period
San Isidro, Malpaso, Chiapas
Mexico
Ceramic
Height. 11.2 cm
diameter: 13.4 cm
Mexico City
Museo Nacional de Antropología
Inv. no. 10-128017

The changes expressed in the forms and decoration of ceramics over hundreds of years has allowed the identification of specific traditions of certain periods and cultural groups. This bowl displays a well-polished, cream-colored surface with an incised band in the middle. As decoration it has designs of concentric lines, and the symbol of *etznab*, one of the days from the Maya calendar.   MCG

211
Miniature Vessel
Early Classic
Provenance unknown
Ceramic
Height: 5.2 cm; diameter: 10.1 cm
Mexico City
Museo Nacional de Antropología
Inv. no. 10-001219

In this ceramic work, modeled with a composite silhouette, the incised decoration forms semicircles repre-

211

senting petals, the placement of which evoke the image of a sacred flower: the water lily, a plant of the nympheaceous family, with wide, round leaves and white or yellow flowers with a wide-open corolla. The symbolism of this plant is twofold: it represents abundance and fertility, phenomena that may be seen in lakes and lagoons where they grow and multiply quickly. Because they are on the surface, with their roots in the water, they belong to water-earth elements, that signify creative fertility, so the image of these aquatic lilies also formed the symbolic glyph of the jaguar and the crocodile, terrestrial and aquatic animals respectively and that indistinctly are represented as carrying the earth on their backs. The water lily was also related with the underworld.   MCM

212
Vessel
Classic period
Ceramic
Height: 11.0 cm; length: 32.0 cm
Guatemala, Museo Nacional
de Arqueología y Etnología
Inv. no. MNAE 6419

Shoe-type vessel. These vessels are characterized by their asymmetrical form. The surface is a brown. It has a handle opposite the point where

212

Ceramic
Height: 21.0 cm
maximum diameter: 18.5 cm
Mexico City
Museo Nacional de Antropología
Inv. no. 10-000132

Tetrapod vessel with handle-spout; its form and type of supports are characteristic of the Protoclassic period. Its body has a composite silhouette; its resist decoration is executed in the "lost wax" technique

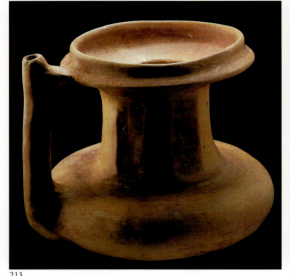

213

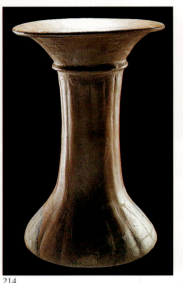

214

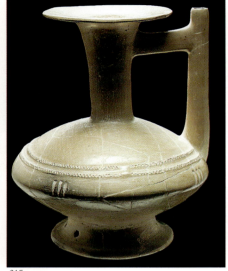

215

the flat rim emerges toward the body of the vessel. The tip of the "shoe" is fairly narrow and elongated and it has a "coffee-bean" figurine; between the two there is a long, appliquéd fillet. The nose and mouth are modeled. This vessel form has been widely used in Guatemala from the Preclassic period until today. Examples have been found in the United States, several Mesoamerican sites, and in South America. Its function is not known with certainty, although these vessels could have been used in a ceremonial or domestic context to cook food, which is how these vessels are still used today in the Department of Huehuetenango in Guatemala. MSB

213
Jar
Late Preclassic period
Chiapas, Mexico
Ceramic
Height: 15.6 cm; width: 19.2 cm
diameter of the mouth: 14.6 cm
Pomoná, Museo de Sitio de Pomoná
Inv. no. 10-389540

This piece is part of the Late Preclassic ceramic complexes of the Maya lowlands, characterized by the standardization of shape and decoration. Similar pieces have been reported at sites such as Tikal, Barton Ramie, Altar de Sacrificios, and Chiapa de Corzo, fairly dispersed sites, which would suggest that the ware serves as a time mark-

er, and does not come from a single location. The jar displays one of the most notable characteristics of this period, which is the preference for monochrome. Colors such as red, black, brown, and cream were often used. As for form, in addition to elegant shapes, a common trait is the dominance of the faceted neck and the hollow handle, forming a channel that allowed liquids to flow through. SPA

214
Florero
Early Protoclassic period
Chiapa de Corzo, Chiapas, Mexico
Ceramic
Height: 35.0 cm; diameter: 22.0 cm
Mexico City
Museo Nacional de Antropología
Inv. no. 10-136

The exquisite shape of this elongated, elegant piece has merited the designation of *florero*, a term referring to tall vessels with small necks resembling a flower vase, without implying that this was its original function. Decorated with vertical grooves, it has a flat base and flaring rim, which together with the similar shape of the lower part of the body, gives it a balanced symmetry. It was found as part of the funerary furnishings of Tomb 7, Mound 1, along with 34 vessels, apparently all imported from different parts of Mesoamerica, which denotes the importance of its context. It is prob-

able that this *florero* was brought from some place in Guatemala, where ceramic wares of this type, with a highly polished red slip, were frequently made and used. LCGS

215
Florero with Spout
Preclassic–Classic period
Playa de los Muertos, Cortés
Honduras
Ceramic
Height: 26.9 cm; width: 21.5 cm
diameter: 13.7 cm
Tegucigalpa, Bodegas Centrales
del Instituto Hondureño
de Antropología e Historia
Inv. no. TGC-C-1181

Monochrome *florero*, flower-vase-shaped vessel, with a spout-type handle, ring-base, long neck, and concave rim with rounded edge. Semi-polished on the outside and smoothed on the inside, it has parallel circular incisions where the spout joins with the body, and very short vertical lines in groups of three on the lower part and on the ring-shaped base. It is important to mention that this is one of the pre-Hispanic forms that continues to be made by hand in orange and black. CJF

216
Usulután-type Vessel
Protoclassic period
Chiapa de Corzo, Chiapas, Mexico

216

with parallel undulating lines interlacing in the center; this decorative technique is known as "Usulután" or "negative" decoration. It is highly possible that it was imported from El Salvador. When the vessel was found, it was originally covered with stucco and painted with a pattern of interlaced geometric designs in red, green, yellow, and purple; unfortunately this layer has not been preserved. This vessel formed part of the funerary furnishings of Tomb 1, Mound 1, one of the richest at the site. LCGS

217
Polychrome Cylindrical Vessel
Early Classic period
Petén, Guatemala
Ceramic
Height: 16.4 cm; diameter: 11.2 cm
Guatemala, Museo Nacional
de Arqueología y Etnología
Inv. no. MNAE 11959

Polychrome cylindrical vessel with red, black, and cream. A thin black band surrounds the vessel just below the rim, followed by another composed of eleven stylized glyphs with details in cream and outlined in black, followed by a thin black band that surrounds the vessel. Under this is a band with a black background and trapezoids painted in cream alternating with three vertical strips of the same color. Two *moan* bird feathers hang from the band on opposite sides of the vessel. These feathers are white with a black tip. The *moan* bird is a sacred animal represented by an owl, and very common in Maya iconography. It was associated with God L, god of the underworld, because he was often show sitting on his headdress. He personifies the time period of the *katun* and the sky.   MSB

218
Polychrome Cylindrical Vessel
Early Classic period
Tikal, Petén, Guatemala
Ceramic
Height: 12.6 cm; diameter: 7.7 cm
Guatemala, Museo Nacional
de Arqueología y Etnología
Inv. no. MNAE 11133

The surface of this vessel is covered with polished cream slip. A thin black line surrounds the vessel just below the rim, followed by a band of glyphs painted in red and a groove around the vessel. The entire lower area is covered with thick vertical grooves decorated with dispersed vegetal designs painted in black. These designs resemble a flower with four pointed petals. The flowers alternate in two rows on the upper and lower part of the grooved area.   MSB

219
Polychrome Cylindrical Vessel
Late Classic period
Provenance unknown
probably southern Campeche
Mexico
Ceramic
Height: 16.5 cm; diameter: 10.4 cm
Campeche, Centro INAH Campeche
Inv. no. 10-566444

This elegant vessel was decorated using the negative or resist painting technique. This batik or resist painting technique involves of covering a slip base with designs made in wax, grease, or clay, and later appling a darker paint bath for firing in a reduction atmosphere, leaving the design in the color of the bottom layer of slip exposed, which in this case is cream. The motifs are strikingly arranged in a diagonal pattern. They seem to refer to the inside of the tentacles of octopuses and profiles of cut shells. The diagonal lines of circles with dots at the center could

217

218

219

220

symbolize the water or the sea. These same motifs have been reported on vessels from Uaxactún, in the Guatemalan Petén. The continuous dialogue between the ancient Maya and their environment allowed some of their motifs to show an almost modern degree of stylization.   YP

220
Polychrome Cylindrical Vessel
Classic period
Tikal, Petén, Guatemala
Ceramic
Height: 12.5 cm; diameter: 8 cm

Guatemala, Museo Nacional
de Arqueología y Etnología
Inv. no. MNAE 11211

The surface of the vessel is covered with well-polished orange slip. The design is divided into three horizontal bands outlined in black, the central one being the thickest; the upper and lower one have several plant motifs resembling a flower with four pointed petals. The color of these alternates between red and black. The central band also has plant designs and the representation of a mat, known in Mayan as *pop*, framed by a black cartouche. The woven mat

was of great importance in the daily life of the Mayas. Being able to sit on one of these implied authority, and often it came to be synonymous with the term throne. Few examples of mats have survived, but impressions of them have been found in ceramics and plaster.   MSB

221
Polychrome Cylindrical Vessel
Late Classic period
Guatemalan lowlands
Ceramic
Height: 16.0 cm; width: 12.5 cm
diameter: 12.0 cm
Guatemala, Museo Popol Vuh
Universidad Francisco Marroquín
Inv. no. MPV 1165

Cream-colored cylindrical vessel
with a flat base. On the inside is a
red, horizontal band and on the
edge, a thin, black band. On the exterior, under the black band, is a red
band followed by two black, horizontal, parallel lines. The decoration
is composed of four vertical panels.
The two main ones, which are
slightly wider, are painted with small
alternating black and white squares
in the form of a checkerboard and
the other two are red, thick, parallel,
vertical bands that separate the
checkerboard panels.   MS

222
Polychrome Cylindrical Vessel
Late Classic period
Dzibilchaltún, Yucatán, Mexico
Ceramic
Height: 27.0 cm; diameter: 20.5 cm
Mexico City
Museo Nacional de Antropología
Inv. no. 10-069163

The size, form the polychrome decoration with symbolic motifs, and
the band of stylized glyphs of this
cylindrical vessel indicates to us that
its use was restricted to the elite. It is
made of finely textured clay, with
red and black applied to an orange
background. This type of decorated
vessel was not as numerous as domestic ceramics and therefore they
were frequently deposited in the
tomb of their owner. The scenes that
appear on ceramics are of great
artistic merit because the motifs included natural, geometric, and
glyphic elements and sometimes
they even pictured portraits of individuals or ritual scenes of great symbolism and complexity.   EGL

223
Polychrome Cylindrical Vessel
Classic period
Petén, Guatemala
Ceramic
Height: 22.0 cm; diameter: 9.0 cm
Guatemala, Museo Nacional
de Arqueología y Etnología
Inv. no. MNAE 13730

Cylindrical vessel with cream, red,
and black polychrome. The surface
is covered with well-polished cream
or buff slip. A red band goes around
the vessel at the rim; another band,
with six glyphs, is framed between
the upper line and a thinner one.
The glyphs are painted red, outlined
in black, and the only recognizable

221

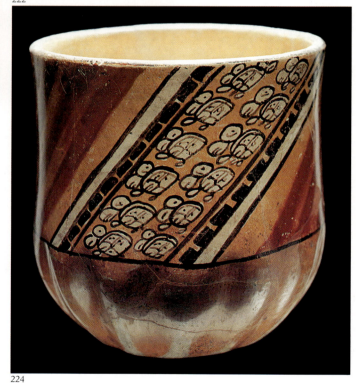

223

222

one is the *ahau* glyph. The custom of
including a glyphic band on the upper part of the vessel was very common during the Late Classic period;
often the names of individuals and
their place of origin were recorded.
There are cases in which the glyphs
serve a purely decorative function
without forming any clause, as in the
present example where they are rep-
etitions. Under this band are six
slanted bands with two different patterns of alternating plant designs.
One consists of interlaced sprouting
vegetation, and the other seems to be
a cord of bell-shaped flowers.   MSB

224
Polychrome Vessel
Late Classic period
El Quiché, Guatemala
Ceramic
Height: 17.0 cm; width: 16.0 cm
diameter: 15.8 cm
Guatemala, Museo Popol Vuh
Universidad Francisco Marroquín
Inv. no. MPV 0143

Vessel with composite silhouette in
the Chamá style. The lower part

has wide grooves which give the
vessel the form of a calabash, while
the upper part is straight. The interior has buff or cream-colored slip
and a black band covers the rim,
while on the outside there are four
diagonal, decorative panels, slanted toward the right. The widest
ones have alternating dark and

light red bands. The other two
panels are decorated with two diagonal rows of pseudo-glyphs
painted in white and outlined in
black. The panels are separated by
a white band and another of black
rectangles. A horizontal black line
separates the straight wall from the
grooved part.   MS

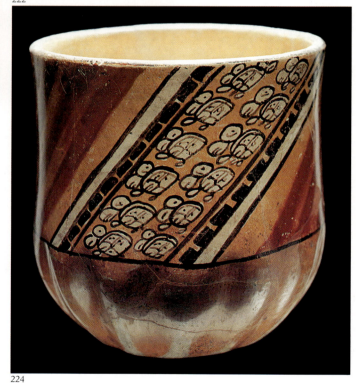

224

225

226

is decorated with alternating red and black panels with stepped frets. The lid has a hand representing the head of an individual, modeled and painted, with a simple headdress in red and black, and circular earplugs. The surface around the handle is buff, or cream-colored. On the handle are black dotted bands and five series of three dispersed dots of the same color. The rim is covered with red slip. Right above the edge is a band of stepped frets in alternating colors of orange, red, and black.   MSB

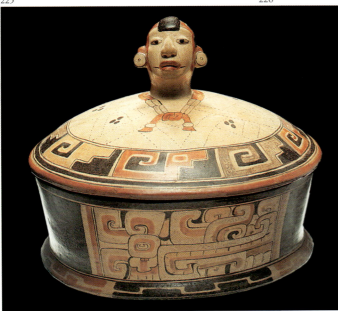

227

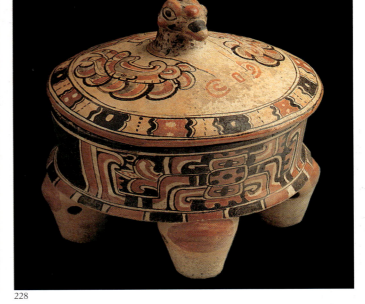

228

225
Polychrome Bowl
Early Classic period
Calakmul, Campeche, Mexico
Ceramic
Height: 35.0 cm
maximum diameter: 40.0 cm
Campeche, Museo Histórico
Fuerte de San Miguel
Baluarte de San Miguel
Inv. no. 10-290540 1/2 and 2/2

During the fourth century, large polychrome bowls with lids with serpentine heads were the most important mortuary vessels in the central Maya region. In the metropolis of Calakmul, this bowl with lid, which formed part of the funerary furnishings of Tomb 1, Structure III, was found. This vessel apparently contained remains of a food made of fermented maize, perhaps *pozol*, for the journey of the tomb's occupant to *Xibalba*. On the lid handle is a quadripartite design, probably symbolizing the cardinal directions. Decoration consists of two large, jawless serpent heads on each half, surrounded by volutes and water symbols, as well as jaguar spots around the handle; the latter probably alluded to the deity known as the Jaguar God of the underworld. The same motif of ser-

pentine heads is repeated on the body of the vessel. The rim at the base again has water symbols, and the lustrous, black background behind the serpentine motifs reinforces the dark, aquatic nature of the underworld.   YP

226
Polychrome Bowl
Early Classic period
Dzibanché, Quintana Roo
Mexico
Ceramic
Height: 21.8 cm
maximum diameter: 38.5 cm
Chetumal
Centro INAH, Quintana Roo
Inv. no. 10-571095 1/2 and 1/2

The main attribute of this funerary vessel is the representation of an owl that serves as the handle of the lid. This nocturnal bird is usually associated with the night and the underworld, and in ancient Mesoamerica it was considered a messenger between humans and the divine. For the Mayas, owls were assistants to the gods of death residing in *Xibalba*, although they were also identified with fertility, perhaps because of an association with rebirth. In some texts, the Early Classic Maya

named the owl of war *kuh*, which means "owl of auguries and omens." In different bellicose representations the owl symbolizes the attributes of the Mexican god Tlaloc, who, in combination with Venus, also constituted a widely recognized metaphor of war. The fact that this funerary vessel displays this bird with his wings extended seems to join his two fundamental attributes: his link with the kingdom of death and warfare. His owner, a woman, would triumph in war even in the world of the dead.   AV

227
Polychrome Basin
Early Classic period
Tikal, Petén, Guatemala
Ceramic
Height with lid: 24.5 cm
diameter: 26.0 cm
Guatemala, Museo Nacional
de Arqueología y Etnología
Inv. no. MNAE 11417

This basin has a ring base and a basal flange. On the outer wall, right below the rim, a black band surrounds the vessel; between this and the basal flange are three stylized serpent heads alternating with three black panels. The basal flange

228
Polychrome Basin
Early Classic period
Tikal, Petén, Guatemala
Ceramic
Height: 20.0 cm
diameter: 18.0 cm
Guatemala, Museo Nacional
de Arqueología y Etnología
Inv. no. MNAE 11131a
and 11131b

Tetrapod basin polychromed in buff or cream, red, black, and gray, with a basal flange and lid. The vessel has lopsided, cylindrical supports with two air holes in each. The upper part of the supports is decorated with a red semicircle. The bowl is decorated with a band of geometric designs with the *kan* cross as the central element. The basal flange is decorated with alternating red and black squares separated by a cream-colored strip. The lid has a zoomorphic handle that represents a bird's head, possibly a turkey; its body, with extended wings, is painted on the surface around it. Near the rim is a band of curvilinear designs in buff or cream alternating with red and black. This style of lid decoration, with zoomorphic handles, was very common during the Early Classic period.   MSB

229
Bichrome Plate
Middle–Late Classic period
Kohunlich, Quintana Roo, Mexico
Ceramic
Height: 8.4 cm
diameter: 35.6 cm
Chetumal
Centro INAH Quintana Roo
Inv. no. 10-390825

This plate formed part of the offering associated with an adult individual buried in one of the main buildings of the compound known as The 27 Steps at Kohunlich. In order to achieve the effect of a central circle at the bottom of the plate, its manufacturers employed two layers of slip (pigment) on the piece. First they applied the red-orange color, on which they placed a circle in beeswax; later they applied black slip and fired the piece. Once they finished this process, they simply removed the layer of wax.   EN and AV

229

Ceramic
Height: 15.25 cm; diameter: 20.7 cm
Chetumal
Centro INAH, Quintana Roo
Inv. no. 10-390820

This vessel was found as part of a funerary offering in the residential complex called The 27 Steps, Building 1. It displays a series of abstract designs made from the application of beeswax or some other easily removable material in those parts of

231

230

230
Cylindrical Vessel
Late Classic period
Tikal, Petén, Guatemala
Ceramic
Height: 12.6 cm
diameter of the rim: 8.7 cm
Guatemala, Museo Nacional
de Arqueología y Etnología
Inv. no. MNAE 11196

The surface of the inside of the vessel is covered with polished, orange slip. On the exterior a red band surrounds the upper part of the vessel, while the rest is covered with polished, black slip. During the Late Classic period, the use of cylinder-shaped vessels with straight walls and decoration in different colors proliferateds, although red, orange, black, and polychrome vessels were predominate. These were used for drinking liquids.   MSB

Ceramic
Height: 12.6 cm; diameter: 14.0 cm
Mexico City .
Museo Nacional de Antropología
Inv. no. 10-006404

This bowl was found as an offering in one of the many burials on the island of Jaina. It is distinguished by its grooves and painted resist decoration; this technique was developed in the Preclassic period in Mesoamerica and it basically consists of applying wax to the areas forming the design, before submerging the recipient in a bath that will give color to the background of the decoration. Characteristically vessels with such negative decoration have a soap-like finish and they were generally intended for ceremonial use. These pieces almost always have two colors, one of which is the color of the clay itself.   CLO

231
Bowl
Late Classic period
Jaina Island, Campeche, Mexico

232
Vessel
Late Classic period
Kohunlich, Quintana Roo, Mexico

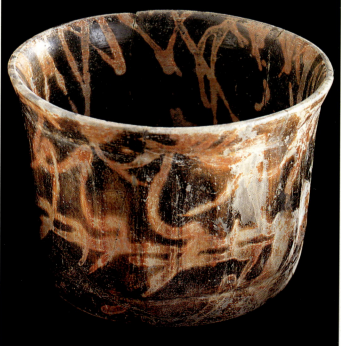

232

233

234

the object where the tonality of the first pigment applied was to be preserved (orange in this case). Later, the piece was covered with a second color (black) and it was fired; as the last step, the wax applied at the beginning of the process was removed.   EN and AV

233
Cylindrical Vessel
Late Classic period
Dzibanché, Quintana Roo, Mexico
Ceramic
Height: 17.3 cm
diameter: 10.3 cm
Chetumal
Centro INAH Quintana Roo
Inv. no. 10-390809

Cylindrical vessels made of the ware called Jojoba Acanalado, as the example presented here, form part of the funerary ceramic tradition that developed in southern Quintana Roo and other regions in the Petén. This piece was part of an offering dedicated to a ruler at Dzibanché, whose body was deposited in a vaulted space of a complex system of chambers located inside Building 2 also referred to as the Building of the Cormorants, which is in fact the most monumental building of the main grouping at the site.   EN and AV

234
Cylindrical Vessel
Middle Classic period
Dzibanché, Quintana Roo

235
Mexico
Ceramic
Height: 20.85 cm
diameter: 10.4 cm
Chetumal
Centro INAH Quintana Roo
Inv. no. 10-390804

This cylindrical vessel was found in the main tomb of the Building of the Lintels at Dzibanché. It has grooves and is an excellent example of the type of ceramic made in southern Quintana Roo around

A.D. 600, as part of the funerary offerings accompanying important individuals. During the Middle Classic period, many of the vessels produced for funerary purposes are characterized by the sobriety and elegance of their forms, which contrasts with the baroque quality of those made for the same purpose during the Early Classic period, as well as with those vessels with rich mythical and historical scenes made during the Late Classic period.   EN and AV

235
Cylindrical Vessel
Late Classic period
Kohunlich, Quintana Roo, Mexico
Ceramic
Height: 10.9 cm
diameter: 9.5 cm
Chetumal
Centro INAH Quintana Roo
Inv. no. 10-390812

This small vessel with grooves, possibly used to drink chocolate or some other liquid, was deposited as an offering to an individual buried in one of the most important buildings of the residential complex known as The 27 Steps of Kohunlich. The fact that it was found in the central chamber of an elegant palace indicates that possibly the individual is one of the main lords that made up the ruling elite of the city around A.D. 650 or 700.   EN and AV

Neighbors

236

237

238

236
Human Pendant
Middle Preclassic period
San Gervasio, Cozumel
Quintana Roo, Mexico
Green stone
Height: 6.8 cm
width: 5.5 cm
Merida, Museo Regional de Yucatán
"Palacio Cantón"
Inv. no. 10-152738

This carved and incised pendant is in the characteristic Olmec style. The form of the head, the slanted eyes, and, above all, the mouth make this identification unquestionable. Despite the fact that this style belongs to the Preclassic period and is rarely found in the northern lowlands, the piece was placed in a Late Classic period Maya tomb at the site of San Gervasio on the island of Cozumel. The tomb contained the remains of two individuals. Among other offerings were shell beads and ceramics. Some of the explanations offered by the excavators for the presence of the pendant in such a late context are the possibilities that it was an heirloom or even that it might have been looted in ancient times from an Olmec burial. On the other hand, it constitutes further evidence of the continuity of sea travel on the part of pre-Hispanic populations. LFS

237
Celt
Middle Preclassic period
Simojovel, Chiapas, Mexico
Green stone
Height: 31.0 cm
width: 9.5 cm
depth: 3.5 cm
Mexico City
Museo Nacional de Antropología
Inv. no. 10-009674

Around the year 800 B.C., there was a great expansion of Olmec traits to locations in Chiapas, such as Chiapa de Corzo, Simojovel, Ocozocoautla, Piedra Parada, Izapa, and even as far away as Uaxactún, Guatemala. In these places, objects have been

239

found that are of well-defined Olmec style, such as the celt from Simojovel. Some researchers have identified the creators of this type of object as Zoque people who inhabited Chiapas and the southern Gulf Coast. Olmec celts were conceived of as offerings. Many are made of smooth, well-polished green stone, always in a petaloid shape suggesting a relationship with forms of vegetation. Some have thin incisions reproducing faces and symbolic elements related to maize and agriculture. MCL

238
Animal Pendant
Last Postclassic period
Edzná, Campeche, Mexico
Green stone
Length: 5 cm
Campeche, Museo Histórico
Fuerte de San Miguel
Baluarte de San Miguel
Inv. no. 10-566433

Small pendant with the possible representation of a hummingbird. This bird was considered by the Mayas to be a manifestation of the

sun god. In some of the sacred books of the Mayas, the young sun is transformed into a hummingbird to suck the honey from the flower, symbolizes sexual union as the fertilizing aspect of the sun. Just as other Mesoamerican groups, the Mayas believed the spirit of a sacrificial victim was reincarnated in the form of this small bird, who later descended to the earth. For some contemporary, Mayan-speaking groups, the sun is transformed into a hummingbird to court the moon. LMC

239
Female Figurine
Middle Preclassic period
South coast of Guatemala
Ceramic
Height: 27.0 cm
width: 14.0 cm
Guatemala, Museo Popol Vuh
Universidad Francisco Marroquín
Inv. no. MPV 0483

Female figurine made of a clay with a gray paste. On her head the figure wears a reddish-brown cap with an oval decoration on the front and another on the back, left portion. The helmet-like headdress goes from the forehead to the nape of the neck. Her face has elongated, with well-defined eyes, a prominent nose, a large mouth and ears, and she wears earplugs perforated in the center. Her arms extend downward and her hands are supported on her knees. Her navel is rendered by a perforation. Her short legs, extended outward toward the front, end in schematically defined feet. MS

240
Human Figurine
Late Preclassic period
Uaxactún, Petén, Guatemala
Jadeite
Height: 25.5 cm
width: 12.5 cm
Guatemala, Museo Nacional
de Arqueología y Etnología
Inv. no. MNAE 924

Anthropomorphic figure carved in jadeite. This was fashioned from a single rounded block of rock. The figure appears seated with crossed legs, arms flexed at the height of the thorax, and hands joined. The eyes are incised in the form of a horizontal rectangle. The details of the flaming eyebrows, decoration on the cheeks, and the hands appear incised. The design on both cheeks is the representation of *kin*. The figure has two circular perforations on the forehead, one on each ear, and twelve in the head. It has six cavities on the arms and six on the legs, perhaps used to hold some ornament. The color of the surface is light green with darker veins. The figurine was found under a stairway leading to Temple A-XVIII at Uaxactún. MSB

240

241

241
Animal *palma*
Late Classic period
Kohunlich, Quintana Roo
Mexico
Stone
Height: 25.0 cm
length: 14.5 cm
Cancún
Museo Arqueológico de Cancún
Inv. no. 10-389624

This is the only *palma* (palm-shaped stone associated with the ball game) found to date in southern Quintana Roo, because they are more characteristic of the Gulf of Mexico region (Veracruz–Tamaulipas), where they are recognized as a cultural element traditionally associated with the Totonac culture. Although it must have been made in another zone, this *palma* was found, possibly as a construction offering, in a substructure of the building known as the Acropolis at Kohunlich, Quintana Roo. The

243

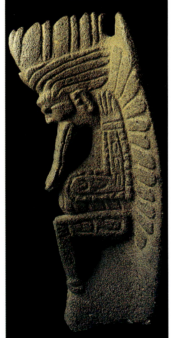

242

piece shows a red *coatí*, an animal that was highly esteemed by the ancient Maya for the quality of its meat.   AV

242
Palma
Late Classic period
Quelepa, Department
of San Miguel, El Salvador
Stone
Height: 49.0 cm
width: 16.5 cm

244

El Salvador
Museo Nacional de Antropología
"Dr. David J. Guzmán"
Inv. no. A2.2-976

Palma sculpted in fine–grained style. It probably represents the Mexican god Quetzalcoatl in his manifestation as Ehecatl, God of the Wind. This *palma* was found at the archaeological site of Quelepa in the Department of San Miguel, in eastern El Salvador. It belongs to the Lepa phase of the Late Classic period, and it was associated with the ball game. The presence in El Salvador of this type of elaborately carved Classic Veracruz artifact suggests that its simultaneans presence in the Guatemalan highlands reflects a regional difference in the ball game. At Quelepa, beginning with the Lepa phase (A.D. 750-950), a series of drastic changes may be noted in material culture.   JMR

243
Votive *hacha*
Terminal Classic or Epiclassic period
Comalcalco, Tabasco, Mexico
Andesite
Width: 19.2 cm; length: 26.6 cm
thickness: 4.8 cm
Comalcalco
Museo de Sitio de Comalcalco
Inv. no. 10-575774

Hachas, just as yokes and *palmas*, have been identified as trappings of the ball game. They could have been used as part of the game, or they could have been placed in a post stuck inside the ball court. *Hachas* are generally objects in the form of a human head, combined with the head of an animal. In this case it is clearly a rabbit crouching on his hind legs, an animal associated with the moon.   RAT

244
Votive *hacha*
Late Classic period
Toniná, Chiapas, Mexico
Jadeite
Height: 21.4 cm; width: 20.5 cm
thickness: 4.9 cm
San Cristóbal de las Casa
Centro Cultural
de los Altos de Chiapas
Inv. no. 10-409790

The presence of votive *hachas*, together with yokes and *palmas*, items associated with the ball game, at different sites at the end of the Classic period, suggests the penetration of groups from the gulf Coast of Mexico into the Maya area. This type of sculpture, in which human or animal heads are represented, has been related with the ball game and with the cult of the dead in the Gulf region. The way in which the piece was carved on a thin slab with the same design on both sides indicates that it could have been inserted into another element. The piece comes from Toniná, a site that dominated the Ocosingo Valley because of its geographic position and route to the Lacandon area. It was a center of redistribution and was in control of exchange routes in the region.   AGC

245
Animal *hacha*
Classic period
Bolivia, Escuintla, Guatemala
Stone
Height: 25.0 cm; width: 21.0 cm
Guatemala, Museo Nacional
de Arqueología y Etnología
Inv. no. MNAE 15352

Ceremonial *hacha* representing the head and part of the body of a stylized serpent. It has a circular perforation in the center and remains of red pigment. The serpent was the most important animal in Mesoamerica, perhaps because of its great diversity in nature; it possessed the broadest and most varied religious symbolism and functions. In *hachas*, serpents are represented in different forms, always with a certain mythological connotation. *Hachas* generally have been found in funerary contexts next to yokes. It is believed that they might have originated on the Gulf Coast of Mexico and that they were adopted by the ancient inhabitants of Guatemala. The majority of the examples found in Guatemala come from the highlands and from several sites in the Department of Escuintla on the southern coast. Other *hachas* have been recovered in the states of Chiapas and Tabasco in Mexico, and in El Salvador and Honduras.   MSB

246
Hacha
Classic period
El Tazumal, Chalchoapa
Department of Santa Ana, El Salvador
Stone
Height: 29.5 cm; width: 21.5 cm
thickness: 3.8 cm
El Salvador, Museo Nacional
de Antropología
"Dr. David J. Guzmán"
Inv. no. A2.2-773

Hacha in roughly rectangular shape, carved in fine-grained stone with a longitudinal perforation. This type of object, associated with the ball game, was carried by athletes as a distinctive element. It has remains of red paint, and an animal design in high relief that possibly represents seven serpent heads. This *hacha* was found in a Late Classic period context at the archaeological site of Tazumal, in the area of Chalchoapa in the western zone of the country. Frequently *hachas* are found in El Salvador and in the Guatemalan highlands that indicate links with Veracruz, and probably the presence of a group from the Gulf Coast of Mexico.   JMR

247
Animal *hacha*
Classic period
Southern coast, Guatemala
Stone

245

246

247

248

Height: 26.0 cm; width: 21.0 cm
Guatemala, Museo Nacional
de Arqueología y Etnología
Inv. no. MNAE 2211

Ceremonial *hacha* representing the head of a deer with pointed ears, exposed tongue, and closed eye, uncommon features in images of this creature. It is believed that it could represent the head of a dead deer. This is one of the most common species in the Maya area. In pre-Hispanic times, deer were associated with deities and rituals of different types. In all examples of *hachas*, deer heads appear in profile and are easily identifiable even if they lack the characteristic ear. The function of these *hachas* is unknown, although they were probably related to the ball game. Nevertheless, no concrete evidence has been found to support this idea.   MSB

248
Animal hacha
Classic period
Southern coast, Guatemala
Stone
Height: 26.5 cm; width: 19.5 cm
Guatemala, Museo Nacional
de Arqueología y Etnología
Inv. no. MNAE 7566

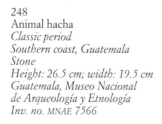
249

Ceremonial *hacha* representing the head of a deer with its characteristic traits. There are remains of red pigment on and around the eye. *Hachas* are sculptures carved on a narrow sheet of hard, dense volcanic stone. Generally, its surface is smooth; the height and width vary depending on the stone. The central motif may be anthropomorphic or animal and replicates the same design on both sides. A few examples have been found that combine two different figures. *Hachas* have one or more perforations; it is unknown if this is for decorative or functional purposes. There are some pieces with remains of red paint and, very rarely, of another color of point. It is believed that they could have been covered completely at the moment they were used. Sometimes other materials were inlaid as decoration.   MSB

249
Yoke
Terminal Classic–Epiclassic period
Balancán, Tabasco, Mexico
Andesite
Width: 35.5 cm; length: 41.9 cm
Comalcalco
Museo de Sitio de Comalcalco
Inv. no. 10-575753

Yokes have been considered by several specialists as symbols of power, whether they were symbolic trophies of a ceremony associated with the ball game, or offerings in human burials, as suggested by archaeological evidence. The central motif of this piece represents a skull with circular earflares, on which there are two interlaced rattlesnakes. Two more skulls are located at the ends, also associated with bones, rattlesnake tails, and bodies and heads of intertwined serpents. The serpentine element indicates a divine and human character. The yokes and *hachas*, (stone belt-like objects and animal or human heads, respectively), believed to have been ball game regalia, excavated at Comalcalco are evidence of a market presence of Gulf Coast cultures, which had extensive commercial exchange with this region.   RAT

250
Human Head Pendant
Early Classic period
Dzibanché, Quintana Roo, Mexico
Jadeite
Height: 2.8 cm
width: 2.2 cm
thickness: 2.8 cm
Chetumal
Centro INAH, Quintana Roo
Inv. no. 10-390933

Small pendant representing the face of an individual with cranial deformation and pyrite inlays in the eyes. The piece was covered with cinnabar, probably at the moment it

250

251

was deposited as an offering. Its maker committed the error of perforating the forehead twice; the error was remedied by insetting three very tiny and perfect plaques of the same material, which are barely visible on the nose and on the back part of the piece. Of particular interest are the typically Teotihuacán traits of the person represented. Pieces similar to this one, although made of ceramic and sometimes forming part of articulated figures, are commonly found in the context of the Xolalpan phase at Teotihuacán, which speaks of the intense contact that existed between that great capital and political centers of the southern Maya lowlands throughout the Early Classic period.   EN and AV

251
Vessel Fragment
Early Classic–Late Classic period
Provenance unknown, probably
Teotihuacán culture, Mexico
Ceramic

Height: 12.0 cm
width: 13.6 cm
Campeche, Museo Histórico
Fuerte de San Miguel
Baluarte de San Miguel
Inv. no. 10-343207

Since the fourth century in the Maya area, the institution of Tlaloc-Venus warfare began with new strategies, weapons, deities, and symbolism that originated in Teotihuacán culture. The icon of Tlaloc, a Teotihuacán deity, appears on monuments of war in stelae in the Maya area. This fragment, probably from a Teotihuacán ceramic vessel, shows a of the Tlaloc-Venus military order, because he wears goggles and holds a circular shield and perhaps a spearthrower in his right hand. His great tasseled headdress is emblematic of emissaries from that city. It is probable that forms similar to Teotihuacán ones were commissioned by the Maya elite from local ceramists to reinforce their status and demonstrate their participation with

Mesoamerican power groups. Nevertheless, this piece, just as others from Kaminaljuyú, seems to be imported from the Mexican highlands. The beautiful and fragile surface of stuccoed and painted cylinder tripods implies that their production was intended for the elite. As a prized personal possession of high-level members of society, its decora-

252

tive themes reflect the occupational, religious, social, and political affiliation of its owners. These vessels have been found in burials and tombs, and could have contained food or other offerings.   SB

252
Polychrome Box
Classic period
Southern coast, Guatemala
Ceramic
Height: 19.0 cm; width: 16.0 cm
length: 22.0 cm
Guatemala, Museo Nacional
de Arqueología y Etnología
Inv. no. MNAE 15829a and 15829b

Rectangular, polychrome, tetrapod box with lid. Its supports and some decorative elements are solid and conical, resembling the thorns of the *ceiba* tree. On one of the two short exterior sides is an appliquéd zoomorphic figure, perhaps a frog with a shell on its back. On the interior are four attached elements: three of them are similar, resembling cotton balls painted in yellow, while the fourth is a human figure with a headdress, earplugs, and pectoral. On the bottom of the box is a complete appliquéd figure with arms stretching upward and legs flexed, wearing a skirt. At the level of the thorax he has a circular perforation forming a small container. The lid has appliquéd elements on three of its sides, which seem to be circular earplugs. On the upper part is an anthropomorphic head with headdress, large circular earplugs, and a necklace with three strings of spherical beads with a shell pendant. Part of the headdress and both earplugs are painted yellow.   MSB

253
Bowl with Human Figurine
Early Classic period
Bécan, Campeche, Mexico
Ceramic
Height of bowl: 16.5 cm
diameter of bowl: 18.0 cm
Merida, Museo Regional de Yucatán
"Palacio Cantón"
Inv. no. 10-251140 0/41

During the explorations of Tulane University and National Geographic at Bécan, this offering was found. It was deposited in Room 3 of Structure XVI-sub. The offering consisted of this cylindrical tripod bowl, from the Sabucán ceramic complex, which has been dated to between A.D. 400 and 550, and the hollow terracotta statuette and ten other figurines, whose garments display great similarities with Teotihuacán representations. The form of the bowl is similar to tripod vessels at Teotihuacán, which suggested some type of contact with this great Mexican city, or else with people associated with it, although the evidence is not definitive on this

254

255

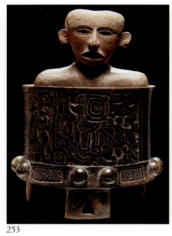

253

point. Figurines similar to those that formed part of this offering are found in elite ritual contexts, and they tend to be made with molds. LFS

254
Tripod Vessel with
Anthropomorphic Supports
Early Classic period
Calakmul, Campeche, Mexico
Ceramic
Height: 30.3 cm; diameter: 16.0 cm
Campeche, Museo Histórico
Fuerte de San Miguel
Baluarte de San Miguel
Inv. no. 10-366406

This piece was found in Tomb 2 of Structure IVB of Calakmul. The modeled, appliquéd decoration of the Balanza group on the lid of this cylinder tripod displays the lower part of the face of a possible ruler. This ruler has a well-defined lower jaw and wears a helmet showing the Principal Bird Deity, as King Vulture, which is one of the earliest icons of power among the Mayas. The same concept is ex-

256

pressed in the bas-relief of a dignitary with the costume of the Principal Bird Deity, with *quincunx* earplugs in Stela 11 from Kaminaljuyú and La Mojarra in Veracruz, emphasizing a new tradition of dynastic government. The anthropomorphic supports with appliquéd decoration possibly represent faces of the deceased with a half-open mouth, a bead between the lips, and a noseplug in the form of two small balls, a popular ornament during the Early Classic period. The small sphere between the lips perhaps refers to the funerary custom of inserting a jadeite bead in the mouth of the deceased, which signified life or death and could serve in the tribulations of the journey in the underworld. SB

255
Vessel with ball game yoke
Early Classic period
Ceramic
Height: 27.9 cm
Purchase
New York

257

The Metropolitan Museum of Art
Mr. Charles S. Payson Gift, 1970
Inv. no. 1970.138

This rare tripod vessel is encircled at the base of the cylinder by a hollow yoke, representing the ball game yoke. The sides of the cylinder and its lid are carved in shallow relief with scenes showing elaborately dressed ball players diving for big balls topped with feathered decoration. Like many stone yokes from the Gulf Coast, the open ends of the yoke have modeled human faces with

closed eyes, perhaps a reference to the sacrifice of the losing player. The ball game, was played throughout Mesoamerica from Olmec times to the conquest, and ball courts have been found at many archaeological sites, usually located near the most sacred structures of the anient cities. The rules and purpose of the game probably changed over space and time. For the Maya of the Classic period the ball game was the ritual reenactment of events that took place in mythical times. Death and sacrifice were frequently the outcome.

256
Tripod Vessel
Early Classic period
Calakmul, Campeche, Mexico
Ceramic
Height with lid: 30.0 cm
diameter: 13.5 cm
Campeche, Museo Histórico
Fuerte de San Miguel
Baluarte de San Miguel
Inv. no. 10-397992 0/2

Tripod vessel of the Balanza group. It shows openwork rectangular slab feet, a modeled anthropomorphic figure applied to the body of the vessel, and a lid displaying the deity called the Principal Bird Deity. One of the most ancient gods of the Mayas, omnipresent in Maya iconography since the Protoclassic period, the Principal Bird Deity is also one of the icons with the earliest public image. It was probably inspired by the King Vulture (*Sarcoramphus papa*), one of the largest birds in Mesoamerica. Some of the attributes associated with the Principal Bird Deity are wings showing a serpent head lacking a lower jaw, a beak resembling a door latch with a knot in the form of a woven straw mat (*pop*, associated with rulers or serpents), and the affix *yax* in the upper part of his headdress, as in this vessel. The Principal Bird Deity has also been identified with Vucub Caquix, the false sun from the beginning of creation, described in the *Popol Vuh*, the sacred book of the Quiché Mayas in the sixteenth century. Opposite the Principal Bird Deity is a spider monkey with an elongated body, wearing a pectoral, perhaps an allusion to Hun Chuen of the *Popol Vuh*, the half-brother of the Hero Twins, who was turned into a spider monkey by them. Monkeys in Maya art are frequently considered to be patrons of artists, scribes, and musicians.   SB

257
Tetrapod Bowl
Early Classic period
Calakmul, Campeche, Mexico
Ceramic
Height: 36.5 cm; diameter 22.7 cm
Campeche, Museo Histórico
Fuerte de San Miguel
Baluarte de San Miguel
Inv. no. 10-342805 0/2

The concave lid depicts a face with closed eyes, wearing a combination helmet-diadem topped off by a human mask. The handle reproduces the headdress and face of the jade-and-shell funerary mask of the individual buried in Tomb 1 of Structure III of Calakmul, which is where this piece was found. A cloth or soft pendant, alluding to sacrifice, hangs from the earplugs. The torso of the figure on the lid has a beaded necklace with a shell pendant characteristic of the Principal Bird Deity or of God D, which ended knotted in a strip of cloth with a fringe at the ends as if a

sacrificial scarf. The torso and shell display *nen*, or shiny mirror signs, implying the positive or divine nature of the individual, or might indicate that he is an ancestor who lives in the supernatural world. The vessel walls are decorated in low relief with two large, jawless serpent heads with small bodies. The four supports seem to repre-

258

sent tapir or peccary heads with the snout downward, which, in the latter case, could be symbols of the pillars of the cosmos at each cardinal point, or the constellation of Gemini . . . for the ancient Maya. Just as the polychromed vessel with lid, this vessel from the funerary furnishings of Tomb 1 contained remains of solid foods, in this case possibly cacao.   SB

258
Relief
Terminal Classic–Early Postclassic period
Chichén Itzá, Yucatán, Mexico
Stone
Height: 65.0 cm; width: 25.0 cm
depth: 26.0 cm
Chichén Itzá, Bodega
del Laboratorio de Arqueología
Inv. no. 10-569629

This narrow relief panel must have formed part of a larger composition framed by a door or a niche. It was discovered in a context of secondary use, as a corner of Structure 3E8 in the Grupo de las Caritas to the northeast of El Castillo. A richly dressed lord extends his right arm, apparently with fist clenched, in front of a sun with a

259

human face, which emits flames that seem to surround the lord. The object that the lord tries to reach or that he has just released could be a ball. On both arms he wears protectors, which are well tied with knots, on his head he wears a turban with a coiled snake and a feather crest. Apart from the bar noseplug and ear ornaments, there is a cut-shell pendant, the famous *chezcoatl*, of the Mexican manifestation of the deity Ehecatl. In front of his body there are flames. If the rules of the game at Chichén Itzá allowed players to hit the ball with the hand or the fist, as is possibly represented here, it would help to explain the size of the playing field and the position of rings in the Great Ball Court (2D1), which would be totally impossible to reach exclusively with hipshots, following the rules at the time of the conquest.   PJS

259
Plaque
Terminal Classic–Early Postclassic period
Chichén Itzá, Yucatán, Mexico
Jadeite
Height: 12.0 cm; width: 12.5 cm
diameter of the perforation: 5.0 cm

Merida, Museo Regional de Yucatán
"Palacio Cantón"
Inv. no. 10-424899

Among the objects recovered from the Sacred Cenote at Chichén Itzá were three jadeite plaques with a central perforation and similar scenes. This piece shows two facing warriors in elaborate attire characteristic of military figures sculpted on the buildings at Chichén Itzá. The warrior on the left, armed with a spear and spearthrower, has a feather and beaded headdress. The left-hand figure wears a "butterfly" motif as a pectoral, which is frequently worn by Itzá or Toltec warriors. His costume is complemented by armlets and wristlets. The figure on the right is also armed with a spearthrower, a feather crest, ear ornaments, and a pectoral; the wrists are decorated with bands. Both look at a third figure who lies in a position of complete surrender, clearly indicating that it is a scene of sacrifice by heart excision, since the reclining man has an opening in his chest. In common with other representations of captives or sacrificial victims, he is naked, but he retains his jewels and elaborate headdress.   LFS

260
Pendant
Terminal Classic–Early Postclassic period
Chichén Itzá, Yucatán, Mexico
Green stone
Height: 5.0 cm; width: 4.8 cm
Merida, Museo Regional de Yucatán "Palacio Cantón"
Inv. no. 10-424844

Flat disks of green stone, measuring from 4.5 to 6 centimeters in diameter, were found in the Sacred Cenote at Chichén Itzá. They all have a small, central perforation that is not part of the design and sometimes there is a second perforation at the end. All disks have a human face and some have been reworked. This disk, with an irregular shape and probably also reworked, uses curved lines to depict the face of an individual whose headdress is formed by two serpent heads with open maws. The serpent was a widely represented animal in Mesoamerican art and at Chichén Itzá; its presence is ubiquitous in stone sculpture, as well as in this type of portable object made of different materials. Plaques of this kind could have been used in diadems, or as a luxurious ornament.   LFS

261
Disk
Early Postclassic period
Tula, Hidalgo, Mexico
Turquoise, pyrite, and wood
Mexico City
Museo Nacional de Antropología
Inv. no. 10-564025

Representations of warriors at Tula and in some Maya cities have disks worn on the back at the level of the waist, known as *tezcacuitlapilli*, which have been related primarily with the sun. This piece was found at Tula, Hidalgo, in the so-called Burnt Palace. It was discovered as part of an offering consisting of branch-and-valve-type seaweed. On top of these was a vest made with rectangular shell plaques, on which rested a plate in which copal had been burned, and on top of the offering was the turquoise disk. The *tezcacuitlapilli* was made with three thousand finely worked turquoise plaques mounted on a wood base. Turquoise trade was acquired from the source that supplied a large part of Mesoamerica, located in New Mexico in the United States, which shows that it was conducted out over long distances. In this case, the distance covered was almost 2000 kilometers to reach the legendary Tula. Also in this magnificent piece are fragments of pyrite that divide the disk into four, probably indicating the cardinal directions, which had a religious significance.   FSM

260

261

262

262
Disk
Early Postclassic period
Chichén Itzá, Yucatán Mexico
Wood, turquoise, shell and coral
Diameter: 24.0 cm
Mexico City
Museo Nacional de Antropología
Inv. no. 10-001253

In the archaeological zone of Chichén Itzá, under the stairway pertaining to the substructure of El Castillo or Temple of Kukulkan, was found a cylindrical stone box that contained a sumptuous offering that included this disk. The piece, mounted on wood, consists of a turquoise, coral, and shell mosaic divided into four sections that depict serpent heads. Although the coral and shell could have been obtained from oceans near the site, the turquoise must have been imported, probably from the southwestern part of the United States. The use of the serpent as a symbol of fertility and other similar connotations was pervasive in Mesoamerican iconography, and especially that of the Maya.   CLO

263
Human Pendant
Postclassic period
Chichén Itzá, Yucatán, Mexico
Gold
Height: 4.7 cm; width: 2.6 cm
Mexico City
Museo Nacional de Antropología
Inv. no. 10-004543

A large number of gold objects from the Postclassic period have been recovered, especially in the Sacred Cenote at Chichén Itzá, where this piece was found. The product of trade, represents a standing, naked man. His hair falls to both sides, forming two long, loose locks with others twisted around his face, and a small lock of hair tied at the forehead completes the headdress. He wears goggles and a buccal mask. In both hands he holds similar objects, which could be stylized offering bags. At the knees he has decorative bands, and the feet are rendered realistically to show that he is barefoot. Based on the technique of manufacture and the style represented, we deduce that it comes from the southern region of Costa Rica or northern Panama.   EGL

264
Animal Bell
Postclassic period
Chichén Itzá, Yucatán, Mexico
Gold
Height: 4.9 cm; width: 3.0 cm
Mexico City
Museo Nacional de Antropología
Inv. no. 10-004573

The majority that have a bell-shaped rattles have been found when dredging the Sacred Cenote of Chichén Itzá, but they also occur at other sites in the Maya area. It is believed that they were a common ornament of the god of death, Yum Cimil, also known as God A, and they are generally associated with him. Due to the technique of manufacture and the style in which many of these objects were made, it is thought that they come from Central America. This example has a bell and a band with three cords decorating the upper part, which serves as the base for the bird crowning the piece. Due to the position of the bird with extended wings, it looks as if it were sustaining the bell with both talons, and carrying it in flight. The plumes of the bird are represented in very fine incised lines.   EGL

265
Animal Bell
Postclassic period
Chichén Itzá, Yucatán, Mexico
Gold
Height: 4.7 cm; width: 4.4 cm
Mexico City
Museo Nacional de Antropología
Inv. no. 10-004538

This gold bell, found in the Sacred Cenote at Chichén Itzá, represents a kneeling monkey eating a fruit held in his right paw, while with the left he holds what could be his extremely long tail, which goes all the way up to his head. The bell itself would be the body of the animal, but it is broken. Monkeys are commonly identified with the wind because

263

265

264

266

267

268

Length 14.1 cm; width: 5.7 cm
Merida, Museo Regional de Yucatán
"Palacio Cantón"
Inv. no. 10-425695

This jadeite plaque found in the Sacred Cenote at Chichén Itzá represents the Feathered Serpent, known as Quetzalcoatl in central Mexico and as Kukulcan in northern Yucatán. At Chichén Itzá, this figure is represented profusely in sculpture. This plaque is made of very fine quality jadeite, carved with a technique unusual among the pieces from the Sacred Cenote. This technique consists of grooves and clean sharp holes and drilled circles, the sides of which were widened to emphasize the forms. The plaque was suspended by way of six small, biconical holes on the upper and lower sides.   LFS

they are of variable humor, going from relaxed to violent or aggressive states, just like the tempestuous wind, which can transform without warning into a hurricane. The face is worked with great realism, and on it is a loop to hang the piece. It was made by techniques of flattening and molding, and the tail by rolling a thick sheet which was shaped into a tube and bent into the position seen here.   EGL

266
Animal Bell
Postclassic period
Chichén Itzá, Yucatán, Mexico
Gold
Height: 7.5 cm; width: 4.2 cm
Mexico City
Museo Nacional de Antropología
Inv. no. 10-004569

In metallurgy, the most highly developed techniques used by Maya goldsmiths were hammering and repoussé. The gold used in the objects made at Chichén Itzá was probably obtained by melting objects previously molded in remote places, for there are no deposits in the Maya area. This bell was found in the Sacred Cenote at Chichén Itzá. It has a composite silhouette, with two bands in the upper part and a decorative element representing a bird, surely some type of eagle judging by the beak and the

feathers on the head, with a highly stylized body and extended tail feathers. The importance of the eagle is evident in images of warriors with eagle and jaguar costumes, symbols of Toltec military orders that appear offering hearts of sacrificial victims at the Temple of the Warriors at Chichén Itzá.   EGL

267
Human Pendant
Postclassic period
Chichén Itzá, Yucatan, Mexico
Gilded copper
Height: 6.5 cm; width: 3.5 cm
Mexico City
Museo Nacional de Antropología
Inv. no. 10-004552

The chemical analysis carried out on metal objects discovered in the Sacred Cenote of Chichén Itzá indicate that the pieces come from

different locations to the south, such as Colombia, Panama, Honduras, and Guatemala, and as far west and north as Chiapas, Oaxaca, and the Valley of Mexico. The copper pieces that contain tin and arsenic come from Oaxaca and the Valley of Mexico, while those that contain only tin come from Honduras. Pure copper objects are from Guatemala and Chiapas. All this testifies to the great territory reached by trade among the Mayas during the Postclassic period. This piece represents a standing, naked man with rattles. The headdress is formed by long locks of loose, wavy hair that fall to both sides of the face, topped by a lock of knotted hair over the forehead. On the upper part it has a flap or ring through whichs the cord passed to suspend it. The figure has ornaments at his knees and his feet are stylized. The figure is dark in color because the gilded copper has not been polished. The body of the figure has small incisions that could be the marks of body scarification so common in this period throughout the region.   EGL

268
Zoomorphic Plaque
Terminal Classic–Early Postclassic period
Chichén Itzá, Yucatán, Mexico
Jadeite

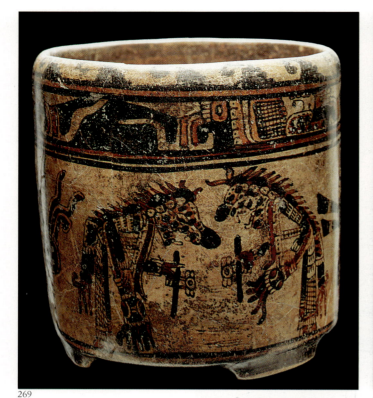

269

270

269
Polychrome Tripod Basin
Late Classic period
Ulúa Valley, Honduras
Ceramic
Height: 19.0 cm; width: 19.0 cm
diameter: 18.5 cm; depth: 17.5 cm
Guatemala, Museo Popol Vuh
Universidad Francisco Marroquín
Inv. no. MPV 0677

271

Tripod cylindrical basin in the Ulúa-Yojoa style, with black, rectangular feet. The inner surface has two horizontal black bands. Under the rim is a series of designs in the form of stepped frets and volutes. Below these is a band with three stylized serpents, framed in black and red lines. The body of each serpent is represented by a square with interlaced lines with connected eyes and mouth. The main scene consists of two figures seated on a jaguar pelt with a shield or standard in front of them, inside a temple stylistically very similar to those that appear in Mixtec codices. In front of each figure, there are standing individuals, dressed in jaguar pelts, and holding a standard and an axe.   MS

270
Tripod Basin
Late Classic period
Western Honduras
Ceramic
Height with supports: 23.5 cm
width: 22.0 cm; diameter: 21.6 cm
depth: 18.8 cm
Guatemala, Museo Popol Vuh
Universidad Francisco Marroquín
Inv. no. MPV 0682

The main decoration consists of three very similar, richly dressed figures.

Their bodies are painted red and in the hand of their extended arms, they hold an object (perhaps a staff or mace). Between the figures are representations of human torsos framed by rectangular bands in red and black, creating the impression of a fragment seen through a window. These figures are richly dressed, with a serpent or lizard headdress, earflares, necklace, and wristlets. Above and below these figures are six unknown symbols. The feet have a red band on the back part, and on the front, symbols representing a temple.   MS

271
Metate with *mano*
Classic–Postclassic period
La Mosquitia, Gracias a Dios
Honduras
Stone
Metate: height: 48.5; width: 52.0 cm
length: 95.8 cm
Mano: length: 92.4 cm; width: 9.4 cm
Tegucigalpa, Bodegas Centrales
del Instituto Hondureño
de Antropología e Historia
Inv. no. TGC-P-858

Ceremonial grinding stone, possibly made of granite. It was found on the surface, not as part of an excavation. It is decorated on the front with an

272

incised serpent head and displays stylized, tripod supports. The flat surface shows no evidence of use as a grinding tool.   CJF

272
Polychrome Cylindrical Vessel
Late Classic period
Sula Valley, Honduras
Ceramic
Height: 19.9 cm; width: 17.5 cm
diameter: 17.0 cm

Tegucigalpa, Bodegas Centrales
del Instituto Hondureño
de Antropología e Historia
Inv. no. TGC-C-1638

Red, black, and orange on cream polychrome vessel with straight walls, flat bottom and base, straight, beveled edge, with a polished interior and an exterior with very fine cream slip. It has horizontal parallel lines encircling the vessel at the rim, body, and base and a band near the

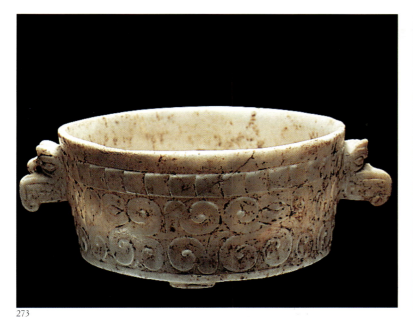

273

274

275

down to the base is engraved on the outside with high and low relief representing many joined, spiral-shaped volutes (known as false glyphs) that give the impression of a single plane. The handles are small, very well-worked mythical jaguars, the features of which are rendered in relief. These vessels are not originally from this location. According to researchers, the production center was in the Sula Valley, so this piece might have been the object of inter-regional exchange, as has been documented at other sites in the La Venta Valley, which maintained intense exchange with sites in central Honduras and outside the country. There are few vessels of this type, particularly those found in an archaeological context and held in government collections.   CJF

276

276
Salúa Polychrome Vessel
Classic period
El Paraíso Valley, Department
of Cuscatlán, El Salvador
Ceramic
Height: 16.1 cm; width: 15.1 cm
El Salvador, Museo Nacional
de Antropología
"Dr. David J. Guzmán"
Inv. no. A1-177

During the Late Classic period, there appears a ware called the Salúa group, probably from the west of Honduras. This ceramic displays a variety of natural and mythological designs painted in black and orange. This cylindrical tripod vessel has rectangular supports, with decoration on its exterior in the form of two panels surrounded by seated, human figures, combined with geometric designs. It was found in the zone of the Valley of El Paraíso and pertains to this ceramic typology of Salúa polychrome. In the valley of El Paraíso, the Late Classic period is a period of resettlement, demographic growth, and political and economic growth. There were several sites in this zone during this period. The ceramics and artifacts found at these sites are similar to those found at El Tazumal and San Andrés, which probably indicates an ethnic unity among the populations in the central and western zone.   JMR

edge of orange-colored stepped frets, followed by another band of highly realistic rattlesnake tails. The main pictorial space displays four panels with individuals apparently dressed in jaguar skins. Each one of them carries a serpent in his left hand and two of them hold spears in the right hand. The figures are painted orange, red, and black on a black background and they wear feather headdresses on their heads. This symbolism in Mesoamerica is related to the elite and the activities of warriors.   CJF

273
Vessel
Late Classic period
Sula Valley, Cortés, Honduras
Alabaster
Height: 9.1 cm; width: 24.5 cm
diameter: 19.2 cm
Tegucigalpa, Bodegas Centrales
del Instituto Hondureño
de Antropología e Historia
Inv. no. TGC-P-260

Tripod vessel with button-shaped supports, straight walls, and high-and-low relief decorations all over the body of the vessel, consisting of false glyphs and volutes representing water. Its two handles are in the shape of a bird believed to represent a macaw.   CJF

274
"Jaguar" Cylindrical Vessel
Late Classic period
El Abra, La Venta Valley
Copán, Honduras
Marble
Height: 17.0 cm; depth: 16.5 cm
diameter: 14.1 cm
Copán, Centro Regional
de Investigaciones Arqueológicas
Inv. no. TGC-M-207

Monochrome cylindrical vessel with straight walls and ring-shaped base integrated into the shape of the vessel, bearing a straight rim with rounded edge. The entire body

275
Chichicaste Vessel
Late Classic period
Chichicaste, Juticalpa
Olancho, Honduras
Ceramic
Height: 26.8 cm; depth: 17.6 cm
diameter: 32.5 cm
Tegucigalpa, Bodegas Centrales
del Instituto Hondureño
de Antropología e Historia
Inv. no. TGC-C-1808

Tripod vessel, polychromed and polished inside and out, with hollow supports. It has been preliminarily classified as the type known as Bold Geometric. Its polychromy consists of orange-on-cream delimiting the central zone, with bands of red in linear designs. The central scene is the body of a serpent exactly where the two heads emerge, to function as handles. This vessel is important because it has stimulated a reconsideration of the zone of Mesoamerican influence, since this type of ceramic had not been found previously in the eastern part of the country.   CJF

277

277
Miniature Figurine
Late Classic period
Provenance unknown
Bone
Height: 6.5 cm; width: 2.5 cm
thickness: 2.0 cm
Mexico City
Museo Nacional de Antropología
Inv. no. 10-001239

Bone was used in the creation of different useful objects, such as spatulas, fish hooks, perforators, and needles. In many burials, stingray spines have also been found that, just as perforators and needles, were used in rites of autosacrifice to extract blood from certain parts of the body. Other objects faithfully reproduce different mythical and historical subjects, such as this miniature figurine that represents a *halach uinic*, the title given to rulers or functionaries who exercised maximum civil authority in ancient Maya society. Noteworthy are the meticulous details, both of the costume and physical traits. The hollow seen in the headdress, above the forehead, perhaps contained an inlaid material. ACM

278
Stela 11
Late Classic period
Acropolis (Structure 18)
Copán Ruinas, Honduras
Stone
Height: 171.0 cm; width: 45.0 cm
Copán, Parque Arqueológico
Ruinas de Copán
Inv. no. CPN-P-37560

Stela 11 is the latest stela depicting a ruler at Copán. Here the 16th ruler, Yax Pasah is dressed as the maize god with foliation sprouting from his head and ceremonial bar. He performed a ritual in his third *katun*. WF

278

279
Pendant
Late Classic period
Unknown location east of Misantha
Nephrite
Height: 7.2 cm
width: 9.5 cm
Berlin, Museum für Völkerkunde
Strebel Collection, 1890, SMPK
Inv. no. IV 13023

Pendants, earrings, necklaces, and armbands made of the highly treasured jadeite and green stone were often very elaborately wrought. The engraved portrait on this asymmetrical pendant seems to represent a prince. The head of the bearded man is shown in profile, his plump body in frontal view. His face has a fiercely glaring expression, and he sits crosslegged on a mat or low throne. The pendant has three holes bored in it. MG

280
Plaque
Classic period
Nebaj, El Quiché, Guatemala
Jadeite
Height: 10.6 cm
ength: 14.6 cm
Guatemala, El Museo Nacional
de Arqueología y Etnología
Inv. no. MNAE 4733

279

280

Plaque carved in jadeite on which are represented two figures, a richly garbed noble and a smaller figure, seated opposite each other and in poses suggesting dialogue. The noble wears a headdress with the figure of a bird and long feathers, circular earplugs with pendants, bracelets, and a pectoral with three anthropomorphic faces, one on each shoulder and a third on the thorax. The individual is seated on a cushion with three human heads alternating with bands and crossed legs; an anklet is on his right leg. On the back part is a seat back, possibly made of a woven mat. A dwarf with arms and legs crossed is seated on the right side of the figure. On the opposite side are series of two anthropomorphic masks. MSB

281
Plaque
Classic period
Mixcoac, Mexico City
Mexico
Jadeite
Height: 5.0 cm
width: 8.9 cm
Mexico City
Museo Nacional de Antropología
Inv. no. 10-001234

The green semirectangular plaque is carved in low relief, and shows, in the center, an individual of very high rank. He is seated frontally, with crossed arms and legs, barefoot, with hair tied back, adorned with two clasps and a comb or something of this nature to hold it down. On the left wrist he wears a bracelet and with his arms he sus-

tains a ceremonial bar in horizontal position, from which emerge serpents on both sides. For some scholars, the bicephalic serpent, as a celestial animal, is the representation of the Milky Way, the main element in the nocturnal sky, and in this sense is another representation of Itzamna, the creator-god among the Mayas. EGL

282
Plaque
Terminal Classic–Early Postclassic period
Chichén Itzá, Yucatán
Mexico
Jadeide
Length: 7.0 cm
width: 9.5 cm
thickness: 9 mm
Merida
Museo Regional de Yucatán
"Palacio Cantón"
Inv. no. 10-424910

One of the most beautiful pieces taken from the Sacred Cenote is this pentagonal jade plaque. It represents a person seated crosslegged and facing toward the right. He wears an elaborate animal headdress from which hang long feathers decorated with beads. As clothing, he wears an *ex* (loincloth in Mayan) and his costume is complemented by ear ornaments, a necklace with an anthropomorphic pendant, bracelets, and anklets. His overall appearance is that of an important dignitary. A double line, interrupted by a cascade of headdress feathers, frames the scene, and on the right side, outside of the frame, part of a large mask can be seen. This piece, together with other similar objects, belong to a tradition that possibly originated in the lower Usumacinta, although it was not necessarily made in that region. These types of plaques are considered to be in the Nebaj style, so named because it was at that site that the first of them was found. LFS

281

282

283

285

284

283
Pendant
Classic period
Nicoya, Guanacaste
Costa Rica
Jadeite
Height: 22.6 cm
width: 3.3 cm
thickness 6.0 cm
San José
Museo del Jade Lic.
Fidel Tristán
Instituto Nacional de Seguros
Inv. no. INS 4439

Pendant with two perforations to suspend the piece horizontally. The main incised figure details a Maya person in profile. It possibly represents a priest or a high ranking individual, based on the attire and accoutrements that he wears. Below the glyphs, there seems to be a macaw, a bird prized for its feathers and coloring.   JVGM

284
Figurine
Late Classic period
Hieroglyphic Stairway
Copán Ruinas, Honduras
Jadeite
Height: 14.5
width: 15.0
thickness: 4.0 cm
Copán

Centro Regional
de Investigaciones Arqueológicas
Inv. no. CPN-J-185

This figurine was placed with three eccentric flints, a ceramic incense burner, and a *Spondylus* shell in the dedicatory cache at the foot of the Hieroglyphic Stairway. It represents a Maya man, simply dressed in loincloth and headband, with his legs slightly bent and his forearms in a horizontal position as on the Copán stelae, where the rulers are shown sustaining the ultimate symbol of divine authority known as the Ceremonial Bar. On the back of the figure's head, the knot in the headband and his hair are identical to the main sign on the "emblem glyph" that identifies the kingdom of Tikal. The dark color, veins of lighter hues, high relief and rounded carving, and make this one of the finest jade objects ever produced in the New World.   WF

285
Figural Pectoral
Late Classic period
Las Sepulturas, Copán
Honduras
Jadeite
Height: 12.7
width: 4.0 cm

thickness: 1.0 cm
Copán, Museo Regional
de Arqueología
Inv. no. CPN-J-158

This piece shows a Maya lord in profile, looking left, with a large bird head forming the centerpiece of his plumed headdress. His pose is that of Late Classic Maya stelae: torso and legs facing front, head in profile looking left (see also Stela 11, no. 278). He stands on the stylized head of a supernatural animal, referred to in Maya studies as a zoomorph. The zoomorph is not unlike any of the large stone altars in the civic-ceremonial center, which many scholars have argued were glorified stools upon which the ruler and other dignitaries stood to make themselves seen and heard in public gatherings. This fine jadeite was placed with a *Spondylus* shell inside a ceramic incense burner as part of a build-ing dedication cache for a religious structure in Plaza H, part of the elite residential Group 9N-8 in the Sepulturas urban ward of Copán.   WF

286

286
Plaque
Late Postclassic period
El Meco, Quintana Roo, Mexico
Bone
Height: 17.2 cm; width: 4.4 cm
thickness: 3.0 cm
Cancún
Museo Arqueológico de Cancún
Inv. no. 10-389669 EM-1-1

This piece of engraved bone was decorated with a scene charged with deep religious symbolism. It represents an anthropomorphic figure in profile wearing sumptuous attire and associated with elements such as the serpent, an ear of maize an and a *kan* glyph. This suggests that it could have been a Postclassic image of God K, or that of a priest with the attributes of this deity. The headdress of the figure consists of a serpent head, whose body also forms part of the symbolic motif; it even seems that the divinity is standing on the serpent and one of his lower extremities extends to form the appendage of the reptile. Opposite the face of the figure is an ear of corn and the *kan* symbol.   ECTA

287
Cylindrical Vessel
Late Classic period
Tikal, Petén, Guatemala
Jadeite
Height: 24.2 cm
diameter: 10.0 cm
Guatemala, Museo Nacional
de Arqueología y Etnología
Inv. no. MNAE 11080a and 11080b

287

Cylindrical vessel made of jadeite mosaic with a lid. This was found as part of the funerary offering of the important ruler, Hasaw Chan Kawil, also known as Ah Cacau, discovered in Temple 1, or the Temple of the Great Jaguar, at Tikal. An animal design emerges from the body of the vessel. The lid has a head wearing a feather headdress and circular earplugs with tubular and spherical pendants, all worked in jadeite. The eyes and mouth are open. A necklace of several irregular spherical beads is seen and a pendant with an incised glyph hangs from the neck. It is believed that this figure is a portrait of the young ruler Hasaw Chan Kawil. The color of the raw material is brilliant green in several shades. According to some specialists, this vessel together with similar one also found at Tikal, represents the culmination of jadeite mosaic work.   MSB

288

288
"Lizard" Pectoral
Late Classic period
Copán Valley, Honduras
Shell
Height: 13.0 cm; width: 5.2 cm
Copán
Museo Regional de Arqueología
Inv. no. CPN-h-77

Found in association with a residence located less than 200 meters north of the Great Plaza of Copán, this object is one of the finest examples of shell-working ever unearthed in Copán, and one of the finest found in Mesoamerica. The profile of a man and his shoulders looks to the left in

289

288a

the center of the pendant or broach, surrounded by jade inlays. He occupies the center of a stylized water lily pad, which also forms the body of a saurian creature whose head is seen in profile at the viewer's right. In the ancient Maya view of the world, the surface of the earth was the back of a giant caiman, floating in an immense sea. The association of water lilies with caimans is an enduring one in nature and in Maya art, and it seems likely that the man's face was that of an ancestor whose remains came to reside in the watery underworld.   WF

288a
Shell
Probably Late Classic
Panabá, Yucatán, Mexico
Shell

Length: 10.2 cm; width: 10 cm
Museo Regional de Antropología
de Yucatán "Palacio Cantón"
Inv. no. 10-290320

Shell was a material utilized in many ways in pre-Hispanic times. It was used for food, in the production of tools, in making musical instruments and in some cases, even as a currency. It has been found in archaeological contexts in a wide variety of shell decorations: ear ornaments, pendants and mosaic pieces. The object displayed here is a beautiful example of shellwork in the Maya area. The original shape of the specimen was exploited and the design was adapted to it, beginning with the frame. The scene displays two seated persons, one of them is turning over an unidenti-

290

fied object. The figure on the right sits on a type of bench or throne, which is placed at a slightly higher level than that of the other figure and which is apparently a symbol of his power. Both men have crossed legs and the bottoms of their feet are visible. They are dressed with loincloths and headdresses with feathers and jewels.   LFS

289
Plaque
Late Classic period
Jaina Island, Campeche, Mexico
Shell
Height: 9.1 cm; width: 6.2 cm
Mexico City
Museo Nacional de Antropología
Inv. no. 10-078166

This shell plaque represents a member of the Maya nobility conducting a ritual. Opposite him is a receptacle from which emerge two sections of what could be the body of a serpent, while opposite the face of the noble appears the head of the reptile. The serpent that he manipulates is a being through which he makes physical contact with the supernatural, introducing himself into the realm of the sacred, which is the aim of all ritual acts.   MCG

290
Figurine Fragment
Late Classic period
Tenam Rosario, Chiapas, Mexico
Ceramic
Height: 19.8 cm
width: 15.2 cm
thickness: 6.5 cm
San Cristóbal de las Casas
Centro Cultural de los Altos
de Chiapas
Inv. no. 10-338430

Many Maya cities are characterized by their pottery production, which includes a large and variety of figurines both modeled and mold-made that exhibit the personal array and wardrobe number the Maya. The majority of these pieces are representations of men and women in elegant poses, either of the elite or priestly

291

292

class. There are human figures with headdresses, such as this example, in the form of a rosette-indicating high status. The piece comes from Tenam Rosario, a site occupied near the end of the Late Classic period.   AGC

291
Animal Sculpture
Terminal Classic–Early Postclassic period
Chichén Itzá, Yucatán, Mexico
Limestone
Height: 64.0 cm
length: 73.5 cm
depth: 54.0 cm
Merida, Museo Regional de Yucatán "Palacio Cantón"
Inv. no. 10-426383

Another example of this type of figure, painted red and with simulated spots made of jadeite circles, was found in the substructure of El Castillo at Chichén Itzá. The jaguar

is a symbol of the underworld. It is common to see rulers represented seated on thrones covered with a jaguar skin. This sculpture was most likely used as a throne or for the placement of offerings.   APC

292
Sculpture
Classic period
Usumacinta Valley, Mexico
Limestone
Height: 125.0 cm; width: 176.0 cm
thickness 25.0 cm
Puebla, Fundación Amparo-Museo Amparo
Inv. no. 52 22MA FA 57 PJ 1372

The arrangement of columns of glyphs and masks in profile that makes up the frame of this extraordinary sculpture indicates that it was complemented by a third panel on the right side, probably containing another figure. Nothing similar to this has been found, although at Piedras Negras, a throne with a piece carved in three dimensions and a relief representing a similar throne have been found. In this piece, the royal couple seems to be represented with total realism, although attention is called to a gnomic deity thus establishing the symbolic dimensions of the scene. It

might be a symbol of divine rule, corresponding to the headdresses, the staffs, or other ritual objects that appear in different compositions at Palenque, which display a dominant figure with male and female companions. The relief commemorates, in a pair of glyphs above the central column, a date that J. Eric S. Thompson places between A.D. 747 and A.D. 799.

Epigraphic reading
It was (9.14.19.11.12 or 9.17.12.6.122) 6 *eb*5 *zotz* [12-April-731 or 30-March-783], Ah Nal Chaan spilled blood . . . Lord Pacal, dedicated his seat, the sacred lord . . .

293
Altar
Late Classic period
Edzná, Campeche, Mexico
Limestone
Height: 17.5 cm
diameter: 24.5 cm
Campeche, Museo Histórico
Fuerte de San Miguel
Baluarte de San Miguel
Inv. no. 10-397886

This small altar, painted red, comes from an offering in a building that was remodeled, probably in the Postclassic period at the small Acropolis at Edzná, Campeche. In the upper part of the altar is rucgkt dressed woman of high status with a flower headdress. Perched on top of the headdresses is a hummingbird, a manifestation of the sun god in its fertility aspect. This bird is frequently found in sculptures, including the headdresses of individuals who appear on Lintel 58 at Yaxchilán, Chiapas. On the body of the altar may be seen seven blocks of glyphs, which confirm that the subject is a woman.   LMC

Epigraphic reading by Alfonso Arellano
on the horizontal surface may be read: lord [of the] mountain,
on the vertical: her altar, precious [of the], Lady Pah, Lady Bapa, Xokil, Lady Shell *Tz'a*, upholder of the cosmos.

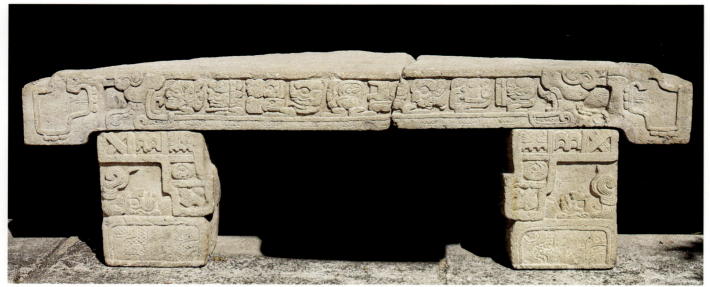

295

294

296

297

294
Piedras Negras Lintel 3
Late Classic period
Piedras Negras, Petén, Guatemala
Stone
Width: 61.0 cm; length: 121.0 cm
Guatemala, Museo Nacional
de Arqueología y Etnología
Inv. no. MNAE 613

On the stela is a courtly scene with several figures on different planes. In the foreground are seven seated men who represent secondary nobles; in the midground are another six figures, standing in groups of three, and in the group to the right is a youth, the son of the ruler, wearing a feather headdress. In the central plane is the ruler, Ruler 4, seated on his throne. This lintel was commissioned by Ruler 6. On it is represented the naming of the future Ruler 5, in which Ruler 4 participated. The text mentions that the ruler Bird Jaguar of Yaxchilán was present. Several are part of the scene panels of glyphs. In one of them is the signature of the sculptors. It is dated 9.15.18.3.13 5 *ben* 16 *chen* (749 A.D.). MSB

Epigraphic reading by Alfonso Arellano
It was 9.15.18.31.3 5 *ben* 16 *chen*, GI reigned over the night, F, the moon was 8 days old, it was the first of the period, X was his name, and he would last 29 days [27-July-749], he completed his first *katun* as lord of the succession of Ruler 4, sacred lord of Piedras Negras. He was seen in a canoe by (Yaxum) Balam, sacred lord of Yaxchilán. His change was on 9.15.18.3.15) 7 *men* 18 *chen* [29-July-749] and he danced(?) with Kawil Ruler 4, divine lord of Piedras Negras; on the day . . . on the plate for cacao Ruler 4, . . . sun . . . then. There passed 8 *tuns*, 8 *uinals* and 2 *kins* then it was the day 9.16.6.11.17 7 *caban* 0 *pax* [26-November-757] when Ruler 4 died, sacred lord of Piedras Negras; 3 days (later) it was 9.16.6.12.0 10 *ahau* 3 *pax* [29-November-757], and they buried him at the Hill of the Shield . . . Then passed 1 *katun* (4 *tuns*, 12 *uinals* y 1 *kin*) and on the day 9.17.6.11.6.1 12 *imix* 19 *zip* [24-March-782] . . . . . . lord of 3 *katuns*, he is Ah Hun . . ., sacred lord of Piedras Negras.
[There are 14 glyphic clauses corresponding to names of the each associated individual. Outstanding is Yaxum Bahlum of Yaxchilán and some names of sculptors.]

295
Hieroglyphic Bench
Late Classic period
Acropolis, Copán, Honduras
Stone
Height: 57.8 cm; width: 185.8 cm
Tegucigalpa, Bodegas Centrales

del Instituto Hondureño
de Antropología e Historia
Inv. no. TGC-P-248

This bench was found in one of the largest structures (9K-47) near the Great Plaza, and its hieroglyphic text is the most enigmatic at Copán. On its supports is engraved the representation of the sun god, between a celestial band and the symbol of the earth below. The text on the bench consists of nine glyphs, without a date nor any historical individuals. These nine glyphs represent the nine Lords of the Night, each one reigning over a nocturnal period. CJF

296
Lintel 24
Height: 109.7 cm; width: 77.3 cm
London, The British Museum
Inv. no. 1886-317

This scene depicts Lord Shield Jaguar and his principal wife Lady Xok engaged in a bloodletting rite that took place on 9.13.17.15.12 5 *eb* 15 *mac* in the Maya calendar, or 28 October A.D. 709. The king stands on the left brandishing a long flaming torch to illuminate the drama that is about to unfold. Kneeling in front of him wearing an exquisitely woven *huipil*, Lady Xok pulls a thorn-lined rope through her

tongue. The rope falls onto a woven basket holding blood-soaked strips of paper cloth.

297
Yaxchilán Lintel 26
Late Classic period
Yaxchilán, Chiapas, Mexico
Limestone
Length: 215.0 cm; width: 85.0 cm
depth: 25.0 cm
Mexico City
Museo Nacional de Antropología
Inv. no. 10-009790

During the reign of Shield Jaguar (late seventh-early eighth century A.D.) the sculptural school of Yaxchilán produced its best carvings, to the extent that many monuments are signed and we know the names of several sculptors. Particularly outstanding are the lintels from Structure 23, showing scenes related to autosacrifice, visions of ancestors emerging from serpent maws and representations such as this one commemorating a marriage alliance between the sovereign and Lady Xok, a lady from the lineage of Calakmul, who offers him the trappings of warfare: a shield and jaguar helmet. The hieroglyphic inscription includes the signature of the sculptor and the dedication date of the monument which is recorded discretely in

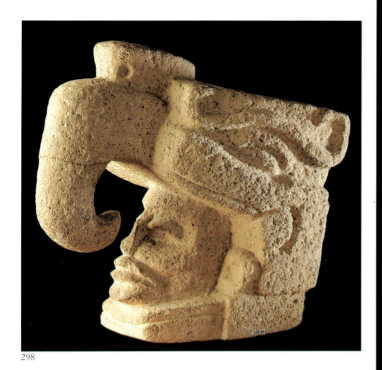

298

299

301

the upper, proper right corner, behind the head of Lord Shield Jaguar. The text in the shape of a T, located between both figures, mentions the name of the Lord and his titles. The inscription continues on the left side of the lintel. TPS

298
Sculpture
Late Classic period
Chimaltenango, Guatemala
Stone
Height: 38.0 cm; width: 46.0 cm
Guatemala, Museo Nacional
de Arqueología y Etnología
Inv. no. MNAE 2084

Sculpture of an anthropomorphic head emerging from the jaws of a zoomorphic deity. It has a receptacle on the upper part. The god seems to be a celestial bird combining elements of a serpent (flaming eyebrow) and bird (beak). The emerging figure has a closed mouth and eyes, a square earplug, and protruding lips. Birds were important in Maya cosmology. The most frequently mentioned is the Celestial Bird, or the Serpent Bird, represented with long feathers and short feet. This lives in the Tree of the World. MSB

299
Anthropomorphic Figure Emerging from a Flower
Classic period
Jaina Island, Campeche, Mexico
Ceramic
Height: 9.5 cm; width: 3.5 cm
Campeche, Museo Histórico
Fuerte de San Miguel
Baluarte de San Miguel
Inv. no. 10-290662

The representation of individuals or animals emerging from flowers or from plant elements is common in Pre-Columbian Maya iconography. The flower produces life. Deities who govern human events also emerge from plants. Deeply knowledgeable about their environment, the Mayas named and classified a large number of plants. Through oral tradition, this wisdom has endured through the centuries and it now constitutes valuable ethnobotanic information. Many rural communities use roots, bark, resin, leaves and fruit from a wide variety of plant species with proven effectiveness for medicinal, nutritional, dyeing, constructive, textile, and other practical purposes. ABC

300
Anthropomorphic Figure
Emerging From a Flower
Classic period
Jaina Island, Campeche, Mexico
Ceramic
Height: 12.0 cm; width: 6.5 cm
Mexico City
Museo Nacional de Antropología
Inv. no. 10-078182

In this piece is whith a hair the bust of a man with crossed arms, shown inside a flower. His body is modeled in detail pronounced chin and half-closed eyes. Although he lacks hair on the upper part of his head, falls on his shoulders. His mouth lacks teeth and his face is covered with wrinkles. These characteristics may indicate an individual of advanced age, or a newborn. Although at Jaina, fine human figurines often refer to real individuals rather than deities, in this case we might find a parallel in a Lacandon cosmogonic myth

narrating the birth of the gods from flowers: "*kakoch* formed the tuberose flower, and he made the gods be born from its blossons." MCG

301
Effigy Vessel
Late Classic period
Ceramic
Height: 18.0 cm
Mexico City
Museo Nacional de Antropología
Inv. no. 10-076519

Among the Mayas, shells were associated with the earth, the underworld and death; but they were also a symbol of life, birth, and water because of their very nature. They were linked with the feminine principle and they were attributes of the goddess of the moon, who was also the goddess of procreation, the earth, and water. In form they display a certain resemblance to the uterus, which came to be the symbol par excellence of birth and resurrection. In ancient Mexican thought it was said that just as the mollusk comes out of its shell, thus emerges man from the womb of his mother. Given the shell's importance, it is not strange in the repertory of Maya iconography to see representations of individuals carrying or emerging from a shell. These individuals, which can display attributes of an old man, perhaps represent God N, who is associated with the *bacabs* and with *Pahuatuns*, bearers of the sky and of the earth. ACM

302

303

305

304

302
Effigy Vessel
Late Postclassic period
Mayapán, Yucatán, Mexico
Ceramic
Height: 20.0 cm
width: 11.5 cm
Merida, Museo Regional
de Yucatán "Palacio Cantón"
Inv. no. 10-347672

This vessel was found as an offering under the floor of a shrine at Mayapán, a densely populated, walled Postclassic site. It belongs to the category of effigy vessels of Chen Mul Modelado ware, which represent frogs, turtles, birds, people in different positions, and even deities. This piece displays a fantastic being, part lizard or alligator and part turtle or shell, from which emerges a human head. The details can still be appreciated thanks to the permanence of the red, blue, yellow, and black colors on the white background. The motif of humans or gods emerging from the maws of animals, often serpents, is recurrent in Maya art and in other Mesoamerican cultures.   LFS

303
Effigy Vessel
Late Postclassic period
Mayapán, Yucatán, Mexico
Ceramic
Height: 18.5 cm; length: 22.0 cm
width: 17.5 cm
Merida, Museo Regional de Yucatán
"Palacio Cantón"
Inv. no. 10-251131

Turtle with human face emerging from its mouth and seated human figure on its head. The figure mounted on the turtle holds in his hands a braided design, a mat for the Mayas, which is found on the back and lateral part of the turtle. This design is a symbol of authority and is related to lineage power. Also, the turtle at Mayapán could have been related to the cult of the ancestors. It should be mentioned that God N or Pahuatun is characterized by the shell or turtle shell that he wears; he is also identified as a *bacab* or upholder of the sky. Perhaps this sculpture represents one of these deities.   APC

304
Bowl
Classic period
Northern Maya area
Ceramic
Height: 10.8 cm
diameter: 23.0 cm
Merida, Museo Regional de Yucatán "Palacio Cantón"
Inv. no. 10-383128

This tripod bowl with rattle supports belongs to the Fine Orange ceramic tradition. The main characteristics of Fine Orange are the fine-textured paste, the lack of temper, the smooth surface, and the orange slip. On occasion there is a second black or white slip, as in this case. The vessel displays a figure with cranial deformation, a feather headdress, necklace, and ear ornaments. Near his left hand, is a vessel of unidentified contents. The man is smoking a long cigar from which a column of smoke arises imparting movement to the scene. Tobacco was often used by Mesoamerican people; even the gods are depicted smoking, such as the Old God L sculpted on one of the panels of the Temple of the Cross at Palenque or several other deities in the *Madrid Codex*.   LFS

305
Sculpture
Preclassic period
Kaminaljuyú, Guatemala
Basalt
Height: 28.5 cm
length of the base: 15.8 cm
Guatemala, Museo Nacional
de Arqueología y Etnología
Inv. no. MNAE 15353

Mushroom with a stylized animal effigy. On the stalk is the face of a coiled serpent with nose upturned. The base is a solid rectangle. According to the classification proposed for these sculptures, this piece corresponds to the "composite type with three-dimensional zoomorphic figure," which is early in relation to other types. "Mushroom-stones," as they are known, are portable objects carved in stone. To date, their function is unknown, although several hypotheses have been put forth. One of these relates them to ceremonies in which hallucinogenic mushrooms were used. Another suggests that they could have been used to mark territorial boundaries. However, there is insufficient archaeological information to support any one of these theories. These sculptures were very common from the Preclassic period to the Late Classic period, although their manufacture was not continuous.   MSB

306
Sculpture
Classic period
Zaragoza
Chimaltenango, Guatemala
Stone
Height: 31.3 cm; width: 18.0 cm
Guatemala, Museo Nacional
de Arqueología y Etnología
Inv. no. MNAE 3595

Mushroom with stylized effigy and sculpted stalk. The cap of the mushroom is flat. It has a tripod base, corresponding to the Late Preclassic period. The majority of "mushroom-stones," as they are known, are made from a single block of volcanic stone (basalt), or occasionally of sandstone. It is common to find this type of sculpture in the Guatemalan highlands, although they have also been found on the southern coast of Guatemala; in Chiapas, Mexico; and in El Salvador. One of the problems in studying these sculptures is that the

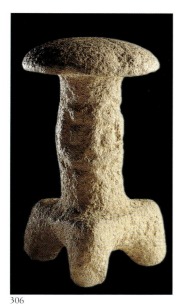

306

307

308

In the Maya area, representations of this animal, especially white-tailed deer, are very common both in ceramic and in sculpture. The upper classes ate deer meat, which they combined with corn tortillas and beans. There is also evidence that in the Guatemalan highlands hunters consumed a ritual dish made of deer meat thickened with maize dough. MSB

308
Adolescent from Cumpich
Terminal Classic period
Cumpich, Campeche, Mexico
Limestone
Height: 93.0 cm
width: 43.0 cm
Mexico City
Museo Nacional de Antropología
Inv. no. 10-009788

At the end of the Classic period, some sites in the Yucatán peninsula display clear evidence of a widespread phallic cult, which seems to have been propagated by groups from the region of the Gulf Coast of Mexico. This piece, which shows a young, naked youth with marked cranial deformation and scarification between the eyebrows and on the cheeks, may be an example of this cult. Although in part mutilated, the body of this figure displays a certain dynamism and calls attention to the size of the genitals. Around his neck, he wears a serpent knotted on his chest, and its broken extremities hang down onto the abdomen, as if a prolongation of the phallus. ACM

309
Kaminaljuyú Stela 9
Middle Preclassic period
Kaminaljuyú, Guatemala
Basalt
Height: 140.0 cm; width: 32.0 cm
Guatemala, Museo Nacional
de Arqueología y Etnología
Inv. no. MNAE 2359

The stela was found in Mound C-III-6. It is an irregular basalt column with a human figure carved to represent a dancer, similar to those known later at Monte Albán, Mexico. The pose is strange from the waist down: the face is shown in profile, but the thorax is depicted frontally. The hands are flexed. The figure wears a headdress with a volute in back, and a circular earplug. From his mouth emerge two volutes rising upward, possibly signifying speech. The stela was found with the bases of two pedestal sculptures that, together with three blocks of basalt, were placed around a large stone slab inside a pit. On the slab were found offerings of ceramics of the period, fine jadeite artifacts, and evidence of burning. MSB

309

origin of the majority of examples is unknown because very few have been found at archaeological excavations, in funerary contexts, or dispersed at sites. Its original function remains unknown. MSB

307
Sculpture
Preclassic period
Kaminaljuyú, Guatemala
Stone

Height: 29.0 cm; diameter: 13.6 cm
Guatemala, Museo Nacional
de Arqueología y Etnología
Inv. no. MNAE 9708

Mushroom with animal effigy of a full-body deer. The features of the head are well defined. The front legs stretch forward, while the back limbs are flexed and display hooves. A groove surrounds the lower part of the mushroom cap. The base is flat, solid and circular.

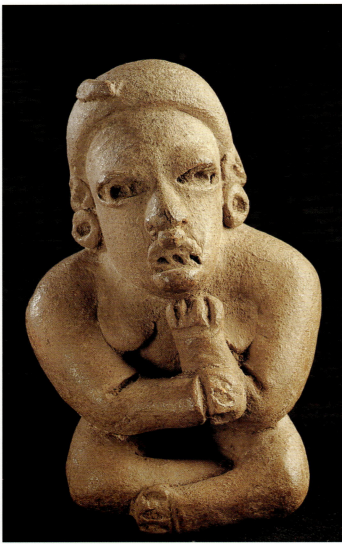

310

311

312

de Yucatán "Palacio Cantón"
Inv. no. 10-490149

This polychrome, hollow female figurine has a stepped fret design crossing her face from ear to ear and on her naked torso. Her legs resemble polychrome, zoomorphic, tetrapod supports typical of the fourth century or the ceramic phases known as Tzakol 1 and 2. Tomb 2 at Yaxuná, where this piece was found, contained thirteen individuals, including several children of both genders. Perhaps one of them was the owner of this figurine. It has been proposed that this tomb perhaps represents the elimination of a lineage or a royal captive and his family, an indication of the violent events of those times.   SB

314
Female Figurine
Late Classic period
Campo Pineda, Sula Valley
Honduras
Ceramic
Height: 22.5 cm
width: 17.0 cm
thickness: 11.0 cm
San Pedro Sula, Cortés
Museo de Antropología
Inv. no. SPS-DBF-91

Monochrome, polished, solid, molded figurine depicting a woman popularly known as the "Speaking Woman." Details are incised and there are remains of stucco and perforations. She is adorned with long bracelets, a necklace with pectoral, and earflares. It is important to note that the three-strand bracelets signify high status, as does her headdress with incisions on the front containing a precious stone.   CJF

315
Mural Painting
Middle–Late Postclassic period
Xcaret, Quintana Roo
Mexico
Stone, stucco, and paint
Height: 46.0 cm
width: 44.0 cm

310
Female Figurine
Preclassic period
San Agustín Acasaguastlán
El Progreso, Guatemala
Ceramic
Height: 10.7 cm
Guatemala
Museo Nacional
de Arqueología y Etnología
Inv. no. MNAE 9702

Figurine that represents a seated woman with arms and legs crossed. She wears a low headdress in the shape of a turban, and circular earplugs. Modeled elements were added to a nucleus of clay to form the head, extremities, and decorative motifs. These figurines may be standing or seated, because the arms and legs were represented in different positions. The faces display considerable detail. The eyes were made with circular impressions and often had ornaments such as headdresses and earplugs.   MSB

311
Duality Figurine
Late Classic period
Campo Pineda, Sula Valley

Honduras
Ceramic
Height: 16.0 cm
width: 4.5 cm
thickness: 9.0 cm
weight: 359,8 gm
San Pedro Sula, Cortés
Museo de Antropología
Inv. no. SPS-DBF-244

Monochrome, polished, solid figurine called a "duality" because the body and lower extremities are animal, while the head is human. It is positioned on its side, half reclining. The face and headdress bear incised decoration, while the nose is appliquéd, and the open mouth displays teeth. The figure wears earplugs, and the simple headdress in particular usually characterizes depictions of women. The single strand of beads of the necklace suggests an individual of low rank.   CJF

312
Female Figurine
Preclassic period
Kaminaljuyú, Guatemala
Ceramic
Height: 25.0 cm

width: 19.0 cm
Guatemala
Museo Nacional
de Arqueología y Etnología
Inv. no. MNAE 10603

The figurine represents a seated woman with crossed arms and extended legs. Her hands are placed on her rounded belly. She wears circular earplugs. Her legs show remains of reddish-brown slip. During the Middle Preclassic period, all figurines were covered with white, red or flesh-colored slip. They were represented in natural positions, with the eyes marked with circular punch marks and the mouth open, with thick lips. The exact function of these figurines in Mesoamerica is unknown; however, it is believed that they could be related to a fertility cult, referring to either the harvest of pregnancy or the breeding of children. This idea is shared by many other cultures worldwide.   MSB

313
Doll
Early Classic period
Yaxuná, Yucatán, Mexico
Ceramic
Height: 22.5 cm; width: 15.0 cm
thickness: 7.0 cm
Merida
Museo Regional

313

314

maximum depth: 16.0 cm
weight: 25.0 kg
Cancún
Museo Arqueológico
de Cancún
Inv. no. 10-229272

The subject matter of Postclassic-period mural painting, as seen here, was mainly religious in character with a strong tendency toward agricultural subjects such as the representation of rites or ceremonies related to rain and the harvest, fundamentally of corn, which was the main staple of the Mayas. This painting was executed in the *fresco secco* technique, also known as the dry fresco technique, using plant and mineral pigments or a mixture of both, as in the case of the distinctive color known as Maya blue. The scene represented here, although incomplete, decorated the interior of a temple at Xcaret and reflects agricultural concerns. Perhaps the central figure is Itzamna, one of the main deities in the Maya pantheon, creator-god and sustainer, from whose arm hangs a bag that could contain an aromatic resin or seeds of corn. The god looks out of the corner of his eye at the representation of a plant behind him, which seems to be a young maize plant, still without ears of corn, but with human traits that could perhaps allude to the tender, young corn and the successful harvest.   MJCU

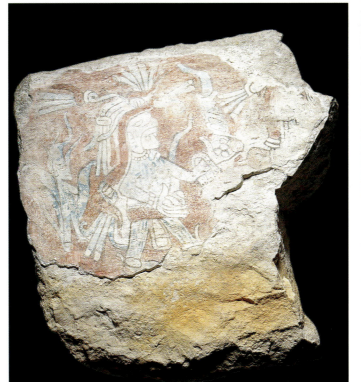

315

316
Ocarina
Middle Classic period
Corruste, Sula Valley, Honduras
Ceramic
Height: 11.7 cm; width: 11.2 cm
thickness: 6 mm

316

Details are incised and appliquéd. The earplugs are unusual because they are not found on other whistles. The figure is animal, possibly a jaguar. Whistles and ocarinas of this type are utensils that are hallmarks of the Middle Classic period in the Sula Valley.   CJF

Tegucigalpa, Bodegas Centrales
del Instituto Hondureño
de Antropología e Historia
Inv. no. TGC-C-245

Monochrome whistle in zoomorphic shape with polished surface.

317

318

From his arms hang copal incense bags and in the left hand he holds a smoking ball of this resin, while in the other he holds the vessel with water that the god spills on the earth. ACM

321
Urn
Late Postclassic period
Mayapán, Yucatán, Mexico
Ceramic
Height: 60.0 cm; width: 34.0 cm
depth: 34.0 cm
Mexico City
Museo Nacional de Antropología
Inv. no. 10-001243

Censers of this type with effigies attached to the front are characteristic of the Late Postclassic period. The most well-known examples come from Mayapán; however, they have appeared, although with some variants, in other parts of the Yucatán peninsula, especially on the east coast. They were made of rough clay, they lack surface polish, and once the effigy was placed on the piece, after firing, they were painted with bright colors that gave them an attractive appearance, although their technical quality is not very satisfactory. The figures were made by assembling different parts of the body (hands, feet, faces, legs, arms, ornaments, etc.) which, thanks to molds, were made in series and were practically the same. At the end, certain traits were added to identify them with some particular deity. Apparently these objects had a double function. They served as recipients to burn copal and they also served as idols of the gods they personified. In this case, the urn bears the representation of Itzamna, the most important god of the Maya pantheon. ACM

322
Censer
Late Postclassic period
Mayapán, Yucatán, Mexico
Ceramic
Height: 57.5 cm; diameter: 35.5 cm
Merida, Museo Regional de Yucatán
"Palacio Cantón"
Inv. no. 10-290437

This incense burner belongs to the ceramic ware known as Chen Mul Modelado and represents the god of corn. His face is yellow and red. The sphere held in his right hand could be copal or corn because the leaves of the maize plant sprout from it. Remains of red, blue, green, and yellow are preserved on this vessel. APC

323
Censer
Late Postclassic period
Mayapán, Yucatán, Mexico

317
Censer Lid
Late Classic period
Moxviquil, Chiapas, Mexico
Ceramic
Height: 20.3 cm
width: 12.9 cm
thickness: 8 cm
San Cristóbal de las Casas
Centro Cultural Ná Bolom
Inv. no. 164PF 144 L2M146

A human face projects from inside the maw of a fantastic animal mask on this hollow incense burner lid. Below the jaw of the face is a hole to allow the smoke to escape from the burner. Scarification can be seen around the lips and on the jaw of the anthropomorphic figure. Volutes around this face represent the teeth of the fantastic animal. TALW

318
Anthropomorphic Figure
Middle Classic period
Los Bordos, Chiapas, Mexico
Ceramic
Height: 39.0 cm
width 23.0 cm
thickness: 28.0 cm
San Cristóbal de las Casas
Centro Cultural de los Altos
de Chiapas
Inv. no. 10-458600

Individual in seated position wearing a mask with jaguar attributes. Based on the pose of the arms, supported on the knees, probably it was originally part of a bowl that functioned as a brazier. During religious ceremonies, different ritual objects intervened. The images of

319

gods, such as the one on this object – perhaps representing the deity of the underworld sun – were frequently accompanied by censers where aromatic resins were burned to feed the deities and communicate with them. AGC

319
Figurine on a Throne
Late Classic period
Palenque, Chiapas, Mexico
Ceramic
Figurine height: 17.0 cm
width: 8.3 cm
throne height: 6.6 cm
width: 13.6 cm
length: 18.6 cm
Palenque, Museo de Sitio
"Alberto Ruz Lhuillier"
Inv. no. 10-458661 0/2

This superbly made piece represents a seated man with crossed legs. He wears a helmet or mask with the image of the ocellated turkey, called *kutz* in Maya. He has a simple hipcloth that still pre-

320

serves traces of blue pigment, as well as wristlets and a beaded necklace. The position of his right arm seems to indicate that he is holding something in front of his face, while his left hand rests on his knee. The figurine was found placed in the center of an altar, also made of clay and painted blue. The scene possibly alludes to the moment when a noble is performing a ritual act. It was found in Tomb 1, Building 3 of Group B at Palenque. AGC

320
Censer
Late Postclassic period
Mayapán, Yucatán, Mexico
Ceramic
Height: 56.0 cm; width: 34.0 cm
Mexico City
Museo Nacional de Antropología
Inv. no. 10-081374

In the Yucatán peninsula, the beginning of the Late Postclassic period coincides with the culmination and predominance of Mayapán. One of the most characteristic ceramic expressions of the site, and of the period, are censers with effigies of deities, such as this piece, representing Chaac, the long-nosed rain god. The entire figure is divided vertically into two colors: blue and reddish brown, a possible allusion to the sky or celestial water and to the earth.

321

322

323

Ceramic
Height: 58.2 cm; width: 36.0 cm
depth: 32.0 cm
Merida, Museo Regional de Yucatán
"Palacio Cantón"
Inv. no. 10-251125

Among the objects of material culture produced by the inhabitants of Mayapán is a painted ceramic, which, despite its lack of slip, was highly attractive, especially for the richness of the appliquéd ornamentation that can be seen on anthropomorphic incense burners. The burners seem to represent gods or priests dressed as deities. This piece depicts Quetzalcoatl, the Feathered Serpent, a fundamental figure in Mesoamerican iconography. He can be identified by the cut shell pectoral, painted blue and outlined in yellow, that hangs from his neck. In each of his hands, raised in front of him, he holds a sphere, which could represent an offering of copal.   APC

324
Censer
Late Classic period
Purulhá, Baja Verapaz, Guatemala
Ceramic
Height: 47.0 cm
width of the base: 30.0 cm
Guatemala, Museo Nacional
de Arqueología y Etnología
Inv. no. MNAE 7892

Polychrome cylindrical censer with a human effigy representing an individual disguised as a quetzal, an identification based on certain human traits such as the eyes and nose.

324

325

The figure has three openwork circles on each side and stands on a plain black base. The quetzal wears a diadem with six crosses, square ear ornaments with small pendants and a necklace of round beads; on the lower part are two small quetzal birds. Different details of the decoration were modeled and appliquéd. This type of vessel was used to burn incense during ceremonies; these many examples display traces of burning. These objects generally consist of two parts: the receptacle, and the lid with air holes for the smoke to escape.   MSB

325
Figurine
Terminal Classic period
Jonuta, Tabasco, Mexico
Ceramic
Height: 22.5 cm
width: 12.0 cm
depth: 7.0 cm
Jonuta
Museo "Omar Huerta Escalante"
Inv. no. MJ-239

Located on the banks of the Usumacinta River, the archaeological zone of Jonuta, Tabasco, now under the streets of the town of the same name, functioned as an important figurine production center. Chemical analyses have shown that many of these, of the so-called Jaina type, were made with the local clays of Jonuta. Similarly, during the Terminal Classic period, hundreds of figurines were produced of fine orangeware, manufactured in molds. The vast majority are whistles and they represent richly dressed individuals with attributes of a wide variety of animals and fantastic beings, as may be appreciated in this extraordinary piece.   TPS

326
Figurine
Late Classic period
Jaina Island, Campeche, Mexico
Ceramic
Height: 13.2 cm
width: 7.0 cm
thickness: 6.0 cm
Mexico City
Museo Nacional de Antropología
Inv. no. 10-223506

Whistle figurine with a mouthpiece on the lower part that also serves as a third support, made with a mold, just as the majority of others found on the island of Jaina. The figure represents a priest with arms raised to the center of his chest; in his right hand he carries a whistle. His garb is characteristic of this type of figure. He wears a cape, painted blue, which covers him to his waist, and a long skirt with a decoration hanging down the front; he has a necklace with spherical beads and a bird mask, probably a turkey. Figurines representing men dressed with bird masks or entire bird costumes with feather decoration are frequent in Jaina burials and in the lower Usumacinta, as well as in the mountainous region of the Tuxtlas in Veracruz.   MCL

327
Figurine
Terminal Classic period
Jonuta, Tabasco, Mexico
Ceramic
Height: 17.0 cm; width: 11.5 cm
depth: 8.0 cm
Jonuta
Museo "Omar Huerta Escalante"
Inv. no. MJ-232

The use of molds to manufacture figurines increased notably during the end of the Classic period. This mass production permitted the existence of identical pieces. Many of them function as whistles and display a more or less flat form when seen from the front, although they have a mouthpiece on the back. This may be seen in the case of this figurine, showing the image of a human body endowed with great dynamism, achieved by the support of the right knee on the ground and the movement of the left arm. The head, which looks toward the left, is covered with a bird mask and an elegant aureole of feathers seems to emerge from the back.   TPS

328
Animal Ocarina
Terminal Classic period
Provenance unknown
Ceramic
Height: 14.0 cm; width: 9.0 cm
depth: 5.2 cm
Villahermosa, Museo Regional
de Antropología "Carlos Pellicer"
Inv. no. A-0663

326

327

328

This zoomorphic ocarina has the remains of white paint. It represents a richly attired figure with a swollen abdomen and an opossum mask. Animals are associated with the gods of the Maya people. Their worship was a form of controlling the forces of nature, and justifying the dualistic concepts of the balance of life: fertility and drought, life and death, earth and sky. Hun Ah Pu Vuch, "One Hunter Opossum," is an animal that caught the attention of the Quiche Maya for its cleverness and the way it reproduces; its gestation period is only thirteen days, a sacred number for the Maya. These and other characteristics of the way the animal nurses must have recalled notions of fertility, prompting the use, of its image.   RP

329
Censer Holder
Late Classic period
Palenque, Chiapas, Mexico
Ceramic
Height: 114.0 cm
maximum width: 60.5 cm
Mexico City
Museo Nacional de Antropología
Inv. no. 10-009789

Objects of this type, called cylinders, tubes, supports, or bases for incense burners, had an important function in ceremonial activities. They are composed of a tubular section that has a rectangular plaque on each side, attached as if fins. In this example the front decoration consists of a series of masks and different symbols, placed one above the other. The main mask displays the complete face of the sun god Kinich Ahau, generally represented blind or cross-eyed; he is placed between other partial masks that serve as a base below and as a headdress in the upper part. This type of decorative element, formed by superimposed masks, is also common in architecture and in the headdresses of some figures.   ACM

330
Censer Base
Late Classic period
Palenque, Chiapas
Mexico
Ceramic
Height: 84.5 cm
width: 30.0 cm
diameter: 28.0 cm

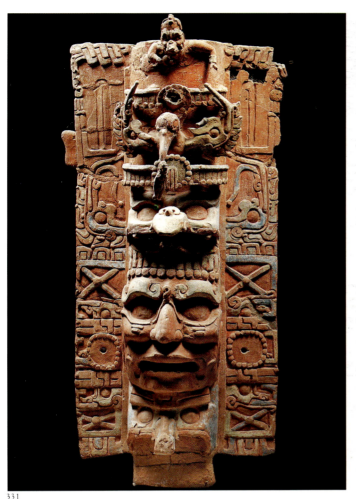

331

329

330

*Palenque, Museo de Sitio
"Alberto Ruz Lhuillier"
Inv. no. 10-479190*

This incense burner base, recovered from recent excavations of Temple XV-C at Palenque, is the example in the best state of preservation and displays the greatest artistic and technical perfection of this ceramic tradition. It is also a representation of complex religious symbolism. Composite censers are objects used to burn aromatic resins during rituals, for which a bowl was placed in the upper part of the pedestal. They were also temporary receptacles of the deities; therefore the central motif of their decoration are the faces of these numens. In the piece displayed here are human features without the attributes of supernatural beings, so perhaps it is the image of a deified ruler.   MCG

331
Censer Base
*Late Classic period
Palenque, Chiapas, Mexico
Ceramic
Height: 92.0 cm; width: 46.0 cm
Palenque, Museo de Sitio
"Alberto Ruz Lhuillier"
Inv. no. 10-458627*

This piece, found as a result of explorations carried out between 1991 and 1994, comes from the Temple of the Foliated Cross. The

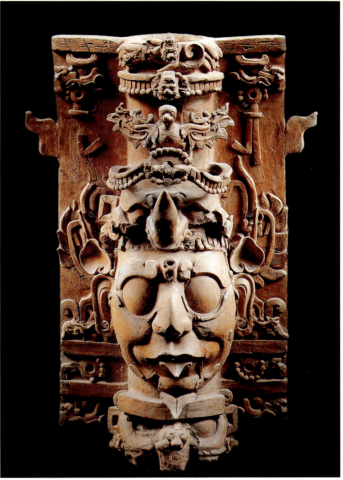

332

use of composite incense burners in the Maya area has a long tradition that goes back to the Late Preclassic period. The most notable characteristics of these objects are the hollow, cylindrical pedestals with two flanges at each side. These traits are preserved until the Late Classic, a period when decoration becomes more complex. The examples recovered in the Group of the Crosses at Palenque are characterized by having masks superimposed on the central face as if a headdress; it also includes birds of different types and figurines of deities at the top. This example displays the face of GIII of the Palenque Triad, a deity that personifies the underworld sun. The bird holds the head of the Maize God in his beak, the same deity who is seen with his head replacing an ear of corn. At the peak stands the image of GII, *kawil*, a deity related to fertility and one of the most important symbols of the ruling nobility.   MCG

332
Censer Base
*Late Classic period
Palenque, Chiapas, Mexico
Ceramic
Height: 105.0 cm; width: 71.0 cm
Palenque, Museo de Sitio
"Alberto Ruz Lhuillier"
Inv. no. 10-458622*

The group of the buildings of the Crosses were the scene of intense ceremonial life, a context in which incense burners were of particular importance. The image of the god represented on this piece is that of the nocturnal aspect of the sun, so that the deity has the ears of a jaguar, the animal with which the trajectory of this star was identified in the underworld. The fact that this deity is one of the most frequently represented tells us that his extensive cult had a very special significance as the ruling class' link with the creative deity of the cosmos. Thus, as the sun is born, dies, and is reborn again in repetitive cycles Maya kings succeeded one another without interrupting the continuity and order of the world.   MCG

333

334

335

333
Anthropomorphic Head
Late Postclassic period
Mayapán, Yucatán, Mexico
Ceramic
Height: 26.0 cm; width: 16.6 cm
Merida
Museo Regional de Yucatán
"Palacio Cantón"
Inv. no. 10-290435

This piece is a fragment from a poly-chrome Chen Mul Modelado ware incense burner. It bears the image of the sun god as the Jaguar God of the underworld, as God GIII of Palenque. There are fangs at the corners of the mouth and a head-dress in the form of a bird.   APC

334
Effigy Vessel
Late Postclassic period
Mayapán, Yucatán, Mexico
Ceramic
Height: 11.0 cm; diameter: 5.2 cm
Merida, Museo Regional de Yucatán
"Palacio Cantón"
Inv. no. 10-290494

Cylindrical tripod vessel with solid supports and a modeled face of Chaac, the long-nosed god. The ware is known as Chen Mul Mode-lado. Undoubtedly representations of this god are abundant in north-ern Yucatán, because the absence of superficial water sources in the region makes rain particularly im-portant for the survival of the com-munity.   APC

335
Censer Fragment
Postclassic period
Provenance unknown
Ceramic
Height: 24.0 cm; width: 15.0 cm
depth: 13.0 cm
Villahermosa, Museo Regional
de Antropología "Carlos Pellicer"
Inv. no. A-0666

This sculpture formed part of a cylinder that perhaps functioned as an incense burner. The representa-tion of faces superimposed one on top of another is common in Maya art, perhaps because it was believed that the main figure took on the at-tributes and thinking power of the superimposed ones, or in this case, of those below the main figure. Al-though the attributes of the faces are not clear, they could represent a deity.   RP

336
Polychrome Cylindrical Vessel
Classic period
La Lagunita, Quiché
Guatemala
Ceramic
Height: 24.1 cm
diameter: 18.5 cm

336
Guatemala
Museo Nacional
de Arqueología y Etnología
Inv. no. MNAE 15361

The supports of this vessel are spherical. The surface is covered with blue stucco; the Mayas seem to have had only one variety of this color, whose tone changed depending one which surface it was applied. These tonalities could be of plant or mineral origin, although studies show that those of mineral origin are more common – this could be due to the perishable nature of plant pigments. The vessel is decorated with a ceremonial scene framed by two red lines. Six figures are represented in a procession. The main wears a mask and is richly dressed; he is followed by figures of lesser rank dressed in simpler garb. In the highland region, figures are represented differently from those in the lowlands because their respective development was independent.   MSB

337
Polychrome Tripod Plate
Classic period
Petén, Guatemala
Ceramic
Height: 8.0 cm
diameter: 33.8 cm
Guatemala
Museo Nacional
de Arqueología y Etnología
Inv. no. MNAE 8458

The supports of this plate are oval-shaped and have two air holes each. The basal flange is crenelated, a common treatment in Late Classic period plates. The crenelated design patterns of the basal flange vary from simple to elaborate. The

337

338

339

surface of the rim and the interior are covered with polished red slip. Two thick black lines surround the vessel near the rim. The surface of the rest of the interior is covered with polished buff or cream-colored slip. A band of abstract designs surrounds the base of the vessel. In the center is a standing figure wearing a simple headdress, a circular ear ornament with pendant, a bead necklace, bracelets, and anklets. On his waist he wears

a wide belt from which gray and red feathers hang. It appears that he is wearing a kind of sash or band made of jaguar pelt.   MSB

338
Polychrome Plate
Late Classic period
Uaxactún, Petén, Guatemala
Ceramic
Height: 7.7 cm
diameter: 35.2 cm

Guatemala
Museo Nacional
de Arqueología y Etnología
Inv. no. MNAE 352

The supports on the plate are conical. The surface is covered with orange slip. In the center, a figure wearing a simple headdress and a skirt seems to be dancing. This interpretation is based on the position of the feet and hands, and the skirt seems to be moving. A band of four sections of glyphs in orange, red, and black surrounds the vessel near the rim. The different sections are separated by two dots, one on top of the other. This piece pertained to the site offerings associated with an elite burial, found at Uaxactún. As part of the burial ritual, the Mayas "killed" many vessels, perforating them in the center as part of the preparation of the deceased and his or her belongings for departure to the underworld.   MSB

339
"Acrobat" Lid
Late Classic period
Acropolis
Copán Ruinas, Honduras
Ceramic
Height: 23.0 cm
diameter: 22.5 cm
Copán, Museo Regional
de Arqueología
Inv. no. CPN-C-698

Lid of a polychromed, anthropomorphic censer showing the full-body of an acrobat. Noteworthy are the representation of a cacao pod in his headdress and the contortion of his legs. This lid was found associated with other censer lids representing Copán rulers, in a tomb beneath the Hieroglyphic Stairway.   CJF

340

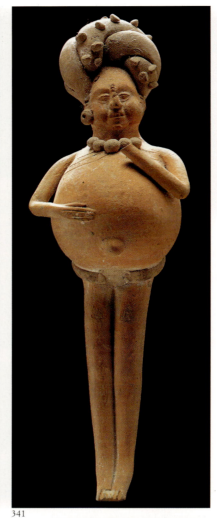

341

343

340
Male Figurine
Late Classic period
Nebaj
Quiché, Guatemala
Ceramic
Height: 21.0 cm
width: 11.0 cm
Guatemala
Museo Nacional
de Arqueología y Etnología
Inv. no. MNAE 4728

Musical instrument in the form of a figurine representing a standing man with an animal headdress and feathers. He wears earplugs, bracelets, and a necklace, possibly made of jadeite based on the color with which they were covered. He has a rattle in each hand and wears a skirt and loincloth with geometric designs. He is painted red and blue on a buff or cream surface. Featherwork has not survived in the Maya area, nevertheless, it may be appreciated in figurines, monuments, and murals such as those of Bonampak, Mexico. The Mayas used feathers from tropical birds, macaws, toucans, and quetzals that lived in the forests of the lowlands. These feathers were considered exotic objects of great value exchanged over wide-ranging territories. MSB

341
Figurine
Late Classic period
Jaina Island, Campeche
Mexico
Ceramic
Height: 18.5 cm
width: 5.8 cm
Mexico City
Museo Nacional de Antropología
Inv. no. 10-078172

Maya figurines show us costumes, ornaments, cultural practices applied to the human body, and social organization. Also evident are representations of pathologies, such as this figurine associated with the first case of hypertrophic osteoarthropathy, related to hepatic cirrhosis. It displays ascites, the great abdominal deformity with the bulging navel caused by chronic liver disease. The characteristics of this pathology were also detected in a skeleton at Jaina, which confirms its presence on the island. The figurine wears an elaborate turban, earplugs, beaded necklace, and a hip cloth. In addition to cranial deformation, he displays scarification between his eyebrows, and it is important to mention that his ribs are marked by incisions and the vertebral column is indicated in a special way. This small sculpture consti-

342

tutes, to date, the most ancient representation of this ailment. POC

342
Ocarina
Terminal Classic–Epiclassic period
Comalcalco, Tabasco, Mexico

Ceramic
Height: 11.7 cm
width: 4.6 cm
thickness: 4.5 cm
Comalcalco, Museo de Sitio
de Comalcalco
Inv. no. 10-575764

This ocarina was found in the north pit of Temple I in the North Plaza at Comalcalco. It represents a dwarf wearing a complicated headdress with sticks or reeds mounted on a turban, which is held by a frontal braid and three small disks. His regalia is complemented by ear pendants, a large slate disk as a pectoral, as well as a loincloth. Dwarfs or *zayam uinicoob* were believed to possess magical, religious powers, with the ability to foretell the future – activities that were of great importance in the daily life of Maya dignitaries, who they permanently accompanied. Dwarfs were widely represented in historical, religious, and political scenes. RAT

343
Ocarina
Terminal Classic–Epiclassic period
Comalcalco, Tabasco
Mexico
Ceramic
Height: 7.0 cm
width: 3.1 cm
thickness: 4.0 cm
Comalcalco, Museo de Sitio
de Comalcalco
Inv. no. 10-575765

Human figurine and musical wind instrument that represents a shaved dwarf with thick lips, fallen chest, and big belly, dressed with a sash and a loincloth. Dwarfs, or *zayam uinicoob*, were considered by the Mayas a, beings with magical powers. Therefore, they were highly regarded by priests, shamans, and high-level Maya dignitaries, who protected them by feeding and maintaining them for life within the court of the royal family. Their representation in different forms of Maya art emphasize their importance in society. RAT

344

345

344
Hand Drum
Early Postclassic period
Nabalam, Yucatán, Mexico
Ceramic
Height: 22.0 cm
width: 21.0 cm
diameter [each]: 9.0 cm
Valladolid, Museo del Centro
Coordinador del INI
No inv. no.

The majority of Maya musical instruments were made, at least in part, from perishable materials. We know about music to a large extent from representations in painting and sculpture, such as the "orchestra" in the Bonampak murals. The majority of figurines are also whistles, ocarinas, flutes, or rattles, but we do not know if they were actually used to play music or whether the sound was a magical voice with which they were endowed as offerings. This small drum with two sections probably belongs to the type of instruments of ritual use, based on drums carried in the left hand of some figures disguised as birds found at Chichén Itzá. The ceramic type is Xcanchakan black/cream from the Terminal Classic period to Early Postclassic period transition. The incisions on the upper part were to attach the skins.   PJS

345
Shell
Classic period
Uaxactún
Petén, Guatemala
Shell
Width: 19.2 cm
length: 41.5 cm
Guatemala, Museo Nacional
de Arqueología y Etnología
Inv. no. MNAE 1945

Shell used as a trumpet. Its four perforations allowed it to be employed as a musical instrument, one of several functions these objects served

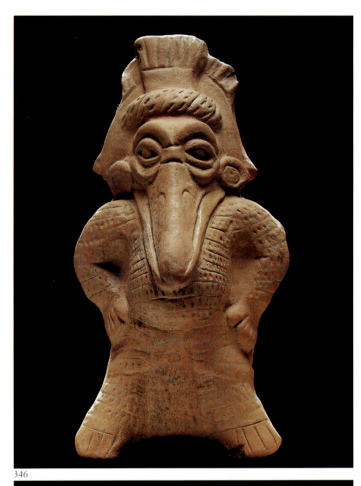

346

347

during the pre-Hispanic period in ritual ceremonies involving music and singing. The nature of music played in Mesoamerica is unknown, but what has been possible to reconstruct comes from the instruments themselves. Representations and descriptions of flutes, rattles, turtle shells that were played with a deer horn, drums, bells and trumpets were the most common. Trumpets could be made of conch shells, wood, or gourds. To date, no evidence of stringed instruments has been found.   MSB

346
Figurine
Terminal Classic period
Jonuta, Tabasco, Mexico
Ceramic
Height: 17.5 cm
width: 9.0 cm
depth: 7.0 cm
Jonuta
Museo "Omar Huerta Escalante"
Inv. no. MJ-235

Because of the costume and animal mask of this figurine, which was used as a whistle, perhaps it represents a shaman invested with bird attributes, in this case, an aquatic bird, perhaps a pelican, because of the robust quality of the beak. Figurines of this type, which tend to represent human bodies covered with skins or feathers of the most varied animals and fantastic beings, fulfilled functions associated with cult activities and religious ceremonies. In this way, thanks to magical thought, man could appropriate the attributes and qualities of animals, plants, and natural forces.   RP

347
Male Figurine
Late Classic period
Jaina Island, Campeche, Mexico
Ceramic
Height: 13.0 cm
width: 5.0 cm
depth: 4.0 cm
Villahermosa, Museo Regional
de Antropología "Carlos Pellicer"
Inv. no. A-0542

The realism and expressive movement shown by this figure of an old man allows us to see the extraordinary skill of Maya artists. The figure must be of high status, based on his beaded necklace and pectoral, as well as his headdress and leg decorations. These elements could indicate that he is a shaman. The shaman played an important role in the life of rulers and in the social fabric of the people. This type of figurine, found on the island of Jaina, is associated with funerary burials. The body ornaments and the loincloth were added using the appliqué technique.   RP

348

348
Symbolic Bone
Late Classic period
Acropolis, Copán Ruinas
Honduras
Bone
Height: 25.0 cm
width: 4.5 cm
Copán
Museo Regional de Arqueología
Inv. no. CPN-H-3791

This incised deer tibia shows the sixteenth and final ruler of Copán, Yax Pasah, being attended by a female consort dressed in a long *huipil*. The text at the bottom of the bone cites his name in the second glyph, and extols his virtues as a long-lived ("3-*katun*") king. The portrait of the monarch bears a striking similarity to that seen on Stela 11, where he is also shown with a beard and a foliated device in his forehead. The bone was found with a number of other offerings in Temple 11 of the Acropolis, at the bottom end of a long vertical shaft which led down from the floor of the temple.   WF

349
Femur
Protoclassic period
Chiapa de Corzo, Chiapas, Mexico
Human bone
Length: 26.5 cm
diameter: 3.3 cm

349

Tuxtla Gutiérrez
Museo Regional de Chiapas
Inv. no. 10-222063

Fragment of a decorated human femur, worked in low relief with a complex design representing four figures, one of them almost entirely destroyed. The most realistic motif is that of a human head seen in profile with a fleshless jaw and a tongue sticking out of its mouth. The hair of the figure hangs in short tufts over the forehead, and long ones beside the ears. The hands and arms seem to indicate that he is swimming, while on the body there are three superimposed

351a   351b

350

disks and the body is covered with a woven mat design, a bar, and two dots.   TALW

350
Eccentric
Classic period
El Palmar, Quintana Roo, Mexico
Flint
Height: 31.0 cm; width: 25.0 cm
thickness: 1.4 cm
Mexico City
Museo Nacional de Antropología
Inv. no. 10-009648

Although eccentrics appear in other Mesoamerican cultures, it was the Maya who achieved maximum artistic expression both for the quality of carving, as well as for the complexity of the figures represented. It should be noted that flint is not worked by percussion, but rather by the delicate technique of pressure that makes it possible to extract small flakes. In the Maya zone, this type of object is frequently found placed as an offering beneath stelae and temples, so that its ceremonial content is clear although its specific function is unknown. This particular example was found under Stela 10 from El Palmar, an archaeological site in the state of Quintana Roo, and despite the elaborate nature of its design, human profiles may be seen at its corners.   CLO

352a

352b

352c

351a-b
Knives
Terminal Classic–Early Postclassic period
Chichén Itzá, Yucatán, Mexico
Silex
Width: 10.3 cm; length: 32.8 cm
width: 10.0 cm; length: 38.5 cm
Merida, Museo Regional de Yucatán
"Palacio Cantón"
Inv. no. 10-425890; 10-425891

These impressive objects were found as an offering inside a stone box under the stairway of El Castillo at Chichén Itzá. These types of bifacial knives were used in human sacrifice; some of them had handles. These examples were worked on both sides.   ABC

352a-b-c
Offering
Late Classic period
Provenance unknown
Obsidian
Length: 5.5 cm, 5.0 cm, 6.5 cm
4.5 cm, 6.0 cm
Belmopan, Bodega
del Departamento de Arqueología
Inv. no. 35/196-1

Resembling the custom of offering flint eccentrics and often in the same context, there are also these forms made of obsidian. Of course, given the greater fragility of the material when submitted to fine working, the resulting forms are rarely as perfect and attractive as those of flint. On the other hand, obsidian has an advantage in that it may be decorated by means of incisions, a possibility often exploited to its fullest. As with flint, the quantity of elements in each offering seems to be nine pieces of obsidian, including hooks, s-shapes, circles, scorpions, and so forth, together with eighteen pieces of flint and a large number of obsidian blades in different

352d

352e

states of conservation, only one of them whole. Obviously, the number nine and multiples of nine (eighteen) were important in the ritual associated with the placement of the offering, perhaps as a reference to the nine levels of the underworld. Until today, rituals of divination, petitions for rain, giving thanks for the harvest, and other rites involve specific numbers of each object offered, whether they are sacrificed animals, ritual beverages, fruit or seeds, genuflections, movements that had to be carried out with the incense burner, etc. The difference with this offering resides in the fact that it is no longer the rulers, but rather the *ah men ob* and curers who are in charge of these acts. PJS

352d
Eccentric
Late Classic period
Acropolis, Copán Ruinas, Honduras
Flint

353

Height: 33.3 cm; width: 15.0 cm
Copán, Centro Regional
de Investigaciones Arqueológicas
Inv. no. CPN-P-112

One of the three magnificently chipped ceremonial lance heads placed under the altar at the dedication of Copán's famed Hieroglyphic Stairway of Structure 10L26, this object is an awesome display of the flint-knapper's art. Called "eccentrics" because of their unusual and elaborate forms, chipped flint and obsidian objects of this type have been found throughout the Maya area, but very few show this much elaboration or technical skill. The artisan started with a larger boulder of flint, and slowly whittled it down to a long, thin, flat object. Thereafter he carefully chipped off small pieces using pressure-flaking, probably employing a deer antler and occasional heat from a fire to ensure greater precision in his work. His mastery of the medium was so complete that this flint-knapper left a tiny remnant of the original exterior of the boulder (known as "cortex") visible at the bottom tip of this lance-head. WF

352e
Eccentric
Late Classic period
Acropolis, Copán, Honduras
Flint
Height: 30.9 cm; width: 12.5 cm
Copán, Centro Regional
de Investigaciones Arqueológicas
Inv. no. CPN-P-113

This flint eccentric was fashioned into a ceremonial lance head. This piece is distinguished by the lanceolate form, with each of the tangs bearing a Maya face in profile. The central face appears in the center of the piece, with the shoulder of that figure shown in profile behind the head. Here it is clear that the central axis of the object was meant to represent the body from this central head and shoulder. Viewed in this way, they form an elaborate headdress for the central figure. The front central flange represents his arms, and the lower flanges bear the heads on his belt assemblage, just as so often depicted in full body portraits of the kings at Copán. Perhaps, then, tak-

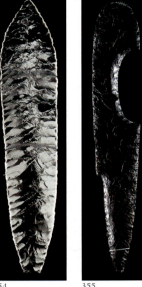

354

355

en together, these lance heads from the Hieroglyphic Stairway cache represent the concept of the Maya ruler as the *axis mundi* of his realm. WF

353
Eccentric
Period unknown
Provenance unknown
Flint
Length: 22.5 cm; width: 14.0 cm
Campeche, Centro INAH Campeche
Inv. no. 10-290656

Semicircular eccentric with a projection that probably topped a ceremonial staff used by a high-ranking individual. Among the Mayas, both gods and mortals bore weapons and at times even these arms were deified. Because the Mayas apparently believed that flint and obsidian were created when lightning hit the earth, they were treated as sacred materials. YP

354
Knife
Late Classic period
Campeche, Mexico
Obsidian
Length: 33.0 cm
width: 6.2 cm
Campeche, Centro INAH Campeche
Inv. no. 10-566394

The use of the volcanic glass obsidian was common in Mesoamerica. It was highly abundant in volcanic regions, but scarce elsewhere. A wide variety of tools was fashioned from

it, above all implements for cutting and scraping. However, it was also made into ritual objects like eccentrics and figurines that were used in certain ceremonies or formed part of offerings in burials of important people. Large knives, delicately carved into bifacial forms, were used in human sacrifice for decapitation or, later, to extract hearts in sacrifice. APC

355
Eccentric
Late Classic period
Palenque, Chiapas, Mexico
Obsidian
Length: 34.0 cm; width: 5.5 cm
Palenque, Museo de Sitio
"Alberto Ruz Lhuillier"
Inv. no. 10-479203

Among the materials used, obsidi-

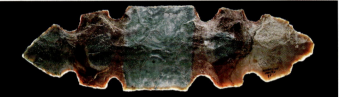

356

an occupied an important place, both for the manufacture of tools (blades, knives, projectile points, scrapers), as well as for the production of different ornaments (earflares, pendants, and beads). Palenque obtained this raw material by way of trade with El Chayal, Guatemala, which is the source for the obsidian of this eccentric. This piece was found as an offering in the Temple of the Cross. Perhaps it had no practical use, but rather was used as a symbol of power by the ruling class. AGC

356
Eccentric
Late Classic period
Xpuhil, Campeche, Mexico
Flint
Length: 21.0 cm; width: 6.5 cm
Campeche, Museo Histórico
Fuerte de San Miguel
Baluarte de San Miguel
Inv. no. 10-290658

Flint eccentric in the form of a ceremonial knife, decorated with alternating blue and red bands, the latter with a rhomboid design. It comes from an offering found in one of the towers of the main building at Xpuhil. Flint was a highly valued material among the ancient Maya to produce tools for practical as well as ceremonial use. There are many deposits in different parts of the peninsula, but one of the richest and most important was at Colhá, Belize, a site that apparently specialized in the production of objects of this material. LMC

357

358

359

shows 18 Rabbit, Uaxaklahun Ubah Kawil on the left, squaring off with the god of number zero, one of the gods of the underworld.   WF

359
Yoke Vessel
Late Classic period
Las Sepulturas, Copán Ruinas
Honduras
Ceramic
Height: 15.1 cm; base: 14.5 cm
diameter: 8.5 cm
Tegucigalpa, Taller de Restauración
Inv. no. CPN-C-719

This drinking vessel has the image of a Maya ball player wearing a yoke and hip protectors. The style of the figure is reminiscent of those which appear on Copador, even down to the details of the headdress. The figure stands apart from the excised background, with finely incised details visible on his clothing and jewelry. The two "pseudo-glyphs" next to him cannot presently be read, but they likely name either the figure or the vessel itself.   WF

360
Ocarina
Classic period
Guatemalan highlands
Ceramic
Height: 11.5 cm
width: 7.3 cm
thickness: 7.0 cm
Guatemala, Museo Popol Vuh
Universidad Francisco Marroquín
Inv. no. MPV 0062

Human figurine representing a ball player. It retains traces of yellow and blue paint applied after firing. The player is standing with arms at his sides and hands on his thighs. On his head he wears a headdress in the form of a bird, perhaps a toucan. He also has earflares, a necklace, a blue yoke, and loincloth with remains of the same color. The face is not well defined, but he has a prominent nose resembling a bird beak. On the back, he seems to wear a cape or mantle, on top of which are the mouthpiece and two holes near the shoulders.   MS

361
Ball player Figurine
Classic period
San Agustín Acasaguastlán
El Progreso, Guatemala
Ceramic
Height: 19.0 cm
width: 8.5 cm
Guatemala, Museo Nacional
de Arqueología y Etnología
Inv. no. MNAE 12161

Musical instrument in the shape of a mold-made human figurine. It represents a standing ball player wearing a tall headdress, possibly with feathers, circular earplugs, a neck-

357
Eccentric
Classic period
Altar de Sacrificios, Petén
Guatemala
Flint
Width: 5.8 cm; length: 13.5 cm
Guatemala, Museo Nacional
de Arqueología y Etnología
Inv. no. MNAE 7825

Flint eccentric with an anthropomorphic figure representing a human face in profile with an open mouth. Eccentrics have been found buried in caches under Maya monuments and buildings. There are several very fine examples from other sites, such as El Palmar, Quintana Roo, Mexico; Quiriguá, Guatemala; and Copán, Honduras. Recently, in the latter city, a cache dating from the Early Classic period was found in the Rosalila structure; the eccentrics recovered there represented very elaborate figures. The precise function of this type of artifact is still unknown.   MSB

358
Marker
Late Classic period
Ball Court II, Copán Ruinas
Honduras
Stone
Diameter: 73.0 cm
thickness: 10.0 cm
Copán, Museo Regional
de Arqueología
Inv. no. CPN-P-185

Ball court II, built in the late sixth century A.D., was discovered to have central markers in the playing alley. Each marker was later capped with a carved disk that corresponded to the Ball court IIb construction at the end of the seventh century A.D. This object was the carved disk placed over the central marker. The scene, framed by a quatrefoil cave opening,

lace with spherical beads, bracelets, a yoke at the waist, and a knee-guard on the right side. Protective padding was used both to hit the ball and to direct it to desired spots. It is believed that yokes used during the game could have been made of leather or wood and that those made of stone were used in rituals before or after the game. Figurines of this type help reconstruct the equipment used for this game. Similarly, they have helped demonstrate that although the ball game was a cultural trait widely shared by Mesoamerican groups, there were regional differences in the way the players dressed and thus also in the way the game was played.   MSB

362
Ball player
Late Classic period
Jaina Island, Campeche, Mexico
Ceramic

Height: 15.0 cm;
width: 11.5 cm
Mexico City
Museo Nacional de Antropología
Inv. no. 10-078175

The ball game was a civic-ceremonial event of religious life, both of the Mayas as well as of other groups in Mesoamerica. It was practiced in a special playing field located in a privileged place in ceremonial centers. The great importance of these events, as well as the ritual symbolism contained in them, is represented in the material elements associated with ball games. The rules of the game did not permit the ball to be touched with the hands; it had to be struck with the forearm, the hip, and the knee, so these parts of the body were protected. In this figurine, found at Jaina, the player is represented with protectors at the waist and arm, covered by a thick, cushioned sleeve.   MCG

360

361

362

364

In the pre-Hispanic period, the ball game had a profound religious and symbolic significance; this practice represented the daily struggle between opposing forces and antagonistic concepts, such as light and darkness, day and night, life and death, etc. The ceremonial or ritual importance of this game may be deduced from the numerous representations of ball players and from the great number of architectonic spaces dedicated to its practice. This disk, used as a ball court marker, comes from La Esperanza, an archaeological site near Chinkultic, Chiapas. On one of its faces, it shows the figure of a ballplayer at the moment of striking a large ball with his hip. The scene is framed by a band of glyphs with the Maya date 9.7.17.12.14 11 *ix* 7 *zotz*, which is the equivalent of A.D. 591.   ACM

363

363
Ball player
Late Classic period
Jaina Island, Campeche, Mexico
Ceramic
Height: 12.8 cm; width: 12.5 cm
Mexico City
Museo Nacional de Antropología
Inv. no. 10-078165

Unlike mold-made figurines, in which uniformity may be achieved, in modeled pieces there is a great vitality and diversity in subjects represented, constituting an important testimony on the customs, activities, and physical appearance of the Classic-period Maya. In this piece, the pose of the figure's arms and legs and the twisting position of his body create the impression of the movement of a ball player as he prepares to strike the ball. His garment is characteristic of a ball player, with a voluminous skirt and a belt to protect him from the impact of the ball. MCG

364
Disk
Late Classic period
La Esperanza, Chinkultic
Chiapas
Mexico
Limestone
Diameter: 56.0 cm
thickness: 13.0 cm
Mexico City
Museo Nacional
de Antropología
Inv. no. 10-080364

366

367

365
Female Figurine
Late Classic period
Jaina Island, Campeche, Mexico
Ceramic
Height: 14.8 cm; width: 6.9 cm
Mexico City
Museo Nacional de Antropología
Inv. no. 10-222282

This beautiful, molded figurine represents a priestess or a woman personifying a deity. It is hollow and on its interior there are small pieces of ceramic that make the piece a rattle. It retains traces of blue, red, and white pigment. The figure wears a dress, the lower part of which has dotted and incised decoration, detailing the type of textile used, and a belt of shells. At the sides of her body are feathers and stepped frets, on the inside of which are what seem to be the ends of long bones: there is a possible head of a femur on her right side. What is most outstanding is her majestic headdress, crowned by a bird with long feathers; on each side of her face is a serpent head, from the jaws of which emerges a human face. The theme of a face emerging from the jaws of a serpent or a fantastic animal is recurrent in Maya iconography; the bicephalic serpent is one of the most important deities in their mythology. On her head, she wears the symbol of a flower. The dotted, circular design, under the petals is the sign *mo*, which may be read as *ni* if it refers to *nicte*, which means flower.   LCGS

366
Statuette Pair
Late Classic period
Provenance unknown
Clay
Height: 11.5 cm
Berlin, Museum für Völkerkunde
Jimeno Collection, 1881, SMPK
Inv. no. IV *Ca 4942*

A statue pair of two contrasting figures, a young woman and a toothless old man. Whereas the old man clasps her in a warm embrace, the young woman holds one arm loosely around her partner, her other hand resting on her lap. This scene is by no means unique. The woman, who is bare-breasted and wears a skirt, is probably the moon-goddess. The old man is likely to be a god of the underworld, who is usually depicted either as completely toothless or as having only one tooth.   MG

367
Jaina Figurine
Late Classic period
Campeche, Mexico
Ceramic
Height: 25.6 cm

368
length: 13.5 cm
diameter: 8.6 cm
Washington, D.C.
Dumbarton Oaks
Research Library Collections
Inv. no. B-195.MAP

In this double-figurine, a young woman and an old man embrace. They stand in three-quarter view, gazing into each other's faces, and each with an arm about the other's waist. She raises her right hand to his face, while he lifts her skirt with his left hand. Both are attired in rich garments; she wears a long skirt, scalloped on the sides of its frontal opening, as well as arm bands, earspools, a tied neck scarf, and a high, elaborately looped headdress on top of her angular coiffure. He wears a skirt and loincloth, earspools, a large beaded necklace, and a full-size deerhead headdress set on folded bands of cloth or leather. Scholars have suggested that these figures represent a theme of the coupling of a young Maya woman with an old dwarf, or the joining of the young, beautiful Moon Goddess with the lecherous Old Sun God.

368
Anthropomorphic Whistle
Late Classic period
Las Sepulturas
Copán Ruinas
Honduras
Ceramic
Height: 13.0 cm
width: 6.5 cm
Tegucigalpa
Bodegas Centrales
del Instituto Hondureño
de Antropología e Historia
Inv. no. CPN-C-780

Polished whistle with two human figures, found in Group 9N-8 of Plaza D at the ruins of Copán. This whistle represents a couple wearing headdresses and simple necklaces. This type of object is not common at Copán, so that it is presumed that it pertained to a group of people from central Honduras, where the production of this type of whistle is more common. CJF

369
369
Stela
Preclassic period
Sacatepéquez, Guatemala
Stone
Height: 103.0 cm
maximum width: 41.0 cm
Guatemala, Museo Nacional
de Arqueología y Etnología
Inv. no. MNAE 2081

Openwork stela worked as a silhouette. It has a stylized mask of a deity with perforations corresponding to eyes, the lower part of the nose and the mouth. It has profile masks on both cheeks. This type of representation was common in art of the period as space filler. As a headdress, the deity wears a stepped pyramid with an offering radiating rays of sunlight at the peak. During the Preclassic period stelae were the splendor of sculpture in the highlands. It is believed that stelae served religious purposes, in part because the majority of them are found with structures dedicated to cult. Another possible reason is that they represent mythical figures and scenes, deities, animals, and places. Despite their religious importance, many stelae were re-used or mutilated. MSB

370
Figure Seated on a Throne
Late Classic period
Jaina Island, Campeche, Mexico

Ceramic
Height: 16.5 cm; width: 9.3 cm
Mexico City, Museo Nacional
de Antropología
Inv. no. 10-001195

This hollow, orange-brown clay figurine represents a figure seated on a throne on a rectangular element, perhaps a litter, with a step in the front and four circular perforations that could correspond to openings for the posts or trunks with which the litter would be carried. His face is fleshless, but his ears are preserved and he wears feathers in them. By way of punching, the texture of the textile is highlighted. The figure wears bracelets, sandals with heel guards, as well as a cape on his shoulders and a short skirt. From his neck hangs a weaving that falls to his knees and is gathered into three bands at the level of his stomach. On his chest he wears what seems to be a duck mask. On his head is a semicircular element, a band knotted in the front, and two applied, spherical elements that could be knots or pompoms. Both the individual and his garb are highly original because his costume and ear ornaments are not typically Maya. It is probable that the fleshless face is a mask and that the figure borne on shoulders, formed part of a ceremony related to death, or that personifies the god of death. LCGS

370

371
371
Tzompantli (Skull Rack)
Postclassic period
Chichén Itzá, Yucatán, Mexico
Limestone
Height: 28.0 cm
width: 30.0 cm; depth: 25.0 cm
Dzibilchaltún
Museo del Pueblo Maya
Inv. no. 10-251120

This slab with the partial representation of two skulls in bas-relief comes from the building known as the *tzompantli*, a platform found in the central part of the site. By analogy with other sites, such as Tula or Tenochtitlan, we know that it served as a structure where stakes with skulls of sacrificial victims were placed. For the Mayas, warriors who died in combat and women who died in childbirth went directly to paradise, which the Franciscan friar Diego de Landa describes as a land where the dead passed a happy, idle life with all imaginable delights in the shade of a giant *ceiba* tree, the sacred *Yaxcheel cab*. LMC

372a

372b

372c

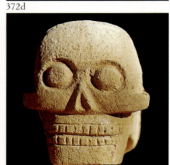

372d

372e

372f

372g

372h

372
Skulls Sculpture
Terminal Classic period
Kabah, Yucatán, Mexico
Limestone
Height: 22.0–29.0 cm
length: 36.0–48.5 cm
depth: 18.0–23.5 cm
Merida, Bodega de Sitio
Arqueológico de Kabah
Inv. no. 10-569620 21; 10-569622 23
10-569624 25; 10-569626 27-28
10-569625; 10-569627
and 10-569628

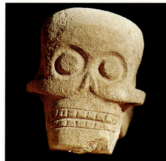

372i

These skulls formed part of the decoration of the frieze on the first level of Structure 1A1, also known as
the Structure of the Red Hands, of
the archaeological zone of Kabah.
This sculpture, together with other
skulls of the same quality and characteristics, was symmetrically distributed on the middle molding of
the building. Their presence on the
frieze, in combination with other
decorative elements such as hand
prints or the zoomorphic entrance
of the second level, indicates that
this precinct was dedicated to rites
associated with death and transit to
the underworld.   RCV

373
Piedras Negras Altar 4 Leg
Late Classic period
Piedras Negras, Petén, Guatemala
Limestone
Height: 72.0 cm
Guatemala, Museo Nacional
de Arqueología y Etnología
Inv. no. MNAE 864c

This altar formed part of a group
with four similar supports. It represents the head of a *cauac* monster or
earth monster, which always has a
zoomorphic appearance and is
characterized by the presence of an

372l

element composed of several joined
circles, similar to a bunch of
grapes, which is the *cauac* glyph.
The creature's eyes are generally
half-open. The *cauac* monster represents stone, because it originates
in the ground, although it may also
be a cave; nevertheless, it never appears as an active figure in a composition. This figure is found in objects or buildings made of stone,
and this support has teeth carved in
stylized form. The *cauac* elements
(bunches of grapes) are repeated
on both eyes and cheeks. The figure has flaming eyebrows and a row
of three glyphs incised in low relief
on its forehead.   MSB

*Epigraphic reading by Alfonso Arel-
lano*
His sculpture of *Ek . . . Ah Tunil*

373

374
Censer Base
Late Classic period
Tapijulapa, Tabasco, Mexico
Ceramic
Height: 37.0 cm; width: 20.0 cm
depth: 21.0 cm
Villahermosa, Museo Regional
de Antropología "Carlos Pellicer"
Inv. no. A-0194

The performance of ritual ceremonies in caves and grottos must
have been limited to only a few people, but the benefits obtained result-

ed in the social, religious, and political cohesion of the people. The effigy figure adorning this incense burner base conceptualizes the Maya notion of duality about life and death,
day and night, and water and fire.
The base represents a priest with the
attributes of the sun god and an animal. The priest stands on the head of
a bat symbolizing night, darkness,
death, and underground water. The
water that for centuries dripped on
the figure formed a coating of calci-
um carbonate, emphasizing his hier-
atic pose.   RP

375

377

374

375
Censer Base
Late Classic period
Tapijulapa, Tabasco, Mexico
Ceramic
Height: 40.0 cm
width: 34.0 cm
depth: 26.0 cm
Villahermosa, Museo Regional
de Antropología "Carlos Pellicer"
Inv. no. A-0002

376

The underworld represents the nocturnal side of the world, described as a dark, inaccessible place, without life. In Maya thought, *Xibalba* is located in the deepest reaches of the earth. Thus, the pre-Hispanic representation of the bat has often come to be associated with a deity who symbolizes the night, darkness, and death. This seated figure carries solar attributes, such as a tooth filed into a T-shape, goggles with a scroll on the nose, and a solar pectoral. A schematized ear of corn in the headdress suggests that the lateral orna-

ments refer to vegetation and life. Cultural expressions of the ancient inhabitants have been recorded in caves located in the mountains of the sierra of Tabasco, the provenance of these incense burner bases, which possibly belong to a tradition begun at Palenque.   RP

376
Urn
Terminal Classic–Early Postclassic period
Ixil Region, El Quiché, Guatemala
Ceramic
Height: 69.0 cm
diameter: 62.0 cm
depth: 61.5 cm
Guatemala, Museo Popol Vuh
Universidad Francisco Marroquín
Inv. no. MPV 4122

Funerary urn without a lid, displaying remains of red, yellow, and white paint. It has four large handles on the body, four small ones at the rim, and a fillet painted white that goes around the urn. The main scene consists of the head

and front paws of a young jaguar emerging from the jaws of the earth monster. The feline has exposed teeth and fangs, and its paws have extended claws. The eyes of the animal are open and the rounded ears are painted white. The monster exhibits the characteristic distended eyes with hanging iris, and a large, open maw, the upper jaw turned upward. On each side of the monster, there are two vertical rows of skulls painted white.   MS

377
Censer Base
Late Classic period
Tapijulapa, Tabasco, Mexico
Ceramic
Height: 63.0 cm; width: 26.0 cm
depth: 13.0 cm
Villahermosa, Museo Regional
de Antropología "Carlos Pellicer"
Inv. no. A-0052

This image represents a figure with zoomorphic extremities, perhaps alluding to a priest with attributes of deities associated with the underworld. He is standing on the head of a bat (*zotz*), a deity related to night and death. This incense burner holder was found in a cave in the sierra of Tapijulapa, in the municipality of Tacotalpa, Tabasco, which corroborates the fact that for Mesoamerican peoples, caves were sacred sites, places of birth, life, and death, as well as the place of cult for a privileged few, because it is there where the fruits of the earth are stored.   RP

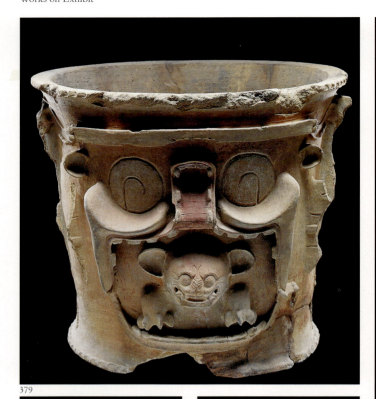

379

378

380

381

378
Urn
Terminal Classic–Early Postclassic period
Ixil Region, El Quiché, Guatemala
Ceramic
Height: 78.0 cm
diameter: 61.0 cm
depth: 73.0 cm
Guatemala, Museo Popol Vuh Universidad Francisco Marroquín Inv. no. MPV 2922

Funerary urn without lid, with remains of red, white, yellow, and orange paint. Below the rim there is a fillet that goes around the body of the urn. Four equidistant handles go from this detail to the rim. There are four more handles on the body of the urn and three modeled anthropomorphic figures equally spaced on the body. The head, fingers, and feet are in high relief, the body only slightly in relief; the faces of the figures have the characteristics of the underworld sun god: round distended eyes with hanging iris, wrinkled aquiline nose, and projecting cheeks. They wear disk ear ornaments and beaded necklaces. The headdress consists of a white, horizontal band, divided by incised lines on which there is another yellow band. Two strips, which possibly represent cloth, emerge from the sides of the headdress.   MS

379
Urn
Terminal Classic–Early Postclassic period
Ixil Region, El Quiché, Guatemala
Ceramic
Height: 59.0 cm
diameter: 69.0 cm
depth: 47.5 cm
Guatemala, Museo Popol Vuh Universidad Francisco Marroquín Inv. no. MPV 2930

Funerary urn without lid, with flaring walls, an everted rim with a fingerprint on the edge and an everted ring-shaped base. The main scene consists of the head and front paws of a jaguar cub emerging from the jaws of an earth monster. The front paws are extended with claws curved upward. The central part of the upper jaw extends upward with the fangs exposed. The monster has rounded ears very similar to those of the jaguar. On top of the monster is a horizontal edge with appliquéd disks at the ends.   MS

380
Urn
Early Postclassic period
Ixil Region, El Quiché, Guatemala
Ceramic
Height: 100.0 cm
width: 65.0 cm
depth: 66.0 cm
diameter: 56.0 cm
Guatemala, Museo Popol Vuh Universidad Francisco Marroquín Inv. no. MPV 1388

Urn with curved, converging walls, flat edge, and pedestal feet with a concave lid. Under the rim there are four handles, and four more on the body. The main decoration of the effigy is a jaguar emerging from the jaws of the earth monster. The head of the animal is painted yellow, its feet red, and its claws white. Its mouth is open and its fangs are exposed, the round eyes lack an iris, and it has a vegetal symbol on the forehead. The eyes of the monster are round and white with the symbol of the distended eye, and the eyebrows have remains of blue paint. The mouth is open, painted red, and the teeth are white. The lid, painted yellow-gray, has a design in relief of a jaguar supported on its four feet, and there are four handles near the edge.   MS

381
Urn
Terminal Classic–Early Postclassic period
Ixil Region, El Quiché, Guatemala
Ceramic
Height: 78.0 cm (with lid 120.0 cm)
diameter: 60.0 cm
depth: 73.0 cm
Guatemala, Museo Popol Vuh Universidad Francisco Marroquín Inv. no. MPV 0007

Funerary urn with lid and eight flat handles, four on the rim and the others in the middle of the body. The lid has a fingerprint on the edge and four small handles that are aligned with the handles on the lip of the urn. On the lid is a modeled head of the underworld sun god, who has open eyes painted

382

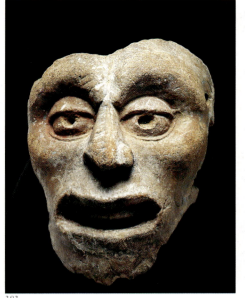

383

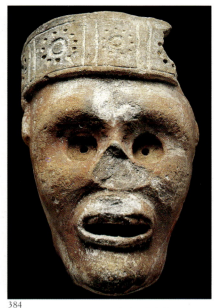

384

385

white, an aquiline nose and disk earflares. On the surface of the lid are four series of three vertical rows, or points that go from the face of the deity to the edge. On the front of the urn is the face of the old sun god in the maw of the earth monster. The aquiline nose with wrinkles and the mouth of the deity are highlighted. The mouth is open and displays filed teeth in the center, and at each side there are upward-curving volutes. The eyebrows, eyes, and cheeks of the figure are painted yellow, and the eyes of the monster are the same as those of the deity. The face is painted as a jaguar pelt with yellow with black spots.   MS

382
Miniature Mask
Late Classic period
Ocozocoautla, Chiapas, Mexico
Wood, bone, leather, shell, pyrite
cinnabar pigment
Height: 5.1 cm
width: 4.2 cm
thickness: 3.0 cm
Tuxtla Gutiérrez
Museo Regional de Chiapas
Inv. no. 10-586516 0/2

Miniature mask in the form of a human skull. It was made of wood with mother of pearl inlay, and was painted red or covered with cinnabar. It has bone teeth and eyes, the latter including a pyrite inlay simulating the iris. Its jaw is articulated and attached to the rest of the piece with thick leather cords. There are perforations and remains of cord at the sides, indicating that there was originally an attached necklace. This piece, together with other objects, formed part of a funerary offering contained in a basket, in which shell beads, cord fragments, cacao, bean, chili, and squash seeds were found, as well as a bone needle.   ELV

383
Human Mask
Late Classic period
Caves to the east of Comitán
Chiapas, Mexico
Ceramic
Height: 14.0 cm
width: 11.7 cm
Comitán
Museo Arqueológico de Comitán
Inv. no. 10-588891

Funerary mask recovered from a cave in the municipality of Trinitaria, in the state of Chiapas. It represents the face of a dead man identified by the typical half-open mouth, emulating the rictus of the corpse. It must have formed part of the garb of an important person, perhaps a shaman, who was buried in the cave. It is common to find in caves this type of element related to death, because in Maya thought, caves were the entrance to the underworld and they functioned as sites for rites of passage, and therefore as places of burial.   ELV

384
Mask
Late Classic period
Cave to the east of Comitán
Chiapas
Mexico
Ceramic
Height: 16.2 cm
width: 10.4 cm
Comitán
Museo Arqueológico de Comitán
Inv. no. 10-588890

Human mask made of clay that still has remains of blue and red paint. It comes from an offering in "El Bailón" cave. Because of the perforations in the headdress, it may have been attached to the face of the corpse, or it might have functioned as a "trophy head" that hung at the chest or belt of the important individual buried in the cave. What stands out is the half-open mouth, emulating the rictus of the deceased. There are circular cavities at the eyes, which must have been occupied by shell or bone disks.   ELV

385
Box with Lid
Late Classic period
Cueva de los Andasolos, Chiapas
Mexico
Ceramic
Height: 19.0 cm
length: 37.5 cm
width: 12.0 cm
Comitán
Museo Arqueológico de Comitán
Inv. no. 10-335333 0/2

On the lid there are three representations of human faces, and the box itself is free of decoration. The images symbolize the life-death duality because the faces of the figures pertain to living beings, with open eyes. On the front, they wear masks with anthropomorphic faces with eyes in half-moon form, which indicates that they are closed and allude to dead individuals. The masks have a simple headdress with a flower over the forehead. They wear a noseplug and the tongue is outside the mouth, while the faces of living beings only wear earplugs. The dualistic conception of the universe was a central part of Mesoamerican religious thought. Life-death duality is derived from the day-and-night cycle of the sun, its disappearance at dusk and its brilliant return at dawn, as well as the alternation of periods of rain and drought.   MCG

386

387

386
Jar
Period unknown
Chocola, Yucatán, Mexico
Carved blackware
Height: 14.0 cm; diameter: 15.0 cm
Washington, D.C., Dumbarton Oaks
Research Library Collections
Inv. no. B-530.63.MAP

This vessel is carved with sunken reliefs that were rubbed or painted with a thick red pigment. On one side of the vessel is a diagonally oriented column of six glyphs. On the other side is a seated, profile figure wearing a loincloth, bracelets, a beaded necklace, and an elaborate headdress; he holds a manikin scepter that displays the complete face of the pendolous-nosed Maya Rain God, Chaac. Recent studies of the figure's "god eye," Roman nose, "Tau tooth," and barbel-like whiskers have identified him as GI of the Palenque triad of gods. On either side of the figure are swirling smoke motifs, one of which ends behind the figure in a fish tail or fin. Within the smoke swirls are also markings commonly found on depictions of marine seashells; because a relationship exists between GI and Chaac, this depiction has been taken by some as further evidence to associate GI with underwater, chthonic deities.

387
Effigy Vessel
Early Postclassic period
La Lagunita, Quiché, Guatemala
Ceramic
Height: 14.0 cm
diameter of the rim: 7.5 cm
Guatemala, Museo Nacional
de Arqueología y Etnología
Inv. no. MNAE 12166

Vessel with anthropomorphic effigy made of Plumbate ware. The body

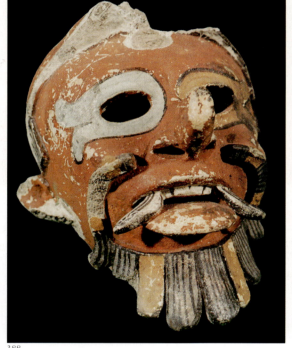

388

389

of the pitcher displays the image of Tlaloc, the Mexican god of rain and lightning. He has rings around his eyes, an aquiline nose, and fangs emerge from the sides of his mouth. These elements were modeled and appliquéd. This type of ceramic was produced on the Guatemalan coastal inlet area around the end of the Late Classic to the Early Postclassic periods. During this later period, it was widely distributed in Mesoamerica and further south. Examples have been found in Hidalgo, Nayarit, and Yucatán in Mexico, and in Guatemala, Honduras, El Salvador, and Panama. It may be noted that this ceramic has a lead-like appearance due to the high temperatures at which it was fired.   MSB

388
Anthropomorphic Face
Late Postclassic period
Mayapán, Yucatán, Mexico
Ceramic
Height: 17.0 cm; width: 15.0 cm
Merida, Museo Regional
de Yucatán "Palacio Cantón"
Inv. no. 10-251128

This incense burner fragment appears to represent the god of merchants, Ek Chuah. The dark red color of the face, the elongated nose, the fangs and beard, in addition to the bands surrounding the eyes, identify this deity. He could have been introduced into Yucatán by Mexicanized merchants. Ek Chuah is also identified with cacao, which

was used as currency in many commercial transactions.   APC

389
Effigy Censer
Late Postclassic period
Zinacantán, Chiapas, Mexico
Ceramic
Height: 12.5 cm; width: 11.0 cm
diameter of the mouth: 7.0 cm
Tuxtla Gutiérrez
Museo Regional de Chiapas
Inv. no. 10-409892

The Mexicas carried out large military ventures of conquest and alliance with different territories in Mesoamerica. Toward the Pacific coast of Chiapas, they achieved control of important

390

391

392

centers that were forced to pay tribute in products that came from different parts of the state of Chiapas, including amber, which came from Simojovel. In Chiapas, no monumental vestiges of Mexica presence have survived, but their influence may be seen in ceramics and minor arts, where new religious concepts were absorbed. Deities such as Quetzalcoatl, Xipe, and Tlaloc were represented in objects such as this censer, displaying the main traits of the rain god, including goggles around the eyes, a mustache, and buccal mask, where several teeth emerge. This type of miniature censer could have been used during the celebration of rituals conducted inside caves dedicated to the gods of rain. MCG

raphy. Found both in caves as well as at archaeological sites, they are part of a widespread tradition of solar images associated with the underworld. The central body of this piece is formed by a cylindrical vessel that has two flat sections referred to as fins or flanges. On the upper part of the rim is seated an anthropomorphic figure representing the Jaguar God of the underworld. He bears on his face the attributes of the sun: a band delimiting the eyes and twisted between the eyebrows. On the lower part of the vessel is an animal and above it is a serpent from whose jaws emerges the face of another young individual, perhaps the deified ruler. MCG

co. These formed part of the decoration of walls, piers, and friezes of many buildings. The realism and expressive quality of this stuccowork is evident in this piece, which must have formed part of an inscription. It represents the face of a deity who is difficult to identify. He has a swollen brow, filed tooth, and a kind of beard that seems to be an extension of a lock of hair that appears over his ear. TPS

"Alberto Ruz Lhuillier"
Inv. no. 10-458672

At Palenque, stuccowork modeled to decorate buildings was exceptional, giving its structures an aesthetic vision distinguishing it from other Maya cities. This piece displays the handling of details to create the face of the sun deity, Kinich Ahau, "Lord Face of the Sun." He has large eyes and his pupils are lightly indicated by a pair of incised lines depicting his crossed eyes. His mouth appears to be half open and from the corners emerge two motifs in the form of filaments. This head could have formed part of the decoration of the frieze or the roofcomb of a building. AGC

390
Effigy Censer
Late Classic period
Comitán, Chiapas, Mexico
Ceramic
Height: 94.5 cm; diameter: 40.6 cm
Tuxtla Gutiérrez
Museo Regional de Chiapas
Inv. no. 10-409817

Censers from the Late Classic period are characterized by complex iconog-

391
Anthropomorphic Profile
Late Classic period
Palenque, Chiapas, Mexico
Stucco and pigment
Height: 13.2 cm; width: 11.0 cm
depth: 4.5 cm
Villahermosa, Museo Regional de Antropología "Carlos Pellicer"
Inv. no. A-0068

The sculptors of Palenque achieved extraordinary images in modeled stuc-

392
Anthropomorphic Head
Late Classic period
Palenque, Chiapas, Mexico
Stucco
Height: 40.5 cm; width: 27.0 cm
Palenque, Museo de Sitio

393

394

This figurine, carved from jadeite, was found in the Temple of the Inscriptions in the sepulcher of Pacal, beside his left foot. The human representation is in seated position, he wears a loincloth and is adorned with a necklace, bracelets, and anklets. From the corners of his mouth emerge two undulating bands and he has a small beard. His eyes are large, squarish, and surrounded by a band. These attributes have made it possible to identify this image as the solar deity, who was closely linked with rulers by ideologically supporting their social rank. MCG

396
"Cacao" Censer Base
Late Classic period
Copán Ruinas, Honduras
Ceramic
Height: 28.3 cm
width: 30.3 cm

393
Bird ornament
Late Classic period
Provenance unknown
Shell
Height: 6.3 cm
New York
The Metropolitan Museum of Art
The Michael C. Rockfeller Memorial
Collection, Purchase
Mrs. Gertrud A. Mellon Gift, 1963
Inv. no. 1978.412.103

The Maya used many materials to create beautiful ornaments for the elite, including a variety of shells obtained by trade from the Caribbean Sea as well as from the Pacific Ocean. Shell is an extremely delicate material and breaks easily. During the Classic period it could only be worked with stone tools in conjunction with sand and water for grinding and polishing, since metal tools were unknown to the Maya. Nonetheless highly specialized artisans succeeded in creating miniature masterpieces in shell, like this ornament in the form of a long-necked waterbird, probably a cormorant. It has massive cut-out talons and spread wings, with the plumage indicated by incision. On its stomach is the profile face of a deity, perhaps that of the Jaguar God of the underworld. He is identified by the scroll above his aquiline nose, known as "cruller," the hook motif in his eye, and the pointed front tooth. Water fowl and shells are associated with the underworld in ancient Maya thought.

394
Anthropomorphic Figurine
Late Classic period
Acropolis, Copán, Honduras
Jadeite
Length: 22.0 cm; width: 7.3 cm
thickness: 2.7 cm; weight: 710 g

395
Copán, Museo Regional
de Arqueología
Inv. no. CPN-J-4112

This handsome example of the Copán Maya jadeworker's art was found in an offering placed beneath the altar at the base of the Hieroglyphic Stairway at the time this impressive ode to the royal ancestors was dedicated. This and a companion jadeite figurine placed with the offering were heirlooms, whose carving style indicates that they were probably carved around the time the dynasty was founded. This piece is a bar pectoral pendant, drilled transversally so that it could be strung and worn on the chest. Pectorals of this same type and size were depicted on all of the sculpted effigies of deceased royal ancestors that decorated the Hieroglyphic Stairway and the temple at its summit. It seems likely that this particular jadeite pendant was used by a number of the ancestors portrayed on the monument, since it was about three hundred years old by the time the fifteenth ruler,

396

Smoke Shell, placed it in the offertory cache. On one side of the pectoral is a very stylized supernatural serpent head. Such creatures were frequently depicted in Classic Maya art as the frame of the sky or at the ends of the double headed scepters worn by Maya kings as symbols of their ability to summon the supernatural forces of their world. WF

395
Figurine
Late Classic period
Palenque, Chiapas, Mexico
Jadeite
Height: 9.0 cm
width: 2.4 cm
Mexico City
Museo Nacional de Antropología
Inv. no. 10-001293

diameter: 25.4 cm
Copán
Museo Regional de Arqueología
Inv. no. CPN-C-4115

Monochrome, unpolished censer base. Its anthropomorphic decoration consists of the mask of a male figure with headdress and ornaments, including the earplugs and necklace of a high-ranking individual. The entire body of the base is decorated with representations of cacao pods. CJF

397
Urn
Late Postclassic period
Dzibanché, Quintana Roo, Mexico
Ceramic
Height: 33.0 cm
diameter: 30.0 cm

Mexico City
Museo Nacional de Antropología
Inv. no. 10-571165

Although there are representations of figures with wings in several regions of Mesoamerica, in the Maya area the most ancient have been found at Izapa, Chiapas. It is also here that the first images of sacrifice by decapitation, associated with a descending god, have been found, and this deity has been interpreted in many ways: as a symbol of the sun setting in the afternoon, rain, lightning, and bees. In general it is linked with ancient fertility rituals, and in the case of the effigy decorating this censer, it is identified with the maize god, also known as God E in Maya codices. It has been suggested that the majority of representations of descending figures personify this deity because they have maize foliage in the headdress and in many cases wings on

398

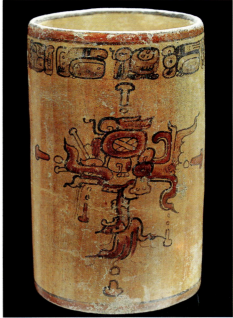

400

397

the arms. In this representation he is shown as a young man who holds a flower in his right hand because he is also the god of vegetation and lord of mountains.   ACM

398
Panel
Late Classic period
Palenque, Chiapas, Mexico
Limestone and paint
Height: 27.4 cm
width: 19.8 cm
thickness: 7.0 cm
Mexico City
Museo Nacional de Antropología
Inv. no. 10-007999

On this panel is carved the face of Bolon Dzacab, known as God K, represented in one of his less-common manifestations without the

cigar on his head, but clearly identified by the sign that he wears on his forehead and by the curving elements surrounding him and emerging from his mouth. The manikin scepter carried by rulers bears the image of God K, whose leg is often transformed into a serpent. This god is associated with lightning and with the act of smoking, an activity of widespread religious significance among the Mayas.   LCGS

399
Anthropomorphic Pendant
Late Classic period
Cobá, Quintana Roo, Mexico
Jadeite
Height: 3.9 cm
width: 1.8 cm
thickness: 6 mm

399

Cancún
Museo Arqueológico de Cancún
Inv. no. 10-389853 1/5

The figurine represents God K, shown seated in profile and is a splendid example of Maya lapidary art. Despite its small size, the artist captured the physical features, costume, and symbolism of the deity with great detail. Within the Maya pantheon God K was one of the gods of greatest importance. He is identified with the corn god and is directly associated with the natural elements linked to agricultural activities, such as rain and thunder. Among his attributes are a long, prominent nose and the representation of one of his feet in the form of a serpent. During the Classic period, many sculptures represent rulers wearing God K on their chest or placed diagonally in the form of a ceremonial or bicephalic bar. Similarly, some individuals carry a manikin scepter (a ritual object) in their hand, topped by a statue of this deity. These objects symbolize the royal origins of who-

ever carries God K and the legitimacy of the individual to occupy the throne.   ECTA

400
Polychrome Cylindrical Vessel
Late Classic period
Tikal area, Guatemala
Ceramic
Height: 19.5 cm; width: 12.0 cm
diameter: 12.0 cm
depth: 19.0 cm
Guatemala, Museo Popol Vuh
Universidad Francisco Marroquín
Inv. no. MPV 0464

Cylindrical vessel with orange-colored slip. It has red, horizontal bands around the rim and the base, outlined in black. Below the rim there is a band with a glyphic series in the Primary Standard Sequence, painted orange and outlined in black. As the central motif, there are two scenes that represent the serpent monster with noseplug, beard, headdress, and stylized earplugs. On the four cardinal directions of the figure, there are phallic designs with what perhaps represent drops of blood and semen.   MS

401

401
"Aquatic Monster" Bird
Late Classic period
Acropolis Structure 26
Copán Ruinas, Honduras
Carved volcanic stone
Height: 73.0 cm; width: 50.0 cm
Copán, Centro Regional
de Investigaciones Arqueológicas
Inv. no. CPN-P-15702

This water bird sculpture is the highest-relief carving uncovered at the ancient Maya site of Copán. It was unearthed during tunnel excavations in the northeast corner of Structure 26, which has the famous Hieroglyphic Stairway on its west side. A small building was found at this locus and given the field name "Híjole" (an exclamation of surprise). When the "Híjole" Structure was buried, a number of mosaic sculptures were placed on or near the bench in the west end of the building's interior. Such activity may have been part of a termination ritual for this and other earlier buildings beneath Structure 26. Similar fragments of water birds were also found in excavations of Structure 22, and it is conceivable that the bird once adorned an earlier version of Temple 22. The water bird is part of larger complex of water symbols that adorned numerous building facades at Copán and other Maya sites. Water was recognized as the giver of life and guarantor of fertility. We understand the scope of water management in Maya society and the role it played in the dynamic structure of daily life. The flamboyant nature of this Late Classic period piece beautifully illustrates the Copán sculptor's ability to master the stone medium and capture the essence of a wild bird intricately linked to our planet's most vital natural element. The dramatic form of the bird was carved from a single block of stone. The soft volcanic tuff from Copán's hillsides lends itself to the fluid lines and open contours that the sculptor achieved. Animated works such as this proliferated during the reign of the thirteenth ruler, from A.D. 695 to 738. A curving hook identifies this as

402

404

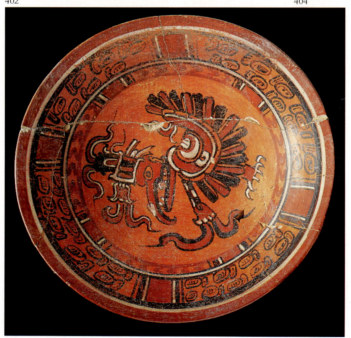

403

a cormorant. Caught in its elongated beak is a flapping fish snatched up from a lagoon or marsh, a favorite haunt of these water birds. The chest of the bird is transformed into a wild-eyed personification head. Similar birds are also found on Classic period vases from the Maya lowlands. WF

402
Polychrome Cylindrical Vessel
Late Classic period
Motagua Valley, Guatemala
Ceramic
Height: 16.0 cm; width: 14.9 cm
diameter: 14.5 cm; depth: 15.4 cm
Guatemala, Museo Popol Vuh
Universidad Francisco Marroquín
Inv. no. MPV 1908

On the inside of the vessel there is a red band under the rim, while on the outside there are horizontal red bands, outlined in black to frame the main elements. Two panels exhibit almost identical representations of God K with two characteristic elements, his prominent nose and the axe over his forehead. There is an unknown element in the form of a wing, tied to the earplug and the headdress. Under the jaw of God K there is an *ahau* glyph with volutes. There are two vertical series of three repeated glyphs, among them the representation of God K. In one of the series, the number 7 precedes the glyph and the number 8 in the case of the other. MS

403
Tripod Bowl
Late Classic period
Provenance unknown
probably Campeche, Mexico
Ceramic
Maximum height: 11.0 cm
diameter 43.0 cm
Campeche, Museo Histórico
Fuerte de San Miguel
Baluarte de San Miguel
Inv. no. 10-398164

This tripod bowl with open walls has a central motif of a version of the Late Classic period Principal Bird Deity, an icon of dynastic power at the beginning of the Maya Classic period. From this time, there are abundant representations of this deity, who often exhibits celestial traits of the god Itzamna. It has been proposed that the Celestial Bird could be the *uay*, the animal spirit-companion of that deity. The Principal Bird Deity has also been identified with Vucub Caquix, the false sun from the beginning of the creation myth in the *Popol Vuh*, the sacred book of the sixteenth century Quiche Maya. In the mythical story of the *Popol Vuh*, the projectile from the blowgun of Hunahpu, one of the Hero Twins, breaks the jaw and teeth of Seven Macaw or Vucub Caquix. In this representation, the Bird Deity wears a pectoral and headdress with unusual volutes, a wing with a stylized serpent eye, a beak with conspicuous fangs, and teeth painted white. SB

404
Pear-shaped Vessel
Early Postclassic period
Edzná, Campeche, Mexico
Ceramic
Height: 33.5 cm; width: 20.7 cm
Campeche, Museo Histórico
Fuerte de San Miguel

Baluarte de San Miguel
Inv. no. 10-397840

Cremation was among the funerary customs of the ancient Mayas. Ashes and bone fragments, the product of incinerating of the cadaver, were deposited in urns or in vessels such as this one from an Early Postclassic period context in Structure 419-3 of the Small Acropolis at Edzná. The motif on the outside represents, by way of a flowery stylized figure, a type of serpent with open maw, a being symbolizing the *cauac* "earth monster" as a devourer. In other words, it is swallowing or it contains the vestiges of a human being, who upon entering the underworld, completes and closes the cycle that began at birth.   ABC

405

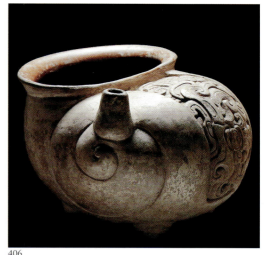

406

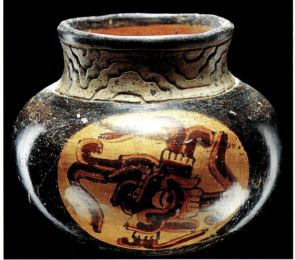

407

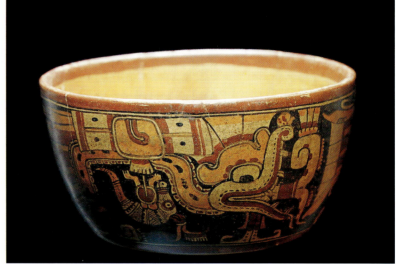

408

405
Tripod Vessel
Late Classic period
Provenance unknown
probably Edzná, Dzibilnocac or Santa Rosa Xtampak, Campeche, Mexico
Ceramic
Height: 8.5 cm; diameter: 28.2 cm
Dzibilchaltún
Museo del Pueblo Maya
Inv. no. 10-290792

The painted decoration on the interior of this tripod bowl with straight, flaring walls, flat bottom, and hollow conical supports characteristic of Cui Naranja Policromo ware, consists of a central motif outlined in black of a bird in profile reserved in the first slip of the vessel, which is orange. The animal wears a feather headdress and a scarf tied at the neck. On the wall is a panel composed of some representations reminiscent of an *ahau*, flanked by bird heads with long beaks. Both the headdress as well as the knot of the scarf, with its *cimi* sign of death and sacrifice held by the bird, indicate its association with death and the underworld, which suggests an almost exclusively funerary function for this ritual vessel. The bird is the mythical *moan* bird, messenger

of the lords of *Xibalba*. This animal has been interpreted as representing the owl, *cui* in Yucatec Maya or more recently as the turkey-buzzard (*Cathartes aura*). The absence of glyphs, the repetitive motifs, and the relatively high number of bowls of this tradition imply a production focused on a wide base of consumers rather than individual pieces commissioned exclusively for the elite.   SB

406
Vessel
Early Classic period
Paraíso, Tabasco, Mexico
Ceramic
Height: 14.2 cm; width: 23.5 cm
diameter: 21.0 cm
Villahermosa, Museo Regional de Antropología "Carlos Pellicer"
Inv. no. A-0072

This exceptional bowl is in the shape of a shell and has a handle that also serves as a spout for pouring. The outer wall is covered by a cream-colored slip, over which can be seen the remains of red paint. The interior is painted with a polished slip of bright orange. In addition, on the upper outer wall of the

vessel is sculpted a stylized serpent head surrounded by volutes. This animal was a sacred symbol associated with priests and leaders, and it is perhaps the main emblem in Maya art. The shell is another element found in the iconography of this culture, and it is associated with the underworld and fertility.   RP

407
Vessel
Late Classic period
Escama de Sabalo
Puerto Cortés, Honduras
Ceramic
Height: 11.7 cm
diameter: 8.8 cm
Tegucigalpa, Bodegas Centrales del Instituto Hondureño de Antropología e Historia
Inv. no. CMG-C-113

Red-and-orange-on-cream polychrome jar, classified within the Ulúa polychromes. It is decorated with an incised or scratched band of stepped frets on the neck and on part of the body. The central figure is incised and represents a serpent, a highly venerated, frequently represented animal among pre-Hispanic cultures.   CJF

408
Feathered Serpent Bowl
Late Classic period
Sula Valley, Honduras
Ceramic
Height: 15.2 cm
width: 11.2 cm
diameter: 4.0 cm
Tegucigalpa
Bodegas Centrales del Instituto Hondureño de Antropología e Historia
Inv. no. SPS-DFB-276

Red, orange, and cream bowl with flaring walls and flat base, polished on the inside and outside with a very fine cream-colored slip. On the exterior there is a wide zone, delimited by fine black lines, of human figures seated with complex headdresses and with signs of speech. There is a representation of a feathered serpent with a combination of a bird and the sign of the earth. The colors, red, orange, black, and cream, contrast with the black base. Decoration ends with a red band near the base. It is classified among the polychromes of the lower Ulúa and was the ceramic most widely traded in the zone.   CJF

409–410
Incense Burner
Late Classic period
Acropolis, Copán Ruinas, Honduras
Stone
Height: 119.5 cm; width: 50.0 cm
Copán, Centro Regional
de Investigaciones Arqueológicas
Inv. no. CPN-P-601 and 602

Incense burners were popular
throughout the Late Classic period
but especially during the reign of
Yax Pasah, the sixteenth ruler. According to David Stuart, the vessels
were called *saclactuns* (white stone
plates) and were used for offerings
of both food and incense during cal-
endrically-timed rituals.   CJF

411
Tetrapod Plate
Protoclassic period
Probably from the Central Maya
Lowlands
Ceramic
Height: 14.0 cm
maximum diameter: 25.5 cm
Mexico City
Museo Nacional de Antropología
Inv. no. 10-079165

Tetrapod plate with slightly flaring
vessel walls and a concave bottom, a
projecting rim along the base and
mammaform supports. This type of
support, diagnostic of the Protoclassic period, is named after its resemblance to women's breasts. The
piece has an orange-colored slip,
which was painted with red and
black designs; the rim and basal
edging are red. On the outer part, in
addition to red bands with dotted
black lines, may be seen a pair of animals whose sole identifiable element is a bifid tongue, perhaps indicating that a serpent is represented.
The designs are framed by two subtle, parallel black lines that create a
band around the piece. The exact
provenance of the plate is not
known, but based on the ceramic
type, it is probably from the central
lowlands.   LCGS

409-410

411

412
Panel with Astronomic Symbols
Terminal Classic–Early Postclassic
period
Chichén Itzá, Yucatán, Mexico
Stone
Height: 73.0 cm
width: 62.0 cm
thickness: 27.0 cm
Chichén Itzá
Museo de Sitio de Chichén Itzá
Inv. no. 10-290178

This comes from a construction
prior to the Venus Platform (Structure 2D4) in the Great Plaza at
Chichén Itzá. On the left is represented the symbol of the planet
Venus, not as a Maya glyph, but
rather by a sign pertaining to cen-

tral Mexico, as a star cut in half
and bound inside a cave. To the
right, accompanied by circles that
add up to the number eight, is a
tie with broken lines that could
refer to the well-known Mexican
ceremony of tying the years. Also
seen is a combination of an interlaced trapeze and a rectangle
which has been called the "Mixtec
year sign," but which also appears
since Teotihuacan times together
with Tlaloc elements in references
to warfare. In the current Venus
Platform, just as in the recently discovered Osario (3C3), we see the
placement of these lateral panels
next to men-bird-serpent and mat
(*pop*) reliefs, the latter symbols of
political power. Judging by extant

loose corners at the site, Chichén
Itzá must have had at least four
Venus platforms.   PJS

413
Small Glyphic Tablet
Terminal Classic–Epiclassic period
Comalcalco, Tabasco, Mexico
Ceramic
Length: 21.3 cm
width: 12.3 cm
thickness: 2.3 cm
Comalcalco
Museo de Sitio de Comalcalco
Inv. no. 10-575771

At many Maya settlements, there
are glyphic texts that serve as a
record for important events for so-

ciety. These historical inscriptions
were carved in stone, modeled in
stucco, or worked in wood. At Comalcalco, the most complete texts
that have been excavated correspond to three small tablets modeled in clay that record the death of
a person at a certain place in A.D.
804 to 846. It is important to note
that on the lower right corner –
cartouche B4 – there is an emblem
glyph of a city that will be identified if this design appears at other
sites; it could perhaps correspond
to that of Comalcalco. The piece
was found on the eastern facade of
Temple I, close to Burial 1 at the
site.   MJGG

*Epigraphic reading by Alfonso Arel-
lano*
In (9.19.15.16.12 8 *eb*) 10 *zip* [4-
March-826] the moon was Twenty-
one days old and the sixth of the period had been completed; the object
of clay was dedicated, his . . . of the
great one of the sun: Wal, sacred
lord of Comalcalco.

414
Stairway Fragment
Classic period
Petén, Guatemala
Stone
Height: 35.5 cm
width: 61.0 cm
Guatemala, Museo Nacional
de Arqueología y Etnología
Inv. no. MNAE 12213

This piece has an inscription composed of two columns of five
glyphs each. Several stairways with
glyphs have been found at different sites in the Maya area, for example, at Copán, Honduras, where
the Stairway narrates the site's
most important historical events
and rulers.   MSB

415

413

412

416

Epigraphic reading by Alfonso Arellano
There passed 15 *tuns*, 3 *uinals*, 12 *kins*, and then it was (9.14.17.11.1 or 9.17.10.6.1) 3 *imix* 4 *zotz* [11-April-729 or 29-March-781] when *batz* was born, Chaan Pahuatun (Smoke Sky Pahuatun) the successor?, then . . .

415
Dupaix Slab
Late Classic period
Palenque
Chiapas

Mexico
Limestone
Length: 41.2 cm
width: 26.8 cm
thickness: 6.5 cm
Mexico City
Museo Nacional
de Antropología
Inv. no. 10-224213

This piece was found by Guillaume Dupaix in 1807. It is one of the six small panels found in the subterranean portion of the Palace. The slab was carved only on one of its sides, where there

are six glyphs that refer to the date of 12 *ahau* 8 *ceh*, which corresponds to the end of *katun* 11 (9.11.0.0.0). This date refers to the period of the rule of Pacal, when the city achieved a level of cultural development never before seen.   MCG

416
Panel Fragment
Late Classic period
Chinikihá, Chiapas, Mexico
Limestone
Height: 60.3 cm
width: 63.5 cm
depth: 11.5 cm
San Cristóbal de las Casas
Museo del Ex Convento
de Santo Domingo
Inv. no. 10-460843

During the Classic period, the Usumacinta River basin was the setting for the rise of great cities such as Ceibal, Altar de Sacrificios, Yaxchilán, and Bonampak, among others. Side by side with these great sites, a number of more mi-

nor centers also flourished, such as Chinikihá, where this sculptural fragment was found, located approximately halfway between Palenque and Piedras Negras. The engraved text begins with two glyphs in the upper row that mark the Calendar Round date 7 *ahau* or *cib*, 13 *pop*. Based on the style of the glyphs, the inscription may be dated to between A.D. 700 and 800. Following this temporal framework, the inscription continues with the first glyph of the lower row, which records, by way of an expression used frequently in texts at Palenque, the enthronement of a ruler called Ah Baak Sak Chak.   TPS

417

418

419

417
Glyphic Cartouche
Late Classic period
Palenque, Chiapas, Mexico
Modeled stucco
Height: 17.0 cm; width: 21.0 cm
Palenque, Museo de Sitio
"Alberto Ruz Lhuillier"
Inv. no. 10-117746

Stucco is a soft mixture of lime and sand that was applied to the surfaces of walls and floors of temples. One of the most outstanding groups of craftsmen at Palenque was that which dominated the technique of modeled stucco. The demand for these workers must have been important because they not only decorated the totality of temples, but also the platforms sustaining them. Work in this technique must have implied knowledge of religious symbolism, although limited on the part of craftsmen because the knowledge and use of calendars and ritual events was in the hands of a small elite group. This modeled glyph formed part of a panel executed in stucco that once decorated the pilasters of the portico of the Forgotten Temple. Based on a hypothetical reconstruction of the placement of the removed glyphs, it has been suggested that it mentions Kan Balam I and Lady Zac Kuk, parents of the great ruler Hanab Pacal II. AGC

418
Glyphic Cartouche
Late Classic period
Palenque, Chiapas, Mexico
Stucco
Height: 12.3 cm; width: 15.0 cm
depth: 3.0 cm
Villahermosa, Museo Regional
de Antropología "Carlos Pellicer"
Inv. no. A-0066

To the south of the Temple of the Foliated Cross are the ruins of Temple XVIII at Palenque. The walls of the now-destroyed building, which was commissioned by Ah Kul Ah Nab, grandson of Pacal, who ruled from A.D. 722 to 763, display a long inscription of glyphs finely modeled in stucco. In this glyphic panel that formed part of the inscription is the face of a fantastic being with squared, crossed eyes, Roman nose, tooth filed into a T-shape, and four-petaled flower on the cheek, all characteristics of the sun god. The glyph functions as a common title that precedes the names of rulers and that can be read a Kinich ("Sun Eye"). Following it is the name of the ruler Ah Kul Ah Nab, of which we can see only the first part, written phonetically with the syllables *ah ku la*. TPS

419
Glyphic Panel
Late Classic period
Palenque, Chiapas, Mexico
Limestone
Length: 161.0 cm; width: 52.0 cm
depth: 6.0 cm
Palenque, Museo de Sitio
"Alberto Ruz Lhuillier"
Inv. no. 10-335198

This sculpture originally covered the north balustrade of the Temple of the Foliated Cross and the texts engraved on it are related to the mythical birth of GII, also called God K or Bolon Dzacab (Nine Generations), one of the gods of the Palenque Triad, considered to be the divine ancestors and protectors of the rulers of this kingdom. GII may be distinguished by his serpentine leg. He is the god of maize and blood, of illustrious lineages as well as of that offered to the gods in self-sacrifice. He is also represented in scenes of accession or expressions of power. On his forehead he has a mirror, symbol of what shines, from which spirals smoke. The glyphic text indicates that the divinity GII was born on 1 *ahau* 13 *mac*, a date in the Calendar Round that corresponds to 1.18.5.4.0 in the Maya Long Count. In terms of our chronology, it is the equivalent of November 8, 2360 B.C. AGC

420
Panel
Late Classic period
Xcalumkin, Campeche
Mexico
Limestone
Height: 77.0 cm
width: 69.0 cm
thickness: 26.0 cm
Campeche
Museo de las Estelas
"Román Piña Chán"
Baluarte de la Soledad
Inv. no. 10-342680

The development of political organization among the ancient Maya seems to have derived during the Early and Late Classic periods from a strict absolutism to a government shared by several nobles of the same lineage. Several historical sources on the Postclassic period seem to confirm this, as well as a few archaeological examples from the Terminal Classic period, as is the case of Xcalumkin, a site 85 kilometers to the northeast of the city of Campeche. At this place, which in days of yore saw the splendor of Puuc architecture, there was no concentration of buildings. The different religious, administrative, and residential groups were distributed in a relatively uniform way. Representations of dignitaries accompanied by hieroglyphic inscriptions also indicate a homogeneity in the distribution of power, goods, and services. ABC

420

421

Epigraphic reading by Alfonso Arellano
Took control, their union [person] · *cahal.*

421
Panel
Late Classic period
Xcalumkin, Campeche
Mexico
Limestone
Height: 51.0 cm
width: 46.5
thickness: 27.0 cm
Campeche
Centro INAH Campeche
Inv. no. 10-290464

This panel with four blocks of glyphs was associated with a sculpture representing one of the lords of Xcalumkin, a city located in the Puuc region of Campeche. The rank of the leader is *cahal*, an office that during the Classic period occupied a level under that of the king, the *ahau*. Their importance within society was great, because sometimes they could govern cities, participate in rites together with the *ahau*, and even commission monuments. The date on which this monument was erected was the second *tun* of the *katun* ending on the date 2 *ahau*, which corresponds to the Long Count date of 9.15.1.0.10 (A.D. 733).   LMC

423

422
Yaxchilán Lintel 48
Early Classic period
Yaxchilán, Chiapas, Mexico
Limestone
Length: 176.0 cm
width: 83.0 cm
thickness: 23.5 cm
Mexico City
Museo Nacional de Antropología
Inv. no. 10-080370

Metaphorically we might say that at Yaxchilán the buildings are books and the lintel of each door is a page volume. The first "page" of Structure 12 (with eight lintels) is this example, which records an Initial Series date, the numbers of

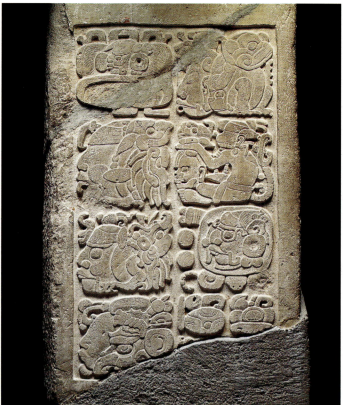

422

which are represented as heads, and four of the time periods (*baktun, katun, uinal,* and *kin*) in full-figure glyphs. The date is 9.4.11.8.16 (A.D. 534) and the day of the ritual calendar is 2 *cib*. The numeral of this date is noted with two dots and a head for the day name. The lunar count, the month (19 *pax*), and the event that occurred on this date were sculpted on the next "page", Lintel 47.   TPS

423
El Zapote Stela 5
Early Classic period
El Zapote, Petén, Guatemala
Stone
Height: 127.0 cm
width: 44.0 cm
Guatemala, Museo Nacional de Arqueología y Etnología
Inv. no. MNAE 7652a

Front side of Stela 5 from El Zapote. This stela is unusual because the front depicts a male figure and the back a female figure. The male wears a headdress with mask and feathers, circular earplugs, a pectoral (which cannot be seen very clearly due to the figure's pose), bracelets, and anklets with spherical beads. He wears a cape and a skirt with a beaded criss-cross design next to a loincloth with several masks. With his right hand, he holds a cartouche with the number 12 and the Teotihuacán year sign. On the lower part an element that may be a censer, from which smoke appears to emerge.   MSB

Epigraphic reading by Alfonso Arellano
It was 9.0.0.0.8 *ahau* 13 *coh*, G9 was the Lord of the Night, F, the moon was 4 days (old) [10-December-435], stood up . . . *awil* . . . on the 8 *tun* (*ahau*) . . . the cloud rose in the sky . . . that of the sun, the great one of the sun [person] . . . he decapitated . . .

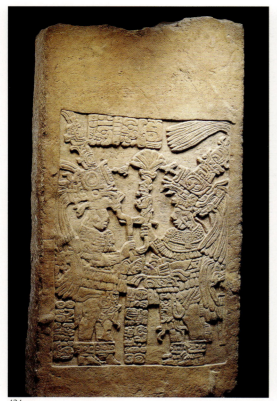

424

426

424
Yaxchilán Lintel 58
Late Classic period
Yaxchilán, Chiapas, Mexico
Limestone
Length: 188.0 cm; width: 75.0 cm
thickness: 31.0 cm
Mexico City
Museo Nacional de Antropología
Inv. no. 10-080371

The Mayas used all available spaces on their buildings, sculptures, and other artistic works to leave a record of the most important individuals, events, and matters of their history. The lintels and stelae of Yaxchilán have always been admired for the fineness of their sculptural art and the beauty of their reliefs, in which scenes depict figures of all types: deities, rulers, warriors, captives, and so forth. With advances in deciphering of Maya hieroglyphic writing in the last four decades, the lintels, among other sculptural monuments, have gained new and greater importance due to the wealth of information contained in their historical records. Thus, we now know that the scene represented on this piece commemorates an important event: a member of the Jaguar lineage, which reigned over Yaxchilán during the Classic period, identified as Shield Jaguar II, fourteenth ruler of the city, participates in a ceremony in which another figure, lord Great Skull, also participated.   ACM

425
Tablet of the Scribes
Late Classic period
Pomoná, Tabasco, Mexico

425

Limestone
Height: 100.0 cm
width: 106.0 cm
depth: 22.5 cm
Pomoná
Museo de Sitio de Pomoná
Inv. no. 10-392507

This piece is not really a tablet, but rather a throneback. It displays two high-rank Maya individuals. The one on the left is Tok Kohol, "Cloud-Puma," the *ahau* or ruler of Pomoná, who wears a God C pectoral exclusive to his rank. The figure on the right is a *cahal*, or first level provincial ruler, who wears the attire characteristic of God N or *Pahuatun*. The glyphic text associated with this *cahal* confirms that he was personified as this deity, because the title 4 *Pahuatun* is recorded. The Mayas believed that they upheld the celestial vault and there was one at each cardinal direction. The lost part of this throneback must have included two other individuals and an Initial Series date that could be reconstructed as 9.17.0.0.0 13 *ahau*, 18 *kumku*, or January 20, A.D. 771. The glyphic text indicates that Tok Kohol celebrated the end of the

katun with a ceremony in which he conducted self-sacrifice, and he sprinkled his blood (*yokaw ch'ahi*) in honor of the deity called *Yax Lo, Hun Ts'an, Na Chan*, "Precious Twin, of the Sole Throne, First Serpent." The inscription confers Tok Kohol with the titles of "Divine Ahau of Pakabul (the original name of Pomoná) and Pourer" (Kul Pakabul Ahau, Bacab). The text adds that the ceremony ended three days later on 3 *akbal*, 1 *uayeb* (*ox lat, iual ut, ox akbal, hun uayeb tsutsah*).   SPA and GB

426
Slab
Late Classic period
Oxkintok, Yucatán, Mexico
Limestone
Height: 84.5 cm
width: 43.0 cm
thickness: 5.5 cm
Mexico City
Museo Nacional de Antropología
Inv. no. 10-136922

Within the Puuc region, Oxkintok was a civic-ceremonial center that was distinguished by its large constructions. Associated with architecture, sculpture was an important medium in which the Maya captured their testimonies in writing. In the Chich Palace of the urban group of Ah Canul, several figures were found on lintels, vault caps, and panels. On this slab is the figure of a woman who wears the costume and ornaments of the ruling group in Maya society. Decoration is based on two elements, one human and the other hieroglyphic

in the form of an inscription saying "she is . . ." which after the name, identifies her as a woman; it is also possible to transcribe a composite title associated with high-rank individuals and the last block, translated "she of the resplendent face." The figure stands frontally with her head in profile; on her head she wears a great headdress formed by a zoomorphic mask adorned with beads and a feather panache; scarification may be seen on her face. For ornaments, she wears multiple bracelets and her left arm is bent, holding a long object, probably a copal bag. She also wears a type of necklace bearing a ceremonial bar, a symbol of power. She wears a skirt held by a band that has an anthropomorphic mask in the middle. On her feet, she wears sandals with heel guards and decorations on the front.   POC

Epigraphic reading by Alfonso Arellano
She is the lady . . . upholder of the cosmos, she of the water lily, she of the solar face.

426bis
Disk
Late Classic period
Toniná, Chiapas, Mexico
Limestone
Diameter: 76.5 cm
thickness: 12.0 cm
Toniná
Sitio Arqueológico de Toniná
No inv. no.

Within the variety of sculpted monuments at Toniná, disks with circular inscriptions and a large glyph in the center are particularly noteworthy. Many of them were erected to commemorate the completion of the 360-day cycle called *tun*, therefore these disks tend to display the glyph of the day *ahau*. Nevertheless, excavated in 1991, in front of the Temple of the Prisoners, this example records a funerary ceremony that occurred on June 17, A.D. 730. The reading begins on the upper part with the introductory glyph and going clockwise, records that a Long Count date begins, composed of 9 *baktun*, 14 *katun*, 13 *tun*, 14 *uinal* and 12 *kin*, which falls on the day 5 *eb* (which is repeated in monumental form in the center of the disk) of the month 10 *yaxkin*. This is followed by three glyphs that record a ceremony linked with the death and burial of the ruler Kinich Baknal Chak, Divine Lord of Toniná.   TPS

427
"The Bundle" Sculpture
Late Classic period
Palenque, Chiapas, Mexico
Limestone
Height: 40.0 cm

426 bis

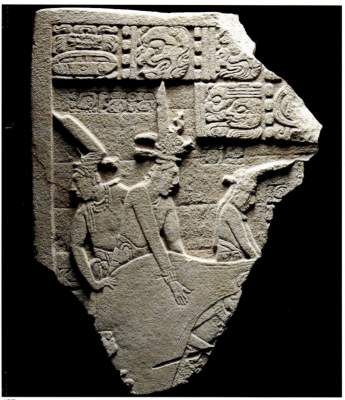

427

428a

length: 29.0 cm
thickness: 5.3 cm
Palenque, Museo de Sitio
"Alberto Ruz Lhuillier"
Inv. no. 10-479218

In this panel fragment from Group XVI, five individuals are represented at the moment they descend a stairway while carrying a bundle, perhaps a mortuary bundle. Three of them are dressed in a very simple way and are distinguished only by the complexity of their conical headdresses. The central figure wears wristlets, earflares, and a necklace, as well as a representation of God K in the front part of his headdress. The glyphic band identifies him as the ruler Akul

428b

Ha Nab III. The style of this type of sculpture is similar to that of Piedras Negras, Guatemala, and to that of the Usumacinta River basin. This masterpiece of Maya art is noteworthy for the natural appearance of the figures and for transmitting a sensation of movement.   AGC

428a-b
"Leiden Plate"
Period unknown
Tikal, Guatemala
Jadeite
Height: 21.7 cm
Leiden
Rijksmuseum voor Volkenkunde
Inv. no. RMV 1403-1193

The Leiden Plate or Leiden Plaque owes its name to the circumstance that the first publications dealing with it appeared in the English language. Actually, it is a pendant made of Middle-American jadeite which was found by chance in 1864 by a Dutch engineer who was in charge of the digging of a canal in the vicinity of Puerto Barrios in Guatemala, where he came across bronze and jadeite objects. The Leiden Plate owes its importance to the fact that one of the oldest known recorded dates of the Maya calendar is engraved on it and has been preserved intact. The text reads as follows: "After the period composed of 8 baktuns, 14 katuns, 3 tuns, 1 uinal, and 12 kins, on the day 1 Eb, when the fifth Lord of the Night ruled and the month Yaxkin commenced, Balam Ahau Chan, ruler of [probably] Tikal, was installed". This refers to the date on which Balam Ahau Chan ascended the throne, in our calendar corresponding with Friday, the 17 September, A.D. 320. The other side shows Balam-Ahau-Chan with such regalia as the double-headed serpent staff, which he holds horizontally in his arms. This headdress is topped by the face of the Jester God, the symbol of royal power. The king stands on a vanquished man whose hands are tied and whose head is turned away. Because the Leiden Plate was found together with small bells made of bronze–which did not come into use until the end of the Classic period–we know that this pendant was looted from a grave by Mayas around that time (A.D. 800-900) and was used and reburied. The possession of a pendant of this kind enhanced the value of the kingship and of the king himself, as Balam Ahau Chan showed by hanging three Leiden plates from the right and left sides of his girdle.

627

429

429
Carved Bone
Late Classic period
Xcalakdzonot, Yucatán, Mexico
Bone
Length: 16.0 cm; diameter: 3.0 cm
Valladolid, Museo del Centro
Coordinador del INI
Inv. no. 59

In the center of a long, possibly human bone, placed horizontally, is a very elaborate, incised, carved glyph. It probably formed part of a necklace or belt group. Both sides have stepped bands at their ends, which perhaps may be interpreted as the ends of short feathers. The main glyph, in its cartouche with a double outline, represents the head of a bat (*zotz* in Maya) and is easily identified by the distinctive, ferocious teeth and the triangular leaf shape of the nose. In addition to obvious associations with the underworld derived from its subterranean habitat and caves, *zotz* was also an important lineage name; as a place glyph, it is intimately related to a center as important as Copán. The bone here was found in a burial at Xcalakdzonot (which means "Double Cenote"), a few kilometers south of Chichén Itzá, together with two polychrome vessels, a flint knife, the head of a monkey, and a human figure carved on a deer bone. Associated ceramics date it to the Late Classic period and establish relations with the Jaina region, Campeche.   PJS

Epigraphic reading by Alfonso Arellano
His sculpture

430
Animal Figurine
with Hieroglyphic Inscription
Late Classic period
Provenance unknown
Bone
Length: 14.5 cm; width: 5.0 cm
Mexico City
Museo Nacional de Antropología
Inv. no. 10-001238

This figurine is undoubtedly one of the great masterpieces made of bone, because by exploiting the form of the bone, perhaps a jaguar femur, the body of a crouching reptile, perhaps an iguana or a lizard, was reproduced. On its belly a hieroglyphic inscription was carved with full-body glyphs, representing numbers and time periods. This animal figurine could represent Itzamna, the most important god of the Maya pantheon, whose name has

430

been translated as "House of the Iguanas." The Mayas conceived of the world as a house, the walls of which were formed by four gigantic iguanas with their heads turned downward, each one of them with a different color according to the cardinal direction to which they corresponded.   ACM

431
Plaques
Early Classic period
Calakmul, Campeche, Mexico
Jadeite
Length: 10.2 cm; width: 6.0 cm
Length: 10.3 cm; width: 6.0 cm
Length: 10.4 cm; width: 6.2 cm
Campeche, Museo Histórico
Fuerte de San Miguel
Baluarte de San Miguel
Inv. no. 10-342887; 10-342888
10-342889

These incised plaques lung from a medallion to form a belt that covered the pelvic area of the individual buried in the funerary chamber of Tomb 1, Structure III at Calakmul. Each plaque has an incised pair of glyphs; the name and titles of the individual may be included on one of them. The group may also correspond to a text similar to what appears on the so-called "Primary Standard Sequence." Because of its location, the character of the in-

431a

431b

432

431c

San José, Museo del Jade Lic.
Fidel Tristán
Instituto Nacional de Seguros
Inv. no. INS 2007

This is an incised pendant or plaque of Maya jadeite. It seems to have been split in the middle. It contains an incised hieroglyphic text on the back part and the portrait of a Maya figure incised on the front. The text has been interpreted as, "he harvested from his tongue" or "the harvest of his tongue," a reference to blood sacrifice from this soft fleshy body part, and ends in the "ear of maize" glyph, which serves to name the jadeite pendant.   JVGM

scription, and the glyphs used, it might correspond to a text of ritual character, and not to a nominal clause.   RCV

Epigraphic reading by Alfonso Arellano
Plaque 1: the moon completed its seating.
Plaque 2: darkness is seated.
Plaque 3: [The Monster of the] sky.

432
Pendant
Classic period
Nicoya, Guanacaste, Costa Rica
Jadeite
Height: 12.8 cm; width: 2.9 cm
thickness: 0.5 cm

433
Disk
Early Classic period
La Fortuna, San Carlos, Costa Rica
Slate
Diameter: 17.0 cm; thickness: 2.0 cm
San José, Museo del Jade Lic.
Fidel Tristán
Instituto Nacional de Seguros
Inv. no. INS 29267

Slate disk incised with Maya hieroglyphs. It was also the base on which to mount a pyrite mirror. According to new interpretations, it briefly tells of the ascent to power of a king: "During the month of *yaxkin* during the month of [?] the king or lord

433

434

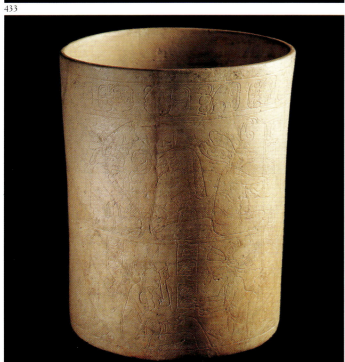

435

436

[?], ninth successor in his lineage, tied the royal band for himself [crowned himself]." JVGM

434
Disk
Classic period
Nicoya, Guanacaste, Costa Rica
Slate
Diameter: 22.0 cm; thickness: 2.0 cm
San José, Museo del Jade Lic.
Fidel Tristán
Instituto Nacional de Seguros
Inv. no. INS 6528

Slate disk with Maya glyphs, which served as a base for a pyrite mirror. It is said that the hieroglyphs narrate the birth of a person or a place ac-

cording to the myth of the *Popol Vuh.* It has been preliminarily interpreted as: "It was separating into two. The place seven-black-precious yellow was born from the carapace of the turtle *uaxaktun* [Uaxactún emblem glyph], he harvested from his tongue its sacred substance [he let blood] the son of the puma-turtle the protected son. Of jaguar divine sun eye or king of *uak* [emblem glyph]." JVGM

435
Cylindrical Vessel
Late Classic period
Tikal, Petén, Guatemala
Ceramic
Height: 24.2 cm; diameter: 18.0 cm

Guatemala, Museo Nacional de Arqueología y Etnología
Inv. no. MNAE 11134

Cylindrical vessel with incised decoration. It has a band of glyphs surrounding the vessel right below the rim. Other vertical columns display glyphs and several ceremonial scenes. The surface is cream-colored. MSB

Epigraphic reading by Alfonso Arellano
The sacred lord Tx'i Te'Chi, [lord] of 3 *katuns* dedicated the inscription of the vessel for *atole enchilado* [?; a chili-laced cornmeal beverage]. [The rest of the glyphic clauses refer to associated figures.]

436
Bowl
Late Classic period
Campeche, Mexico
Onyx marble
Height: 11.6 cm; diameter: 15.8 cm
Washington, D.C., Dumbarton Oaks

Research Library Collections
Inv. no. B-147.MAS

This delicate bowl is carved from a single piece of translucent, white banded onyx marble. An incised hieroglyph text encircles the outer rim, while fluting separates three panels with seated figures on the vessel walls below. One of the figures is a bearded man who sits in a conventionalized serpent mouth. He wears elaborate garments and holds a ceremonial bar with supernatural faces emerging from each end; Head Seven of the "Seven and Nine Zoomorphic Heads" pair emerges from one end, while a supernatural saurian head emerges from the other. The next figure is an elaborately garbed woman seated in a serpent mouth; in her right hand she offers the other head of the "Seven and Nine Zoomorphic Heads" pair. The third figure is also elegantly dressed, but does not sit within a serpent mouth. He holds a saurian head similar to that emerging from one end of the bar held by the bearded figure.

437a

437

438

439

437a
Disk
Late Classic period
Guaymil, Campeche, Mexico
Slate
Diameter: 9.5 cm
Cologne
Rautenstrauch-Joest-Museum
Inv. no. 49640

A row of glyphs round the edge; in the middle, in the same very flat relief, the squat, plump form of a dwarf. Particularly noteworthy are the feather ornaments which embellish both arms.   GSS

437
"Scribe" Vessel
Late Classic period
Copán Ruinas, Honduras
Ceramic
Height: 17.0 cm
base: 16.2 cm
diameter: 14.5 cm
Tegucigalpa
Bodegas Centrales
del Instituto Hondureño
de Antropología e Historia
Inv. no. CPN-C-918

This represents the finest example extant of incised Surlo ceramics. Four seated figures and a band of hieroglyphs were first incised by a masterly hand, then the background area was coated with a thin slip that fired slightly whiter than the original burnished surface. The text is a superlative example of the Primary Standard Sequence, and states that this was a vessel used for drinking cacao. The four figures are of noble bearing and station, and are exquisitely rendered. One represents a Maya artist, shown carving a face which he holds in his left hand. Wrapped around his waist and extending out in back of the artist is a device that has been likened to a computer print-out, complete with Maya numbers in the form of bars and dots.   WF

438
Vessel in Plant Form
Early Classic period
Acanceh, Yucatán, Mexico
Ceramic
Height: 14.1 cm; diameter: 17.5 cm
Merida, Museo Regional de Yucatán
"Palacio Cantón"
Inv. no. 10-426169

In each one of the sections of this beautiful ceramic vessel is an incised glyph, totaling five complete glyphs and one half glyph. The text is the usual one that appears on this type of object, in which the type of receptacle, its contents, and its owner are mentioned. It should be noted that in this case the contents of the receptacle, transcribed as *"b'ukuts cacao"* (*bu-ku-tsi 2ka-[ka]-wa*), refers to one of the different types of cacao beverages consumed by the Mayas. The same substance, *b'ukuts*, appears as one of the offerings given to the rain god, Chaac, in one of the texts in the Dresden Codex. The vessel pertains to the ware known as Timucuy Naranja, which is characterized by a smoothed, slipped surface and which dates from A.D. 300 to 600. Although its provenance is not entirely clear, there is a reference that indicates it was found at Acanceh, an important Early Classic period city in the northern Yucatán peninsula.   LFS

Epigraphic reading by Alfonso Arellano
Its squash sculpture . . .

439
Bowl with Hieroglyphic Inscription
Late Classic period
Probably from Maxcanú, Yucatán
Mexico
Ceramic
Height: 9.0 cm; diameter: 21.0 cm
Valladolid, Museo del Centro
Coordinador del INI
No inv. no.

In recent years, great strides have been made in the decipherment of Maya hieroglyphs, not only in public inscriptions and codices, but also in the reading of short texts recorded on vessels and other portable objects of personal use. A large portion of these writings have turned out to be fairly prosaic: they give the name of the vessel shape; its function in daily life, for example: "an open cylindrical vessel for cacao"; and the name or title of its owner, who it probably had to accompany to the other life. This dark brown bowl, with composite silhouette, belongs to this type of vessel. It has a glyphic inscription below the rim. Based on verbal indications, it comes from the region of Maxcanú, Yucatán, and it belongs, therefore, to the provisional ceramic type called Haabín-gubiado-inciso of the Late Classic period. The individual referred to could be a functionary from Oxkintok or another nearby site. PJS

440
Bowl
Late Classic period
Provenance unknown
Ceramic
Height 13.0 cm; diameter: 13.5 cm
Dzibilchaltún, Museo del Pueblo Maya
Inv. no. 10-347230

This bowl with slightly converging walls, straight edge, and flat base, has a panel of gouged and incised glyphs under the rim, outlined by black bands. The entire body has modeled and excavated decoration, resembling stems, probably alluding to a plant element such as a gourd. Naturalistic representations are very frequent in Maya ceramics, so that they constituted a visual language by way of the culture and time, since the artist established a continuous dialogue between himself and the cosmological beliefs that were the basis of his civilization.   YP

440

443

441

442

444

Fuerte de San Miguel
Baluarte de San Miguel
Inv. no. 10-339735

High-ranking Maya officials possessed numerous objects as personal property. Among these items were costume elements, headdresses, footwear, jewelry and even vessels. In receptacles similar to the one presented here, the hieroglyphic band found beneath the rim contains the name of the owner of the object, as well as a reference to the vessel's use. It was common to use these to drink *atole*, a cornmeal gruel beverage, or to consume chocolate. The other glyphic elements on the vessel's outer wall can refer to an event or specific ceremony for which the piece was made. Knowing that few common people were literate, craftsmen, who also knew glyphs, had to maintain a close relationship with the elite in power.   ABC

Epigraphic reading by Alfonso Arellano
He rose [his sculpture?] [name of the individual] he of the band, he of the weight of the tree . . .

441
Shell
Late Classic period
Simojovel, Chiapas, Mexico
Bivalve shell
Length: 11.7 cm; width: 6.2 cm
thickness: 1.5 cm
Tuxtla Gutiérrez
Museo Regional de Chiapas
Inv. no. 10-409798

By way of a complex system of morphosyllabic writing, Maya scribes left a record of the most significant events from the lives of their rulers. For this purpose, they turned to different techniques, and used the most varied of materials. Among these materials were objects carved from bivalves and other shells. Today it is known that the Mayas held these mollusks in great esteem, not only because of their form, texture, and color, but also for their symbolism, linked with water, fertility, and the underworld. This finely incised shell, worked on both sides, comes from the Simojovel region, an amber-producing zone in the state of Chiapas. On the interior, it displays the image of a hunchbacked individual with a glyph on his back; the inscription on the back, in addition to recording two dates from the Calendar Round, refers to Kinich Hanab Pacal, the Divine Lord of Palenque.   TPS

442
Vessel
Late Classic period
Campeche, Mexico
Travertine
Height: 11.0 cm
diameter: 12.0 cm
thickness: 3-6 mm
Cologne
Rautenstrauch-Joest-Museum
No inv. no

Cylindrical vessel with a smooth bottom; the outer surface is evenly fluted up to about 1 centimeter below the slightly protruding rim, creating the illusion that the vessel tapers towards the top. Spaced out round the middle of the wall are six cartouches with glyphs in very fine relief; the meaning of the glyphs has yet to be interpreted. Originally the vessel was painted; traces of red are visible in the cartouches. A number of other travertine vases of the Maya are known which have preserved a certain amount of their paint; one rarely finds all the paint intact, not surprisingly given the *a secco* technique of application. The present specimen is remarkable for its perfect state of preservation; it was recovered unbroken. The extraordinarily thin wall and the glyphs carved in fine relief are a testimony to the masterly skill of this unknown Mayan artist.   GSS

443
Cylindrical Vessel
Classic period
Northeastern Campeche, Mexico
Ceramic
Height: 20.5 cm; diameter: 11.0 cm
Campeche, Museo Histórico

Epigraphic reading by Alfonso Arellano
1st band: Lord (?)
Columns: Lord Jaguar (?)

444
Vessel with Reliefs
Early Classic period
Santa Rita Corozal
Corozal District, Belize
Calcite
Height: 8.0 cm; diameter: 14.0 cm
Belmopan, Bodegas,
del Departamento de Arqueología
Inv. no. 35/203-2:152

This extraordinary limestone vessel comes from the tomb of an Early Classic ruler buried in Structure 7. Four medallions in relief decorate an outer panel: two are occupied by representations of an old man, God N identified with *bacabs*, *Pauahtuns*, upholders of the sky, patrons of the four directions of the world, and protectors of scribes. The other two medallions display a hieroglyphic inscription with three cartouches each. The style of this inscription is typical of the Early Classic period and forms a single text referring to the function of the vessel (*y-uch'ib*) to drink cacao.   PJS

445

447

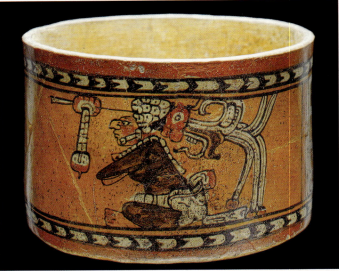

446

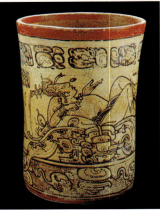

448

445
Bowl
Classic period
Yucatán, Mexico
Probably stone
Height: 8.6 cm; diameter: 15.9 cm
Washington, D.C., Dumbarton Oaks
Research Library Collections
Inv. no. B-208.MAP

Taking the shape of a carved gourd, the bowl originally was incised with three sunken oval cartouches containing reliefs, separated by rectangular, incised cartouches of large glyphs. The two surviving oval cartouches each contain a figure, a woven throne, and a small rectangle of incised glyphs. In one of the ovals, a figure with headdress sits on a throne and points to a necked jar embellished with a jawless "zip monster." In the other oval, the figure appears to be swimming above the throne while a water bird plucks at the "jeweled Ahau" headdress, and two overlapping rectangular vessels float in front of the figure's arms. Each of the figures wears composite earspools and a beaded

necklace, bracelets, anklets, and a belt. They also each display tatoo-like earth markings, and cacao pods grow from various places on their bodies. The fragment of the third oval cartouche shows a similar headdress and two cacao pods, indicating that a similar figure once existed in this space. Scholars have suggested that the figures represent vegetation deities.

446
Polychrome Basin
Late Classic period
Chamá area of Quiché, Guatemala
Ceramic
Height: 13.0 cm; width: 19.5 cm
diameter: 19.2 cm; depth: 12.6 cm
Guatemala, Museo Popol Vuh
Universidad Francisco Marroquín
Inv. no. MPV 0084

Cylindrical basin with flat bottom with decoration typical of the Chamá style. Two seated figures in profile may be seen, cross-legged and leaning slightly forward. One of them is supported by the palms of

his hands, while the other has his arms crossed in front of the body. The two wear white loincloths, necklaces, and ear ornaments. The white headdress has an effigy of a lizard or serpent decorated with feathers and volutes. Between the figures are two vertical panels of glyphs, painted orange and outlined in black on a white background. The glyphs are somewhat carelessly drawn, which is characteristic of the Chamá style. The first of them seems to be a representation of the calendrical day sign *etznab*, but it has a diagonal painted on the cartouche. The other two glyphs probably represent the calendrical signs *muluc* and *ahau*.   MS

447
Plate
Classic period
Chiapas, Mexico
Ceramic
Height: 6.3 cm; diameter: 29.6 cm
Pomoná, Museo de Sitio de Pomoná
Inv. no. 10-422277

This polychromed piece is characteristic of the Petén area during the Classic period. It displays a glyphic text near the rim, in which the so-called Standard Primary Sequence can be seen. This type of inscription was widely used in Maya funerary vessels; it expresses terms related to the burial ritual, the type of ceramic used and the contents of the offering. The plate shows the head of the Water Lily Jaguar, a Maya mythological being whose distinctive trait is the water lily that he wears on his forehead and the plant growth that emerges from his maw. In this example, his eye is formed by the Maya day glyph *ix*, "jaguar." The Water Lily Jaguar is an aspect or personification of God GIII of the Palenque Triad, an entity that represents the underworld sun, in other words the Sun of the Region of the Dead. An unusual feature is the kind of feather head-

dress gracefully framing the head of the animal; the long, exuberant feathers follow the circular rim of the plate and endow the composition with harmony and an exquisite sense of movement.   GB and SPA

448
"Codex-type" Cylindrical Vessel
Late Classic period
Calakmul, Campeche, Mexico
Ceramic
Height: 14.0 cm; diameter: 9.5 cm
Mexico City
Museo Nacional de Antropología
Inv. no. 10-566398

This vessel formed part of an offering dedicated to an important individual in Tomb 1, Structure II, Building 2H at Calakmul. It is noteworthy for its beauty and perfection, the fineness and mastery of the drawing, and for the symbolism of the scene and the inscription framing it. The position of the figure reminds us of that of the slab from Pacal's tomb in the Temple of the Inscriptions at Palenque. The figure painted on this vessel is reclining on a mask floating on a band with elements symbolizing the underworld. One might surmise that it represents the ruler falling into the world of the dead, and hope for his subsequent resurrection.   ACM

449

449
"Blom Plate"
Late Classic period
Chetumal, Quintana Roo, Mexico
Ceramic
Height: 7.3 cm; diameter: 44.5 cm
Merida, Museo Regional de Yucatán
"Palacio Cantón"
Inv. no. 10-455136

The Blom Plate was named after American archaeologist Frans Blom, who made its existence known in an article published in 1950 by the Carnegie Institution of Washington, D.C. The plate, which was found during excavations to construct the airport in Chetumal, Quintana Roo, remained in a private collection in Oaxaca City until 1985, when it was donated to the Museo Regional de Yucatán "Palacio Cantón". It is probable that the scene depicted on the interior of this vessel recalls a story from the *Popol Vuh*, the sixteenth-century sacred book of the Quiche Maya in which the Hero Twins, Hunahpu and Xbalanque, shoot Vucub Caquix, a mythical bird who proclaimed himself the Sun and Moon. Irritated by his arrogance, the twins wait for him to climb up into his favorite fruit tree and they shoot him with their blowguns, knocking him down and killing him. This time the Hero Twins are not portrayed as hunters with special hats, but rather as twins with distinctive diadems. Both have circles or black spots on the body and they have already shot the projectile from their respective blowguns at Vucub Caquix, who appears with a fantastic bird headdress with a long, skeletal neck. Although the patches of jaguar pelt characteristic of Xbalanque are not present, the twin on the left is seated on a throne in the form of a cushion covered with jaguar skin, which allows him to be identified. The glyphs that surround the other half of the plate form a dedicatory text that is known as the Primary Standard Sequence: "Saw dedicate . . . [lord]? 8 Muanil his writing [of] Coc Ch'ax."   SB

450
Inkpots
Late Classic period
Las Sepulturas, Copán, Honduras

451

Ceramic
Different dimensions
Copán, Centro Regional
de Investigaciones Arqueológicas
Inv. no. CPN-C-110

These bottles have been found in a large area of eastern Guatemala, western El Salvador, and western Honduras, particularly Copán where they are most abundant. They are fashioned from the same cream clay of Copador, and usually bear modeled decoration pressed from a mold. In several examples the bottles were found with red pigment

450   452

(either cinnabar or hematite) inside. Their function as pigment bottles is somewhat intriguing given that they are never themselves painted.   WF

451
Polychrome Cylindrical Vessel
Late Classic period
Guatemalan lowlands
Ceramic
Height: 23.2 cm; width: 10.5 cm
diameter: 10.0 cm; depth: 22.4 cm
Guatemala, Museo Popol Vuh
Universidad Francisco Marroquín
Inv. no. MPV 0366

Cream-colored cylindrical vessel with an orange band around it covering the rim, and another around the base. Near the edge is a horizontal band of glyphs painted light orange and outlined in a darker tone. Below is a scene with two major figures, standing and seen in profile, richly dressed with elaborate feathered headdresses, tubular and circular beaded necklaces, loincloths, anklets, wristlets, and knee ornaments. Opposite each person there is a dwarf with a loincloth and black headdress that seems to be helping the individual get dressed. Behind each main figure is the head of God K, and in the headdress of one of them, another representation of the same god in miniature. Two vertical panels of five glyphs separate the scenes; a fish is next to each panel.   MS

452
Vessel
Late Classic period
Motagua Valley, Guatemala
Ceramic
Height: 18.0 cm; width: 15.5 cm
diameter: 11.0 cm
depth: 17.0 cm
Guatemala, Museo Popol Vuh
Universidad Francisco Marroquín
Inv. no. MPV 0659

Vessel with composite silhouette and ring-shaped base. It has red specular hematite paint applied to

the relief. At the neck is a horizontal band with a series of glyphs that form a Primary Standard Sequence with an initial sign, God N, Bat, Wing quincunx, Rodent. On each one of the flat sides is a medallion; one displays a seated Maya noble with his legs crossed, wearing a loincloth, necklace, and earplugs, and holding an object from which volutes emerge. His hair is tied back. The other medallion shows a mask of a deity with multiple fangs, possibly an earth monster. The impression of the neck and body was made with a mold.   MS

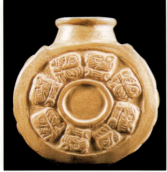

453

453
Monochrome Jar
Classic period
El Tazumal, Chalchuapa
Department of Santa Ana
El Salvador
Ceramic
Height: 7.3 cm
width: 7.0 cm
El Salvador
Museo Nacional de Antropología
"Dr. David J. Guzmán"
Inv. no. A1-2900

Monochrome jar in the form of a short-necked disk, with decoration on both sides consisting of Maya glyphs in high relief. On its sides is a series of oblique, excavated channels. Its interior contains remains of cinnabar. This type of object corresponds to the Late Classic period, and it was found at the archaeological site of El Tazumal, in the area of Chalchoapa in the western zone of the country. It is probable that the same merchants who brought obsidian and jadeite from the region's source in the Motagua Valley used this type of jar to transport pigments, such as cinnabar and hematite. These small ceramic vessels, which are often called "perfume bottles," generally had cylindrical shapes and were of standardized size, which indicates that their distribution was probably conducted under a centralized economic authority.

JMR

454
Rectangular Jar or "Perfume Bottle"
Classic period
El Tazumal, Chalchuapa
Department of Santa Ana
El Salvador
Ceramic
Height: 12.5 cm
width: 6.9 cm
thickness: 5.7 cm
El Salvador
Museo Nacional de Antropología
"Dr. David J. Guzmán"
Inv. no. A1-2798

Polychrome, sculpted jar with rectangular shape, flat base, and four panels decorated on two of its sides with ceremonial scenes. These consist of figures in seated position and animals, and the other two sides display ten glyphs on

454

456

each side, with remains of red paint or cinnabar, and white. This piece was found at the archaeological site of El Tazumal in the area of Chalchuapa in western El Salvador. These jars were used during the Late Classic period to store and transport pigments such as cinnabar and hematite. Generally they were standardized in cylindrical form, which is why they are also referred to as "perfume bottles."

JMR

455
Male Figurine
Late Classic period
Ceramic
Height: 16.0 cm
width: 7.5 cm
depth: 9.5 cm
Mexico City
Museo Nacional de Antropología
Inv. no. 10-076516

Despite the fact that it does not come from the island of Jaina, this sculpture, worked in orange-colored clay, displays the unequivocal style of objects found there. These figurines are magnificent examples of the refined art of the Mayas, and they reflect the human sense of sculpture, highlighting man in activities from daily life, as well as in exceptional activities that take place within the religious and political world. This image is of a high-ranking leader.

MCL

455

457

456
Female Figurine
Late Classic period
Jaina Island, Campeche, Mexico
Ceramic
Height: 15.9 cm
width: 10.1 cm
Mexico City
Museo Nacional de Antropología
Inv. no. 10-078723

Recent archaeological studies have confirmed data from historical sources, both for the Mayas as well as for the Mexican highlands, referring to the social importance of artists and scribes in charge of drawing codices and painting polychrome vessels. These individuals are recognized as artists for their abilities and profound intellectual knowledge in the realms of hieroglyphic writing, the calendar, cosmogony, religion, and in general a vast knowledge of history. Although to date no names of women scribes have been identified, nevertheless there is the possibility that this figurine represents one. She is seated and holds on her right leg an object that has been identified as a codex.

ACM

457
The Scribe
Late Classic period
Structure 9N-82, Las Sepulturas
Copán Ruinas, Honduras
Stone
Height: 57.0 cm
width: 37.0 cm
Copán
Museo Regional de Arqueología
Inv. no. CPN-P-3446

The simian facial features and shell paint pots inserted in the headband above his ears identify this deity as the patron of Maya scribes and artists. In his left he holds a sectioned conch-shell inkpot, and in his right a paint brush. The inverted water lily around his neck ties him to the watery realm and perhaps doubles as a symbol representing this residential area. He wears a netted hair piece with *cauac* markings of the earth's surface at its corners. Scribes were held in great esteem among the Classic Maya; their profession appears to have been passed down a family line. This exceptional

449

449
"Blom Plate"
Late Classic period
Chetumal, Quintana Roo, Mexico
Ceramic
Height: 7.3 cm; diameter: 44.5 cm
Merida, Museo Regional de Yucatán
"Palacio Cantón"
Inv. no. 10-455136

The Blom Plate was named after American archaeologist Frans Blom, who made its existence known in an article published in 1950 by the Carnegie Institution of Washington, D.C. The plate, which was found during excavations to construct the airport in Chetumal, Quintana Roo, remained in a private collection in Oaxaca City until 1985, when it was donated to the Museo Regional de Yucatán "Palacio Cantón". It is probable that the scene depicted on the interior of this vessel recalls a story from the *Popol Vuh*, the sixteenth-century sacred book of the Quiche Maya in which the Hero Twins, Hunahpu and Xbalanque, shoot Vucub Caquix, a mythical bird who proclaimed himself the Sun and Moon. Irritated by his arrogance, the twins wait for him to climb up into his favorite fruit tree and they shoot him with their blowguns, knocking him down and killing him. This time the Hero Twins are not portrayed as hunters with special hats, but rather as twins with distinctive diadems. Both have circles or black spots on the body and they have already shot the projectile from their respective blowguns at Vucub Caquix, who appears with a fantastic bird headdress with a long, skeletal neck. Although the patches of jaguar pelt characteristic of Xbalanque are not present, the twin on the left is seated on a throne in the form of a cushion covered with jaguar skin, which allows him to be identified. The glyphs that surround the other half of the plate form a dedicatory text that is known as the Primary Standard Sequence: "Saw dedicate . . . [lord]? 8 Muanil his writing [of] Coc Ch'ax."   SB

450
Inkpots
Late Classic period
Las Sepulturas, Copán, Honduras

451

450

Ceramic
Different dimensions
Copán, Centro Regional
de Investigaciones Arqueológicas
Inv. no. CPN-C-110

These bottles have been found in a large area of eastern Guatemala, western El Salvador, and western Honduras, particularly Copán where they are most abundant. They are fashioned from the same cream clay of Copador, and usually bear modeled decoration pressed from a mold. In several examples the bottles were found with red pigment

(either cinnabar or hematite) inside. Their function as pigment bottles is somewhat intriguing given that they are never themselves painted.   WF

451
Polychrome Cylindrical Vessel
Late Classic period
Guatemalan lowlands
Ceramic
Height: 23.2 cm; width: 10.5 cm
diameter: 10.0 cm; depth: 22.4 cm
Guatemala, Museo Popol Vuh
Universidad Francisco Marroquín
Inv. no. MPV 0366

Cream-colored cylindrical vessel with an orange band around it covering the rim, and another around the base. Near the edge is a horizontal band of glyphs painted light orange and outlined in a darker tone. Below is a scene with two major figures, standing and seen in profile, richly dressed with elaborate feathered headdresses, tubular and circular beaded necklaces, loincloths, anklets, wristlets, and knee ornaments. Opposite each person there is a dwarf with a loincloth and black headdress that seems to be helping the individual get dressed. Behind each main figure is the head of God K, and in the headdress of one of them, another representation of the same god in miniature. Two vertical panels of five glyphs separate the scenes; a fish is next to each panel.   MS

452
Vessel
Late Classic period
Motagua Valley, Guatemala
Ceramic
Height: 18.0 cm; width: 15.5 cm
diameter: 11.0 cm
depth: 17.0 cm
Guatemala, Museo Popol Vuh
Universidad Francisco Marroquín
Inv. no. MPV 0659

Vessel with composite silhouette and ring-shaped base. It has red specular hematite paint applied to

452

the relief. At the neck is a horizontal band with a series of glyphs that form a Primary Standard Sequence with an initial sign, God N, Bat, Wing quincunx, Rodent. On each one of the flat sides is a medallion; one displays a seated Maya noble with his legs crossed, wearing a loincloth, necklace, and earplugs, and holding an object from which volutes emerge. His hair is tied back. The other medallion shows a mask of a deity with multiple fangs, possibly an earth monster. The impression of the neck and body was made with a mold.   MS

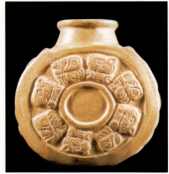

453

453
Monochrome Jar
Classic period
El Tazumal, Chalchuapa
Department of Santa Ana
El Salvador
Ceramic
Height: 7.3 cm
width: 7.0 cm
El Salvador
Museo Nacional de Antropología
"Dr. David J. Guzmán"
Inv. no. A1-2900

Monochrome jar in the form of a short-necked disk, with decoration on both sides consisting of Maya glyphs in high relief. On its sides is a series of oblique, excavated channels. Its interior contains remains of cinnabar. This type of object corresponds to the Late Classic period, and it was found at the archaeological site of El Tazumal, in the area of Chalchoapa in the western zone of the country. It is probable that the same merchants who brought obsidian and jadeite from the region's source in the Motagua Valley used this type of jar to transport pigments, such as cinnabar and hematite. These small ceramic vessels, which are often called "perfume bottles," generally had cylindrical shapes and were of standardized size, which indicates that their distribution was probably conducted under a centralized economic authority. JMR

454
Rectangular Jar or "Perfume Bottle"
Classic period
El Tazumal, Chalchuapa
Department of Santa Ana
El Salvador
Ceramic
Height: 12.5 cm
width: 6.9 cm
thickness: 5.7 cm
El Salvador
Museo Nacional de Antropología
"Dr. David J. Guzmán"
Inv. no. A1-2798

Polychrome, sculpted jar with rectangular shape, flat base, and four panels decorated on two of its sides with ceremonial scenes. These consist of figures in seated position and animals, and the other two sides display ten glyphs on

454

456

each side, with remains of red paint or cinnabar, and white. This piece was found at the archaeological site of El Tazumal in the area of Chalchuapa in western El Salvador. These jars were used during the Late Classic period to store and transport pigments such as cinnabar and hematite. Generally they were standardized in cylindrical form, which is why they are also referred to as "perfume bottles." JMR

455
Male Figurine
Late Classic period
Ceramic
Height: 16.0 cm
width: 7.5 cm
depth: 9.5 cm
Mexico City
Museo Nacional de Antropología
Inv. no. 10-076516

Despite the fact that it does not come from the island of Jaina, this sculpture, worked in orange-colored clay, displays the unequivocal style of objects found there. These figurines are magnificent examples of the refined art of the Mayas, and they reflect the human sense of sculpture, highlighting man in activities from daily life, as well as in exceptional activities that take place within the religious and political world. This image is of a high-ranking leader. MCL

457

456
Female Figurine
Late Classic period
Jaina Island, Campeche, Mexico
Ceramic
Height: 15.9 cm
width: 10.1 cm
Mexico City
Museo Nacional de Antropología
Inv. no. 10-078723

Recent archaeological studies have confirmed data from historical sources, both for the Mayas as well as for the Mexican highlands, referring to the social importance of artists and scribes in charge of drawing codices and painting polychrome vessels. These individuals are recognized as artists for their abilities and profound intellectual knowledge in the realms of hieroglyphic writing, the calendar, cos-

455

mogony, religion, and in general a vast knowledge of history. Although to date no names of women scribes have been identified, nevertheless there is the possibility that this figurine represents one. She is seated and holds on her right leg an object that has been identified as a codex. ACM

457
The Scribe
Late Classic period
Structure 9N-82, Las Sepulturas
Copán Ruinas, Honduras
Stone
Height: 57.0 cm
width: 37.0 cm
Copán
Museo Regional de Arqueología
Inv. no. CPN-P-3446

The simian facial features and shell paint pots inserted in the headband above his ears identify this deity as the patron of Maya scribes and artists. In his left he holds a sectioned conch-shell inkpot, and in his right a paint brush. The inverted water lily around his neck ties him to the watery realm and perhaps doubles as a symbol representing this residential area. He wears a netted hair piece with *cauac* markings of the earth's surface at its corners. Scribes were held in great esteem among the Classic Maya; their profession appears to have been passed down a family line. This exceptional

449

449
"Blom Plate"
Late Classic period
Chetumal, Quintana Roo, Mexico
Ceramic
Height: 7.3 cm; diameter: 44.5 cm
Mérida, Museo Regional de Yucatán
"Palacio Cantón"
Inv. no. 10-455136

The Blom Plate was named after American archaeologist Frans Blom, who made its existence known in an article published in 1950 by the Carnegie Institution of Washington, D.C. The plate, which was found during excavations to construct the airport in Chetumal, Quintana Roo, remained in a private collection in Oaxaca City until 1985, when it was donated to the Museo Regional de Yucatán "Palacio Cantón". It is probable that the scene depicted on the interior of this vessel recalls a story from the *Popol Vuh*, the sixteenth-century sacred book of the Quiche Maya in which the Hero Twins, Hunahpu and Xbalanque, shoot Vucub Caquix, a mythical bird who proclaimed himself the Sun and Moon. Irritated by his arrogance, the twins wait for him to climb up into his favorite fruit tree and they shoot him with their blowguns, knocking him down and killing him. This time the Hero Twins are not portrayed as hunters with special hats, but rather as twins with distinctive diadems. Both have circles or black spots on the body and they have already shot the projectile from their respective blowguns at Vucub Caquix, who appears with a fantastic bird headdress with a long, skeletal neck. Although the patches of jaguar pelt characteristic of Xbalanque are not present, the twin on the left is seated on a throne in the form of a cushion covered with jaguar skin, which allows him to be identified. The glyphs that surround the other half of the plate form a dedicatory text that is known as the Primary Standard Sequence: "Saw dedicate . . . [lord]? 8 Muanil his writing [of] Coc Ch'ax." SB

450
Inkpots
Late Classic period
Las Sepulturas, Copán, Honduras

451

Ceramic
Different dimensions
Copán, Centro Regional
de Investigaciones Arqueológicas
Inv. no. CPN-C-110

These bottles have been found in a large area of eastern Guatemala, western El Salvador, and western Honduras, particularly Copán where they are most abundant. They are fashioned from the same cream clay of Copador, and usually bear modeled decoration pressed from a mold. In several examples the bottles were found with red pigment

(either cinnabar or hematite) inside. Their function as pigment bottles is somewhat intriguing given that they are never themselves painted. WF

451
Polychrome Cylindrical Vessel
Late Classic period
Guatemalan lowlands
Ceramic
Height: 23.2 cm; width: 10.5 cm
diameter: 10.0 cm; depth: 22.4 cm
Guatemala, Museo Popol Vuh
Universidad Francisco Marroquín
Inv. no. MPV 0366

Cream-colored cylindrical vessel with an orange band around it covering the rim, and another around the base. Near the edge is a horizontal band of glyphs painted light orange and outlined in a darker tone. Below is a scene with two major figures, standing and seen in profile, richly dressed with elaborate feathered headdresses, tubular and circular beaded necklaces, loincloths, anklets, wristlets, and knee ornaments. Opposite each person there is a dwarf with a loincloth and black headdress that seems to be helping the individual get dressed. Behind each main figure is the head of God K, and in the headdress of one of them, another representation of the same god in miniature. Two vertical panels of five glyphs separate the scenes; a fish is next to each panel. MS

452
Vessel
Late Classic period
Motagua Valley, Guatemala
Ceramic
Height: 18.0 cm; width: 15.5 cm
diameter: 11.0 cm
depth: 17.0 cm
Guatemala, Museo Popol Vuh
Universidad Francisco Marroquín
Inv. no. MPV 0659

Vessel with composite silhouette and ring-shaped base. It has red specular hematite paint applied to

452

the relief. At the neck is a horizontal band with a series of glyphs that form a Primary Standard Sequence with an initial sign, God N, Bat, Wing quincunx, Rodent. On each one of the flat sides is a medallion; one displays a seated Maya noble with his legs crossed, wearing a loincloth, necklace, and earplugs, and holding an object from which volutes emerge. His hair is tied back. The other medallion shows a mask of a deity with multiple fangs, possibly an earth monster. The impression of the neck and body was made with a mold. MS

453

453
Monochrome Jar
Classic period
El Tazumal, Chalchuapa
Department of Santa Ana
El Salvador
Ceramic
Height: 7.3 cm
width: 7.0 cm
El Salvador
Museo Nacional de Antropología
"Dr. David J. Guzmán"
Inv. no. A1-2900

Monochrome jar in the form of a short-necked disk, with decoration on both sides consisting of Maya glyphs in high relief. On its sides is a series of oblique, excavated channels. Its interior contains remains of cinnabar. This type of object corresponds to the Late Classic period, and it was found at the archaeological site of El Tazumal, in the area of Chalchoapa in the western zone of the country. It is probable that the same merchants who brought obsidian and jadeite from the region's source in the Motagua Valley used this type of jar to transport pigments, such as cinnabar and hematite. These small ceramic vessels, which are often called "perfume bottles," generally had cylindrical shapes and were of standardized size, which indicates that their distribution was probably conducted under a centralized economic authority. JMR

454
Rectangular Jar or "Perfume Bottle"
Classic period
El Tazumal, Chalchuapa
Department of Santa Ana
El Salvador
Ceramic
Height: 12.5 cm
width: 6.9 cm
thickness: 5.7 cm
El Salvador
Museo Nacional de Antropología
"Dr. David J. Guzmán"
Inv. no. A1-2798

Polychrome, sculpted jar with rectangular shape, flat base, and four panels decorated on two of its sides with ceremonial scenes. These consist of figures in seated position and animals, and the other two sides display ten glyphs on

454

456

each side, with remains of red paint or cinnabar, and white. This piece was found at the archaeological site of El Tazumal in the area of Chalchoapa in western El Salvador. These jars were used during the Late Classic period to store and transport pigments such as cinnabar and hematite. Generally they were standardized in cylindrical form, which is why they are also referred to as "perfume bottles." JMR

455
Male Figurine
Late Classic period
Ceramic
Height: 16.0 cm
width: 7.5 cm
depth: 9.5 cm
Mexico City
Museo Nacional de Antropología
Inv. no. 10-076516

Despite the fact that it does not come from the island of Jaina, this sculpture, worked in orange-colored clay, displays the unequivocal style of objects found there. These figurines are magnificent examples of the refined art of the Mayas, and they reflect the human sense of sculpture, highlighting man in activities from daily life, as well as in exceptional activities that take place within the religious and political world. This image is of a high-ranking leader. MCL

455

457

456
Female Figurine
Late Classic period
Jaina Island, Campeche, Mexico
Ceramic
Height: 15.9 cm
width: 10.1 cm
Mexico City
Museo Nacional de Antropología
Inv. no. 10-078723

Recent archaeological studies have confirmed data from historical sources, both for the Mayas as well as for the Mexican highlands, referring to the social importance of artists and scribes in charge of drawing codices and painting polychrome vessels. These individuals are recognized as artists for their abilities and profound intellectual knowledge in the realms of hieroglyphic writing, the calendar, cosmogony, religion, and in general a vast knowledge of history. Although to date no names of women scribes have been identified, nevertheless there is the possibility that this figurine represents one. She is seated and holds on her right leg an object that has been identified as a codex. ACM

457
The Scribe
Late Classic period
Structure 9N-82, Las Sepulturas
Copán Ruinas, Honduras
Stone
Height: 57.0 cm
width: 37.0 cm
Copán
Museo Regional de Arqueología
Inv. no. CPN-P-3446

The simian facial features and shell paint pots inserted in the headband above his ears identify this deity as the patron of Maya scribes and artists. In his left he holds a sectioned conch-shell inkpot, and in his right a paint brush. The inverted water lily around his neck ties him to the watery realm and perhaps doubles as a symbol representing this residential area. He wears a netted hair piece with *cauac* markings of the earth's surface at its corners. Scribes were held in great esteem among the Classic Maya; their profession appears to have been passed down a family line. This exceptional

Man

figure was found in the fill of the final construction of Structure 9N-82, a building whose facade displays other sculpted scribal images. The importance placed on the scribal profession in association with this building has led to the conclusion that it was the residence of scribes for several generations. WF

458
Brick with the Image of a Person
Terminal Classic–Epiclassic
period
Comalcalco, Tabasco, Mexico
Ceramic
Length: 36.5 cm; width: 26.1 cm
thickness: 4.0 cm
Comalcalco, Museo de Sitio
de Comalcalco
Inv. no. 10-575769

This piece, just as number 10-575770 was located as part of the masonry that formed the vault of Structure 2 of the Great Acropolis of Comalcalco. They have very similar dimensions and the ends are almost identical. In both cases, the representation decorating the pieces is similar: the profile of an individual, a design that is repeated in more than 200 excavated bricks. This is one of the decorative motifs found most frequently in the archaeological record, which seems to indicate that the rich garb worn by important members of Maya society was an attraction for the common people as well. MJGG

459
Brick with the Image of a Person
Terminal Classic–Epiclassic
period
Comalcalco, Tabasco, Mexico
Ceramic
Length: 24.6 cm
width: 17.1 cm
thickness: 2.3 cm
Comalcalco, Museo de Sitio
de Comalcalco
Inv. no. 10-575768

The clayworkers who modeled and fired the many bricks that would became the basis of important buildings, were also, at time, the creators of the decoration. In these pieces are abundant representations of high, ranking individuals shown in profile, always with jewelry, a headdress, or complex clothing, in addition to the characteristic cranial deformation. There are also impressions of hands and textiles, a diversity of animals, some scenes, and even isolated glyphs and numerals. On occasion, the motifs resemble texts, such as naive copies of original inscriptions that the rural population of Comalcalco would see on the facades of buildings in the main plaza.

458

461

459

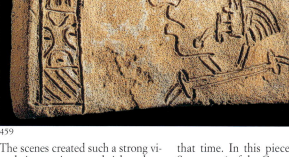

460

The scenes created such a strong visual impression on brickworkers that, when the clay was wet, they traced hundreds of iconographic elements with a pointed object, probably unaware of the real significance of them. MJGG

460
Brick with the Image of a Person
Terminal Classic–Epiclassic
period
Comalcalco, Tabasco, Mexico
Ceramic
Length: 36.0 cm
width: 22.4 cm
thickness: 3.4 cm
Comalcalco, Museo de Sitio
de Comalcalco
Inv. no. 10-575775

On decorated bricks from Comalcalco, representations of richly dressed individuals are common. On some occasions, they are shown carrying out some activity that gives us an idea of the world of

that time. In this piece, found in Structure 1 of the Great Acropolis, an individual with accentuated Maya traits consumes some type of food from a receptacle, probably *pozol* with cacao, the traditional cornmeal beverage that continues to be a fundamental part of the diet of modern Chontals. RAT

461
Brick with the Image of a Person
Terminal Classic–Epiclassic
period
Comalcalco, Tabasco, Mexico
Ceramic
Height: 37.7 cm; width: 25.7 cm
thickness: 4.3 cm
Comalcalco, Museo de Sitio
de Comalcalco
Inv. no. 10-575770

Part of the cultural traits associated with the ancient Maya were intentional modification of the body, such as cranial deformation, praticed by men and women, which gave

greater height and depth to the face of the individual, and perforation of earlobes to hold elaborate ear ornaments in different materials and forms, which complemented the strands of beads worn around the neck. Another important appurtenance to the ornaments or garb of the people was the arrangement of the hair, which preferentially is gathered at the neck, adorned with beads, cloth, or feathers, as is the case of the individual in this piece found in Structure 2 of the Great Acropolis of Comalcalco. MJGG

462
Figurine Fragment
Late Classic period
Jaina Island, Campeche
Mexico
Ceramic
Height: 11.0 cm; width: 8.0 cm
depth: 6.5 cm
Villahermosa, Museo Regional
de Antropología "Carlos Pellicer"
Inv. no. A-0594

The head is from a figure made of the ceramic type known as Fine Orange ware. Despite erosion, it is possible to admire the delicacy with which the details of the face were worked, especially the gentle swelling of the half-open eyelids. At the forehead, the hairstyle has a stepped arrangement around the face, and the figure has a headdress made of two bands of clay added after modeling. The cross-shape may refer to the center and four directions of the universe. The straight, flat forehead is evidence of cranial deformation that was practiced on children when they were only a few months old. Small boards were placed on the head that resulted in frontal occipital pressure to elongate the head.   RP

463
Human Head
Terminal Classic–Epiclassic period
Comalcalco, Tabasco, Mexico
Ceramic
Height: 16.0 cm; width: 11.7 cm
depth: 14.0 cm
Comalcalco, Museo de Sitio
de Comalcalco
Inv. no. 10-575760

Architectonic nails were important elements in pre-Hispanic construction, where they took on different shapes and materials, in addition to fulfilling different constructive and decorative purposes. At Comalcalco, several examples have been found that indicate their use within the nuclear area of the settlement. This piece was found on the north facade of Temple III-A of the North Plaza of Comalcalco. It represents the head of an individual with tabular oblique cranial deformation and a simple hairstyle. What stands out on his face is the presence of scarification at the corners of his mouth, highlighting the stereotypical physical features of the Chontal Mayas of Comalcalco.   RAT

464
Fragment of a Censer Base
Late Classic period
Palenque, Chiapas
Mexico
Ceramic
Height: 19.6 cm; width: 10.1 cm
Palenque, Museo de Sitio
"Alberto Ruz Lhuillier"
Inv. no. 10-988898 0/4

462

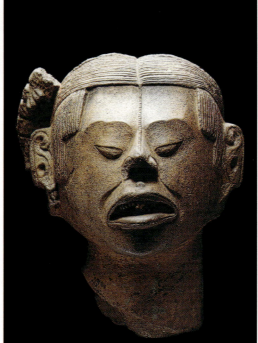

465

464

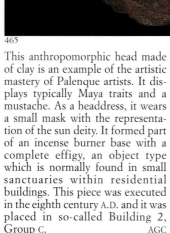

463

This anthropomorphic head made of clay is an example of the artistic mastery of Palenque artists. It displays typically Maya traits and a mustache. As a headdress, it wears a small mask with the representation of the sun deity. It formed part of an incense burner base with a complete effigy, an object type which is normally found in small sanctuaries within residential buildings. This piece was executed in the eighth century A.D. and it was placed in so-called Building 2, Group C.   AGC

465
Fragment of a Human Figurine
Late Classic period
Venustiano Carranza, Chiapas
Mexico
Ceramic

Height: 14.0 cm; width: 11.5 cm
thickness: 9.0 cm
Tuxtla Gutiérrez
Museo Regional de Chiapas
Inv. no. 10-409601

Head of a hollow, human figurine that displays the so-called style of the "Upper Tributaries of the Grijalva River," identified at Maya sites in the Comitán Valley and in the region of La Trinitaria, Chiapas. The shape of the colture is outstanding, depicted with fine, incised lines and clay applications to simulate a braid that must have wound around the upper part of the head. Also noteworthy is the filing of the upper incisors into a T shape, perhaps representing *ik*, or the Maya symbol of movement and the wind, as well as a line of scarification that goes from the hair to

the tip of the nose. These elements of personal beautification, as well as the cranial deformation, suggest that figurines of this type represent individuals of high status with to noble lineages.   ELV

466
Figurine
Late Classic period
Jaina Island, Campeche, Mexico
Ceramic
Height: 12.0 cm; width: 9.0 cm
depth: 5.0 cm
Villahermosa, Museo Regional
de Antropología "Carlos Pellicer"
Inv. no. A-0593

Human figurines are evidence of ancient Maya physiognomy, characteristics of their dress and ornament, as well as their social cus-

466

468

467

toms. Alteration of appearance by means of tattooing or scarification was a form of permanent body ornament that indicated status and beautified the individual. There is scarification or tattooing on this face, on the center of the chin and at the corners of the mouth, in the form of a line of dots. The headdress looks as though it could represent a braid of yarn placed on a simple, stepped hairstyle that resembles the base of pyramids. Knowledge of the techniques that

were developed for the manufacture of figures is also part of the information that figurines can offer us. Some were mold-made, and only the added decorations in appliqué differentiate them. RP

467
Human Mask
Late Classic period
Palenque, Chiapas, Mexico
Stucco
Height: 24.4 cm; width: 18.9 cm

thickness: 11.2 cm
Mexico City
Museo Nacional de Antropología
Inv. no. 10-228046

There are numerous images of Maya men in different materials: clay, stucco, stone, etc. These often display cranial deformation, scarification or dental mutilation, alterations to the body that were practiced to beautify and distinguish one from another group or to indicate rank or social status. This head, which realistically portrays the face of an adult, is an excellent example of the Maya physical type. Due to the characteristics of the back part of this piece, it probably originally decorated a structure or temple. ACM

468
Votive *hacha*
Late Classic period
Palenque, Chiapas, Mexico
Green stone
Height: 18.4 cm; length: 17.3 cm
thickness: 6.0 cm
Palenque, Museo de Sitio
"Alberto Ruz Lhuillier"
Inv. no. 10-458684

Although this type of votive *hacha* was developed mainly by people inhabiting the central coast of Ver-

acruz as part of the ball game cult, at Palenque several sculptures have been found that have led to the idea that the site was occupied by people from the Gulf Coast of Mexico near the end of the time Palenque functioned as a city. In fact, this group of outsiders could have been one of the causes of its demise. This piece was found in Building 3, Group XVI. AGC

469

469
Face
Late Classic period
Palenque, Chiapas, Mexico
Stucco
Height: 9.9 cm; length: 11.0 cm
thickness: 4.5 cm
Palenque, Museo de Sitio
"Alberto Ruz Lhuillier"
Inv. no. 10-117742

Important Maya cities such as Palenque were the seat of rulers, priests, and administrators in charge of overseeing the movement of the universe, building temples and palaces, and conserving mythical and historical memory. From Palenque, work in agricultural fields was directed from here, and tribute was organized, as was trade and warfare. It was the place where specialized craftsmen resided, those who produced sacred objects, such as the images of the gods or else articles of adornment for priests and nobles, as well as those who sculpted stone or modeled stucco. This piece representing a human face exhibits the ability of these artists to execute portraits in stucco with great detail. AGC

470
Human Profile
Possibly Late Classic period
Jaina Island, Campeche, Mexico
Stucco
Height: 20.2 cm; width: 13.0 cm
thickness 3.0 cm
Merida, Museo Regional de Yucatán
"Palacio Cantón"
Inv. no. 10-424571

This piece modeled in stucco depicts a typical Maya profile with aquiline nose, cranial deformation, hair gathered on top of the head, and pendants hanging from the ears. The fragment comes from the island of Jaina off the coast of Campeche in the western littoral of the Yucatán peninsula. This small island was modified by its pre-Hispanic inhabitants, who leveled and filled the ground to construct stone buildings. Jaina is famous for the wide variety of clay figurines found there representing all sorts of people from Maya society. The figurines are generally found in funerary contexts from the Classic period. Stucco was a material common-

470

472

ly used by the lowland Maya since the Middle Preclassic period. It was used to coat buildings and modeled into fine reliefs that decorated the facades of buildings, as in the case of Palenque, Chiapas, and Acanceh, Yucatán. LFS

471
Human Profile
Late Classic period
Palenque, Chiapas, Mexico
Stucco
Height: 16.4 cm
maximum width: 11.0 cm
thickness: 4.0 cm
Mexico City
Museo Nacional de Antropología
Inv. no. 10-223526

This human head in profile is an excellent example of the type of cranial deformation known as tabular oblique, which the Mayas practiced in the pre-Hispanic period. This example is adorned by a headdress formed by narrow bands that interlace and hold the hair,

471

which is not visible. The facial features are indicated by incisions and shallow relief: the eye is smooth and almond-shaped, the nose straight, and the mouth with well-defined lips that are slightly open, which allows us to see part of the teeth. This fragment of modeled stucco, a perfect example of the Classic Maya profile, probably formed part of a panel or frieze of a structure. ACM

472
Male Head
Late Classic period
Palenque, Chiapas, Mexico
Stucco
Height: 43.0 cm; width: 17.0 cm
Mexico City
Museo Nacional de Antropología
Inv. no. 10-001285

Stucco and stone sculpture reached its maximum expression in human representations at Palenque. They are notable for their perfection of anatomical proportions, the portrait-like character of the images, and the tremendous dynamism that many of them express. This head corresponds to that of an adult male with fine features, whose nose seems to extend over his forehead, resulting in cranial deformation that produced the well-known Maya profile. It was found on the floor of the funerary chamber of the Temple of the Inscriptions, under the sarcophagus, together with several vessels and another head, probably feminine, that formed part of the funerary offering of Pacal, ruler of Palenque. It is possible that both heads had been removed from complete sculptures, simulating decapitation sacrifice associated with the maize cult. ACM

473

473
Female Head
Late Classic period
Palenque, Chiapas, Mexico
Stucco
Height: 32.0 cm; width: 20.0 cm
thickness: 15.0 cm
Mexico City
Museo Nacional de Antropología
Inv. no. 10-001284

This human head probably formed part of a complete sculpture. Due to the fineness of its features and the closed eyes, it seems to represent an adult deceased woman. It displays cranial deformation, a half-open mouth, and perforated earlobes. The hair is arranged in loose locks, cut in stepped form, and the upper part is held by a diadem composed of rectangular plaques that could represent the sun as a four-petaled flower. The sculpture formed part of a mortuary offering together with several vessels and a male head with similar characteristics; it was found on the floor of the funerary chamber in the Temple of the Inscriptions, under the monolith where the

474

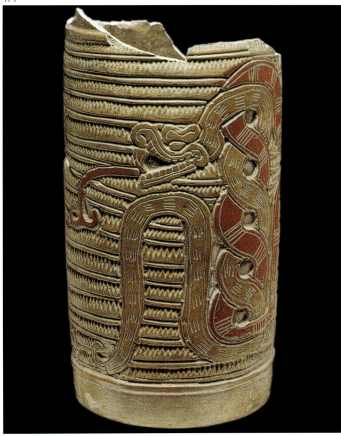

475

476

Ceramic
Height: 25.0 cm; width: 12.8 cm
diameter: 12.8 cm; depth: 23.5 cm
Guatemala, Museo Popol Vuh
Universidad Francisco Marroquín
Inv. no. MPV 0313

This vessel is a good example of the tall vessels from the Tiquisate region in Guatemala, during the Late Classic period. It is cylindrical and has a well-polished, light brown slip. The piece has grooved horizontal bands, within which there are incisions in the form of teeth or a comb. The main decoration consists of two scenes of interlaced serpents. Each group has a serpent painted in red specular hematite, and the other in light brown, with open maw and exposed teeth and fangs. The serpents of one of the groups display a long, bifurcated tongue. MS

476
Human Head
Late Classic period
Palenque, Chiapas, Mexico
Stucco
Height: 14.0 cm; width: 14.0 cm
depth: 8.5 cm
Villahermosa, Museo Regional
de Antropología "Carlos Pellicer"
Inv. no. A-0061

Stuccowork illustrates the talent of Maya artists, who with extraordinary ability modeled and attached stucco to architecture, from majestic masks to detailed human figures expressing movement in their forms. Each deity represented was charged with symbolism; proof of this may be seen in Maya sculptures such as this example, in which the perfection of facial features expresses the reality of an old man. RP

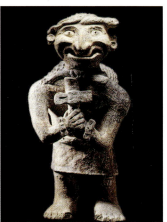

477

477
Censer
Late Classic period
Los Bordos, Chiapas, Mexico
Ceramic
Height: 50.0 cm
width: 26.5 cm
depth: 23.5 cm
Tuxtla Gutiérrez
Museo Regional de Chiapas
Inv. no. 10-456466

This censer was found near the canyon of the La Venta River, around the archaeological site of Mirador. It represents an old woman carrying a basket on her back. She wears two knotted serpents on her head and her neck, while her staff and wrists also have knots. The woman smiles and her open mouth is in the form of a U. According to Agrinier, this image is reminiscent of the goddess of the moon represented in the Dresden Codex. He mentions that her attributes are related to the goddess of weaving, as well as the fact that the object was found in a cave. MCG

crypt of the ruler of Palenque, known as Pacal, was excavated. It is probable that these heads were removed from complete sculptures, perhaps simulating a sacrifice by decapitation, associated with the maize cult. ACM

474
Bowl
Late Classic period
Provenance unknown
Ceramic
Height: 10.2 cm; diameter: 19.0 cm
Merida, Museo Regional de Yucatán
"Palacio Cantón"
Inv. no. 10-290423

Relatively common in Maya ceramics are low-walled bowls in which

two very similar or identical figures are represented wearing only a loincloth, a necklace or pectoral, and usually provided with spectacular headdresses. Recently, many images on ceremonial ceramics have been interpreted as episodes from the *Popol Vuh*, the Quiche Maya mythical saga from Guatemala. The seated figures, duplicated on opposite sides of this vessel, have been identified as Hunahpu and Xbalanque, heroes of the narrative and also known as the Hero Twins. APC

475
Cylindrical Vessel
Late Classic period
South coast of Guatemala

478

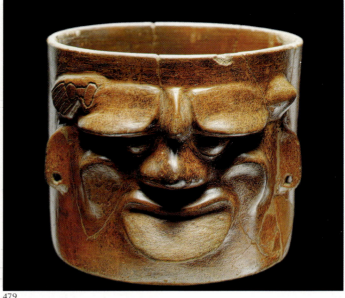

479

480

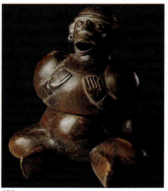

481

478
Effigy Vessel
Early Postclassic period
Chinkultic, Chiapas, Mexico
Ceramic
Height: 15.8 cm
maximum width: 23.0 cm
diameter: 11.2 cm
Tuxtla Gutiérrez
Museo Regional de Chiapas
Inv. no. 10-338428

Effigy vessel that represents a seated, smiling old man. It is representation of the ceramic type known as Plumbate in form and decoration, where it is common to find motifs related to flora, fauna, and deities of Nahuatl groups. Plumbate ware is considered a marker of the arrival of Toltec groups from Central Mexico to the Maya area. This vessel bears a representation of Huehueteotl, the old fire god, whose cult began in the Basin of Mexico before the Christian era. What stand-out in this piece is the craftsman's treatment of the face to highlight characteristics of happiness and age-traits of the fire god. This vessel and another almost identical one formed part of a funerary offering deposited at Chinkultic at the end of the Early Postclassic period.   ELV

479
Effigy Vessel
Late Classic period
Motagua Valley, Guatemala
Ceramic
Height: 16.5 cm; width: 21.5 cm
diameter: 18.0 cm; depth: 15.5 cm
Guatemala, Museo Popol Vuh
Universidad Francisco Marroquín
Inventory number: MPV 0878

Bowl with straight walls and flat bottom, dark brown in color and covered with a thick, polished, reddish brown slip. The vessel represents the face of an individual, possibly an old man. It display sagging eyelids, a wide nose, protruding lips and projecting cheeks. There is a modeled element projecting, between the eyebrows, one at the edge of the left eyelid and a decorative symbol at the edge of the other. The ears are perforated for the insertion of ear ornaments.   MS

480
Effigy Vessel
Early Classic period
Uaxactún, Petén, Guatemala
Ceramic
Height: 21.5 cm
width of the base: 20.2 cm
Guatemala, Museo Nacional
de Arqueología y Etnología
Inv. no. MNAE 214

Vessel representing a seated individual with hands near the chest and whose thumbs form a ring. His legs are flexed and he faces looks forward with eyes and mouth closed; the hair takes the form of bangs, and he wears a headdress consisting of a band tied with a knot in front and circular earplugs. The face and remainder of the body are decorated with incised, white hatched lines in bands. The vessel is composed of two pieces covered with polished black-brown slip; it comes apart at the level of the torso. This type of vessel was very common during the Early Classic period.   MSB

481
Effigy Vessel
Early Classic period
Uaxactún, Petén, Guatemala
Ceramic
Height: 22.5 cm; width: 19.0 cm
Guatemala, Museo Nacional
de Arqueología y Etnología
Inv. no. MNAE 200a and 200b

The figure is seated, with hands over the chest and legs open and flexed. The face is covered by a zoomorphic mask, perhaps of a monkey with an open mouth. He wears a headdress in the form of a diadem, circular ear ornaments, and bracelets. The arms, thorax, and belly are of a robust individual. The vessel is composed of two pieces whose surfaces are covered with polished, dark brown slip.   MSB

482
Effigy Vessel
Postclassic period
Provenance unknown
Ceramic
Height: 15.5 cm
diameter: 10.5 cm
Guatemala, Museo Nacional
de Arqueología y Etnología
Inv. no. MNAE 5759

Vessel with human effigy made of Plumbate ware. It was produced in the area of the volcano Tajumulco. It has the face of an old man with a diadem and circular earplugs; its details include wrinkles, sunken areas under the eyes, a toothless mouth, prominent cheekbones, and a beard. Representations of old men were common in the Plumbate tradition and Mesoamerican iconography as a whole. This type of piece was used for consuming liquids during ceremonies.   MSB

483
Effigy Vessel
Classic period
La Lagunita, Quiché, Guatemala.
Ceramic
Height: 25.0 cm
width: 21.5 cm
Guatemala, Museo Nacional
de Arqueología y Etnología
Inv. no. MNAE 11756a and 11756b

The figure is seated, facing forward with arms crossed over the chest and legs crossed. The eyes are closed and the mouth half-open, so it is possible to see two teeth. He wears a rectangular headdress with an incised design, circular earplugs and ornaments on arms and legs. The figure wears a loincloth tied as a rectangular element in the front. The vessel is composed of two pieces, both of buff or cream color.   MSB

484
Effigy Vessel
Early Postclassic period
Frontera Hidalgo, Chiapa
Mexico
Ceramic
Height: 6.1 cm; lenght: 6.1 cm
width: 7.1 cm
Tuxtla Gutiérrez
Museo Regional de Chiapas
Inv. no. 10-409833

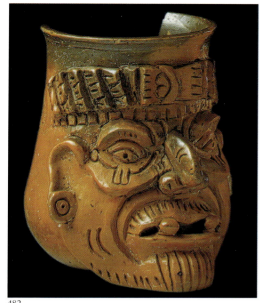

482

483

484

485a

485c

485b

485d

Vessel fragment with the image of a human head. It pertains to the so-called Tohil Plumbate ceramic tradition, characterized by the grayish, iridescent tones of the surface of objects. This piece must have formed part of an effigy vessel that alluded to an old man, perhaps the representation of Huehueteotl, the old fire god among the Toltecs. In this vessel, the ancient craftsman successfully rendered the aged characteristics of the face, the lack of several teeth, and the grooves resembling wrinkles on the cheeks and forehead. Ceramic objects such as this vessel fragment, produced locally on the coast of Chiapas, are evidence of the arrival of Nahuatl-speaking groups to the south of Mesoamerica around the year A.D. 1300.   ELV

485
Group of Clay Figurines
Late Classic period
Lubaantún, Toledo District, Belize
Ceramic
29/180-1:106: height: 5.0 cm
width: 2.0 cm
29/180-1:22: length: 6.39 cm
width: 4.81 cm
thickness: 1.4 cm
29/180-1:143: length: 6.3 cm
width: 4.85 cm
thickness: 3.3 cm
29/180-1:48
Belmopan, Bodegas
del Departamento de Arqueología
Inv. no. 29/180-1:106, 29/180-1:22
29/180-1:143, 29/180-1:48

Apart from Jaina and Jonuta on the Gulf Coast, Lagartero in Chiapas, and Alta Verapaz in Guatemala, there was Lubaantún, in southern Belize, where the art of manufacturing clay figurines reached a peak of development. Although these do not enjoy as much fame as other figurines, they are of great interest because they were made with their own characteristic style. Unfortunately, erosion has notably affected them to the extent that they lack slip or paint, and we can only see the reddish color of the paste. The frontal part of the majority of Lubaantún figurines are relatively flat, perhaps made in molds, while on the back part there is a mouthpiece that allowed them to function as whistles and ocarinas. Although there are varied representations, there are recurrent themes, such as the images of dwarfs, rulers seated on thrones, and warriors, the latter group identified by a helmet covering the entire head and allowing them to see through a narrow, horizontal slit. These helmets and a certain type of glove may also be used by ballplayers. In this group of four figurines are included two rulers seated on thrones decorated with hieroglyphic inscriptions. The others are a warrior with typical garb and the fragment of another figure representing the image of Tlaloc combined with the so-called Teotihuacán year sign, a symbol of war among the Classic period Maya.   PJS

486

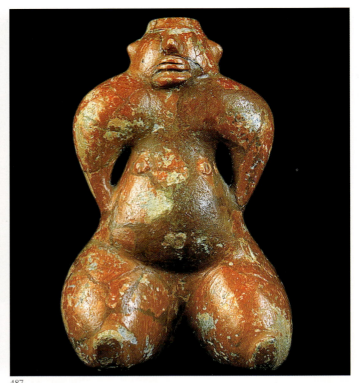

487

486
Effigy Vessel
Late Classic period
Guajilar, Chiapas, Mexico
Ceramic
Height: 20.3 cm; width: 14.2 cm
depth: 18.5 cm
Tuxtla Gutiérrez
Museo Regional de Chiapas
Inv. no. 10-338427

Vessel with lid in the form of a kneeling person with hands folded over the right knee and face resting on the stet hands. The thorax, hips, and legs form the body of the vessel, while the lid corresponds to the shoulders, arms, hands, and head. The facial features display what is perhaps a dead man, because the eyes are closed.   TALW

487
Effigy Vessel
Middle–Late Preclassic period
Kichpanhá (Kates Lagoon)
Orange Walk District, Belize
Ceramic
Height: 23.0 cm; width: 15.0 cm
Belmopan, Bodegas
del Departamento de Arqueología
Inv. no. 34/198-1:3

This vessel was recovered after the destruction of a Preclassic period mound of Kichpanhá, an archaeological site located in northern Belize. The exaggeration of certain physical traits and the absence of clothing or distinctive ornaments of a dignitary or of a deity leads us to think that it is the representation of vanquished enemies or slaves in images of the Classic period. From the same Middle Preclassic period structure, and associated with a

488

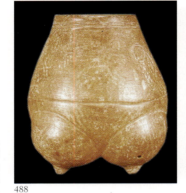

489

burial, there is a bone instrument decorated with an inscription composed of eight glyphs. This could have been used in ceremonies of self-sacrifice conducted by the individual buried there. The inscription, magnificently rendered, is the first documented in the Maya lowlands.   PJS

488
Negative Usulután Vessel
Late Preclassic period
Possibly from the Western Zone
El Salvador
Ceramic
Height: 17.5 cm; diameter: 15.4 cm
El Salvador, Museo Nacional
de Antropología
"Dr. David J. Guzmán"
Inv. no. A1-40

Negative or resist Usulután ware is characteristic of the Preclassic period. It appears in different shapes and styles at sites from this time, and it is one of the most widely traded wares in the region. Researchers who have studied this ceramic have reported its relationship with the

Caynac ceramic complex, defined on the basis of local stratigraphy, typological analysis, and comparison with other already established ceramic sequences. This Preclassic complex has been represented mainly at the site of El Trapiche in the area of Chalchoapa in the western zone of the country, thereby relating it to the ceramics of Kaminaljuyú during the Miraflores and Arenal phases, the Usulután type predominating. Most of this ware has been found in hiding places in the plaza and in the fill of the ramp of the mound, one at El Trapiche and at other sites of this period. The bichrome, tetrapod vessel with hollow, mammiform supports corresponds to the Usulután resist type, with decoration of two appliquéd circles in high relief and incised lines.   JMR

489
Negative or Resist Usulután Ware
Late Preclassic period
Department of Usulután, El Salvador
Ceramic
Height: 13.3 cm; width: 26.3 cm

El Salvador, Museo Nacional
de Antropología
"Dr. David J. Guzmán"
Inv. no. A1-3438

The region of Chalchuapa, according to researchers, maintained a close relationship with sites in the Maya lowlands. Usulután ware, which may be distinguished by its negative or resist decoration, was probably produced in the region of Chalchuapa and it came to be one of the main articles of trade in the Maya zone. As one of the main centers of this cultural nexus, the position of Chalchuapa was not peripheral with respect to the Maya area in the Late Preclassic period, but rather it was one of the largest sites in southeastern Mesoamerica. Clearly the description of the bichrome, tetrapod bowl with mammiform supports with rattles pertains to the ware known as Batik Usuluteco, from the Late Preclassic period. Its decoration is based on narrow, straight and undulating parallel lines made with wax. During its firing, the wax evaporates, leaving the negative decoration.   JMR

490

492

491

493

490
Vessel
Middle Preclassic period
Cuello, Orange Walk District, Belize
Ceramic
Diameter: 16.6 cm; height: 10.5 cm
diameter of the base: 10.6 cm
Belmopan, Bodegas
del Departamento de Arqueología
Inv. no. 33/199-3:131

Cuello is an archaeological site located in northern Belize that in recent years has sparked debate on the first evidence of groups using ceramics in the Maya lowlands. In the beginning, a series of radiocarbon dates led to the conclusion that the first local ceramic complex, called Swasey, was a thousand years older than other known early complexes. Later, new data have modified this impression, placing the dates of this ceramic between 1000 and 800 B.C. Nevertheless, now that these dates have been clarified, Cuello is one of the best studied early settlements. Evidence from this site allows us to see the beginnings of the development of more complex ceremonial and adminis-

trative life. Among the vessels recovered at this site, this basin, with flaring walls, reinforced edges, and a surface covered with a thick red slip, sturts out. PJS

491
Large Jar
Late Preclassic period
Kaminaljuyú, Guatemala
Ceramic
Height: 13.1 cm
width: 12.8 cm
diameter: 10.1 cm
depth: 12.4 cm
Guatemala, Museo Popol Vuh
Universidad Francisco Marroquín
Inv. no. MPV 1396

Large jar with globular body, short flaring neck, inward curving walls and two equidistant handles on the body. A white slip covers the entire piece. Two horizontal panels below the handles with vertical grooves were made before applying the slip, and in the middle part of the body, two medallions with geometric motifs were made with thick incisions after applying the slip. MS

492
Manatee Bowl
Postclassic period
Santa Elena, Isla de la Bahia
Honduras
Ceramic
Height: 8.8 cm
diameter: 15.0 cm
Tegucigalpa, Bodegas Centrales
del Instituto Hondureño
de Antropología e Historia
Inv. no. TGC-C-1805

Monochrome bowl with handles and irregular zoomorphic supports crossed by incised lines on the base and the body. This ceramic was found in the Department of Colón, and characterizes the beginning of the Postclassic period in the eastern zone and coast of Honduras. CJF

493
Campana Polychrome Vessel
Classic period
Provenance unknown
Ceramic
Height: 9.7 cm
width: 24.4 cm

El Salvador
Museo Nacional
de Antropología
"Dr. David J. Guzmán"
Inv. no. A1-506

This type of ceramic has been found at archaeological sites from the Late Classic period (A.D. 600–950) It probably originated in Honduras, but it came to be very popular in El Salvador, and possibly this piece was produced there. Its use was always related to ceremonial contexts, notably in tombs and in ritual offerings. This ceramic is distinguished by its use and by certain forms, especially shallow tripod bowls, such as this polychrome Campana tripod with hemispherical supports with rattles. It is decorated on its interior with bands and glyphs and with a central figure representing a human head in profile with open mouth and possibly a feathered headdress. To date, most of this ware has been found in tombs at Tazumal and around the mountain El Zapote in El Salvador and Asanyamba. JMR

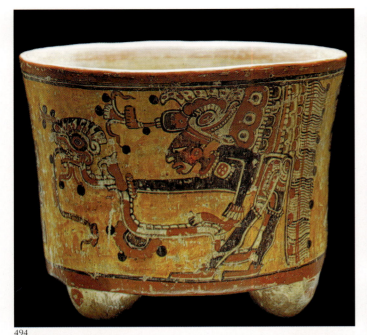

494

496

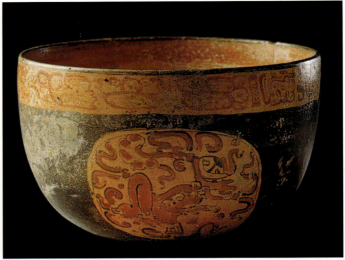

495

497

494
Serpent Bowl
Late Classic period
Sula Valley, Honduras
Ceramic
Height: 12.7 cm; base: 10.0 cm
diameter: 15.7 cm
San Pedro Sula, Cortés
Museo de Antropología
Inv. no. SPS-DBF-200

Cream ceramic with red, orange, and black polychrome. Tripod vessel with conical supports, flat base and bottom, with straight walls and rounded rim, polished both inside and outside, with a very fine cream-colored slip. The decoration consists of a red band on the rim covering the interior and exterior, followed by two parallel, horizontal black lines around the circumference. A zone bears designs of stylized serpents with bird heads, which are grabbed by a black zoomorphic figure with a very complex headdress with mythical and plant elements. It has a series of symbolic red and black glyphs and has been classified among the most complex Ulúa polychrome wares. Remains of this type have been found at sites always within the Sula Valley "Campo Dos" and "Dos Caminos."   CJF

495
Polychrome Basin
Late Classic period
Uaxactún, Petén, Guatemala
Ceramic
Height: 12.5 cm; diameter: 18.6 cm
Guatemala, Museo Nacional
de Arqueología y Etnología
Inv. no. MNAE 304

A red band surrounds the vessel beneath the rim. On an orange ground is a series of glyphs outlined in red. Under these, the surface is covered with black slip. On one side of the vessel is a medallion on an orange background, with the representation of a stylized zoomorphic figure and volutes in red and black all around. During the Late Classic, the art of decorating vessels with polychrome glyphs reache its maximum splendor.   MSB

Epigraphic reading by Alfonso Arellano
(was decorated) his vessel for cacao (of lord . . .)

496
Tripod Basin
Terminal Classic period
Uxmal, Yucatán, Mexico
Ceramic

Height: 12.5 cm
diameter: 21.5 cm
Merida, Museo Regional de Yucatán
"Palacio Cantón"
Inv. no. 10-290424

This bowl, deposited as an offering in the Great Pyramid at Uxmal, belongs to the ceramic group known as Ticul Pizarra Delgada, characterized by its fine texture, slip the same color as the paste, and a polished surface finish less lustrous than other types of slateware. The shapes of this ware are almost always hemispherical bowls, cylindrical vessels, tripod plates and jars. The city of Uxmal was an important political and economic center in the western part of the modern state of Yucatán, Mexico, between the years 800 and 1000 A.D.   LFS

497
Polychrome Tetrapod Plate
Protoclassic
Tikal, Petén, Guatemala
Ceramic
Height: 13.4 cm
diameter: 38.0 cm
Guatemala, Museo Nacional
de Arqueología y Etnología
Inv. no. MNAE 11130

Polychrome tetrapod plate with large, hollow mammiform supports. Each one has a rattle, a flat button on its tip and two long, vertical air holes that reach this point. This type of support, named because their shape resembles a breast, is characteristic of the Late Preclassic to the Early Classic (Protoclassic period) transition throughout the Maya area and varies in size and decoration. The interior is covered with a polished orange slip; on the wall is a clear red band, on its lower side, by a thin black line. The decoration consists of a band of geometric designs in black and red. On the upper lower part of the vessel are three black triangles, one flaming half-medallion with abstract designs on the interior, and black triangles on the other side. Because they are reflective surfaces the semicircular designs have been interpreted as suns with mirrors.   MSB

498
Tripod Cylindrical Vessel
Late Classic period
Cara Sucia, Department
of Ahuachapán, El Salvador
Ceramic
Height: 22.1 cm; width: 16.4 cm
El Salvador, Museo Nacional

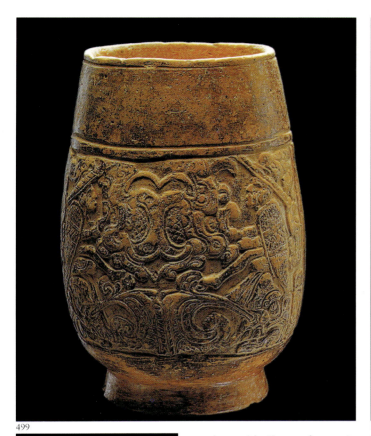

499

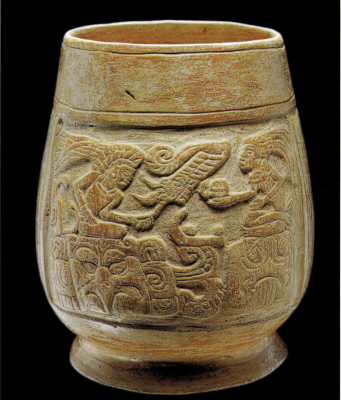

500

498

de Antropología
"Dr. David J. Guzmán"
Inv. no. A1-317

This bichrome, tripod cylindrical vessel decorated on the outside with two panels of ceremonial scenes and a series of glyphs sculpted in high and low relief, was found at the pre-Hispanic site of Cara Sucia, in the coastal zone of the Department of Ahuachapán. This sculpted ceramic ware is typical of the collapse of Classic Maya civilization. At the site of Cara Sucia, the Terminal Classic occupation (A.D. 700–905) represents an extension of Cotzumalguapa culture, which has its center of distribution in the zone of Escuintla, on the southeastern Pacific coast of Guatemala. Cara Sucia shows con-nections with Cotzumalguapa in sculpture, architecture, ceramic, and figurines during the Late Classic period, although the Cotzumalguapa culture also has strong ties with Veracruz. JMR

499
Cylindrical Vessel
Late Classic period
Copán Ruinas, Honduras
Ceramic
Height: 16.8 cm; diameter: 8.5 cm
Copán, Centro Regional
de Investigaciones Arqueológicas
Inv. no. CPN-C-359

The exhibit contains nine examples of Copador derived from the two locales – Copán and El Salvador – where it is most frequently found. It is distinguished by the use of a glittering red paint made of specular hematite, and by certain characteristic red design motifs. The latter include glyphic figures, human beings, and birds, and occasionally monkeys, frogs, and other mammals make an appearance. Vessel forms are generally simple and include composite-silhouette bowls, vases, and effigy jars; there is a marked correspondence between these forms and the types of designs placed on them. The pottery is considered to have been produced for serving vessels. It was a popular pottery type that cut across social lines, and is found in the households and burials of all classes and walks of life in ancient Copán. The paste is a fine soft cream, sometimes painted orange before the application of designs. Before firing, the ware is bur-nished, and a luster is still evident on most vessels. The known range of this ware is wide, extending east to west from the Ulúa Valley in Honduras to Chiquimulilla and Tisquisate in Guatemala, and north to south from the middle Motagua Valley in Guatemala to central and western El Salvador. There is de-bate about the actual production area of Copador. To date no one has located the white-firing clay source or the source for the specular red hematite. John Longyear speculated that it was manufactured in Copán and exported to other areas, primarily El Salvador. Marilyn Beaudry is in agreement with this, even after her paste analysis did not conclusively show that the paste matched other examples known to be of Copán Valley production. WF

500
Pabellón Ware Vase
Late Classic period
Copán Valley, Honduras
Ceramic
Height: 14.8 cm; base: 13.7 cm
diameter: 12.3 cm
Tegucigalpa, Bodegas Centrales
del Instituto Hondureño
de Antropología e Historia
Inv. no. CPN-C-919

This vessel belongs to Pabellón modeled vessels that were pro-duced on the western edge of the Maya lowlands at the end of the Classic period. The scene on the exterior panels was produced from a mold, and shows two human fig-ures facing each other. The pear-shaped form is diagnostic of this class of cylinder, which uses an ar-chaistic ring-base to lend an aura of antiquity to this mass-produced ware. WF

503

504

501

501
Polychrome Cylindrical Vessel
Late Classic period
Uaxactún, Petén, Guatemala.
Ceramic
Height: 18.5 cm; diameter: 11.2 cm
Guatemala, Museo Nacional
de Arqueología y Etnología
Inv. no. MNAE 318

Cylindrical polychrome vessel with
pedestal base and stucco. It has two
equal, opposing bands; one surrounds the vessel right below the
rim and the other appears at the
juncture of the vessel wall and base.
The background of both is eroded
green. The upper band has two
parallel red lines around the upper
part. Under these lines is a row of
red triangles with the base on the
upper part. The lower band displays two parallel red lines on the
lower part and a row of red triangles on these lines. Between both
bands is a brown area in with parallel bands of opposing, incised, diagonal lines in the background
which give the impression of arrows or a mat design. On this
ground and opposite the vessel are
two stucco panels, both with the
ahau glyph in red, (on a white
ground and the other blue), preceded by the numeral 8 in red and
white. The pedestal base has openwork stepped frets painted in alternating red and blue.   MSB

502

502
Copador Vessel
Classic period
El Tazumal, Chalchuapa
Department of Santa Ana
El Salvador
Ceramic
Height: 7.7 cm; width: 16.6 cm
El Salvador, Museo Nacional
de Antropología
"Dr. David J. Guzmán"
Inv. no. A1-194

Many of the objects recovered from
tombs at El Tazumal form part of
the complex known as Payú ceramics from the Late Classic period, a
time of strong links to Copán.
What stands out is the ceramic
presence of the groups known as
Copador and Gualpopa, both

probably made in the area of
Copán, but the latter possibly was
introduced originally from El Salvador. This ceramic is distinguished by its characteristic figures
of "swimmers," pseudo-glyphs and
geometric motifs painted in red
and black on an orange and beige
ground. This ceramic type resembles the polychrome bowl of Copador type found at the archaeological site of El Tazumal in the
area of Chalchoapa in the west of
the country. The distribution of this
ware extended from western El Salvador to the region of Copán and
the central zone of Honduras,
which indicates that there was a
fairly sophisticated trade network
that joined these zones during the
Late Classic period. The name of

this ware is a contraction of Copán
and El Salvador, a reference to its
zone of distribution.   JMR

503
Bichrome Basin
Classic period
Tikal, Petén, Guatemala
Ceramic
Height: 5.7 cm; diameter: 11.5 cm
Guatemala, Museo Nacional
de Arqueología y Etnología
Inv. no. MNAE 11303

The surface of this vessel is covered with highly polished red slip.
Its outer surface is decorated with
two alternating geometric designs;
one is a large square with a smaller
one in the center, surrounding the
representation of the *kan* cross.
The other design is composed of
a square with two opposing triangles on its vertical sides and two
parallel horizontal bands in the
center.   MSB

504
Polychrome Basin
Classic period
Petén, Guatemala
Ceramic
Height: 10.0 cm; diameter: 10.6 cm
Guatemala, Museo Nacional
de Arqueología y Etnología
Inv. no. MNAE 11781

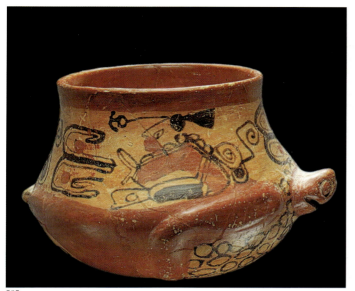

505

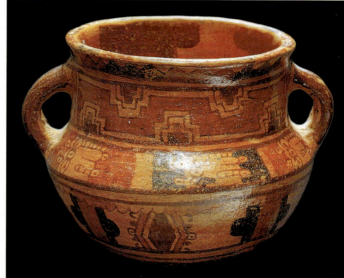

506

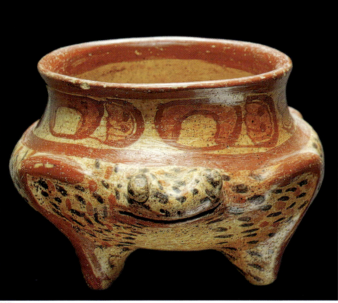

507

508

The inside of the vessel is covered with eroded brown slip and the outside with buff or cream-colored slip. A black band surrounds the vessel near the rim. Under this band, is another, orange-colored band, its upper and lower edges delimited with thin black lines. Below these bands are an orange-colored zigzag and undulating black bands, in addition to rectangles divided into opposing triangles, one with its base on the orange band and the next on the base of the vessel, thus alternating in succession. These triangles are framed by orange and undulating black lines. MSB

505
Jar
Late Classic period
Copán Valley, Copán Ruinas
Honduras
Ceramic
Height: 8.8 cm
width: 14.0 cm
diameter: 8.8 cm

Copán, Centro Regional
de Investigaciones Arqueológicas
Inv. no. CPN-C-436

Jar with zoomorphic decoration made of Copador-type ware; it has been classified within polychrome types. It is burnished with red and black on orange. The entire vessel represents a frog, an animal frequently represented at Copán both in stone as well as in ceramics, because it is regarded as a harbinger of rain. CJF

506
Jar
Late Classic period
Copán, Honduras
Ceramic
Height: 10.3 cm
width: 14.3 cm
diameter: 10.4 cm
Copán
Centro Regional
de Investigaciones Arqueológicas
Inv. no. CPN-C-551

Ulúa-type ceramic jar with two handles. This composite-silhouette vessel has a sunken base in red and black on orange polychrome. It is decorated on the outside with linear designs over a system of stepped frets, a very common element at the end of the Late Classic period at Copán. CJF

507
Vessel
Late Classic period
Las Sepulturas, Copán Ruinas
Honduras
Ceramic
Height: 9.2 cm
width: 16.9 cm
diameter: 11.2 cm
Copán, Centro Regional
de Investigaciones Arqueológicas
Inv. no. CPN-C-594

Copador ware with zoomorphic handles representing the heads of two frogs joined at the belly in what is the central part of the ves-

sel. The body is represented by red and black spots; the feet of the frogs end in supports, which are conical and solid. On the neck of the vessel is a band of symbolic glyphs. CJF

508
Vessel
Late Classic period
Copán Valley, Honduras
Ceramic
Height: 12.1 cm
width: 14.0 cm
diameter: 10.2 cm
Copán, Museo Regional
de Arqueología
Inv. no. CPN-C-744

Polychrome vessel with double silhouette and two handles joining the neck with the body. Stepped fret designs decorate the body. This is an example of Ulúa polychrome ware imported to Copán at the end of A.D. 800, when it was deposited in a tomb. CJF

509

509
Censer
Postclassic period
Nebaj, Quiché, Guatemala
Ceramic
Height: 24.7 cm
diameter: 23.8 cm
Guatemala, Museo Nacional
de Arqueología y Etnología
Inv. no. MNAE 4628

Red and blue bichrome tripod censer with lateral flanges. Each support has the representations of a different face. On the rim is a band adorned with circular impressions. On the front part is a modeled, appliquéd figure, painted blue with details in red. He wears a headdress, circular earplugs, a pectoral, and loincloth, and his hands rest on his abdomen. The surface is painted with slanted, alternating blue and red lines. This piece was used to burn *pom* (copal incense) and other aromatic substances during ceremonies.   MSB

510
Effigy Vessel
Classic period
Petén, Guatemala
Ceramic
Height: 22.0 cm; diameter: 25.4 cm
Guatemala, Museo Nacional
de Arqueología y Etnología
Inv. no. MNAE 11777

On the front of the vessel is the face of the sun god framed by four circles, four half circles, and a series of small spherical beads. This god is generally represented with a large nose and square eyes. Often his upper teeth are filed into a T-shape. He is represented depending on the time of day: as young when he rises, or as old when he sets. The sun god appears in several buildings at different archaeological sites; for example, in the Acropolis at Quiriguá.   MSB

511
Urn
Late Classic period
Quiché, Guatemala
Ceramic
Height: 33.5 cm
diameter: 33.0 cm
Guatemala, Museo Nacional
de Arqueología y Etnología
Inv. no. MNAE 13779

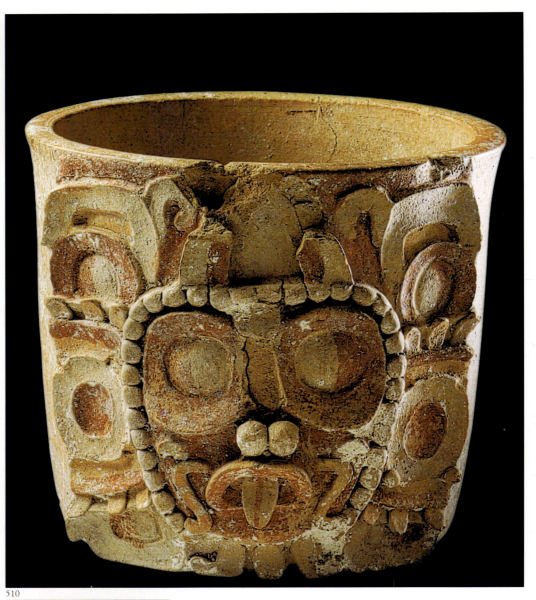

510

511

This cylindrical urn has lateral flanges, while its edges have fingerprints at the base and the rim. The front part is decorated with a modeled appliquéd face with open eyes and mouth, where two filed teeth are seen. The figure also has circular earplugs. On the upper part are the ears of a feline, perhaps a jaguar. Representations of this animal, as sun god, are very common on this type of piece. It preserves traces of white and blue stucco, while the surface is red in color, just like the paste. Urns were used during the Late Classic and Early Postclassic periods for placing the deceased in a flexed position inside. Some have a lid, which is also decorated. Many examples of these urns have been found in the area of ixil in the Department of Quiché.   MSB

512
Urn
Late Classic period
Quiché, Guatemala
Ceramic
Height: 38.5 cm
diameter of the rim: 39.5 cm
Guatemala, Museo Nacional
de Arqueología y Etnología
Inv. no. MNAE 11019

Anthropomorphic cylindrical urn with lateral flanges; the edge has fingerprints. On the front, framed by two fillets, one above and one below, is a modeled, appliqued face with open eyes and mouth, which shows teeth filed into T-shape. Among the Mayas, dental mutilation has been very common from pre-Hispanic times to the present. They used several techniques for this purpose, including filing certain teeth and inlaying stones such as jadeite. The headdress is composed of a horizontal band, an ear of corn, and two maize leaves. The band and leaves are painted blue. The figure has circular ear ornaments with tubular pendants similar to the beads of his necklace, in addition to a spherical bead at the center, all painted blue. The surface is red, the same color as the paste. There are remains of white paint.   MSB

513
Tripod Vessel
with Anthropomorphic Lid
Early Classic period
Santa Rita Corozal
Corozal District, Belize
Ceramic
Diameter of lip: 21.8 cm
height: 10.5 cm
diameter: 19.0 cm
Belmopan, Bodegas
del Departamento de Arqueología
Inv. no. 35/203-2:159

Santa Rita Corozal, an archaeological site located at the northern

512

514

with fingerprints, one near the rim and the other above it. The surfaces surrounding the handle and the bands are covered with white paint and between the bands is red color. This type of urn was made from the Early Classic period until the Postclassic period. In Nebaj, several similar pieces were found, decorated with human as well as animal effigies. Based on the contexts in which they were found and because they contained funerary offerings, it can be determined that their function was ceremonial.   MSB

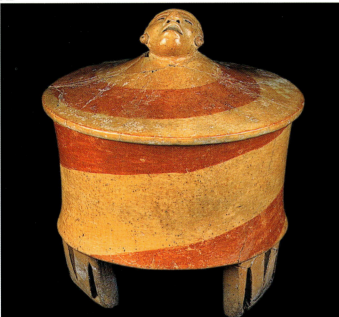

513

end of Belize, derives its fame mainly from the fact that it was the capital of Chactemal, a flourishing Maya state at the time of Spanish contact. Despite its almost entire destruction as a result of the conquest and above all by the modern city of Corozal, which occupies the majority of this settlement, tombs, offerings, and mural paintings, as well as abundant and varied trade articles recovered in archaeological excavations at this site, testify to their wealth as described in sixteenth-century sources. This tripod vessel, executed in a Teotihuacan shape but clearly Maya in style, comes from the tomb of a ruler buried in Structure 7 with a rich offering that included a flint eccentric, *Spondylus* shell, stingray spine, jadeite mask, eight ceramic vessels, a stone vessel, and remains of a possible codex.   PJS

514
Urn with Lid
Late Classic period
Nebaj, Quiché, Guatemala
Ceramic
Height: 21.6 cm; diameter: 18.5 cm
Guatemala, Museo Nacional
de Arqueología y Etnología
Inv. no. MNAE 4630

Bichrome tripod urn with lid and rectangular supports. The basin has two bands with fingerprints, one at the juncture of the vessel wall and base, and the other on the rim. Both are covered with white paint and the area between them is covered with red paint, while the interior, exterior, and base of the piece are covered with white paint. The red handle of the lid is the face of an individual who wears a twisted band as a headdress, has coffee-bean shaped eyes, and wears circular earplugs. The lid has two bands

Timeline

Timeline				EARLY **Preclassic**	First stable settlements based on cultivation of maize First pottery production
Maya civilization Northern lowlands					
Central lowlands				 *Dart point*	
Southern highlands					

For the corresponding dates in the western calendar we have used the GTM 584285 system (Goodman, Thompson Martinéz)

2000 B.C.	1900	1800	1700	1600

Other American civilizations

Spear point from site at Cinega Creeks

2000 ca. First metalworking in Peru

1800 ca. Diffusion of pottery in Peru

Europe

2030 ca. England: Stonehenge
2000-1450 ca. Minoan civilization Knossos and Phaistos
2000 ca. Brettany megalithic at Carnac

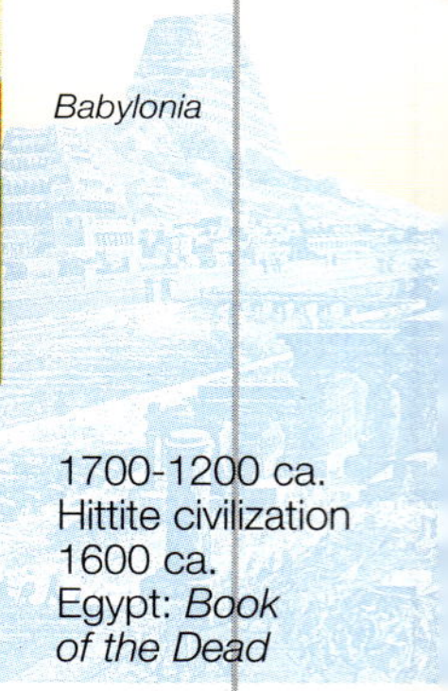

Babylonia

Middle East Africa

Blue bird, fresco in the palace of Knossos

1792-1750 Hammurapi unites Mesopotamia foundation of the Babylonian empire *The Gilgamesh saga*

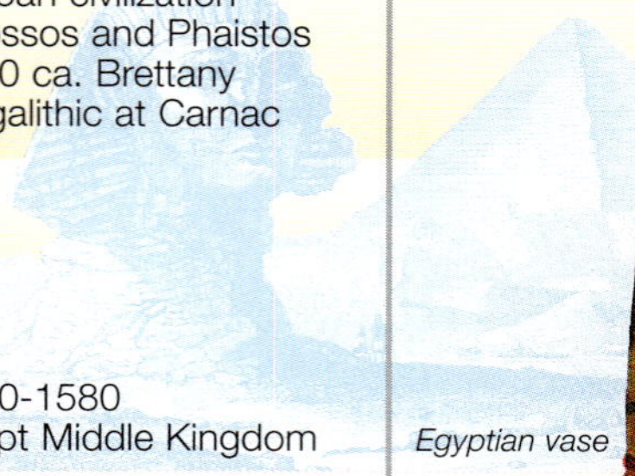

2160-1580 Egypt Middle Kingdom

Egyptian vase

1700-1200 ca. Hittite civilization
1600 ca. Egypt: *Book of the Dead*

Far East
India, Tibet, China Mongolia

Diagram of Fu-hi Book of the ethical rules, politics and principal rules of life

1767-1123 China: Shang dynasty

Japan

Ceramic bowl
Belize

Litic sculpture
Kaminaljuyú, Guatemala

Tetrapod plate
ceramic

Ceramic jar
Chiapas, Mexico

Manatí sculpture

1600   1500   1400   1300   1200   1100

1250 ca. Start
in Peru of Guanape
civilization

1200-600 Olmec civilization

1500 ca.
Crete and Greece
Linear B script

Cuneiform writing

1600-1200 ca.
Mycenaean civilization

*Babylonian solar
quadrant*

*Abu Simbel
Ramses II
Tomb*

1580-1090
Egypt: New Kingdom
Valley of Kings

1500 ca.
Cuneiform Hittite
sculpture in Anatolia

*Pharaoh
Amenhotep III*

1304 ca.
Egypt
Ramses II
Pharaoh

1200 ca.
first five
books
of the Bible

1500 ca.
Ideographic writing
in China

1600 ca. China: *I Ching*
or Book of Changes

1500-800 ca.
India: Vedic period

1122-249 ca.
China: Chou dynasty

Writing evolution in China

Timeline	Early Preclassic				

Maya civilization

Northern lowlands

Central lowlands

Southern highlands

*Female figurine
San Agustín Acasaguastlán
El Progreso, Guatemala*

*Simojovel celt
Chiapas, Mexico*

*Stela 9 at Kaminaljuyú
Guatemala*

1100 B.C.	1000	900	800	700

Other American civilizations

900 ca.
Foundation of La Venta
Olmec capital

Europe

Middle East Africa

1100-700 ca
Phoenicians
in the
Mediterranean
basin
diffusion
of alphabet

*Documentary stone
of King Nabuchadnezzar I*

900 ca.
Arrival of
Etruscan
in Italian
peninsula

*Etruscan mural
Tarquinia*

965-928 ca.
Solomon, king
of the Jews
Song of Solomon

814 The Phoenicians
found the colony
of Carthage

776 First Olympic
Games
753 Foundation of
Rome; Seven Kings
750 ca. First
written version
of Homeric texts

*Kalak, Black Obelisk
of Shalmaneser III*

Far East
India, Tibet, China
Mongolia

900 ca. India:
start of *Upanishad*
sacred texts

Japan

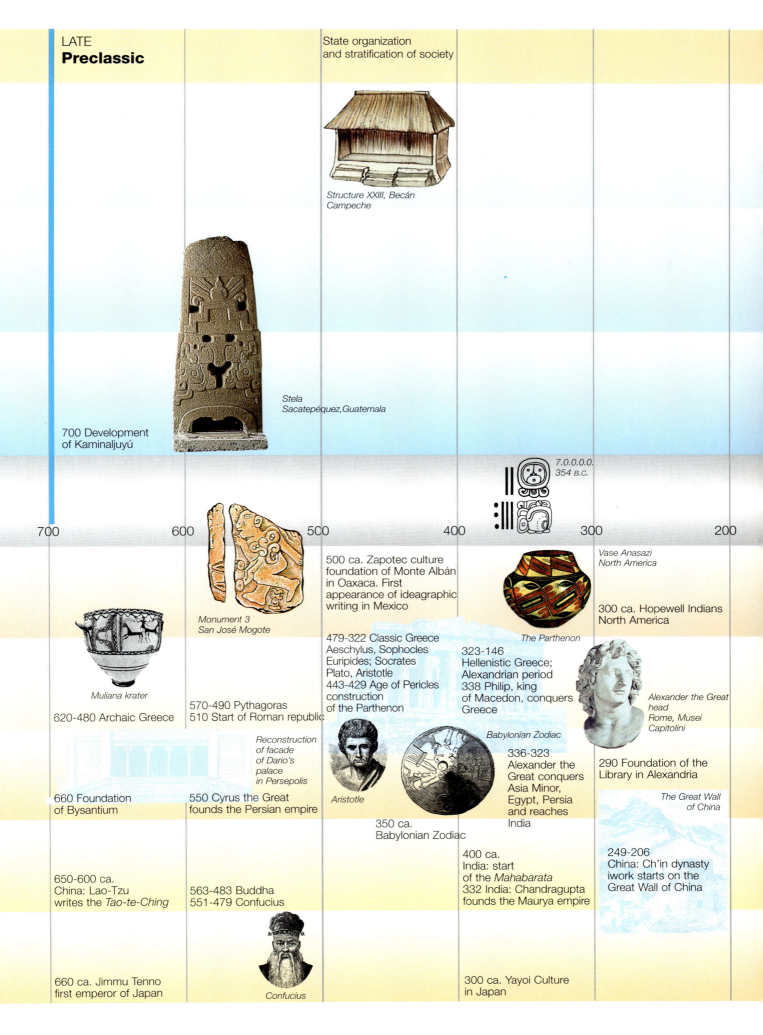

LATE
Preclassic

State organization
and stratification of society

*Structure XXIII, Becán
Campeche*

*Stela
Sacatepéquez, Guatemala*

700 Development
of Kaminaljuyú

7.0.0.0.0.
354 B.C.

700	600	500	400	300	200

500 ca. Zapotec culture
foundation of Monte Albán
in Oaxaca. First
appearance of ideagraphic
writing in Mexico

*Vase Anasazi
North America*

300 ca. Hopewell Indians
North America

*Monument 3
San José Mogote*

479-322 Classic Greece
Aeschylus, Sophocles
Euripides; Socrates
Plato, Aristotle
443-429 Age of Pericles
construction
of the Parthenon

The Parthenon

323-146
Hellenistic Greece;
Alexandrian period
338 Philip, king
of Macedon, conquers
Greece

Muliana krater

620-480 Archaic Greece

570-490 Pythagoras
510 Start of Roman republic

Aristotle

Babylonian Zodiac

336-323
Alexander the
Great conquers
Asia Minor,
Egypt, Persia
and reaches
India

*Alexander the Great
head
Rome, Musei
Capitolini*

290 Foundation of the
Library in Alexandria

*Reconstruction
of facade
of Dario's
palace
in Persepolis*

660 Foundation
of Bysantium

550 Cyrus the Great
founds the Persian empire

350 ca.
Babylonian Zodiac

*The Great Wall
of China*

249-206
China: Ch'in dynasty
iwork starts on the
Great Wall of China

650-600 ca.
China: Lao-Tzu
writes the *Tao-te-Ching*

563-483 Buddha
551-479 Confucius

400 ca.
India: start
of the *Mahabarata*
332 India: Chandragupta
founds the Maurya empire

660 ca. Jimmu Tenno
first emperor of Japan

Confucius

300 ca. Yayoi Culture
in Japan

Timeline

Early Preclassic

Maya civilization

Northern
lowlands

Central
lowlands

162 Foundation
of Tikal
and Uaxactún

Southern
highlands

7.10.0.0.0.
157 B.C.

8.0.0.0.0.
41 A.D.

200 B.C.   100   0   100 A.D.   200

Other
American
civilizations

200 ca. Teotihuacán

Mural in Teotihuacán

The Colosseum

Europe

146
Siege of Corinth
Greece falls
to Roman dominion

Julius Caesar
48 Julius Caesar
conquers Gaul

*Fresco in the
Villa of Mysteries
Pompeii*

75-80 Rome
work begins
on the
Colosseum

118-125 Rome:
construction of the Pantheon

Middle East
Afirca

149-146
Third Punic War
Carthage
distinguishes itself

Christ monogram

Birth of Jesus

70 Titus
son of Vespasian
destroys the Temple
of Jerusalem

Petra

Far East
India, Tibet
China, Mongolia

112 ca. Silk Road links
China to the west
through the Middle East

65 China: first Buddhist
communities
documented

100-400 India
Gandhara art flourishes

Chinese old zodiac

Japan

292 Diffusion of hieroglyphic script and use of calendar. Introduction of vigesimal system and zero

600 Influx of the culure of Teotihuacán

*Incense-holder
Palenque, Chiapas, Mexico*

*Funerary mask
jadeite and conch
Tikal, Petén, Guatemala*

First calendar inscription
on Stela 29, Tikal

*Copan, 4th ruler
Culx, 485-495 A.D.*

*"The Queen
of Uxmal"
architectural tenon
Uxmal, Yucatán, Mexico*

Peack of development of
Tikal, Yaxchilán, Bonampak
Copán and Palenque

*Tripod vase, ceramic
Usumacinta, Mexico*

8.10.0.0.0.
238 A.D.

9.0.0.0.0.
435 A.D.

9.10.0.0.0.
633 A.D.

200   300   400   500   600   700

300 ca. Teotihuacán
Sun Pyramid
350-500 ca.
Mochica Culture in Peru

600-650 ca.
Fall of Teotihuacán

Runic inscription

313 Edict of Constantine
giving freedom to Christians
395 End of unity
for the Roman Empire

410 Visigoths in Italy
sack of Rome
476 Fall of the western
Roman Empire
486 Clovis I founds
the Frankish kingdom

493-553 Theodoric
in Ravenna
Ostrogoth kingdom
534 Justinian issues
the *Corpus iuris civilis*
568-774
Longobards in Italy

697 Venice
election of the first doge

Constantine

622 Muhammad flees
to Medina
634 Arab expansion
begins

Muhammad

520 India: invention of
decimal numeration system

Persian plate

265-420
China: Ts'in dynasty

320-550 India
Gupta Empire founded
by Chandragupta I

*Deity, wood sculpture
from the Asoka period
(552-710)*

620-907 China
T'ang dynasy

300 ca. Japan
Kofun culture

552-710 Japan
Asoka period

Timeline	*Late Classic*	850-1000 "Collapse of Maya system"	EARLY **Postclassic**	Migration of coastal peoples from Gulf of Mexico with their political and cultural legacy

Maya civilization

Northern lowlands

Uxmal Tortuga house

Tripod vase Calakmul Campeche Mexico

Puuc style Uxmal, Sayil Labná

Zoomorph sculpture Chichén Itzá, Yucatán Mexico

Chichén Itzá, El Castillo

Central lowlands

Figurine Palenque Chiapas Mexico

Building 33 in Yaxchilán

Pottery production in Jaina

Censer lid "Acrobat" ceramic Copán Ruinas, Honduras

Sculptured facade, Tikal

Southern highlands

Policrom vessel Chamá area Quiché Guatemala

Building "B" at Xpuhil

10.0.0.0.0. 830 A.D.

10.10.0.0.0. 1027 A.D.

700 A.D.	800	900	1000	1100

Other American civilizations

Tula, Temple of the morning star Toltec culture

750 ca. Foundation of Tula, Toltec capital

1000 Kingdom of Chimú in Peru

Europe

711 Arabs invade the Iberian peninsula
732 Battle of Poitiers blocks Arab expansion in Europe

CONSEQUENTI
Caroline writing

Monogram of Charlemagne

800 Rome: Charlemagne crowned emperor of the Holy Roman Empire

Edoardo I, king of England

962 Otto II, emperor

1016 Normans enter southern Italy
1054 Great Schism of the Western and Eastern churches
1066 Normans conquest of Britain

Middle East Africa

800 ca. Kanem kingdom in the Chad lands

1096-1099 First crusade

Far East
India, Tibet China, Mongolia

700-1067 Ghana Empire

Incense burner from Sung era

960-1279 China Sung dynasty

1045 China: invention of movable type
1100 ca. Apogee culture in Cambodia; construction of the Angkor Vat temple

Japan

710-794 Japan Nara period
794-1185 Japan: Heian period transfer of capital from Nara to Kyoto

Shinto deity sculpture in painted wood

Go-Shiricawa 77th emperor of Japan, 1128-1192

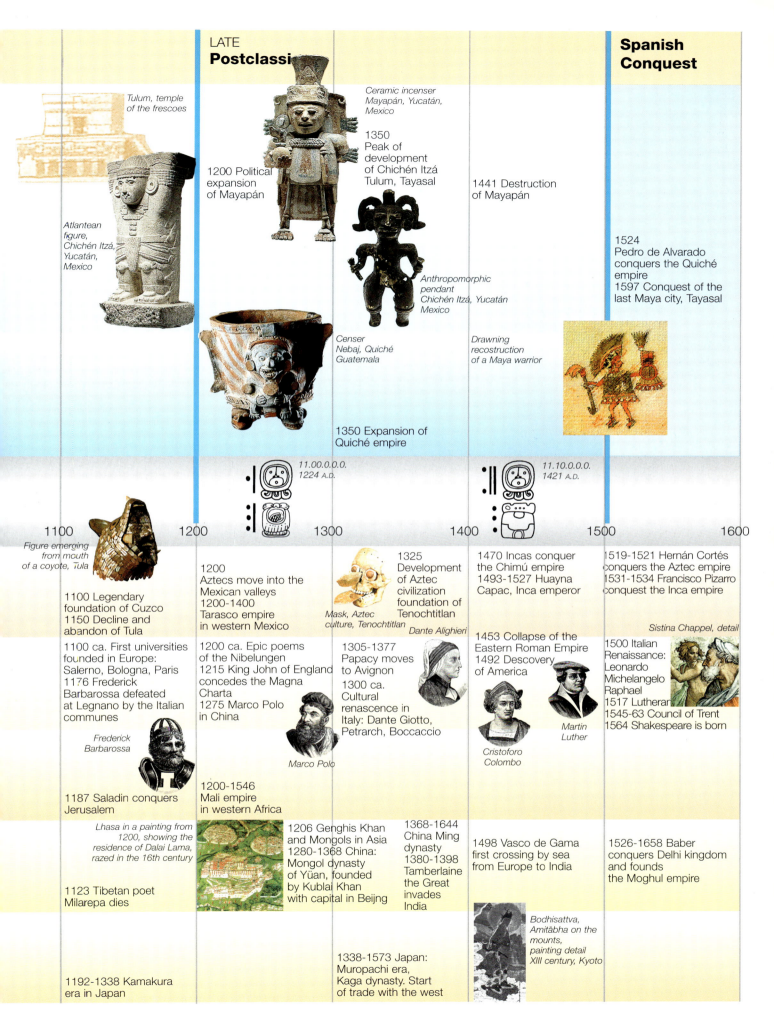

Tulum, temple of the frescoes

Atlantean figure, Chichén Itzá, Yucatán, Mexico

Ceramic incenser Mayapán, Yucatán, Mexico

1200 Political expansion of Mayapán

1350 Peak of development of Chichén Itzá Tulum, Tayasal

1441 Destruction of Mayapán

1524 Pedro de Alvarado conquers the Quiché empire
1597 Conquest of the last Maya city, Tayasal

Anthropomorphic pendant Chichén Itzá, Yucatán Mexico

Censer Nebaj, Quiché Guatemala

Drawning recostruction of a Maya warrior

1350 Expansion of Quiché empire

11.00.0.0.0. 1224 A.D.

11.10.0.0.0. 1421 A.D.

1100   1200   1300   1400   1500   1600

Figure emerging from mouth of a coyote, Tula

1100 Legendary foundation of Cuzco
1150 Decline and abandon of Tula

1200 Aztecs move into the Mexican valleys
1200-1400 Tarasco empire in western Mexico

Mask, Aztec culture, Tenochtitlan

1325 Development of Aztec civilization foundation of Tenochtitlan

Dante Alighieri

1470 Incas conquer the Chimú empire
1493-1527 Huayna Capac, Inca emperor

1519-1521 Hernán Cortés conquers the Aztec empire
1531-1534 Francisco Pizarro conquest the Inca empire

Sistina Chappel, detail

1100 ca. First universities founded in Europe: Salerno, Bologna, Paris
1176 Frederick Barbarossa defeated at Legnano by the Italian communes

1200 ca. Epic poems of the Nibelungen
1215 King John of England concedes the Magna Charta
1275 Marco Polo in China

1305-1377 Papacy moves to Avignon
1300 ca. Cultural renascence in Italy: Dante Giotto, Petrarch, Boccaccio

1453 Collapse of the Eastern Roman Empire
1492 Descovery of America

1500 Italian Renaissance: Leonardo Michelangelo Raphael
1517 Lutheran
1545-63 Council of Trent
1564 Shakespeare is born

Frederick Barbarossa

Marco Polo

Cristoforo Colombo

Martin Luther

1187 Saladin conquers Jerusalem

1200-1546 Mali empire in western Africa

Lhasa in a painting from 1200, showing the residence of Dalai Lama, razed in the 16th century

1206 Genghis Khan and Mongols in Asia
1280-1368 China: Mongol dynasty of Yüan, founded by Kublai Khan with capital in Beijng

1368-1644 China Ming dynasty
1380-1398 Tamberlaine the Great invades India

1498 Vasco de Gama first crossing by sea from Europe to India

1526-1658 Baber conquers Delhi kingdom and founds the Moghul empire

1123 Tibetan poet Milarepa dies

Bodhisattva, Amitābha on the mounts, painting detail XIII century, Kyoto

1192-1338 Kamakura era in Japan

1338-1573 Japan: Muropachi era, Kaga dynasty. Start of trade with the west

Glossary
Maya Gods
Entries References
Index of the names

Glossary

by
Adriana Konzevik Cabib
Antonio Benavides
Sol Levin Rojo
with the collaboration of
Mario Humberto Ruz
Raúl del Moral
Tomás Pérez
and Michela Craveri

A

ACROPOLIS
[from Greek] Group of elevated buildings resulting from constructions superimposed through time.

ACHIOTE
[from the Nahuatl *achtli*; in Yucatec Mayan, *kiwi* or *kuxub*] Plant (*Bixa Orellana*) from whose seeds an edible red dye is extracted.

ADELANTADO
Title granted by the Spanish crown to those men who led exploratory and conquest expeditions to new territories

AGOUTI
[In Yucatec Mayan, *tsub*] Rodent (*Dasyprocta punctata*), of the size of a cat, with edible flesh.

AGUACATECA
Language and ethnic group name, in the area of northwest Guatemala.

AH ATANZAH
[Yucatec Mayan] Matchmaker.

AH CANUL
[Yucatec Mayan] Literally, the guardian. This is the name the Cocom used to refer to foreign mercenaries they hired in Mayapán for their protection. A Maya political entity in the north during the Classic period was also known by this name.

AH CHEMBAL UINICOOB
[Yucatec Mayan; singular *ah chembal uinic*] Plebeians or commoners.

AH CUCH CAB
[Yucatec Mayan] Representative of the *batab* in the council of the *batabil*.

AH HOLPOPOOB
[Yucatec Mayan; singular *ah holpop*] Functionaries who mediated between the commoners and the great lords. Literally, "those at the head of the mat."

AH KIN
[Yucatec Mayan; also *ah 'kin*; plural: *ah kinoob*] Designation for priests. It means "he of the Sun."

AH KIN CHEL
[Yucatec Mayan, also Ah'kin Chel] Maya political and territorial entity of the sixteenth century located at the center of the north coast of Yucatán.

AH KUL
[Mayan; plural: *ah kuloob*] Delegate or assistant to the *batab*. Sacred lord.

AH MEN OR AHMEN
[Yucatec Mayan, also *ah'men*] Ritual specialist, who also serves as a doctor. He was also called by the apocope *h-men*.

AH POLOM
See *polom*

AH POP
[Yucatec Mayan] "Lord of the Mat," or ruler.

AH TEPAL
[Yucatec Mayan] Lord, sovereign, majesty, he who reigns or should reign; title referring to a god.

AH TOOC
[Yucatec Mayan, also *ah tok*] Bloodletter by office, surgeon.

AHAU
[Mayan, also *ahaw*] Lord, divine may, ruler, or king.
Name of the last day of the month *tzolkin*.

AK
[Yucatec Mayan] For the Mayas, the earth has the round shape of the carapace of a turtle, an animal of great symbolic value for its ability to live both on earth as well as in water. Its shell also served as a musical instrument.

AKALCHE
[Yucatec Mayan] Low terrain that is flooded in the rainy season.

ALMEHEN
[Yucatec Mayan, plural: *almehenoob*] Of the noble lineage, both on the mother's side (*al*: born son) as well as on the father's side (*mehen*: created son).

ALMUD
[from Arabic] Colonial measure of volume for seeds.

AMATE
[Mexicanism, from Nahuatl *amatl*; in Mayan, *huun*, or *copo* in Yucatec Mayan] Tree (*Ficus sp.*) from the bark of which paper is made. Maya codices that have survived are made of *amate* paper.

AMATL
[Nahuatl] See *amate*.

AMBER
Transparent yellowish fossil resin was used as a precious stone. The Simojovel region of Chiapas was the main source of amber in Mesoamerica. This resource is still exploited.

ANTEOREJERAS
Ornaments for eyes.

APPLIQUÉ
Decorative technique that consists of attaching small modeled elements to a surface.

ARROBA
Weight measurement equivalent to 11-12 kilograms. As a measure of capacity, it is used to measure oils, its equivalence varying considerably in different regions.

ATLANTEAN FIGURES
Stone sculptures, generally with arms extended upward, which served as a support or as a column. The name is derived from Greek mythology.

ATLATL
[Nahuatl; *hulche* in Mayan] Spearthrower.

ATOLE
[word of Nahuatl origin; *ul* in Mayan] Thick drink prepared with cooked cornstarch and water, typical of Mesoamerica and still consumed today.

AVOCADO
[*aguacate* in Spanish, from the Nahuatl *auacatl*; in Yucatec Mayan, *on*] Tree (*Persea americana*) with oily, pulpy, perfumed edible fruit of the same name. It is an evergreen species originally from America.

AZTECS
[in Nahuatl] Indigenous group of Central Mexico that came from Aztlán to establish Tenochtitlan. In the sixteenth century they dominated large portions of what today is Mexico.

B

BAAT
[Yucatec Mayan] Stone axe.

BACAB
[Mayan] One of the four deities who upheld the sky in Maya cosmovision.

BACAL
See *olote*.

BAKTUN
[Mayan, also *bak'tun*] Calendric cycle in the Long Count, of 400 years with 360 days each. Period of twenty *katuns*.

BALAM
[Yucatec Mayan] Jaguar, American feline (*Felis onca*) with spotted fur . The Mayas associated it with political power, deities, warfare, night, the underworld, and even today it is used as a family name.

BALCHE
[Yucatec Mayan, also *balche'*] Tree (*Lonchocarpus spp.*) from which bark was fermented with honey and water to make an alcoholic beverage of the same name, generally used in ceremonies .

BALL GAME
Ritual game the playing fields have an I-shape and are delimited on the sides by twin buildings with walls sloping toward the playing area, equipped with stone rings or markers on which the rubber ball bounced. Two teams played apparently hitting the ball only on the hips, the buttocks, the elbows and knees. The game could represent war, the struggle between good and evil, or the movements of the stars. When the players were war captives, they could be sacrificed after the game.

BATAB
[Mayan; plural, *bataboob*] Title given to rulers or minor political heads who were under the *halach uinic*.

BATABIL
[Mayan] *Señorío* or territory ruled by a *batab*.

BAYAL
Palm tree.

BERIMBAU
[word of South American origin] Musical instrument with a single string with a gourd as a resonance box, mounted on an arc.

BOCH
[Yucatec Mayan] Woman's headdress. *Mantilla*, hat.

BOLON DZACAB
See manikin scepter.

BOOT STONE
Cut stone block used in the construction of Maya vaults in the Puuc region and at Chichén Itzá. It is cut in the form of a boot.

BUUL
[Mayan, also *bu'ul*] Bean (*Phaseolus vulgaris*).

C

CABAN
[Yucatec Mayan, also *cabam*] One of the twenty Maya days.

CACAO
[Mayan] Seeds of the tree *Theobroma cacao*, an American species, from which chocolate is extracted. The seeds were used widely by the Maya, not only as a food product but also as a currency.

CACTLI
[Nahuatl] See *xanab*.

CAHAL
See *sahal*.

CAKCHIQUEL
Maya ethnic and language group from the highlands of Guatemala.

CALENDAR WHEEL
[*Xiuhmolpilli* among the Aztecs] Period of 52 years, the dates of which are represented by a numeral plus a day glyph and a numeral plus a month glyph.

CALUAC
[Yucatec Mayan] Title given to tribute collector.

CAP STONE
The stone that closes the false arch or Maya vault. It is also called the key or lid.

CANKIN
See *kankin*.

CARGA
Colonial period measure for the trade of different products, especially seeds. It refers to 24,000 units of the product in question. As a measurement of volume, it was generally the equivalent of 181.5 liters. A *carga* of cacao, in turn, was generally the equivalent of 37 kilograms.

CASTE WAR
Armed movement that took place in the Yucatán peninsula, headed by Maya indigenous groups who tried to gain independence from the Mexican government. It lasted from the middle of the nineteenth century to the beginning of the twentieth.

CAUAC
[Mayan] Monster associated with the earth in Maya mythology . The name of the penultimate day of the month of the Maya *tzolkin* calendar.

CAZABE
[Americanism] Manioc or tapioca flour bread or roll.

CEH
[Mayan] Deer. Month in the Maya calendar *haab*.

CEHACHE
Indigenous Maya ethnic group from the southcentral and north of Guatemala. Maya ethnic group in the fourteenth and seventeenth centuries, today extinct. They were also called the Mazatecs or "people of the deer" (from the Nahuatl word *mazatl*, deer). Cehache also refers to the territory where they lived.

CEHPECH
Sixteenth century political and territorial entity located on the northeastern coast of Yucatán.

CEIBA
[In Mayan, *yaaxche*, or tree of the center, which comes from *yaax*: green, happiness] Sacred tree (*Ceiba sp.*) of Maya mythology, considered to be the *axis mundi*.

CENOTE
[*dzonot* in Yucatec Mayan] Natural deposit of freshwater, the product of the collapse of underground caves. These are very common water sources in the limestone surface of the Yucatán peninsula. Sometimes they were also reused as funerary deposits or as dumps. The sacred cenote at Chichén Itzá is also known as the Well of Sacrifice.

CHAC
[Mayan] Red color. Large. Strong. Downpour.

CHAC MOOL
[Mayan, also *Chacmol*] Name of a reclining anthropomorphic sculpture on which offerings for the gods were placed during the Early Postclassic. The name means "red jaguar"and was coined by Le Plongeon, who found the first example in the Temple of the Jaguars at Chichén Itzá in 1875. These sculptures are characterized by a figure stretched out with head turned to one side, the legs drawn up, and a vessel on the belly.

CHAKAN
[Yucatec Mayan] Savannah, flat territory. Name for a Maya territorial political entity in the Classic period.

CHALCHIHUITL
[Nahuatl] Name given to precious green stones of jade or jadeite, also called *chalchihuites*. See also jadeite.

CHAY KIN
[Yucatec Mayan, also *Ch'ay Kin*] "Lost days" of the Maya calendrical system.

CHAYA
[from the Yucatec Mayan chay] Edible plant (*Cnidoscolus chayamansa*).

CHE
[lowlands Mayan, equivalent in the highlands is *te*] Staff, stick, rod. Tree.

CHECHEM
[Yucatec Mayan] Hardwood tree (*Metopium brownei*), the resin of which is highly toxic .

CHEL
[Yucatec Mayan, also *ch'el*] Surname. Term designating people of white skin and light hair. Yucatecan magpie-jay (*Cyanocitta yucatanica* or *Cissolopha yucatanica*).

CHEN
[Yucatec Mayan, also *ch'en*] Well. Month in the Maya civil calendar.

CHENES
Architectural style characterized by profuse decoration of facades. Characteristic of the northeast region of Campeche.

CHÍA
Seed that was and is still used to prepare a refreshing drink, and the oil of which is used to shine gourds.

CHIC KABAN
[Yucatec Mayan] Pre-Hispanic celebration in honor of Kukulcan in which images of the gods were blessed. Some people dressed as buffoons and collected gifts.

CHICOZAPOTE
American hardwood tree (*Manilkara zapota*) that was often used in pre-Hispanic constructions. Chewing gum was obtained from its resin and its sweet, round fruit is edible.

CHIKINCHEL
[Mayan, also Chik'in Che'el or Chiquinchel] Maya province recorded during the sixteenth century.

CHILAM BALAM, BOOKS OF
The so-called *Books of Chilam Balam* form an important part of indigenous literature. They were written after the Spanish conquest and the material that they contain is highly heterogeneous. Their diverse contents cover several of the phases of the Maya people of Yucatán. Among the topics covered are religious (both purely indigenous as well as Christian translated into Mayan), historical, medical, chronological, ritual, astronomical, and astrological practices.

CHIM
[Mayan] Fiber bag. Surname that has become Chin.

CHOL
[from Mayan] Maya language and ethnic group of northern Guatemala and Chiapas, and since several decades ago, also the Mexican states of Tabasco and Campeche.

CHOLTÍ
Together with Chol, Chontal, and Chortí, this formed part of the family or group of Cholan languages. It disappeared more than a century ago.

CHOM
[Yucatec Mayan, also *kuch*] See turkey buzzard.

CHONTAL
[from Nahuatl *chontalli*, foreigner] Maya ethnic group that originally inhabited northeastern Tabasco and southwestern Campeche. Its language is derived from the Cholan family of languages. Today this language is spoken in Tabasco.

See *putun*

CHORTÍ
[From Quiché] Maya ethnic group and language from southeastern Guatemala and western Honduras. Its language derives from the Cholan family of languages.

CHU
[Yucatec Mayan] See gourd.

CHUJ
Maya language and ethnic group.

CHUL
[Mayan] Flute or shawm.

CHULTUN
[Yucatec Mayan] Underground receptacle to catch rainwater. It was partially carved in the rock to give it a bell or bottle-shaped form and it held several tens of thousands of liters.

CIB
[Yucatec Mayan] Wax, candle, copal. Sixteenth of the twenty Maya day names of the *tzolkin*.

CINNABAR
Mercury oxide or mercuric sulfite, both of a brilliant red color. A mineral widely used in Maya funerary contexts on corpses, precious objects, and vessels.

CIRICOTE
[In Yucatec Mayan, *kopte*] Tree (*Cordia dodecandra*) native to America with edible fruit, and wood used for furniture and beams.

CIZIN
[Yucatec Mayan and Lacandón, also *quizin* or *kizin*] Death, although among today's Maya it means devil. It seems that it was a deity of the underworld that the Spaniards considered the devil.

COA
[Nahuatl] Planting stick.

COCO KABA
[Mayan, also *koko kaba*] Nickname, alias, humorous name.

COCOM
Dynasty that ruled Mayapán (c. 963–1471) and exercised political control over a large part of the Yucatán peninsula. The Xius finally defeated them.

CODEX
[from the Latin *codex*] Ancient manuscript. There exist pre-Hispanic manuscripts on leather or treated bark, as well as Colonial ones on paper or cloth of European origin.

CODZ POP
[Mayan, also *Codz Poop*] Literally, "rolled straw mat"; name of an important building at Kabah, Yucatán.

COHUNE
See *mop*.

COJOLITE
[From the Nahuatl *coxolitli*, also *cojolita*; in Yucatec Mayan, *kox*] Black bird (*Penelope purpuracens*) that resembles a pheasant.

COL
Tangle, bend, something twisted. Possibly derived from the Nahuatl word *colli*, which means grandfather.

COLOMCHE
[Yucatec Mayan, also *colomche'*] Dance of the reeds.

COPAL
[from the Nahuatl *copalli*; in Yucatec Mayan, *pom*] Incense extracted from a resinous shrub (*Protium copal*).

COSTUMBRE
Literally "custom," this is the word that different contemporary Maya groups use to refer to the complex of traditions inherited from their ancestors.

COTÓN
[Mopán] Garment with sleeves, made of wool or cotton, characteristic of the Maya groups of the highlands.

COUOH
[Mayan] A black, poisonous spider (*Euripelma sp.*)

CRUZOOB
[From the Spanish *cruz*, combined with the Mayan plural suffix, *oob*] "Those of the Cross." Refers to Maya indigenous groups who fought in the so-called Caste War. They said they received instructions from sacred crosses that talked to them.

CUCH
[Mayan] Weight, it also refers to the weight of the obligation of occupying a public office. Government.

CUCHTEEL
[Yucatec Mayan, also *cuuchteel*] Neighborhood. Subjects. People or family under one's responsibility.

CUM
[Mayan, also *c'um*] Squash, calabash, or gourd (*Cucurbita sp.*)

CUMKU OR CUMHU
[Mayan] See *kumku*.

CUPUL
[Mayan] Possibly derived from a variety of *kup*, or jícama (*Calopogonium coeruleum*), consumed in times of food shortage. Ruler of the Chichén Itzá region in the sixteenth century, belonging to the dynasty of the same name.

CUUCHCABAL
[Yucatec Mayan, also *cuchcabal*] Maya political, territorial entity. The Spaniards translated it as "province."

D

DZUL
[Yucatec Mayan] Man with white skin. Name applied, by extension, to Europeans and other foreigners.

E

ECCENTRIC
Flint or obsidian objects, possibly used in ceremonies as they have been frequently found in funerary offerings. Called eccentrics for their unusual and complex shape.

EHECATL
[Nahuatl] Wind god of Nahuatl mythology.

EMBLEM GLYPH
Maya glyphs representing an important political entity.

ENAGUA
Long, female garb worn underneath or instead of skirts.

ENCOMIENDA
Spanish colonial institution dedicated to the extraction of tributes and native labor. In Yucatán it remained in force until the end of the eighteenth century.

EPIGRAPHY
The study and decipherment of ancient inscriptions.

ESGRAFIADO
Ceramic decorative technique of fine incisions on the surface finish.

ESUQ
[Mayan] Among the highland Maya, the name of the skirt worn under a blouse.

ETZNAB
[Yucatec Mayan, also *etz'nab* or *edznab*] One of the twenty Maya day names of the *tzolkin*.

EX
[Yucatec Mayan] Loincloth.

F

FALSE ARCH
[Also called the Maya arch or Maya vault] Unlike the true arch, the Maya arch was made so that weight was transferred to the sustaining walls. This method does not permit the roofing of large spaces, but it facilitates the conservation of the structure.

FANEGA
[also *hanega*] Colonial period measurement. Used measure surfaces, it is the equivalent of 6600 square meters; used to measures volume it is 22.5–55.5 liters, depending on the region, the product, and the period.

FINE ORANGE CERAMICS
Archaeological term first coined in English. Receptacles of fired clay, the presence of which serves as a diagnostic to determine a context of the Terminal Classic period. Originally from the northeast of Tabasco, this ware did not contain temper. One of its tactile characteristics is its gesso-like surface.

FLINT
A variety of quartz of great hardness with which different implements were manufactured.

G

GLYPH
Figure, character, or hieroglyph in Maya writing.

GOURD
[In Yucatec Mayan, chu] A certain fruit, usually *Lagenaria siceraria*. Also, its rind, emptied and dried, used as a receptacle to carry liquids.

GRAFFITO
[Italian, in plural, *graffiti*] Motif scratched into a finish (stucco, ceramic, stone, etc.). Its execution is after the conclusion of the work and not part of the original plan.

H

HA
[Yucatec Mayan; also *haa'*, *ja*, or *a'*] Water.

HAAB
[Mayan, also *ha'ab*] The Maya nineteen-month solar calendar. Eighteen of the months had twenty days and one additional month had only five days to add up to a total of 365 days.

HACIENDA
Large, landed estate or group of lands for economic exploitation in the eighteenth century.

HALACH UINIC
[Mayan] Literally, "true man." Great lord or ruler of a powerful political entity.

HAMMOCK
Wide strip of net that is hung by the ends and is used as a bed or swing. It was introduced to the Yucatán peninsula from the Antilles.

HANAL PIXAN
[Yucatec Mayan] Literally, "food of the souls." It refers to the offering of food prepared for the spirits of the dead.

HEADDRESS
See *penacho*.

HENEQUEN
[In Yucatec Mayan, *ki*] Agave (*Agave* sp.), the resistent fiber of which is used to make cords, ropes, and other products.

HERO TWINS
Epic figures from the *Popol Vuh*: Hunahpu and Xbalanque. They are also called the Divine Twins. They are represented on some polychrome vessels.

HETZMEK
[Yucatec Mayan] Ceremony in which a child is placed astride at the mother's waist for the first time, after naming the godfather. In the course of this rite, tiny utensils are placed in the child's hands to prefigure future work tasks.

HIATUS
[Latin] Literally, "a gap" or void, referring to a period in Maya history (approximately A.D. 534–593) in which recorded events and erected monuments ceased in many cities. It possibly had some relationship with the fall of the great city of Teotihuacán.

HOLCAN
[Mayan] Warrior.

HOLCAN OKOT
[Yucatec Mayan] Dance of the warriors.

HOTUN
[Yucatec Mayan] Maya period of five years.

HUEHUETL
[Nahuatl; *pax* in Yucatec Mayan]. Percussion instrument made from a hollowed-out trunk, leaving a thin wall to be struck with sticks or drumsticks.

HUIPIL
[Nahuatl; also *hipil*. In Yucatec Mayan, *kub*] Embroidered upper garment Mesoamerican indigenous item of clothing equivalent to the dress.

HUITZ
See *uits*.

HULCHE
[Yucatec Mayan] See *atlatl*.

HUN
[Mayan] Word referring to the numeral one.

HUN CHUEN
[Quiché] Half-brother of Hero Twins in the *Popol Vuh*.

HUNAHPÚ
[Also Junajpú] One of the Hero Twins.

HUNAL
[Mayan] Headdress or headband for the hair.

HUUN
[Mayan, also *hu'un*] See *amate*.

I

ICATZ
[Mayan] Tied bundle. In its glyphic representation this sometimes has a sacred significance; in others, it refers to merchants.

ICHCAHUIPIL
[Nahuatl] Shirt cushioned with cotton for warfare.

IK
[Yucatec Mayan, also *ik'*] Breath of life. Glyph that represents the wind, its form resembling that of the letter T. Symbol of virility, breath of the wind that animates the flame of creation. It is also the name of the second day.

INITIAL SERIES
Group of five calendrical elements that indicate a date written in the Long Count.

INTENDENCIA
Territorial division in New Spain that allowed for control of internal administration.

ITSAT
[Mayan, also *its'at*] Artist.

ITZ OR ITS
[Mayan] Witch.

ITZÁ
Literally, "water witch." Refers to the lineage of different groups that burst into the northern Yucatán peninsula beginning in the tenth century and caused major repercussions in the region, exercising political control at different locations. The Itzá lineage is spoken of at Chichén Itzá and at several regions of the peninsula and Guatemalan Petén. Also in northern Belize, where they were called the *tsul uinicoob* until the sixteenth century. Surname.

IXBALANQUÉ
See Xbalanqué.

IXIK
[Mayan, also *ix ik 'al*] Important Lady, honored woman.

IXIL
Ethnic and language group assigned to the Mam group. Its speakers inhabit northwest Guatemala.

IXIMCHÉ
[Mayan, also Ixi'mche'] Capital of the Cakchiquels. Plant (*Casearia nitisa*) used for fodder; also a shrub (*Citharexylom schotii*).

J

JA
[Mayan] See *ha*.

JACALTEC
Language ascribed by some linguists to the Kanjobalan branch. Although the majority of its inhabitants live in Guatemala, they are also in Chiapas.

JADEITE
Generic term applied to different minerals of great hardness and tonalities of green (nephrite, jadeite, chloromelanite, etc.). Jade had great economic and symbolic value in the ancient world, and was widely used in jewelry.

JAGUAR
See *balam*.

JUNAJPÚ
See Hunahpú.

K

KABAL
[Yucatec Mayan, also *k'abal*] Lathe, wooden disk used by potters to spin pieces being made.

KAHAL
[Mayan] See *sahal*.

KALOMTE
[Mayan, also *Kalomte'*] Noble or governmental title.

KAN
[Yucatec Mayan. Also *can*] Serpent. Name of the fourth day. Number four. Surname.

KANJOBAL
Maya ethnic group and language from the Guatemalan highlands.

KANKIN
[Mayan, also *cankin*] Month of the Maya calendar *haab*.

KATUN
[Mayan, also *k'atun*] Long Count cycle of twenty years of 360 days.

KAUIL
[Yucatec Mayan, also *k'auil* or

k'awil] Surname. Food. A type of black bird (*Megaquiscalus major macrourus*).

KAYAB
[Mayan] Month of the Maya calendar *haab*.

KEEHEL UAH
[Yucatec Mayan] See *tamal*.

KEKCHÍ
[Also Quekchí or Kekché] Language of the Quichean group.

KIZIN
See *cizin*.

KIKCHE
[Yucatec Mayan] See rubber tree.

KIN
[Yucatec Mayan, also *k'in*] Sun. To reign. Feast day. Day of the *tzolkin*.

KITAM
[Yucatec Mayan, also *k'itam*] Collared peccary or wild pig. In the Yucatán peninsula there are three species (*Pecari sp.*). Also means "bad odor."

KOX
[Yucatec Mayan] See *cojolite*.

KUB
[Mayan, also *k'ub*] See *huipil*.

KUCH
[Yucatec Mayan, also *k'uch* or *chom*] See turkey buzzard.

KUCHE
[Mayan, also *k'uche'*] Tropical cedar (*Cedrella mexicana*).

KUK
[Yucatec Mayan, also *k'uk'*] Quetzal. Sprout. Descendence. Plant angle. Surname.

KUL AHAU
[Mayan, also *K'ul Ahau*] "Sacred Lord," referring to the ruler who has taken possession.

KUMKU
[Mayan, also *cumku* or *kumk'u*] Pottery kiln. Eighteenth and final month of the Maya calendar.

KUTS
[Mayan, also *k'uts'*] Tobacco.

KUTZ
[Mayan] Wild turkey (*Agriocharis ocellata*).

KUUM
[Yucatec Mayan, also *k'u'um*; in Nahuatl, *nixtamatl*] Corn softened in water with lime to grind it afterwards.

L

LACANDÓN
Almost-extinct Maya ethnic group and language. The Lacandons inhabit the mountains of the upper courses of the Usumacinta river in the state of Chiapas, Mexico.

LAHUNTUN
[Yucatec Mayan] Period of ten years.

LEC
[Yucatec Mayan, also *lek*] Gourd, emptied and dried, (*Crescentia cujete*) that serves to store tortillas, fruit, seeds, and other objects.

LEYES DE INDIAS
Corpus of laws issued by the Spanish crown to govern their American colonies.

LINTEL
Upper or horizontal closing beam of doors and windows.

LOINCLOTH
[In Nahuatl, *maxtlatl*; in Yucatec Mayan, *ex*] Male garb consisting of a strip of cloth tied to cover the genitals.

LONG COUNT
Maya calendrical system in which dates do not repeat.

M

MAAXOOB
[Yucatec Mayan] Spider monkeys (*Ateles sp.*). Equivalent to the *ozomatli* of the Aztecs.

MAC
[Mayan, also *mak*] Month of the Maya civil calendar.

MACAW
A bird larger than a parrot with a long tail and vividly colorful plumage. The predominantly green macaw is *Ara militaris*, while the predominantly red one is *Ara macao*.

MALACATE
[From Nahuatl *malacatl*] Small piece of stone or ceramic that serves as a support for the spindle or stick when it is spun or twisted to make thread.

MAM
Ethnic group and language of the Mame group, which lives in the Guatemala highlands and in the Sierra Madre of Chiapas.

MAMEY
Tree (*Mammea americana* or *Pouteria sapota*). Its fruit, of the same name, has a hard rind and a sweet, reddish pulp. It can weigh up to 1 kg.

MANIKIN SCEPTER
[In Mayan, *Canhel, Bolom Dzacab*, or *Bolom Dz'acab*, "perpetual thing"] Insignia of political power, the equivalent to the scepter or staff of authority.

MANO
See *metate*.

MAT
See *petate*.

MAXTLATL
[Nahuatl] See loincloth.

MAYA
Ethnic group and language of the Maya group; the term is used to apply such peoples of Mexico, Guatemala, and Belize.

MAYA VAULT
See false arch.

MAYACIMIL
[Mayan] From *Cimi*, god of death. Epidemic, the "easy death," pestilence, mortality.

MAYANCE
Related to or belonging to the complex of ethnic groups of Maya origin.

MAYUT
[Pocomam] Wooden framework adorned with feathers that was worn on the back.

MECAPAL
[From Nahuatl *mecapalli*] Leashes or ropes that are held across the forehead to support a very heavy weight on the back.

MEMBRANES
Vibratile covers for drums, made of leather.

METATE
[From Nahuatl *metatl*] Wide, flat grinding stone with or without supports. It is complemented by a *mano*, a long, cylindrical piece of stone with which grain or fruit was ground.

MILPA
[Nahuatl] Land where maize and sometimes other plants are cultivated. Cornfield.

MIXTEC
[Nahuatl] Ethnic group and language mainly of the state of Oaxaca, Mexico.

MOAN
[Mayan, also *muan*] Mythical bird. Surname.
Mochó - See Motozintleco.

MOL
[Mayan] Month of the Maya calendar *haab*.

MONOCHROME CERAMICS
Receptacles of fired clay displaying only one color.

MOP
[Yucatec Mayan] Corozo palm (*Attalea cohune*). The combination of two words, *cohune* and "ridge," evolved to give rise to the name Kohunlich.

MOPÁN
Maya language and ethnic group of Belize and Guatemala.

MOTOZINTLECO
OR MOTOCINTLECO
[Also Mochó] Ethnic and language group of Maya affiliation, close to Mam, restricted to a neighborhood in Motozintla, Chiapas.

MUAN
[Mayan, also *moan*] Fifteenth month of the Maya calendar.

MULTEPAL
[Mayan] A coalition government or one with several political heads.

N

NA
[Yucatec Mayan] House or temple. Surname.

NA'
[Yucatec Mayan] Mother.

NAAL KABA
[Mayan] Maternal surname, maternal lineage.

NAB
[Yucatec Mayan] Water lily (*Nynphacea ampla*). References to *nab* may be related to the sea, lakes, or other bodies of water. Associated with the jaguar and with the underworld.

NAHUAL
[Nahuatl] See *uay*.

NAHUA
Great family of ethnic groups or people who inhabit northern Mexico and El Salvador.

NAHUATL
[Also Nahua] Linguistic variant of the family of Nahua ethnic groups.

NICTE
[Yucatec Mayan] Flower name frequent for frangipani or *Plumeria spp.*

NOCH
[Yucatec Mayan] Gourd or dried calabash, used as a receptacle.

O

OBSIDIAN
Black, gray, or greenish volcanic glass with which cutting implements were made in pre-Hispanic times.

OCARINA
Musical wind instrument, generally made of clay.

OCNA
[Yucatec Mayan] Great annual festival in honor of the rain gods.

OKOFAISÁN
[Mexicanism *kambul* in Yucatec Mayan] Species of pheasant (*Crax rubra*) common in the Yucatán peninsula.

OKOT
[Yucatec Mayan] Dance.

OLMEC
Culture that developed several centuries before the Common Era, in the region today occupied by the Mexican states of Tabasco and southern Veracruz. It had great influence in the origins of Maya and Zapotec (Oaxaca) culture; in fact, it is known as the Mother Culture.

OLOTE
[From Nahuatl *olotl*; in Yucatec Mayan, *bacal*] Corn cob.

OPOSSUM
See *tlacuache*.

P

PAAL KABA
[Yucatec Mayan] The part of a child's name that precedes the family name.

PACUM CHAC
[Yucatec Mayan] Festival of warriors in honor of the god Cit Chac Coh, held in the month of *pax*.

PAHUATUN
[Yucatec Mayan; also *pawatun*, *pahuahtun*, or *pauahtun*] Deities of the winds that inhabit each one of the cardinal directions and that correspond to different colors.

PALM or *PALMITO*
Plant common in Spain, used to make brooms and mats. The stalk is edible.

PALMA
Accessory that formed part of the accoutrements of the ball player. It was worn in front of the body, inserted into the yoke. These have been represented in stone, richly carved with decorations.
Also a broom.

PATI
[Yucatec Mayan, also *patí*] Narrow, rough cotton cloths, measuring two *varas* and a half in length, with which tribute was paid. The textile *vara* was the equivalent of 0.826 meters.

PAX
[Yucatec Mayan] See *huehuetl*. Also, month in Maya calendar *haab*.

PECH
[Yucatec Mayan] Surname. Also, a tick or chigger.

PENACHO
A kind of headdress. Headgear made of feathers of different birds that was used by rulers, priests, and other important functionaries in ancient Mesoamerican cultures.

PENTACOOB
[Yucatec Mayan, also *p'entacoob* or *ppentacoob*] Male slaves.

PETATE
[From Nahuatl *petatl*; in Yucatec Mayan, *pop*] Mat woven in palm, which among the Mayas was a symbol of political power, since it represented the community or the group of people in a jurisdiction and the lord himself that presided over them.

PETÉN
Geographic region covering the south of the Yucatán peninsula and northern Guatemala, where it still names a Department or State. Name given to the first Maya architectural style. Literally, it means "island," and today, in the peninsular coast, it designates a place with fresh water and trees.

PIB
[Yucatec Mayan] Technique of food preparation consisting of cooking food underground.

PIK
[Yucatec Mayan] Long side-skirt worn under the blouse. Large, flying bedbug that transmits the disease known as *Chagas*. The number 8000.

PIPIL
[From Nahuatl *pipilotl*] Groups of Nahuatl-speakers who emigrated to Central America.

PIOCHA
[Mexicanism] Beard cut to a point.

PIXOM
[Mayance] Wrapped headdress.

PLUMBATE CERAMICS
Receptacles made of clay fired for a long time at a high temperature, which display a notably lustrous, almost metallic surface, in gray, olive green, and orange colors. They are diagnostic of the Early Postclassic period, when they were widely distributed, although they originate on the Pacific Coast.

POCOMAM
[Also Pocomán] Maya ethnic group and language from eastern Guatemala.

POCOMCHÍ
[Also Pocomché] Mayan language from the Guatemala highlands.

POLOM
[Yucatec Mayan, also *p'olom or ah p'olom*] Professional merchant or trader.

POLYCHROME CERAMICS
Receptacles made of fired clay, displaying several colors of decoration.

POM
[Mayan] See *copal*.

POP
[Mayan, also *poop*] See *petate*. Month in the Maya calendar *haab*.

POPOL NA
[Yucatec Mayan] "House of Mats," that is, House of Council or of the coalition government.

POPOL VUH
[Quiché] Book written around 1557 in the Quiché language, but using the Latin alphabet and some Biblical references that have been "Mayanized." Its three parts refer to the creation and origins of man, the adventures of the Hero Twins, and news on the origins of native peoples of Guatemala. It literally means "Book of the Community" or of Council.

POZOL
[From Nahuatl *pozolli*, in Yucatec Mayan, *keyem*] Beverage made of cooked corn mixed with water.

PRIMARY STANDARD SEQUENCE (PSS)
Hieroglyphic inscription on some polychrome vessels that contain information on the type of piece, its function, owner, and sometimes the artist who made it.

PROVINCIA
Geographic and political space of different extent depending on the strength of the political entity to which it pertained. Historical sources refer to several types of indigenous "provincias" in the sixteenth century.

PUK AK
[Yucatec Mayan, also *p'uk ak*] Resin to burn.

PUTUN
[Yucatec Mayan] See Chontal.

P'UTUN
[Yucatec Mayan] Chili. Small, dwarf.

PUUC
[Yucatec Mayan] Literally "mountain range." Southwestern region of Yucatán and northeastern Campeche characterized by natural elevations rarely taller than 100 meters.

Architectural style present in this region, which is characterized by its geometric ornamentation.

PYRITE
Iron sulphur, shiny and hard enough to be used as a flint. Polished, it was used as a mirror.

Q

QUECHQUEMITL
[Nahuatl] Triangular garment that covers the female torso.

QUETZAL
[From Nahuatl *quetzalli*] Bird from Central American jungles, with iridescent-green and scarlet-red feathers, highly prized for the creation of fine garments and headdresses.

QUICHÉ
[also Kiché] Ethnic group and language of the Maya family from the highlands of Guatemala.

QUINCUNX
Distinctive hieroglyph of the planet Venus.

R

RABINAL ACHÍ
Maya theatrical and dance presentation from Guatemala that narrates the capture and sacrifice of a Quiché warrior.

REPARTIMIENTO
Spanish colonial institution by means of which the natives were economically exploited through the forced contribution of labor or by the forced acquisition of European goods.

REPOUSSÉ
Metallurgical technique resulting in high-relief motifs made by hammering.

REPÚBLICA DE INDIOS
During the colonial period, the jurisdiction ruled by native *caciques*, or chiefs, *corregidores*, and protectors of Indians, generally subjects of the *encomienda*.

RÍO BEC
Archaeological region and architectural style characterized by the use of tall towers with false stairways and crowned by simulated temples. It has been reported mainly in southeast Campeche and southern Quintana Roo.

ROOFCOMB
Decoration on top of a temple or important building, consisting of a solid or openwork wall to which figures, symbols, and hieroglyphs are added in painted stucco.

RUBBER TREE
[in Yucatec Mayan, *kikche*] Tree (*Castilla elastica*) from which the resin, latex, which was used to make balls for the ball game, is extracted. Its Mayan name means "blood tree" because of the red color of its resin. It was also burned as an offering.

S

SABACIL THAN
[Yucatec Mayan] Festivities conducted in small towns during the last three months of the solar year to request prosperity from the gods. They were sponsored by well-to-do people.

SACA
[Yucatec Mayan, also *sacab* or *zaca'*] Refreshing maize drink made of cooked maize without lime, which is ground and then dissolved in cold water. It is consumed in several ceremonies and occasionally outside of this context.

SACAN
[Yucatec Mayan] Maize dough. Poorly cooked bread.

SACBE
[Yucatec Mayan, in plural *sacbeoob*] Literally, "white path," a white stone causeway, built by hand. The Milky Way was also called by this name, and was perhaps considered a road to the underworld.

SACRIFICIAL WELL
One name for the sacred cenote of Chichén Itzá. See *cenote*.

SAHAL
[Mayan, also *cahal* or *kahal*] Title for a minor ruler, similar to a *batab*.

SAHCAB
[Yucatec Mayan, also *sascab* or *zaccab*] Limestone gravel or cement that is used for construction. It is the equiva-

lent of sand. Sometimes it refers to sand containing ground shell.

SANDSTONE
Variety of soft stone formed by marine sedimentation.

SASCABERA
[From Yucatec Mayan] Quarry where *sahcab* is extracted.

SASTUN
[Yucatec Mayan] Literally "transparent land." Sacred stone with which Maya shamans predict the future and diagnose the etiology of illnesses.

SCARIFICATION
Alteration of the skin by means of incisions that, when they heal, form raised designs.

SEVEN MACAW
See Vucub Caquix.

SHAMAN
[In Yucatec Mayan ahmen] In some religions of Asia and America, a ritual specialist who communicates with the nature spirits and is a curer. The Maya name means "he who comprehends" (the cause of the illness or the cure).

SHORT COUNT
Maya calendrical system whose dates of twenty years are represented abbreviated with the corresponding number of *katun*. see *xiuhmolpilli*

SLATE
Fine-grained metamorphic rock. Slateware is a ceramic of great resistance with wide distribution in the Yucatán peninsula during the Late Classic and Early Postclassic.

SLIP
Bath of liquid clay that covers the surface of a ceramic and results in a smooth finish after firing.

SOFFIT
Slight projection that marks the beginning of the Maya vault.

SOLOMECA
Dialect or dialectical variant of the Mame group. It is spoken in Guatemala.

SOTS
[Yucatec Mayan] See *zotz*.

SPONDYLUS SP.
[Latin] Scientific name of a genus of marine mollusk, the valves of which were used in the manufacture of ornaments and offerings. They were highly prized for their red color. Small pieces were used as currency.

STANDARD BEARER
Anthropomorphic or zoomorphic figure in stone intended to hold the pole of a banner.

STELA
Rectangular monolith with figures and hieroglyphs in relief on one or several of the sides. There were also plain stelae; their information was painted and it has been lost.

STEPPED FRET
[In Nahuatl, *xicacoliuhqui,* "twisted gourd"] Symbolic motif commonly used on objects and architecture in ancient Mesoamerica.

STUCCO
Mixture of lime, *sahcab,* and water, with a consistency and hardness similar to that of gesso. It was widely used for surfacing masonry and decorating the facade of Pre-Columbian buildings.

SUBSTRUCTURE
Construction covered by a later building.

T
TAH KIN
[Yucatec Mayan] Expression meaning "excrement of the Sun," referring to gold. Today it is used to allude to money.

TAMAL
[From Nahuatl *tamalli;* in Yucatec Mayan, *keehel uah*] Corn dough wrapped in a leaf and steamed. It can contain meat or other ingredients.

TAPIR
Mammal (*Tapirus bairdi*), also called *anteburro* or *danta,* with a long snout like a trunk, that inhabits swampy regions. Today, Maya speakers use its name, *tzimin,* for horses, due to their resemblance to the tapir.

TE
[Highland Mayan] See *che.*

TECOMATE
[From Nahuatl *tecomatl*] Receptacle, bowl. Jar without a neck.

TEMAZCAL
[Also *temascal,* from Nahuatl *temazcalli.* In some Mayan languages, it is called *puz,* in others, *ika*] Sweatbath to purify the body before moking an offering or participating in a ceremony. This type of bath is still used in Mexico for cosmetic or medicinal purposes, and for sexual activities.

TEMPER
Material added to clay to increase its flexibility.

TILMA
[From Nahuatl *tilmatli*] Cotton cloth used as a tunic by the natives of Central Mexico. Among the Mayas, there were several types of cotton capes, including the *zoyem* and the *kubul.*

TLACUACHE
[From Nahuatl *tlacuatl;* in Yucatec Mayan, *och*] Small American marsupial, also known as the opossum (*Oposum virginianus*).

TOJOLABAL
Maya ethnic group and language of the Chuj group, from Chiapas, Mexico.

TOLTEC
[Nahuatl] Cultivated, civilized person or craftsman. Name given to the inhabitant of the city Tollan. The indiscriminate use of the term and its extension to ethnic groups has led to serious confusion.

TORTILLA
[*Uah* in Yucatec Mayan; *tlaxcalli* in Nahuatl] Portion of cooked maize, made into a flat, circular bread. Basic in the Mexican diet and cooking, it is an inheritance from the cultures of Mesoamerica.

TSOTS
[Yucatec Mayan] Hair. Surname.

TSUN
[Yucatec Mayan] Thin, lean, gaunt.

TURKEY BUZZARD
[*zopilote* in Spanish from the Nahuatl *zopilotl;* in Yucatec

Mayan *chom* or *kuch*] Large bird of prey (*Coragyps atratus*) with black plumage.

TUN
[Yucatec Mayan] Period of one year.
Surname.
Also, stone.

TUNKULUCHU
[Yucatec Mayan] Owl.

TUP
[Yucatec Mayan] Earflare.

TUTUL XIU
[Mayan] According to some historical sources, the founding group of several cities including Uxmal and Maní, both in Yucatán.

TUZANTEC
Group with affinity to the Mames who inhabit Tuzantán, Chiapas.

TZEC
[Yucatec Mayan, also *zec*] Skull. Stony ground. Fifth month of the Maya calendar *haab.*

TZELTAL
Maya language and ethnic group of the Chiapan highlands.

TZIMIN
[Mayan] See tapir.

TZOLKIN
[Mayan] Sacred year of 260 days that was not divided into months; it was a succession of days that was formed by adding the numbers 1 to 13 to twenty different hieroglyphs. Literally, it meant "the count of the days."

TZOMPANTLI
[Nahuatl] Literally "skull wall." Wooden structure on which skulls of sacrificial victims were placed in horizontal rows. There are representations of this in masonry with sculpted skulls or skulls in relief.

TZOTZIL
Maya language and ethnic group of the highlands of Chiapas.

TZUTUHIL
Maya language of the Quiché group that is spoken in Guatemala.

U
U KAHLAY KATUNOOB
[Yucatec Mayan] Literally "the song of the katuns."

U LEE HAAS
[Yucatec Mayan] Banana leaf. This plant (*Musa sp.*) was introduced to America during the colonial period. Originally the word *haas* designated the red mamey (*Pouteria sapota*).

UAH
[Yucatec Mayan, in Nahuatl, *tlaxcalli*] Corn *tortilla.*

UAY
[Mayan; *nahual* in Nahuatl] Animal protector of an individual. The term also refers to witches who can change form, adopting that of his or her animal protector. In the beginning the word referred also to a certain type of dream or vision "with a message."

UAYEB
[Yucatec Mayan] Month of the Maya calendar *haab.*

UH
[Mayan] Necklace. Moon.

UINAL
[Mayan] Period of twenty days.

UINIC
[Yucatec Mayan] Man.

UITS
[Mayan; also *wits* or *huitz*] Sacred mountain; by extension, a pyramidal base. The hilly zone to the south of the Puuc hills is also called *Uits.*

UL
[Yucatec Mayan] See *atole.*

UNDERWORLD
Key concept in Mesoamerican cosmology. For the Mayas, the underworld was the destination for everyone after death; in some Maya cosmovisions, it is the place of definitive residence. It could be reached by way of caves, and was related to subterranean waters. Apparently, during the colonial period, priests portrayed it as hell, giving it a connotation as a frightening place.

UO
[Yucatec Mayan] Certain species of frog. Second month of the Maya calendar.

URN
Receptacle of different shapes to contain relics, ashes, or prized objects.

USPANTEC
Language and ethnic group of the Quiché group, spoken in Guatemala.

V

VUCUB CAQUIX
[Quiché, also Vucup Caquix] False sun at the beginning of creation, according to the *Popol Vuh*. He is also known as Seven Macaw.

W

WAH
See *uah*.

WITS
See *uits*.

X

XAMACH
[Yucatec Mayan; in Nahua, *comalli*] Large ceramic plate used to cook tortillas or bread on the coals. Also known as a *comal*.

XANAB
[Yucatec Mayan] Sandals, shoes. See *cactli*.

XBALANQUÉ
[Quiché, also Ixbalanqué] One of the Hero Twins of the *Popol Vuh*.

XIBALBA
[Quiché Mayan] The underworld; it means "the place of fear." It was a place of transition or permanent residence after death.

XICOLLI
[Nahuatl] Sleeveless tunic generally used by warriors.

XIU
[Chontal Mayan] A lineage that struggled for hegemony with the Cocom. Surname. Herb or grass in general.

XIUHMOLPILLI
[Nahuatl] Calendar wheel.

XMA KABA KIN
[Yucatec Mayan] Unnamed days.

XMUCANÉ
[Quiché; also recorded as Ix- mucané] Grandmother of the divine twins, according to the *Popol Vuh*.

XPIYACOC
[Quiché; also recorded as Ix- piyacoc] Grandfather of the divine twins, according to the *Popol Vuh*.

XUL
[Yucatec Mayan] Planting stick. End. Month of the Maya calendar *haab*.

Y

YAAXCHE
[Mayan] See ceiba.

YATAN
[Yucatec Mayan, also *yatanbil*] Wife of...

YAX
[Yucatec Mayan] Month in Maya civil calendar. Center. Green. The first.

YAX BALAM
[Also Yex Balam] Character in the *Popol Vuh*.

YAXCHEEL CAB
[Yucatec Mayan] First tree in the world, associated with a giant ceiba.

YAXKIN
[Yucatec Mayan] Month in the Maya calendar.

YOKE
Piece in the shape of a U, which was worn around the waist and formed part of the attire of ball players. It was used to protect the central part of the body from the impact of the ball. There are representations of yokes in carved stone, although it is believed that the original pieces were made of wood.

Z

ZAC
[Yucatec Mayan] Month in the Maya calendar *haab*. White.

ZACCAB
[Mayan] See *sahcab*.

ZACAN
[Mayan] Ground corn.

ZAC POL
[Yucatec Mayan] Literally, "white head." Carnivorous mammal also known as the *tayra or cabeza de viejo* (*Eira barbara*). It gets this name from an architectural group on the island of Jaina.

ZAPOTE
[From Nahuatl] Leafy tree bearing a round, sweet fruit of the same name.

ZEC
[Yucatec Mayan] See *tzec*.

ZIP
[Yucatec Mayan] Month of the Maya calendar.

ZOQUE
Western neighbors of the Mayas of Tabasco and Chiapas. There are discrepancies among linguists; while some say the Zoque are linguistically unrelated to the Mayas, others affirm that there is a Proto-Maya-Zoquean group.

ZOTZ
[Yucatec Mayan, also *zot'z*, *zodz*, or *sots*] Bat. Fourth month of the Maya calendar.

Maya Gods

by Liwy del Carmen
Grazioso Serra

GOD A

Ah Puch "Fleshless One," Cizin (Kisin-Cisin) "Stinking One," "Flatulent One" (in contemporary Yucatec Maya) or Yum Cimil "Lord of Death" is the deity of death, associated with night time and disease. He is the patron of the day Cimi and of the number 10.

GOD B

Chaac is the god of rain and water. He is related to the serpent. Quadruple deity of the Mayas that is associated with the colors of the four directions (Chac Xib Chac-red-east, Sac Xib Chac-white-north, Ek Xib Chac-black-west and Kan Xib Chac-yellow-south). He is the patron of the number 13 and of the day Ik.

GOD C

Deity of celestial character associated with the day Chuen and with the monkey. He is related with the pole star and with the constellation of Ursa Minor. He is also called Ah Chicum Ek, "Guiding Star."

GODS CH (**Is something missing here??? I've never heard of Gods Ch...)

On their faces they have jaguar pelt spots and a glyph very similar to that of the day Chicchan.

GOD D

Itzamna, god of the sky. His zoomorphic representation is the dragon. He goes by different names, Chicchan "Biting Serpent," Itzam Cab Ain "Terrestrial Crocodile Dragon," Chac Mumul Ain "Great Muddy Crocodile" and Canhel "Dragon" as the vital principle of the sky; he may be represented as a bicephalic dragon, a serpent-bird, and as a winged, feathered serpent. (He is related to the solar god.)

GOD E

In colonial sources, there is no agreement on his name. He is considered the maize deity, patron of the number 8 and his glyph is that of the day Kan, corn. Authors have given him different names Yum Kaax "Lord of the Harvest," Ah Uax-ac Yol Kawil and Itzamna Kawil "The Eight Heart of Abundance of Our Sustenance," Ah Mun "Not Ripe Corn," Sac Uan Nal "New White Kernal that Opens" and Bolon Mayel.

GOD F

Buluc Chabtan, his image appears related to human sacrifice and death by violence. He seems to be the patron of the day Manik.

GOD G

Kinich Ahau, solar god, in the Yucatán he is called Kin "Sun-day-time," Ah Kinchil "With Sun Face" and Kinich Ahau "Lord Solar Eye." (He is a manifestation of Itzamna.) He is related to several animals, such as the jaguar (Dead Sun in the Underworld), the deer and the hummingbird (the Sun's sexual energy) and the eagle (warrior character of the Sun); his epiphany is as the macaw (Kinich Kukmo). He is the patron of the number 4 and of the day Muluc, he has the Kin glyph on his head.

GOD H

Young male who has a glyph on his face like an inverted ahau surrounded by circles. He may have serpent skin markings.

GODDESSES I AND O

They are closely linked and may be different aspects of the same deity. Both are feminine representations, Goddess I is a young woman and Goddess O is old. Goddess I, Ixchel "She of White Skin" is the mother goddess associated with the moon, medicine, childbirth and labors characteristic of women. She has been related to the new moon.

Goddess O, Ixchebel Yax, who also may be called Ixchel, is the companion of God D, as well as patroness of weaving and painting. She has been related with the full moon and with the spider. As a young goddess, she represents medicine and childbirth and as an old goddess, earth, divination, weaving and vegetation.

GOD K

Bolon Dz'acab "Nine Generations" is a manifestation of the celestial dragon. He is closely related to ruling lineages, he is the god of the manikan scepter. He has also been called Kawil "second maize harvest." Because of his serpentine leg, he is linked with Huracán "One-Legged Thunderbolt" and with lightning.

GOD L

He is an old man, generally carrying a staff, jaguar skin and he may be smoking. It has been said that he is the "Old God," "God of Fire" but in reality he is a shaman.

GOD M

Ek Chuah "Black Scorpion," has been identified as the god of merchants. He is the patron of cacao.

GOD N

He is almost always represented as an old man. He is associated with the underworld and as Pauahtun, quadripartite bearer of the world and upholder of the sky.

GOD P

He wears the Tun glyph in his headdress and he has been associated with agriculture and frogs.

CABRACÁN (Kabraqan kab=two, ru=his and aqan=foot or leg)

His name means "He of Two Legs," according to the indigenous population of the highlands. Cabracán is who produced earthquakes by striking the earth with his feet. He is the god of earthquakes and cataclysms.

HURACÁN (Hunrakan or Juraqan, jun=one, r'aqan=his leg or foot)

His name means "He of Only One Foot," for the indigenous population of the highlands (Quichés and Cakchiquels, mainly) this deity by moving his foot with force caused strong winds and storms. God of storms, cyclones and hurricanes. He is also called Caculhá Huracán, "One Leg Thunder."

HUNAHPÚ AND XBALANQUÉ

They are the hero twins of the Popol Vuh. Xbalanqué (Ixbalanqué) means Nocturnal Jaguar, Hunahpú is a calendrical date that is the equivalent in Yucatec to One Ahau (the last day of the twenty days).

HUN HUNAHPÚ

Father of Hunahpú and Xbalanqué, his name is One One Ahau.

HUN CAMÉ "One Death" and VUCUB CAMÉ "Seven Death"

Quiché deities of death and disease.

VUCUB CAQUIX

Bird monster, fantastic being defeated by the twins of the Popol Vuh, deity of the underworld.

GUCUMATZ (Kukumatz)

Also called "Heart of the Sky," he is the Feathered Serpent.

KUKULCÁN

Quetzal Serpent or Feathered Serpent, he is also the celestial dragon.

ACOSTA, JORGE
1940
"Exploraciones en Tula, Hgo." *Revista Mexicana de Estudios Antropológicos*, no. 4, México, 172–94
1941
"Los últimos descubrimientos arqueológicos en Tula, Hgo." *Revista Mexicana de Estudios Antropológicos*, no. 5, México, 239–48
1944
"La Tercera Temporada de Exploraciones Arqueológicas en Tula, Hgo." *Revista Mexicana de Estudios Antropológicos*, no. 6, México, 125–54
1945
"Las Cuartas y Quintas Temporadas de Exploraciones Arqueológicas en Tula, Hgo.", *Revista Mexicana de Estudios Antropológicos*, no. 7, México, 23–64
1952
"Exploraciones Arqueológicas en Chichén Itzá, Yucatán 1951." *Anales del INAH*, Vol. VI, 34, México
1954
"Exploraciones Arqueológicas efectuadas en Chichén Itzá, Yucatán." *Anales del INAH*, Vol. IV, México, 39
1956
"Resumen de las Exploraciones Arqueológicas en Tula, Hgo., durante las VI, VII y VIII Temporadas, 1946–1950." *Anales del INAH*, Vol. VIII, México, 27–115
1956–57
"Interpretación de algunos de los datos obtenidos en Tula relativos a la época tolteca." *Revista Mexicana de Estudios Antropológicos*, no. 14, México, 75–110
1957
"Resumen de los Informes de las Exploraciones Arqueológicas en Tula, durante las VI, VII, VIII Temporadas, 1946–1950." *Anales del INAH*, no. 8, México, 37–115
1960
"Las Exploraciones en Tula, Hgo. durante la XI Temporada, 1955." *Anales del INAH*, no. 11, México, 39–72
1961
"La Doceava Temporada de Exploraciones en Tula, Hgo." *Anales del INAH*, no. 13, México, 29–58
1964
"La Decimotercera Temporada de Exploraciones en Tula, Hgo." *Anales del INAH*, no. 16, México, 45–76
1974
La Pirámide de El Corral en Tula, Hgo. Proyecto Tula, Part I. Colección Científica, 15. México: INAH, Departamento de Monumentos Prehispánicos, 27–49

ADAMS, RICHARD E.W.
1971
The ceramics of Altar de Sacrificios. Papers of the Peabody Museum of Archeology and Ethnology. Vol. 63, 1. Cambridge, Mass.: Harvard University

AGRINIER, PIERRE
1960
The Carved Human Femurs from Tomb 1, Chiapa de Corzo, Chiapas, México. Papers of the New World Archaeological Foundation, no. 6. Publication 5. California, Orinda
1975
Mound 1A, Chiapa de Corzo Chiapas, México. A Late Preclassic Architectural Complex. Papers of the New World Archaeological Foundation, no. 37. California, Orinda, NWAF
1975
Mounds 9 and 10 at Mirador, Chiapas, México. Papers of the New World Archaeological Foundation, no. 37. Provo, Utah: NWAF-Brigham Young University

AGUILERA, PABLO; MARIA DEL MAR DE
1991
"El arte de la piedra. Evolución y Expresión." In *Oxkintok, Una Ciudad Maya de Yucatán.* Madrid: Misión Arqueológica de España en México, Ministerio de Cultura España, fig. 4

ALCINA, JOSÉ
1979
Die Kunst des Alten Amerika. Freiburg

ÁLVAREZ, LUIS; LANDA MARÍA G.; JOSÉ L. ROMERO
1988
"Los ladrillos decorados de Comalcalco." *Antropológicas*, no. 2. México: UNAM, Instituto de Investigaciones Antropológicas, 5–12
1990
Los ladrillos de Comalcalco. México: Instituto de Cultura de Tabasco

ANDERS, FERDINAND; JANSEN M.; ET AL.
1994
Calendario de pronósticos y ofrendas, Lista explicativa del llamado Códice Cospi. Códices mexicanos VIII. Graz-México: Akademische Druck und Verlagsanstadt-Fondo de Cultura Económica

ANDREWS, E. WYLLYS V
1965
Explorations in the Gruta de Chac Yucatán México, Archaeological Investigations on The Yucatán Peninsula. Publication 31. Middle American Research Institute. New Orleans: Tulane University, 12, 16, figs. 3, 6
1970
Balankanche, Throne of the Tiger Priest. Publication 32. Middle American Research Institute. New Orleans: Tulane University

ANDREWS, E. WYLLYS V; HAMMOND, NORMAN
1990
"Redefinition of the Swasey Phase at Cuello, Belize." *American Antiquity*, Vol. 55, 3, Washington, 570–84

ANDREWS, ANTHONY P.; ROBLES CASTELLANOS, FERNANDO (ED. BY)
1986
Excavaciones arqueológicas en El Meco, Quin-

tana Roo, 1977. Colección Científica, 158. México: INAH

ARDREN TRACI; BENNETT, SHARON; FREIDEL, DAVID; JOHNSTONE, DAVID; CHARLES SHULER
1994
"Final Report of the 1993 Field Season." Typescript. Mérida, Yucatán: Archivo de la Ceramoteca del Centro INAH

ARELLANO HERNÁNDEZ, ALFONSO; ET AL.
1997
Los mayas del periodo Clásico. México: CNCA, Jaca Book

ARMIJO TORRES, RICARDO; MILLÁN RUIZ, YAZMÍN E.
in press
"Tecnología arquitectónica y uso de espacios en la Gran Acrópolis de Comalcalco." In *Memorias del Tercer Congreso Internacional de Mayistas*. México: UNAM

AYALA FALCÓN, MARICELA
1994
"The history of Toniná through its inscriptions." Ph. D. Dissertation. Austin: University of Texas Press

BALL, JOSEPH W.
1975
"Cui Orange Polychrome: A late Classic Funerary Type from Central Campeche, Mexico." In *Studies in Ancient Mesoamerica II*, no. 27, Berkeley: Archaeological Research Facility, 32–39
1975
"A regional ceramic sequence for the Rio Bec Area." In *Archaeological Investigation on the Yucatán Península*. Publication 31. New Orleans: Tulane University, Middle American Research Institute, 113–17, fig. 3
1977
The Archaeological Ceramics of Becan, Campeche, Mexico. Publication 43. Middle American Research Institute, National Geographic Society-Tulane University, Program of Research in Campeche. New Orleans: Tulane University, 67, 85
1978
Archaeological Pottery of the Yucatán Campeche Coast. Publication 46. Middle American Research Institute. New Orleans: Tulane University, 46–146

BALSER, CARLOS
1974
El jade de Costa Rica. San José: Imprenta Lehmann

BAUDEZ, CLAUDE F.; MATHEWS, PETER
1978
"Capture and sacrifice at Palenque." In *Tercera Mesa Redonda de Palenque*. Ed. by Merle Greene Robertson. Vol. IV

BECQUELIN, PIERRE; BAUDEZ, CLAUDE F.
1975

"Une cité Maya de l'âge Classique: Toniná." *Archeologie*, no. 80, Paris
1982
Toniná, une cité Maya du Chiapas. Vol. V, Tomes II-III. Paris: Mission Archéologique et Ethnologique Française au Mexique, Collection Études Mésoaméricaines, 6–3

BENAVIDES C., ANTONIO
1981
Cobá. Una ciudad prehispánica de Quintana Roo. México: Centro Regional del Sureste, INAH
1997
Edzná. Una ciudad prehispánica de Campeche. México: INAH-University of Pittsburgh

BENSON, ELISABETH P.
1967
The Maya World. New York

BEYER, FAHMEL BERND
1988
Mesoamérica Tolteca, sus cerámicas de comercio principales. México: UNAM, Instituto de Investigaciones Antropológicas

BEYER, HERMANN
1965
"Mito y simbolismo del México antiguo." In *El México Antiguo*. Vol. X. México: Sociedad Alemana Mexicanista, 197

BLOM, FRANZ
1982
Las ruinas de Palenque, Xupá y Finca Encanto. México: INAH

BLOM, FRANZ; DUBY, GERTRUDE
1957
La Selva Lacandona, Andanzas arqueológicas. Editorial Cultura T.G.

BOUCHER, SYLVIANE
1995
"El Arte de la Guerra entre los Antiguos Mayas." Thematic guide. Mérida, Yucatán: Archivo de la Ceramoteca del Centro INAH

BOUCHER, SYLVIANE; PALOMO, YOLY
1997
"Iconos de Poder de la Tumba de un Gobernante de Calakmul del Siglo Sexto." VII Encuentro de los Investigadores de la cultura Maya. Campeche
n.d.
"Vasijas Polícromas Mayas del Museo Palacio Cantón." Manuscript. Mérida, Yucatán: Archivo de la Ceramoteca del centro INAH
in press
"Informe de la cerámica de excavación en Sayil, 1987–88." Mérida, Yucatán

BRAINERD, GEORGE
1958
The Archaeological Ceramics of Yucatán. Anthropological Records. Vol. 19. Berkeley: University of California, 194, 234–35, 296–97, fig. 90b

1976
The Archaeological Ceramics of Yucatán. Anthropological Records. Vol. 19. Berkeley: University of California

BRAY, WILLIAM
1977
"Maya Metalwork and Its External Connections." In *Social Process in Maya Prehistory, Essays in Honour of Sir J. Eric S. Thompson.* Ed. by N. Hammond. New York: Academic Press, 365–403

BRUCE, ROBERTO; ROBLES, CARLOS; RAMOS CH., ENRIQUETA
1971
Los lacandones. Cosmovisión maya. México: INAH, Departamento de Investigaciones Antropológicas

BRUNHOUSE, ROBERT
1973
In Search of the Maya: The First Archaeologists. Albuquerque: University of New Mexico Press, 136–65

BRYANT, DOUGLAS D.
1980
"The Early Classic Period at Ojo de Agua, Chiapas, México." Manuscript. Archives of The New World Archaeological Foundation. Provo, Utah-San Cristóbal de las Casas: Brigham Young University

CABELLO, CARRO PAZ
1992
Política investigadora de la época de Carlos III en el área maya. Descubrimiento de Palenque y primeras excavaciones de caracter científico. Según documentación de Calderón, Bernasconi, Del Río y otros. Colección Nuestro Mundo, no. 21, Serie Arte y Cultura. Madrid: Ediciones de la Torre

CAMPAÑA, LUZ EVELIA
1995
"Una tumba en el templo del buho, Dzibanche." *Arqueología Mexicana,* Vol. III, no. 14, México

CARDÓS DE MÉNDEZ, AMALIA
1965 and 1997
Catálogo de la colección maya. Unpublished. México: Sub Dirección de Arqueologia del MNA
1983
Los Mayas, Museo Nacional de Antropología. 1st ed. México: G.V. Editores
1987
Estudio de la colección de escultura maya del Museo Nacional de Antropología. México: INAH, 14, 33, 59–66, 83, 96, 109, 138, 141, 150, 171, 180, 182, 184
1988
Los mayas. Museo Nacional de Antropología. México: G.V. Editores, 34

CARDÓS DE MÉNDEZ, AMALIA; ET AL.
1985
Tejedores de voces. A Arte do México Antigo. Belém: Fundacao das Descobertas, Centro Cultural de Belém
1986
El juego de pelota. Una tradición prehispánica viva. Museo Nacional de Antropología, Sociedad de Amigos del Museo. México: INAH-SEP, 24
1990
Arte precolombino de México. Madrid: Olivetti-Electra, 24
1993
Die Welt der Maya. Wien: Kunsthistorisches Museum, 26, 42, 66, 92, 94

CARRASCO, RAMÓN V.; BOUCHER, SYLVIANE
1994
"Calakmul: Espacios Sagrados y Objetos de Poder." *Arqueología Mexicana,* no. 10, México, 32–38

CHASE, ARLEN F.
1992
"Elites and the Changing Organization of Classic Maya Society." In *Mesoamerican Elites: An Archaeological Assessment.* Ed. by D.Z. Chase and A.F. Chase. Norman: University of Oklahoma Press, 30–49

CHASE, ARLEN F.; RICE, PRUDENCE M. (ED. BY)
1985
The Lowland Maya Postclassic. Austin: University of Texas Press

CHEVALIER, JEAN; GHEERBRANT, ALAIN
1991
Diccionario de los símbolos. Barcelona: Editorial Herder, 154, 232, 750

CIREROL, MANUEL
1947
El Castillo, misterios del Templo Piramidal Maya de Chichén Itzá. México: Editorial y Talleres Pluma y Lápiz

CIUDAD REAL, ANDRÉS (ED. BY); ET AL.
1990
Los Mayas: el esplendor de una civilización. Madrid

CIUDAD RUIZ, ANDRÉS (ED. BY); ET AL.
1990
Los mayas: el esplendor de una civilización. Colección Encuentros, Sociedad estatal Quinto Centenario. Madrid: Turner libros, 198, 234

CLANCY, FLORA; COGGINS, CLEMENCY C.; CULBERT, PATRICK; GALLENKAMP, CHARLES; HARRISON, PETER D.; SABLOFF, JEREMY A.
1985
Maya Treasures of an Ancient Civilization. Albuquerque Museum. New York: Abrams Inc.

COBEAN, ROBERTO H.
1990
La cerámica de Tula, Hidalgo. Colección Científica, México: INAH, 482, 485

COE, MICHAEL D.

1968

"San Lorenzo and the Olmec Civilization." In *Dumbarton Oaks Conference on the Olmec.* Ed. by E.P. Benson. Washington, D.C.: Trustees for Harvard University, 41–78

1980

The Maya. London

1988

The Maya. London: Thames and Hudson, 87

1989

"The Hero Twins: Myth and Image." In *The Maya Vase Book*, Vol. 1. New York: Kerr Associates, 161–84

1992

Breaking the Maya Code. London: Thames and Hudson, 235

1995

El desciframiento de los glifos mayas. México: Fondo de Cultura Económica

COE, WILLIAM R.

1959

Piedras Negras Archaeology: Artifacts, Caches of Burials. The University Museum, Museum Monograph, 18, Philadelphia: University of Pennsylvania

1972

"Cultural Contact Between the Lowland Maya and Teotihuacan as Seen from Tikal, Peten, Guatemala." In *XI Mesa Redonda, Sociedad Mexicana de Antropología*, Vol. 2. México, 257–271

1980

"Caches and Offertory Practices of the Maya Lowlands." In *Handbook of the Middle American Indians*, USA, Vol. 2, Part I, 462–69

COGGINS, CLEMENCY CHASE

1983

The Stucco Decoration and Architectural Assemblage of Structure 1-sub, Dzibichaltun, Yucatán, México. Publication 49. Middle American Research Institute. New Orleans: Tulane University

1984

Cenote of Sacrifice. Austin: University of Texas Press, 70

COGGINS, CLEMENCY C.; ET AL.

1989

El Cenote de los Sacrificios. México: Fondo de Cultura Económica, 53, 159–67

CONNOR, JUDITH

1983

"The Ceramics of Cozumel, Quintana Roo, Mexico." Ph. D. dissertation, University of Arizona

CORSON, CHRISTOPHER

1977

"Stylistic Evolution of Jaina Figurines." In *Pre-Columbian Art History, Selected Readings.* Corty-Collins and Stern, Peek Publications

DELGADO, AGUSTÍN

1965

"Terracota de Jaina." In *El Arte de Jaina, Artes de México.* México

DEMAREST, ARTHUR A.

1986

The Archaeology of Santa Leticia and the Rise of Maya Civilization. Publication 52. Middle American Research Institute. New Orleans: Tulane University

1988

"Political Evolution in the Maya Borlderlands." In *The Southeast Maya Zone.* Ed. by E. Boone and G. Willey. Washington, D.C.: Dumbarton Oaks, 335–94

DESMOND, L.G.; MESSENGER, P.H.

1988

A Dream of Maya: Augustus and Alice Le Plongeon in Nineteenth Century in Yucatán. Albuquerque, 90–98

DIANE, Z.; CHASE, ARLEN F.

1986

Offerings to the Gods: Maya Archaeology at Santa Rita, Corozal. Orlando: University of Central Florida

FASH, WILLIAM L.

1991

"Scribes, warriors and kings." In *The City of Copan and the Ancient Maya.* London: Thames and Hudson, 121

FERNÁNDEZ DEL VALLE, PATRICIA

1992

"Vestigios arqueológicos en la ciudad de Mérida." *Revista i'inaj*, no. 5, December 1991-March 1992. México: CNCA-INAH, 31–41

FONCERRADA DE MOLINA, MARTA; CARDÓS DE MÉNDEZ, AMALIA

1988

Las figurillas de Jaina, Campeche, en el Museo Nacional de Antropología. México: UNAM, Instituto de Investigaciones Estéticas, INAH

FORSYTH, DONALD W.

1983

Investigations at Edzna, Campeche, Mexico. Papers at the New World Archaeological Foundation, no. 46, 2 Voll. Provo, Utah

FREIDEL, DAVID; SCHELE, LINDA; PARKER, JOY

1993

Maya Cosmos. Three Thousand Years on the Shaman's Path. New York: William Morrow and Co., 276–86, 300–303

GALLEGOS GÓMORA; JUDITH, MIRIAM

1996

Miniguía Museo de Sitio de Comalcalco. México: INAH

1997

"Forma, materiales y decoración. La arquitectura de Comalcalco." In *Los investigadores de la Cultura Maya 5*, México: Universidad Autónoma de Campeche, 213–32

GALLARETA, TOMÁS; ANDREWS, ANTHONY
1984
El proyecto arqueológico Isla Cerritos. Boletín de la ECAUADY, year 10, 59, 3–29

GANN, THOMAS
1900
"Mounds in Northern Honduras." In *19th Annual Report of the Bureau of American Ethnology*, Part II. Washington, D.C.: Smithsonian Institution, 655–91
1919
"The Maya Indians of Southern Yucatan and Northern British Honduras." Bulletin, 64, Washington, D.C.: Smithsonian Institution, Bureau of American Ethnology

GARCÍA CAMPILLO, JOSÉ MIGUEL
1991
"Edificios y Dignatarios: La Historia Escrita de Oxkintok." In *Oxkintok, Una Ciudad Maya de Yucatán*. Madrid: Misión Arqueológica de España en México, Proyecto Oxkintok, 1986–1991, 56–76
1992
"Informe Epigráfico sobre Oxkintok y la Cerámica Chocholá." In *Oxkintok 4*. Misión Arqueológica de España en México, Ministerio de Cultura España, 185–200
1995
"Nuevos monumentos esculpidos en el norte de la región Puuc, Kuxub y Xburrotunich." *Mexicon XVII*, no. 6, Möckmül, 106–11

GARCÍA COOK, ÁNGEL
1982
Análisis tipológico de artefactos. Colección Científica, 116. México: INAH

GARZA, TARAZONA; KURJAK, EDWARD
1980
Atlas Arqueológico del Estado de Yucatán. Vol. 1, México: INAH

GARZA CAMINO, MERCEDES DE LA
1995
Aves sagradas de los Mayas. México: UNAM, Facultad de Filosofía y Letras, Centro de Estudios Mayas del Instituto de Investigaciones Filológicas, 9, 58–62, 103

GENDROP, PAUL
1983
Los estilos río Bec, Chenes y Puuc en la arquitectura maya. México: UNAM

GIBSON, ERIC C.; C. SHAW, LESLIE; R. FINAMORE, DANIEL
1986
"Early Evidence of Maya Hieroglyphic Writing at Kichpanha, Belize." In *Working Papers in Archaeology*, no. 2, San Antonio: Center for Archaeological Research, The University of Texas at San Antonio

Gids
1961

Gids voor her Rijksmuseum voor Volkenkunde tc Leiden. Leiden

GREENE ROBERTSON, MERLE; RANDS, ROBERT L.; GRAHAM, JOHN A.
1972
Maya Sculpture. From the Southern Lowlands, the Highlands and Pacific Piedmont Guatemala, México and Honduras. Berkeley: Berkeley Lederer, Street and Zeus
1976
"Physical Deformities in the Ruling Lineage of Palenque, and the Dynastic Implications." In *The Art, Iconography and Dynastic History of Palenque*. Part III. Ed. by M. Greene Robertson. California: Pre-Columbian Art Research, Pebble Beach, 59–86
1983
The sculpture of Palenque. Vol IV. The Cross Group, the North Group, the Olvidado, and other pieces. New Jersey: Princeton University Press

GRUBE, NIKOLAI
1990
"The Primary Standard Sequence on Chocholá Style Ceramics." In *The Maya Vase Book*. Vol. 2. Justin Kerr, 320

GRUBE, NIKOLAI; ET AL.
1992
Die Welt der Maya: Archaeologische Schatze aus drei Jahrkausenden. Mainz aus Rhein: Phillip von Zabern

GUERRERO M., J.V.
n.d.
"El contexto de Jade en Costa Rica." *Revista Vínculos*, Vol. 12, 69–81

GUERRERO M., J.V.; SOLÍS, FELIPE
1997
Los pueblos antiguos de la zona Cañas-Liberia, del año 300 al 1500 d.C. San José: Editorial Varitec

GUSSINYER, JORDI
n.d.
"Primera temporada de salvamento arqueológico en la Presa de la Angostura." *Revista ICACH*, no. 4, Tuxtla Gutiérrez, 35–42

HAMMOND, NORMAN
1972
"Classic Maya Music. Part 1: Maya Drums." *Archaeology*, 25, no. 2, New York, 121–31
1975
Lubaantun, A Classic Maya Realm. Peabody Museum Monographs, no. 2. Cambridge, Mass.: Harvard University
1977
"The Earliest Maya." *Scientific American*, Vol. 236, 3, New York, 116–33
1982
La civilización Maya. Madrid: ediciones Itsmo
1990
Ancient Maya Civilization. New Brunswick, New Jersey: Rutgers University Press, 123

HAMMOND, NORMAN (ED. BY)
1973
British Museum, Cambridge University: Corozal Project 1973 Interim Report. Cambridge, Centre of Latin American Studies, University of Cambridge, 68, figg. 79–80

HELLMUTH, NICHOLAS M.
1987
Monster Und Menschen und Der Maya Kunst. Graz: Akademische Druck

HERNÁNDEZ SASTRÉ, RUTILO
1997
"Análisis del material arqueozoológico procedente de las excavaciones de la zona arqueológica de Comalcalco, Tabasco, México." Unpublished dissertation, México: Universidad Juárez, Autónoma de Tabasco

JOYCE, THOMAS A.
1932
"The 'eccentric flints' of Central America." *Journal of the Royal Anthropological Institute*, Vol. 62, XVII–XXVI, London
1933
"The pottery-whistle figurines of Lubaantun." *Journal of the Royal Anthropological Institute*, Vol. 63, XV–XXV, London

KIDDER, A.; JENNINGS, J.; SOOK, EDWIN
1946
Excavations at Kaminaljuyu, Guatemala. Washington, D.C.: Carnegie Institution of Washington, 126–33

KENNEDY EASBY, ELIZABETH; SCOTT, JOHN F.
1970
Before Cortés. Sculpture of Middle America. New York: The Metropolitan Museum of Art, 174

KINGSBOROUGH, LORD
1831
Antiquities of México: comprising facsimiles of ancient mexican paintings and hieroglyphs together with the monuments of New Spain by M. Dupaix. Voll. IV–V, London: Robert Havell and Colnaghi, Son and Co. Publ.

KOSAKOWSKY, L.J.
1987
"Preclassic Maya Pottery at Cuello, Belize." In *Anthropological Papers of the University of Arizona*, no. 47. Tucson: University of Arizona Press

KOWALSKI, JEFF KARL
1987
The House of the Governor: A Maya Palace of Uxmal, Yucatán, México. Cap. 10. Norman: University of Oklahoma Press

KUBLER, GEORGE
1982
"Serpent and Atantean Columns: Symbols of Maya-Toltec Polity." *Journal of the Society of Architectural Historians XLI*, no. 2, 104–106

LAGUNAS RODRÍGUEZ, ZAID
1985
"La exploración de la Tumba 1 de la zona arqueológica de Calakmul, Campeche." *Información*, no. 3.9, Campeche: Universidad Autónoma del Sudeste, 70–97

LANDA, DIEGO DE
1986
Relaciones de las cosas de Yucatán. Mérida: Consejo editorial de Yucatán, 67–69
1992
Relaciones de las cosas de Yucatán. México: Editorial Dante

LAPORTE M., JUAN PEDRO
1989
"Alternativas del Clásico Temprano en la relación Tikal-Teotihuacan: Grupo 6C-XVI, Tikal, Petén, Guatemala." Ph. D. Dissertation in Anthropology. México: UNAM, 22

LE PLONGEON, ALICE
1887
"Dr. Le Plongeon Latest and Most Important Discoveries among the Ruined Cities of Yucatán." *Scientific American 18*, Suppl. 448, 7143–147

LEE, THOMAS A. JR.
1969
The Artifacts of Chiapa de Corzo, Chiapas, México. Papers of the New Archaeological Foundation, no. 26. Provo, Utah: Brigham Young University, 105–106, 162–64, figg. 60, 119a, 121a
1974
Mound 4 Excavations at San Isidro, Chiapas, México. Papers of the New World Archaeological Foundation, no. 34, Provo, Utah: Brigham Young University, V
1988
"Las ofrendas de Guajilar, Chiapas, México." Manuscript, archives of the New World Archaeological Foundation. Provo, Utah-San Cristóbal de Las Casas: Brigham Young University

LEYNAAR, T.J.J.; PARSONS, L.A.
1988
Ulama, The Ball Game of the Mayas and Aztecs. Leiden

LIMON, EMMA; BAUTISTA, JOSEFINA
1989
"Alteraciones orbitrarias debidas a craneoestenosis prematura." *Revista Mexicana de Oftalmología*, Vol. 63, 1, México, 3–7

LOWE, GARETH W.
1962
Mound 5 and minor excavations, Chiapa de Corzo, Chiapas, México. Papers of the New World Archaeological Foundation, no. 12. Provo, Utah: Brigham Young University
1970
"The upper Grijalva Basin Maya Project." Typescript. Provo, Utah: Brigham Young University
1983

"Los olmecas, mayas y mixe-zoques." In *Antropología e historia de los mixe-zoques y mayas*. México: UNAM

LOWE, GARETH W.; AGRINIER, PIERRE
1960
Mound 1, Chiapa de Corzo, Chiapas, México. Papers of the New World Archaeological Foundation, no. 8. Provo, Utah: Brigham Young University

LOWE, GARETH W.; LEE, THOMAS A.; MARTÍNEZ E., EDUARDO
1982
Izapa: An Introduction to the Ruins and Monuments. Papers of the New World Archaeological Foundation, no. 31, Provo, Utah: Brigham Young University

MARCUS, JOYCE
1976
Emblem and state in the classic maya lowlands. Washington, D.C.: Trustees for Harvard University, Dumbarton Oaks Research Library and Collection
1987
The Inscriptions of Calakmul, royal marriage at a maya city in Campeche, México. Technical Report, 21. Ann Arbor: University of Michigan Museum of Anthropology

MARQUINA, IGNACIO
1964
Arquitectura Prehispánica, INAH-SEP, 800, 854, figg. 428, 474

MARTÍ, SAMUEL
1961
Canto, danza y música precortesianos. México: FCE
1968
Instrumentos musicales precortesianos. 2nd ed. México: INAH, 23–29

MARTÍNEZ LAVÍN, MANSILLA; PIJOÁN Y OCHOA, PINEDA
1994
Evidence of Hypertrophic Osteoarthropathy in Human Skeletal Remains from Prehispanic Mesoamerica. Annals of Internal Medicine. USA, Vol. 120, 3. 238–41

MAUDSLAY, ALFRED P.
1887 and 1902
Biologia Centrali-Americana: Archaeology. Vol. IV. London

MAYER, K.H.
1981
Classic Maya Relief Columns. California: Ancona Books, 25

MCANANY, PATRICIA A.
1995
Living with the Ancestors. Kinship and Kingship in Ancient Maya Society. Austin: University of New Mexico Press

MEDIZ BOLIO, ANTONIO
1973
Libro del Chilam Balam de Chumayel. México: UNAM, Biblioteca del Estudiante Universitario

MILLER, MARY ELLEN
1988
El arte de Mesoamerica, de los Olmecas a los Aztecas. México: Diana
1989
"The History of the Study of Maya Vase Painting." In *The Maya Vase Book*. Vol. 1. Justin Kerr

MILLER, MARY ELLEN; TAUBE, KARL
1993
The Gods and Symbols of Ancient Mexico and the Maya. London: Thames and Hudson, 99–100, 111, 117–18, 128, 134–37, 146–48, 152–53, 156, 175–84

MONTOLIU, MARIA
1978
"Algunos aspectos del venado en la religion de los mayas de Yucatán." In *Estudios de Cultura Maya*. Vol. X. México: UNAM

MORA, DAVID
1995
"Descifran glifos mayas encontrados en Costa Rica." *Boletín del Museo Nacional de Costa Rica*, Vol. 13, 2

NÁJERA, MARTHA ILIA
1987
El don de la sangre en el equilibrio cósmico. México: UNAM, Instituto de Investigaciones Filológicas

NEFF, HÉCTOR
1991
"Los orígenes de la producción de la cerámica plomiza.". In *La Economía del Antiguo Socomusco, Chiapas*. México: UNAM-UAC, B. Vooehies, 205–25

NORMAN, V. GARTH
1976
Izapa Sculpture; Part 2: Text. Papers of the New World Archaeological Foundation, no. 30, Provo, Utah: Brigham Young University

PAXTON, MEREDITH
1983
"Eine Palma aus Kohunlich, Quintana Roo, Mexiko im Museum von Cancun." *Mexicon*, Vol. V, 4, Graz, 60

PEÑA, AGUSTÍN
1985
"El Vaso de Zoh Laguna." *Boletín de la Escuela de Ciencias Antropológicas de la Universidad de Yucatán*, no. 74, Mérida, 3–17

PEÑAFIEL, ANTONIO
1890
Monumentos del arte mexicano antiguo. Ornamentación, mitología, tributos y monumentos... Vol. I. Berlin: A. Asher

PENDERGAST, DAVID M.
1969
Altun Ha, British Honduras (Belize): The Sun God's Tomb. Art and Archaeology Occasional Papers, 19. Toronto: Royal Ontario Museum
1979 (I)–1982 (II)
Excavations at Altun Ha, Belize, 1964–1970. Voll. I–II, Archaeological Monographs. Toronto: Royal Ontario Museum
1981
"Lamanai, Belize: Summary of Excavation Results, 1974–1980." *Journal of Field Archaeology*, Vol. 8, 1, Boston, 29–53
1985
"Stability Through Change: Lamanai, Belize, from the Ninth to the Seventeenth Century." In *Late Lowland Maya Civilization*. Ed. by J.A. Sabloff and E.W. Andrews V. Alburquerque: University of New Mexico Press, 223–49

PÉREZ CAMPA, MARIO
1990
La exposicion de la civilizacion maya. Tokio, 151

PINCEMIN, SOPHIA
1994
Entierro en el palacio. Colección Arqueología, Campeche: Universidad Autónoma de Campeche

PIÑA CHÁN, ROMÁN
1964
"Jaina, Campeche." *Boletín INAH*, no. 16, México, 4–8
1964
El Pueblo del Jaguar. México: Museo Nacional de Antropología-INAH
1968
Jaina. La casa en el agua. México: INAH
1970
Informe preliminar de la reciente exploración del Cenote sagrado de Chichén Itzá. Serie Investigaciones, no. 24. México: INAH
1985
Quetzalcóatl, Serpiente emplumada. Lecturas Mexicanas, no. 69. México: Fondo de Cultura Económica
1985
Cultura y Ciudades Mayas de Campeche. Gobierno del Estado de Campeche, 24
1987
Chichén Itzá, la Ciudad de los Brujos del agua. México: Fondo de Cultura Económica
1993
Una visión del México Prehispánico. México: UNAM, 154

PIÑA CHÁN, ROMÁN; FOLAN, WILLIAM J.
1997
"Un cajete polícromo proveniente del Cenote Sagrado de Chichén Itzá." In *Los Investigadores de la Cultura Maya*. Vol. 5. Campeche: Universidad Autónoma de Campeche, 274–83

POLLOCK, H.E.D.
1980
The Puuc. An architectural survey of the hill country of Yucatán and northern Campeche, México. Memoirs of the Peabody Museum of Archaeology and Ethnology. Vol. 19. Cambridge, Mass.: Harvard University, 196–97, 201, figg. 372–73

PROSKOURIAKOFF, TATIANA
1950
A Study of Classic Maya Sculpture. Publication 593. Carnegie Institution of Washington, Washington, D.C.
1961–64
Historical data in the inscriptions of Yaxchilan. Estudios de Cultura Maya. Voll. 3–4. México: UNAM
1974
Jades from The Cenote of Sacrifice, Chichén Itzá, Yucatán. Peabody Museum of Archaeology and Ethnology. Cambridge, Mass.: Harvard University, 78, 102, 117, 119, 135, 149, 158, 175, 181, 399, figg. 37–39, 44, 48, 49a, 57, 64b, 73, 84, 88–89
1993
Historia Maya. Siglo XXI. Colección América Nuestra, 42. México

REENTS-BUDET, DORIE
1997
"Los maestros pintores de ceramica maya." *Arqueología Mexicana*, no. 28, México: Editorial Raíces, 20–29

REENTS-BUDET, DORIE; BALL, J.; BISHOP, R.; FIELDS, V.; MACLEOD, M.
1994
Painting the Maya Universe: Royal Ceramics of the Classic Period. Durham: Duke University Press, 43, 48, 115–39, 240–41, 244–48, 348, 358

REPETTO TIÓ, BEATRÍZ
1985
Desarrollo Militar de los Mayas. Colección Raices. México, Yucatán: Maldonado Editores, 34

RICE, PRUDENCE M.
1991
"Specialization, Standarization and Diversity: A Retrospective." In *The Ceramic Legacy of Anna O. Sheppard*. Ed. by R.L. Bishop and F.W. Lange. Niwot: University Press of Colorado, 257–79

RICE, PRUDENCE M.; SHARER, ROBERT M. (ED. BY)
1987
Maya Ceramics: Papers from the 1985, Maya Ceramic Conference. 2 Voll. Oxford: British Archaeological Reports, International Series, no. 345

ROBERTSON, R.A.; FREIDEL, D.A. (ED. BY)
1986
Archaeology at Cerros, Belize, Central America. Vol. I. Dallas: Southern Methodist University Press, 123–24

ROBLES CASTELLANOS, FERNANDO
1980
La secuencia cerámica de la Región de Cobá. México: Escuela nacional de antropología, 221, 226

1990

La secuencia cerámica de la región de Cobá, Quintana Roo. Colección Científica, 184. México: INAH

ROMERO, JOSÉ LUIS
1990

Tierra y agua, no. 1, México: Instituto de Cultura de Tabasco, 7--14

RUGGERONI, DANTE A.; MOREIRA, MARÍA E.
1985

"El danzante alado de Comalcalco." In *Expresión, Cultura y Recreación*, January-February, no. 4, México: Órgano informativo de la Secretaría de Educación, 12–16

RUPPERT, KARL
1952

Chichen Itzá Architectural notes and plans. Washington, D.C., 38

RUZ LHUILLIER, ALBERTO
1952–53

"Presencia atlántica en Palenque, Huastecos, Totonacos y sus vecinos." *Revista Mexicana de Estudios Antropológicos*, Vol. XIII, 2, 3, México
1952a

"Exploraciones en Palenque: 1950." *Anales del INAH*, Vol. V, 33, Colección México, 25–45, fig. 5, XXVII
1952b

"Palenque, fuente inagotable de Tesoros arqueológicos." *México de Hoy*, Vol. IV, 48
1952c

"Estudio de la Cripta del Templo de las Inscripciones en Palenque." *Tlatoani*, Vol. I, 5–6, México, 3–28
1952d

"Investigaciones arqueológicas en Palenque." *Cuadernos Americanos*, XI, 6, México, 149–65
1955

"Exploraciones en Palenque: 1952." *Anales del INAH*, Vol. VI, Part I, 34, offerta 1, México: INAH, 89
1962

Chichén-Itzá: Comentarios a un Ensayo. Estudios de Cultura Maya. Vol. II. México: UNAM, Facultad de Filosofía y Letras
1973

El Templo de las Inscripciones. Palenque. Colección Científica del INAH, no. 7. México
1987

Frente al Pasado de Los Mayas. México: Secretaría de Educación Pública
1989

Costumbres funerarias de los antiguos mayas. México: Fondo de Cultura Económica

SAHAGÚN, BERNARDINO DE
1956

Historia General de las Cosas de la Nueva España. Vol. III. México: Editorial Porrúa, 187

SANDERS, WILLIAM T.
1960

Prehistoric ceramics and settlement patterns in Quintana Roo, Mexico. Publication 606, Contribution 60. Carnegie Institution of Washington, Washington, D.C.

SCARBOROUGH, V.L.; WILCOX, D.R. (ED. BY)
1991

Maya Mesoamerican Ballgame. Tucson: University of Arizona Press

SCHELE, LINDA
1982

Maya Glyphs. The Verbs. Austin: University of Texas Press

SCHELE, LINDA; FREIDEL, DAVID
1990

A Forest of Kings. The Untold Story of the Ancient Maya. New York: William Morrow and Co., 156–57, 414, 417

SCHELE, LINDA; FREIDEL, DAVID; PARKER, JOY
1993

Maya Cosmos. New York: William Morrow and Co.

SCHELE, LINDA; MILLER, MARY ELLEN
1986

The Blood of Kings. Dinasty and Ritual in Maya Art. Fort Worth, Texas: Kimbell Art Museum, 45, 54, 68–71
1992

The Blood of Kings, Dynasty and Ritual in Maya Art. London: Thames and Hudson

SCHMIDT, PETER J.
1989

"Cantón Naranja Polícromo. Un Tipo Cerámico de la región de los Chenes." In *II Coloquio Internacional de Mayistas.* Vol. ?. México: CEM-UN-AM, 411–26
1990

"Chichén Itzá y la prosperidad en Yucatán." In *México. Esplendores de Treinta Siglos.* New York: The Metropolitan Museum of Art, 189, 190, 195, 196
1995–96

Informe y Memoria del Proyecto Chichén Itzá. México

SELER, EDWARD
1960–61

"Gesammelte Abhandlungen zur Amerikanischen Sprach und Altertumskunde." In *Obras completas.* 5 Voll. [1902–1923]. Graz

SHARER, ROBERT J.
1994

The Ancient Maya. 5th ed. Stanford: Stanford University Press, 369–76, 386–87, 530–32, 542, 659–62, 698, 709, 719

SHARER, ROBERT J.; GROVE, DAVID C. (ED. BY)
1989

Regional Perspectives on the Olmec. School of American Research. Cambridge, Mass.: Cambridge University Press

SILVA, CARLOS; LINARES, ELISEO
1993

"El Tapesco del Diablo." *Arqueología Mexicana*, August-September, Vol. 1, 3, 76–78
in press
"Cuevas arqueológicas del río La Venta, Chiapas." In *Memorias de IV coloquio de investigadores mayistas*. Campeche: Instituto de Investigaciones Históricas y Sociales de la Universidad Autónoma de Campeche

SMITH, ROBERT E.
1955
Ceramic sequence at Uaxactun, Guatemala. Vol. 1. Publication 20. Middle American Research Institute. New Orleans: Tulane University, 59, 66
1957
"Tohil Plumbate and Classic Maya Polychrome Vessels in the Marquez Colection." *Notes on Middle American Archaeology and Ethnology*, March, no. 129
1971
The pottery of Mayapan including studies of ceramic material from Uxmal, Kabah, and Chichén Itzá. Voll. I–II. Papers of the Peabody Museum of Archaeology and Ethnology. Vol. 66. Cambridge, Mass.: Harvard University, Vol. I: 18–19, 21, 26–32, 48; Vol. II: 48, 87, 96–97, figg. 58h, 64n

SMITH, ROBERT E.; GIFFORD, J.C.
1980
"Pottery of the Maya Lowlands." In *Handbook of the Middle American Indians*. Vol. 2. Part I, 498–534

SMITH, ROBERT E.; PIÑA CHAN, ROMÁN
1962
Vocabulario sobre Cerámica. México: INAH

SOLÍS, FELIPE; SODI, FEDERICA
1985
"El Puuc y otros elementos de filiación maya, en Tula y Tenochtitlan." In *II Coloquio Internacional de Mayistas*. México: Instituto de Investigaciones Estéticas, CEM-UNAM

SOTO M., ZULAY
1997
Catálogo de Arte Precolombino Costarricense del Museo del Jade, Lic. Fidel Tristán. Instituto Nacional de Seguros

SOUSTELLE, JACQUES
1983
Los Olmecas. México: Fondo de Cultura Económica

SPINDEN, HERBERT
1975
A Study of Maya Art. New York: Dover Publications, 74, 133, figg. 94, 186

STUART, DAVID
1988
"The Rio Azul Cacao Pot: Epigraphic Observations on the Function of a Maya Ceramic Vessel." *Antiquity 62*, no. 234, Oxford, 153–57

SUÁREZ DÍEZ, LOURDES
1977
Tipología de los objetos prehispánicos de concha. Colección Científica, 54. México: INAH
1981
Técnicas prehispánicas en los objetos de concha. Colección Científica, 14, 2nd ed. México: INAH

TATE, CAROLYN E.
1992
Yaxchilan. The Design of a Maya Ceremonial City. Austin: University of Texas Press, 41–44, 169, 260

TAUBE, KARL ANDREAS
1988
"The Ancient Yucatec New Year Festival: the Liminal Period in Maya Ritual and Cosmology." Thesis of Yale University, 59–62, 107–10, figg. 19c, 35–36, 69
1992
"The Major Gods of Ancient Yucatán." In *Studies in Pre-Columbian Art and Archaeology*, no. 32. Washington, D.C.: Dumbarton Oaks Research Library and Collection, 37–38, 64–69, 79–88, 94

TEDLOCK, DENNIS
1985
Popol Vuh. New York: Simon and Schuster

THOMPSON, J. ERIC S.
1939
The moon goddess in Middle America, with notes on related deities, Publication 509. Carnegie Institution of Washington, Washington, D.C., 148
1952–53
"Relaciones entre Veracruz y la Región Maya, Huastecos, Totonacas y sus vecinos." *Revista Mexicana de Estudios Antropológicos*, Vol. XIII, 2–3, México
1957
Deities portrayed on censers at Mayapan. Current Report 40. July 1957. Cambridge: Carnegie Institution of Washington, Department of Archaeology, 599–632, fig. 1j
1960
Maya Hieroglyphic Writing an Introduction. University of Oklahoma Press, 73–74
1962
Grandeza y decadencia de los mayas. México: Fondo de Cultura Económica
1970
Maya History and Religion. Norman, Oklahoma, 187, 212–33, fig. 4
1975
Historia y Religión de los Mayas. Siglo XXI. México, 177, 166, 258, 306–19, 370
1979
Historia y Religión de los Mayas. Siglo XXI, 3rd ed. México
1986
Historia y Religión de los Mayas. Siglo XXI, 7th ed. México, 137–59
1988
Grandeza y decadencia de los mayas. México: Fondo de Cultura Económica

TOZZER, ALFREDO
1957
Chichén Itzá and its Cenote of Sacrifice: a comparative study of contemporaneus Maya and Toltec. Cambridge: Peabody Museum

VALENTINI, P.J.D.
n.d.
To Mexican Chalchihites, the Humboldt Celt and the Leiden Plate. Proc. Amer. Antiquarian Soc. New Series, 5, 1, 283–302

VELÁZQUEZ MORLET, ADRIANA; *ET AL.*
1988
Zonas arqueológicas, Yucatán. México: INAH

WEBSTER, DAVID
1989
The house of the bacabs, Copan, Honduras. Washington, D.C.: Dumbarton Oaks Research Library and Collection, 68

WILK, RICHARD R.
1988
"Maya Household Organization: Evidence and Analogies." In *Household and Community in the Mesoamerican Past.* Ed. by R. Wilk and W. Ashmore. Albuquerque: University of New Mexico Press, 135–51

WILLEY, G.R.; CULBERT, T. PATRICK; ADAMS, R.E.W. (ED. BY)
1967
"Maya Lowland Ceramics: a Report from the 1965 Guatemala City Conference." *American Antiquity,* Vol. 32, 3, 298–315

WILLIAM L. RATHJE
1973
"El descubrimiento de un jade olmeca en la Isla de Cozumel, Quintana Roo, México." In *Estudios de Cultura Maya.* Vol. IX. México: UNAM, 85–91

WRIGHT, T.C.
1978
"The fallic temple of Xunantunich." *Belizean Studies,* no. 3, Belize City, 1–6

YADEUN, JUAN
1992
Toniná. El laberinto del inframundo. México: Gobierno del Estado de Chiapas
1993
Toniná. México. Citibank-Ediciones El Equilibrista

References for the section on Maya Gods

CRUZ CORTES, NOEMÍ
1995 Ixchel, diosa madre entre los mayas yucatecos. Thesis for a Licentiate Degree in History, Faculty of Philosophy and Letters, UNAM, Mexico.

HERBRUGER, JR., ALFREDO
AND EDUARDO DÍAZ BARRIOS
1956 *Método para aprender a hablar, leer y escribir la lengua Cakchiquel.* Tipografía Nacional, Guatemala.

MORLEY, SYLVANUS G.
AND GEORGE W. BRAINERD
1983 *The Ancient Maya,* 4th edition, revised by Robert Sharer, California, Stanford University Press.

SANDOVAL, LISANDRO
1941 *Semántica Guatemalense o Diccionario de Guatemaltequismos.* Tomo I (A-K). Tipografía Nacional, Guatemala.

SOTELO , LAURA ELENA
1998 Los dioses antropomorfos en el Códice Madrid, Doctoral dissertation in Mesoamerican Studies, Faculty of Philosophy and Letters, UNAM, Mexico.

A

Abaj Takalik 79; 87; 309; 360
Acanceh 132
Achi 20
Achiotes 344
Acropolis, Copán 339; 340; 345; 347; 350; 351; 353; 354
Agua Caliente 91
Aguateca 332
Aguateca, language
Aguilar, Jerónimo de 451; 483
Agurcia Fasquelle, Ricardo 26; 337
Ah Canul 457
Ah Chuen, Monkey God 249; 265
Ah Kan Ek 490
Ah Kin Canul 387
Ah Kin Chel 457
Ah Kin see Kinich Ahau
Ah Puch, God A 243; 244; 245
Ahau 186; 332
Ahau Can 172
Ahau Itzamná
Ahuachapán, Dept. of 93
Akab Dzib, Chichén Itzá 402; 431; 436
Aké 132; 133; 135
Akumal 152; 459
Almendaríz 30
Alom 175
Altar de Sacrificios 75; 357; 359; 364
Altar Master 271; 274
Altar 10, Uxmal 407
Altar 41, Copán 237
Altar D', Copán 353
Altar F', Copán 353
Altar G1, Copán 341; 353; 237
Altar G2, Copán 353; 237
Altar G3, Copán 353; 237
Altar H', Copán 353
Altar I', Copán 353
Altar K, Copán 353
Altar L, Copán 353
Altar O, Copán 353; 237
Altar P, Quirigá 243
Altar Q, Copán 340; 353
Altar R, Copán 353
Altar S, Copán 353
Altar T, Copán 353
Altar U, Copán 353
Altar V, Copán 353
Altar W', Copán 353
Altar X, Copán 352
Altar Y, Copán 353
Altar Z, Copán 353
Altun Ha 208; 254; 255; 275; 279; 427
Alvarado, Pedro de 23

Alvaro Obregón Park, Soconusco 79
Amatenango del Valle 309; 505
Ambergris Cay 454
America 19; 21; 45; 159; 260; 361; 460
Anales de los Cakchiquels 190
Andrews IV, E. Wyllys 339; 454
Andrews, Anthony P. 26; 451; 454
Andrews, George 401
Angostura 309
Archaelogical Park, Copán see Parque Arquelógico, Copán
Archaeological Project of the Copáan Acropolis see Proyecto Arquelógico Acrópolis de Copán
Art Museum, Princeton 271; 274
Ashmore, Wendy 71
Asia 271
Atlantic Ocean 34; 73; 85; 94
Atlas Arqueológico de Yucatán 401
Aubin 214
Audiencia Real of Guatemala 29
Aveni, Anthony 204
Ayala Falcón, Maricela 26; 179; 194; 195
Ayax, Moreno 75
Aztecs 207; 402; 445

B

Bacab, God N, Pahuatun 411: 414; 439
Bacalar see Salamanca de Bacalar
Baden 34
Bahía de la Ascensión 451
Baja Verapaz 309; 312
Bajío, phase 96
Balamcanché 473
Balamkú 131
Balancán 75; 76; 162
Ball Court IIb, Copán 353
Ball Court III, Copán 91; 339; 352
Ball Court, Cobá 136
Ball Court, Iximché 314
Baluarte de San Miguel, Campeche see Museo Histórico Fuerte de San Miguel, Baluarte de San Miguel, Campeche
Barra, phase 73; 75; 94; 96; 309
Batz Ek 382
Baudez, Claude F. 337
Becán 105; 106; 112; 135; 281; 360; 427; 457
Bejucal 377
Belize 20; 25; 26; 39; 40; 42; 43; 45; 46; 47; 48; 53; 73; 75; 85; 104; 131; 153; 208; 210; 254; 275; 280; 357; 360;

377; 427; 454; 455; 460; 463; 466; 473; 484; 488; 489; 490; 505
Belize River see Río Belize
Belma 451; 479
Benavides C., Antonio 26; 131
Bench Register, Bonampak 306
Berlin, Heinrich 21; 24; 186; 321
Bernasconi, Antonio 30; 31
Bibliothèque Nationale, Paris 214
Bird Jaguar 184; 305
Bishop, Ronald L. 280
Bitol 175
Blom Plate 217; 220; 275; 279
Blood Moon 222
Bodega de Sitio Arqueológico de Kabah, Kabah 414
Bolon Dzacab, God K 236; 241; 243; 244; 299; 300; 353; 406; 445
Bolonchén, cave of 245
Bolontikú, Nine Deity 235
Bonampak 21; 37; 132; 160; 188; 197; 232; 244; 297; 304; 306; 307; 324;
Bonampak Murals 297; 299; 304; 306; 307
Books of Chilam Balam see Libros de Chilam Balam
Boston 170; 279; 280
Boucher, Sylviane 281
Bourbons 496
Bricker, Harvey M. 193; 204
Bricker, Victoria R. 26; 193; 204
British Museum, London 53; 197; 304
Buena Vista 459
Butz' Chan, Smoke Serpent, Smoke Sky 353

C

Cabo Catoche 451
Cacakal 453
Cacaxtla 430
Caddy 30
Cakchiquel 19; 20; 23; 71; 162; 163; 164; 165; 168; 170; 445
Calakmul 21; 26; 36; 69; 110; 112; 132; 188; 189; 226; 254; 255; 279; 281; 286; 287; 292; 295; 322; 323; 325; 328; 334; 360; 369; 373; 374; 377; 380; 381; 382; 384; 457
Calkiní 387; 399; 479
Callender Jr., D.W. 106
Calotmul 479
Cambridge University, Cambridge 34
Campeche 20; 39; 43; 45; 47; 48; 53; 66; 70; 73; 85; 105; 106; 110; 131; 132; 133; 135; 136; 145; 153; 156;

159; 166; 168; 170; 212; 255; 260; 265; 267; 269; 279; 281; 295; 324; 333; 357; 360; 373; 374; 377; 381; 382; 385; 387; 394; 396; 397; 398; 406; 407; 427; 439; 445; 457; 464; 466; 484; 490; 505

Can Pech 479

Canché Balam 453

Cancuen 323

Cancún 60; 152; 452; 453; 454; 459

Candelaria 55

Canek, Jacinto see Canek, Jacinto Uk de los Santos

Canek, Jacinto Uk de los Santos 493

Canhel, Dragon 236; 237; 243

Cansahcab 133

Canul 387; 399; 471

Capilla de Indios, Dzibilchaltún 71

Cara Sucia 93

Caracol 361; 369; 377; 382

Caracol Structure see El Caracol, Chchén Itzá

Caribbean 39; 43; 73; 88; 106; 126; 357; 359; 360; 361; 451; 452; 455; 459; 463; 466

Carlos III 30

Carlson, John B. 204

Carnegie Institution, Washington 36; 37; 123; 126; 194; 373; 401; 453; 454

Carr 106

Carrasco V., Ramón 26; 281; 373

Castañeda 30

Caste War 29; 32; 36; 452; 493; 501

Castillo, Chichén Itzá see El Castillo, Chichén Irzá

Catherwood, Frederick 31; 32; 33; 337; 401; 483; 452; 484

Catholic Action 501

Cauac 241

Cauac Sky 88

Ce Acatl Topiltzin 237

Cehache 473

Cehpech 401; 457

Ceibal 21; 34; 36; 75; 321; 322; 357; 359; 366; 369; 370; 385

Celestial Dragon 235; 236; 237; 241

Celestial Monster 406

Celestún 399

Cenote di Xtoloc, Chichén Itzá 431

Cenote of Mayapán 128

Cenote of Oxtoloc 125

Cenote of Sacrifice, Chichén Itzá 30; 123; 249; 254; 255; 259; 260; 265

Cenozoic 357

Center of Mexican and Central American Studies see Centro de Estudios Mexicanos y Centro-Americanos

Central Acropolis, El Mirador 103

Central Acropolis, Tikal 106; 107

Central America see Mesoamerica

Central American Federation 31

Centre National de la Recherche Scientifique, Francia 337

Centro Cultural de los Altos de Chiapas, San Cristóbal de las Casas 66

Centro de Estudios Mexicanos y Centro-Americanos 340

Centro de Investigaciones Históricas y Sociales de la Universidad Autonoma del Campeche 281

Centro INAH Quintana Roo, Chetumal 328

Centro INAH Campeche, Campeche 168; 170; 255; 280; 333; 490

Centro INAH Yucatán, Merida 280; 281

Cerro Chino 344

Cerro de las Mesas 75; 344

Cerro Palenque 91; 93

Cerros 88; 131; 360; 454; 455

Chaac, God B 201; 210; 236; 238; 241; 243; 312; 401; 406; 409; 413

Chaan Muan 306

Chac 443

Chac Mool 32; 145; 409; 432; 443; 473

Chac Mumul Ain, Great Muddy Crocodile 236; 241

Chac Xib Chac 409; 436; 470

Chacbolay 414

Chacchob 106

Chacmool 453; 454

Chacmultún 136; 405

Chacsinkin 79

Chaculá 314

Chakan 457; 473

Chaktemal see Chetumal

Chalcatzingo 87

Chalchuapa 76; 79; 86; 87; 88; 91; 309

Chamá 170; 312

Chamá Sierra 314

Chamelecón 91

Champotón 212; 466

Chan Bahlum 297; 299; 300; 302

Chancenote 479

Chantuto 309

Charles V 209

Charnay, Désiré 32; 497

Chauac Ha 479

Chel 471

Chenes, style 106; 135; 152; 153; 210; 241; 406; 446

Chetumal 29; 220; 275; 279; 328; 454; 459; 460; 466; 473; 479; 484; 489; 490

Chiapa de Corzo 76; 89; 96; 180; 181; 183; 373

Chiapas 19; 20; 23; 26; 27; 29; 30; 31; 32; 34; 36; 39; 40; 41; 42; 43; 45; 46; 47; 48; 49; 53; 59; 66; 73; 76; 81; 85; 89; 94; 96; 132; 136; 160; 168; 172; 179; 181; 186; 188; 189; 207; 209; 210; 212; 214; 219; 235; 244; 260; 263; 267; 300; 304; 309; 310; 314; 317; 321; 324; 325; 330; 357; 427; 444; 446; 459; 460; 466; 469; 495; 496; 497; 498; 499; 501; 502; 505

Chicanná 135

Chicchan, Serpent Biter 235

Chichankanab 401

Chicharras, phase 96

Chichén Itzá 21; 23; 26; 29; 30; 32; 33; 34; 46; 69; 70; 79; 85; 123; 126; 132; 136; 145; 148; 165; 166; 174; 193; 194; 195; 197; 199; 200; 204; 210; 237; 249; 254; 255; 259; 263; 265; 402; 403; 409; 412; 416; 427; 430; 431; 432; 436; 439; 441; 443; 444; 445; 446; 457; 460; 463; 469; 470; 471; 473; 479; 489

Chichén see Chichén Itzá

Chichén-Puuc, style 439

Chichén-Tolteco, style 439

Chichicastenango 317; 493

Chichimecs 446

Chicoasén 309

Chicomecóatl 470

Chikinchel 473

Chilam Balam see Libros de Chilam Balam

Chimaltenango 70; 152; 265; 309

Chinkultic 21; 310; 312

Chiquibul 357

Chiquilá 459

Chivacavé 309

Chixoy 75; 309

Chocholá, style 463

Chol 19; 20

Cholti 20

Chontal 20; 23; 70; 153; 162; 445; 495

Chontalpa 23; 370; 402

Chorotegas 94

Chorti 20; 92

Chuchumatán 309; 310; 314

Chuitinamit 317

Chuitixtiox 317

Chuj 20

Chumayel 237; 243; 244; 488

Chunyaxché 152; 454; 459

Ciudad Real 29; 30; 484

Ciudad Real, Antonio de 30
Clay, London T. 280
Closs, Michael 203
Clovis 357
Cobá 29; 34; 53; 121; 123; 125; 126; 132; 133; 136; 152; 180; 183; 455; 463; 469
Cochuah 166; 471
Cocom 23; 469; 471; 473
Códice de Calkiní 387
Códice Vindobonensis Mexicanus 1 217
Codz Pop, Kabah 131; 136; 241; 401; 413; 414
Coe, Michael 277; 279
Coggins, Clemency Chase 26; 249
Cold House 223
Colhá 357
Cologne 464
Colombia 444
Columbus, Christopher 29; 460
Comalcalco 51; 97; 132; 155; 168; 183
Comayagua 86; 91; 94; 349
Complejo de los Monos, El Mirador
Complex of the Monkeys, El Mirador 103
Compound of the Paintings, Cobá 152
Conil 450; 459
Consejo de Indios, Spain 209
Conservation Analytical Laboratory (cal) 280
Convent of Izamal 484
Copador, style 91
Copán 21; 26; 29; 30; 31; 32; 34; 48; 66; 69; 75; 86; 88; 91; 92; 94; 96; 110; 126; 131; 132; 133; 135; 176; 194; 195; 196; 208; 226; 227; 232; 243; 246; 249; 255; 259; 312; 321; 322; 324; 335; 337; 338; 339; 340; 341; 344; 345; 347; 349; 350; 351; 352; 353; 354; 427; 467
Copán Archaeological Project see Proyecto Arqueológico Copán
Copán Project see Progetto Arquelógico Copán
Copán River 75; 337
Copán Ruinas 92; 337; 349
Copanaguastla 168
Copanaguastlecs 170
Corozal Bays 484
Cortés, Hernán 29; 71; 212; 436; 451; 483; 488; 490
Costa Rica 79; 93; 94; 463
Coto, Fray Tomás de 163; 165; 168
Cotzumalguapa 93; 444
Coxoh 20; 94

Cozumel 71; 79; 81; 245; 451; 452; 454; 455; 459; 460; 463; 479; 483; 488; 490
Cross Group, Palenque see Group of the Cross, Palenque
Cruz, Noemi 245
Cu Ix 352
Cuadros, phase 94; 96
Cuajilor 317
Cuello 75; 357; 359
Cueva de la Garrafa 267
Cueva de La Media Luna 96
Cueva del Lazo 97
Cuevo el Tapesco del Diablo 172
Culbert, T. Patrick 110
Culubá 136
Cumtún 436
Cupul 29; 471
Cuyamel 82
Cuzcachapa 86

D

Dampier, William 387
Dark House 222; 223
Dávila, Alonso 484
De Vos, Jan 27; 495
Death God 244
Del Río 30
Delgado, Diego 490
Denison, John 373
Denon, Vivant 31
Dominguez Carrasco, María del R. 281
Doña Marina 483
Dos Pilas 323; 332; 334; 366; 369; 384
Double Bird 377; 382
Dragon (see also Canhel) 235; 236; 238; 241; 243
Dresden 190; 194; 199; 200; 201; 202; 204; 207; 208; 209; 210; 211; 212; 214; 237; 238; 241; 243; 246
Dresden Codex 190; 194; 199; 200; 201; 202; 204; 207; 208; 209; 210; 211; 212; 214; 237; 238; 241; 243; 246
Dumbarton Oaks Research Library and Collections, Washington D.C. 66; 79; 250
Dunning, Nicholas 401; 407
Dupaix 30; 179
Dupaix Slab 179
Dzan 480
Dzibanché 26; 123; 128; 132; 381
Dzibilchaltún 71; 85; 86; 136; 373; 403; 427; 473; 489
Dzibilnocac 156

Dzibiltún 133
Dzidzantún 479
Dzitbalché 172
Dzuluinicoob, New River 55; 466; 473

E

Eagle Platform, Chichén Itzá 431; 436
Earthquake 219; 220; 221; 223
Eastern Patio, Acopolis, Copán 340; 345
Ecab 451; 454; 459
Edmonson, Munro S. 203
Edzná 21; 132; 133; 136; 145; 152; 403; 445
Egypt 31
Ehecatl 237
Eighteen Rabbit, see Uaxaclahun Ubah C'amil
Ek Chuah 170; 312
Ekbalam 132; 152; 479; 480
El Altar 454
El Baúl 360; 444
El Bosque 86; 339; 344; 354
El Cafetal 96
El Caracol, Chichén Itzá 125; 193; 194; 195; 204; 409; 436
El Carmen see Hacienda El Carmen
El Cascabel, El Mirador 103
El Castillo of Kukulcan, Mayapán 476
El Castillo, Chichén Itzá 123; 126; 148; 427; 431; 436
El Cerrón Grande 88
El Chayal 463
El Meco 152; 451; 452; 454; 459
El Memorial de Sololá 19; 190; 235; 317
El Mercado, Chichén Itzá 123; 431
El Mesak 87
El Mirador 26; 60; 66; 76; 88; 96; 103; 104; 105; 106; 131; 207; 281; 286; 287; 358; 360; 373; 374; 377; 427
El Mundo Perdido, Tikal see Mundo Perdido Complex, Tikal
El Naranjal 133
El Osario, Chichén Itzá 125; 431
El Perical 88
El Perú 323; 384
El Portón 60
El Progreso 85
El Puente 132
El Quiché 51; 176; 250; 309; 310; 312; 314; 317; 319; 445
El Rey 459
El Salvador 20; 25; 39; 40; 45; 53; 73; 76; 79; 85; 86; 87; 88; 89; 91; 93; 94; 280; 309; 314; 345; 427; 505

El Señor de Petén 328
El Sitio 79
El Tajín 145
El Tigre Complex El Mirador 103;
    131; 360; 374
El Trapiche 86; 88
El Vergel 309
Eliade, Mircea 183
Emiliano Zapata 75; 76
Endless Walk 97
England 25; 34; 210
Escobedo, Hector L. 26; 357
Escuintla 93
Europe 25; 27; 31; 32 ; 271; 322
Expedición Científica Mexicana 454

F

Farfán, Juan 175
Fash, Barbara 338; 350
Fash, William 338; 341; 344; 350; 353
Feathered Serpent 436; 444
Fernández, Miguel Angel 454
Finca Acapulco 309
Fire House 223
First Father see Hunapu and Hun Nal
    Ye
First Pacal 300
First Tree of the World see Yaxcheel
    Cab
Flanders 484
Flores 33; 34
Florescano, Enrique 26; 217
Folan, William 218
Forest, The see El Bosque
Forsyth 104
France 337
Freidel, David 126; 204
Fuensalida, Bartolomé de 490
Fundación Amparo/Museo Amparo,
    Puebla 60

G

G I 186; 302; 303; 360
G II 186; 302; 303; 360
G III 186; 302; 303; 360
Galindo, John see Galindo, Juan
Galindo, Juan 30; 31; 32; 33
García de Palacio, Diego 29; 30
Garza, Mercedes de la 19; 26; 235
Garzón, Juan 489
Gates 210
Germany 25; 29; 34; 209
Gibbs, Sharon L. 204
Globus, magazine 401

God A see Ah Puch
God B see Chaac
God D see Itzamna
God E see Maize God
God G see Kinich Ahau
God K see Bolon Dzacab
God N see Bacab
Goddess I see Ix Chel
Goddess O see Ixchebel Yax
Gómez Panaco, José 162
Gómez-Pompa, Arturo 26; 39
González de la Mata, Rocío 26; 451
Gordon, George B. 337
Gotze, Johann Christian 209
Graham, Elizabeth 489
Graham, Ian 26; 29
Great Acropolis, Calakmul 384
Great Acropolis, Comalcalco 51
Great Ballcourt, Chichén Itzá 123; 126
Great Jaguar Claw see Yukum Yichak
    Kak
Great Muddy Crocodile see Chac Mu-
    mul Ain
Great Palace, Three-Story Palace, Say-
    il 112; 401; 414; 416
Great Plaza, Calakmul 381; 385
Great Plaza, Copán 337; 339
Great Plaza, Tikal 106; 107
Great Pyramid, Mundo Perdido Com-
    plex, Tikal see Structure 5C-54,
    Tikal
Grijalva River see Río Grijalva
Grijalva, Juan de 29; 71; 451
Grolier Club, New York 210
Grolier Codex 202; 208; 210; 211; 212
Group 9N-8, Copán 349; 354
Group 9N-82, Copán 349
Group H, Tikal 107
Group H, Uaxactún 377
Group of the Cross, Palenque 302; 360
Group of the Initial Series Xcalumkín
    407
Grube, Nikolai 322; 323
Guajilar 310
Guatemala 19; 20; 23; 25; 26; 27; 29;
    30; 31; 32; 33; 34; 39; 40; 41; 42; 43;
    45; 47; 51; 53; 59; 60; 66; 70; 73; 75;
    79; 81; 85; 87; 91; 93; 94; 103; 104;
    107; 132; 152; 153; 164; 166; 168;
    170; 176; 188; 191; 195; 208; 209;
    217; 221; 226; 243; 250; 259; 265;
    280; 281; 286; 297; 309; 310; 312;
    314; 315; 317; 319; 323; 325; 328;
    330; 337; 344; 357; 360; 364; 366;
    369; 370; 380; 402; 497; 427; 436;
    444; 446; 460; 463; 469; 484; 489;

490; 493; 495; 498; 501; 503; 505
Guatemala City 33; 66
Guaytán 88
Gucumatz 175; 236; 237
Guerrero, Gonzalo de 29; 451
Gulf of Mexico 20; 23; 43; 53; 60; 73;
    75; 76; 87; 94; 96; 136; 156; 249;
    309; 361; 387; 402; 427; 439; 445;
    451
Gumarcah 23

H

Habsburgs 496
Hacienda El Carmen 86; 87
Hall, Jay 340; 341
Hanal see Hinal
Hartung, Horst 204
Harvard University, Cambridge, Mass.
    249; 254; 255; 260; 337; 338
Hasaw Chan Kawil 384
Hazard 106
Healey, Giles 37
Heart of the Sky see Huracán
Hernández de Cordoba, Francisco 71;
    451; 483
Hero Twins 126; 174; 218; 219; 220;
    221; 222; 223; 224; 226; 229; 277;
    279; 303; 360; 412
Hidalgo 444; 445; 460
Hieroglyphic Stairway, Copán 96; 339;
    350; 353
Hieroglyphic Stairway 2, Yaxchilán
    189
Hieroglyphic Stairway 6, Copán 353
Hieroglyphic Stairway 7, Copán 353
Hieroglyphic Stairway 8, Copán 353
Hieroglyphic Stairway 9, Copán 352
Hieroglyphic Stairway 18, Copán 352
Hieroglyphic Stairway 55, Copán 352
Hinal 387
Hocabá 457; 479
Hochob 135; 145
Holmes, William 452
Holmul 361
Hondo River see Río Hondo
Honduras 20; 23; 25; 29; 30; 39; 40; 41;
    42; 43; 53; 73; 85; 86; 88; 89; 91; 92;
    93; 94; 126; 132; 135; 176; 194; 196;
    208; 227; 243; 249; 255; 280; 312;
    337; 340; 345; 347; 349; 353; 354;
    427; 460; 467; 484; 489; 505
Hormiguero 135
Hotaling 204
House A, Palenque 302
House D, Palenque 300

House E, Palenque 297; 299; 302; 304
House of the corn grinders, Chichén Itzá 431
House of the deer, Chichén Itzá 431
House of the Governor, Uxmal 197; 198; 203; 401; 402; 404; 409; 411
House of the Turtles, Huxmal 411
Houston, Stephen 322
Huaxtecs 166; 172
Huehuetán 209
Huehuetenango 310; 314
Humboldt, Alexander von 30
Hun Ahau 279; 243
Hun Came, One Death 221; 244
Hun Chaan Mah Kina 377
Hun Hunahpu 221; 222; 228; 360; 412
Hun Nal Ye, One Maize Revealed 227; 228; 229; 230; 232; 233
Hunab Ku, One God 237
Hunac Ceel 470
Hunahpu 126; 174; 175; 220; 221; 222; 223; 224; 229; 232; 233; 277; 279; 360
Hunchavin 314
Huracán, Lightning of a Leg, Heart of the Sky 243

I

Ichpaatún 106; 459
Ikil 436
Ilopango 66; 88; 91
INAH see Instituto Nacional de Antropología e Historia, Mexico City
Instituto Hondureño de Antropología e Historia, Tegucigalpa 48; 82; 96; 176; 347
Instituto Nacional de Antropolgía e Historia (INAH), Mexico City 37; 79; 280; 391; 394; 395; 454
Instituto Nacional de Antropología e Historia, Campeche see Centro inah Campeche
Isla Ceritos 70; 444
Isla de Sacrificios 444
Isla del Carmen 466
Isla Mujeres 452; 454
Iturbide 495
Itzá 19; 20; 23; 33; 85; 402; 403; 409; 416; 432; 445; 457; 469; 473; 484; 488; 489; 490; 493
Itzam Cab Ain, Terrestrial Crocodile Dragon 236; 241
Itzam Yeh, Principal Bird Deity 406
Itzamna Kinich Ahau, Lord Solar Eye

of the Dragon 209; 238
Itzamna, God D 22; 135; 222; 236; 237; 238; 243; 245; 483
Itzimté 401; 407; 416
Ix Chel, Goddess I 244; 245; 246; 406
Ixchebel Yax, Goddess O 245; 246
Ixil 20; 132; 427
Iximché 71; 152; 265; 314; 317; 319
Ixtapa 317
Ixtepeque 88; 91
Izabal Lake 88; 309
Izamal 132; 133; 238; 439; 463; 484
Izapa 20; 59; 79; 96; 132; 219; 237; 241; 309; 360; 373

J

Jacaltec 20
Jaguar Claw 188; 384; 385
Jaguar House 223
Jaina Island 25; 159; 170; 260; 265; 267; 269; 387; 391; 394; 395; 396; 397; 398; 399; 490
Jamaica 451
Janus 201
Jataté 76; 309
Jester God see Sak Hunal
Jicaque 73
Jiquipilas 76; 207
Jones, Grant D. 27; 126; 436; 483
Joya de Cerén 91
Juchitán 76
Junaipú see Hunahpu
Junquillo, style 136
Justeson, John S. 204

K

Ka Wil 236; 243
Ka Wil Chaan, Stormy Sky 377
Ka'an, Sky, dynastic elite 88; 377
Kabah 21; 32; 70; 131; 132; 136; 241; 401; 402; 403; 405; 413; 414; 416; 457
Kalomte 332
Kam Manahan 354
Kaminaliuyú 21; 60; 66; 69; 85; 88; 91; 160; 309; 310; 315; 345; 360; 373; 427
Kan II 382
Kan Xul Hok 297
Kan Xul see Kinich Hok Chitam
Kanal Ikal 297; 299
Kang 97
Kanhobal 20
Kayal 136

Kekchi 20
Kelley, David 186
Kilmartin, J.O. 123
Kin, Sun-Day-Time 238
King of Kabah 413; 414
Kinich Ahau Itzamna see Itzamna Kinich Ahau
Kinich Ahau, God G, Lord Solar Eye 236; 238; 243; 350; 351
Kinich Akul Anab 329
Kinich Hanab Pacal, Pacal the Great 22; 25; 254; 297; 298; 299; 300; 302; 304; 329; 332
Kinich Hok Chitam 322
Kinich Yax Kuk Mo, Quetzal Macaw 88; 340; 344; 345; 351; 352; 353
Kinichná 128
Kinick Kakmo, Sun-Eye-Fire-Macaw 133; 238
Kisin 243
Kisteil 493
Knorosov, Yuri 24; 208; 212; 215
Knot-Eye Jaguar 324
Kohunlich 26; 112; 122; 123; 131
Kom 414
Kowalski, Jeff Karl 26; 401
Ku Hix Kab 377; 381; 382
Ku Hix see Ku Hix Kab
Kubler, George 300
Kuhl Kan Ahau, Serpent Head 377; 380; 381; 382; 384; 385
Kukulcan 236; 237; 391; 436; 470; 471; 476
Kul Ahau 322; 324; 332; 407; 410; 416
Kumarcaaj 317

L

La Blanca 87
La Entrada 132
La Iná 454
La Lagunita 51; 75; 310
La Mosquitia 347
La Pasadita 324
La Pimienta 490
La Trinitaria 267
La Venta 73; 75; 76; 79
Labná 70; 136; 145; 401; 402; 405; 414; 457; 483
Labná Arch 145; 483
Lacandon, language 20
Lacandons 33; 34; 36; 37; 162
Lacanhá 324
Lady 1 Deer 217
Lady 6 Sky 334
Lady Katun 334

Lady Xoc 334
Ladyville 357
Lagartero 267
Laguna de Términos 23; 399; 427
Laguna Zope 76
Lamanai 26; 104; 105; 360; 466; 489; 490
Landa, Fray Diego de 29; 34; 160; 162; 174; 209; 212; 235; 241; 436; 439; 446; 473; 476; 477; 486
Lara, Eusebio de 33
Larios Villalta, Rudy 338; 350
Las Margaritas 317
Las Palomas 55
Las Sepulturas, Copán 75; 86; 339; 344; 349; 350; 354
Las Ventanas, Copán 30
Las Victorias 79
Le Plongeon, Alice 452
Le Plongeon, Augustus 32; 452
Leiden 196
Leiden Plate 196
Lempa 53; 73
Lenca 73; 88
Ley Federal de Reforma Agraria 136
Libros de Chilam Balam 19; 190; 235; 237; 243; 244; 469; 486; 488
Lightning of a Leg see Huracán
Linde, John H. 204
Lintel 1, Structure 23, Yaxchilán 304
Lintel 2, Bonampak 188
Lintel 3, Piedras Negras 323
Lintel 3, Temple IV, Tikal 237
Lintel 5, Structure 23, Yaxchilán 304
Lintel 7, Structure 23, Yaxchilán 304
Lintel 15, Structure 23, Yaxchilán 304
Lintel 17, Structure 23, Yaxchilán 304
Lintel 24, Structure 23, Yaxchilán 53; 190; 304
Lintel 25, Structure 23, Yaxchilán 304; 305
Lintel 26, Structure 23, Yaxchilán 304; 321; 330
Lintel 32, Structure 23, Yaxchilán 304
Lintel 41, Structure 23, Yaxchilán 197
Lintel 53, Structure 23, Yaxchilán 304
Lintel 54, Structure 23, Yaxchilán 304
Lo de Vaca 88
Locona-Ocós, phase 87
Loltún, cave of 360
London 29; 32; 33; 34; 53; 197; 304
Looper, Mathew 344
Lopez Mateos 96
Lord 1 Deer 217
Lord Chaac 402; 407; 409; 410; 411; 416

Lord Solar Eye of the Dragon see Itzamna Kinich Ahau
Los Higos 132
Los Naranjos 88
Los Tapiales 309
Lothrop, Samuel K. 145
Lounsbury, Floyd 186; 203; 204
Lowe, Gareth W. 96
Lower Temple of the Jaguars, Chichén Itzá 412
Lubaantún 366
Lunar Goddess 247
Lundell, Cyrus 373
Luti 471

M

Ma Cuch 381
Machaquilá 325
Madrid 159; 165; 180; 190; 207; 208; 212; 213; 214; 241; 245; 246
Madrid Codex 159; 165; 180; 190; 207; 208; 212; 213; 214; 241; 245; 246
Mah Kina Ahau Pop 187
Main Ball Court, Uxmal 402; 407; 411
Main Group, Copán 337; 338; 344; 347; 349; 354
Main Palace, Labná 401
Maize God, God E 244; 246; 299
Maize Goddess 297
Maler, Teobert 34; 36; 133; 401; 452
Malpaso 76; 96
Mam 20
Manatí 73
Maní 457; 479
Manos Rojas 135
Marcus, Joyce 323
Marker Stone, Xukpi 352
Mars 196; 200; 202; 204; 208; 210; 212
Martin, Simon 279; 322; 323
Martínez, Alejandro 280
Mason-Spinden, Expedition 454
Mat Head 352
Matacapan 427
Matheny, Ray T. 103
Mathews, Peter 186; 187
Maudslay, Alfred 29; 33; 34; 36; 337
Maxcanú 401
Maximilian I 34
Maya 19; 20; 21; passim
Maya Polichrome Ceramics Project (mpcp) 280
Mayapán 23; 26; 70; 71; 106; 125; 126; 128; 152; 214; 399; 445; 457; 463; 469; 470; 471; 473; 476; 479; 483; 486; 493

Mayapán League 457
Mazatán 73; 79
Megalithic style 133
Memorial de Sololá see El Memorial de Sololá
Méndez, Modesto 33
Mercado, Chichén Itzá see El Mercado, Chichén Itzá
Merida 46; 81; 94; 136; 165; 166; 197; 217; 220; 279; 427; 430; 432; 439; 444; 457; 463; 479; 484; 488; 489; 490
Mesoamerica 20; 21; 23; 34; 39; 53; 70; 73; 75; 79; 81; 87; 88; 94; 103; 165; 166; 179; 194; 196; 201; 203; 207; 212; 215; 217; 232; 237; 249; 259; 260; 297; 298; 309; 334; 340; 373; 427; 430; 432; 445; 488; 495
Metropolitan Museum of Art, New York 259
Mexican Scientific Expedition see Expedición Científica Mexicana
Mexico 20; 23; 25; 29; 30; 31; 32; 34; 39; 43; 53; 55; 69; 70; 71; 73; 85; 86; 94; 96; 103; 104; 105; 132; 136; 160; 170; 180; 184; 208; 259; 260; 271; 275; 279; 281; 309; 334; 341; 357; 360; 380; 401; 427; 439; 444; 445; 451; 460; 463; 464; 466; 483; 486; 495; 503; 505
Mexico City 39; 49; 59; 60; 73; 76; 79; 89; 159; 160; 162; 163; 172; 179; 210; 235; 238; 255; 265; 267; 269; 295; 312; 321; 324; 325; 330; 332; 387; 391; 394; 395; 396; 397; 398; 409; 436; 439; 443; 460; 463; 469; 483; 486; 493
Mezcalapa, Río Grande de Chiapas 76
Michael C. Rockefeller Memorial Collection, Metropolitan Museum of Art, New York 259
Michoacán 445
Milky Way 164; 197
Miller, Mary Ellen 306
Millon, René 105
Mirador see El Mirador
Mirador Temple, Sayil 414
Mirones y Lescano, Francisco 490
Mixco Viejo 70; 152; 317
Mixe-Zoque 73; 74; 76; 81; 96; 209; 357
Mixteca-Puebla Compex 445
Mixtecs 207; 217; 225
Mochó 20
Moctezuma 209
Molina, Alonso de 172

Monjas annex, Chichén Itzá *see* Las Monjas, Chichén Itzá

Monjas, Chichén Itzá *see* Nunnery, Chichén Itzá

Monte Albán 179

Monte Alto 79

Montejo the jounger, Francisco de 29

Montejo, Francisco de 23; 29; 209; 451; 483; 484

Monument 26, Toniná 325

Monument 27, Toniná 324

Moon 21; 22; 196; 197; 198; 199; 208; 210; 224; 245; 247; 363

Moon Jaguar 353

Mopan 20; 33

Mopán 357

Morelos 87

Morley, Sylvanus 24; 29; 36; 181; 337; 453

Mosaic, style 136

Motagua *see* Río Motagua

Motolinía, Fray Toribio de 309

Motul de san José 34; 322; 377; 402; 479

Muchuppipp 166

Mulchic 403; 406; 459

Mundo Perdido Complex, Tikal 105; 189

Mundo Perdido Marker, Tikal 189

Museo "José Gómez Panaco", Balancán 162

Museo Arqueológico de Cancún, Cancún 60; 459

Museo de América, Madrid 207; 212; 213; 241; 245; 246

Museo de la Escultura, Copán 351

Museo de sitio "Alberto Ruz Lhuillier", Palenque 60; 263; 459

Museo de sitio, Chichén Itzá 69; 441

Museo de sitio, Comalcalco 51; 97; 155; 168; 183

Museo de sitio, Pomoná 60; 334

Museo de sitio, Uxmal 473

Museo del Centro Coordinator del INI, Valladolid 255

Museo del Prado, Madrid 159; 165

Museo del Pueblo Maya, Dzibilchaltún 473; 489

Museo del Soconusco, Tapachula 81

Museo Histórico Fuerte de San Miguel, Baluarte de San Miguel, Campeche 66; 156; 373; 374; 377; 382; 396; 457

Museo Nacional de Antropología, Mexico City 39; 49; 59; 60; 73; 76; 89; 159; 160; 162; 163; 172; 179; 210; 235; 238; 255; 265; 267; 269; 295; 312; 321; 324; 325; 330; 332; 387; 391; 394; 396; 397; 398; 409; 436; 439; 443; 460; 463; 469; 483; 486; 493

Museo Nacional de Arqueología y Etnología, Guatemala 51; 60; 70; 81; 85; 91; 93; 164; 168; 176; 250; 265; 310; 314; 317; 319; 323; 325; 330; 357; 364; 366; 369; 370; 484

Museo Popol Vuh, Guatemala 59; 309

Museo Regional de Antropología "Carlos Pellicer", Villa Hermosa 99

Museo Regional de Antropología de Yucatán "Palacio Cantón" 81; 94; 165; 166; 217; 220; 279; 427; 430; 432; 439; 441; 457; 463; 479

Museo Regional de Arqueología, Copán 259; 339; 467

Museo Regional de Chiapas, Tuxtla Gutierrez 79; 172; 267; 310; 466

Museo Regional de Soconusco, Tapachula 79

Museum of Archaeology and Anthropology, University of Pennsylvania 107

Museum of Fine Arts, Boston 170; 279; 280

Museum of Mankind, London 29; 33; 34

Museum of the City of Balancán 76

Museum of the Ruins, Copán *see* Museo Regional de Copán Ruinas, Copán Ruinas 92; 349

Mutul 332

Muyil 152; 454; 455; 459

N

Nacajuca 495

Naco 94

Nadzcaan 133

Nahuail 314

Nahuas 225; 237

Nahuatl 179; 436; 483;

Nakbé 60; 104; 243; 286; 357; 358; 359; 360; 373; 374; 377

Nalda, Enrique 26; 103

Naranjo 36; 321; 322; 323; 328; 334; 366; 369; 381

National Institute of Anthropology and History of Mexico *see* Instituto Nacional de Antropologia e Historia, Mexico City

National Liberation Army 502

Nebaj 176; 208; 251; 310; 312; 317; 319

New River *see* Dzuluinicoob

New York 32; 208; 259

Nicaragua 93; 94

Nicoya 79

Nine Deity *see* Bolontikú

Nito 88; 460

Nohku 453

Nohoch Mul, Cobá 152

Nojpat 132; 403; 413; 416

Nojpetén 488; 490

Nonoalco-Zuyuá 399

Nonoualco 402

North Acropolis, Tikal 107; 374; 377

North America 32; 43; 207

North Structure, Nunnuery Quadrangle, Uxmal 404

Northern River Lagoon 454

Nucuchtunich 133

Nuevo, River *see* Dzuluinicoob

Nuñez de la Vega, don Francisco 209

Nunnery Quadrangle, Uxmal 401; 402; 404; 407; 411; 412; 416; 431; 436

Nunnery, Chichén Itzá 125; 197; 199; 200

O

O'Neal 123

Oaxaca 53; 60; 76; 87; 94; 96; 170; 179; 334; 373; 439

Obregón, Alvaro 79

Ocós, phase 94; 96; 309

Ocosingo 76

Ocote 96; 97

Ocozocuatla 76; 79; 96; 466

Ojo de Agua 79; 81; 309

Ojochi, phase 94; 96

Olmec Relief of Xoc 76

Olmecs 60; 73; 75; 76; 79; 81; 85; 87; 207 249; 250; 309

Ometeotl 237

One Ahan *see* Hunapu

One Artisan 221

One Death *see* Hun Came

One God *see* Hunab Ku

One Monkey 221

Orbita, Juan de 490

Ordóñez y Aguiar, Ramón 30

Orefici, Giuseppe 26; 85

Osario, Chichén Itzá *see* El Osario, Chichén Itzá

Oval Palace Tablet, Palenque 297; 298; 302

Oxchuc 209

Oxkintok 136; 403; 427; 439; 445

Oxkutzcab 489
Oxlahuntikú , Thirteen Deity 235
Oxtoloc 125

P

PAAC *see* Proyecto Arqueológico Acrópolis de Copán
Paamul 459
PAC *see* Proyecto Arquelógico Copán
Pacal *see* Kinich Hanab Pacal
Pacal the Great *see* Kinic Hanab Pacal
Pachá 490
Pacheco 484; 489
Pachuca 445
Pacific Ocean 34; 43; 45; 56; 59; 60; 66; 73; 76; 79; 81; 85; 94; 181; 209; 212; 309; 345; 427; 444; 445
Padre Piedra 76
Pahuatun *see* Bacab
Palace, Palenque 31; 297; 299; 302
Palacio Cantón, Yucatán *see* Museo Regional de Antropología de Yucatán, "Palacio Cantón", Merida
Palacio n. 1, Tikal 32
Palazzo Grassi, Venezia 25
Palenque 19; 21; 22; 25; 30; 31; 33; 34; 46; 60; 132; 136; 160; 179; 186; 224; 225; 232; 235; 236; 238; 244; 226; 227; 237; 243; 254; 260; 263; 297; 298; 299; 300; 302; 304; 305; 321; 322; 324; 329; 332; 366; 382; 459
Palenque Triad (*see also* G I, G II and G III) 186; 302; 303
Pampa El Pajón 79
Panama 94; 96; 460; 463
Panel of Xalumkin 333
Paredes, J. Hector G. 26; 309
Paris 31; 190; 197; 198; 208; 214; 215
Paris Codex 190; 197; 198; 208; 214; 215
Parker, Joy 126
Parque Arqueológico, Copán 337; 339; 341
Parque Museo La Venta, Villahermosa 79
Pasión, River *see* Río de la Pasión
Patio of the Jaguars, Copán *see* Eastern Patio, copán
Pauahtun *see* Bacab
Peabody Museum of Archaelogy and Ethnology, Harvard University, Cambridge, Mass. 34; 36; 249; 254; 255; 260
Pech 471
Pellicer, Carlos 99

Pendergast, David 489
Pennsylvania State University 337; 347
Pérez, Juan Pío 214
Pérez-Suárez, Thomás 26; 73
Perigny, Maurice de 133
Petén 26; 31; 33; 34; 36; 37; 43; 47; 75; 81; 91; 93; 112; 122; 131; 132; 133; 136; 152; 153; 175; 196; 209; 212; 221; 259; 297; 323; 325; 328; 330; 357; 358; 363; 366; 373; 377; 380; 381; 384; 385; 427; 445; 466; 473; 488; 490; 493
Petén Itzá, lake 33; 34; 436; 484; 488; 490; 493
Petexbatun 332; 381
Peto 79
Philip II 29
Piedra Parada 96
Piedras Negras 21; 34; 36; 132; 199; 254; 297; 305; 321; 322; 323; 324; 330; 334; 366; 407
Pier B, House D, Palenque 300
Pier D, House A, Palenque 302
Pier D, House D, Palenque 300
Pijijiapan 76; 309
Piña Chán, Román 26; 387
Pipil 73; 94; 314
Placencia Lagoon 454
Platform N10-43, Lamanai 104
Playa del Carmen 152; 453; 454; 459
Plaza de las Estelas, Copán 337; 341
Pleistocene 309
Plumajillo 76
Pocam 209
Poco Uinic 199
Pocomam 20; 166
Pocomchi 20; 162
Pocvicuc 75
Polé 454; 459
Pollock, Harry 401
Polochic 309
Pomoca 75
Pomoná 60; 132; 322; 324; 334
Ponce, Alonso 30
Popol Na 350; 411
Popol Vuh 19; 22; 23; 126; 174; 175; 190; 217; 218; 219; 220; 221; 222; 224; 225; 226; 228; 229; 235; 236; 237; 241; 243; 244; 255; 277; 279; 303; 317; 360; 412
Popolá 479
Popoluca 96
Primary Standard Sequence (PSS) 279; 280; 292
Princeton 271; 274
Principal Bird Deity *see* Itzam Yeh

Project for the Study of Mosaic Sculpture *see* Proyecto para el Estudio de la Escultura en Mosaico
Proskouriakoff, Tatiana 21; 135; 186; 321; 337
Proto-Puuc, phase 136
Proyecto Arqueológico Acrópolis de Copán (PAAC) 338
Proyecto Arqueológico Copán (PAC) 75; 337
Proyecto para el Estudio de la Escultura en Mosaico 338
PSS *see* Primary Standard Sequence
Puebla, valley of 60; 444
Puebla-Tlaxcala 427; 430
Pueblo Moderno 341; 344
Puerto Morelos 459
Puleston, Dennis E. 106
Punta Pájaros 454
Punta Piedra 454
Putnam, Frederick W. 34
Putun 23; 70; 212; 370; 399; 445;
Puuc, phase 135; 136; 145; 152; 153; 210; 241; 401; 402; 403; 404; 405; 406; 407; 411; 414; 443; 444; 445; 446
Puuc, region 53; 70; 110; 112; 133; 401; 402; 403; 406; 407; 409; 411; 413; 414; 416; 432; 457
Pyramid of Cobá 125
Pyramid of Edzná 133
Pyramid of Kinich Kakmo, Izamal 133
Pyramid of the Masks, Kohunlich 131
Pyramid of the Sun, Teotihuacan 105
Pyramid of the Tiger, El Mirador 103; 104; 105
Pyramid Structure E-VII-sub, Uaxactún 131; 360; 374

Q

Qaholom 175
Quelepa 88
Quetzalcoatl 237; 391; 436
Quetzal-Serpent 236; 237
Quezada, Sergio 26; 469
Quiche 19; 20; 23; 71; 195; 219; 224; 226; 235; 236; 244; 303; 360; 488
Quiché, region *see* El Quiché
Quintana Roo 20; 36; 42; 45; 47; 48; 53; 73; 81; 85; 106; 121; 122; 125; 126; 131; 132; 133; 136; 145; 149; 152; 183; 210; 220; 275; 279; 328; 357; 381; 427; 451; 452; 453; 454; 455; 459; 463; 484; 505
Quiriguá 21; 34; 88; 94; 132; 183; 232; 243; 312; 321

R

Rabinal 317
Rabinal Achí 317
Raised-Up-Sky-Place 227
Rautenstrauch-Joest Museum, Cologne 464
Razor House 223
Reastern Coast, Style 145; 152
Red House, Chichén Itzá 431; 436
Reents-Budet, Dorie 26; 271
Relación de Tekantó y Tepankán 432
Relationes Histórico-Geográficas 166; 175
Retalhuleu, Dept. of 79
Rijksmuseum voor Volkenkunde, Leiden 196
Río Azul 271; 281; 361; 363
Río Bec 66; 384
Río Bec, style 106; 112; 133; 135; 153; 155; 241; 373; 406; 446
Río Belize 55; 490
Río Cara Sucia 86
Río de la Pasión 34; 55; 75; 323; 357; 369; 370
Río Dulce 88
Río Grande de Chiapas *see* Mezcalapa
Río Grijalva 20; 56; 76; 85; 94; 96; 309; 314
Río Hondo 55; 460; 484
Río La Venta 96; 97; 172
Río Motagua 56; 75; 88; 132; 153; 249; 254; 309; 312; 463
Río Pelo 85
Río Sucio 91
Ritual de los Bacabes 190
Robertson, Merle Green 26; 297; 304
Rockefeller Michael C. 259
Rockefeller Nelson A. 259
Rodríguez Girón, Zoila 26; 309
Rome 34
Room 1, Bonampak 306
Room 2, Bonampak 306; 307
Room 3, Bonampak 306
Rosalila *see* Rosalila Temple, Copán
Rosalila Temple, Copán 131; 350; 351; 353
Rosetta Stone 31
Rosny, León de 214
Royal City *see* Ciudad Real
Royal Geographical Society, London 31
Royal Library, Saxony 209
Roys, Ralph 24
Ru Bey Palama 164
Ruler 1, Naranjo 381

Ruler 3, Piedras Negras 334
Ruppert, Karl 36; 373
Ruz, Alberto 24; 26; 299
Ruz, Mario Humberto 159

S

Sabloff, Jeremy A. 26; 53; 110; 112
Sacalum 490
Sacapulas 317
Sacatepéquez 309
Sächsische Landesbibliothek, Dresden 207; 209; 211; 238; 241; 243; 246
Sací 479
Sacred Cenote, Chichén Itzá 23; 431; 439; 444
Sacred Precinct, El Mirador 104
Sáenz, Josué 210
Sahagún, Bernardino de 172
Sak Hunal, Jester God 299; 384; 407
Saksus 490
Salamá 75
Salamanca de Bacalar 484; 488; 489; 490
Salamanca de Xelhá 451
Salinas La Blanca 79
Salúa, style 92
San Agustín Acasaguastlán 208
San Andrés 33; 91; 92
San Cristobal de las Casas 30; 66; 499; 502
San Gervasio 455; 459
San Isidro 49; 76; 96; 309
San Jerónimo, valley of 309
San José Mogote 87
San Juan, phase 96
San Lorenzo 73; 76; 79; 94
San Mateo Ixtatán 314; 317
San Miguel 459
San Miguel Pakchén 133
San Pedro 29
San Pedro Mártir River 76; 357
Sánchez de Aguilar, Pedro 172
Sanders, William T. 337; 347; 454
Santa Elena 407
Santa Marta, cave of 309
Santa Rita 88
Santa Rita Corozal 459; 460; 463; 466
Santa Rosa Xtampak 135
Santayana, George 241
Santo Ton 314
Saxony 209
Sayaxché 34
Sayil 21; 26; 70; 110; 111; 112; 136; 401; 407; 413; 414; 416; 457
Sayil Project 111

Sayosal 387
Schele, Linda 126; 186; 204; 344
Schellhas, Paul 235
Schield Jaguar 304
Schmidt, Peter J. 26; 427
Sepulchers, The *see* Las Sepulturas
Serpent Biter *see* Chicchan
Serpent Head *see* Kul Kan Ahau
Seven Death *see* Vucub Came
Seven Hunahpu 221
Seven Macaw *see* Vucub Caquix
Seville 29; 451
Sharer, Robert 339; 345; 353
Sheets, Payson D. 92
Sibun 490
Sierra Madre 43; 309
Sierra Maya 40
Siete Muñecas, Dzibilchaltún 86
Siltepec 267
Simojovel 73; 76
Sin Cabeza 79
Sinanché 166
Sittee River 490
Sky, dynastic elite *see* Kaían
Smithsonian Institution 280
Smoke Jaguar, Smoke Imix, God K 353
Smoke Spiral, Squirrel, Smoke Conch Shell 353
Smoking Frog 188; 377; 381
Société Geographique de Paris, Parigi 31
Society of Antiquaries, Londra 32
Soconusco 45; 73; 79; 170; 444; 445; 460
Sotuta 457; 479; 493
South Acropolis, Yaxchilán 305
South America 31; 207
South Structure, Nunnery Quadrangle, Uxmal 411; 412
Spain 19; 166; 200; 496
Spinden, Herbert 24
Stela 1, Bonampak 244
Stela 1, Cobá 180; 183
Stela 1, Copán 88; 353
Stela 2, Chiapa de Corzo 181; 183
Stela 2, Copán 353
Stela 2, Machaquilá 325
Stela 3, Caracol 382
Stela 3, Copán 353
Stela 3, Piedras Negras 199
Stela 4, Caracol 382
Stela 4, Copán 353
Stela 4, Uaxactún 377
Stela 5, Copán 353
Stela 5, Uaxactún 188; 377

Stela 6, Copán 353
Stela 6, Piedras Negras 330
Stela 7, Copán 353
Stela 8, Copán 353
Stela 9, Copán 353
Stela 9, Kaminaljuyú 315
Stela 10, Copán 353
Stela 11, Copán 353
Stela 11, Yaxchilán 184
Stela 12, Copán 353
Stela 13, Copán 353
Stela 14, Uxmal 407; 409; 410
Stela 15, Copán 88; 352
Stela 18, Copán 352
Stela 18, Tikal 377
Stela 19, Copán 353
Stela 25, Izapa 219; 237
Stela 25, Naranjo 381
Stela 29, Tikal 377
Stela 31, Tikal 188
Stela 33, Calakmul 382
Stela 34, Copán 353
Stela 39, Tikal 189; 191
Stela 50, Izapa 59
Stela 51, Calakmul 325
Stela 63, Copán 352
Stela 66, Calakmul 384; 385
Stela 114, Calakmul 381
Stela A, Copán 353
Stela B, Copán 349; 353
Stela C, Copán 135; 353
Stela C, Quirigá 183
Stela D, Copán 241
Stela E, Copán 352
Stela F, Copán 353
Stela H, Copán 353
Stela J, Copán 353
Stela M, Copán 241; 243; 353
Stela N, Copán 337
Stela of Xochicalco 430
Stela P, Copán 353
Stephens, John Lloyd 29; 31; 32; 33; 337; 401; 452
Stingray Lagoon 454
Stromsvik, Gustav 337
Structure 1, Bonampak 307
Structure 1, Mulchic 406
Structure 1, Uolantún 188
Structure 2, Calakmul
Structure 5-C2, Cerros 131
Structure 5C-54, Great Pyramid of the Mundo Perdido Complex,Tikal 105; 360
Structure 5D-22, Tikal 131
Structure 5D-33-3, Tikal 131
Structure 10L-11, Copán 339; 344; 353

Structure 10L-16, Copán 340; 345; 350; 351; 353
Structure 10L-18, Copán 350; 353
Structure 10L-22, Copán 227; 350; 351; 353
Structure 10L-22A, Copán 227; 350; 353
Structure 10L-26, Copán 350; 351; 353
Structure 10L-26-sub, Copán 352
Structure 21A, Copán 353
Structure 23, Yaxchilán 304
Structure 34, El Tigre Complex, El Mirador 131; 374
Structure 40, Yaxchilán 305
Structure 45, Tulum 452
Structure IIB, Calakmul 385
Structure III, Calakmul 110; 381
Structure IV, Calakmul 381; 382
Structure IVB, Calakmul 374; 377; 381; 385
Structure V, Calakmul 382
Structure VII, Calakmul 254
Structure X, Calakmul 385
Structure XIII, Calakmul 385
Structure E-VIIsub, Uaxactún see Pyramid E-VIIsub, Uaxactún
Structure N10-43, Lamanai 360
Stuart, David 186; 187; 321
Sula Valley 85; 91; 94; 349
Sun Eye Resplendescent Quetzal-Macaw see KinichYax Kuk Mo
Sun-Eye-Fire-Macaw see Kinich Kakmo
Sweet, Henry N. 29; 33

T

Ta Itza 23
Tabasco 20; 39; 40; 43; 46; 47; 48; 51; 53; 70; 73; 75; 76; 79; 81; 85; 94; 96; 99; 153; 162; 163; 168; 207; 212; 259; 357; 445; 463; 483; 484; 495; 505
Tabasqueño 135
Tablet of the Foliated Cross, Palenque 412
Tablet of the Scribes, Pomoná 334
Tacaná 39; 43
Tamalcab 459
Tancah 152; 451; 453; 454; 455; 459
Tapachula 79; 81
Tapachulteco, style 96
Tapijulapa 99
Tapir see Hun Chaan Mah Kina
Tapir Complex, El Mirador 104
Tapir Pyramid, El Mirador 104

Tate, Carolyn 304
Taube, Karl Andreas 237; 243
Tayasal 366
Tazumal 88; 91; 92
Teeple, John S. 204
Tegucigalpa 48; 82; 96; 176; 347
Tehuantepec 53; 73; 94; 427
Tejeda, Antonio 37; 306
Temple 10L-16, Copán see Structure 10L-16, Copán
Temple 10L-26, Copán see Structure 10L-26, Copán 350
Temple 16, Copán see Structure 10L-16, Copán
Temple 22, Copán see Structure 10L-22, Copán
Temple 26, Copán see Structure 10L-26, Copán
Temple 33, Yaxchilán 304
Temple I, Comalcalco 183
Temple I, Tikal 103; 106; 363; 384
Temple II, Tikal 106; 363
Temple IV, Tikal 107; 110; 237; 366
Temple XII, Palenque 244
Temple of the Chaac Mool, Chichén Itzá 409
Temple of the Hieroglyphic Jambs, Chichén Itzá 402
Temple of the Masks, Kohunlich 122
Temple of the Panels, Chichén Itzá 431; 436
Temple of the Sun, Palenque 302; 303; 304
Temple of the Foliated Cross, Palenque 34; 243; 302; 303
Temple of the Three Lintels, Chichén Itzá 402
Temple of the Cross, Palenque 34; 224; 236; 237; 302; 303
Temple of the Inscriptions, Palenque 22; 107; 110; 297; 298; 300; 302; 382
Temple of the Warriors, Chichén Itzá 123; 148; 237; 431; 436; 473
Temple of the Tiger , El Mirador 104
Templo de la Cruz, Palenque see Temple of the Cross, Palenque
Templo de las Inscripciones, Palenque see Temple of the Inscriptions, Palenque
Templo de los Guerreros, Chichén Itzá see Temple of the Warriors, Chichén Itzá
Tenam Puente 314
Tenampúa 94
Tenochtitlán 19; 23; 103; 483
Tenosique 75; 76

Teotihuacan 21; 69; 85; 91; 92; 96; 103; 105; 128; 345; 361; 427; 432; 445
Tepeu 175
Terrestrial Crocodile Dragon *see* Itzam Cab Ain
Terrestrial Dragon *see* Itzam Cab Ain
Tezcatlipoca 470
The Market, Chichén Itzá *see* El Mercado, Chichén Itzá
Thirteen Deity *see* Oxlahuntikú
Thompson, J. Eric S. 24; 203; 210; 445
Thousand Columns, The, Chichén Itzá 123; 431; 436
Three Towers Structure, Xpuhil 135
Three-Story Palace, Sayil *see* Great Palace, Sayil
Ticul 40; 401
Tierra Blanca 75
Tiger Complex *see* El Tigre Complex
Tihosuco 479
Tikal 21; 26; 32; 33; 34; 36; 60; 66; 69; 85; 88; 103; 105; 106; 107; 110; 112; 126; 131; 132; 188; 189; 191; 196; 237; 255; 276; 282; 321; 322; 323; 328; 332; 334; 345; 357; 358; 359; 360; 361; 363; 366; 369; 370; 374; 377; 381; 382; 384; 427
Tintal 104; 226; 359; 360
Tipuj 466; 488; 489; 490
Tiquisate 79
Título de Totonicapán 22; 190
Tixchel 466
Tlaloc 314; 361; 395; 413; 470; 473
Tlaxcala 430
To ? ni Uch Kawil 384
Tohil, phase 94; 96
Tojolabal 20; 94
Tok, phase 87
Tollan Xicotitlán 444
Toltecs 70; 85; 96; 236; 444; 446
Tomb 2, Structure IVb, Calakmul 374
Tomb 4, Structure II, Calakmul 384
Tonalá 76
Tonalámatl 179
Tonalpohualli 179
Toniná 76; 189; 244; 297; 322; 324; 325; 329
Topoxté 31; 276; 282
Torre, Tomás de la 170; 189
Totonacs 207
Tourtellot, Gair 10; 110; 112
Tower of Palenque 33
Tozzer, Alfred 34; 36
Tres Lagunas 133
Tres Micos Complex, El Mirador 103
Tres Zapotes 73

Trinidad 75
Tropic of Cancer 194
Tropic of Capricorn 194
Trujillo Colón, Cuyamel 82
Tsul Uinicoob 484; 489; 490
Tula 70; 145; 444; 445; 460
Tulane University 110; 339
Tulum 29; 106; 112; 122; 126; 128; 149; 152; 214; 451; 452; 453; 454; 459; 466
Tupak 454
Tut, Ambrosio 33
Tutil 128
Tutz, Ambrosio *see* Tut, Ambrosio
Tuxtla Gutiérrez 46; 79; 172; 267; 310; 466
Tuxtlas 427
Tuzantec 20
Twin Pyramid Complex, Tikal 107
Two Headed Dragon 406
Tzacol 175
Tzacualli 105
Tzamaneb 317
Tzeh 471
Tzeltal 19; 20; 94; 162; 164; 165; 168; 170; 209; 214; 502; 505
Tzotzil Maya 19; 20; 76; 94; 168; 189; 503
Tzotzil Uinic 189
Tzum 132
Tzutuhil 19; 20; 23; 163; 168; 486
Tzutzuculi 76; 309

U

U Cit Tok 353
U-? Kaan 382
U-? Kan 382
Uapala 88
Uaxaclahun Ubah Cíauil, 18 Coniglio 88; 353
Uaxactún 21; 36; 81; 91; 93; 106; 131; 164; 188; 189; 194; 208; 358; 359; 360; 361; 373; 374; 377
Ucareo 445
Ulúa 53; 73; 89; 91; 92; 460
UNESCO 353
United Nations High Commission for Refugees 501
United States of America 25; 322; 444; 505
Università di Tulane dove 454
University of Pennsylvania 107; 339
University of Queensland 340
Uo 209
Uolantún 189

Ursúa y Arizmendi, Martín de 490
Uspantec 20
Usulután, stile 88; 89; 96
Usumacinta 20; 34; 36; 55; 56; 75; 76; 132; 153; 254; 297; 304; 305; 309; 322; 324; 335; 357; 366; 381; 444; 445
Utatlán 71; 152
Uxmal 21; 23; 26; 30; 32; 55; 70; 132; 136; 197; 203; 204; 401; 402; 403; 404; 405; 406; 407; 409; 410; 411; 412; 413; 414; 416; 457; 463; 469; 473
Uxmal Queen 409

V

Vaillant, George C. 445
Valdés, Juan Antonio 26; 357
Valdivia Expedition 451
Valladolid 255; 484; 490
Varea 165
Varejonal 96
Vatican 209
Venice 27
Venus 21; 29; 190; 197; 198; 201; 202; 203; 204; 208; 210; 211; 363; 395; 411; 445; 446
Venus Platform, Chichén Itzá 126; 431; 436
Veracruz 76; 94; 96; 145; 181; 212; 260; 394; 395; 399; 444; 451; 463; 483; 505
Verapaz 94; 96; 160; 309; 484
Viejo Chamula 317
Viel, René 340; 341
Vienna 209
Vienna Codex *see* Códice Vindobonensis Mexicanus I
Villa Madero 136
Villa Real *see* Ciudad Real
Villahermosa 79; 99
Vucub Came, Seven Death 221; 244
Vucub Caquix, Seven Macaw 217; 218; 219; 220; 221; 222; 237; 241

W

Wakan-Chan 224
Waldeck 30
War of Castes *see* Caste War
Washington D. C. 36; 37; 66; 79; 194; 250; 453
Waterlily Jaguar 352
Waterloo 31

Waymil 484; 489
Webster, David L. 106
West Structure, Nunnery Quadrangle, Uxmal 411; 412
Western Court, Palenque 33
Western Patio, Acropolis, Copán 339; 340
Whiting, Thomas A. Lee 26; 207
Wild Cane Cay 454; 463
Willey, Gordon 337
Wizard Pyramid, Uxmal 409

X

Xalá 454; 459
Xamanhá 454; 459
Xamanzama 451; 454; 459
Xbalanque 126; 174; 220; 222; 223; 224; 229; 277; 360
Xcalakdzonot 255
Xcalumkín 136; 324; 333; 401; 406; 407
Xcaret 152; 454; 459
Xcochá 406
Xculoc 406
Xelhá 106; 152; 427; 451; 453; 454; 455; 459
Xibalba 126; 220; 221; 222; 223; 224; 226; 227; 228; 229
Xicalanco 427; 466
Ximénez, Fray Francisco 189; 317
Xinca 73
Xipe 391
Xiu 23; 402; 403; 469; 471
Xkanacol 136
Xkipché 416
Xma Kaba Kin 194

Xmucane, First Mother 126; 175; 218
Xoc 76; 190
Xochicalco 145; 432
Xpiyacoc 175; 218
Xpuhil 135
Xpulyaxché 133
Xtelhú 145
Xunantunich 366

Y

Yahaw Te Kinich 377; 382
Yajalón 210
Yarumela 86; 88
Yax Balam 279
Yax Kuk Mo see Kinich Yax Kuk Mo
Yax Pak see Yax Pasah
Yax Pasah, Yax Pac, Dawn 344; 349; 354
Yaxcabá 145
Yaxcheel Cab, First Tree of the World 411; 412
Yaxchilán 21; 22; 34; 36; 53; 110; 132; 184; 189; 190; 197; 243; 265; 297; 304; 305; 321; 322; 324; 330; 366; 381; 384; 407
Yaxhá 36; 369
Yaxhoom 133
Yaxuná 126; 132; 469
Ychak Kak see Yukum Ychak Kak
Yoc 309
Yohaltún 136
Yojoa, phase 92; 349
Yucatán 19; 20; 23; 26; 27; 29; 32; 33; 34; 39; 40; 45; 46; 53; 70; 73; 79; 81; 85; 86; 94; 110; 111; 112; 122; 125; 128; 131; 132; 133; 135; 136; 145;

148; 153; 160; 165; 166; 175; 209; 210; 212; 214; 217; 220; 235; 236; 237; 238; 241; 249; 254; 259; 263; 279; 280; 281; 321; 324; 357; 371; 373; 385; 401; 402; 404; 405; 406; 409; 411; 414; 416; 427; 430; 432; 436; 439; 441; 443; 444; 445; 446; 451; 457; 459; 460; 463; 466; 469; 470; 471; 473; 476; 479; 480; 483; 484; 486; 488; 489; 490; 493; 495; 497; 501; 505
Yucatecs 34; 162; 163; 165; 235; 241; 497; 500
Yukom ? Tok 384; 385
Yukom 382; 384
Yukum Yichak Kak, Great Jaguar Claw 384
Yulá 145
Yum Cimil 244

Z

Zac Kuk 297; 300
Zacpol, White Head 387
Zacualpa 310
Zaculeu 152; 310; 317
Zama 451; 454; 459
Zapatista National Liberation Army 502; 503
Zapotecs 60; 207
Zapotitán 91
Zinacantán 168; 170; 189
Zinacantecans 189
Zipacna 219; 220; 221; 222; 241
Zoque 86; 87; 94; 96; 170; 207; 314
Zoqui see Zoque
Zuyuá 399; 479

Photos credits

Ricardo Agurcia: 351

Claudio Ansaloni/action press photo agency: 352

Archivio INAH: 105, 238, 240, 241 above, 242, 244 to left, 245 to right, 246 above

Archivio RCS: 359. Entries: 77, 78, 137, 457

Andrea Baguzzi: 51 below, 70 below, 84, 90, 93, 164, 170, 176 to left, 265, 310, 314 to left, 316, 317, 318, 326, 356, 367, 368, 369, 370. Entries: 10, 11, 25, 38, 45, 46, 47, 48, 61, 143, 153, 170, 208, 220, 223, 228, 230, 245, 247, 248, 287, 298, 305, 306, 307, 310, 312, 324, 336, 337, 338, 340, 345, 357, 361, 369, 387, 414, 423, 435, 480, 481, 482, 483, 495, 497, 503, 504, 509, 510, 511, 512, 514

D. Beyl: 91, 336, 337, 339 to left, 345, 348, 354

Carlos Blanco,Proyecto México/INAH: 416

Francesco Böhm: Schede: 86 bis, 426 bis

Victor Boswell/National Geographic Society: 356, 369 to left

Adela Breton: 436, 442

Victoria R. Bricker, Harvey M. Bricker: 197 (from: Linda Schele, Mary Ellen Miller 1986), 200 (from original drawing of Carnegie Institution of Washington), 201 (from: Förstermann 1880), 202 above (from: Förstermann1880)

D. Bryant/Marka: 108-109

Hiller Burger/Peabody Museum: 246 below, 248, 254, 255 to left, 261

Ramón Carrasco: 385

André Cabrioler,Proyecto México/INAH: 110, 381

Michael Calderwood/Raíces: 366

Rodrigo Castillo/Fundación G. E T., Guatemala: 252-253

José Pablo Fernández Cueto-Subdireción de Etnografia MNA/INAH: 500, 501, 502, 503, 504

Dolores Dahlhaus: Entry: 370

Rafael Doniz: 81 above to left

Fulvio Eccardi/Sierra Madre: 43 above, 45

J. Espinosa: 338

Fototeca Nacional del INAH, Pachuca: 112 above, 407 to right, 496

Roberto García Moll, Proyecto México/INAH: 307

Mercedes de la Garza: 237

Gabriel Gasca/INAH: 199 above (from: John Montgomery)

Rocío Gonzalez: 455

Merle Greene: 298, 299, 300, 301, 302, 304, 305, 306

Ignacio Guevara, Proyecto México/INAH: 78

David A. Harvey:National Geographic Society: 134, 340

Ibañez y Sora. Fototeca Nacional del INAH en Pachuca: 494

Otis Imboden/National Geographic Society: 364-365

Lou Just/Sierra Madre: 172 to left

Guillermo Kahlo. Fototeca Nacional del INAH en Pachuca: 499 above

Justin Kerr Associates: 170, 174-175, 270, 271, 272-273, 274-275, 276-277, 280-281, 282-283, 284-285, 286-287, 288-289, 290-291, 292-293

Ricardo Mata/Fundación G. E T.: 363 to left

Alfred Maudslay: 46

Joe Miells: 66 above

George F. Mobley/National Geographic Society: 361, 362

Carlos Ontiveros: 241 below

Tomás Pérez: 79, 81 below, 267 to left,314, 319

Jorge Pérez de Lara: 102, 127, 145, 202-203, 204, 210, 213, 267 to left, 295, 296, 342-343, 344, 363 above, 401, 486, 488. Entry: 183

Román Piña Chan: 387, 391, 394 to left, 395, 399

Proyecto México/INAH: 131, 135 to left, 146-147, 214

Rheinisches Bildarchiv Köln: 465. Entries: 437a, 442

Antonio W. Rieke. Fototeca Nacional del INAH en Pachuca: 497 to right

Emilio Rivera/INAH: 88, 104, 152, 194 below, 196 below

Patricio Robes Gil/Sierra Madre: 47, 160

René Ruiz/INAH: 85, 121, 125, 194 above, 322, 329, 360, 407 to left, 410, 414 below, 430 to left, 431

T. W. Ruttledgez: National Geographic Society: 358

Jeremy Sabloff: 111

Bob Schalkwijk: 64-65

Linda Schele: 196 above to right

W. Schneider-Schültz: Entries: 98, 110, 279, 366

Henry N. Sweet: 28, 33 below

Alfred Tozzer: 36

Raúl Velázquez: 218-219 below (from Justin Kerr), 220 below (from Francis Robicksek and Donald M. Hales), 221 (from Francis Robicksek and Donald M. Hales), 222-223 (from Shattenhuit de Nieuwe Wereld), 224-225 above (from Michael Coe 1982), 225 (from David Freidel, Linda Schele, Joe Parker), 226 below (from Maudslay), 226-227 (from Michael Coe), 228-229 (from David Freidel, Linda Schele, Joe Parker), 230-231 (from Michael Coe), 232 (from Francis Robicksek and Donald M. Hales), 233 (from Francis Robicksek and Donald M. Hales)

Michel Zabé: Cover, between p.16 and p.17, 38, 40-41, 43 below, 46 to left, 48, 49, 50, 51 above, 53, 55, 58, 59, 60, 61, 62, 63, 64-65, 66 below, 67, 68, 69, 70 above, 71, 72, 77, 80, 81 to right, 82, 86-87, 89, 92, 94, 95, 96, 97, 98, 112 below, 113-120, 122-123, 124, 128, 130, 133, 136, 137-144, 148-149, 150-151, 155, 156, 158, 161, 162, 163, 165 below, 166-169, 171, 172 to right, 173, 176, 178, 182, 192, 194 to left, 195 above, 198, 199 below, 201, 202 above, 207, 209, 216, 220 above, 235, 239, 255 to right, 256, 257, 259, 262, 263, 264, 266, 267 to right, 268, 278, 294, 297, 308, 309, 311-313, 315, 323-325, 327,328,331-334, 339, 341, 346, 347, 372, 373, 375-379, 382, 383, 386, 388, 389, 390, 392, 393, 394 to right, 396, 397, 398, 400, 402-406, 408, 409, 411, 412-413, 414 above, 415-429, 430 to left, 432-435, 437-441, 443, 444, 451-454, 456, 457, 459-463, 466-479, 482, 484, 485, 487, 489, 491, 492, 493, 498, 513, 514, 515 to right, 516, 517, 518 above and-below to left, 519 above and to right, 521. Entries: 2-9, 13-22, 24, 26-34, 37, 39-44, 49-60, 62-75a, 76, 79-86, 87, 89-97, 99-109, 111-136, 138-142, 144, 146-152, 155, 156, 157, 160-163, 165, 168, 169, 171182, 184-188, 190-195, 197-200, 203-207, 209-219, 221, 222, 224-227, 229, 231-241, 243, 249-254, 256-273, 275, 277,280-286, 288-295, 297, 299-304, 308, 309, 311, 313, 316323, 325-335, 339, 341-344, 346-351, 352 d-e, 353-356, 360, 362-365, 368, 371-377, 379, 381-385, 389-392, 395-400, 402-408, 411-413, 415-422, 424-427, 429, 430, 431, 437, 438-441, 443, 446-452, 455, 456, 458-479, 484, 486, 491, 492, 494, 496, 499-501, 504-508

MAPS AND RECONSTRUCTION DRAWING

Consultoría Creativa: 8-9, 39, 42, 44, 54, 56-57, 74, 153, 154, 179, 180, 181, 183, 184, 185, 186, 187, 188, 189, 190, 191, 193, 218 sopra, 236, 243, 244 sopra, 245 a sinistra, 247, 274, 380, 459, 464, 480

Flavio Guberti / Break Point: Timeline Design

This catalogue has been published with the support of Cartiere Burgo
and it is printed on R4 New Matt Satin 130 g/m² paper manifactured by Cartiere Burgo

Fotocomposizione Grande - Monza (Milan)

Printed in August 1998
by Arti Grafiche A. Pizzi - Cinisello Balsamo (Milan)